MANAGEMENT ACCOUNTING

MANAGEMENT ACCOUNTING

[For Undergraduate, Postgraduate, MBA of all Indian Universities and Professional Courses Like ICWA and ICAI]

R.S.N. PILLAI
M.A., M.Com., LLB
Prof. & Head of the Department of Commerce
Arignar Anna College, Aramboly
Kanyakumari

BAGAVATHI
M.A., M.Com.
240, Chidambaranagar,
Nagercoil
Kanyakumari

S Chand And Company Limited
(ISO 9001 Certified Company)

S Chand And Company Limited

(ISO 9001 Certified Company)

Head Office: D-92, Sector–2, Noida – 201301, U.P. (India), Ph. 91-120-4682700

Registered Office: A-27, 2nd Floor, Mohan Co-operative Industrial Estate, New Delhi – 110 044, Phone: 011-49731800

www.**schandpublishing.com**; e-mail: **info@schandpublishing.com**

Marketing Offices:

Chennai	:	Ph: 23632120; chennai@schandpublishing.com
Guwahati	:	Ph: 2738811, 2735640; guwahati@schandpublishing.com
Hyderabad	:	Ph: 40186018; hyderabad@schandpublishing.com
Jalandhar	:	Ph: 4645630; jalandhar@schandpublishing.com
Kolkata	:	Ph: 23357458, 23353914; kolkata@schandpublishing.com
Lucknow	:	Ph: 4003633; lucknow@schandpublishing.com
Mumbai	:	Ph: 25000297; mumbai@schandpublishing.com
Patna	:	Ph: 4011400; patna@schandpublishing.com

First Edition 1996
Subsequent Editions and Reprints 1997, 99, 2000, 2001, 2002, 2003, 2004, 2006, 2007, 2008 (Twice), 2009; Revised Edition 2010, 2011, 2012, 2013, 2014, 2015, 2016 (Twice), 2018 (Twice), 2020, 2021, 2022 (Twice), 2023, 2024 (Twice), 2025

Reprint 2026

ISBN: 978-81-219-1062-0 **Product Code:** H8MAC48ACCN10ENAD10R

PRINTED IN INDIA

By Shri Shyamlal Printing Press Private Limited, Plot 20/4, Site-IV, Industrial Area Sahibabad, Ghaziabad – 201 010 and Published by S Chand And Company Limited, A-27, 2nd Floor, Mohan Co-operative Industrial Estate, New Delhi – 110 044.

PREFACE TO THE FOURTH REVISED EDITION

It gives us great pleasure to present the new edition of **Management Accounting** book which has been thoroughly revised and updated. A distinct feature of this book is that it provides a penetrating and comprehensive analysis of the concepts, theories and techniques in a simple and lucid style. Accounting, besides providing data for published financial statements for external use, is an important source of financial information for internal decision-making. The purpose of this book is to explain the way in which accounting information can be used by the managers in performing their managerial functions of planning and controlling.

The main aim of this book is to facilitate easy understanding of the matter at one reading without any tediousness in grasping the theories and illustrations. Almost all the illustrations have been added at appropriate places and replacing the old ones. All the theoretical questions and practical problems given at the end of each chapter have been selected from the latest University and Professional Examinations of different universities. All the practical problems contain the answers just below the exercise, within brackets.

This edition of the book has paid equal importance to both theory and practice.This book contains 333 solved illustrations, 134 theoretical questions, 215 objective type questions and 347 practical problems, with answers.

We hope that both students and teachers will find this book highly useful. Students and teachers are invited to offer their suggestions for improving the standard of this book.

We are thankful to the Management Team and the Editorial Department of S. Chand & Company Ltd. for all help and support in the publication of this book.

R.S.N. PILLAI
BAGAVATHI

Kanyakumari

PREFACE TO THE FIRST EDITION

We have great pleasure in placing the book 'Management Accounting' before the esteemed readers. The book, a humble contribution of ours to the existing literature on Management Accounting, is primarily meant for the students of commerce. Management Accounting is generally regarded as a difficult subject, but the readers of this book will realise that it is not so. We do not claim any originality, but we have taken pains to present the subject in a simple language and in a most systematic manner. Each and every point has been explained at length. The book is the fruit of a long period of teaching experience. The aim of this book is to introduce the subject with clarity and to enable the students, beginners as well as advanced learners, to understand and master the problems without much difficulty.

The special feature of the book is that the concepts have been elaborately explained step by step with minute details and suitable illustrations at the appropriate places. We have heavily drawn on the syllabi of various universities and professional bodies. Theoretical questions and 234 practical problems have been given with answers.

We hope that both students and teachers will find this book highly useful. We will be much grateful to those who send us constructive suggestions for improving the standard of the book. We take this opportunity to offer our sincere thanks to M/s. S. Chand & Company, New Delhi, for bringing out this book in its excellent form.

R.S.N. PILLAI
BAGAVATHI

CONTENTS

INTRODUCTION

MANAGERIAL USES OF FINANCIAL STATEMENTS

Chapter 1

Management Accounting

Development of Accounting; Accounting Principles; Accounting Concepts; Accounting Conventions; Financial Accounting; Meaning; Functions of Financial Accounting; Users of Financial Accounting Information; Limitation of Financial Accounting; Cost Accounting; Meaning; Functions of Cost Accounting; Limitations of Cost Accounting; Management Accounting; Evolution; Meaning; Definition; Nature or Characteristic of Management Accounting; Scope of Management Accounting; Objectives (Purposes) of Management Accounting; Functions of Management Accounting; Distinction between Financial Accounting and Management Accounting; Distinction between Management Accounting and Cost Accounting; Tools of Management Accounting; Conventions of Management Accounting; Need and Importance of Management Accounting; Users of Management Accounting Information; Limitation of Management Accounting; Installation of Management Accounting System; Management Accountant; Functions of Management Accountant; Duties of Management Accountant; Objective Type Questions; Theoretical Questions.

Development of Accounting

Book-keeping is as old as money itself. The necessity of book-keeping and accountancy, in the early periods, arose mainly due to the fact that memory of human beings is limited. They cannot remember various pieces of information for ever. Transactions related to business have become so important that their recording became a necessity. The need for keeping such records, in a clear and systematic manner, is the basis which gives rise to the subject—book-keeping. Book-keeping includes recording of journal, posting in ledgers and balancing of accounts. All the records before the preparation of Trial Balance is the whole subject matter of book-keeping. Thus, book-keeping may be defined as the science and art of recording transactions in money or money's worth so accurately and systematically, in a certain set of books, regularly, that the true state of businessman's affairs can be correctly ascertained. Here it is important to note that only those transactions related to business are recorded which can be expressed in terms of money. The work of book-keeping is usually entrusted to junior employees, who maintain various books of accounts—journal, subsidiary books, ledgers etc.—can be called as book-keepers. The books of original records, by themselves, do not give an idea of the company's financial position. When one has to make a judgment regarding the financial position of the firm, the information contained in these books has to be analysed and interpreted. According to American Institute of Certified Public Accountants, "Accounting is the art of recording, classifying and summarising in a significant manner and in terms of money, transactions and events which are of a financial character and interpreting the results thereof."

Accounting has been clearly defined as "the measurement and communication of financial and economic data". Accounting is as old as money itself. The science of accounting is still in the evolutionary process. Accounting refers to the discipline of recording and classifying the monetary effects of business transactions and events of an enterprise for the purpose of analysing, and finally reporting the result to a variety of interested parties. Accounting is the language effectively employed to communicate the financial information of a business unit to various parties interested in its progress, such as, proprietors, creditors, employees, consumers, government, debenture-holders etc.

It is now well-recognised that accountancy is largely independent professionally and that in every individual enterprise, there is an important place and work for accountancy apart from production and commercial activities of management. The role of book-keeper is to record and process the data in the accounting system. Much of this may be described as data processing in contrast with the job of an accountant, which is much broader. Finance is closely related to accounting, for it depends upon recording, reporting and measuring of business transactions. Through these activities, the financial data becomes understandable to a businessman. Much of modern business management has only been made possible by accounting information. Business is finance-oriented. It is the process of using money to make money. Management is a process of converting information into action and accounting is a source of most of the information that is used for this purpose. Management is heavily dependent on accounting for operating facts.

Accounting Principles

The development of accounting principles has been closely associated with the growth of business. When the business was small, the accounting was needed only for the owner. But, when the business grows in size and begins to function through stiff competition, uncertainty and risk, the businessman has to divert his attention to the problems of policies. And thus, ownership and management have gone into two different hands. Each accounting system was intended to serve more limited range purposes, and hence there was no need for many of the concepts, which are important to-day. Accounting, a man-made art, designed to aid man in achieving certain aims. Accounting principles, if they are generally accepted, must be practically applicable. That is, there should be proper balance between theory and practice. Good accounting theory is consistent with good business practice. Unlike the principles of physics, chemistry etc., accounting principles were not deducted from basic axioms nor their validity is verifiable through experiments. Even though accounting is based upon the principles, there is no universally accepted list of such principles, prepared by accountants. There is no agreement even among the accountants as to the significance of *Principles*. No List of universally accepted principles can be prepared but still certain principles are drawn which are accepted by most of the accountant. According to the terminology of AICPA, the nature of the generally accepted accounting principles is in the following statements :

> "Accountants are generally agreed that accounting principles cannot be derived from or proven by the laws of nature. They are rather in the category of conventions or rules developed by man from experience to fulfil the essential and useful needs and purposes in establishing reliable financial and operating information control for business activities. In this respect, they are similar to principles of commercial laws and other social disciplines."

The committee on terminology of the AICPA states the following as to the meaning of "Accounting Principles".

> "It is desirable that the accountant conceives of his work as a complex problem to be solved and of his statements as creative works of art, and that he reserves to himself the

freedom to do his work with the cannons of art constantly in mind and as his skill, knowledge and experience best enables him. Every art must work according to a body of applicable rules, but it also must reserve the right to depart from the rules, whenever it can thereby achieve a better result".

It is left to the best judgement of the accountant to record the events without ignoring the generally accepted accounting principles. For correct understanding of the principles, it is necessary to know the several concepts and conventions, even though they are subject to criticism. These principles are often divided into two broad categories : (1) Accounting Concepts and (2) Accounting Conventions.

ACCOUNTING CONCEPTS

There are some assumptions on which accounting is based. Accounting is the language of business. Business firms communicate their affairs and financial positions to the outsiders through the medium of accounting, which is the language of business in the form of financial statements. To make the language convey the same meaning to all interested parties, accountants have agreed on a number of concepts which they try to follow. The messages so communicated should easily be understood by the people for whom it is intended. Accounting concepts can be described as something which signifies a general notion regarding accounting principle. The assumptions, so made, are most natural and are not forced ones. A concept is a self-evident proposition *i.e.,* something taken for granted. There is no authoritative list of these concepts. The following are some of the accounting concepts that are quite popular in accounting.

1. Money Measurement Concept

Only those transactions, which can be expressed in monetary terms, are recorded in accounting though their quantitative records may also be kept. All business transactions should be expressed only in money. Thus transactions, which cannot be expressed in money, will not be recorded in accounting books. Thus, labour-management relations, sales policy, labour unrest, effectiveness of competition etc., which are of vital importance to business concern, do not find place in accounting. Another limitation of this concept makes the assumption that the money value is constant. It is contrary to fact as there are fluctuations in the money value. For instance, a land, purchased for Rs 10,000 in 2009, may cost four or five times in 2010. This is because of fall in money value. Thus this concept ignores the qualitative aspect of things : and the impact of inflationary changes is not adjustable in this principle.

2. Business Entity Concept or Enterprise Concept

Business is treated as separate from the proprietor. This concept is important and implies that a business is separate and distinct from the persons who supplied capital to the firm. All transactions of the business are recorded in the books of the firm. If business affairs and private affairs are mixed, the true picture of the business will not be available. The proprietor is treated as a creditor to the extent of his capital. Capital is thus a liability to the firm and the proprietor is the creditor of the business. The proprietors—sole trader, partners of a partnership firm etc.—may draw amount out of the business and this reduces the liability of the firm. Because of this concept, financial position of the business can be easily found out and earning capacity of the firm can be easily ascertained. It is important to note that transactions of the business affairs and private affairs are separated for recording only and in law, no such distinction is recognised except for an incorporated company.

3. Going Concern Concept or Continuity Concept

This concept relates with the long life of the business. A business is intended to continue for an indefinitely long period. For all practical purposes, a business firm comes under going concern concept, when there is no evidence to the contrary. All firms that continue to operate on a profitable footing are treated as going concerns. Accordingly, continuity of activity is assumed, thus accounting reports are fashioned as a going concern, just as against liquidation. The current disposal value is irrelevant for a continuing business. Thus under this assumption fixed assets are recorded at original cost and are depreciated in a proper manner. In Balance Sheet market price of fixed assets are not considered. While preparing final accounts, record is made for outstanding expenses and pre-paid expenses with the assumption that the business will continue. This concept will no longer exist when an accountant is asked to prepare a statement of financial position when the concern is about to be liquidated, in which case the assets will be valued at their current values and the liabilities at the value at which they have to be met.

4. Cost Concept

Under this concept fixed assets are recorded in the account books at the price at which they are acquired. The price paid to acquire the assets is termed as cost and this cost is the basis for all the subsequent accounting for the asset. When an asset is acquired for Rs 5,000, it is recorded in the account books at Rs 5,000 even though the market value may be different. But the asset is shown in balance sheet year after year, at cost price minus depreciation. This value is called book value. If the business pays nothing for an item it acquired, then this will not appear in the accounting records as an asset. Thus, all such events are ignored which affect the business but have no cost, for example, a favourable location, a good reputation with its customers, market standing etc. The value of an asset may change but the cost remains the same. The cost and value of an asset might be the same when it is purchased. The 'cost' should not be confused with 'value'. The book value of an asset as recorded do not reflect their real value. They do not signify that the values noted therein are the values for which they can be sold. Similarly, value of assets at the time of replacement may certainly be more than their cost.

5. Dual Aspect Concept (Accounting Equation Concept)

This concept signifies that every business transaction involves a two-fold aspect—(*a*) the yielding of benefit and (*b*) the giving of the benefit. For an exchange of value, two parties are required—a giver and a receiver. Thus, a firm sells goods worth Rs 100, the two simultaneous implications on the *seller* are (1) forgoing goods worth Rs 100 and (2) receipt of cash Rs 100. And those on the purchaser would be (1) receipt of goods for Rs 100 and (2) forgoing cash Rs 100. Every transaction affects two accounts and entails two-fold simultaneous effect on each party. Thus a giver necessarily implies a receiver and a receiver necessarily implies a giver and each transaction affects receiving account and giving account equally. Technically speaking, "for every debit, there is a credit". Therefore, we can say that every debit must have a corresponding credit and vice versa. This is the only system of modern account keeping. The underlying principle of Double Entry is very simple but wonderfully effective. "Double Entry book-keeping is a system of accounting by which receiving and giving aspects of each transaction are recorded at a time." As such transaction affects giving account and receiving account equally, the assets of a business entity will always be equal to its equities *i.e.,*

Total Assets = Total Liabilities

Total Assets = Capital + Outsiders' liabilities

Capital = Total assets – Outsiders' liabilities

6. Accounting Period Concept

Accounting is a continuous process in any business undertaking. Every businessman wants to know the result of his investment and efforts at frequent intervals. Accountants choose some shorter period to measure the result. Therefore, one year has been, generally, accepted as the accounting period. It may be 3 months, 6 months or 2 years also. This period is called accounting period. Financial period chosen, in this regard, should be neither too long nor too short. Closing day of the accounting period is known as accounting date. At this date, accountant prepares income and position statements, shows the business operations, brings the changes of positions since the construction of last statements. The financial reports prepared facilitate to make good decision, corrective measures, expansion etc. On the basis of income and position statement, financial position and earning capacity of one year can be compared with another. Their comparison helps the business for expansion. The outsiders too draw various conclusions. One year accounting period is recognised by law and the taxation is assessed annually. Reports to the outsiders are provided on this accounting period.

7. Matching Concept

According to this concept, it is necessary to match the expenses incurred during the accounting period with the revenues recognised during the same period. Since profit is an excess of revenue over expenses, it becomes necessary to bring together all revenues and expenses pertaining to a particular period. In other words, expenses incurred in an accounting year should be matched with the revenues recognised in that year. Again, only such expenses as incurred in generating revenues during the period should be deducted from those revenues for deriving the amount of income or profit during the period. The object of accounting is that accounting record be made in such a manner that cost may be compared with revenue. If the accounting method does not facilitate the comparison, then accounting method is considered unsatisfactory. Neither receipt of cash for revenue nor payment of cash for expenses is necessary. What is necessary is this that they must accrue in the current year so that the incurred expenses are matched against the realised revenue. American Institute of Certified Public Accountants' Committee on Accounting Procedure states that "it is plainly desirable to provide, by charging in the current income statement, properly classified, for all foreseeable costs and losses applicable against current revenues, to the extent that they can be measured and allocated to fiscal periods with reasonable approximation." All costs incurred during the period are taken. Similarly, expenses paid in advance are excluded from the total costs incurred to arrive at the expired costs. By application of this concept, proprietor can easily know about the profit/loss and he can make effort to increase earning capacity.

8. Realisation Concept

This concept revolves around the determination of the point of time when revenues are earned. A business firm invests money to purchase or manufacture goods for sale. To earn profit, sales have to be made. There can be no profit without realisation of sale proceeds. According to realisation concept, which is also known as the "revenue recognition concept", revenue is considered as being earned on the date on which it is realised *i.e.,* the date on which goods and services are transferred to customers either for cash or for credit. "Credit transactions create debtors and the promise of debtors to make payment is sufficient for the purpose of realising revenue." The realisation concept is important in ascertaining the exact profit earned during a period in a business concern. This concept is very important as it prevents firms from inflating their profits by recording sales and incomes that are likely to accrue.

9. Objectivity Concept

This concept implies that all accounting transactions should be evidenced and supported by business documents *i.e.,* invoices, vouchers etc. The evidence substantiating the business transactions should be objective *i.e.,* free from the bias of the accountant or others. These supporting documents form the basis for record of entries and of audit. Accounting record based on documentary evidence is readily and objectively verifiable and therefore universally acceptable.

ACCOUNTING CONVENTIONS

Conventions in accounting have been evolved and developed to bring about uniformity in the maintenance of accounts. Conventions denote customs or traditions or usage which are in use since long. To be clear, these are nothing but unwritten laws. The accountants have to adopt the usage or customs, which are used as a guide in the preparation of accounting reports and statements. These conventions are also known as doctrine. Following are the important accounting conventions in use.

1. Convention of Disclosure

This convention requires that accounting statements should be honestly prepared and all significant information should be disclosed therein. That is, while making accountancy records, care should be taken to disclose all material information. Here the emphasis is only on material information and not on immaterial information. This convention assumes greater importance in respect of corporate organisations where the management is divorced from ownership. That is why forms of Balance Sheet and Profit and Loss accounts are prescribed in Schedule VI of the Companies Act, 1956; so that significant information may not be left out to be disclosed. The purpose of this convention is to communicate all material and relevant facts of financial position and the results of operations, which have material interests to proprietors, creditors and investors. Sometimes, there may be time gap between the preparation of Balance Sheet and its publication and if there are material events—bad debts, destruction of plant or machinery etc., which occurred in the time gap, may also be known to users—proprietors, creditors etc. In short, full disclosure of all relevant facts in accounts is a necessity in order to make accounting record useful. Therefore, full disclosure is a very healthy convention, and is important.

2. Convention of Consistency

Rules and practices of accounting should be continuously observed and applied. In order to enable the management to draw conclusions about the operation of a company over a number of years, it is essential that the practices and methods of accounting remain unchanged from one period to another. Comparisons are possible only if a consistent policy of accounting is followed. If there are frequent changes in the treatment of accounts there is little or no scope for reliability. Comparison of accounting period with that in the past is possible only when the convention of consistency is adhered to. According to Anthony, "the consistency requires that once a company had decided on one method, it will treat all subsequent events of the same character in the same fashion unless it has a sound reason to do otherwise." This convention plays its role particularly when alternative accounting practice is equally acceptable. Moreover, consistency serves to eliminate personal bias. But if a change becomes desirable, the change and its effect should be clearly stated in the financial statements. Accounts should lend themselves easily to comparisons and contrasts. This convention increases accuracy and comparability of accounting information for prediction or decision making. This convention does not prohibit changes. If there is any change, its effect should be clearly stated in the financial statements.

3. Convention of Conservatism

"Anticipate no profit and provide for all possible losses" is the essence of this convention. Future is uncertain. Fluctuations and uncertainties are not uncommon. Conservatism refers to the policy of choosing the procedure that leads to under-statements as against overstatement of resources and income. The consequences of an error of understatement are likely to be less serious than that of an error of overstatement. For example, closing stock is valued at cost or market price whichever is lower. This is a convention of caution or playing safe and is adhered to while preparing financial statements. Showing a position better than what it is, is not permitted. Moreover, it is not proper to show a position substantially worse than what it is. Following are the examples :

(*a*) The value of an asset should not be overestimated.

(*b*) The value of a liability should not be underestimated.

(*c*) The profit should not be overestimated.

(*d*) The loss should not be underestimated.

Such conservatism is generally accepted to present a true and fair value of business in the financial statements.

4. Convention of Materiality

American Accounting Association defines the term materiality as "An item should be regarded as material if there is reason to believe that knowledge of it would influence the decision of informed investor." It refers to the relative importance of an item or event. Materiality of an item depends on its amount and its nature. Theoretically, all items, large or small, should be treated alike. Materiality convention implies that the economic significance of an item will to some extent affect its accounting treatment. Materiality in its essence is of relative significance. In the sense that some of the unimportant items are either left out or included with other items. For instance, acquisition of items like fountain pen, stapler, pin cushion, punching machine etc., can be treated as part of assets, when considering their durability and span of life. But, it is not necessary to maintain separate ledgers. Such low cost items can be treated as expense for the period. Therefore, unimportant items are either left out or merged with other items. The reason for this different treatment lies in the magnitude of their amount. The dividing line between material and immaterial varies according to the company, the circumstances of the transactions and economic significance. It should also be noted that an item considered to be material for one business firm, may be immaterial for another firm. Similarly, an item of material in a year may not be material in the subsequent years. Similarly, most of the companies publish their financial statements in whole rupees—round figures, by ignoring paise. Omission of paise is immaterial *i.e.,* insignificant when figures appear in lakhs. In short, all material information should be disclosed that is necessary to make the financial statements clear and understandable.

The aim of this book is to cover the main areas of management accounting. However, to have a clear understanding of the subject—management accounting—it is a must to have sound knowledge of financial accounting and cost accounting. This is because a greater part of management accounting is concerned both with financial accounting and cost accounting. Accounting can be broadly classified into three type (*a*) Financial Accounting, (*b*) Cost Accounting and (*c*) Management Accounting. Each one supplements the other. Financial accounting provides the basis for cost accounting as well as management accounting and in the ultimate analysis, management accounting includes part of cost accounting. Thus, conclusions drawn by Management Accountant depend to a large extent upon the accuracy with which financial and cost records are kept. Management Accounting is just next step to both financial accounting and cost accounting and mainly based on the results exhibited by these accounts. Some of the weaknesses of financial and cost accounting system have paved the way for the development of Management Accounting system. Before we take up the topic of management accounting, it is necessary to understand what is financial accounting and cost accounting. After this, our main topic—Management Accounting—is taken up in detail.

FINANCIAL ACCOUNTING

Meaning

American Institute of Certified Public Accountants has defined 'Financial Accounting' as "the art of recording, classifying and summarising in a significant manner and in terms of money transactions and events which are in part atleast of a financial character and interpreting the result thereof." Accounting is often referred to as the language of business. Financial Accounting records business transactions taking place during the accounting period with a view to prepare financial statements. One of the important objectives of accounting is to measure the "profit of the business" and to ascertain the "financial position of the business." Thus Income and Expenditure or Profit and Loss Account is prepared for a particular period to determine the profitability of the concern and Balance Sheet is prepared on a particular date and it determines the financial position of the concern.

Functions of Financial Accounting

The progress and reputation of any business is built upon sound financial footing. There are a number of parties who are interested in the accounting information relating to business. Accounting is the language employed to communicate financial information of a concern to parties—Owners, Management, Creditors, Employees, Investors, Government, Consumers etc. The final accounting providing information regarding the status of the business and results of its operations. The following are main functions, in brief :

1. Record Keeping Function : The primary function of accounting relates to recording, classification and summary of financial transactions—journalisation, posting, and preparation of final statements. These facilitate to know *operating results* and *financial positions*. The purpose of this function is to report regularly to the interested parties by means of financial statements. Thus accounting performs historical function *i.e.,* attention on the past performance of a business; and this facilitates decision-making programme for future activities.

2. Managerial Function : Decision-making programme is greatly assisted by accounting. The managerial function and decision-making programmers, without accounting, may mislead. The day-to-day operations are compared with some predetermined standard. The variations of actual operations with pre-determined standards and their analysis are possible only with the help of accounting.

3. Legal Requirement Function : Auditing is compulsory in case of registered firms. Auditing is not possible without accounting. Thus accounting becomes compulsory to comply with legal requirements. Accounting is a base and with its help various returns, documents, statements etc., are prepared.

4. Language of Business : Accounting is the language of business. Various transactions are communicated through accounting. There are many parties—owners, creditors, government, employees etc., who are interested in knowing the results of the firm and this can be communicated only through accounting. The accounting shows a real and true position of the firm or the business.

5. Interpretation Function : This aspect helps in unfolding the total financial picture of an undertaking and investing the same with more meaning. Interpretation part is very important for decision-making. The recorded financial data is interpreted in a manner that the end-users can make a meaningful judgement about the financial condition and profitability of the business operations.

Users of Financial Accounting Information

The progress and reputation of any business firm is built upon the sound financial footing. There are a number of parties who are interested in the accounting information relating to business. Accounting is the language employed to communicate financial information of a concern to such parties. The users of accounting information may be grouped into two classes—Internal users and External users. Internal users are owners, management, employees etc. External users are creditors, investors, Government, consumers etc.

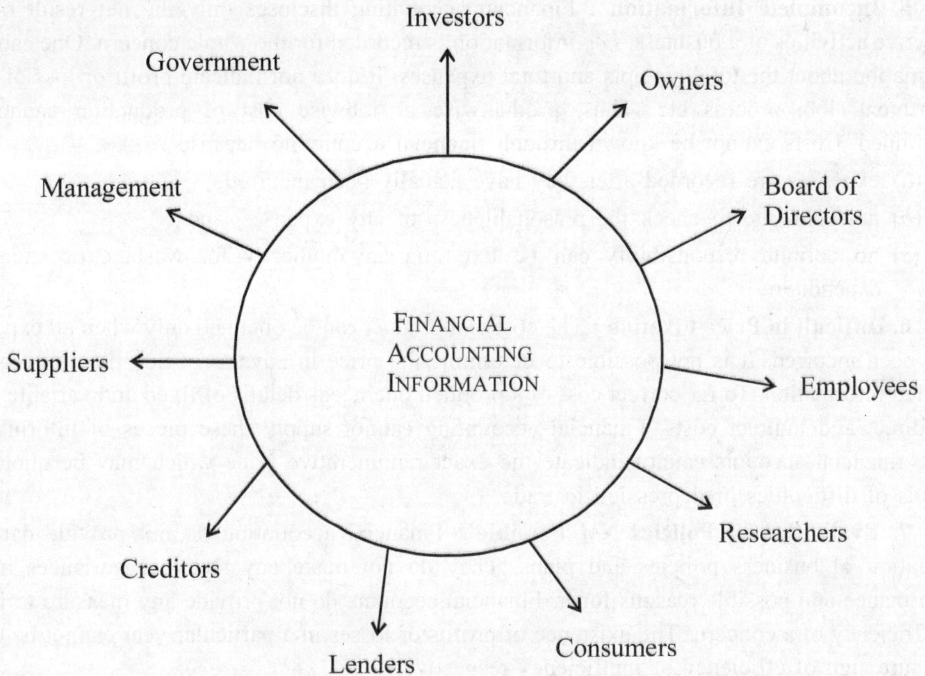

USERS OF FINANCIAL ACCOUNTING INFORMATION

Limitation of Financial Accounting

Financial accounting like any other branch of knowledge, is not without limitations. The growth and complexities of modern business have brought the limitations of financial accounting

1. Varying Informational Needs : The informational needs of the different levels of management vary widely. The Profit and Loss Account and Balance Sheet considered as a "movie" and a "still photograph" of a company respectively have been an end in themselves. The story they tell is already out of date. Financial accounting can only give information about what has happened and not about what will happen. Because financial accounting is historical in nature.

2. Monetary Nature : Financial position of a business concern is affected by several factors—economic, social, financial etc. but only financial factors are recorded in financial accounting. Social and economic factors are not taken into account. That is, transactions of non-monetary nature do not find place in accounting. It excludes qualitative elements like management reputation, employee morale, labour strike etc.

3. Recording Actual Cost : Cost concept is found in financial accounting. Price changes are not considered. Money value is bound to change often from time to time. Financial accounting records only actual costs. Thus, assets are shown at going concern value which has nothing to do with the realisable or replacement value of the assets. This limitation of financial accounting reduces their utility.

4. Technological Revolution : With the advancement in science and technology minute and detailed break up of all types of data concerning various types of business unit have become a must for the management in its day to day functioning. But, it is clear that simple structure of financial accounting is in a position to supply only elementary information.

5. Incomplete Information : Financial accounting discloses only the net result of the collective activities of a business, *i.e.,* information is recorded for the whole concern. One can find information about the total receipts and total expenses. It does not indicate profit or loss of each department, job, process etc. Thus, productwise or jobwise cost of production cannot be determined. Costs cannot be known through financial accounting because :

(*a*) expenses are recorded after they have actually been incurred,

(*b*) no technique to check the reasonableness of any expenses, and

(*c*) no definite responsibility can be fixed on any authority for wastage or excessive expenditure.

6. Difficult in Price Fixation : The cost of a product can be obtained only when all expenses have been incurred. It is not possible to determine the price in advance. Price fixation requires detailed information. To fix correct cost of a product, one needs details of fixed and variable costs and direct and indirect costs. Financial accounting cannot supply these pieces of information. Thus, financial accounts cannot indicate the exact remunerative price which may be quoted in periods of difficulties or depression in trade.

7. Evaluation of Policies Not Possible : Financial accounting do not provide data for evaluation of business policies and plans. They do not make any study of variances in the performance and possible reasons for it. Financial accounts do not provide any measure to judge the efficiency of a concern. The existence of profits or losses in a particular year cannot be taken as a sure sign of efficiency or inefficiency respectively.

8. No Help in Decision Making : Financial accounting do not help in decision making. They do not provide adequate information to enable the management to compare the probable effect of alternative courses of action such as introduction of new product, replacement of labour by machines etc. There are three levels of management—top, middle and lower. The type of information required by each level of management is different. Due to the historic nature of accounting data available from financial accounts, it is not of much helpful to the management.

9. Only Quantitative Information. Financial accounting considers only those factors which are of being quantitatively expressed. The policies and plans of the government have a direct bearing on the working of the business. The concept of welfare state has resulted in increased government interference in all sectors of the national economy. Therefore, management has to take account of government decisions over and above factors operating as a result of normal economic considerations. Financial accounting, being concerned with objectively quantifiable information, is unable to take them into account.

10. Personal Bias. Accounting policies are framed by Accountants. They differ on the use of accounting principles. Although a number of conventions and postulates have been propounded in accountancy, their use is greatly affected by the personal judgement of Accountants. It is often found that financial statements prepared by two different persons of the same concern gives different results and this may purely be due to varying personal judgement in using or applying a particular convention. For instance, inventory cost may be ascertained by FIFO or LIFO, stock may be valued at cost price or market price, amount kept for the reserve for doubtful debts, methods of depreciation on fixed assets, allocation of expenses between revenue and capital etc. Hence it is subjective factor that prevails in accounting and objective factor is ignored.

LIMITATIONS OF FINANCIAL ACCOUNTING

1. It is historical in nature.
2. It tells "What has happened" but not "What will happen".
3. Non-monetary transactions are not considered.
4. It fails to record price level changes.
5. It cannot supply information in fixing prices of output.
6. Immaterial pieces of information are not recorded.
7. There is a lack of unanimity on the use of accounting principles.
8. It is subjective factor, that prevails in Accounting:
   [objective factor is ignored.]
9. It fails to convey the impact of qualitative factors—Management Reputations, Employee morale etc.
10. Specific information is not usually available, say product-wise, department-wise etc.
11. Appraisal of policies not possible.

The financial accounting sometimes gives vague solutions to the following questions:

1. Is there any way to decrease the waste to the minimum ?
2. What is the actual cost of the product manufactured ?
3. Is it possible to increase or reduce the selling price ? If so, to what extent ?
4. Which products give profit and which one incur loss ?
5. Can the expenses be cut down in order to minimise the cost of production ? If so, how and to what extent ?
6. Can the firm earn more profits ?
7. Is it possible to split the cost of production into each element of cost ?
8. Is the capital effectively employed ?
9. How is the amount locked up in the inventories ?
10. Is it possible to know departmentwise profit or loss ?

Financial accounting was able to cope up with the needs of business in the initial stages when business was not so complex. But the growth and complexities of modern business have made financial accounting highly inadequate. Management accounting is free from the above limitations of financial accounting though it makes use of information that is drawn from financial accounting.

COST ACCOUNTING

Meaning

In a way, management accounting is an extension of cost accounting. It is one of the important element of accounting information bearing on the problems of internal managerial control. Financial accounts are unable to meet information needs about the cost structure of a product. It is important to develop an accounting system by which cost information may be developed and income determined. Cost accounting is the process of ascertaining cost from the point at which expenditure is incurred or committed to the establishment of its ultimate relationship with cost centres and cost units. It measures the operating efficiency of an enterprise. It is an internal aspect of the organisation.

To understand the meaning of cost accounting, a few definition have been given as under:

1. "Costing is the classifying, recording and appropriate allocation of expenditure for the

determination of the cost of products or services and for the presentation of suitably arranged data for purposes of control and guidance of the management. It includes the ascertainment of the cost of every order, job, contract, process, service or unit as may be appropriate. It deals with the cost of production, selling and distribution."

—Wheldon, Harold J.

2. "Cost accounting is the provisions of such analysis and classification of expenditure as will enable the total cost of any particular unit of production to be ascertained with reasonable degree of accuracy and at the same time to disclose exactly how such total cost is constituted." **—Bigg, Walter W.**

3. "The application of costing and cost accounting principles, methods and techniques to the science, art and practice of cost control and ascertainment of profitability. It includes the presentation of information derived therefrom for purpose of managerial decision-making." **—The Institute of Cost and Management, London**

Functions of Cost Accounting

The main functions of cost accounting can be summarised as follows:

1. It enables the management to ascertain the *cost* of product, job, contract, service or unit of production so as to develop cost standard.
2. Cost data are useful in the determination of *selling price* or quotation.
3. The object is to *minimise the cost* of manufacturing. Comparison of actual cost with standards reveals the discrepancies—variances.
4. The determination of *profitability* of each product, process, department etc. is the main object.
5. The central theme is to provide information, largely in the area of costs, which will be useful in *controlling the operations* of a business in a broad sense.

Limitation of Cost Accounting

Cost accounting like other branches of accountancy is not an exact science but is an art which has developed through theories and accounting practices based on reasoning and common sense. These practices are not static but changing with the change of time. Cost accounting lacks a uniform procedure. There is no stereotyped system of cost accounting applicable to all industries. There are widely recognised cost concepts but understood and applied differently by different industries. Cost accounting can be used only by big concerns.

MANAGEMENT ACCOUNTING

Evolution

Accounting refers to the discipline of recording and classifying the monetary effects of business transactions and events of an enterprise for the purpose of analysing, and finally reporting the result to a variety of interested parties. Since financial accounting has been to meet the aims and objectives of the persons (share-holders, creditors etc.) outside the concern, it was being considered that Accountant's primary duty was to record and to prepare final accounts. Though financial accounting conveys meaningful information to the outsiders, it fails to communicate valuable and varied information to the management. The evolution of Joint Stock Company form of organisation has resulted in large-scale production and separation of ownership and management. Thus with the increase in the size and complexity of business due to a variety of factors like large-scale operation, application of sophisticated modern technology, management has become more complex and cumbersome. To cope up with the increasing needs of large scale business, the modern managers need meaningful and timely data for making decisions. Decision-making, in any business organisation, is a primary function of management. The financial accounts prepared by accountant are important treasure house of facts and information but in their traditional form, Profit and Loss Account, Balance Sheet etc., they are unable to convey any meaningful information. Financial accounting furnishes a good deal of factual information which in their raw form are unable to prove to be of significant use to the busy management of a large scale organisation. At present, the tempo of our thinking and way of life in general having become faster, technological changes taking place day-by-day, economic and social values being obsolete over the night. Under these circumstances, management can no longer afford to wait upto the end of the year to know the relationship and problems arising from the day-to-day transactions. The correct information regarding the effect of each business transaction must be gathered from week to week or month to month. This has changed the accounting form a mere device of recording to a powerful tool of forecasting, budgeting, budgetary control etc. Thus financial accounting has been supplemented with financial and cost control, budgeting and budgetary control and also production, planning and control besides reporting on business performance. Probably, it has led to the development of the technique which is now commonly known as Management Accounting or Management Accountancy. In fact, when accounting assumes the function of providing adequate information for management needs, it is called Management Accounting.

Meaning

In ordinary language, any system of accounting which assists management in carrying out its functions more efficiently may be termed as Management Accounting. The term Management Accounting refers to accounting for the management *i.e.,* accounting which provides necessary information to the management for discharging its functions. Management Accounting is the presentation of accounting information in such a way as to assist management in the creation of policy and in the day-to-day operation of undertaking. The functions of management are planning, organising, directing and controlling. Thus, management accounting provides information to management so that planning, organising, directing and controlling of business operations can be done in an orderly manner.

Definition

Management Accounting is also known as "Management Oriented Accounting" or "Accounting for Management." In common parlance Management Accounting refers to the modern concept of accounts as an effective tool in the hands of the management as against the traditional package of accounts. Here are some definitions of Management Accounting.

> "Management Accounting is concerned with accounting information that is useful to management." **—Robert N. Anthony**
>
> "Management Accounting is the term used to describe the accounting methods, systems and techniques which, coupled with special knowledge and ability, assist management in its task of maximising profits or minimising losses." **—J. Batty**
>
> "Any form of accounting which enables a business to be conducted more efficiently can be regarded as management accounting."
>
> **—Institute of Chartered Accountants of England and Wales**
>
> "Such of its techniques and procedures by which accounting mainly seeks to aid the management collectively have come to be known as management accounting."
>
> **—The Institute of Chartered Accountants of India**
>
> "Management accounting is accounting for effective management." **—Bose**
>
> "Management Accounting includes the methods and concepts necessary for effective planning, for choosing among alternative business actions and for control through the evaluation and interpretation of performances."
>
> **—The American Accounting Association**

"Management accounting is an integral part of management concerned with identifying, presenting and interpreting information used for :

1. Formulating strategy
2. Planning and controlling activities
3. Decision taking
4. Optimising the use of resources
5. Disclosure to shareholders and others external to the entity
6. Disclosure to employees
7. Safeguarding assets"

The ICMA (UK)

Nature or Characteristic of Management Accounting

It is concerned with accounting information which is useful to management in maximising profits or minimising losses. The following are the main characteristics of Management Accounting.

1. Forecasting : It is concerned with future. It is not confined only to the collection of historical data or facts but also attempts to highlight upon "What should have been." That is, it helps in planning for the future because decisions are always taken for future course of action. All techniques of it are concerned with future.

2. Supply Information : It provides information to the management and not decisions. It can inform but it cannot prescribe. The way in which the data is used depends upon the efficiency of the management.

3. Increase in efficiency : It is basically concerned with "the problem of choice." A comparative study of various related alternative plans have to be undertaken and only that alternative is normally selected which seems to be more attractive and profitable.

4. Techniques and Concepts : It uses special techniques and concepts to make accounting data more useful. It makes a study of costs by dividing the total costs into fixed, semi-variable and variable components. The techniques usually used includes marginal costing, break-even analysis, uniform costing etc.

5. Cause and Effect Analysis : It attempts to examine the "Cause" and "Effect" of different variables. For instance, if there is a loss, the reasons for the loss are probed. Similarly, if there is a profit, the factors directly influencing the profitability are also studied. This may be the reason that management accounting is called as science.

6. No Fixed Norms : It has no set of rules and formats like double entry system of book-keeping. Though the tools of management accounting are the same but their use differs from concern to concern. The analysis of data depends upon the person using it.

7. Assists Management : It assists management in several ways in its functions but does not replace it. It is an integral part of business management. It provides all assistance to management in all of its functions. By providing the accounting information in the required form, and at the required time, it enables management to perform its functions effectively.

8. Achieving of Objectives : The principal objective of management accounting is "to serve the needs of management" or "to enable manager to manage better." To take more intelligent decision, he is able to get the necessary data through accounting procedures by responsibility accounting, direct costing and other approaches. Management accounting provides means for bringing meaningful knowledge promptly to the management for their use.

Scope of Management Accounting

The scope or field of management accounting is very wide and broad based and it includes within its fold, a variety of aspects of business operations. The main aim is to help management in its functions of planning, directing and controlling. The following are some of the areas of specialization included within the ambit of management accounting.

1. Financial Accounting : Financial accounting is the general accounting which relates to the recording of business transactions in the books of prime entry, posting them into respective ledger accounts, balancing them and preparing a trial balance. Then a Profit and Loss Account showing the results of the business and also a Balance Sheet depicting assets and liabilities of the business concern are prepared. This in turn forms the basis for analysis and interpretation for furnishing meaningful data to the management. Hence management accounting cannot obtain full control and coordination of operations without a well designed financial accounting system.

2. Cost Accounting : Costing is a branch of accounting. It is the process and technique of ascertaining costs. Planning, decision-making and control are the basic managerial functions. The cost accounting system provides the necessary tools such as Standard Costing, Budgetary Control, Inventory Control, Marginal Costing etc. for carrying out such functions efficiently.

3. Budgeting and Forecasting : Budgeting means expressing the plans, policies and goals of the enterprise for a definite period in future. Forecasting, on the other hand, is a prediction of what will happen as a result of a given set of circumstances. Targets are set for different departments and responsibility is fixed for achieving these targets. The comparison of actual performance with budgeted figures will give an idea about the performance of departments.

4. Statistical Methods : Statistical tools such as graphs, charts, diagrams, pictorial presentation, index numbers etc. make the information more impressive, comprehensive and intelligible: other tools such as time series, regression analysis, sampling technique etc. are highly useful for planning and forecasting.

5. Inventory Control. It includes control over inventory from the time it is acquired till its final disposal. Inventory control is significant as it involves large sums. The management should determine different levels of stocks—Minimum Stock Level, Maximum Stock Level, Re-ordering Stock Level, for inventory control. The study of inventory control will be helpful for taking managerial decisions.

6. Interpretation of Data : Analysis and interpretation of financial statements are important parts of management accounting. Financial statements may be studied in comparison to statements of earlier periods or in comparison with the statements of similar other firms. After analysing, the interpretation is made and the reports drawn from these analysis are presented to the management in a simple language.

7. Reporting : The interpreted information in the form of quantitative expression must be communicated to those who are interested in it or to whom it carries vital importance. At the same time these data should be communicated within reasonable time. Delay in passing on the data makes the data useless and obsolete. The reports may cover Profit and Loss Account, Cash and Fund Flow Statement, Stock Reports etc. Reports may be sent monthly, quarterly, half yearly etc.

8. Internal Audit : It needs devising a system of internal control by establishing internal audit coverage for all operating units. Internal audit helps the management in fixing responsibility of different individuals.

9. Tax Accounting : Income statements are prepared and tax liabilities are calculated. The management is informed about tax burden from Central Government, State Government and Local Authorities. This includes the computation of taxable income as per tax law, filing of returns etc. Apart from this, some of the Acts which have their influence on management decisions are the Companies Act, The Controller of Capital Issues Act, MRTP Act etc.

10. Methods and Procedures : This includes maintenance of proper data processing and other office management services, reporting on best use of mechanical and electronic devices. It provides statistical data to the various departments of the organisation. It undertakes special cost studies and estimations, reports on cost-volume-profit relationships, under changing conditions.

Objectives (Purposes) of Management Accounting

The primary objective of management accounting is to enable the management to maximise profits or minimise losses. The fundamental object of management accounting is to assist management in their functions of formulating policies, making decisions, planning activities and controlling business operations. The evolution of management accounting has given a new approach to the function of accounting. The main objectives or purposes of management accounting can be summarised as follows :

1. Planning and Policy Formulation : Planning is one of the primary functions of management. It involves forecasting on the basis of available information, setting goals, framing policies, determining the alternative courses of action and deciding on the programme of activities to be undertaken. Management accounting can help greatly in these processes. Management accounting facilitates for the preparation of statements in the light of past results and gives estimation for the future.

2. Help in the Interpretation process : The main object of management accounting is to present financial information to the management. Financial information is of technical nature. Therefore, the financial information must be presented in such a way that it is easily understood, apart from simple language. The management accounting presents accounting information in an intelligible manner and explains with the help of statistical devices like charts, diagrams, graphs, index numbers etc.

3. Helps in Decision-making : Management accounting makes decision-making process more modern and scientific by providing significant information relating to various alternatives in terms of cost and revenue. With the help of techniques provided by management accounting, data relating to cost, price, profit and savings for each of the available alternatives are collected and analysed and provides a base for taking sound decisions.

4. Controlling : Management accounting is a useful device of managerial control. Management accounting devices like standard costing and budgetary control are helpful in controlling performance. The actual results are compared with pre-determined objectives. Cost control is effected through the use of standard costing and departmental control is made possible through the use of budgets. The management is able to control performance of each and every individual with the help of management accounting devices.

5. Reporting : One of the primary objectives of management accounting is to keep the management fully informed about the latest position of the concern. This facilitates management to take proper and timely decisions. The object of management accounting is to provide data. It presents the different alternative plans before the management in a comparative manner. The performance of various departments is also regularly communicated to the top management.

6. Motivating : Delegation increases the job satisfaction of employees and encourage them to look forward. So it serves as a motivational device. Targets are laid down for employees. The setting of goals, planning the best and economical course of action, measuring the results etc. increase the effectiveness of the organisation and motivate the workers.

7. Helps in Organising : "Return on Capital Employed" is one of the tools of management accounting. Since management accounting stresses more on budget centres, investment centres, cost centres and profit centres, with a view to control costs and responsibilities, it also contributes to principles of decentralisation to a greater extent. All these aspects are helpful in setting up effective and efficient organisation framework.

8. Coordinating Operations : Management accounting helps in overall control and coordination of business operations. It provides tools which are helpful in coordinating the activities of different sections or departments. Budgets are important means of coordination.

Functions of Management Accounting

Management accounting is closely associated with the process called "Management Control." Management Control is the process of assuring that resources are obtained and used effectively and efficiently in the accomplishment of an organisation's objectives. The basic function of management accounting is to assist the management in performing its functions effectively. Management accounting is a part of accounting. It has developed out of the need for making more and more use of accounting for taking managerial decisions. Management accounting functions may be said to include all activities with collecting, processing, interpreting and presenting data to management. The manner in which management accounting satisfies the requirements of the management for arriving at appropriate business decisions may be described as follows:

1. Modification of Data : Accounting data as such are not suitable for managerial decision-making and control purposes. Management accounting modifies the available accounting data by rearranging in such a way that it becomes useful for management. The modification of data in similar groups makes the data more useful and understandable. For example, sales figures for different months may be classified, to know the total sales made during the period, product-wise, salesmen-wise and territory-wise.

2. Planning and Forecasting : Under the process of planning, management formulates policies and executes plans to achieve the desired objectives. Management accounting can help greatly in this process. Planning and forecasting are essential for achieving business objectives. The most important function of management accounting is to make short-term and long-term forecasts and planning the future operations of the business. Management accounting provides necessary information and data for forecasting. It uses various techniques such as budgeting, standard costing, marginal costing, fund flow statement, trend ratio, correlation etc. These are important tools of management accounting in planning.

3. Financial Analysis and Interpretation : The accounting data is analysed and interpreted meaningfully for effective planning and decision-making. The interpretation is most important function of management accounting. The top management people are not always well-versed in accounting techniques. They may not understand the financial data in its raw form. Management accounting selects useful data, analyses it and presents the interpretation before management in a non-technical manner alongwith comments and suggestions. Thus, analysis and interpretation of data are considered as backbone of management accounting.

4. Communication : Management accounting is an important medium of communication. Different levels of management (top, middle and lower) need different types of information. The top management needs concise information at relatively long intervals, middle management needs information regularly and the lower management are interested in detailed information at short-intervals. Management accounting establishes communication within the organisation and with outside world.

5. Facilitate Managerial Control : Management accounting is very useful in controlling performance. Management accounting enables all accounting efforts to be directed towards the attainment of goals efficiently by controlling the operations of the company more effectively. The standards of various departments and individuals are set up. The actual performance is recorded and variations are calculated. This process enables the management to assess the performance of everyone in the organisation.

6. Use of Qualitative Information : Mere financial data and its analysis and interpretation are not sufficient for decision-making purposes. Management accounting does not confine itself merely to financial data to assist the management in decision-making process but frequently draws upon various sources other than accounting for qualitative information which cannot be converted into monetary terms. For this purpose, engineering records, case studies, special surveys, productivity reports etc. are greatly relied upon.

7. Decision-Making : Management accounting furnishes accounting data and statistical information required for the decision-making process which vitally affects the survival and the success of the business. Management accounting supplies analytical information regarding various alternatives and the choice of management is made easy.

8. Coordinating : Coordination is the essence of managerial activity. The targets and performances of different departments are communicated to the management from time to time. Different tools such as budgeting, financial analysis and interpretation etc. are provided. It helps to increase the efficiency of various sections thereby increasing profitability of the concern. The supply of adequate information at the proper time will increase the efficiency of the management.

Distinction between Financial Accounting and Management Accounting

Financial accounting and management accounting are closely interrelated since management accounting draws out a major part of the information from financial accounting and modifies the same for managerial use. Financial accounting is concerned with the recording of day-to-day transactions of the business. Finally the concern find out profit or loss for a period through the Profit and Loss Account and judge the financial position by preparing Balance Sheet. The main concern of management accounting is to provide necessary information—quantitative as well as qualitative—to the management for planning and control. Despite the close inter-relationship that exists, there are certain points of difference between the two and they are discussed below :

1. Objective : The primary objective of financial accounting is to make periodical reports to owners, creditors and government but in management accounting the objective is to assist internal management. Thus, the former involves external reporting and the latter involves internal reporting. The financial accounting is primarily an external reporting system while management accounting is primarily an internal reporting system.

2. Nature of Data Used : Financial accounting is concerned with historical records relating to past whereas management accounting is mainly concerned with the future plans and policies. That is, financial accounting makes use of data which is historical, quantitative, monetary and objective, while management accounting uses data which is descriptive, statistical, subjective and relates to the future.

3. Subject Matter : Financial accounting deals with the position of the business as a whole *i.e.,* the financial statements report mostly the overall performance or position of the business. But management accounting deals with assessing the activities of different units, departments or divisions. Management accounting is limited in its coverage—deals with vital and significant activities.

4. Flexibility : In financial accounting, attempts are being made to prepare accounts in accordance with the standards fixed by and/or suitable for external parties. On the other hand, management accounting considers the standards fixed by management itself. Thus management accounting is free in its approach and flexible as compared to the rigidities of the financial accounting principles and rules.

5. Legal Compulsion : Financial accounting has more or less become compulsory or statutory for every business. But a business is free to install or not to install a system of management accounting. Thus management accounting is adopted on voluntary basis to increase the managerial efficiency.

6. Periodicity of Reporting : Under management accounting, immediate and prompt communication of data is very much required. In fact, if data are received too late or they are not upto date, they would not be considered as valuable for the use of management. Prompt and quick communication of information and keeping them upto date are not required under financial accounting. The period of reporting is much longer in financial accounting as compared to management accounting.

7. Precision : Under financial accounting, it is necessary to record the transactions with perfect accuracy and precision. All transactions are therefore, recorded at actual amount involved. As the information is meant for internal use, there is less emphasis on precision in the case of management accounting. Sometimes, approximated figures are much more significant and valuable than actual figures, because the objective of these figures is to find out the trend in business and not to disclose accurate financial position.

8. Unit of Account : Financial accounting recognises the whole business concern as one "unit of account." Financial statements prepared at the end of a year highlight upon the operating results and position of the business as whole. While, management accounting is concerned, in addition to overall position, with assessing the results of the activities of those divisions which are set up in the process of organisation.

9. Coverage : Financial accounting covers entire range of business activity while management accounting considers only parts of activity which are relevant to management for decision-making. In financial accounting only those events and transactions are recorded which can be expressed in money. On the other hand, management accounting touches and deals with non-monetary events such as competition, technical changes, change in the value of money. Financial accounting is *static* in nature whereas management accounting is *dynamic* in nature.

10. Publication and Audit : Financial statements like Profit and Loss Account and Balance Sheet are published for the use of general public. They are audited by practicing chartered accountants while there is no such provision in management accounting. All the reports, statements and forecasts made by management accounting are for the internal use of management only.

11. Accounting Principles : Financial accounting are governed by the generally accepted principles and conventions. No such set of principles are followed in management accounting. Management accounting is used for taking policy decisions. The form and method of presenting figures differs from concern to concern.

12. Methodology : Management accounting and financial accounting both differ on the methodology also. In financial accounting records are maintained in the form of revenue, income and expenditure, personal accounts and property accounts etc. In management accounting, costs and revenue are mostly reported by responsibility centres or profit centres.

Distinction between Management Accounting and Cost Accounting

Management accounting and cost accounting are two important branches of accounting. Management accounting and cost accounting involves presentation of accounting information in a manner that facilitates a prudent planning, correct decision-making and effective controlling of day-to-day operations. Cost accounting is not a mere tool for cost ascertainment and cost recording, it is also a good tool for cost control, ascertainment of profitability and for management decision-making. Most of the cost accounting concepts are freely used in management accounting for assisting the management. The deficiency of financial accounting has resulted in the emergence of cost accounting system. Cost accounting is not independent of the financial accounting, but is an expanded phase of financial accounting. The functions of management accounting and cost accounting are complementary in nature. Cost accounting deals primarily with cost data only. Management accounting involves the consideration of both costs and revenues. Although there appeared to be overlapping of areas between cost accounting and management accounting, the following distinctions between the two are observed :

1. Object : The primary objective of cost accounting is to determine and to record the cost of producing a product or providing a service. The purpose of management accounting is to provide information to the management for planning and coordinating the activities of the business.

2. Nature : Cost accounting is based on past and present facts and figures while management accounting deals with future projections and plans, on the basis of past and present cost data.

3. Principles : Certain principles and procedures are followed in the system of costing. But no such principles and procedures are being followed in management accounting. The information is prepared and presented as is required by the management.

4. Data Used : Only quantitative aspect is recorded in cost accounting while management accounting uses both quantitative and qualitative information.

5. Parties : The facts and data, provided by cost accounting, are preferred by both internal as well as external parties whereas the information furnished by management accounting is useful only to the management.

Cost accounting evolved out of financial accounting while management accounting evolved out of cost accounting. In fact, both the systems are complementary in nature. Management accounting without a system of cost accounting would certainly lose its significance. In the same way, cost data and information would be of no use for the management in the absence of management accounting. A good system of cost accounting is very helpful for management accounting. The scope of cost accounting in comparison to management accounting is limited. Management accounting draws heavily on cost data and other information derived from cost accounting.

Tools of Management Accounting

As we know, Management accounting is concerned with accounting information that is useful to management. Management accounting, as an accounting service to management through its various functions, has to employ a number of tools, techniques and methods. No one technique can satisfy all managerial needs. With gradual development of this subject, a number of new tools and techniques have been developed either replacing the old ones or in addition to them. The important tools and techniques used in Management accounting are discussed below :

1. Financial Planning : Financial planning involves determining both long-term and short-term financial objectives of the firm, formulating financial policies and developing the financial procedures to achieve the objectives. Every firm has to take a decision about the sources of raising funds. The funds can be raised either through issue of share capital or through raising loans. Again a decision is to be taken about the type of capital *i.e.,* equity share capital or preference share capital. When it decides to raise fund through loans, it is to be decided whether the loan is of short-term or long-term nature. The proportion between share capital and loan capital should also be decided. All these decisions are important for financial planning.

2. Analysis of Financial Statements : "The analysis and interpretation of financial statements are an attempt to determine the significance and meaning of the financial statement data so that a forecast may be made of the prospects for future earning, ability to pay debt and probability of a sound dividend policy." The technique of financial analysis includes comparative financial statements, ratios, fund flow statements, trend analysis etc. These are important tools.

3. Historical Cost Accounting : The statement of actual costs after they have been incurred is called Historical cost accounting. Although these are of limited value, they are essential in order to operate a standard costing system.

4. Standard Costing : Standard costing is an important tool of cost control which is one of the main objectives of management accounting. This involves the technique of preparation of standard costs, their comparison with actual costs and analysis of the differences *i.e.,* variances to their causes and point of incidence. It is the most effective method available for controlling performances and costs.

5. Budgetary Control : One of the essential features of modern management is planning and control. There are a number of devices which help in controlling. The most widely used device for managerial control is "budget." It is a quantitative expression of plan of action. The actual performance is recorded and compared with the pre-determined targets. Finding out deviation is an important tool for planning.

6. Marginal Costing : This is a method of costing which is concerned with changes in costs resulting from changes in the volume of production. Marginal costing is helpful for measurement of profitability of different lines of production.

7. Decision Accounting : Decision-making is the primary function of top management. Decision taking involves a choice from various alternatives. Decisions are taken after studying the alternative data in terms of costs, prices and profits furnished by management accounting and exercising the best choice after considering other non-financial factors.

8. Revaluation Accounting : Revaluation accounting is also an important tool of management accounting. This term is used to denote the methods employed for overcoming the problems connected with fixed asset replacement in a period of rising prices. It ensures the maintenance and preservation of the capital of the enterprise.

9. Ratio Accounting : Ratio accounting signifies the technique and methodology of analysis and interpretation of financial statements by means of accounting ratios derived from such statements. Ratio accounting includes trend analysis, comparative financial statements, inter-period comparisons, ratio analysis, fund flow statements etc. The analysis and interpretation of financial statements result in the presentation of information that will aid to business executives, investors, creditors etc.

10. Control Accounting : It consists of techniques of standard costing, budgetary control, control reports and statements, internal check, internal audit and reports, it is in this field that the management has scope to display ingenuity in the analysis, interpretation and presentation of information at all levels of management.

11. Internal Auditing : Internal auditing is an independent appraisal activity within an organisation for the review of accounting, financial and other operations as a basis for protective and constructive service to management. It is a type of control tool which functions by measuring and evaluating the effectiveness of other types of control. It deals primarily with accounting and financial matters but it may also properly deal with matters of an operating nature.

12. Management Information System : One of the primary functions of the management accounting of an enterprise is to provide management at all levels with necessary factual data and information so as to enable them to carry out the functions of planning, controlling and decision-making effectively. With the development of electronic devices for recording and classifying data, reporting to management has considerably improved. Feedback of information and responsive actions can be used as control techniques.

13. Statistical Techniques : There is a large number of statistical and graphical techniques which are used in management accounting. Some common examples are master chart, chart of sales and earnings, investment chart etc.

Conventions of Management Accounting

Conventions refer to the "rule of the game" of management accounting that help and guide a Management Accountant in performing his duties. Management accounting like all other social sciences, is partly a science and partly an art. The common practices, which have been adopted by the management accountants to deal with special problems from time to time, have taken the form of conventions. The new practices on the basis of their qualities of "commonness" are called conventions. These conventions may be taken as guidance while using management accounting and they are :

1. Accounting concerns itself with the recording of business transactions only.
2. As far as possible, costs and revenues should be properly matched.
3. Profits should be credited on realisation basis while losses should be provided in advance.
4. The methods, procedures and principles should be consistent.
5. The principle of matching costs with revenues should be strictly followed.
6. The accounting records should be kept as objective as possible.
7. The entire accounting information, past, present or future, in any form should be designed to meet the particular needs of the business.
8. The principle of reporting of exceptions should be followed when presenting information to the management.
9. The object of "control at source accounting" should be followed. It means that the control mechanism should be established at the points where costs are incurred.
10. A profit cannot be said to be earned unless the capital employed is maintained intact in real terms.
11. For measuring the efficiency of business, technique of measuring the return on capital employed should be adopted.
12. The management information should be fully integrated.
13. Overhead costs should be apportioned to the cost centres and recovered by products. The basis for recovery may be either the benefit received for fixed costs or responsibility incurred for variable costs.
14. Management accounting must attempt to show whether the resources of the business are most effectively utilized.
15. Responsibility should be identified on the basis of the distinction between controllable and non-controllable costs.
16. Management accounting should be forward looking *i.e.,* it should lay a great emphasis on the anticipation of problems.
17. The means of recording accounting information, presenting it to management, should be most appropriate.
18. Reports and statements should not be used as a substitute for personal contact with the persons at the higher levels of authority.

The above list of conventions is fairly long but not exhaustive. The main reasons for it, is this, that the science of management accounting is a growing, an inexact one. In the times to come, there may be new additions to this list or some of it may be dropped too.

Need and Importance of Management Accounting

Management accounting is the application of appropriate accounting techniques and concepts in processing historical and projected economic data of a business entity to assist its management in implementing plans for realising its objectives. In the present complex industrial world, management accounting has become an integral part of the management. It guides and advises management at every step. The following are the advantages of management accounting :

1. It increases the efficiency of various business functions. The targets of different departments are fixed in advance. The achievement of these goals is a tool for measuring their efficiency.
2. The activities of the concern are planned in a systematic manner. Various operations can be planned with the help of accounting information—budgeting and forecasting.
3. The different tools of management accounting have provided validity, objectivity and reliability in business management.
4. Different techniques of management accounting help in effective control of business operations. The maximum utilisation of capital and maximum return on capital invested in business becomes feasible through application of accounting techniques.
5. It creates harmony in the relationship between the management and employees. It enables the management to improve its services to its customers.
6. The management aims to control the cost of production and at the same time increase the efficiency of employees. When cost of production is reduced, it will increase the profit.
7. The business gets rid of seasonal and cyclical fluctuations on account of the use of management accounting.
8. Unacceptable standards or sub-standards, which are often responsible for unhealthy and bad relations between management and employees, can be removed by the use of management accounting. There arise improved and more healthy relations.
9. The use of management accounting may control or even eliminate various types of wastages, production defectives etc.
10. Management accounting helps in communicating upto date information to various parties interested in successful working of the business organisation.

Users of Management Accounting Information

The objective of management accounting is to record, analyse and present financial data to the management in such a way that it becomes useful and helpful in planning and running business operations systematically and effectively. Anyone who needs information to plan, to control, to coordinate, to decide and to manage an organisation becomes the user of management accounting.

A **production manager** would require information about production-efficiencies, output ratio, quality measures, different raw materials stock-levels, wastage rate etc.

A **sales manager** would require information about sales-trends, profitability, finished goods stock levels, stock turnover rate, salesman's performance, sales volumes etc.

A **human resource manager** would require information about absenteeism rates, sickness levels, employee turnover rates, recruitment costs, etc.

A **director or high level manager** would require information as a guide for the future. It enables the management in performing managerial functions efficiently and effectively. Management accounting as an accounting service to the management through its various functions has to employ a number of tools, techniques and methods—standard costing, Budgetary control, Marginal costing, Ratios, Statistical techniques etc.

Limitation of Management Accounting

Management Accounting is a recent discipline and therefore, it is in the process of development. Hence, it suffers from all the limitations of a new discipline. Some of these limitations are :

1. Limitations of Basic Records : Management accounting is mainly concerned with the rearrangement or modification of data. It derives its information from financial accounting, cost accounting and other records. The correctness of the management accounting depends upon the correctness of these basic records: that is, their limitations are also the limitations of management accounting.

2. Persistent Efforts : The conclusions and decisions drawn by the management accountant are not executed automatically. Thus, there is need for continuous and coordinated efforts of each management level to execute these decisions.

3. Management Accounting is only a Tool : Management accounting should never be considered as an alternate or substitute for management. This is a mere tool for management. Ultimate decisions and corrective steps or measures are being taken by management and not by management accountant.

4. Costly Installation : It is very costly. The installation of management accounting system needs a very elaborate organisation and numerous rules and regulations. This results in heavy investment which only big concerns can afford.

5. Personal Bias : The interpretation of financial information depends upon the capacity of interpreter as one has to make a personal judgement. Personal prejudices and bias affect the objectivity of decisions.

6. Resistance : The installation of management accounting involves basic change in organisational set up. New rules and regulations are also required to be framed which affect a number of personnel and hence there is a possibility of resistance from some quarters or the other.

7. Evolutionary Stage : Management accounting is only in a developmental stage. It has not reached the final stage. Its conventions are not as exact and established as of other branches of accounting. Being an inexact science, its results depend to a very great extent upon the intelligent interpretation of the data for managerial use.

8. Provides only Data : The main function of management accounting is to provide data and not decisions. It can only inform, not prescribe. This limitation should also be kept in mind while using the techniques of management accounting.

9. Broad-based Scope : The scope of management accounting is wide and broad based and this creates many difficulties in the implementation process. Management requires information from both accounting as well as non-accounting sources. This creates many problems and bring a degree of inexactness and subjectivity in the conclusion obtained through it.

10. Not an alternation to Administration : Management accounting is a tool of management, not an alternative of management. It cannot replace the management or administration.

Installation of Management Accounting System

The installation of Management Accounting system in a comprehensive way in an organisation should be done under the guidance of Management Accountant, who is also known as Controller of Accounts, Accounts Manager, Finance Director etc. The following steps will have to be taken for installation of an efficient and effective management accounting system :

1. Organisational manual for the entire organisation must be drafted and adopted. This will clearly explain the duties and responsibilities of each level of management. This prevents over-lapping of functions, powers and responsibilities.
2. Proformas for various types of statements and reports must be designed and prescribed.
3. Financial Accounts and Cost Accounts should be classified, codified and integrated.
4. Cost centres, investment centres, profit centres and budget centres should be clearly set up.
5. The techniques of standard costing are introduced for setting up standards and recording the performance so that reasons for variations are ascertained and corrective measures are taken in time.

6. The system of budget, budgeting, budgetary control should be introduced in the organisation.
7. Requisite staff should be recruited, trained and placed them on the work in the system.
8. Every day new challenges are faced. Because business is operated under changing economic, political and social environment. The operational research technique will be essential to cope up with the need of the hour.

Management Accountant

The officer who is entrusted with Management Accounting function in an organisation is known as Management Accountant. He plays a significant role in the decision-making process of an organisation. The organisational status or position of Management Accountant varies from concern to concern depending upon the pattern of management system in that concern. He may be considered as executive in some concern, while he may be a member of Board of Directors in case of some other concern. Normally he occupies a key position in the organisation heading the accounting department. In large concerns, his designation may be that of a "Controller", "Management Accountant", "Chief Accountant", "Chief Accounts Officer", "Finance Controller" etc. He is responsible for the installation, development and efficient functioning of the management accounting system. He plays an important role in gathering, compiling, reporting and interpreting internal accounting information. He designs the frame work of the financial and cost control reports that provide each management level with the most useful data at the most appropriate time. The Management Accountant, sometimes described as Chief Intelligence Officer because apart from top management, no one in the organisation perhaps knows more about the various functions of the organisation than him. Tandon has explained beautifully the position of Management Accountant in the following line:

"The management accountant is exactly like the spokes in a wheel, connecting the rim of the wheel and the hub receiving the information. He processes the information and then returns the processed information back to where it came from."

A controller or management accountant can exercise better influence and control more by his personality, mental equipment, industrial background, competence and integrity than by virtue of his holding the office.

Functions of Management Accountant

Management Accountant is considered to be a part of the management team since he has the responsibility for collecting vital information, both from within and outside the company. The functions of the controller have been laid down by the Controllers' Institute of America. They are typical of the functions of any management accountant by whatever name he is called. These functions are :

1. To establish, coordinate and administer, as an integral part of management, an adequate plan for the control of operations. Such a plan would provide, to the extent required in the business cost standards, expense budgets, sales forecasts, profit planning, and programme for capital investment and financing, together with necessary procedures to effectuate the plan.
2. To compare performance with operating plan and standards and to report and interpret the results of operation to all levels of management, and to the owners of the business. This function includes the formulation and administration of accounting policy and the compilation of statistical records and special reports as required.
3. To consult with all segments of management responsible for policy or action concerning any phase of the operations of business as it relates to the attainment of objectives, and the effectiveness of policies, organisation structures, procedures.

4. To administer tax policies and procedures.
5. To supervise and coordinate preparation of reports to Government agencies.
6. To assure fiscal protection for the assets of the business through adequate internal control and proper insurance coverage.
7. To continuously appraise economic and social forces and government influences, and interpret their effect upon business.

It may be noted that these seven functions of a Controller are broad enough to include all phases of policy and organisation within the controller's jurisdiction.

Duties of Management Accountant

The primary duty of Management Accountant is to help management in taking correct policy-decisions and improving the efficiency of entrepreneurial operations. He performs a staff function and also has line authority over the accountants. If management accountant feels that a decision likely to be taken by the management based on the information tendered by him shall be detrimental to the interest of the concern, he should point out this fact to the concerned management, of course, with tact, patience, firmness and politeness. On the other hand, if the decision taken happens to be wrong one on account of inaccuracy, biased and fabricated data furnished by the management accountant, he shall be held responsible for wrong decision taken by the management.

Controllers Institute of America has defined the following duties of Management Accountant or Controller :

1. The installation and interpretation of all accounting records of the corporation.
2. The preparation and interpretation of the financial statements and reports of the corporation.
3. Continuous audit of all accounts and records of the corporation wherever located.
4. The compilation of costs of distribution.
5. The compilation of production costs.
6. The taking and costing of all physical inventories.
7. The preparation and filing of tax returns and to the supervision of all matters relating to taxes.
8. The preparation and interpretation of all statistical records and reports of the corporation.
9. The preparation as budget director, in conjunction with other officers and department heads, of an annual budget covering all activities of the corporation for submission to the Board of Directors prior to the beginning of the fiscal year. The authority of the Controller, with respect to the veto of commitments of expenditures not authorised by the budget shall, from time to time, be fixed by the Board of Directors.
10. The ascertainment currently that the properties of the corporation are properly and adequately insured.
11. The initiation, preparation and issuance of standard practices relating to all accounting matters and procedures and the co-ordination of system throughout the corporation including clerical and office methods, records, reports and procedures.
12. The maintenance of adequate records of authorised appropriations and the determination that all sums expended pursuant thereto are properly accounted for.
13. The ascertainment currently that financial transactions covered by minutes of the Board of Directors and/or the Executive committee are properly executed and recorded.
14. The maintenance of adequate records of all contracts and leases.
15. The approval for payment (and/or countersigning) of all cheques, promissory notes and other negotiable instruments of the corporation which have been signed by the treasurer

or such other officers as shall have been authorised by the by-laws of the corporation or from time to time designated by the Board of Directors.

16. The examination of all warrants for the withdrawal of securities from the vaults of the corporation and the determination that such withdrawals are made in conformity with the by-laws and/or regulations established from time to time by the Board of Directors.
17. The preparation or approval of the regulations or standard practices, required to assure compliance with orders of regulations issued by duly constituted governmental agencies.

Objective Type Questions

(A) Choose the correct answer to the following :

1. Financial accounting deals with :
(a) Determination of costs.
(b) Determination of profits.
(c) Determination of prices.

2. Financial accounts record only :
(a) Actual figures.
(b) Budgeted figures.
(c) Standard figures.

3. The use of management accounting is :
(a) Compulsory.
(b) Optional
(c) Obligatory

4. Going concern concept assumes :
(a) Business as a going concern.
(b) Business as a dissolving concern.
(c) Business on realising values.

5. The cost concept records the figures at :
(a) Market values :
(b) Actual amount paid.
(c) Actual amount or market value whichever is loss.

6. Businessentity concept distinguishes between :
(a) Individual and business.
(b) Business and business.
(c) Owners.

7. Accounting concepts are based on :
(a) Certain assumptions.
(b) Certain facts and figures.
(c) Certain accounting records.

8. The primary goal of management accounting is to :
(a) Interpret the financial data.
(b) Record all business transactions.
(c) Provide information for planning, decision-making etc.

Ans: **1.** (b) **2.** (a) **3.** (b) **4.** (a) **5.** (b)
6. (a) **7.** (b) **8.** (c)

(B) State whether the following statements are true or false :

1. Money measurement concept ignores qualitative aspects of things.
2. Convention of disclosure requires important information to be disclosed in statements.
3. The avoidance of insignificant things will not affect accounting results.
4. Going concern concept cannot be used when the life of the concern is certain.
5. Management accounting provides decisions to the management.
6. Management accounting deals only with that information which is useful to the management.
7. Management accounting deals with both quantitative and qualitative information.
8. Publication of management accounting statements is not compulsory.
9. In management accounting only those figures are used which can be measured in monetary terms.
10. Management accounting is concerned only with the present state of the business concern.

Ans: True : 3, 4, 6, 7 and 8
False : 1, 2, 5, 9 and 10.

THEORETICAL QUESTIONS

1. Describe the meaning of "Accounting Principles." What are their essential features ?
2. What do you understand by basic accounting concepts and conventions ? Describe important conventions in brief.
3. What is meant by "Accounting Entity ?" What is the necessity of assuming existence of this entity ?
4. What is the place of conservatism and consistency in accounting ?
5. "The convention of consistency is necessary for making the financial statements comparable." Discuss.
6. What are the limitations of accounting principles.
7. "While financial accounting is external, cost accounting is internal to the business." Explain. [*B.Com. Punjab*]
8. What is cost accounting ? State briefly the scope of cost accounting.
9. "Cost accounting is an aid to management." Discuss the main points in support of this statement."
10. Discuss the limitations of cost accounting. [*B.Com. Bangalore*]
11. Differentiate between financial accounting and cost accounting.
12. "Management Accounting is accounting for effective management." Explain this statement.
13. Explain the characteristic features of Management Accounting. [*B.Com. Saugar*]
14. Give an outline of the scope and objectives of Management Accounting.
15. Discuss the scope and importance of Management Accounting. How does it differ from Financial Accounting. [*B.Com. Delhi*]
16. List out the main tools of Management Accounting.
17. What are the functions of a Management Accountant ? [*B.Com. M.S.*]
18. Discuss the utility of Management Accounting.
19. Explain the importance of Management Accounting as a tool of management decision-making. [*M.Com. Madras*]
20. How does Management Accounting help planning and control functions in an organisation? [*B.Com. Madurai*]

21. What are the tools and techniques used in Management Accounting ?

22. Describe fully the limitations of Financial Accounting and point out how Management Accounting helps in overcoming them. [*B.Com. Bombay*]

23. Describe the limitations of Management Accounting. [*B.Com. Bombay*]

24. State the position you would recommend for the Management Accountant to occupy in the organisational structure.

25. "Management Accounting is the best tool for the management to achieve higher profits and efficient operations". Discuss. [*B.Com. Jabalpur*]

Chapter 2

Analysis and Interpretation of Financial Statements

Introduction; Balance Sheet; Title; Basic Divisions of Balance Sheet; Form of Balance Sheet; Balance Sheet Equation; Profit and Loss Account; Forms; Persons Interested in Financial Statement; Nature of Financial Statements; Limitation of Financial Statement; Essentials of Good Financial Statements; Analysis and Interpretation; Tools of Financial Analysis (Methods); Comparative Financial Statement; Procedure for Interpretation; Objectives of Analysis and Interpretation; Common Size Statement; Trend Analysis; Objective Type Questions; Theoretical Questions; Practical Problems.

Introduction

Shareholders, Managers, Tax Authorities and other interested groups seek answers to the following important questions about a firm :

* What is the financial position of the firm at a given point of time ?
* How did the firm perform financially over a given period of time ?

To answer the above questions, one has to prepare two major financial statements - the Balance Sheet and the Income Statement. The Balance Sheet shows the financial position or condition of the firm at a given point of time. It provides a snapshot and may be regarded as a static picture. The Income Statement or Profit and Loss Account reflects the performance of the firm over a period of time. In other words, "Financial Statements are prepared for the purpose of presenting a periodical review or report on the progress by the management and deal with (*a*) the status of investments in the business and (*b*) the results achieved during a period under review." The statement disclosing *status of investments* is known as Balance Sheet and the statement showing *the result* is known as Profit and Loss Account.

A firm communicates financial information to the users through financial statements and reports. The financial statements contains summarised information of the firm's financial affairs, organised systematically. They are means to present the firm's financial situation to users. The preparation of the financial statements is the responsibility of top management. The two basic financial statements prepared for the purpose are the two statements, that is, Balance Sheet and Profit and Loss Account. As these statements are used by investors and financial analysts to examine the firm's performance in order to make investment decisions, they should be prepared very carefully and contain as much information as possible.

Recently a number of schedules are also being used to supplement the data and information contained in the above statements. Thus, Schedule of Fixed Assets, Schedule of Debtors, Schedule of Creditors, Schedule of Reserves etc. are some of the schedules which are generally attached to the statements. The schedules are considered as part of the statements for the purpose of analysis and, in fact, they constitute the first step towards the analysis of certain data in financial statements. The financial statements are prepared from the accounting records maintained by the firm. The generally accepted accounting principles and procedures are followed to prepare these statements. It seems quite desirable to discuss the nature of each of the financial statements.

Balance Sheet

The Balance Sheet comprises of a list of assets, liabilities and capital at a given date. It is static in character because it tells about the financial position of a business as on a certain date. At the same time, business is dynamic while Balance Sheet is static. It records only periodic changes rather than continuous ones. More specifically, Balance Sheet contains information about resources and obligations of a business entity and about owners' interests in the business at a particular point of time. Thus, the Balance Sheet of a firm prepared on 31st December reveals the firm's financial position on this specific date. In simple language or in a layman's language, a Balance Sheet may be called as a statement of equality in which equality is established by representing assets values on one side and the values of liabilities and owners' fund on the other side of it. "The Balances Sheet is a statement which reports the property's value-owned by the enterprise and the claims of the creditors and owners against these properties". The amount of value is obtained by posting and balancing the individual accounts of each item.

Title

A Balance Sheet is called by different names. Generally the following titles are used in respect of a Balance Sheet :

1. Balance Sheet or General Balance Sheet
2. Statement of financial position or condition
3. Statement of Assets and Liabilities
4. Statement of Resources and Liabilities
5. Statement of Assets, Liabilities and Owners' Fund, etc.

However, the title "Balance Sheet" is mostly used. Let us look at a few definitions :

"Balance Sheet is a classified summary of the ledger balances remaining after closing all revenue items into the Profit and Loss Account." **—Cropper**

"The Balance Sheet is a statement which reports the values owned by the enterprise and the claims of the creditors and owners against these properties." **—Howard**

"Balance Sheet is a screen picture of the financial position of a going business at certain moment." **—Francis**

A clear and correct understanding of the basic divisions of the Balance Sheet and the meanings which they signify and the amount which they represent is very essential for the proper interpretation of financial statements. The various items of the Balance Sheet for the purpose of analysis may be grouped into the following categories :

Basic Divisions of Balance Sheet

Assets	*Liabilities*
1. Current Assets	1. Current Liabilities
2. Fixed Assets	2. Non-current Liabilities
3. Intangible Assets	3. Net Worth
4. Other Assets	
5. Deferred Expenditure	

The important functions served by a Balance Sheet are :

(1) It gives a concise summary of the firm's resources and liabilities and owners equity.

(2) It is a measure of the firm's liquidity.

(3) It is a measure of the firm's solvency.

A brief discussion regarding the meaning, nature and contents of various groups of Balance Sheet is given below :

1. Current Assets

"The goods of the merchant yield him no revenue profit till he sells them for money and the money yields him as little till it is again exchanged for goods." His capital is continuously going from him in one shape and returning to him in another and it is only by means of such circulation or successive exchanges that it can yield him any profit. Such a capital can be properly called circulating capital. The term Current Assets, in the words of Alexander Wall, "are such assets as in the ordinary and natural course of business move onward, through the various processes of production, distribution and payment for goods, until they become cash or its equivalent, by which debts may be rapidly and immediately paid." Current Assets are the assets acquired through cash and easily convertible into cash during the normal course of business. The normal course takes a period of one year. The accounting period is of one year duration. In other words, Current Assets are those resources of the firm which are either held in the form of cash or are expected to be converted into cash within the accounting period or the operating cycle of the business. The operating cycle is the time period which is taken to convert raw materials into finished goods, sell finished goods, and convert receivables into cash. All assets which are acquired for reselling during the course of business, are to be treated as Current Assets. For instance, furniture purchased by a furniture dealer will be treated as Current Asset : whereas furniture purchased by a hotel-owner will be treated as non-current asset. Thus, it is clear that the nature *i.e.,* current asset or non-current asset is to be decided with reference to its objective of acquisition and not to its name by which it has been termed in the accounting system. Generally, the operating cycle is equal to or less than the accounting period. The following are generally included in Current Assets :

1. Cash in hand and at Bank
2. Book debts (or Debtors or Accounts Receivables)
3. Bills Receivables (or Notes Receivables)
4. Stocks—Raw Materials, Work-in-progress, Finished Goods
5. Government and other marketable securities
6. Advance Payments

2. Fixed Assets

Fixed assets are those assets which are acquired for the purpose of using them in the conduct of business operations and not for reselling to earn profit. They are of such a nature that they will be used over a considerable period of time, and are not meant for resale. Since these are not for reselling, these assets are not readily convertible into cash in the normal course of business operations. Some examples of assets coming into the fixed asset categories are :

1. Land
2. Buildings
3. Plant, Machineries, Equipment etc.
4. Furniture and Fixtures
5. Leasehold Improvements etc.

The above list is not exhaustive one. A number of other assets may be included in the list, if they are acquired primarily for the purpose of continuous use in the business operations.

3. Intangible Assets

Fixed Assets may be either tangible or intangible. The tangible assets have a definite physical existence. They can be seen and can, if necessary, be sold separately. The intangible assets cannot be seen though their existence has some effect, often very material, on the profit-earning capacity of the business. While the tangible assets often have a value as things apart from their profit-earning capacity, the intangible assets usually have no physical value whatever. They are not available for the payment of the debts of a going concern. They depreciate greatly in case of liquidation. Intangible assets represent the firm's rights and include the following :

1. Patents and Trademarks
2. Copyright, Formula, Licence etc.
3. Goodwill etc.

Patents are the exclusive rights granted by the Government enabling the holder to control the use of an invention. *Copyrights* are the exclusive rights to reproduce and sell literary, musical and artistic works. *Franchises* are the contracts giving exclusive rights to perform certain functions or to sell certain services or products. *Goodwill* represents the excessive earning power of a firm due to special advantages that it possesses. Costs of intangible fixed assets are amortised over their useful lives.

4. Other Assets

All other assets which cannot be included in any of the above categories are grouped as Other Assets. These assets possess a tangible form but these are not directly used in the operations of business. Such assets may be :

1. Investments excluding marketable securities
2. Non-trade Debtors
3. Fund earmarked for assets.

5. Deferred Expenditures

There are certain expenditures which are not incurred repeatedly or which are not of recurring nature and which do not arise from the present operations. These expenditures contribute income or benefit in the future years also. These expenditures are written off gradually over several years of operations, treating each year's share in such expenditure as a charge on operational profit for that year. The amount of such expenditure not written off at a point of time is shown as an asset in the Balance Sheet at that point of time. Prepayments for services or benefits for period longer than the accounting period are referred to as deferred charges and include advertising expenditure, preliminary expenses etc.

6. Current Liabilities

Current liabilities include such debts and obligations or charges which are payable either at demand or within one year from the date of Balance Sheet. All short-term obligations generally due and payable within one year, are described as Current Liabilities. All long-term loans and borrowings may take the character of current liabilities as and when they become due for payment. Typical examples of current liabilities are :

1. Trade Creditors or Accounts Payables
2. Bills Payables or Notes Payables
3. Short-term Public Deposits
4. Outstanding or accruals

5. Short-term Loans
6. Bank overdraft but not bank loan
7. Provision for Taxes
8. Unclaimed Dividends
9. Current maturity of long-term debt due payable within the Period of the current year.

7. Non-Current Liabilities

These are also called Long-Term liability or debt. All such liabilities payable over a longer period of time, say after one year, are known as Non-current liabilities. Some examples of such liabilities are :

1. Loan on Mortgage
2. Debentures or Bonds
3. Bank Loan
4. Loans from Financial Institutions etc.

8. Net Worth

The financial interests of owners are called owners' equity. The owners' interest is residual in nature, reflecting the excess of the firm's assets over its liabilities. It has several names, such as Net Assets, Shareholders' Fund, Owners' Equity, Net Capital Employed etc. What remains after deducting all liabilities (both current and long-term) from total assets is called Net Worth or Shareholders' Fund. As liabilities are the claims of outside parties, owners' equity represents owners' claim against the business entity as of the Balance Sheet date. The nature of the owners' claim is not same as the claims of creditors. Creditors' claim are defined and have to be met within a specified period. The claim of owners changes and the amount payable to them can be determined only when the firm is liquidated. In the beginning stage, owners' equity arises on account of the funds invested by them. But it changes due to the earnings of the firm and their distribution. The firm's earnings (or losses) do not affect creditors' claims. Owners' equity will increase when the firm makes earnings and retains whole or a part of it. If the losses are incurred by the firm, owners' claim will be reduced. Shareholders' equity or capital has two parts (*i*) Paid up share capital, and (*ii*) Reserves and surplus (retained earnings), *i.e.,* representing undistributed profits.

1. Preference Share Capital
2. Equity Share Capital
3. General Reserve
4. Capital Reserve
5. Other Reserves and undistributed profits

Form of Balance Sheet

A Balance Sheet reflects the financial position of a firm. Balance Sheet can be prepared in the Account Form or the Report Form. The Account form of Balance Sheet has two sides. The right hand side lists the various assets and left hand side shows the liabilities and owners' equity. The total of the two sides are equal *i.e.,* Total Assets = Total Liabilities + Owners' Equity. The Balance Sheet does not convey anything very special, as the two sides must always balance.

In the Report Form of Balance Sheet, the figures should be arranged properly. Usually instead of two-columns (T Form) statement as ordinarily prepared, the statement is prepared in single-vertical column form. A specimen is given below :

Report Form of Balance Sheet

Balance Sheet As On.......

Last Year				
	NET ASSETS EMPLOYED :			
	Fixed Assets	—		
	Less: Depreciation	—		—
	Investments at cost			
	Current Assets			
	Cash	—		
	Bank	—		
	Sundry Debtors			
	Less : Reserve	—		
	Stock	—		
	Bills Receivable	—	—	
	Less: Current Liabilities :			
	Sundry Creditors	—		
	Bills Payable	—		
	Provisions	—		
	Others	—	—	—
	TOTAL			—
	Equity Funds:			
	Share Capital		—	
	Reserves & Surplus		—	—
	Loan Funds:			
	Debentures		—	
	Loan Funds		—	—
	TOTAL			—

Balance Sheet Equation

Both sides of the Balance Sheet should be equal. That is, the assets must be equal to liabilities plus owners' capital. We can express this equality of the Balance Sheet in an equation form. The equation is known as Balance Sheet Equation, also known as Accounting Equation. The relationship can be expressed in the following equation.

Total Assets = Total Liabilities + Owners' Equity

We have noted earlier that Owners' Equity is a residue *i.e.,* it is the difference between assets and liabilities. Thus :

Total Assets – Total Liabilities = Owners' Equity

We can obtain more equations if we elaborate the above equation. For instance,

Liquid Assets = Current Assets – Stock of all types

Working Capital = Current Assets – Current Liabilities

Capital Employed = Total Assets – Current Liabilities

The equation can be technically stated as "for every debit there is an equivalent credit." As a matter of fact the entire system of double entry book-keeping is based on this concept.

Profit and Loss Account

The Balance Sheet, as we know it, is a pictorial presentation of the financial health of a business on a certain date. "It fails to indicate whether a concern is making or losing money." This financial statement merely indicates the resources and liabilities of a business enterprise at a particular date. In short, the Balance Sheet is nothing but a snapshot of the financial condition of a business at a given moment. But every transaction has immediate and direct impact on the items of the Balance Sheet and items do change due to this impact.

The earning capacity and potential of the firm are reflected by the Income Statement *i.e.*, Profit and Loss Account. The Profit and Loss Account is the "Score-board" of the firm's performance during a particular period of time. The Profit and Loss Account may also be called by various names, such as :

1. Statement of Income and Earned Surplus
2. Income Statement
3. Statement of Revenue and Expenses
4. Profit and Loss Account
5. Operating Statement etc.

The Profit and Loss Account presents the summary of revenues, expenses and net income or net loss of a firm for a period of time. It serves as a measure of the firm's profitability. Net income which is an indicator of the firm's profitable operations, is the amount by which the revenues earned during a period exceed the expenses incurred during that period. If the firm's operations prove to be unprofitable, total expenses will exceed total revenues and the difference is referred to as net loss. Revenues are the amounts which the customers pay to the firm for providing them the goods and services. Profit and Loss Account is an explanation of the impact of profit-seeking operations on shareholders' equity. The statement of Profit or Loss is the condensed and classified record of the gains or losses causing changes in the owners' interest in the business for a period of time. A comparison of earnings and expenses incurred in the earning of those incomes is made in this statement and the difference between the two is known as net profit or loss. The Indian Companies Act 1956 fails to prescribe any legal proforma for Profit and Loss Account, as it has prescribed for Balance Sheet. As a result, the Profit and Loss Account is being prepared in varying form due to diversity in the nature of industry and also in business interest. Again Profit and Loss Account in the statement form can be prepared in two ways for the purpose of analysis.

(a) Single Step Form

In Single Step Form records all revenues (Operating or non-operating) and all expenses (operating or non-operating) in one stroke. The items of revenues and expenses are not grouped into distinct heads or sub-heads. A specimen is given below :

Statement of Revenues and Expenses

Revenues:	*Rs.*	*Rs.*
Sales	—	
Interest on Securities	—	
Dividends	—	
Miscellaneous	—	
		—
Less: Expenses :		
Deducted from Revenues :		
Cost of Goods sold	—	
Administrative Expenses	—	
Selling & Distribution	—	
Financial Expenses	—	
Interest on Debenture	—	
Tax Provisions etc.	—	—
Net Profit (+)/Net Loss (–)		—

(b) Multi Step Method

Multistep income statement gives more useful information. Each item of revenue and expenses are considered step by step. It makes a distinction between operating revenue and non-operating revenue. This method of preparing the statement of incomes and expenses are much useful for the purposes of analysis and interpretation. A specimen is given below:

Operating Income Statement for the period ending.....

	Rs.	Rs.
Gross Sales	—	
Less: Returns	—	
Net Sales for the year (A)		—
Less: Cost of Sales: (B)		
Raw Materials consumed	—	
Direct Wages	—	
Manufacturing Expenses	—	
Finished Goods etc.	—	
Total	—	—
Less: Closing Stock		—
Gross Profit (A) – (B) = (C)		—
Less: Operating Expenses (D)		
Administration	—	
Selling & Distribution	—	—
Net Operating Profit (C) – (D) = (E)		—
Add: Non-Trading Income:		
Interest Received	—	
Dividend Received	—	—
Less: Non-trading expenses:		
Discount Allowed	—	
Interest Paid	—	—
Earning before Interest & Tax (F)		
Less: Interest on Debentures etc.		—
Earning before Tax (G)		—
Less: Tax		—
Net Profit after Interest & Tax (H)		—
Appropriation:		
Dividends	—	
Transfer to Reserve	—	
Balance to Balance Sheet	—	
Total (H)	—	

Steps :

1. Items of operating revenue (sales minus returns) and cost of goods sold are considered first, which gives gross profit or gross margin. That is, Gross Profit = Sales minus Cost of goods sold.
2. Secondly, all operating expenses are deducted from Gross Profit and the difference is known as operating profit. (Operating expenses consisting of general, administrative, selling and depreciation).
3. Thirdly, non-operating incomes as addition and non-operating expenses as deduction are taken up to the operating profit. This gives net profit before tax.

4. Fourthly, provision for tax and interest are deducted from the Net Profit and the balance is known as Net Profit after tax and interest.

The Profit and Loss Account upto net operating profit may be expressed in equation form, thus :

Gross Profit = Sales – Cost of Goods Sold

Net Operating profit = Gross Profit – Operating Expenses

Net Operating profit = Sales – (Cost of Sales + Operating Expenses)

Sales – Net Operating Profit = Cost of Sales + Operating Expenses

Sales = Cost of Sales + Operating Expenses + Net Operating Expenses

Financial statements are the result of accounting process involves recording, classifying and summarising business transactions. Financial statements are organised, collection of data according to logical and consistent accounting procedures. Its purpose is to convey an understanding of some financial aspect of a business firm.

Persons Interested in Financial Statement

The following are the groups who like to make use of financial statements :

(1) Owners : The owners provide funds or capital for the organisation. They possess curiosity in knowing whether the business is being conducted on sound lines or not and whether the capital is being employed properly or not. Owners, being businessmen, always keep an eye on the returns from the investment. Comparing the accounts of various years helps in getting good pieces of information.

(2) Management : The management of the business is greatly interested in knowing the position of the firm. The accounts are the basis, on which the management can study the merits and demerits of the business activity. Thus, the management is interested in financial statements to find whether the business carried on is profitable or not. The financial statements are the "eyes and ears of management and facilitate in drawing future course of action, further expansion etc."

(3) Creditors : Creditors are the persons who supply goods on credit, or bankers or lenders of money. It is usual that these groups are interested to know the financial soundness before granting credit. The progress and prosperity of the firm, to which credits are extended, are largely watched by creditors from the point of view of security and further credit. Profit and Loss Account and Balance Sheet are nerve centres to know the soundness of the firm.

(4) Employees : Payment of bonus depends upon the size of profit earned by the firm. The more important point is that the workers expect regular income for the bread. The demand for wage rise, bonus, better working conditions etc., depend upon the profitability of the firm and in turn depend upon financial position. For these reasons, this group is interested in financial statements.

(5) Investors : The prospective investors, who want to invest their money in a firm, of course wish to see the progress and prosperity of the firm, before investing their money, by going through the financial statement of the firm. This is to safeguard the investment. For this purpose, this group is eager to go through the accounting statements which enable them to know the safety of investment.

(6) Government : Government keeps a close watch on the firm which yield good amount of profits. The state and central governments are interested in the financial statements to know the earnings for the purpose of taxation. At present most of the business concerns are organised and operated in the form of Joint Stock Companies. One of the main features of company form of organisation is that there is distinction between providers of capital and those entrusted with the actual operation and the management of the business. Just to safeguard the interest of former class, the government is interested in the financial statements.

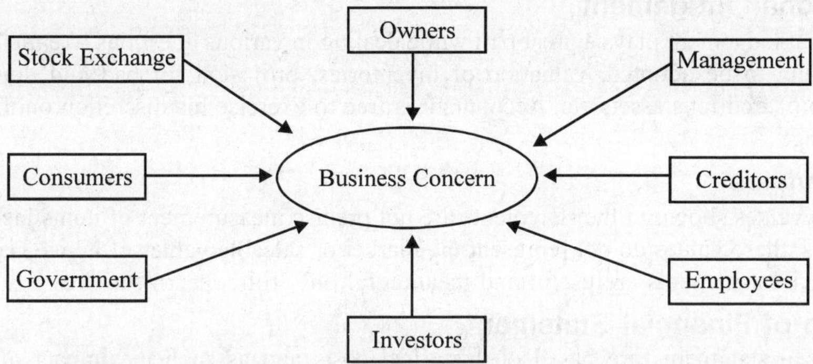

Users of financial information relating to a business organisation

(7) Consumers : These groups are interested in getting the goods at reduced price. Therefore, they wish to know the establishment of proper accounting control, which in turn will reduce the cost of production, in turn less price to be paid by the consumers. Researchers are also interested for interpretation.

(8) Stock Exchange : The financial statements are the blue prints of financial affairs. These statements facilitate the stock exchange to protect the investors' interests or to watch as a watch-dog of corporate investors.

Professional societies like Chambers of Commerce, Indian Accounting Associations, Employers' Association, Banks, Financial institutions etc. are deeply interested in such statements of business concerns.

Nature of Financial Statements

Financial statements are prepared for the purpose of presenting a periodical review or report on progress by the management and deal with the status of investment in the business and the results achieved during the period under review. According to the American Institute of Certified Public Accountants, financial statements reflect "a combination of recorded facts, accounting conventions and personal judgements and the judgements and conventions applied affect them materially." This implies that data exhibited in the financial statements are affected by recorded facts, accounting conventions and personal judgements.

(a) Recorded Facts

Record is made only of those facts which can be expressed in monetary terms. Facts which have not been recorded in the financial books are not depicted in the financial statements. Thus, the recorded facts consist of such data as the amount of cash on hand and in the bank, the amount due from customers, the cost of fixed assets, the amounts payable to creditors etc. As the price level *i.e.,* cost, as on the date of acquiring fixed assets is, as a rule, stated in the accounts rather than the replacement cost; the Balance Sheet does not show the financial position of a business in terms of current economic conditions though, in some cases, appraised values might be substituted for cost. Certain factors which may affect the financial position of a business, are not shown in the accounting records. Such items—purchase and sale contracts, claims for refunds, guarantee etc. appear as footnotes to Balance Sheet.

(b) Accounting Conventions

In spite of the accounting standards laid down by the various accounting bodies, managements of concerns are free to choose an accounting policy suited to their concern. Accounting policies differ with regard to valuation of inventory, depreciation, research, development etc. Further provision is made for expected losses but expected profits are ignored.

(c) Personal Judgement

Personal judgement plays a great part while dealing in various questions like method and rate of depreciation to be adopted, valuation of inventories, provision for bad and doubtful debts, amortization of fictitious assets etc. Accountant is free to exercise his discretion on many matters on accounting.

(d) Postulates

Rupee values shown in the statements are not precise measurement of items incorporated in them. That is, these values do not represent the market or saleable values of items. Data disclosed by the financial statements are useful and meaningful only till concern survives.

Limitation of Financial Statement

Financial statements are based on historical costs and as such the impact of price level changes is completely ignored. They are interim reports. The basic nature of financial statements is historic. These statements are neither complete nor exact. They reflects only monetary transactions of a business. The statements furnish only information and that too in the form of figures. Figures won't speak in themselves and it is the duty of the analyst to make these figures speak of good or bad of the business affairs. Generally the following limitations may be noted :

1. The financial position of a business concern is affected by several factors—economic, social and financial, but only financial factors are being recorded in these financial statements. Economic and social factors are left out. Thus the financial position disclosed by these statement is not correct and accurate.
2. The profit revealed by the Profit and Loss Account and the financial position disclosed by the Balance Sheet cannot be exact: they are essentially interim reports. Exact position can be known when the business is liquidated *i.e.,* after it has put down its shutters.
3. Facts which have not been recorded in the financial books are not depicted in the financial statements. Only quantitative factors are taken into account. But qualitative factors—such as reputation and prestige of the business with the public, the efficiency and loyalty of its employees, integrity of management etc. which are equally important for the business success, are not capable of being translated in terms of money, and as such, they do not appear in the financial statements.
4. The rupee of 2007, as for example, does not mean the same as the rupee of 2009 or the rupee of 2010. The existing accounting system results in over-statement of profits in times of inflation and under-statement in depression. The existing historical accounting is based on the assumption that the value of monetary unit, say rupee, remains constant and accordingly assets are recorded by the business at the price at which they are acquired and the liabilities are recorded at the amounts at which they are contracted for. But monetary unit is never stable under inflationary conditions. This instability has resulted in a number of distortions in the financial statements and is the most serious limitation of historical accounting. The price level changes are not taken into account and as such financial statements prepared on a historical cost basis fail to give realistic and correct picture of the state of affairs of a firm.
5. Many items are left to the personal judgement of the accountant. For instance, provision of depreciation, stock valuation, bad debts provision etc. depend on the personal judgement of accountant.
6. On account of convention of conservation the income statement may not disclose true income of the business since probable losses are considered while probable incomes are ignored.
7. The fixed assets are shown at cost less depreciation on the basis of "going concern concept." But the value placed on the fixed assets may not be the same which may be realised on their sale.

8. The data contained in the financial statements are dumb; they do not speak themselves. It is also worth while to note that human judgement is always involved in the interpretation of statements. It is the analyst or user who provides tongue to those data and make them to speak. It rarely happens that the users of financial statements may have the same opinion and meaning in respect of a particular accounting figure.
9. Information conveyed by these statements may not be comparable on account of difference between dates of preparation of these statements. Different methods of accounting followed by different concerns or difference in the nature of business of different concerns etc. may render the financial statements of two concerns impossible or difficult for the purpose of comparison.

Essentials of Good Financial Statements

Different parties have interest in the financial statements with different objectives. It may not be possible to the concerns to construct the statements to suit every interested person. However, such statements should have atleast the following essentials :

1. Figures which are incorporated in financial statements, should be readily and easily available from the books of accounts of the concern. The size of the form of financial statements should not be abnormally too large.
2. The form should not be complex in nature. The various terms used should be in simple and common language. The form should have suitable columns for additions and deductions and it must arrest and retain the attention of users.
3. It must facilitate easy comparison. In addition to the figures of previous years, it is also essential that uniformity in the form is maintained from year to year. This is for easy comparison.
4. The form and contents of the form should be designed in such a way that the attention of the readers is automatically drawn and directed to most significant items.
5. All facts should be presented in such a way that required items and figures are easily obtained for calculating various accounting ratios, to be used by the analysts.
6. The information contained in the financial statements should be such that a true and correct idea is taken about the financial position of the concern.
7. The comparable figures will make the statements more useful. The results of financial analysis should be in a way that can be compared to the previous years' statements. The comparison of the figures will enable a proper assessment for the working of the concern.

Analysis and Interpretation

Financial statements are prepared primarily for decison-making. The statements are not an end in themselves, but are useful in decision making. Financial analysis is the process of determining the significant operating and financial characteristics of a firm from accounting data. The profit and Loss Account and Balance Sheet are indicators of two significant factors—Profitability and Financial Soundness. Analysis of statement means such a treatment of the information contained in the two statements as to afford a full diagnosis of the profitability and financial position of the firm concerned. Financial statement analysis is largely a study of relationship among the various financial factors in a business as disclosed by a single set of statements and a study of the trends of these factors as shown in a series of statements. The main function of financial analysis is the pinpointing of the strength and weakness of a business undertaking by regrouping and analysis of figures contained in the financial statements, by making comparisons of various components and examining their content. The financial statements are the best media of documenting the results of managerial efforts to the owners of the business, its employees, its customers and the public at large, and thus become excellent tools of the public relations.

Anaylsis includes : (*a*) Breaking financial statements into simpler ones, (*b*) Regrouping, (*c*) Rearranging the figures given in financial statements and (*d*) Finding out ratios and percentages. Thus all process which help in drawing certain results from the financial statements are included in analysis. The data provided in the financial statements should be methodically classified and compared with figures of previous period or other similar firms. Thereafter, the significance of the figures is established. The work of an accountant in making analysis of financial statements is the same as that of a pathologist, who takes a drop of blood and analyse it to point out its various components and gives a report on the basis of his analysis. Similarly, an accountant makes analysis of each item appearing in financial statements and then gives a report on the basis of his analysis. Analysis only establishes a relationship between various amounts mentioned in Balance Sheet and Profit and Loss Account. After making analysis of the financial statements, the next step is to use mind for forming an opinion about the enterprise. This is the interpretation stage. The technique is called "Analysis and Interpretation" of financial statements. Analysis consists in breaking down a complex set of facts or figures into simple elements. Interpretation, on the other hand, consists in explaining the real significance of these simplified statements. Interpretation includes both analysis and criticism.

To interpret means to put the meaning of statement into simple terms for the benefit of a person. Interpretation is to explain in such a simple language the financial position and earning capacity of the company which may be understood even by a layman, who does not know accounting. The analysis and interpretation of financial statements requires a comprehensive and intelligent understanding of their nature and limitations as well as the determination of the monetary valuation of the items. The analyst must grasp what represent sound and unsound relationship reflected by the financial statements. Interpretation is impossible without analysis. "Interpretation is not possible without analysis and without interpretation analysis has no value". Analysis and interpretation act as a bridge between the art of recording and reporting financial information and the act of using this information. Analysis refers to the process of fact finding and breaking down complex set of figures into simple components while interpretation stands for explaining the real significance of these simplified components. Interpretation is a mental process based on analysis and criticism.

George O. May points out the following uses of financial statements :

1. As a report of stewardship;
2. As a basis for fiscal policy;
3. To determine the legality of dividends;
4. As a guide to advise dividend action;
5. As a basis for granting of credit;
6. As informative for prospective investors in an enterprise;
7. As a guide to the value of investment already made;
8. As an aid to Government supervision;
9. As a basis for price or rate regulation;
10. As a basis for taxation.

Tools of Financial Analysis (Methods)

A financial analyst can adopt the following tools for analysis of the financial statements : These are also termed as methods of financial analysis.

1. Comparative Financial Statements
2. Common Size Statements
3. Trend Ratios or Trend Analysis

4. Statement of changes in Working Capital
5. Fund Flow and Cash Flow Analysis
6. Ratio Analysis

The first three methods are discussed in this chapter. Remaining methods have been discussed in separate chapters.

COMPARATIVE FINANCIAL STATEMENT

The preparation of comparative financial and operating statement is an important device of horizontal financial analysis. As their very name suggests, comparative financial statements are statements of the financial position of a business so designed as to provide time perspective to the consideration of various elements of financial position embodied in such statements. Generally, Balance Sheet and Income Statement which alone are prepared in a comparative form because they are the most important statements of financial position. In these statements figures for two or more periods are placed side by side to facilitate comparison. These statements render comparison between two periods of time and exhibit the magnitude and direction of historical changes in the operating results and financial status of a business. Financial statements of two or more firms may also be compared for drawing inferences. This is known as inter-firm comparison. The statement also provides for columns to indicate the change from one year to another in absolute terms and also in percentage form.

Procedure for Interpretation

1. Ascertain the purpose and the extent of analysis and interpretation.
2. Study the available data contained in financial statements.
3. Get additional information, if needed.
4. Arrange the data in useful manner.
5. Prepare comparative statements, ratios etc.
6. Interpret the facts revealed by the analysis.
7. The interpretation drawn from the analysis are presented.

Objectives of Analysis and Interpretation

The following are the main objectives of analysis and interpretation of financial statements :

1. To estimate the earning capacity of the firm.
2. To assess the financial position of the firm.
3. To decide about the future prospects of the firm.
4. To know the progress of the firm.
5. To judge the solvency of the firm.
6. To measure the efficiency of operations.
7. To determine debt capacity of the firm.
8. To assess the financial performance of the firm.
9. To have comparative study.
10. To help in making future plans.

Past performance is often a good indicator of future performance. The decision makers are futuristic and are always concerned with the future. Financial statements which contain information on past performances are analysed and interpreted as a basis for forecasting future rates of return and for assessing risks. The trends of past sales, expenses, net income, return on investment etc. offer a means for judging management's past performance and are possible indicators of future performance. The analysis of current position shows where the business stands today. Managers may use the ratios prediction model to assess the solvency position of their firms and thus they can take appropriate corrective actions.

Analysis of financial statements should always be tuned to the objective. People use financial statements for satisfying their particular curiosity. Financial accounts are interpreted by different persons in different ways according to their objects. For instance same financial statement may be very good for one : ordinarily good for the other and worst for the third. This is because their views and objects of interpretation differ. For instances : (1) A prospective shareholder would like to know whether the business is profitable and is progressing on sound lines. (2) A supplier who would like to transact business with the firms may be interested in the company's ability to honour its short-term commitments. (3) A financier would like to be satisfied with safety and reliability of return on his investment. Thus, the object of the analysis determine the extent, depth and nature of analysis. The following illustrations make clear understanding :

Illustration 1

From the following Profit and Loss Account and Balance Sheet of Ramco Ltd. for the year ended 2009 and 2010, you are required to prepare a comparative income statement and a comparative Balance Sheet.

PROFIT AND LOSS ACCOUNT

	2009	*2010*		*2009*	*2010*
	Rs.	Rs.		Rs.	Rs.
To Cost of Goods sold	6,000	7,500	By Net Sales	8,000	10,000
To Operating Expenses :					
Administrative	200	200			
Selling	300	400			
To Net Profit	1,500	1,900			
	8,000	10,000		8,000	10,000

BALANCE SHEET as on 31st December

	2009	*2010*		*2009*	*2010*
Bills Payable	500	750			
Sundry Creditors	1,500	2,000	Cash	1,000	1,400
Tax Payable	1,000	1,500	Debtors	2,000	3,000
6% Debentures	1,000	1,500	Stock	2,000	3,000
10% Preference Capital	3,000	3,000	Land	1,000	1,000
Equity Capital	4,000	4,000	Buildings	3,000	2,700
Reserves	2,000	2,450	Plant	3,000	2,700
			Furniture	1,000	1,400
	13,000	15,200		13,000	15,200

(*B.Com. MS*)

Solution:

RAMCO Limited
COMPARATIVE INCOME STATEMENT
For the years ended 31st Dec. 2009 and 2010

	2009	*2010*	*Increase (+) or Decrease (–)*	
			Absolute 2010	*Percentage 2010*
Net Sales	8,000	10,000	+ 2,000	+ 25
Less :Cost of goods sold	6,000	7,500	+ 1,500	+ 25
Gross Profit	2,000	2,500	+ 500	+ 25
Less :Operating Expenses:				
Administrative	200	200	—	—
Selling	300	400	+ 100	+ 33.3
Total Operating Expenses	500	600	+ 100	+ 20
Operating Profit	1,500	1,900	+ 400	+ 26.7

The above statement shows that though the sales have gone up in 2010, the rate of gross profit remains at 25%. The cost of goods sold and its percentage remains at 75%. Administrative expenses remains the same, but selling expenses have been increased. This is due to the increase in sales. The rate of net profit is also increased.

RAMCO Ltd.
COMPARATIVE BALANCE SHEET
As on 31st Dec. 2009 and 2010

	2009	*2010*	*Increase (+) or Decrease (–)*	
			Absolute 2010	*Percentage 2010*
Assets:				
Current Assets :				
Cash	1,000	1,400	+ 400	+ 40
Debtors	2,000	3,000	+ 1,000	+ 50
Stock	2,000	3,000	+ 1,000	+ 50
Total Current Assets :	5,000	7,400	+ 2,400	+ 48
Fixed Assets :				
Land	1,000	1,000	—	—
Buildings	3,000	2,700	– 300	– 10
Plant	3,000	2,700	– 300	– 10
Furniture	1,000	1,400	+ 400	+ 40
Total Fixed Assets	8,000	7,800	– 200	– 2.5
Total Assets	13,000	15,200	+ 2,200	+ 17
Liabilities and Capital				
Current Liabilities :				
Bills Payable	500	750	+ 250	+ 50
Sundry Creditors	1,500	2,000	+ 500	+ 33.3

Taxes Payable	1,000	1,500	+ 500	+ 50
Total Current Liabilities	3,000	4,250	+ 1250	+ 41.7
Long-term Liabilities :				
6% Debentures	1,000	1,500	+ 500	+ 50
Total Liabilities	4,000	5,750	+ 1,750	+ 43.75
Capital and Reserves :				
10% Preference Capital	3,000	3,000	—	—
Equity Capital	4,000	4,000	—	—
Reserves	2,000	2,450	+ 450	+ 22.5
Total Shareholders Funds	9,000	9,450	+ 450	5
Total Liabilities and Capital	13,000	15,200	2,200	17

Common Size Statement

Financial statements when read with absolute figures are not easily understandable. They are even misleading. Each item of assets is converted into percentage to Total Assets and each item of Capital and Liabilities is expressed to Total Liabilities and Capital Fund. Thus the whole Balance Sheet is converted into percentage form. Such converted Balance Sheet is known as Common-Size Balance Sheet. When Balance Sheets of the same concern for several years or when Balance Sheets of two or more than two concerns for the same year are converted into percentage form and presented as such, they are known as Comparative Common-Size Balance Sheets. Again, in Profit and Loss Account Sales figure is assumed to be equal to 100 and all other figures are expressed as percentage to sales. Similarly, in Balance Sheet the total of assets or liabilities is taken as 100 and all the figures are expressed as percentage of the total.

Illustration 2

The following is the Profit and Loss Account of Sun Ltd. for 2009 and 2010 :

PROFIT AND LOSS ACCOUNT
for the year ended 31st December

	2009	*2010*		*2009*	*2010*
	Rs.	*Rs.*		*Rs.*	*Rs.*
To Cost of Sales	4,63,250	4,83,899	By Sales	7,21,456	8,34,250
To Administrative			*Less*: Returns	11,588	13,903
Expenses	46,531	54,137		7,09,868	8,20,347
To Selling Expenses	91,823	1,15,632	By Other		
			Incomes :		
To Interest Paid	4,275	3,500	Interests	3,795	2,620
To Loss on sale			Discounts	4,250	3,792
of fixed items	1,254	350	Profit on sale		
			(Land)	3,000	—
To Income Tax	43,038	80,390			
To Net Profit	70,742	88,851			
	7,20,913	8,26,759		7,20,913	8,26,759

Prepare the above data in a suitable comparative form both in absolute way and in common size.

(*B.Com. Madurai*)

Solution :

(*a*) COMPARATIVE PROFIT AND LOSS ACCOUNT

	2009 *Rs.*	*2010* *Rs.*	*Increase (+)/Decrease (–)*	
			Amount *Rs.*	*%*
Sales	7,21,456	8,34,250	+ 1,12,794	+ 15.7
Less : Returns	11,588	13,903	+ 2,315	+ 20.0
	7,09,868	8,20,347	+ 1,10,479	+ 15.6
Less : Cost of sales	4,63,250	4,83,899	+ 20,649	+ 4.5
Gross Margin	2,46,618	3,36,448	+ 89,830	+ 36.4
Less : Administrative Expenses	46,531	54,137	+ 7,606	+ 16.3
Balance	2,00,087	2,82,311	+ 82,224	+ 41.0
Less: Selling Expenses	91,823	1,15,632	+ 23,809	+ 25.9
Net operating profit	1,08,264	1,66,679	+ 58,415	+ 54.0
Add : Other Incomes	11,045	6,412	– 4,633	– 42.0
	1,19,309	1,73,091	+ 53,782	+ 45.0
Less: Other Expenses	5,529	3,850	–1,679	– 30.0
Net profit before tax	1,13,780	1,69,241	+ 55,461	+ 48.7
Less: Tax	43,038	80,390	+ 37,352	+ 86.8
Net profit after tax	70,742	88,851	+ 18,109	+ 25.6

(*b*) COMPARATIVE COMMON SIZE PROFIT AND LOSS ACCOUNT

	2009		*2010*	
	Amount	*%* *Rs.*	*Amount*	*%* *Rs.*
Sales	7,21,456	101.6	8,34,250	101.7
Less: Returns	11,588	1.6	13,903	1.7
Net Sales	7,09,868	100.0	8,20,347	100.0
Less: Cost of Sales	4,63,250	65.3	4,83,899	59.0
Gross Margin	2,46,618	34.7	3,36,448	41.0
Less: Administrative Expenses	46,531	6.5	54,137	6.6
Balance	2,00,087	28.2	2,82,311	34.4
Less: Selling Expenses	91,823	12.9	1,15,632	14.0
Net Operating Profit	1,08,264	15.3	1,66,679	20.4
Add: Other Incomes	11,045	1.6	6,412	0.7
	1,19,309	16.9	1,73,091	21.1
Less: Other expenses	5,529	0.8	3,850	0.5
Net Profit before Tax	1,13,780	16.1	1,69,241	20.6
Less: Income Tax	43,038	6.0	80,390	9.8
Net Profit After Tax	70,742	10.1	88,851	10.8

Illustration 3

From the following Balance Sheet, prepare a Common-size statement :

	2009	*2010*
Assets :	*Rs.*	*Rs.*
Cash	27,000	31,500
Debtors	2,20,000	2,11,000

Stock	1,00,000	1,26,000
Prepaid Expenses	11,000	21,000
Bills Receivables	10,000	10,500
Fixed Assets	6,35,000	6,50,000
	10,03,000	10,50,000
Liabilities & Capital:		
Share Capital	6,58,000	7,00,000
Long-term Debt	2,25,000	2,00,000
Sundry Creditors	42,000	50,000
Other Liabilities	78,000	1,00,000
	10,03,000	10,50,000

(*B.Com. MS*)

Solution :

COMPARATIVE COMMON-SIZE BALANCE SHEET

	2009	*2010*
Assets :		
Current Assets :		
Cash	2.7	3.0
Debtors	21.9	20.1
Stock	10.0	12.0
Prepaid Expenses	1.1	2.0
Bills Receivables	1.0	1.0
Total Current Assets	36.7	38.1
Fixed Assets	63.3	61.9
Total Assets	100.0	100.0
Liabilities & Capital :		
Current Liabilities:		
Sundry Creditors	4.2	4.8
Other Liabilities	7.8	9.5
Total Current Liabilities	12.0	14.3
Long-Term Liabilities :		
Long Term Debt	22.4	19.0
Capital & Reserves :	34.4	33.3
Share Capital	65.6	66.7
Total Liabilities & Capital :	100.0	100.0

Illustration 4

The summary of Balance Sheet data in respect of A Ltd. and B Ltd. is as under :

	A Ltd.	*B Ltd.*
	Rs.	*Rs.*
Buildings	1,00,000	4,50,000
Machinery	3,00,000	7,50,000
Share Capital	4,50,000	14,50,000
Retained Earnings	50,000	33,000
Debtors	1,15,000	1,60,000
Stocks	60,000	2,17,000
Cash	10,000	5,000
Prepaid Expenses	5,000	3,000

Creditors	91,000	1,00,000
Liability for Expenses	9,000	17,000
Preliminary Expenses	10,000	15,000

Prepare Common-size Balance Sheets

Solution :

COMPARATIVE COMMON-SIZE BALANCE SHEETS

	A Ltd.	*B Ltd.*
Assets :		
Current Assets :		
Cash	1.7	0.3
Debtors	19.1	10.0
Prepaid Expenses	0.8	0.2
Stocks	10.0	13.6
Total Current Assets	31.6	24.1
Fixed Assets :		
Buildings	16.7	28.1
Machinery	50.0	46.9
	98.3	99.1
Preliminary Expenses	1.7	0.9
Total Assets	100.0	100.0
Liabilities and Capital :		
Current Liabilities		
Creditors	15.2	6.3
Liability for Expenses	1.5	1.0
Total Current Liabilities	16.7	7.3
Capital and Reserves :		
Share Capital	75.0	90.6
Retained Earnings	8.3	2:1
Total Capital & Reserves	83.3	92.7
Total Liabilities & Capital	100.0	100.0

Trend Analysis

The Comparative and Common-size statements suffer from a major limitation *i.e.,* absence of a basic standard to indicate whether the proportion of an item is normal or abnormal. Trend analysis overcomes this limitation. This method is also an important and useful technique of financial statement analysis. The calculation of trend ratio involves the ascertainment of arithmetical relationship which each item of several years to the same item of base year. Thus, one particular year out of many years is taken as base. The value of one particular item out of several items shown in the financial statements are converted into ratio or percentage taking of that item in base year as equal to 100.

Illustration 5

From the following data relating to the purchase of a firm, prepare Trend Percentages and Trend Ratios.

Year	*Purchases ('00,000)* *Rs.*
2005	1,672
2006	1,789

2007	1,873
2008	1,923
2009	2,123
2010	1,463

Solution :

(a) Trend Percentages :

Year	*Decrease/Increase (in %)* *(Base Year = 2005)*
2005	—
2006	+ 7
2007	+ 12
2008	+ 15
2009	+ 27
2010	– 12.5

The above type of analysis cannot be regarded as good in the sense that it contains plus and minus signs. A better way will be to express the figures for each year as a percentage to the value of base year.

(b) Trend Ratios :

Year	*Trend Ratios (in %)*
2005	100
2006	107
2007	112
2008	115
2009	127
2010	87.5

Illustration 6

From the following figures, compute trend percentage and comment, using 2005 as the base year :

('000)

Year	*Sales*	*Cost of goods sold*	*Profit before tax*
	Rs.	*Rs.*	*Rs.*
2005	600	360	120
2006	680	414	138
2007	840	512	186
2008	960	574	204
2009	1040	600	228
2010	1200	666	300

(*B. Com. MS*)

Solution :

TREND PERCENTAGE (Base year : 2005)

('000)

Year	Sales		Cost of goods sold		Profit before Tax	
	in Rs.	*Trend %*	*in Rs.*	*Trend %*	*in Rs.*	*Trend %*
2005	600	100	360	100	120	100
2006	680	113	414	115	138	115
2007	840	140	512	142	186	155

2008	960	160	574	159	204	170
2009	1040	173	600	167	228	190
2010	1200	200	666	185	300	250

Comments :

1. There is steady growth in sales and profit before tax, after the base year.
2. The increase in sales and profit is satisfactory. The increase in profit is more than proportionate to the increase in sales. A minute study of trend shows that the profitability is sound.

(A) Choose the correct answer to the following :

1. Financial accounts provide a summary of :
(a) Assets.
(b) Liabilities.
(c) Accounts.

2. Financial statements are :
(a) Estimates of facts.
(b) Recorded facts.
(c) Anticipated facts.

3. Retained earnings statements depicts :
(a) Appropriation of profits.
(b) Estimated profits.
(c) Estimated costs.

4. The term current assets does not include :
(a) Payments in advance.
(b) Bills Receivables.
(c) Long term deferred charges.

5. The fixed assets include :
(a) Stock-in-trade.
(b) Furniture.
(c) Payments in advance.

6. Operating profit to sales gives us :
(a) Gross Profit Ratio.
(b) Net Profit Ratio.
(c) Operating profit ratio.

7. Financial statements convey to different parties :
(a) Financial information.
(b) Market information.
(c) Price information.

8. The tools of financial statement analysis are :
(a) Comparative financial statement.
(b) Commonsize statement.
(c) Trend ratio.
(d) All these.

Ans: **1.** (c) **2.** (b) **3.** (a) **4.** (c) **5.** (b) **6.** (c) **7.** (a) **8.** (d)

(B) State whether the following statements are true or false.

1. Financial statements are prepared on the basis of realisable values.
2. A company is required to public its accounts every year.
3. Certain assumptions are necessary to prepare financial statements.
4. Financial statements accomplish only external reporting.
5. Accounting concepts and conventions govern the preparation of the financial statements.
6. The position statement or the Balance Sheet reflects the financial position of a concern over a period of time.
7. Preparation of financial statements is the ultimate object of accounting.
8. Analysis and interpretation of financial statements is only a post mortem examination of events expressed in terms of money.
9. Analysis of financial statements is a study of relationships among the various financial factors in a business.
10. Interpretation of financial statements depends upon the purpose for which it is made.

Ans: True : 2, 3, 5, 8
False : 1, 4, 6, 7, 9, 10.

THEORETICAL QUESTIONS

1. What do you understand by Analysis and interpretation of Financial Statements ? *(B.Com. Agra)*
2. Discuss the objects of Financial Statement Analysis. *(B.Com. MS)*
3. Explain the methods of Financial Statement Analysis. *(B.Com. Mysore)*
4. Explain the special features of Common-Size Statements.
5. What is meant by Ratio Analysis.
6. Are there any limitations on the interpretation of Financial Statements. *(B.Com. Madras)*
7. What is Balance Sheet ? Is it really a statement of financial. Position of a business concern ? *(B.Com. MS)*
8. What is trend analysis ?
9. Describe the characteristics of good or ideal financial statement.
10. "Financial statements suffer from a number of limitations" Discuss. *(B.Com. Madurai)*

PRACTICAL PROBLEMS

1. From the following Balance Sheet of a Company, you are required to prepare a common-size Balance Sheet.

BALANCE SHEET as on 31st Dec.

Liabilities	*Rs.*	*Assets*	*Rs.*
Equity Share Capital	1,25,000	Plant & Machinery	2,00,000
Preference Share Capital	50,000	Furniture	12,140
Reserves	55,000	Current Assets	1,69,500
Profit & Loss A/c	35,000		
Current Liabilities	1,16,640		
	3,81,640		3,81,640

2. From the following statements, prepare common-size analysis of the company.

BALANCE SHEET as on 31st Dec.

Liabilities	*Rs.*	*Assets*	*Rs.*
Share Capital	13,16,000	Cash	54,000
Fixed Liabilities	4,50,000	Debtors	4,40,000
Sundry Creditors	84,000	Stock	2,00,000
Other Liabilities	1,56,000	Prepaid Expenses	22,000
		Bills Receivable	20,000
		Fixed Assets (Net)	12,70,000
	20,06,000		20,06,000

INCOME STATEMENT for the year ended 31st Dec.

Net Sales		Rs. 25,38,000
Cost of Goods sold		14,22,000
Gross Profit		11,16,000
Selling Expenses :	7,20,000	
Administrative Expenses	1,84,000	9,04,000
Operating Profit		2,12,000
Other Incomes		26,000
		2,38,000
Other Expenses		40,000
Income before Tax		1,98,000
Tax		68,000
Income After Tax		1,30,000
Loss on Sale of Security		96,000
Surplus		34,000

(*B.Com. MS*)

3. Convert the following Income Statement into common-size income statement and comment on the prevailing conditions.

	2009	*2010*
	Rs.	*Rs.*
Gross Sales	15,300	18,360
Less : Returns	300	350
	15,000	18,010
Less : Cost of Sales	9,100	10,125
Gross Profit	5,900	7,885
Operating Expenses :		
Selling Expenses	3,000	3,300
Administrative Expenses	1,500	1,700
Total Operating Expenses	4,500	5,000
Operating Profit	1,400	2,885
Other Incomes	150	200
	1,550	3,085
Other expenses	200	300
	1,350	2,785

4. From the following Profit and Loss Accounts and Balance Sheets for the year ended 31st Dec. 2009 and 2010, prepare comparative income statements and comparative Balance Sheets.

PROFIT AND LOSS ACCOUNT

(In lakhs of Rs.)

	2009	2010		2009	2010
	Rs.	Rs.		Rs.	Rs.
To Cost of Sales	600	750	By Net Sales	800	1,000
To Administrative Expenses	20	20			
To Selling Expenses	30	40			
To Net Profit	150	190			
	800	1,000		800	1,000

BALANCE SHEETS

Liabilities	2009	2010	*Assets*	2009	2010
	Rs.	Rs.		Rs.	Rs.
Bills Payables	50	75	Cash	100	140
Sundry Creditors	150	200	Debtors	200	300
Tax Payable	100	150	Stock	200	300
6% Debentures	100	150	Land	100	100
10% Preference shares	300	300	Buildings	300	270
Equity Shares	400	400	Plant	300	270
Reserves	200	245	Furniture	100	140
	1,300	1,520		1,300	1,520

(*M.Com. Punjab*)

5. From the following profit and Loss account and Balance Sheet, prepare a comparative income statement and a comparative Balance Sheet.

PROFIT AND LOSS ACCOUNT
for the year ended 31st Dec., 2010

(In lakhs of Rs.)

	2009	2010		2009	2010
	Rs.	Rs.		Rs.	Rs.
To cost of goods sold	500	640	By sales	700	900
To *Operating Expenses :*					
Administrative	20	20			
Selling	30	40			
To Net Profit	150	200			
	700	900		700	900

Balance Sheet as on 31st Dec., 2010

	2009	2010		2009	2010
	Rs.	Rs.		Rs.	Rs.
Bills Payable	50	75	Cash	50	70
Tax Payable	100	150	Debtors	300	450
Creditors	150	200	Stock	100	200
15% Debentures	100	150	Land	100	120
12% Preference Shares	200	200	Buildings	250	225
Equity Capital	300	300	Plant	200	180
Reserves	200	250	Furniture	100	80
	1,100	1,325		1,100	1,325

(*B.Com. Madurai*)

Chapter 3

Ratio Analysis

Introduction; Meaning of Ratio; Mode of Expression; Steps in Ratio Analysis; Importance of Ratio Analysis; Nature of Ratio Analysis; Importance of Ratios; Limitations of Ratio Analysis; Interested Parties; Classification of Ratios; Balance Sheet Ratios; Current Ratio; Significance of Current Ratio; Problems of Window Dressing; Limitations of Current Ratio; Net Working Capital Ratio; Quick Ratio; Cash Position Ratio (Absolute Liquidity Ratio); Proprietary Ratio; Significance of Proprietary Ratio; Capital Gearing Ratio; Significance of Capital Gearing Ratio; Debt-Equity Ratio; Reserves to Equity Share Capital Ratio; Solvency Ratio; Security Ratio; Revenue Statement Ratios (Profit and Loss Account Ratios); Gross Profit Ratio; Operating Ratios; Expenses Ratio; Net Profit Ratio; Profitability Ratios Related to Investments; Combined Ratios; Activity Ratios or Turnover Ratios; Inventory (Stock) Turnover; Debtors Turnover Ratio; Creditors Turnover Ratio; Working Capital Turnover Ratio; Fixed Assets Turnover Ratio; Capital Turnovers; Profit Cover Ratios; Interest Coverage; Dividend Coverage; Equity Shareholders Coverage; Standard of Comparison; Projections through Ratios; Du Pont Chart; Miscellaneous; Cautions in using Ratio Analysis; Objective Type Questions; Theoretical Questions; Practical Problems.

The Balance Sheet and Profit and Loss Account are the basic financial statements of a business enterprise. They undoubtedly, provide useful financial data regarding the operations of a firm. Financial statements contain a wealth of information which, if properly analysed and interpreted, can provide valuable insights into a firm's performance and position. The information contained in the financial statements is used by management, creditors, investors and others to form judgement about the operating performance and other financial position of the firm. Financial statement analysis may be done for a variety of purposes, which may range from a simple analysis of short-term liquidity of the firm to a comprehensive assessment of strength and weakness of the firm in various areas. However, they fail to present all the useful financial data required for decision-making, specially financing decisions by the management. A Balance Sheet reports the firm's assets and liabilities at a point of time. The Profit and Loss Account presents the summary of items relating to the revenue and the expenses of a firm during a particular period of time. Neither of these shows the nature of the transactions entered into during the period to finance the firm's operations. Nevertheless, they provide some extremely useful information. *The Balance Sheet is a mirror of the financial position of a firm*. It reveals the assets the firm owns, the liabilities it is to pay to outsiders and the amount of internal liabilities in terms of capital supplied by the owners at a particular point of time. The *Profit and Loss Account shows the results of business activities or operations during a certain period of time, usually a year*. It presents the summary of income obtained and the costs incurred by the firm during a year. Thus, the financial statements provide a summarised view of the operations of a firm. Much can be learnt about a firm from careful examination of its financial statements. The analysis of financial statements is an important aid to financial analysis. Of the various methods of financial statement analysis, Ratio Analysis is by far the most widely used. Ratio analysis is based on different ratios which are calculated from the accounting data contained in the financial statements. Different ratios are used for different purposes. Financial analysis depends to a very large extent on the use of ratios though there are other equally important tools of such analysis.

Introduction

The company's financial information is contained in Balance Sheet and Profit and Loss Account. The figures contained in these statements are absolute and sometimes unconnected with one another. An absolute figure does not convey much meaning. However, it is only in the light of other information that the significance of a figure is realised. For instance, Mr. X weighs 50Kg. Is he fat ? We cannot give answer unless we know his age and height. Similarly a company's profitability cannot be known unless together with the amount of profit, the capital employed is also seen. The relationship of these two figures expressed mathematically is called a RATIO. The ratio refers to the numerical or quantitative relationship between two variables or items. A ratio is calculated by dividing one item of the relationship with the other. The ratio analysis is one of the most useful and common method of analysing financial statements. As compared to other tools of financial analysis, the ratio analysis provides very useful conclusions about various aspects of the working of an enterprise. The need for ratio arises due to the fact that absolute figures are often misleading. Absolute figures are certainly valuable but their value increases manifold if they are studied with another through ratio analysis. Ratios enable the mass of data to be summarised and simplified. Ratio analysis is an instrument for diagnosis of the financial health of an enterprise. Ratios, in fact, are full of meaning and communicate the relative importance of the various items appearing in the Balance Sheet and Profit and Loss Account.

Meaning of Ratio

A ratio is only a comparison of the numerator with the denominator. The term ratio refers to the numerical or quantitative relationship between two figures. A ratio is the relationship between two figures, and obtained by dividing the former by the latter. Ratios are designed to show how one number is related to another. It is worked out by dividing one number by another.

Ratio analysis is an important and age old technique of financial analysis. The data given in financial statements, in absolute form, are dump and are unable to communicate anything. Ratios are relative form of financial data and very useful technique to check upon the efficiency of a firm. Some ratios indicate the trend or progress or downfall of the firm.

Mode of Expression

(*i*) RATE, which is the ratio between the two numerical facts over a period of time, for example, stock turnover is three times a year.

(*ii*) PURE RATIO OR PROPORTION which is arrived at by the simple division of one number by another, for example, Current Asset to Current Liability ratio is 3 : 1.

(*iii*) PERCENTAGE which is a special type of rate expressing the relationship in hundred. It is arrived at by multiplying the quotient by 100, for example, gross profit is 30% of sales.

These alternative methods of expressing items which are related to each other are, for purposes of financial analysis, referred to as ratio analysis. In other words, ratios, as a tool of financial management, can be expressed as (*i*) Pure Ratio (*ii*) Percentage and (*iii*) a stated comparison between numbers. Each method of expression has a distinct advantage over the other. The analyst will elect that mode which will best suit his purpose and convenience.

It should be noted that computing ratios do not add any information not already inherent in the figures. What the ratios do is that they reveal the relationship in a more meaningful way so as to enable us to draw conclusions from them. A single figure by itself has no meaning but when expressed in terms of a related figure it yields significant inferences. For instance, a firm earns Rs. 3,00,000 as net profit. This fact throws no light on its adequacy or otherwise. The figure of net profit has to be considered in relation to sales or capital employed or other variables. Then a meaningful conclusion can be drawn by converting the figures into meaningful comparable forms and removes the difficulty of drawing inferences on the basis of absolute figures. As a quantitative tool, it enables the analyst to draw conclusions or answers to questions such as : Are the net profit adequate ? How does it stand in relation to capital ? What does it represent by way of return on capital employed ? etc.

Steps in Ratio Analysis

The first task of the financial analyst is to select the information relevant to the decision under consideration from the statements and calculates appropriate ratios.

The second step is to compare the calculated ratios with the ratios of the same firm relating to past or with the industry ratios. This step facilitates in assessing success or failure of the firm.

The third step involves interpretation, drawing of inferences and report-writing. Conclusions are drawn after comparison in the shape of report or recommended course of action.

Importance of Ratio Analysis

The inter relationship that exists among the different items appeared in the financial statements, are revealed by accounting ratios. Ratio analysis of a firm's financial statements is of interest to a number of parties, mainly, shareholders, creditors, financial executives etc. Shareholders are interested with earning capacity of the firm : creditors are interested in knowing the ability of firm to meet its financial obligations ; and financial executives are concerned with evolving analytical tools that will measure and compare costs, efficiency, liquidity and profitability with a view to make intelligent decisions.

The importance of ratio analysis are discussed below, in brief :

1. Aid to measure General Efficiency: Ratios enable the mass of accounting data to be summarised and simplified. They act as an index of the efficiency of the enterprise. As such they serve as an instrument of management control.

2. Aid to measure Financial Solvency: Ratios are useful tools in the hands of management and other concerned to evaluate the firms performance over a period of time by comparing the present ratio with the past ones. They point out firm's liquidity position to meet its short term obligations and long term solvency.

3. Aid in Forecasting and Planning: Ratio analysis is an invaluable aid to management in the discharge of its basic function such as planning, forecasting, control etc. The ratios that are derived after analysing and scrutinising the past result, helps the management to prepare budgets to formulate policies and to prepare the future plan of action etc.

4. Facilitate decision-making: It throws light on the degree of efficiency of the management and utilisation of the assets and that is why it is called surveyor of efficiency. They help management in decision-making.

5. Aid in corrective Action: Ratio analysis provides interfirm comparison. They highlight the factors associated with successful and unsuccessful firms. If comparison shows an unfavourable variance, corrective actions can be initiated. Thus, it helps the management to take corrective action.

6. Aid in Intra Firm Comparison: Intra firm comparisons are facilitated. It is an instrument for diagnosis of financial health of an enterprise. It facilitates the management to know whether the firm's financial position is improving or deteriorating by setting a trend with the help of ratios.

7. Act as a Good Communication: Ratios are an effective means of communication and play a vital role in informing the position of and progress made by the business concern to the owners and other interested parties. The communications by the use of simplified and summarised ratios are more easy and understandable.

8. Evaluation of Efficiency: Ratio analysis is an effective instrument which, when properly used, is useful to assess important characteristics of business—liquidity, solvency, profitability etc. A study of these aspects may enable conclusions to be drawn relating to capabilities of business.

9. Effective Tool: Ratio analysis helps in making effective control of the business—measuring performance, control of cost etc. Effective control is the keynote of better management. Ratio ensures secrecy.

10. Act as a Barometer: Ratios serve as barometer for the future. Ratios have predictory value. They are helpful in planning the business activities for a future. They indicate direction in which adjustment should be made in budget or in performance to bring both closer to one another.

Figures, in their absolute forms, shown in the financial statements are neither significant nor able to be compared. In fact, they are dump. But ratios have power to speak.

Nature of Ratio Analysis

Ratio analysis is a powerful tool of financial analysis. A ratio is defined as "the indicated quotient of two mathematical expressions" and as "the relationship between two or more things". In financial analysis, a ratio is used as an index or yardstick for evaluating the financial position and performance of a firm. Analysis of financial statements is a process of evaluating relationship between component parts of financial statements to obtain a better understanding of the firm's position and performance. Financial analysis is used as a device to analyse and interpret the financial health of enterprise. The absolute accounting figures reported in the financial statements do not provide a meaningful understanding of the performance and financial performance of a firm. An accounting figure conveys meaning when it is related to some other relevant information. Just like a doctor examines his patient by recording his body temperature, blood pressure etc., before making his conclusion regarding the illness and before giving his treatment, a financial analyst analyses the financial statements with various tools of analysis before commenting upon the financial health or weaknesses of an enterprise. A ratio is known as a symptom like blood pressure, the pulse rate or the temperature of an individual. It is with the help of ratios that the financial statements can be analysed more clearly and decisions are drawn from such analysis. The point to note is that a ratio indicates a quantitative relationship, which can be, in turn, used to make a qualitative judgement. Such is the nature of all financial ratios.

IMPORTANCE OF RATIOS

1. Ratios act as an index of *efficiency of a firm.*
2. They serve as an instrument of *management control.*
3. They are useful in *evaluating performance.*
4. They facilitate and help in *forecasting future events.*
5. They help management in exercising *effective dicisions.*
6. They help management to take *corrective actions.*
7. They facilitate *intra firm comparisons.*
8. They play effective role for *easy and clear communications.*
9. They ensure *secrecy.*
10. They facilitate *inter-firm comparisons.*

Limitations of Ratio Analysis

Ratio analysis is, as already mentioned, a widely-used tool of financial analysis. It is because ratios are simple and easy to understand. But they must be used very carefully. They suffer from various limitations. For instance, financial statements suffer from a number of limitations and may therefore, affect the quality of ratio analysis. If due care is not taken, they might confuse rather than clarify the situation. Different firms may use these terms in different senses or the same firm may use them to mean different things at different times. Some of the limitations of the ratio analysis are given below :

1. Differences in Definitions : Comparisons are made difficult due to differences in definitions of various financial terms. Lack of standard formula for working out ratios makes it difficult to compare them. They are worked out on the basis of different items in different industries.

2. Limitations of Accounting Records : Ratio analysis is based on financial statements which are themselves subject to limitations. Thus, ratios calculated on the figures given in the financial statements, also suffers from similar limitations.

3. Lack of Proper Standards : It is very difficult to ascertain the standard ratio in order to make proper comparison. Because, it differs from firm to firm, industry to industry. Apart from this, it may also have happened that in one firm, a current ratio of 2 : 1 is found to be quite satisfactory, whereas in another firm 2.5 : 1 may be unsatisfactory. Again, a high current ratio may not necessarily mean sound liquid position when current assets include large inventory or inventory consisting of obsolete items.

4. No Allowances for Price Level Changes : Due to changes in price level of various years, comparison of ratios of such years cannot give correct conclusions. A change in the price level can seriously affect the validity of comparisons of ratios computed for different time periods. For instance, a firm which has purchased an asset at a lower price, will show a higher return, than the firm which has purchased the asset at a higher price.

5. Changes in Accounting Procedure : Comparison between two variables prove worth provided their basis of valuation is identical. But in reality, it is not possible, such as methods of valuation of stock (FIFO or LIFO) or charging different methods of depreciation on fixed assets etc. Thus, if different methods are followed by different firms for their valuation, then comparison will practically be of no use.

6. Qualitative Factors are ignored : Ratios are tools of quantitative analysis only and normally qualitative factors which may generally influence the conclusions derived, are ignored while computing ratios. For instance, a high current ratio may not necessarily mean sound liquid position when current assets include a large inventory consisting of mostly obsolete items. Therefore, it is very difficult to generalise whether a particular ratio is *good* or *bad.*

7. Limited use of Single Ratio : A single ratio would not be able to convey anything. Ratios can be useful only when they are computed in a sufficient large number. If too many ratios are calculated, they are likely to confuse instead of revealing meaningful conclusions.

8. Background is overlooked : When inter-firm comparison is made, they differ substantially in age, size, nature of product etc. When an inter-firm comparison is made, these factors are not considered. Therefore, ratio analysis cannot give satisfactory results.

9. Limited Use : Ratio analysis is only a beginning and gives just a fraction of information needed for decision-making. Ratio analysis is not a substitute for sound judgement. But ratios are tools to aid in applying judgement. Conclusions drawn from the ratio analysis are not sure indicators of *bad* or *good* management. They merely convey certain observations which need further investigations, otherwise wrong conclusions may be drawn. Computation of ratios are not useful unless they are interpreted.

10. Personal Bias : Ratios have to be interpreted and different people may interpret the same ratio in different ways. Ratios are only means of financial analysis but not an end in themselves. Ratios are simple to understand and easy to calculate. Therefore, there is a tendency to over employ them. It should be clearly noted that ratios are only tools and the personal judgement of analyst is more important. The analyst has to carry further investigations and exercise his judgement in arriving at a correct diagnosis.

11. Arithmetical Window Dressing : Window-dressing means manipulation of accounts in a way so as to conceal vital facts and present the statements in a way to show better position than what it actually is. By doing so, it is possible to cover up bad financial position. Therefore, ratios based on such figures are not reliable.

12. Changing Policies : Ratios are computed on the basis of past result. Past is not an indicator of future. Ratios computed from historical data are used for predicting and projecting the likely events in the future. Such ratios may provide a glimpse of firm's past performance. But forecast for the future may not be correct as several other factors like management policies, market conditions etc. may induce future operations.

Ratios are only a post-mortem of what has happened between two Balance Sheet dates. The position in the interim period is not revealed by ratio analysis. Besides, they give no clue to future. Ratio analysis suffers from serious limitations. The analyst should not be carried away by its oversimplified nature, easy computation with a high degree of precision. They are as good as data itself.

The analyst must have comprehensive but practical knowledge and experience about the concerns whose statements have been used for calculating these ratios. Ratios are not an end in themselves but they are means to achieve a particular end. Another limitation is that of standard ratio with which the actual ratios may be compared. Generally, there is no such ratio which may be treated as standard for the purpose of comparison, because conditions of one concern differ significantly from those of another concern. The analyst must be able to examine the nature of the data carefully. If accounting data lack uniformity particularly definitional uniformity, then ratios calculated on the basis of them will be misleading. Ratio analysis is one of the many techniques of analysis and interpretation. Thus, while attempting to draw any conclusion on this basis, other techniques should also be used.

Interested Parties

Ratio analysis of a firm's financial statements is of interest to a number of parties, mainly, share-holders, creditors, debtors, firm's own management etc. People in various walks of life are at present interested in ratio analysis though in different ways and fashion and each, however, from his own angle. The type of ratio analysis, its nature and dimension differ from party to party according to their objectives of financial analysis. Different ratios are used to signify different trends in the working of the firm. However, the table given below would help the students to have a rough idea. Parties interested and application of different ratios, in short, are given below :

Parties Interested	*Application of Ratios*	*To Test*
I. Creditors (Short-term) Investors Money Lenders	1. Current Ratio 2. Liquid Ratio 3. Absolute Liquid Ratio 4. Proprietary Ratio 5. Assets to Proprietorship Ratio 6. Debt-Equity Ratio 7. Capital Gearing Ratio	Liquidity and Solvency

II. Shareholders Creditors (Long-term) Government Purchasers of Enterprise Employees	1. Gross Profit Ratio 2. Net Profit Ratio 3. Operating Ratio 4. Return on capital employed 5. Dividend Ratio 6. Earning per Share 7. Dividend per Share	Profitability
III. Share-holders and Outsiders	1. Capital Gearing Ratio 2. Equity Capital Ratio 3. Long-term Loans to Net Worth	Capital Structure
IV. Management	All types of Ratios	Management Efficiency

Classification of Ratios

Financial ratios have been classified in several ways. A number of standpoints may be used as base for classifying the ratios. It is a matter of great surprise that no uniformity has been achieved in this regard. Different authors have classified the ratios in varying groups. To illustrate, the short-term creditors' main interest is in the liquidity position or short-term solvency of the firm: long-term creditors are more interested in the long-term solvency and profitability analysis and the analysis of the firm's financial conditions; management is interested in evaluating every activity of the firm because they have to protect the interests of all parties. Thus accounting ratios may be classified on the following bases leading to somewhat overlapping categories.

(A) Classification by Statements

The Traditional classification is based on those statements from which information is obtained for calculating the ratios. The ratios are classified as follows:

CLASSIFICATION BY STATEMENTS

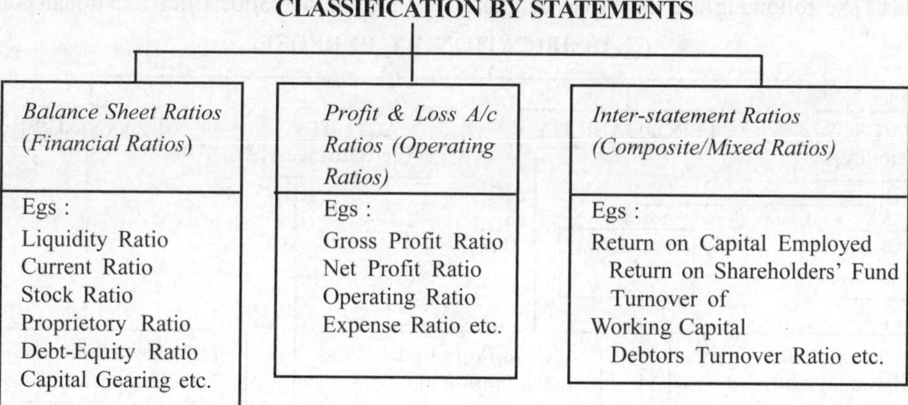

(B) Classification by Users

This classification is based on the parties who are interested in making the use of ratios.

CLASSIFICATION BY USERS

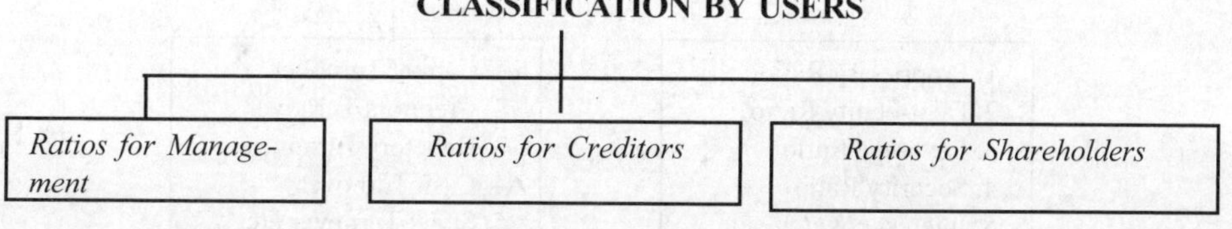

Egs:	Egs:	Egs:
Operating Ratio Debtors Turnover Stock Turnover Solvency Ratio Return on Capital etc.	Current Ratio Solvency Ratio Fixed Asset Ratio Creditors Turnover etc	Yield Rate Proprietary Ratio Dividend Rate Capital Gearing Return on Capital Fund etc.

(C) Classification According to Importance

This basis of classification of ratios has been recommended by the British Institute of Management. They are of two types.

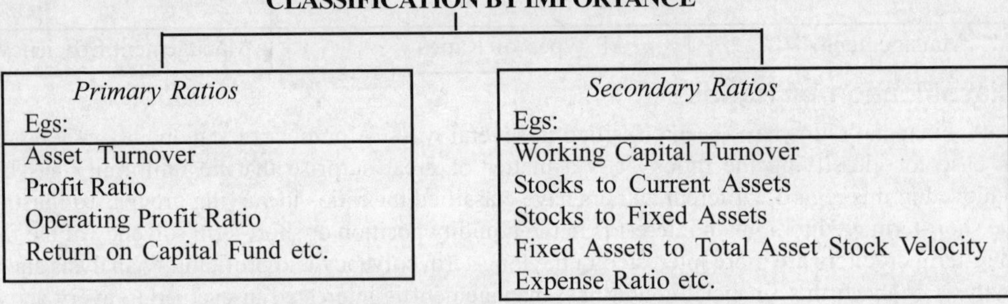

(D) Classification by Purpose/Function

This is a classification based on the purpose for which an analyst computes these ratios. The modern approach of classifying the ratios is according to the purpose or object of analysis. Normally, ratios are used for the purpose of assessing the profitability and sound financial position. Thus, ratios according to the purpose are more meaningful. There can be several purposes which can be listed. For analysis, it is customary to group the purposes into broad headings. The following are the broad categories of accounting ratios from functional point of view :

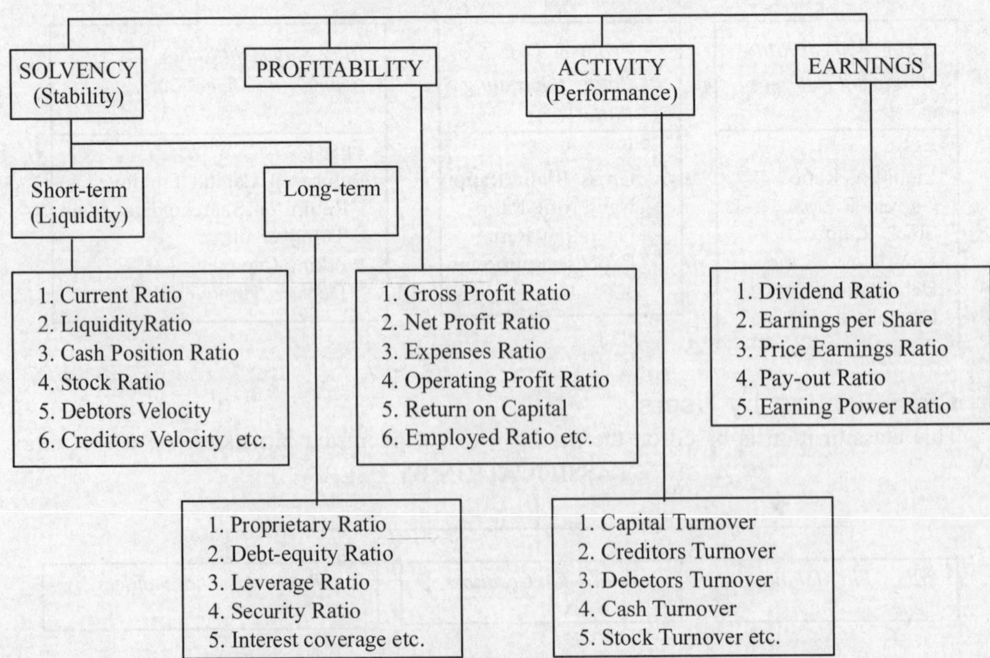

BALANCE SHEET RATIOS

1. Current Ratio

Current Ratio is the most common ratio for measuring liquidity. Being related to working capital analysis, it is also called the working capital ratio. Current ratio expresses relationship between current assets and current liabilities. *The current ratio is the ratio of total current assets to total current liabilities*. It is calculated by dividing current assets by current liabilities, or

$$\text{Current Ratio} = \frac{\text{Current Assets}}{\text{Current Liabilities}}$$

Current assets are those, the amount of which can be realised within a period of one year. That is, the current assets of a firm represent those assets which can be in the ordinary course of business converted into cash within a period not exceeding one year. Following are normally treated as current assets :

1. Cash in Hand
2. Cash at Bank
3. Debtors
4. Bills Receivable
5. Prepaid Expenses
6. Money at call and short notice
7. Stock
8. Sundry Supplies
9. Other amounts receivable within a year

Current liabilities are those amounts which are payable within a period of one year. Following are normally treated as current liabilities :

1. Creditors
2. Bills Payable
3. Bank Overdraft
4. Expenses Outstanding
5. Interest Due or Payable
6. Reserve for unbilled Expenses
7. Instalment payable on long term-loans
8. Any other amount which is payable in short period. (One year)

The current ratio of a firm measures its short-term solvency *i.e.,* its ability to meet short-term obligations. As a measure of short-term current financial liquidity, it indicates the rupees of current assets available for each rupee of current liability/obligation. *The higher the current ratio, the larger the amount of rupees available per rupee of current liability, the more the firm's ability to meet current obligations and the greater the safety of funds of short-term creditors.*

Significance of Current Ratio

Current ratio provides a margin of safety to the creditors. *In a sound business, a current ratio of 2 : 1 is considered an ideal one.* If current assets are equal to current liabilities, position is not good even though it appears that after realising all the amount of current assets, current liabilities can be paid off. This means the firm has no working capital. Working capital is excess of current assets over current liabilities. The current ratio must not only be equal to current liabilities but should leave a comfortable margin of working capital after paying of the current debts. The reason in favour of prescribing current ratio as 2 : 1 or 2 for 1 is that all the current assets do not have the same liquidity, or in short, all current assets cannot be immediately converted into cash for a number of reasons. For instance, debts may not be realised in full, credit sales may be higher than the cash sales etc. If goods are always sold for cash, a small margin will suffice. But in case of credit sales, margin will have to be increased. Therefore, the demand for a 100% margin of current assets over current liabilities, as a precautionary measure, is preferred. Secondly, prescribing the current ratio as 2 : 1 or 200% facilitates to keep the surplus as working capital even if all current liabilities are paid off :

Current ratio is an index of the firm's financial stability *i.e.,* an index of technical solvency and an index of the strength of working capital, which means excess of current assets over current liabilities. A high current ratio is an assurance that the firm will have adequate funds to pay current liabilities and other current payments. Significance of Current Ratio, in brief:

1. Current ratio indicates the firm's ability to pay its current liabilities *i.e.,* day-to-day financial obligations.
2. It shows short-term financial strength.
3. It is a test of credit strength and solvency of a firm.
4. It indicates the strength of the working capital.
5. It indicates the capacity to carry on effective operations.
6. It discloses the over-trading or under-capitalisation.
7. It shows the tendency of over-investment in inventory.
8. Higher ratio *i.e.,* more than 2 : 1 indicates sound solvency position.

NB : Bank Overdraft : Overdraft arrangement facility with the bank is more or less permanent. Therefore, it is argued that this should be excluded when current ratio is calculated. At the same time, it can also be argued that overdraft facility may be cancelled by the bank at any time. Thus, it is advisable to include bank overdraft in current liabilities.

9. Lower ratio *i.e.,* less than 2 : 1 indicates inadequate working capital.
10. It discloses the quantity of working capital position.

Precautions : While calculating the Current Ratio, the following guidelines may be noted:

1. Reasonable valuation should be made in case of current assets and current liabilities. The amount of bad debts and doubtful debts should be deducted from the amount of debtors. The amount of obsolete stock, if any, should also be deducted from the stock. The reserves and other accounts related to the valuation of currents are deducted from the total current assets.
2. Loose tools though called current asset are not included.
3. Investments which are easily marketable and are meant to be sold for cash should be treated as current assets.
4. Fictitious assets such as, preliminary expenses, Discount on Issue of Shares, advances made for purchase of fixed assets etc. are to be excluded.
5. Long-term liabilities, if they are repayable within a year, should be treated as a current liabilities.
6. Bank overdraft, unless specially stated as a permanent arrangement, should be treated as a current liability.
7. All Bills Receivable, whether discounted or not, should be treated as current assets and at the same time, discounted bills should be treated as current liability.

Problems of Window Dressing

Window-dressing as used here refers to the practice of manipulating the current assets and current liabilities in a manner so as to present a more favourable current ratio than the actual one. This may be done by manipulating the value of inventory, recording in advance cash receipts of next year, treating a short-term obligation as long term debt etc. In such cases, the current ratio will not be representative of the actual position.

Limitations of Current Ratio

Current ratio suffers from the following weaknesses :

1. While current liabilities are fixed in the sense that they have to be paid in full in all circumstances the current assets are subject to shrinkage in value, possibility of bad debts, unsalability of inventory and so on. Moreover, some of the current assets are more liquid than others : cash is the most liquid of all, receivables are more liquid than inventories etc. Different components of current assets have not the same degree of liquidity. The limitation of current ratio arises from the fact that it is a *quantitative* rather than a *qualitative* index of liquidity. A qualitative measure takes into account the proportion of various types of current assets to the total current assets. All current assets are treated alike but they are not equally or readily realisable in cash.
2. Ratios are computed from the figures taken from Balance Sheet. The current assets and current liabilities might be manipulated to show a better liquidity and solvency position of a firm, through a high current ratio, by the name of window-dressing. A high current ratio, therefore, will be of no significance, if the same is the product of window dressing.
3. Even if the ratio is favourable, the firm may be in financial trouble because of more stocks, work-in-progress etc. which are not easily convertible into cash. Therefore, the current ratio, is not a conclusive index of the real liquidity of a firm.
4. It is a crude measure of financial liquidity as it does not take into account the liquidity of the individual components of current assets.
5. Ratio analysis gives only a good basis for quantitative analysis of financial problems. But at the same time, it suffers from qualitative aspects.

2. Net Working Capital Ratio

Net working capital is not a ratio. The difference between current assets and current liabilities is called net working capital. The term current assets refers to assets which in the normal course of business get converted into cash over a short period, usually not exceeding one year. Current liabilities are those liabilities which are required to be paid in short period, normally a year. It is a measure of company's liquidity position. Generally it is understood that between two firms, the one having a larger net working capital has the greater ability to meet its current obligations. But this is not necessarily so. The measure of liquidity is a relationship, rather than the difference between current assets and current liabilities. At the same time, it measures the firm's potential reservoir of funds.

$$\text{Net Working Capital Ratio} = \frac{\text{Net Working Capital}}{\text{Net Assets}}$$

3. Quick Ratio

Quick ratio is also known as *liquid ratio or acid test ratio or near money ratio*. It is the ratio between quick or liquid assets and quick liabilities. As pointed out, the current ratio in the study of solvency may be sometimes misleading due to high ratio of stock to current assets. This ratio is calculated by dividing the quick assets by the current liabilities.

$$\text{Liquid Ratio} = \frac{\text{Quick or Liquid Assets}}{\text{Liquid or Current Liabilities}}$$

$$= \frac{\text{Current Assets} - (\text{Stock and Prepaid Expenses})}{\text{Current Liabilities} - \text{Bank Overdraft}}$$

It indicates the relation between strictly liquid assets whose value is almost certain on the one hand, and strictly liquid liabilities on the other. The term quick assets refers to current assets which can be converted into cash immediately or at a short notice without diminution of value.

Liquid assets comprise all current assets minus stock and prepaid expenses. Liquid liabilities comprise all current liabilities minus bank overdraft. Stock is excluded from liquid assets on the ground that it is not converted into cash in the immediate future ; prepaid expenses by their very nature are not available to pay off current debts : and at the same time bank overdraft is excluded on the ground that it is not required to be paid off in the immediate future.

A comparison of current ratio with liquid ratio would give an indication regarding inventory position.

Example :

	X Ltd.	Y Ltd.
Current Ratio	2 : 1	2 : 1
Liquidity Ratio	1 : 1	0.5 : 1

Both the companies show satisfactory working capital position as the current assets are two times the current liabilities. However, the liquidity ratio of Y Ltd. has gone far below than that of X Ltd. It can be concluded that Y Ltd. is over stocking. Thus, *less the quick ratio, higher the incidence of inventory in inflating the current ratio. The higher the quick ratio, lower the incidence of inventory in inflating the current ratio.*

As pointed out earlier, current ratio may be misleading, in spite of a favourable current ratio, a firm may not be able to pay off its creditors in time due to larger proportion of stock in current assets. In such a case liquid ratio will be more reliable and a safer guide. Generally speaking, *an acid test ratio of 1 : 1 is considered satisfactory* as a firm can easily meet all current claims. If the ratio is less than 1 : 1, that is, liquid assets are less than current liabilities, the financial position of the concern shall be deemed to be unsound. On the other hand, if the ratio is more than 1 : 1, the financial position of the concern is sound and good. The acid test ratio provides, in a sense, a check on the liquidity of a firm as shown by its current ratio. The quick ratio is a more rigorous and penetrating test of the liquidity position of a firm. The interpretation that can be placed on the current ratio (2 : 1) and acid test ratio (0.7 : 1) is that a large part of the current assets of the firm is tied up in slow-moving and unsaleable inventories and slow-paying debts. Both the current ratio and quick ratio should be considered in relation to the industry average to infer whether the firm's short-term financial position is satisfactory or not.

Significance of Quick Ratio, in brief :

1. It is the true test of business solvency.
2. Higher ratio *i.e.,* more than 1 : 1 indicates sound financial position.
3. Lower ratio *i.e.,* less than 1 : 1 indicates financial difficulty.
4. This is an important ratio of financial institutions.
5. It is a stringent test of liquidity.
6. It gives better picture of firm's ability to meet its short-term debts out of short-term assets.
7. If the current ratio is more than 2 : 1 but liquid ratio is less than 1 : 1 it indicates excessive inventory.
8. It is more of a qualitative nature of test.

Illustration 1. The following is the Balance Sheet of a firm :

	Rs.		*Rs.*
Share Capital	30,000	Fixed Assets	16,500
Creditors	8,000	Cash	1,000
Bills Payable	2,000	Book Debts	6,000
Provision for Tax	3,500	Bills Receivables	2,000
		Stock	17,500
		Prepaid Expenses	500
	43,500		43,500

Comment upon the liquidity of the firm.

Solution :

(1) Current Ratio $= \dfrac{\text{Current Assets}}{\text{Current Liabilities}}$

$= \dfrac{\text{Rs. } 27{,}000}{\text{Rs. } 13{,}500}$

$= \mathbf{2 : 1}$

(2) Liquid Ratio $= \dfrac{\text{Liquid Assets}}{\text{Current Liabilities}}$

$= \dfrac{\text{Rs. } 9{,}000}{\text{Rs. } 13{,}500}$

$= \mathbf{0.67 : 1}$

Current Assets :	
Cash	Rs. 1,000
Book Debts	6,000
B/R	2,000
Stock	17,500
Prepaid Exp.	500
	27,000

Current Liabilities :	
Creditors	Rs. 8,000
Bills Payable	2,000
Provision for Tax	3,500
	13,500

Comments :

Current ratio is 2 : 1 which is considered satisfactory. But quick ratio is below the optimum ratio of 1 : 1, indicating that the liquidity position of the firm is not satisfactory. The firm can meet its current obligations only to the extent of 67%. However, a detailed analysis of stock is necessary before drawing a final conclusion. Any way, the fact is that firm's liquid assets are not sufficient.

Illustration 2. The following figures are extracted from the Balance sheet of X Ltd. as on 31st December:

	2009 Rs.	*2010* Rs.
Stock	25,000	40,000
Debtors	10,000	16,000
Cash at Bank	5,000	4,000
Creditors	8,000	15,000
Bills Payable	2,000	3,000
Provision for Taxes	5,000	7,000
Bank Overdraft	5,000	15,000

Calculate the Current Ratio and Acid Test Ratio for the two years and commend on the liquidity position of the Company. [*B.Com. Calicut*]

Solution :

Current Assets :

= Stock + Debtors + Cash at Bank

= Rs. 25,000 + Rs. 10,000 + Rs. 5,000 = Rs. 40,000 (2009)

= Rs. 40,000 + Rs. 16,000 + Rs. 4,000 = Rs. 60,000 (2010)

Current Liabilities :

= Creditors + Bills Payable + Provision for Taxes + Overdraft

= Rs. 8,000 + Rs. 2,000 + Rs. 5,000 + Rs. 5,000 = Rs. 20,000 (2009)

= Rs. 15,000 + Rs. 3,000 + Rs. 7,000 + Rs. 15,000 = Rs. 40,000 (2010)

Liquid Assets = Rs. 10,000 + Rs. 5,000 = Rs. 15,000 (2009)

= Rs. 16,000 + Rs. 4,000 = Rs. 20,000 (2010)

Liquid Liabilities

= Rs. 8,000 + Rs. 2,000 + Rs. 5,000 = Rs. 15,000 (2009)

= Rs. 15,000 + Rs. 3,000 + Rs. 7,000 = Rs. 25,000 (2010)

$$\text{Current Ratio} = \frac{\text{Current Assets}}{\text{Current Liabilities}}$$

$$2009 = \frac{\text{Rs. } 40{,}000}{\text{Rs. } 20{,}000} = 2:1$$

$$2010 = \frac{\text{Rs. } 60{,}000}{\text{Rs. } 40{,}000} = 1.5:1$$

$$\text{Acid Test Ratio} = \frac{\text{Liquid Assets}}{\text{Liquid Liabilities}}$$

$$2009 = \frac{\text{Rs. } 15{,}000}{\text{Rs. } 15{,}000} = 1:1$$

$$2010 = \frac{\text{Rs. } 20{,}000}{\text{Rs. } 25{,}000} = 0.8:1$$

Comment :

In 2009, the Current Ratio is 2 : 1. It implies that for every one rupee of current liabilities, 2 rupees of current assets are available to meet them. In other words, the current assets are two times the current liabilities. The liquidity position is also satisfactory. A ratio of 2 : 1 (2 times current assets of current liabilities) is considered satisfactory as a rule of thumb. A firm with higher current Ratio has better liquidity short-term solvency. It provides a margin of safety to the creditors. Acid Test Ratio is also satisfactory.

In 2010, both the ratios have fallen below the standards. The current assets are just equal to the current liabilities and the stock has gone to Rs. 40,000. Therefore, the company, in 2010, will not be able to meet its immediate commitments. Besides, the liquid position has also fallen below the standard (1 : 1). As such, the liquidity position of the company is not satisfactory. Its short-term solvency is threatened. An Acid Test Ratio of 1 : 1 is considered satisfactory as a firm can easily meet all current claims. The interpretation that can be placed on the Current Ratio and Acid Test Ratio is that a large part of current assets of the firm is tied up in inventories.

4. Cash Position Ratio

(Absolute Liquidity Ratio)

It is a variation of quick ratio. When liquidity is highly restricted in terms of cash and cash equivalents, this ratio should be calculated. Liquidity ratio measures the relationship between cash and near cash items on the one hand, and immediately maturing obligations on the other. The inventory and the debtors are excluded from current assets, to calculate this ratio.

$$\text{Cash Position Ratio} = \frac{\text{Cash + Marketable Securities}}{\text{Current Liabilities}}$$

Generally, 0.75 : 1 ratio is recommended to ensure liquidity. This test is more rigorous measure of a firm's liquidity position. If the ratio is 1 : 1, then the firm has enough cash on hand to meet all current liabilities. This type of ratio is not widely used in practice.

5. Proprietary Ratio

Proprietary Ratio relates the shareholders funds to total assets. It is a variant of the debt equity ratio. This ratio shows the long-term or future solvency of the business. It is calculated by dividing shareholders funds by the total assets.

$$\text{Proprietary Ratio} = \frac{\text{Shareholders' Fund}}{\text{Total Assets or Total Resources}}$$

Preference share capital and equity share capital plus all reserves and surplus items are called shareholders' fund. Total assets includes all assets including goodwill. The acceptable norm of the ratio is 1 : 3. The ratio shows the general strength of the company. It is very important to creditors as it helps them to find out the proportion of shareholders' funds in the total assets used in the business. Higher ratio indicates a secured position to creditors and a low ratio indicates greater risk to creditors. A ratio below 50% may be alarming for the creditors since they may have to lose heavily in the event of company's liquidation on account of heavy losses.

Proprietary Ratios are also further analysed into the following manner :

(*i*) Ratio of Fixed Assets to Proprietors' Funds.

(*ii*) Ratio of Current Assets to Proprietors' Funds.

(*i*) Fixed Assets to Proprietors' Fund Ratio

This shows the relationship between fixed assets and shareholders' funds. The purpose of this ratio is to calculate the percentage of the owners funds invested in fixed assets.

$$\text{Fixed Assets to Shareholders Fund} = \frac{\text{Fixed Assets}}{\text{Proprietors' Funds}}$$

The fixed assets are valued at their depreciated book value. Internal equities in Debt Equity ratio are the proprietors' funds. If the ratio is greater than one, it means that creditors obligation have been used to acquire a part of the fixed assets.

(*ii*) Current Assets to Proprietors Fund Ratio

It shows the relationship between current assets and shareholders' funds. The purpose of this ratio is to calculate the percentage of shareholders' funds invested in Current assets

$$\text{Current Assets to Proprietors Fund} = \frac{\text{Current Assets}}{\text{Proprietors' Funds}}$$

This ratio can be expressed in percentage or as a proportion. Different industries have different norms and hence the ratio should be carefully studied. Fixed assets to proprietors ratio and this ratio should be studied for a meaningful analysis.

Significance of Proprietary Ratio:

1. It indicates long-term solvency of the firm.
2. It shows the proportion of assets financed by the proprietors.
3. It is a test of long-term credit strength.
4. Higher ratio, say more than 75% shows lesser dependence on external sources. (*i.e.,* sound financial position)
5. Lower ratio, say less than 60% shows more dependence on external sources (*i.e.,* unsound financial position)
6. It shows the general financial strength of the firm.
7. It determines the extent of trading on equity.
8. It measures the extent of protection available to creditors.

6. Capital Gearing Ratio

Capital Gearing Ratio is also known as Capitalisation Ratio or Leverage Ratio. Closely related to solvency ratios is the capital gearing ratio which is mainly used to analyse the capital structure of a company. The term Capital Gearing or Leverage normally refers to the proportion between *the fixed interest or dividend bearing funds and non-fixed interest or dividend bearing funds*. The former includes funds supplied by debenture-holders and preference shareholders and the latter includes equity shareholders' fund, including reserves and surplus.

$$\text{Capital Gearing} = \frac{\text{Fixed Interest Bearing Funds}}{\text{Equity Share-holders' Funds}}$$

The capital gearing ratio shows the mix of finance employed in the business. It indicates the proportion between owners' funds and non-owners funds (Preference shares plus long-term debt). This proportion is by definition known as leverage. If the ratio is high, the capital gearing is said to be high and if the ratio is low, the gearing is said to be low. The extent to which capital is geared shows the speed with which the enterprise is accelerating towards the corporate goal. High gearing means more speed and low gearing means less speed. Further, high gearing means trading on thin equity and low gearing is known as trading on thick equity.

Highly geared capital structure may be indicative of under-capitalisation which means that the amount of capital is disproportionate to the needs measured by the volume of activity. A capital gearing ratio of low order indicate trading on thick equity and it indicate over-capitalisation. This ratio is important to the company and the prospective investors. It must be carefully planned as it affects the company's capacity to maintain a uniform dividend policy during difficult trading periods. The capital gearing also reveals the suitability or otherwise of the company's capitalisation, that is :

$$\text{Equity Capital} = \text{Loan Capital} = \text{Even Gear}$$
$$\text{Equity Capital} > \text{Loan Capital} = \text{Low Gear} = \text{Over Capitalisation}$$
$$\text{Equity Capital} < \text{Loan Capital} = \text{High Gear} = \text{Under Capitalisation}$$

Company's financial strength can also be known from the following ratios :

(*i*) Total Investments to Long-term Liabilities
(*ii*) Current Liabilities to Proprietors Fund
(*iii*) Reserve to Equity Capital Ratios.

Significance of Capital Gearing Ratio :

1. It aids in regulating a balanced capital structure in a company.
2. It analyses the capital structure of a company.
3. Low gearing indicates trading on equity.

4. It is useful to ascertain whether a company is practising "trading on equity" and if so, to what extent is done.

Illustration 3

	Rs.
Equity Share Capital	10,00,000
10% Pref. Share Capital	5,00,000
18% Debentures	8,00,000
Loan at 15% (Long period)	1,40,000
Current Liabilities	3,00,000
General Reserve	8,00,000

Find out Capital Gearing from the above particulars.

Solution:

Capital Gearing Ratio

$$= \frac{\text{10\% Pref. Cap.} + \text{18\% Deb.} + \text{Long Period Loan}}{\text{Equity Capital} + \text{General Reserve}}$$

$$= \frac{\text{Rs. } 5{,}00{,}000 + \text{Rs. } 8{,}00{,}000 + \text{Rs. } 1{,}40{,}000}{\text{Rs. } 10{,}00{,}000 + \text{Rs. } 8{,}00{,}000}$$

$$= \frac{\text{Rs. } 14{,}40{,}000}{\text{Rs. } 18{,}00{,}000}$$

$$= 0.8$$

Since the ratio is less than one, it is low geared.

7. Debt Equity Ratio

The financing of total assets of a business concern is done by owners' equity (also known as internal equity) as well as outside debts (known as external equity). How much fund has been provided by the owners and how much by outsiders in the acquisition of total assets is a very significant factor affecting the long-term solvency position of a concern. In other words, the relationship between borrowed funds and owners' capital is a popular measure of the long-term financial solvency of a firm. This relationship is shown by the debt-equity ratio. This ratio indicates the relative proportions of debts and equity in financing the assets of a firm. This ratio is calculated in various ways.

It is also known as External-Internal Equity Ratio. Debt-Equity ratio is determined to ascertain soundness of the long-term financial policies of the company. This ratio relates all external liabilities to owners' recorded claims. Debt-equity ratio is calculated as follows :

(*i*) $\text{Debt-equity Ratio} = \frac{\text{External Equities}}{\text{Internal Equities}}$ or

(*ii*) $\text{Debt-Equity Ratio} = \frac{\text{Outsiders Funds}}{\text{Shareholders Funds}}$

As a long-term financial ratio it may be calculated as follows :

(*i*) $\text{Debt-Equity Ratio} = \frac{\text{Total Long – term Debts}}{\text{Total Long – term Funds}}$ or

(*ii*) $\text{Debt-Equity Ratio} = \frac{\text{Total Long–term Debts}}{\text{Shareholders' Funds}}$

The term external equities refers to the total outside liabilities. The term internal equities refers to all claims of preference shareholders and equity shareholders such as share capital and reserves and surplus. Outside fund refers to all short-term debts like mortgage, bills etc. When long-term financial ratio is calculated, term debts like debentures are to be considered. Shareholders' funds refer to preference share capital, equity share capital, capital reserve, revenue reserve, reserves for contingencies, sinking fund for renewal of a fixed asset or redemption of debentures etc. less fictitious assets.

As acceptable norm for this ratio is considered to be 2 : 1. A higher debt-equity ratio is allowed in the case of capital-intensive industries, a norm of 4 : 1 is used for fertiliser and cement units and a norm of 6:1 is used for shipping units.

Whatever way the debt-equity ratio is calculated, it shows the extent to which debt financing has been used in the business. A high ratio shows that the claims of creditors are greater than those of owners. A very high ratio is unfavourable from the firm's point of view. This introduces inflexibility in the firm's operations due to the increasing interference and pressures from creditors. A High debt company, also known as highly leveraged or geared, is able to borrow funds on very restrictive terms and conditions. A low debt-equity ratio implies a greater claim of owners than creditors. From the point of view of creditors, it represents a satisfactory capital structure of the business since a high proportion of equity provides a larger margin of safety for them.

Illustration 4

Calculate debt-equity ratio from the following :

	Rs.
Total Assets	2,60,000
Total Debt	1,80,000
Current Liabilities	20,000

Solution :

Shareholders Fund = Total Assets – Total Debts
= Rs. 2,60,000 – Rs. 1,80,000
= Rs. 80,000

Long-term Debt = Total Debt – Current Liabilities
= Rs. 1,80,000 – Rs. 20,000
= Rs.1,60,000

$$\text{Debt Equity Ratio} = \frac{\text{Long-term Debts}}{\text{Shareholders' Funds}}$$

$$= \frac{\text{Rs. } 1,60,000}{\text{Rs. } 80,000} = 2:1$$

Illustration 5

Calculate the debt-equity ratio from the following :

	Rs.
Capital employed	24,00,000
Long-term Debt	16,00,000

Solution :

Shareholders' Fund = Capital Employed – Long-term Debt
= Rs. 24,00,000 – Rs. 16,00,000
= Rs. 8,00,000

$$\text{Debt Equity Ratio} = \frac{\text{Long-term Debts}}{\text{Shareholders' Funds}}$$

$$= \frac{\text{Rs. } 16,00,000}{\text{Rs. } 8,00,000} = 2:1$$

Illustration 6

	Rs.
Preference Share Capital	3,00,000
Equity Share Capital	11,00,000
Capital Reserve	5,00,000
Profit & Loss Account	2,00,000
6% Debentures	5,00,000
Sundry Creditors	2,40,000
Bills Payable	1,20,000
Provision for Taxation	1,80,000
Outstanding creditors	1,60,000

Calculate Debt-Equity Ratio.

(*B.Com. Agra*)

Solution :

$$\text{Debt-Equity Ratio} = \frac{\text{External Equities}}{\text{Internal Equities}}$$

$$= \frac{\text{Rs. } 12,00,000}{\text{Rs. } 21,00,000}$$

$$= 0.57 \text{ or } 4 : 7$$

It means that for every four rupees worth of the creditors' investment, the shareholders have invested seven rupees. That is external debts are equal to 57% of shareholders' fund.

Ratio of Fixed Assets to Current Assets

This ratio differ from industry to industry. This ratio is calculated as follows :

Increase in this ratio means that trading is slack or mechanisation has been used. A decline in the ratio means that debtors and stocks are increased too much or fixed assets are more intensively used. If current assets increase with the corresponding increase in profit, it will show that the business is expanding.

Illustration 7 The following is the Balance Sheet of a company as on 31st March :

Liabilities	*Rs.*	*Assets*	*Rs.*
Share Capital	2,00,000	Land and Buildings	1,40,000
Profit & Loss Account	30,000	Plant and Machinery	3,50,000
General Reserve	40,000	Stock	2,00,000
12% Debentures	4,20,000	Sundry Debtors	1,00,000
Sundry Creditors	1,00,000	Bills Receivable	10,000
Bills Payable	50,000	Cash at Bank	40,000
	8,40,000		8,40,000

Calculate :

(1) Current Ratio

(2) Quick Ratio

(3) Inventory to working Capital

(4) Debt to Equity Ratio

(5) Proprietary Ratio
(6) Capital Gearing Ratio
(7) Current Assets to Fixed Assets

Solution :

(1) $\text{Current Ratio} = \dfrac{\text{Current assets}}{\text{Current Liabilities}}$

$= \dfrac{\text{Rs. } 3{,}50{,}000}{\text{Rs. } 1{,}50{,}000} = \mathbf{2.33:1}$

(2) $\text{Quick Ratio} = \dfrac{\text{Liquid Assets}}{\text{Liquid Liabilities}}$

$= \dfrac{\text{Rs. } 1{,}50{,}000}{\text{Rs. } 1{,}50{,}000} = \mathbf{1:1}$

(3) $\text{Inventory to Working Capital} = \dfrac{\text{Inventory}}{\text{Working Capital}}$

$= \dfrac{\text{Rs. } 2{,}00{,}000}{\text{Rs. } 2{,}00{,}000} = \mathbf{1:1}$

(Working Capital = Current Assets – Current Liabilities
= Rs. 3,50,000 – Rs. 1,50,000 = Rs. 2,00,000)

(4) $\text{Debt to Equity Ratio} = \dfrac{\text{Long-term Debts}}{\text{Shareholders' Fund}}$

$= \dfrac{\text{Rs. } 4{,}20{,}000}{\text{Rs. } 2{,}70{,}000} = \mathbf{1.56:1}$

(Or)

$= \dfrac{\text{Long-term Debts}}{\text{Shareholders' Fund + Long-term Debts}}$

$= \dfrac{\text{Rs. } 4{,}20{,}000}{\text{Rs. } 2{,}70{,}000 + 4{,}20{,}000} = \mathbf{0.6:1}$

(5) $\text{Proprietary Ratio} = \dfrac{\text{Shareholders' Fund}}{\text{Total Assets}}$

$= \dfrac{\text{Rs. } 2{,}70{,}000}{\text{Rs. } 8{,}40{,}000} = \mathbf{0.32:1}$

(6) $\text{Capital Gearing Ratio} = \dfrac{\text{Fixed Interest Bearing Securities}}{\text{Equity Share Capital}}$

$= \dfrac{\text{Rs. } 4{,}20{,}000}{\text{Rs. } 2{,}00{,}000} = \mathbf{2.1:1}$

(7) $\text{Current Assets to Fixed Assets Ratio} = \dfrac{\text{Current Assets}}{\text{Fixed Assets}}$

$= \dfrac{\text{Rs. } 3{,}50{,}000}{\text{Rs. } 4{,}90{,}000} = \mathbf{0.71:1}$

8. Reserves to Equity Share Capital Ratio

It reveals the policy pursued by the company with regard to growth and distribution of dividends. A very high ratio indicates a conservative dividend policy and increased ploughing back of profit. Higher the ratio, better will be the position.

$$\text{Reserve to Equity Capital Ratio} = \frac{\text{Revenue Reserves}}{\text{Equity Capital}}$$

9. Solvency Ratio

It is also known as Debt ratio. It is a difference of 100 and proprietary ratio. This ratio is found out between total assets and external liabilities of the company. External liabilities mean all long period and short period liabilities.

$$\text{Solvency Ratio} = \frac{\text{Total Liabilities}}{\text{Total Assets}}$$

Solvency generally refers to the capacity or ability of the business to meet its short-term and long-term obligations. If a company is in a position to pay its long-term liabilities easily, it is said to possess long term solvency. If a company's financial position is strong to pay current liabilities, it is regarded as short term solvency. There are circumstances arising to find out solvency of the company for very short period for immediate solvency, for example, Liquidity Ratio and Absolute Liquid Ratio.

It measures the proportion of total assets provided by the firm's creditors. If total assets are far more than external liabilities, the company is treated as solvent. A company is solvent if it can meet its outside liabilities out of its total assets. Higher the ratio, the greater amount of firm's creditors' money that is being used to generate profits for the firm's owners.

10. Security Ratio

Fixed liabilities usually take the form of debentures, preferably, secured on fixed assets of the company. The market value or depreciated book value of the fixed assets, should be taken into account at the date of calculation of this ratio. A ratio of 1.5 : 1 is considered good.

Illustration 8

From the following balance sheet of a company you are required to calculate: Current Ratio and Solvency Ratio.

BALANCE SHEET as on 31st December

Share Capital	10,00,000	Fixed Assets	12,00,000
Fixed Liabilities	5,00,000	Current Assets	8,00,000
Current Liabilities	5,00,000		
	20,00,000		20,00,000

[*B.Com., Punjab*]

Solution :

(1) $$\text{Current Ratio} = \frac{\text{Current Assets}}{\text{Current Liabilities}}$$

$$= \frac{8,00,000}{5,00,000} = \mathbf{1.6 : 1}$$

(2) $$\text{Solvency Ratio} = \frac{\text{Outside Liabilities}}{\text{Total Assets}} \times 100$$

$$= \frac{5,00,000+5,00,000}{20,00,000} \times 100 = \mathbf{50\%.}$$

Illustration 9 From the following Balance Sheet, compute the following ratios :

1. Current Ratio
2. Liquid Ratio
3. Absolute Liquid Ratio
4. Proprietary Ratio
5. Assets-proprietorship Ratio
   (*i*) Fixed Assets to Proprietors' Equity
   (*ii*) Current Assets to Proprietors' Equity
6. Debt-Equity Ratio
7. Stock to Current Assets Ratio
8. Stock to Working Capital Ratio
9. Current Assets to Working Capital Ratio
10. Current Assets to Liquid Assets Ratio
11. All long-term funds to Working Capital Ratio
12. Tangible Assets to Working Capital Ratio
13. Capital Gearing Ratio

BALANCE SHEET As on 31st December

Liabilities	*Rs.*	*Assets*	*Rs.*
Equity Share Capital	2,00,000	Plan and Machinery	2,00,000
10% Preference Share Capital	1,00,000	Land and Buildings	2,00,000
20% Debentures	1,00,000	Stock	1,50,000
Reserves and Surplus	1,00,000	Debtors	50,000
Loan (long-term)	50,000	Cash	1,00,000
Creditors	1,00,000		
Bank Overdraft	50,000		
	7,00,000		7,00,000.

Solution :

Computation of required components :

1. *Current Assets* :

	Rs.
Stock	1,50,000
Debtors	50,000
Cash	1,00,000
	3,00,000

2. *Current Liabilities* :

	Rs.
Creditors	1,00,000
Bank Overdraft	50,000
	1,50,000

3. *Liquid Assets* :

	Rs.
Debtors	50,000
Cash	1,00,000
	1,50,000

4. *Liquid Liabilities* :

	Rs.
Creditors	1,00,000

5. *Absolute Liquid Assets* :

	Rs.
Cash	1,00,000

6. *Proprietors Equity* :

	Rs.
Equity Share Capital	2,00,000
10% Preference Share Capital	1,00,000
Reserves and Surplus	1,00,000
	4,00,000

7. *Total Fixed/Tangible Assets* :

	Rs.
Plant and Machinery	2,00,000
Land and Buildings	2,00,000
	4,00,000

8. *Total Debts* :

	Rs.
20% Debentures	1,00,000
Loan (Long-term)	50,000
Current Liabilities	1,50,000
	3,00,000

9. *Working Capital* :
Current Assets – Current Liabilities
Rs. 3,00,000 – Rs. 1,50,000 = **Rs. 1,50,000**

10. *Long-term Funds* :

	Rs.
10% Pref. Share Capital	1,00,000
20% Debentures	1,00,000
Loan	50,000
	2,50,000

11. *Total Assets* :
Fixed Assets + Current Assets
Rs. 4,00,000 + Rs. 3,00,000 = **Rs. 7,00,000**

1. Current Ratio $= \frac{\text{Current Assets}}{\text{Current Liabilities}} = \frac{\text{Rs. } 3{,}00{,}000}{\text{Rs. } 1{,}50{,}000} = \mathbf{2:1}$

2. Liquid Ratio $= \frac{\text{Liquid Assets}}{\text{Liquid Liabilities}} = \frac{\text{Rs. } 1{,}50{,}000}{\text{Rs. } 1{,}00{,}000} = \mathbf{1.5:1}$

3. Absolute Liquid Ratio $= \frac{\text{Absolute Liquid Assets}}{\text{Liquid Liabilities}}$

$$= \frac{\text{Rs. } 1{,}00{,}000}{\text{Rs. } 1{,}00{,}000} = \mathbf{1:1}$$

4. Proprietary Ratio $= \frac{\text{Proprietors' Equity}}{\text{Total Assets}} = \frac{\text{Rs. } 4{,}00{,}000}{\text{Rs. } 7{,}00{,}000} = \mathbf{0.57:1}$

5. Asset Proprietorship Ratio

(*i*) *Fixed Assets to Proprietor?s Equity*: $\frac{\text{Fixed Assets}}{\text{Proprietors? Equity}}$

$$= \frac{\text{Rs. 4,00,000}}{\text{Rs. 4,00,000}} = \mathbf{1:1}$$

(*ii*) *Current Assets to Proprietors' Equity*: $\frac{\text{Current Assets}}{\text{Proprietors? Equity}}$

$$= \frac{\text{Rs. 3,00,000}}{\text{Rs. 4,00,000}} = \mathbf{0.75:1}$$

6. Debt-Equity Ratio = $\frac{\text{Total Debts}}{\text{Proprietors' Equity}}$

$$= \frac{\text{Rs. 3,00,000}}{\text{Rs. 4,00,000}} = \mathbf{0.75:1}$$

7. Stock to Working Capital Ratio = $\frac{\text{Stock}}{\text{Working Capital}}$

$$= \frac{\text{Rs. 1,50,000}}{\text{Rs. 1,50,000}} = \mathbf{1:1}$$

8. Stock to Current Asset Ratio = $\frac{\text{Stock}}{\text{Current Assets}}$

$$= \frac{\text{Rs.1,50,000}}{\text{Rs. 3,00,000}} = \mathbf{0.5:1}$$

9. Current Assets to Working Capital Ratio

$$= \frac{\text{Current Assets}}{\text{Working Capital}} = \frac{\text{Rs. 3,00,000}}{\text{Rs.1,50,000}} = \mathbf{2:1}$$

10. Current Assets to Liquid Asset Ratio:

$$= \frac{\text{Current Assets}}{\text{Liquid Assets}} = \frac{\text{Rs. 3,00,000}}{\text{Rs. 1,50,000}} = \mathbf{2:1}$$

11. All Long-term funds to Working Capital Ratio:

$$= \frac{\text{All Long-term Funds}}{\text{Working Capital}} = \frac{\text{Rs. 2,50,000}}{\text{Rs. 1,50,000}} = \mathbf{1.67:1}$$

12. Tangible Assets to Working Capital Ratio:

$$= \frac{\text{Tangible Assets}}{\text{Working Capital}} = \frac{\text{Rs. 4,00,000}}{\text{Rs. 1,50,000}} = \mathbf{2.67:1}$$

13. Capital Gearing Ratio:

$$= \frac{\text{Pref. Shares + Debentures}}{\text{Equity Share Capital}} = \frac{\text{Rs. 2,00,000}}{\text{Rs. 2,00,000}} = \mathbf{1:1}$$

REVENUE STATEMENT RATIOS (PROFIT & LOSS ACCOUNT RATIOS)

Profit earning is the main objective of each business concern. A company should earn profits to survive and to grow over a long period. A measure of profitability is the overall measure of efficiency. Profitability should be distinguished from profits. Profits refers to the absolute quantum of profit whereas profitability refers to the ability to earn profits. Profitability is a measure of efficiency and control. It is the main objective of every concern to earn maximum profit not only in absolute terms but also in relative terms. Profit is an absolute measure of earning capacity and profitability is the relative measure of earning capacity.

Profit is the engine that drives the business enterprise. Profit is an index of economic progress. Profits are the test of efficiency and a measure of control to the management. It is a measure of the worth of owners investment. It is the margin of safety to creditors. It is a source of fringe benefits to employees. Profit is a measure of tax paying capacity to the Government. To Customers, it is a hint for demand for price cuts. Operation ratios and activity ratios or efficiency ratios are calculated to measure the profitability of an enterprise. Operating ratios relate to income statement and activity ratios are mixed ratios.

Poor operational performance may result in poor sales and, therefore, low profits. Low profitability may be due to lack of control over expenses resulting in low profits. Profitability ratios are employed by management in order to assess how efficiently they carry on business operations. Profitability is the main base for liquidity as well as solvency. Creditors, banks and financial institutions are interested in profitability ratios since they indicate liquidity or capacity of the business to meet interest obligations and regular and improved profits enhance the long term solvency position of the business. Owners are interested in profitability for they indicate the growth of and also the rate of return on their investments.

Profit is the difference between total revenues and total expenses over a period of time. Profitability reflects the final result of a business operation. Profit is the ultimate output of a company and it will have no future if it fails to make sufficient profits. Therefore, the financial manager should continuously evaluate the efficiency of its company in terms of profits. Profitability analysis comprises the study of sales, analysis of cost of goods sold, analysis of gross margin on sales, analysis of operating expenses, analysis of operating profit and analysis of profit in relation to sales and capital. There are two types of profitability ratios. They are Profit margin ratios and rate of return ratios. Profit margin ratios show the relationship between profit and sales. Rate of return ratios reflect the relationship between profit and investments. Profitability ratios can be determined on the basis of either sales or investments. Many ratios are being used in such type of analysis which are as under :

1. Gross Profit Ratio

The Gross Profit Ratio is also known as Gross Margin Ratio, Trading Margin Ratio etc. It is expressed as a "Per Cent Ratio." The difference between Net Sales and Cost of Goods Sold is known as Gross Profit. Gross profit is highly significant. The earning capacity of the business can be ascertained by taking the margin between cost of goods sold and sales. It is very useful as a test of profitability and management efficiency. It is generally contented that the margin of gross profit should be sufficient enough to recover all operating expenses and other expenses and also leave adequate amount as Net Profit in relation to sales and owners' equity. Thus, in a trading business, gross profit is net sales minus trading cost of sales.

Cost of Goods Sold

$$= \begin{bmatrix} \text{Opening} \\ \text{Stock} \end{bmatrix} + [\text{Purchases}] - \begin{bmatrix} \text{Closing} \\ \text{Stock} \end{bmatrix} + \text{All direct expenses}$$

(All direct expenses means the expenses relating to purchases *i.e.,* all expenses charged to Trading Account)

Cost of Goods Sold, in the case of manufacturing concern, is the sum of the cost of raw materials used, wages, direct expenses and all manufacturing expenses. Net sales means total sales minus sales return.

$$\text{Gross Profit Ratio} = \frac{\text{Gross Profit}}{\text{Net Sales}} \times 100$$

or

$$= \frac{\text{Sales} - \text{Cost of Goods Sold}}{\text{Net Sales}} \times 100$$

Gross profit ratio shows the gap between revenue and trading costs. Maintenance of steady gross profit ratio is important. An analysis of Gross Profit Margin should be carried out in the light of information relating to purchasing, increasing or reducing the sales price of goods sold by mark up and mark downs, credit and collections and merchandising policies.

If Gross Profit Ratio is deducted from 100, then the balance will represent the ratio between Cost of Sales and Sales *i.e.,* direct operating ratio. This ratio also indirectly highlights upon the margin of gross profit of the concern.

A higher ratio may be the result of one or all of the following :

1. Increase in the selling price of goods sold without any corresponding increase in the cost of goods sold.
2. Decrease in the cost of goods sold without corresponding decrease in selling price.
3. Both selling price and cost of goods sold may have changed, the combined effect being increase in gross margin.
4. Out of sales-mixes, product having higher gross profit margin, should have been sold in larger quantity.
5. Under-valuation of opening stock or over-valuation of closing stock.

On the other hand, if the Gross Profit Ratio is very low, it may be an indicator of lower and poor profitability. A lower ratio may be the result of the following factors :

1. Decrease in the selling price of goods sold, without corresponding decrease in cost of goods sold.
2. Increase in cost of goods sold without any increase in selling price.
3. Unfavourable purchasing policies.
4. Over-valuation of opening stock or under-valuation of closing stock.
5. Inability of management to improve sales volume.

Normally, the Gross Profit Ratio should remain the same from year to year, because cost of sales will normally vary directly and in the same proportion with sales. Higher ratio is better. The financial manager must be able to detect the causes of a falling gross margin and initiate action to improve the situation. A ratio of 25% to 30% may be considered good.

2. Operating Ratios

This ratio establishes the relationship between total operating expenses and sales. Total operating expenses include cost of goods, administrative expenses, financial expenses and selling expenses. Cost of goods sold are also known as direct operating expenses and the rest are known as other operating expenses. Operating ratios are generally expressed in percentages.

$$\text{Operating Ratio} = \frac{\text{Cost of goods sold} + \text{Operating Expenses}}{\text{Net Sales}} \times 100$$

Cost of goods sold = Opening stock + Purchases – Closing stock

$$\text{Operating expenses} = \begin{Bmatrix}\text{Administrative} \\ \text{Expenses}\end{Bmatrix} + \begin{Bmatrix}\text{Financial} \\ \text{Expenses}\end{Bmatrix} + \begin{Bmatrix}\text{Selling} \\ \text{Expenses}\end{Bmatrix}$$

Operating profit ratio can be computed by subtracting the operating ratio from 100. It is an important ratio. It is used to discuss the general profitability of the concern. A business concern is said to be efficient if it is able to keep up the cost of goods sold and other operating expenses as low as possible in relation to the net sales effected.

This ratio shows the operational efficiency of the firm. Lower operating ratio shows the higher operating profit and vice versa. For manufacturing concern an operating ratio between 75% and 80% is expected.

$$\text{Material Consumed Ratio} = \frac{\text{Materials Consumed}}{\text{Net Sales}} \times 100$$

Conversion Cost Ratio (Manufacturing Expense Ratio)

$$= \frac{\text{Manufacturing Expenses} - \text{Material Cost}}{\text{Net Sales}} \times 100$$

3. Expenses Ratio

The expenses is also known as supporting ratios to operating ratio. It becomes imperative that each aspect of cost of sales and/or operating expenses should be analysed in detail just to find out as how far the concern is able to save or is making over expenditure in respect of different items of expenses. For this, relationship of each item of expenses to sales is established. Thus these ratios reveal the relation of different expenses to net sales. There are many expenses ratio. The following are a few :

(*a*) $\text{Factory Expenses Ratio} = \frac{\text{Factory Expenses}}{\text{Net Sales}} \times 100$

(*b*) $\text{Administrative Expense Ratio} = \frac{\text{Administrative Expense}}{\text{Net Sales}} \times 100$

(*c*) $\text{Selling Expense Ratio} = \frac{\text{Selling Expense}}{\text{Net Sales}} \times 100$

(*d*) $\text{Particular Expense Ratio} = \frac{\text{Particular Expense}}{\text{Net Sales}} \times 100$

These ratios are compared with the same ratios of the previous year or some standard ratios determined by the management. The lower the ratio, the greater is the profitability.

Example :

Cost of goods sold	Rs. 1,80,000
Other operating expenses	Rs. 30,000
Net Sales	Rs. 3,00,000

Find operating ratio and operating profit ratio.

Solution :

$$\text{Operating Ratio} = \frac{\text{Rs. }1{,}80{,}000 + \text{Rs. }30{,}000}{\text{Rs. }3{,}00{,}000} \times 100 = 70\%$$

Operating Profit Ratio = 100% – 70% = 30%

4. Net Profit Ratio

It is also called Net Profit to Sales Ratio (= Profit margin). The profit margin is indicative of management's ability to operate the business with sufficient success not only to recover from revenues of the period, the cost of merchandise or services, the expenses of operating the business and the cost of borrowed funds, but also to leave a margin of reasonable compensation to the owners for providing their capital at risk. Higher the ratio of net operating profit to sales, better is the operational efficiency of the concern.

$$\text{Net Profit Ratio} = \frac{\text{Net Profit}}{\text{Net Sales}} \times 100$$

This ratio is used to measure the overall profitability and hence it is very useful to proprietors. It is an index of efficiency and profitability when used with gross profit ratio and operating ratio.

Illustration 10 From the following particulars found in the Trading, Profit and Loss Account of A Company Ltd., work out the operation ratio of the business concern :

TRADING ACCOUNT OF A COMPANY LTD.
for the period ending December 31

Dr. *Cr.*

Expenses	*Rs.*	*Incomes*	*Rs.*
To Opening Stock	1,400	By Net Sales	10,000
To Purchases	6,400	By Closing Stock	600
To Direct Expenses	300		
To Gross Profit	2,500		
	10,600		10,600

PROFIT AND LOSS ACCOUNT OF A COMPANY LTD.
for the period ending December 31

Dr. *Cr.*

Expenses	*Rs.*	*Incomes*	*Rs.*
To Operating Expenses:		By Gross Profit	2,500
(a) Administrative Expenses	1,600		
(b) Selling and Distribution Expenses	300		
To Financial Expenses	100		
To Net Profit	500		
	2,500		2,500

Solution :

$$\text{Operating Ratio} = \frac{\text{Cost of goods sold and other operating expenses}}{\text{Net sales}} \times 100$$

	Rs.
Cost of Goods Sold :	
Opening Stock	1,400
Purchases	6,400
Direct Expenses	300
	8,100
Less Closing Stock	600
Cost of Goods Sold	7,500

Operating Expenses :	Rs.
(a) Administrative Expenses	1,600
(b) Selling and Distribution Expenses	300
(c) Financial Expenses	100
Operating Expenses	2,000

$$\text{Operating ratio} = \frac{7{,}500 + 2{,}000}{10{,}000} \times 100 = 95\%$$

Illustration 11. Alpha Manufacturing Co. has drawn up the following Profit and Loss Account for the year ended 31st March.

	Rs.		Rs.
To Opening Stock	26,000	By Sales	1,60,000
To Purchases	80,000	By Closing Stock	38,000
To Wages	24,000		
To Manufacturing Expenses	16,000		
To Gross Profit c/d	52,000		
	1,98,000		1,98,000
To Selling & Dist. Expenses	4,000	By Gross Profit b/d	52,000
To Administrative Expenses	22,800	By Compensation for acquisition of land	4,800
To General Expenses	1,200		
To Value of furniture lost by fire	800		
To Net Profit	28,000		
	56,8000		56,8000

You are required to find out :

(a) Gross Profit Ratio

(b) Net Profit Ratio

(c) Operating Ratio

(d) Operating Net Profit to Net Sales Ratio [C.A. Inter]

Solution :

(a) $\text{Gross Profit Ratio} = \frac{\text{Gross Profit}}{\text{Net Sales}} \times 100$

$$= \frac{52{,}000}{1{,}60{,}000} \times 100 = 32.5\%$$

(b) $\text{Net Profit Ratio} = \frac{\text{Net Profit}}{\text{Net Sales}} \times 100$

$$= \frac{28{,}000}{1{,}60{,}000} \times 100 = 17.5\%$$

(c) $\text{Operating Ratio} = \frac{\text{Cost of Goods Sold + All operating Exp.}}{\text{Sales}} \times 100$

(Cost of goods sold = Opening Stock + Purchases + Direct Expenses
That is Rs. 26,000 + 80,000 + 24,000 + 16,000 – 38,000 = 1,08,000)

(Operating Expenses = Rs. 4,000 + 22,800 + 1,200 = 28,000

$$\text{Operating ratio} = \frac{1,08,000 + 28,000}{1,60,000} \times 100 = 85\%$$

(*d*) Operating Net Profit to Net Sales Ratio

$$= \frac{\text{Operating Net Profit}}{\text{Sales}} \times 100$$

$$= \frac{28,000 + 800 - 4,800}{1,60,000} \times 100 = 15\%$$

Illustration 12 The following figures relate to the trading activities of Hind Traders Limited for the year ended 30th June.

	Rs.
Sales	5,20,000
Purchases	3,22,250
Opening Stock	76,250
Closing Stock	98,500
Sales returns	20,000
Selling and Distribution expenses :	
Salaries	15,300
Advertising	4,700
Travelling	2,000
Administrative expenses :	
Salaries	27,000
Rent	2,700
Stationery, Postage etc.	2,500
Depreciation	9,300
Other Charges	16,500
Provision for Taxation	40,000
Non-operating Income :	
Dividend on Shares	9,000
Profit on Sales of Shares	3,000
Non-operating expenses :	
Loss on Sale of Assets	4,000

You are required to

(*a*) Arrange the above figures in a form suitable for analysis, and

(*b*) Show separately the following ratios :

(1) Gross Profit Ratio

(2) Operating Ratio

(3) Operating Profit Ratio

(4) Net Profit Ratio [*C.A. Final & B.Com., Guru Nanak*]

Solution :

REVENUE STATEMENT OF HIND TRADERS LTD.

for the year ended 30th June

		Rs.	*Rs.*
Sales		5,20,000	
Less : Sales Returns		20,000	5,00,000
Less : Cost of Goods Sold :			
Opening Stock	76,250		
Purchases	3,22,250	3,98,500	

Less : Closing Stock		98,500	3,00,000
Gross Profit			2,00,000
Less : Operating Expenses :			
Selling and Distribution Expenses :			
Salaries	15,300		
Advertising	4,700		
Travelling	2,000	22,000	
Administrative Expenses :			
Salaries	27,000		
Rent	2,700		
Stationary, Postage etc.	2,500		
Depreciation	9,300		
Other Charges	16,500		
Provision for Taxation	40,000	98,000	1,20,000
Operating Profit			80,000
Add : Non-operating Income :			
Dividend on Shares	9,000		
Profit on Sale of Shares	3,000	12,000	
Less : Non-operating Expenses :			
Loss on Sale of Assets		4,000	8,000
Net Profit			88,000

(1) Gross Profit Ratio $= \frac{\text{Gross Profit}}{\text{Net Sales}} \times 100 = \frac{2,00,000}{5,00,000} \times 100 = 40\%$

(2) Operating Ratio $= \frac{\text{Cost of Goods Sold + Operating Expenses}}{\text{Net Sales}} \times 100$

$$= \frac{3,00,000 + 1,20,000}{5,00,000} \times 100 = 84\%$$

(3) Operating Profit Ratio $= \frac{\text{Operating Profit}}{\text{Sales}} \times 100 = \frac{80,000}{5,00,000} \times 100 = 16\%$

(4) Net Profit Ratio $= \frac{\text{Net Profit}}{\text{Sales}} \times 100 = \frac{88,000}{5,00,000} \times 100 = 17.6\%$

Illustration 13. The following is the summarised Profit and Loss Account of Taj Products Ltd. for the year ended 31st December.

PROFIT AND LOSS ACCOUNT

	Rs.		*Rs.*
Opening stock of Materials	99,500	Sales	8,50,000
Purchase of Materials	3,20,000	Stock of Materials (Closing)	89,000
Direct Wages	2,25,250		
Manufacturing Expenses	14,250	Stock of Finished Goods (Closing)	60,000
Selling & Distribution		Non-operating Income Interest	3,000
Expenses	30,000	Profit on sale of Shares	6,000
Administrative Expenses	1,50,000		

Finance Charges	15,000		
Non-operating Expenses:			
Loss on sale of Assets	4,000		
Net Profit	1,50,000		
	10,08,000		10,08,000

Work out the following ratios :

(1) Gross Profit Ratio
(2) Net Profit Ratio
(3) Operating Ratio
(4) Cost ratios (to cost of Production)
  (*i*) Materials consumed Ratio
  (*ii*) Labour Cost Ratio
  (*iii*) Production Overhead Cost Ratio.

(*B.Com. Madurai Kerala, MS.*)

Solution:

		Rs.
Gross Sales (*a*)		8,50,000
Less : Cost of Goods Sold :	Rs.	
Opening Stock of Materials	99,500	
Add : Materials purchased	3,20,000	
	4,19,500	
Less : Stock of materials (Closing)	89,000	
Materials Consumed : (*b*)	3,30,500	
Direct Wages	2,25,250	
Manufacturing Expenses	14,250	
Cost of Production (*c*)	5,70,000	
Less : Closing Stock of Finished Products	60,000	
Cost of Goods sold (*d*)		5,10,000
Gross Profit (*e*)		3,40,000
Less : Administrative Expenses	1,50,000	
Selling and Distribution	30,000	1,80,000
Net Operating Profit before Interest and Taxation : (f)		1,60,000
Add : *Non-operating Incomes (g)*		
Interest	3,000	
Profit on sale of shares	6,000	9,000
		1,69,000
Less : Loss on sale of Assets	4,000	
Finance Charges	15,000	19,000
Income before Taxation (h)		1,50,000

$$(1)\ \text{Gross Profit Ratio} = \frac{\text{Gross Profit}}{\text{Net Sales}} \times 100$$

$$= \frac{\text{Rs. } 3{,}40{,}000}{\text{Rs. } 8{,}50{,}000} \times 100 = 40\%$$

(2) Net Profit Ratio $= \dfrac{\text{Net Profit}}{\text{Net Sales}} \times 100$

$$= \frac{1,60,000}{\text{Rs. } 8,50,000} \times 100 = 18.82\%$$

(3) Operating Ratio $= \dfrac{\text{Cost of Goods Sold + Operating Expenses}}{\text{Net Sales}} \times 100$

$$= \frac{\text{Rs. } 5,10,000 + \text{Rs. } 1,80,000}{\text{Rs. } 8,50,000} \times 100 = 81.18\%$$

(4) (*i*) Material Consumed Ratio $= \dfrac{\text{Material Consumed}}{\text{Cost of Product}} \times 100$

$$= \frac{\text{Rs. } 3,30,500}{\text{Rs. } 5,70,000} \times 100 = 57.98\%$$

(*ii*) Labour cost ratio $= \dfrac{\text{Labour Cost}}{\text{Cost of Production}} \times 100$

$$= \frac{\text{Rs. } 2,25,250}{\text{Rs. } 5,70,000} \times 100 = 39.52\%$$

(*iii*) Production Overhead Ratio $= \dfrac{\text{Production Overhead}}{\text{Cost of Production}} \times 100$

$$= \frac{\text{Rs. } 14,250}{\text{Rs. } 5,70,000} \times 100 = 2.5\%$$

Profitability Ratios Related to Investments

The profitability of the firm is also measured in relation to investments. The term investment may refer to total assets, capital employed or the owners' equity. The efficiency of an enterprise is judged by the amount of profits. But sometimes the conclusion drawn on the basis of profit-to-sales ratios may be misleading. Because it is possible that profit in terms of sales is sufficient but sales with regard to capital may be inadequate. Therefore, the state of efficiency cannot be judged by the volume of profits alone: we have to consider the size of investment alongwith profit. The shareholders can measure the success of a firm in terms of profit related to capital employed. The efficiency can only be judged by calculating return on capital employed or with investments. The volume of profit depends to a great extent upon the volume of investments. Investments are represented by those assets which are acquired for conducting the business operations, mainly production and sales and the size of investments (asset) certainly affects the volume of profit. The important categories of such ratios are discussed below :

(i) Return on Assets

Profitability can be measured in terms of relationship between net profit and assets. This ratio is also known as profit-to-assets ratio. It measures the profitability of investments. The overall profitability can be known.

$$\text{Return on Assets} = \frac{\text{Net Profit}}{\text{Total Assets}} \times 100$$

There are various approaches possible to define net profits and assets, according to the purpose and intent of the calculation of the ratios.

(ii) Return on Capital Employed

This is the second type ROI (Return on Investment). This is also known as Return on Investment or Rate of Return. The prime objective of making investments in any business is to obtain satisfactory return on capital invested. It indicates the percentage of return on the capital employed in the business and it can be used to show the efficiency of the business as a whole.

$$\text{Return on Capital Employed} = \frac{\text{Operating Profit}}{\text{Capital Employed}} \times 100$$

The term capital employed refers to long-term funds supplied by the creditors and owners of the firm. It can be computed in two ways. First, it is equal to non-current liabilities (Long-term liabilities) plus owners' equity. Alternatively, it is equivalent to net working capital plus fixed assets. Thus, the capital employed basis provides a test of profitability related to the sources of long-term funds. A comparison of this ratio with similar firms, with the industry average and over time would provide sufficient insight into how efficiently the long-term funds of owners and creditors are being used. The higher the ratio, the more efficient use of the capital employed.

(iii) Return on Shareholders Equity

This ratio establishes the profitability from the shareholders point of view.

$$\text{Return on Shareholder' Equity} = \frac{\text{Net Profit}}{\text{Shareholders Fund}} \times 100$$

The term Net Profit as used here, means net income after payment of interest and tax including net non-operating income (*i.e.* Non-operating income minus non-operating expenses). It is the final income that is available for distribution as dividends to shareholders. Shareholders' funds include both preference and equity share capital and all reserves and surplus belonging to shareholders.

Illustration 14. From the following Balance Sheet and additional information, you are required to calculate :

(*i*) Return on Total Resources
(*ii*) Return on Capital Employed
(*iii*) Return on Shareholders' Fund

BALANCE SHEET as on 31st Dec.

	Rs.		*Rs.*
Share Capital (Rs. 10)	8,00,000	Fixed Assets	10,00,000
Reserves	2,00,000	Current Assets	3,60,000
8% Debentures	2,00,000		
Creditors	1,60,000		
	13,60,000		13,60,000

Net operating profit before tax is Rs. 2,80,000. Assume tax rate at 50%. Dividend declared amounts to Rs.1,20,000. (*B.Com. MS.*)

Solution.

(*i*) $\text{Retrun on Total Resources} = \frac{\text{Profit after Tax}}{\text{Total Assets}} \times 100$

$$= \frac{\text{Rs.}1,40,000}{\text{Rs.}13,60,000} \times 100 = 10.29\%$$

(*ii*) Return on Capital Employed

$$= \frac{\text{Profit before Tax \& Interest}}{\text{Capital Employed}} \times 100$$

$$= \frac{\text{Rs.2,96,000}}{\text{Rs.12,00,000}} \times 100 = 24.7\%$$

(*iii*) Return on Shareholders' Fund

$$= \frac{\text{Profit after Tax}}{\text{Shareholders Fund}} \times 100$$

$$= \frac{\text{Rs.1,40,000}}{\text{Rs.10,00,000}} \times 100 = 14\%$$

Illustration 15. A company has capital of Rs.10,00,000; its turnover is 3 times the capital and the margin on sales is 6%. What is the return on investment. (*M.Com. Delhi*)

Solution.

$$\text{Capital Turnover Ratio} = \frac{\text{Sales}}{\text{Capital}}$$

$$3 = \frac{\text{Sales}}{\text{Rs. 10,00,000}}$$

$$\text{Sales} = \text{Rs. 30,00,000}$$

$$\text{Rate of Return on Investment} = \frac{\text{Gross Profit}}{\text{Investment}} \times 100$$

$$= \frac{\text{Rs. 1,80,000}}{\text{Rs. 10,00,000}}$$

$$= 18\%$$

$$\text{Gross Profit} = 6\% \text{ of Rs. 30,00,000}$$

$$= \text{Rs. 1, 80,000}$$

COMBINED RATIOS

Activity Ratios or Turnover Ratios

This category of ratios include those ratios, which highlight upon the activity and operational efficiency of the business concern. The funds of creditors and owners are invested in various kinds of assets to generate sales and profits. The better the management of assets, the larger the amount of sales. *Activity ratios*, also referred to as *turnover ratios* or *asset management ratios*, measure how efficiently the assets are employed by the firm. These ratios indicate the speed with which assets are being converted or turned over into sales. The efficiency with which the assets are used would be reflected in the speed and rapidity with which assets are converted into sales. Activity ratios, thus, involve a relationship between sales and various assets and presume that there exist an appropriate balance between sales and the various assets. The efficiency of a firm depends, to a large extent, on the efficiency with which its assets are managed and utilised. Activity ratios are concerned with measuring the efficiency in asset management. These ratios are also called *efficiency ratios*.

The liquidity ratios and leverage ratios, it may be recalled, are relevant for the short-term and long-term creditors of the firm. The profitability ratios are useful in assessing the profitability of a firm to its owners as also operational efficiency of a firm. The efficiency of a firm depends, to a large extent, on the efficiency with which its assets are managed and utilised. Thus, the activity ratios are concerned with measuring the efficiency in asset management. An activity ratio may, therefore, be defined as a test of the relationship between sales and various assets of a firm.

Every business concern formulates certain policies with regard to the operation of the business and then it acquires financial resources in the form of fixed and current assets, which are being constantly used in the operation of the concern. The success or failure of the concern depends upon proper and judicious use of these resources.

To examine the efficiency and profitability in making use of these resources certain ratios are being used and they are collectively called as *Activity Ratios or Performance Ratios*.

It is significant to note that these ratios are always expressed as *turnover or in number of times i.e.* rate of turning over or rotation. These are also known as *velocities*. Several activity ratios can be calculated to judge the effectiveness of asset utilisation. The following are the important and widely used ratios :

INVENTORY (STOCK) TURNOVER

This is also known as Stock Velocity. This ratio is calculated to consider the adequacy of the quantum of capital and its justification for investing in inventory. A firm must have reasonable stock in comparison to sales. It is the ratio of cost of sales and average inventory. This ratio helps the financial manager to evaluate inventory policy. This ratio reveals the number of times finished stock is turned over during a given accounting period. This ratio is used for measuring the profitability. The various ways in which Stock Turnover Ratios may be calculated are as follows :

$$(i)\ \text{Stock Turnover Ratio} = \frac{\text{Cost of Goods Sold}}{\text{Average Inventory at cost}}$$

$$\text{(or) } (ii)\ \qquad = \frac{\text{Net Sales}}{\text{Average Inventory at cost}}$$

$$\text{(or) } (iii)\ \qquad = \frac{\text{Net Sales}}{\text{Average Inventory at selling price}}$$

$$\text{(or) } (iv)\ \qquad = \frac{\text{No. of Units Sold}}{\text{Average No. of Units in Stock}}$$

Stock turnover ratio can be calculated by employing any one of the above formulae. The first and third formulae are considered more reasonable. The second can be used when the cost of goods sold is not known. The fourth formula is used to eliminate the effect of changing prices.

$$\text{Average Stock} = \frac{\text{Opening Stock} + \text{Closing Stock}}{2}$$

Cost of goods sold may be calculated as under :

(*i*) *In case of Trading Concerns* :

$$\text{Cost of goods sold} = \left\{ \begin{matrix}\text{Opening}\\ \text{Stock}\end{matrix} + \text{Purchases} + \begin{matrix}\text{Direct}\\ \text{Expenses}\end{matrix} \right\} - \text{(Closing Stock)}$$

(*ii*) *In case of Manufacturing concerns* :

$$\text{Cost of Goods sold} = \left\{ \begin{matrix}\text{Total}\\ \text{Cost}\end{matrix} + \begin{matrix}\text{Opening Stock}\\ \text{of Finished goods}\end{matrix} \right\} - \left\{ \begin{matrix}\text{Closing Stock of}\\ \text{Finished goods}\end{matrix} \right\}$$

$$\text{Total Cost} = \left\{ \begin{matrix} \text{Raw Materials} \\ \text{Consumed (cost)} \end{matrix} + \text{Labour Cost} + \text{Overheads Cost)} \right\}$$

(*iii*) *In all cases where Gross Profit is known* :

Cost of goods Sold = Sales – Gross Profit

This ratio indicates whether investment in inventory is within proper limit or not. The quantum of stock should be sufficient to meet the demands of the business but it should not be too large to indicate unnecessary lock-up of capital in stock and danger of stock-items obsolete and getting it wasted by passing of time.

The inventory turnover ratio measures how quickly inventory is sold. It is a test of efficient inventory management. To judge whether the ratio of a firm is satisfactory or not, it should be compared over a time on the basis of trend analysis.

Illustration 16. Calculate Stock Turnover Ratio.

Opening Stock	Rs. 20,000
Closing Stock	Rs. 10,000
Purchases	Rs. 50,000
Wages	Rs. 3,000
Carriage Inward	Rs. 2,000
Freight Outward	Rs. 5,000

(*M.Com. Madras*)

Solution:

Cost of Goods Sold = Opening Stock + Purchases + Wages + Carriage Inward – Closing Stock

= Rs. 20,000 + Rs. 50,000 + Rs. 3,000 + Rs. 2,000 – Rs. 10,000

= Rs. 65,000

$$\text{Average Stock} = \frac{\text{Opening Stock + Closing Stock}}{2}$$

$$= \frac{\text{Rs. } 20{,}000 + \text{Rs. } 10{,}000}{2}$$

= Rs. 15,000

$$\text{Stock Turnover Ratio} = \frac{\text{Cost of Goods Sold}}{\text{Average Stock}}$$

$$= \frac{\text{Rs. } 65{,}000}{\text{Rs. } 15{,}000}$$

= **4.3 Times**

Illustration 17. Ram & Company supplies you the following information regarding the year ended 31st December.

Cash Sales	Rs. 80,000
Credit Sales	Rs. 2,00,000
Return inward	Rs. 10,000
Opening Stock	Rs. 25,000
Closing Stock	Rs. 30,000

Gross Profit Ratio is 25%

Find out Inventory Turnover. (*B.Com. Madurai*)

Solution :

$$\text{Inventory Turnover} = \frac{\text{Cost of goods sold}}{\text{Average Inventory at cost}}$$

Net Sales = Rs. 80,000 + Rs. 2,00,000 – Rs. 10,000

Rs. = 270,000

Cost of Goods sold = Sales – Gross Profit

= Rs. 2,70,000 – (25% of Rs. 2,70,000)

= Rs. 2,70,000 – Rs. 67,500

= Rs. 2,02,500

$$\text{Average Inventory} = \frac{\text{Rs. } 25{,}000 + \text{Rs. } 30{,}000}{2}$$

= Rs. 27,500

$$\text{Inventory Turnover} = \frac{\text{Rs. } 2{,}02{,}500}{\text{Rs. } 27{,}500} = 7.36 \text{ Times}$$

Significance

A high Inventory turnover ratio is better than a low ratio. A high ratio implies good inventory management and an indication of under-investment. It will adversely affect the ability of a firm to meet customers' demand. At the same time, a higher ratio reflects efficient business activities.

A low inventory turnover ratio is dangerous. It is an indication of excessive inventory and over investment in inventory. A low ratio may be result of inferior quality goods, stock of unsaleable and absolete goods. A lower ratio reflects dull business and suggests that some steps should be taken to push up sales.

Illustration 18 Compute Inventory Turnover for each of the three years shown below and give your comments on the results :

	2008	2009	2010
	Rs.	*Rs.*	*Rs.*
Cost of goods sold	7,60,417	8,54,413	9,55,817
Average Inventory	3,36,420	3,08,243	3,10,412

Solution :

$$\text{Inventory Turnover Ratio} = \frac{\text{Cost of Goods Sold}}{\text{Average Stock}}$$

$$2008 = \frac{\text{Rs. } 7{,}60{,}417}{\text{Rs. } 3{,}36{,}420} = 2.26 \text{ times}$$

$$2009 = \frac{\text{Rs. } 8{,}54{,}413}{\text{Rs. } 3{,}08{,}243} = 2.77 \text{ times}$$

$$2010 = \frac{\text{Rs. } 9{,}55{,}817}{\text{Rs. } 3{,}10{,}412} = 3.08 \text{ times}$$

Comment :

It is seen from the above calculations, that there is a continuous increase in the Stock Turnover Ratios. There is good progress in respect of sales policy. The company was able to sell

Rs. 2.26 by investing rupee one in stock, in 2008; the same sales amounted to Rs. 2.77 by investing rupee one in stock in 2009 and increased its sales to Rs. 3.08 at cost keeping its investment in stock at Re. one in 2009. This is an indicator of good sales policy.

Illustration 19 The following is the Profit and Loss Account of Burn Ltd.

	Rs.		*Rs.*
To Opening Stock :			
Materials	60,000	By Sales	12,70,000
Finished Goods	80,000	By Closing Stock :	
		Materials	70,000
To Purchase (Raw Materials)	6,00,000	Finished Goods	1,00,000
To Wages	3,00,000		
To Factory Expenses	1,00,000		
To Other Expenses	2,00,000		
To Net Profit	1,00,000		
	14,40,000		14,40,000

You are required to calculate the following :

(*i*) Stock Turnover

(*ii*) Raw Materials Turnover

(*iii*) Average material holding (*B.Com. Bhopal, Agra, Madurai*)

Solution :

$$(i) \text{ Stock Turnover} = \frac{\text{Cost of Sales}}{\text{Average Stock}} = \frac{\text{Rs.}11{,}70{,}000}{\text{Rs.}\ 90{,}000} = \mathbf{13\ times}$$

$$(ii) \text{ Raw Materials Turnover} = \frac{\text{Raw Material Consumed}}{\text{Average Stock of Raw Materials}}$$

$$= \frac{\text{Rs.}\ 5{,}90{,}000}{\text{Rs.}\ 65{,}000} = \mathbf{9.08\ times}$$

$$(iii) \text{ Average Material Holding} = \frac{365}{\text{Raw Material Turnover}}$$

$$\text{(Turnover Period)} = \frac{365}{9.08} = \mathbf{40\ days}$$

Workings :

(1) Cost of sales

= Total Cost + Opening Stock of Finished Goods – Closing Stock of finished goods

= Rs. 11,90,000 + Rs. 80,000 – Rs. 1,00,000 = Rs. 11,70,000

$$(2) \text{ Average Stock} = \frac{\text{Opening Stock} + \text{Closing Stock}}{2}$$

Average stock of finished goods

$$= \frac{\text{Rs.}\ 80{,}000 + \text{Rs.}1{,}00{,}000}{2} = \text{Rs.}\ 90{,}000$$

Average stock of Raw Materials

$$= \frac{\text{Rs.}\ 60{,}000 + \text{Rs.}\ 70{,}000}{2} = \text{Rs.}65{,}000$$

(3) Raw Materials Consumed

= Opening Stock + Purchase – Closing Stock

= Rs. 60,000 + Rs. 6,00,000 – Rs. 70,000

= Rs. 5, 90,000

DEBTORS TURNOVER RATIO

This is also called "Debtors Velocity" or "Receivable Turnover". A firm sells goods on credit and cash basis. When the firm extends credits to its customers, book debts (Debtors or Account Receivable) are created in the firm's account : debtors expected to be converted into cash over short period and thus included in current assets. Debtors includes the amount of Bills Receivables and Book Debts at the end of accounting period. It is most essential that a reasonable quantitative relationship between Outstanding Receivables and Sales should always be maintained. If the firm has not been able to collect its debtors within a reasonable time, its funds are unnecessarily locked up in Receivables. In such case short-term loans have to be arranged for paying off its current liabilities. The liquidity position of the firm depends on the quality of debtors to a great extent. Financial analysts employ two ratios to judge the quality or liquidity of debtors—Debtors Turnover and Average Collection Period."

The question of account receivables arises only against credit sales. Debtors Turnover establishes the relationship between Net Sales of the year and Average Receivables. That is, it measures the number of times the Receivables rotate in a year in terms of sales. It shows how quickly debtors are converted into cash.

$$\text{Debtors Turnover} = \frac{\text{Credit Sales}}{\text{Average Debtors}}$$

$$\text{Average Debtors} = \frac{\text{Opening Balance} + \text{Closing Balance}}{2}$$

The purpose of this ratio is to measure the liquidity of the Receivables or to find out the period over which Receivables remain uncollected.

To solve the difficulty arising out of the non-availability of the information in respect of credit sales and average debtors the alternative method is to calculate the Debtors Turnover in terms of the relationship between Total Sales and Closing Balance of Debtors. Thus :

$$\text{Debtors Turnover} = \frac{\text{Total Sales}}{\text{Closing Debtors}}$$

It is important to note that the first approach to the computation of the debtors turnover is superior. The effect of adopting the second approach would be to inflate the Debtors Turnover ratio.

The second type of the ratio for measuring the liquidity of a firm's debtors is the average collection period. This ratio is, in fact, interrelated with, and dependent upon, the Receivable Turnover Ratio. Debt collection period is calculated by any of the following ratios :

(*a*) $\dfrac{\text{Months (or Days) in a year}}{\text{Debtors Turnover}}$

(*b*) $\dfrac{\text{Average Debtors} \times \text{Months (or Days) in a year}}{\text{Net Credit Sales for the year}}$

(*c*) $\dfrac{\text{Accounts Receivable}}{\text{Average Monthly or Daily Credit Sales}}$

Illustration 20 Calculate opening debtors and closing debtors in the following case:

	Rs.
Cash Sales	1,00,000
Cost of Goods sold	3,00,000
Gross Profit	1,00,000

Debtors Turnover Ratio 3 times

Closing debtors were Rs. 1,00,000 in excess of opening debtors.

(*B.com. Calicut*)

Solution :

Total Sales = Cost of Goods sold + Gross Profit
= Rs. 3,00,000 + Rs. 1,00,000
= Rs. 4,00,000

Credit Sales = Total Sales – Cash Sales
= Rs. 4,00,000 – Rs. 1,00,000
= Rs. 3,00,000

Debtors Turnover Ratio

$$= \frac{\text{Net Credit Sales}}{\text{Average Debtors}} = 3$$

$$= \frac{\text{Rs. 3,00,000}}{\text{Average Debtors}} = 3$$

Average Debtors = Rs. 3,00,000 ÷ 3 = Rs. 1,00,000

$$\text{(or)} \quad \frac{\text{Opening Debtors} + \text{Closing Debtors}}{2} = \text{Rs. 1,00,000}$$

(or) Opening Debtors + Closing Debtors = Rs. 1,00,000 × 2 = Rs. 2,00,000

OD + CD = Rs. 2,00,000 (A)

CD – OD = Rs. 1,00,000 (B)

Adding both (A) and (B), wer get:

2 CD = Rs. 3,00,000

CD = Rs. 3,00,000 ÷ 2

CD = Rs.1,50,000

OD = Rs. 1,50,000 – Rs. 1,00,000
= Rs. 50,000

Therefore, Opening Debtors = Rs. 50,000
Closing Debtors = Rs. 1,50,000

Illustration 21 B. Raj and Co. sells goods on cash as well as credit (though not on deferred instalment terms). The following particulars are extracted from their books of accounts for the calendar year 2010.

	Rs.
Total Gross Sales	1,00,000
Cash Sales (included in above)	20,000
Sales Returns	7,000
Total Debtors for Sales as on 31.12.2010	9,000
Bills Receivable on 31.12.2010	2,000
Provision for doubtful debts on 31.12.2010	1,000
Total creditors on 31.12.2010	10,000

Calculate the average collection period

(*C.A., B.Com., Agra*)

Solution :

	Rs.
Net Credit Sales for 2010	
Total Gross Sales	1,00,000
Less : Cash Sales	20,000
Credit Sales	80,000
Less : Sales Returns	7,000
Net credit sales	73,000

$$\text{Average Collection Period} = \frac{\text{Debtors + Bills Receivables}}{\text{Net Credit Sales}} \times 365$$

$$= \frac{9,000 + 2,000}{73,000} \times 365$$

$$= \textbf{55 days}$$

Illustration 22 Calculate Debtors Velocity from the following details :

Opening Balance of Debtors Rs. 10,000
Credit Sales during the year Rs. 20,000
Sales Returns Rs. 1,000
Discount on Sales Rs. 50
Cash collected from Debtors during the year Rs. 5,000
Bad Debts Rs. 500
Bad Debt Provision at 10%

Solution :

The following components are needed to find Debtors Velocity :

1. Net Sales = Gross Sales – (Sales Returns + Discount on Sales)
= Rs. 20,000 – (Rs. 1,000 + Rs. 50)
= Rs. 18.950

2. Net Debtors on Closing = Opening Debtors
Add : Credit Sales
Less : Cash Collection
Less : Sales Returns
Less : Sales Discount

Rs. 10,000 + Rs. 20,000 – (Rs. 5,000 + Rs. 1,000 + Rs. 50) = Rs. 23,950

3. $\text{Average Debtors} = \frac{\text{Opening Debtors + Closing Debtors}}{2}$

$$= \frac{\text{Rs. } 10,000 + \text{Rs. } 23,950}{2} = \text{Rs. } 16,975$$

4. $\text{Average Daily Sales (Credit)} = \frac{\text{Rs. } 18,950}{365} = \text{Rs. } 52$

1. Debtors Turnover (Time)

$$= \frac{\text{Net Sales}}{\text{Average Debtors}} = \frac{\text{Rs. } 18,950}{\text{Rs. } 16,975} = 1.12 \text{ Times}$$

2. $\text{Collection Period} = \frac{365}{1.12} = 326 \text{ days}$

3. Debtors Turnover (Percentage)

$$= \frac{\text{Average}}{\text{Net Sales}} = \frac{\text{Rs. }16{,}975}{\text{Rs. }18{,}950} \times 100 = 89.58\%$$

4. Collection period (Days)

$$= \text{Debtors Turnover (percentage)} \times 365 = 89.58 \times 365 = 326 \text{ Days}$$

5. Collection period

$$= \frac{\text{Average Debtors}}{\text{Average Daily Sales}} = \frac{\text{Rs. }16.975}{\text{Rs. }52} = 326 \text{ Days}$$

Note : Bills Receivable from the buyer of fixed assets, should be excluded.

Bad and doubtful debts and their provisions are not deducted from the total debtors in order to avoid the impression that a larger amount of receivables have been collected.

Significance

A turnover ratio of 8 signifies that debtors get converted into cash 8 times in a year. The average collection period of 1.5 months implies that debtors are collected in 45 days. The average collection period ratio measures the quality of debtors since it indicates the rapidity or slowness of their collectibility. The shorter the average collection period, the better the quality of debtors. The higher the Turnover Ratio and the shorter the average collection period, the better the trade credit management and the better the liquidity of debtors. That is, high Turnover Ratio and short collection period imply prompt payment on the part of debtors. On the other hand, low Turnover Ratio and long collection period reflects that payments by debtors are delayed.

AGEING SCHEDULE

The average collection period measures the quality of debtors in an aggregative way. We can have a detailed idea of the quality of debtors through the Ageing Schedule. The ageing schedule breaks down debtors according to the length of time for which they have been outstanding. An example is given below :

Outstanding period (days)	*Amount of Outstanding Debtors*	*Percentage of Total Debtors*
0 – 30	48,000	36%
31 – 60	52,000	39%
61 – 90	24,000	18%
Above 91	10,000	7%
Total	1,34,000	100%

The Ageing Schedule breaks down debtors according to length of time and quality of debtors. The Average Collection Period measures the quality of debtors in an aggregative way while Ageing Schedule very clearly spots out the slow paying debtors. From the classification, it is clear that 36% of the amounts outstanding are not more than a month old, 39% may be more than a month but less than 2 months, and so on. It also reveals that with some of the accounts the firm has serious problems of collection.

CREDITORS TURNOVER RATIO

This is also known as Accounts Payable or Creditors Velocity. A business firm usually purchase on credit goods, raw materials and services from other firms. The amount of total payables of a business concern depends upon the purchases policy of the concern, the quantity of purchases and suppliers' credit policy. Longer the period of outstanding payable is, lesser is the problem of working capital of the firm. But when the firm does not pay off its creditors within time, it may have adverse effect on the business.

Creditors Turnover indicates the number of times the payable rotate in a year. It signifies the credit period enjoyed by the firm paying Creditors. Accounts payable include Sundry Creditors and Bills Payable.

Payables Turnover shows the relationship between Net Puchases for the whole year and Total Payable (Average or Outstanding at the end of the year)

$$\text{Creditors Turnover Ratio} = \frac{\text{Net Credit Purchase}}{\text{Average Accounts Payable}}$$

$$\text{Average Payment Period} = \frac{\text{Months in a year}}{\text{Creditors Turnover Ratio}}$$

$$\text{(or)} \quad = \frac{\text{Average Accounts Payable} \times \text{Months in a year}}{\text{Credit purchases in the year}}$$

$$\text{(or)} \quad = \frac{\text{Average Accounts Payable}}{\text{Average Monthly credit purchases}}$$

Net Purchase = All Credit Purchases – Purchase Returns

A higher ratio shows that the creditors are not paid in time. A lower ratio shows that the business is not taking the full advantage of credit period allowed by the creditors.

Illustration 23

A trading company purchases goods on cash as well as on credit terms. The following particulars are available :

	Rs.
Total purchases	5,81,000
Cash purchases	30,000
Purchase returns	51,000
Creditors at the end	1,05,000
Bills payable at the end	60,000
Reserve for discount on creditors	10,000

Calculate average payment period. *(B. Com. Ms, Barathiar)*

Solution :

$$\text{Average Payment Period} = \frac{\text{Average Accounts Payable}}{\text{Net Credit Purchases}} \times \text{Months in a year}$$

$$= \frac{1,65,000}{5,00,000} \times 12 = 3.96 \text{ months}$$

$$\text{(or)} \quad = \frac{1,65,000}{5,00,000} \times 360 \text{ days} = 118.8$$

(or) = 119 days

Not Credit purchase = Total Purchase – [Cash Purchases + Returns]

= Rs. 5,81,000 – (30,000 + 51,000)

= Rs. 5,00,000

Accounts payable = Rs. 1,05,000 + 60,000 = Rs, 1,65,000

Illustration 24 From the following figures calculate the Creditors Turnover Ratio and the Average payment period of Accounts Payable:

Credit purchases in 2010 Rs. 10,00,000

Creditors on 1.1.2010	Rs. 2,00,000
Creditors on 31.12.2010	Rs. 1,00,000
Bills Payable on 1.1.2010	Rs. 40,000
Bills Payable on 31.12.2010	Rs. 60,000

Solution :

$$\text{Creditors Turnover Ratio} = \frac{\text{Net Credit Purchase}}{\text{Average Accounts Payable}}$$

$$= \frac{\text{Rs. } 10,00,000}{\text{Rs. } 2,00,000} = 5 \text{ Times}$$

Average Payment Period (Credit Period enjoyed)

$$= \frac{\text{Months in a year}}{\text{Creditors Turnover Ratio}}$$

$$= \frac{12}{5} = 2.4 \text{ Months}$$

$$(or) \quad = \frac{\text{Average Accounts Payable} \times \text{Months in a year}}{\text{Credit Purchase in the year}}$$

$$= \frac{\text{Rs. } 2,00,000}{\text{Rs.} 10,00,000} \times 12 = 2.4 \text{ Months}$$

$$(or) \quad = \frac{\text{Average Accounts Payable}}{\text{Average Monthly Credit purchases}}$$

$$= \frac{\text{Rs. } 2,00,000}{\text{Rs. } 83,333} = 2.4 \text{ Months}$$

$$\frac{\text{Rs.} 10,00,000}{12} = \text{Rs. } 83,333$$

WORKING CAPITAL TURNOVER RATIO

This ratio is a measure of the efficiency of the employment of the working Capital. It indicates the number of times the working capital is turned over in the course of a year. This ratio finds out the relation between cost of sales and working capital. It helps in determining the liquidity of a firm in as much as it gives the rate at which inventories are converted to sales and then to cash.

$$\text{Working Capital Turnover Ratio} = \frac{\text{Cost of Sales}}{\text{Net Working Capital}}$$

(Net Working Capital = Current Assets – Current Liabilities)

Higher sales in comparison to working capital means overtrading and lower sales in comparison to working capital means undertrading. A Higher Working Capital Turnover Ratio shows that there is low investment in working capital and there is more profit.

Illustration 25 Calculate working capital Turnover Ratios from the following:

Current Assets	Rs. 6,00,000
Current Liabilities	Rs. 1,20,000
Credit Sales	Rs. 12,00,000
Cash Sales	Rs. 2,60,000
Sales Returns	Rs. 20,000

(*M.Com. Jabalpur*)

Solution :

Net Sales = Cash Sales + Credit Sales – Sales Returns
= Rs. 2,60,000 + Rs. 12,00,000 – Rs. 20,000
= Rs. 14,40,000

Working Capital = Current Assets – Current Liabilities
= Rs. 6,00,000 – Rs. 1,20,000
= Rs. 4,80,000

Working Capital Turnover Ratio

$$= \frac{\text{Net Sales}}{\text{Working Capital}}$$

$$= \frac{\text{Rs. } 14{,}40{,}000}{\text{Rs. } 4{,}80{,}000}$$

= 3 Times

Illustration : 26 Calculate Working Capital Turnover Ratio from the following.

Capital Employed	Rs. 6,00,000
Net Fixed Assets	Rs. 4,00,000
Cost of Goods Sold	Rs. 20,00,000
Gross Profit	Rs. 4,00,000

(*M.Com.Banaras*)

Solution :

Net Sales = Cost of Goods Sold + Gross Profit
= Rs. 20,00,000 + Rs. 4,00,000
= Rs. 24,00,000

Working Capital = Capital Employed – Net Fixed Assets
= Rs. 6,00,000 – Rs. 4,00,000
= Rs. 2,00,000

Working Capital Turnover Ratio

$$= \frac{\text{Net Sales}}{\text{Working Capital}}$$

$$= \frac{\text{Rs. } 24{,}00{,}000}{\text{Rs. } 2{,}00{,}000}$$

= 12 Times

FIXED ASSETS TURNOVER RATIO

It is also known as Sales to Fixed Asset Ratio. This ratio measures the efficiency and profit earning capacity of the firm. Higher the ratio, greater is the intensive utilisation of fixed assets. Lower ratio means under-utilisation of fixed assets.

$$\text{Fixed Asset Turnover Ratio} = \frac{\text{Cost of Sales}}{\text{Net Fixed Assets}}$$

(Net Fixed assets = Value of assets – Depreciation)

Illustration : 27 Calculate Fixed Assests Turnover Ratio from the following.

Capital Employed	Rs. 2,00,000
Working Capital	Rs. 40,000
Cost of goods sold	Rs. 6,40,000
Gross Profits	Rs. 1,60,000

(*M.Com.Banaras*)

Solution :

Net Sales = Cost of Goods sold + Gross Profit
= Rs. 6,40,000 + Rs. 1,60,000
= Rs. 8,00,000

Net Fixed Assests = Capital Employed – Working Capital
= Rs. 2,00,000 – Rs. 40,000
= Rs. 1,60,000

Fixed Assets Turnover Ratio

$$= \frac{\text{Net Sales}}{\text{Net Fixed Assets}}$$

$$= \frac{\text{Rs. 8,00,000}}{\text{Rs. 1,60,000}}$$

= 5 Times

CAPITAL TURNOVERS

Sometimes the efficiency and effectiveness of the operations are judged by comparing the cost of sales or sales with amount of capital invested in the business and not with assets held in the business, though in both cases the same result is expected. Capital invested in the business may be classified as Long-term and Short-term capital or as fixed capital and working capital or Owned Capital and Loaned Capital. All Capital Turnovers are calculated to study the uses of various types of capital.

$$\text{Total Capital Turnover} = \frac{\text{Cost of Shares}}{\text{Total Capital Employed}}$$

(Total Capital = Total Assets)

$$\text{Capital Turnover} = \frac{\text{Cost of Sales}}{\text{Capital Employed}}$$

Capital Employed = Shareholders' Fund + Long-term Loans
(or) = Total Assets – Current Liabilities

$$\text{Owned Capital Turnover} = \frac{\text{Cost of Sales}}{\text{Shareholder's Fund}}$$

Lower ratio shows lower profit and higher ratio shows higher profit.

Profit Cover Ratios

The coverage ratios measure the relationship between what is normally available from operations of the firms and the claims of the outsiders. We illustrate below the important coverage ratios :

Interest Coverage

This is also known as Interest Cover Ratio or Debt Service Ratio. This ratio measures the debt servicing capacity of a firm in so far as fixed interest on long-term loan is concerned. That is, the relationship between *Earnings Before Interest and Tax* (EBIT) and fixed interest charges. It is expressed in percentage or number of times.

$$\text{Interest Coverage} = \frac{\text{EBIT}}{\text{Fixed Interest Charges}}$$

This ratio shows how many times the interest charges are covered by EBIT out of which they will be paid. The coverage ratio may be interpreted with reference to its degree. Higher the ratio, better is the position of long-term creditors. It also highlights the ability of the firm to raise additional funds in future.

Dividend Coverage

It measures the ability of a firm to pay dividend on preference shares which carry a stated rate of return. The ratio, like the Interest Coverage Ratio, reveals the safety margin available to preference shareholders. Higher the coverage, better is the position. This ratio is the ratio, expressed in number of times, of net profits after taxes. Thus :

$$\text{Dividend Coverage} = \frac{\text{Net Profit after Tax and Interest}}{\text{Preference Dividend}}$$

Equity Shareholders Coverage

It indicates the number of times the Equity dividends are covered by the Net Profit, *i.e.* Net Profit after charging Interest, Tax and Preference Dividend. The higher the coverage, the better will be the financial strength and the fairer the return for the shareholder since maintenance of dividend is assured.

Equity shareholders Coverage

$$= \frac{\text{Net Profit after interest, Tax and Preference Dividend}}{\text{Equity Dividend}}$$

Illustration 28 The Capital of a Company is as follows :

	Rs.
9% Preference Shares of Rs.10 each	3,00,000
Equity Shares of Rs.10 each	8,00,000
	11,00,000

The Accountant has ascertained the following information :

Profit (after tax at 60%) Rs. 2,70,000.

Depreciation Rs. 60,000

Equity dividend paid 20%

Market Price of equity share Rs. 40.

You are required to state the following, showing the necessary workings :

(*a*) Dividend yield on the equity shares.

(*b*) Cover for the preference and equity dividends.

(*c*) Earnings for equity shares.

(*d*) Price-earnings ratio (*CA*)

Solution :

(*a*) *Dividend yield on the Equity Shares :*

$$= \frac{\text{Dividend per share}}{\text{Market Price per share}} \times 100$$

$$= \frac{\text{Rs. 2 (\textit{i.e.} 20\% of Rs.10)}}{\text{Rs. 40}} \times 100 = \mathbf{5\%}$$

(*b*) *Dividend Coverage Ratio* :

(*i*) *Preference Shares* $= \dfrac{\text{Profit After Taxes}}{\text{Dividend Payable to Pref. Shareholders}}$

$= \dfrac{\text{Rs. } 2,70,000}{\text{Rs. } 27,000} = \textbf{10 Times}$

(Rs. 27,000 is 9% of Rs. 3,00,000)

(*ii*) *Equity* $= \dfrac{\text{Profit After Taxes} - \text{Pref. Share dividends}}{\text{Dividend Payable to Equity Shareholders at Rs. 2 per share}}$

$= \dfrac{\text{Rs. } 2,70,000 - \text{Rs. } 27,000}{\text{Rs. } 1,60,000 \ (80,000 \times \text{Rs. } 2)}$

$= \dfrac{\text{Rs. } 2,43,000}{\text{Rs. } 1,60,000} = \textbf{1.518 Times}$

(*c*) *Earnings for Equity Shares* :

$= \dfrac{\text{Earnings available to Equity Shareholders}}{\text{Number of Equity Shares}}$

$= \dfrac{\text{Rs. } 2,43,000}{80,000} = \textbf{Rs. 3.0375 per share}$

(*d*) *Price-earning Ratio* :

$= \dfrac{\text{Market Price Per Share}}{\text{Earnings Per Share}}$

$= \dfrac{\text{Rs. } 40}{\text{Rs. } 3.0375}$

$= \textbf{13.168 Times}$

A few more ratios are given below :

Ratio	*Compution Formula*	*Purpose*
1. Earning per Equity Share	$\dfrac{\text{Profit available for Equity Shareholders}}{\text{No. of Equity Shares}}$	Shows the amount of earnings attributable to each equity share.
2. Dividend Yield	$\dfrac{\text{Dividend per Share}}{\text{Market Price per Share}}$	Shows the rate of return to shareholders in the form of dividends based on the market price of the share.
3. Price Earning Ratio	$\dfrac{\text{Market Price of a Share}}{\text{Earning per Share}}$	A measure for determining the value of a share. It is also used to measure the rate of return expected by investors.
4. Fixed Interest Coverage	$\dfrac{\text{Operating Income}}{\text{Annual Interest Expense}}$	Shows the margin of coverage of interest requirements.
5. Dividend per Share	$\dfrac{\text{Dividend paid to Equity Shareholders}}{\text{No. of Equity Shares}}$	Net distributed profit, after interest and preference share dividend, belongs to equity shareholders. This is a measure of profitability.
6. Dividend	$\dfrac{\text{Dividend per Share}}{\text{Earning per Share}}$ (OR)	It indicates the proportion of earnings

Payout Ratio	$\frac{\text{Total Dividend to Equity Shareholders (Cash Dividend)}}{\text{Total Net Profit available to Equity Shareholders}}$	available to Equity shareholders. When this ratio is deducted from 100, it will give the percentage of profit retained.

Standard of Comparison

The ratio analysis involves comparison for useful interpretation of the financial statements. Interpretation of financial statements of a firm with the help of ratios becomes significant and meaningful. The ratios should be compared with some standard ratios. When actual ratios have been found out, they should be compared with some such ratios which may be termed as an ideal ratio. These ideal ratios are called *standard ratios*. These standards may be of the following types, but selection of standards depends on the nature and circumstances of the firm and choice of management.

(1) Average Historical Ratios

Ratios are calculated from the past financial statements of the same firm. The easiest way to evaluate the performance of a firm is to compare its present ratios with the past ratios. This standard can be used only in those cases where past data are available. This standard or normal ratios are suitable when there is no change in the accounting policies and procedures. It does not make room for changes.

(2) Ratios of Selected Firms

Another way of comparison is to compare the ratios of one firm with some selected firms in the same industry at the same point of time. The financial ratios of the nearest competitor for the current period may be accepted as Standard or Normal Ratios. A firm can easily resort to such a comparison, as it is not difficult to get the published financial statements of the similar firms. But these ratios, as Standards, have the hazards that nearest competing firm, from the financial statements of which, the standard ratios are to be derived, may not be a normal or comparable firm as it may differ with regard to product-mix, manufacturing process, age, size, location, customers, accounting system, financial policies etc.

(3) Ratios of the Industry to which the Firm Belong

To determine the financial condition and performance of a firm, its ratios may be compared with average ratios of the industry of which the firm is a member. Such ratios are important standards in view of the fact that each industry has its characteristic which influence the financial and operating relationships. The average ratios will be meaningless and the comparison futile, if the firms within the same industry widely differ in their accounting policies and practices.

(4) Absolute Standard Ratios

Experts have laid down some standards after making numerous experiments in various companies and at various places. On the basis of such standards, ratios have been found out, and these ratios are called Standard Ratios or Absolute Ratios or Ideal Ratios. They are used all over the world, that is, such ratios are regarded as standard ratios everywhere. Due margin should be given for variations at the time of interpretation.

PROJECTIONS THROUGH RATIOS

The ratio analysis can also be used in making future projections regarding various items of Income Statement and Balance Sheet. Proforma statements can be drawn which may help the management in evaluating the actual performance. For this purpose, past account data are used for the calculation of various accounting ratios, taking into account the expected changes. Thus Standard ratios are prepared. These Standard Ratios are used in making forecasts in respect of several items of Income Statement and Balance Sheet. We have to find out various items by interpolations and extrapolations. At this stage, knowledge of ratio calculations and great skill of reasoning are needed. The following examples will clearly explain the whole process by which we can make future projections and to prepare proforma statements.

Illustration 29 From the following particulars, draw up the Balance Sheet of the company :

Current Ratio	2.5
Quick Ratio	1.5
Net Working Capital	Rs. 30,000
Stock Turnover Ratio (Cost of Sales/Closing Stock)	6 Times
Gross Profit Ratio	20%
Fixed Assets-Turnover Ratio (Cost of sales)	2 Times
Debtors Turnover Ratio	2 Times
Fixed Assets to Shareholders' Net Worth	0.8
Reserves & Surplus to Capital	0.5
Long-term Loans	Rs.15,000

(*B.Com. Nagpur*)

Solution :

BALANCE SHEET As on ....

Liabilities	*Rs.*	*Assets*	*Rs.*
Share Capital	50,000	Fixed Assets	60,000
Reserves	25,000	Stock	20,000
Long-term Loans	15,000	Debtors	25,000
		Bank	5,000
Current Liabilities	20,000		
	1,10,000		1,10,000

Workings :

(1) *Current Liabilities* :

Current Ratio = 2.5 : 1

Current Assets – Current Liabilities = Working Capital

2.5 – 1 = 1.5 = Rs. 30,000

1 = Rs. 20,000

Current Liabilities = **Rs. 20,000**

Current Assets = Rs. 20,000 × 2.5 = **Rs. 50,000**

(2) *Stock* :

Liquid Liabilities = Current Liabilities

$$\text{Liquid Assets} = \text{Rs. Rs. } 20{,}000 \times 1.5 = \text{Rs. } 30{,}000$$

Stock = Current Assets – Liquid Assets

= Rs. 50,000 – Rs. 30,000

= **Rs. 20,000**

(3) *Fixed Assets* :

$$\text{Stock Turnover Ratio} = \frac{\text{Cost of Sales}}{\text{Stock}} = 6 \text{ Times}$$

$$\text{Cost of Sales} = \text{Rs. } 20{,}000 \times 6 = \text{Rs. } 1{,}20{,}000$$

Gross Profit Ratio = 20%

$$\text{Sales} = \frac{\text{Rs. } 1{,}20{,}000}{80} \times 100 = \text{Rs. } 1{,}50{,}000$$

Fixed Assets Turnover Ratio = 2

$$\text{Fixed Assets} = \frac{\text{Cost of Sales}}{2}$$

$$\text{Fixed Assets} = \frac{\text{Rs. } 1,20,000}{2} = \text{Rs. } 60,000$$

(4) *Debtors* :

$$\text{Debtors Turnover Ratio} = \frac{\text{Receivables} \times 12}{\text{Sales}}$$

$$2 \text{ Months} = \frac{\text{Debtors} \times 12}{1,50,000}$$

Debtors = **Rs. 25,000**

(5) *Bank* :

Bank = Liquid Assets – Debtors
= Rs. 30,000 – Rs. 25,000
= **Rs. 5,000**

(6) *Shareholders' Net Worth* :

$$0.80 = \frac{\text{Fixed Assets}}{\text{Shareholders' Net Worth}}$$

$$0.80 \times \text{Shareholders' Net worth} = \text{Fixed Assets}$$

$$\text{Shareholders' Net Worth} = \frac{\text{Rs. } 60,000}{0.80} = \textbf{Rs. 75,000}$$

(7) *Reserves & Surplus* :

Reserves and Surplus to Capital = 0.5 : 1

Shareholders' Net Worth = Capital and Reserves and Surplus

Actual Shareholders' Net Worth is Rs.75,000 which is equal to 1.5

$$\text{So, Reserves \& Surplus} = \frac{\text{Rs. } 75,000 \times 0.5}{1.5} = \textbf{Rs.25,000}$$

$$\text{Capital} = \frac{\text{Rs. } 75,000 \times 1}{1.5} = \textbf{Rs. 50,000}$$

Illustration 30. Given :

Receivables Turnover = 4
Payables Turnover = 6
Inventory Turnover = 8
Capital Turnover Ratio = 2 Times
Fixed Assets Turnover Ratio = 8 Times
Gross Profit Ratio = 25%

Gross profit during the year amounted to Rs. 80,000. There is no long-term loan or overdraft. Reserves and surplus amount to Rs. 28,000. Ending inventory of the year is Rs. 2,000 above the beginning inventory. Notes receivable amount to Rs. 5,000 and notes payable are Rs. 2,000.

Prepare a Balance Sheet on the basis of the information given above.

(*M.Com. Delhi, Madurai*)

Solution :

$$\text{Gross Profit Ratio} = \frac{\text{Gross Profit}}{\text{Sales}}$$

$$25\% = \frac{\text{Rs. } 80{,}000}{\text{Sales}}$$

$$\text{Sales} = \frac{\text{Rs. } 80{,}000}{25\%}$$

$$= \text{Rs. } 3{,}20{,}000$$

$$\text{Cost of Sales} = \text{Sales} - \text{Gross Profit}$$

$$= \text{Rs. } 3{,}20{,}000 - \text{Rs. } 80{,}000 = 2{,}40{,}000$$

$$\text{Inventory Turnover} = \frac{\text{Cost of Goods Sold}}{\text{Average Inventory}}$$

$$8 = \frac{\text{Rs. } 2{,}40{,}000}{\text{Average Inventory}}$$

$$\text{Average Inventory} = \frac{\text{Rs. } 2{,}40{,}000}{8}$$

$$= \text{Rs. } 30{,}000$$

$$\text{Average Inventory} = \frac{\text{Opening Inventory} + (\text{Opening Inventory} + \text{Rs. } 2{,}000)}{2}$$

$$\text{Rs. } 30{,}000 = \frac{2 \text{ Opening Inventory} + \text{Rs. } 2{,}000}{2}$$

$$\text{Rs. } 60{,}000 = 2 \text{ Opening Inventory} + \text{Rs. } 2{,}000$$

$$\text{Rs. } 58{,}000 = 2 \text{ Opening Inventory}$$

$$\text{Opening Inventory} = \frac{\text{Rs. } 58{,}000}{2}$$

$$= \text{Rs. } 29{,}000$$

$$\text{Closing Inventory} = \text{Rs. } 29{,}000 + \text{Rs. } 2{,}000 = \text{Rs. } 31{,}000$$

$$\text{Receivable Turnover} = \frac{\text{Sales}}{\text{Trade Debtors}}$$

$$\text{Trade Debtors} = \frac{\text{Rs. } 3{,}20{,}000}{4} = \text{Rs. } 80{,}000$$

$$\text{Accounts Receivables} = \text{Trade Debtors} - \text{Notes Receivables}$$

$$= \text{Rs. } 80{,}000 - \text{Rs. } 5{,}000$$

$$= \text{Rs. } 75{,}000$$

$$\text{Purchases} = \text{Cost of Sales} + \text{Rs. } 2{,}000 \text{ (Excess Closing Inventory)}$$

$$= \text{Rs. } 2{,}40{,}000 + \text{Rs. } 2{,}000$$

$$= \text{Rs. } 2{,}42{,}000$$

$$\text{Payable Turnover} = \frac{\text{Purchases}}{\text{Trade Creditors}}$$

$$6 = \frac{\text{Rs. } 2{,}42{,}000}{\text{Trade Creditors}}$$

$$\text{Trade Creditors} = \frac{\text{Rs. } 2{,}42{,}000}{6}$$

$$= \text{Rs. } 40{,}333$$

$$\text{Account Payable} = \text{Trade Creditors} - \text{Notes Payable}$$

$$= \text{Rs. } 40{,}333 - \text{Rs. } 2{,}000$$
$$= \text{Rs. } 38{,}333$$

$$\text{Fixed Assets Turnover} = \frac{\text{Cost of Sales}}{\text{Fixed Assets}}$$

$$8 = \frac{\text{Rs. } 2{,}40{,}000}{\text{Fixed Assets}}$$

$$\text{Fixed Assets} = \frac{\text{Rs. } 2{,}40{,}000}{8}$$
$$= \text{Rs. } 30{,}000$$

$$\text{Capital Turnover Ratio} = \frac{\text{Cost of Sales}}{\text{Capital}}$$

$$2 = \frac{\text{Rs. } 2{,}40{,}000}{\text{Capital}}$$

$$\text{Capital} = \frac{\text{Rs. } 2{,}40{,}000}{2}$$
$$= \text{Rs. } 1{,}20{,}000$$

$$\text{Share Capital} = \text{Capital Employed} - \text{Reserves} + \text{Surplus}$$
$$= \text{Rs. } 1{,}20{,}000 - \text{Rs. } 28{,}000$$
$$= \text{Rs. } 92{,}000$$

BALANCE SHEET As on..........

Liabilities		*Rs.*	*Assets*	*Rs.*
Shareholders' Fund :			Fixed Assets	30,000
Share Capital	92,000		Current Assets :	
Reserves and Surplus	28,000	1,20,000	Inventory	31,000
			Accounts	75,000
			Notes Receivables	5,000
Current Liabilities :		38,333	Cash/Bank	19,333
Accounts Payable			(Balancing Figure)	
Notes Payable		2,000		
		1,60,333		1,60,333

Illustration 31 Following are the ratios relating to the trading activities of National Traders, for the year ended on 31st December.

Debtors Velocity	3 Months
Stock Velocity	8 Months
Creditors Velocity	2 Months
Gross Profit Ratio	25%
Gross Profit for the year	Rs. 4,00,000
Closing Stock is Rs.10,000, above the opening stock	
Bills Receivable	Rs.25,000
Bills Payable	Rs.10,000

Find out (*a*) Sales
(*b*) Sundry Debtors
(*c*) Closing Stock
(*d*) Sundry Creditors

(*B.Com. Madurai, Agra*) (*CA*)

Solution :

(1) Sales :

Gross Profit Ratio *i.e.* 25% = Rs. 4,00,000

$$\text{Sales} = \text{Rs. } 4{,}00{,}000 \times \frac{100}{25} = \textbf{Rs. 16,00,000}$$

(2) Sundry Debtors :

Debtors Velocity = 3 Months

So, Debtors Turnover Ratio = 4

$$\text{Debtors Turnover Ratio} = \frac{\text{Credit Sales}}{\text{Closing Debtors + Bills Receivable}}$$

(OR)

$$\text{Closing Debtors + Bills Receivable} = \frac{\text{Credit Sales}}{\text{Debtors Turnover Ratio}}$$

$$= \text{Rs. } \frac{16{,}00{,}000}{4}$$

Closing Debtors + Bills Receivable = Rs. 4, 00,000

Closing Debtors = Rs. 4,00,000 – Rs. 25,000 = **Rs. 3,75,000**

(3) Closing Stock :

Stock Velocity = 8 Months

So, Stock Turnover Ratio = 1.5 or 12 ÷ 8

$$\text{Stock Turnover} = \frac{\text{Cost of Goods Sold}}{\text{Average Stock}}$$

$$1.5 = \frac{\text{Rs. } 12{,}00{,}000}{\text{Average Stock}}$$

Average Stock = Rs. 8,00,000

Opening Stock + Closing Stock = Rs. 8,00,000 ×2 = Rs. 16,00,000

$$\text{Opening Stock} = \frac{\text{Rs. } 16{,}00{,}000 - \text{Rs. } 10{,}000}{2}$$

Opening Stock = Rs. 7,95,000

Closing Stock = Rs. 7,95,000 + Rs. 10,000 = **8.05.000**

(4) Sundry Creditors :

$$\text{Creditors Turnover} = \frac{\text{Credit Purchases}}{\text{Creditors + Bills Payable}}$$

$$6 = \frac{\text{Rs. } 12{,}10{,}000^{*}}{\text{Creditors + Bills Payable}}$$

---

* Credit Purchases :

Cost of Goods = Opening Stock + Purchases – Closing Stock

Rs. 12,00,000 = Rs. 7,95,000 + Purchases – Rs. 8,05,000

Purchases = **Rs. 12,10,000**

$$\text{Creditors + Bills Payable} = \text{Rs. } \frac{12,10,000}{6}$$

Creditors + Rs. 10,000 = Rs. 2,01,667

Creditors = Rs. 2,01,667 – Rs. 10,000 = **Rs. 1,91,667**

Illustration 32 Using the following accounting variables, construct the Balance Sheet :

Gross Profit (20% of sales)	Rs.60,000
Shareholders' Equity	50,000
Credit sales to Total Sales	80%
Total Assets Turnover	3 Times
Stock Turnover	8 Times
Average collection period	18 days
(A year = 360 days)	
Current Ratio	1.6 : 1
Long Term Debt to Equity	40%

BALANCE SHEET As on

	Rs.		Rs.
Creditors	?	Cash	?
Long-term Debt	?	Debtors	?
		Inventory	?
Shareholders' Fund	?	Fixed Assets	?
	?		?

(*B.Com. MS, Madras, Jabalpur*)

Solution :

1. *Total Sales*:

$$\text{Gross Profit Ratio} = \frac{\text{Gross Profit}}{\text{Sales}} \times 100$$

$$20 = \frac{\text{Rs. } 60,000}{\text{Sales}} \times 100$$

Total Sales = Rs. 3,00,000

Credit Sales = 80% of Rs. 3,00000 = Rs. 2,40,000

2. *Debtors* :

$$\text{Average Collection Period} = \frac{\text{Debtors}}{\text{Credit sales}} \times \text{No. of days}$$

$$\text{Debtors} = \frac{\text{Average Collection Period}}{\text{No. of days}} \times \text{Credit Sales}$$

$$= \frac{18}{360} \times 2,40,000 = \textbf{Rs. 12,000}$$

3. *Total Assets* :

$$\text{Turnover to Total Asset Ratio} = \frac{\text{Turnover}}{\text{Total Assets}}$$

$$3 = \frac{\text{Rs. } 3,00,000}{\text{Total Assets}}$$

Total Assets = **Rs. 1,00,000**

4. *Inventory* :

$$\text{Inventory Turnover} = \frac{\text{Cost of Sales}}{\text{Inventory}}$$

$$8 = \frac{\text{Rs. 2,40,000}}{\text{Inventory}}$$

Inventory = **Rs. 30,000**

5. *Long-term Debt* :

Long-term Debt = 40% of Equity Capital
= 40% of Rs. 50,000 = **Rs. 20,000**

6. *Creditors :*

Creditors = Total Assets – (Equity Capital + Long-term Debt)
= Rs. 1,00,000 – (Rs. 50,000 + Rs. 20,000) = **Rs. 30,000**

7. *Current Assets* :

$$\text{Current Ratio} = \frac{\text{Current Assets}}{\text{Current Liabilities}}$$

$$1.6 = \frac{\text{Current Asset}}{\text{Rs. 30,000}}$$

Current Asset = **Rs. 48,000**

8. *Cash* :

Cash = Current Assets – (Debtors + Stock)
= Rs. 48,000 – (Rs. 12,000 + Rs. 30,000) = **Rs. 6,000**

BALANCE SHEET As on ....

	Rs.		*Rs.*
Creditors	30,000	Cash	6,000
Long-term Debt	20,000	Debtors	12,000
Shareholders' Equity	50,000	Inventory	30,000
		Fixed Assets (Balancing Figure)	52,000
	1,00,000		1,00,000

Illustration 33 Assume that a firm has owners' equity of Rs. 1,00,000. The ratios for the firm are :

Current Debt to Total Debt	0.40
Total Debt to owners' equity	0.60
Fixed Assets to owners' equity	0.60
Total Assets Turnover	2 Times
Inventory Turnover	8 Times

Complete the following Balance Sheet, given the information above.

Equities	*Rs.*	*Assets*	*Rs.*
Current Debt	.....	Cash	.....
Long-term Debt	.....	Inventory	.....
Total Debt	.....	Total Current Assets	.....
Owners' Equity	.....	Fixed Assets	.....
Total Equity	.....	Total Assets	.....

(*M.Com. Lucknow, Delhi, kolkata*)

Solution.

Equities	*Rs.*	*Assets*	*Rs.*
Current Debt	24,000	Cash	60,000
Long-term Debt	36,000	Inventory	40,000
Total Debt	60,000	Total Current Assets	1,00,000
Owners' Equity	1,00,000	Fixed Assets	60,000
Total Equity	1,60,000	Total Assets	1,60,000

Workings :

1. Total Debt = 0.60 × Owners' Equity

$$= 0.60 \times \text{Rs.}1,00,000$$
$$= \text{Rs. } 60,000$$

2. Fixed Assets = 0.60 × Owners' Equity

$$= 0.60 \times \text{Rs.}1,00,000$$
$$= \text{Rs. } 60,000$$

3. Total Equity = Total Debt + Owners' Equity
Rs. 60,000 + Rs. 1,00,000
= Rs. 1,60,000

4. Total Assets = Current Assets + Fixed Assets (Must be equal to
= Rs. 1,60,000). Fixed Assets = Rs. 60,000

Current Assets = Rs. 160,000 – Rs. 60,000 = Rs. 1,00,000

5. Sales :

$$\text{Asset Turnover or } 2 = \frac{\text{Sales}}{\text{Assets}}$$

$$2 = \frac{\text{Sales}}{\text{Rs. } 1,60,000}$$

$$\text{Sales} = \text{Rs.}160,000 \times 2 = \text{Rs.}\ 3,20,000$$

6. Inventory :

$$\text{Inventory Turnover or } 8 = \frac{\text{Sales}}{\text{Inventory}}$$

$$8 = \frac{\text{Rs. } 3,20,000}{\text{Inventory}}$$

$$\text{Inventory} = \frac{\text{Rs. } 3,20,000}{8} = \text{Rs.}\ 40,000$$

7. Cash = Current Assets – Inventory
= Rs. 1,00,000 – Rs. 40,000 = Rs. 60,000

8. Current Debt = $0.40 \times$ Total Debt = $0.40 \times$ Rs. 60,000 = Rs. 24,000

9. Long-term Debt = Total Debt – Current Debt = Rs. 60,000 – Rs. 24,000 = Rs. 36,000

Illustration 34 From the following details, prepare statement of propritory funds with as many details as possible :

1.	Stock velocity :	6
2.	Capital turnover ratio based on cost of sales :	2

3. Fixed Assets turnover ratio based on cost of sales : 4
4. Gross profit turnover ratio : 20%
5. Debtors velocity : 2 months
6. Creditors velocity : 73 days

Other details :

(*a*) The groos profit was Rs. 60,000

(*b*) Reserves and surplus comes to Rs. 20,000

(*c*) Closing stock was Rs. 5,000 in excess of opening stock.

(*B. Com. Madurai, Ms, Bharathidasan*)

Solution :

STATEMENT OF PROPRIETORY FUND

		Rs.
Fixed Assets		60,000
Current Assets :		
Cash	16,500	
Debtors	50,000	
Stock	42,500	
	1,09,000	
Less : Current Liabilities :		
Creditors	49,000	60,000
		1,20,000
Represented by :		
Share Capital	1,00,000	
Reserves and Surplus	20,000	
		1,20,000

Workings :

1. Sales :

When gross profit is Rs. 20, sales is Rs. 100.

When groos profit is Rs. 60,000 sales = $\frac{\text{Rs. } 60,000}{20} \times 100$ = Rs. 3,00,000

2. Stock :

Cost of goods sold = Sales – Gross Profit

Rs. 3,00,000 – Rs. 60,000 = Rs. 2,40,000

$$\text{Stock velocity} = 6 = \frac{\text{Cost of goods sold}}{\text{Average Stock}}$$

$$6 = \frac{\text{Rs. } 2,40,000}{\text{Average Stock}}$$

$$\text{Average stock} = \frac{\text{Rs. } 2,40,000}{6} = \text{Rs. } 40,000$$

Total stock = Rs. 40,000 × 2 = Rs. 80,000

Less : Excess stock 5,000

75,000

$$\text{Opening stock} = \frac{\text{Rs. } 75,000}{2} = \text{Rs. } 37,500$$

Closing stock = 37,500 + Rs. 5,000 = **Rs. 42,500**

3. *Debtors* :

$$2 = \frac{\text{Accounts Receivable}}{\text{Credit Sales}} \times 12$$

$$2 = \frac{\text{Accounts Receivable}}{3,00,000} \times 12$$

$$\text{Accounts Receivable} = \frac{\text{Rs. } 3,00,000}{12} \times 2 = \textbf{Rs. 50,000}$$

4. *Creditors* :

$$73 = \frac{\text{Accounts Payable}}{\text{Credit Purchase}} \times \text{No. of days}$$

$$73 = \frac{\text{Accounts Payable}}{2,45,000} \times 365$$

$$\text{Accounts Payable} = \frac{\text{Rs. } 2,45,000}{365} \times 73 = \textbf{Rs. 49,000}$$

(Rs. 2,45,000 = Rs. 2,40,000 + Rs. 42,500 – 37,500)

5. *Share Capital* :

$$\text{Capital Turnover Ratio} = 2 = \frac{\text{Cost of Sales}}{\text{Proprietory Fund}}$$

$$2 = \frac{\text{Rs. } 2,40,000}{\text{Proprietory Fund}}$$

$$\text{Proprietory Fund} = \frac{\text{Rs. } 2,40,000}{2} = 1,20,000$$

Less : Reserve and Surplus 20,000

1,00,000

6. *Fixed Assets*

$$\text{Fixed Assets Turnover Ratio} = \frac{\text{Cost of Sales}}{\text{Fixed Assets}}$$

$$4 = \frac{\text{Rs. } 2,40,000}{\text{Fixed Assets}}$$

$$\text{Fixed Assets} = \frac{\text{Rs. } 2,40,000}{4} = \text{Rs. } 60,000$$

7. *Cash :* Balancing figure

BALANCE SHEET

	Rs.		*Rs.*
Share capital	1,00,000	Fixed Assets	60,000
Reserve & Surplus	20,000	Stock	42,500
Creditors	49,000	Debtors	50,000
		Cash (Balancing figure)	16,500
	1,69,000		1,69,000

Illustration 35 From the following information, make out a statement of Proprietors' Fund with as many details as possible :

1.	Current Ratio	2.5
2.	Liquid Ratio	1.5
3.	Proprietary Ratio Fixed Assets/Proprietors' Fund)	0.75
4.	Working Capital	Rs. 60,000
5.	Reserves and Surplus	Rs. 40,000
6.	Bank Overdraft	Rs. 10,000
7.	There is no long-term Loan or Fictitious assets.	

(*B.Com. Madurai, Jabalpur, Delhi, Agra*)

Solution :

STATEMENT OF PROPRIETORS' FUND

			Rs.	*Rs.*
Proprietors' Fund :				
Capital			2,00,000	
Reserves and Surplus			40,000	2,40,000
Represented by :				
Fixed Assets			1,80,000	
Current Assets :				
Stock		Rs. 40,000		
Liquid Assets		60,000		
		1,00,000		
Less : Current Liabilities				
Overdraft	Rs. 10,000			
Creditors	30,000	40,000	60,000	2,40,000

Workings :

1. Let X be the Current Liabilities.

Current Assets – Current Liabilities = Working Capital

$$2.5X - X = 60,000$$

$$1.5X = \text{Rs. } 60,000$$

$$X = \text{Rs. } 40,000$$

2. Current Liabilities = **Rs. 40,000**

Current Assets = Rs. 40,000 × 2.5 = **Rs. 1,00,000**

3. $$\text{Liquid Ratio} = \frac{\text{Liquid Assets}}{\text{Current Liabilities}}$$

$$1.5 = \frac{\text{Liquid Assets}}{\text{Rs. } 40,000}$$

Liquid Assets = **Rs. 60,000**

4. Stock = Current Assets – Quick Assets

= Rs. 1,00,000 – Rs. 60,000 = **Rs. 40,000**

5. Proprietors' Funds = Fixed Assets + Current Assets – Current Liabilities

= Rs. 1,80,000 + Rs. 1,00,000 – Rs. 40,000

= **Rs. 2,40,000**

6. Reserves and Surplus are given as Rs. 40,000

7. Capital = Rs. 2,40,000 – Rs. 40,000 = **Rs. 2,00,000**

8. Fixed Assets is 0.75 of Proprietors' Fund

$$\text{Rs. } 2,40,000 \times 0.75 = \mathbf{1,80,000}$$

9. Overdraft given as **Rs, 10,000**

10. Creditors = Rs. 40,000 – Rs. 10,000 = **Rs. 30,000**

Illustration 36 Given :

Current Ratio = 2.8

Acid Test Ratio = 1.5

Working Capital = Rs. 1,62,000

Find out :

(1) Current Assets

(2) Current Liabilities

(3) Liquid Assets

(4) Stock

M.Com. Chennai, B.Com. Madurai, Andhra, Calicut

Solution :

$$\text{Current Ratio} = \frac{\text{Current Assets}}{\text{Current Liabilities}}$$

$$2.8 = \frac{\text{Current Assets}}{\text{Curent Liabilities}}$$

Working Capital = Current Assets – Current Liabilities

Rs. 1,62,000 = 2.8 – 1

Rs. 1,62,000 = 1.8

$$1.\quad \text{Current Assets} = \frac{\text{Rs. } 1,62,000}{1.8} \times 2.8 = \text{Rs. } 2,52,000$$

$$2.\ \text{Current Liabilities} = \frac{\text{Rs. } 1,62,000}{1.8} \times 1 = \text{Rs. } 90,000$$

$$\text{Acid Test Ratio} = \frac{\text{Liquid Assets}}{\text{Current Liabilities}}$$

$$1.5 = \frac{\text{Liquid Assets}}{\text{Rs. } 90,000}$$

3. Liquid Assets = Rs. 90,000 × 1.5 = Rs. 1,35,000

Liquid Assets = Current Assets – Stock

Rs. 1,35,000 = Rs. 2,52,000 – Stock

4. Stock = Rs. 2,52,000 – Rs. 1,35,000

= Rs. 1,17,000

Illustration 37. The following balances are extracted fron the account of AB Ltd. in respect of the accounting year ended on 31st March, 2010 :

	Rs.
Sales (2009-2010)	1,00,00,000
Fixed Assests (31.3.2010)	25,00,000
Bank overdraft (31.3.2010)	2,50,000
Long-term debt (31.3.2010)	15,00,000
Equity shares (Rs 10 each) (31.3.2010)	5,00,000
Reserves and surplus (31.3.2010)	25,00,000

Forecasts for 2010 - 2011

(*i*) Sales will increase by 20%. They will spread evenly throughout the year. There will be no further increase in sales in the following year.
(*ii*) Year-end cash balance should be a minimum of 4% of annual sales.
(*iii*) Inventory Turnover-8 times.
(*iv*) Additional capital expenditure will eaual depreciation.
(*v*) Sundry creditors-1 month's purchase.
(*vi*) Upper limit of bank borrowings – Rs 10,00,000.
(*vii*) Accruals – 3% of sales.
(*viii*) Gross margin - 40% of sales.
(*ix*) Net profit margin (after tax) – 8% of sales.
(*x*) Average collection period – 2 months.
(*xi*) Income tax – 40%.
(*xii*) Redemption of long-term debt at the end of the year – Rs 3,75,000.
(*xiii*) Purchases – 50% of the cost of goods sold.

From the above information, prepare a proforma profit and loss account for the year ended 31 March, 2011 and a proforma balance sheet as on that date. All relevant working are to be shown.

Solution :

Proforma Profit & Loss Account
for the year ended 31 March 2011

	Rs.
Sales : (Rs. 1,00,00,000 × 120%)	1,20,00,000
Less : Cost of goods sold (60%)	72,00,000
Gross Profit (40%)	48,00,000
Loss : Expense : Rs. 48,00,000 – (Rs. 6,40,000 + Rs 9,60,000)	32,00,000
Profit before Tax	16,00,000
Less : Tax (40%)	6,40,000
Net Profit (8% of Rs. 1,20,00,000)	9,60,000

Proforma Balance Sheet as on 31 March 2011

	Rs.		*Rs.*
Equity shares (Rs 10)	5,00,000	Fixed Assets (net)	25,00,000
Reserves and Surplus		Current Assests	
Rs (25,00,000 + 9,60,000)	34,60,000	Inventory (2)	9,00,000
		Debtors (3)	20,00,000
		Cash	4,80,000
		(40% of Rs 1,20,00,000)	

Long-term debt Rs (15,00,000 – 3,75,000)	11,25,000		
Accruals (3% of sales)	3,60,000		
Sundry creditors (1)	3,00,000		
Bank overdraft (balancing)	1,35,000		
	58,80,000		58,80,000

(1) 50% of goods sold $\times \frac{1}{12}$ = Rs. 36,00,000 $\times \frac{1}{12}$ = Rs. 3,00,000

(2) $\frac{\text{Rs. } 72,00,000}{8}$ = Rs. 9,00,000

(3) Rs. 1,20,00,000 $\times \frac{2}{12}$ = Rs. 20,00,000

Illustration 38. In projecting the financial plan of firm, the use of the following accounting ratios is made :

Estimated Annual Sales	Rs.2,00,000
Sales to Net Worth	2.5
Current Debt to Net Worth	25%
Total Debt to Net Worth	60%
Current Ratio	3.6 Times
Net Sales to Inventory	4 Times
Average Collection Period (A year = 360 days)	36 days
Fixed Assets to Net Worth	70%

On the above basis, prepare Proforma Balance Sheet of the firm.

(*B.Com. Delhi, Lucknow, Indore*)

Solution :

PROFORMA BALANCE SHEET

	Rs.		*Rs.*
Share Capital	80,000	Fixed Assets	56,000
Long-Term Loan	28,000	Inventory	50,000
Current Liabilities	20,000	Debtors	20,000
		Cash at bank	2,000
	1,28,000		1,28,000

Workings :

1. Net Worth :

$$\text{Sales to Net Worth} = \frac{\text{Sales}}{\text{Net Worth}}$$

$$2.5 = \text{Rs. } \frac{2,00,000}{\text{Net Worth}}$$

$$\text{Net Worth} = \frac{\text{Rs. } 2,00,000}{2.5} = \text{Rs. } 80,000$$

Net Worth = Rs. 80,000

2. Current Liabilities :

Current Debt to Net worth = 25%

Current Liabilities = 25% of Rs. 80,000 = Rs. 20,000

3. Total Debt = 60% of Rs. 80,000 = Rs. 48,000
4. Long-Term Debt = Rs. 48,000 – Rs. 20,000 = Rs. 28,000
5. *Current Assets* :

$$3.6 = \frac{\text{Current Assets}}{\text{Rs. } 20{,}000}$$

Current Assets = Rs. 72,000

6. *Inventory* :

$$\text{Inventory} = \frac{\text{Rs. } 2{,}00{,}000}{4} = \text{Rs. } 50{,}000$$

7. Liquid Assets = Current Assets – Inventory
= Rs. 72,000 – Rs. 50,000 = Rs. 22,000

8. Debtors :

$$\text{Average Collection Period} = \frac{\text{Debtors}}{\text{Sales}/360}$$

$$36 = \frac{\text{Debtors} \times 360}{\text{Rs. } 2{,}00{,}000}$$

Debtors = Rs. 20,000

9. Cash = Rs. 22,000 – Rs. 20,000 = Rs. 2,000
10. Fixed Assets = 70% of Rs. 80,000 = Rs. 56,000

Illustration 39 From the following information presented by a firm for the year ended 31st December, prepare the Balance Sheet :

Sales to Net Worth	5 Times
Current Liabilities to Net Worth	50%
Total Debts to Net Worth	60%
Fixed Assets to Net Worth	60%
Current Ratio	2
Sales to Stock	10 Times
Debtors' Velocity	9 Times
Annual Sales	Rs.15,00,000
Cash Sales	40% of Sales

[*M.Com. MS, Punjab, Kolkata, Madurai*]

Solution :

BALANCE SHEET As on 31st December

Liabilities	*Rs.*	*Assets*	*Rs.*
Proprietors' Fund	3,00,000	Fixed Assets	1,80,000
Long-Term Debt	30,000	Current Assets :	
Current Liabilities	1,50,000	Stock	1,50,000
		Debtors	1,00,000
		Bank (Balancing Figure)	50,000
	4,80,000		4,80,000

Workings :

(1) *Net Worth* :

$$\text{Sales to Net Worth} = 5 = \frac{\text{Sales}}{\text{Net Worth}} = \frac{\text{Rs. } 15{,}00{,}000}{\text{Net Worth}}$$

$$\text{Net Worth} = \frac{\text{Rs. } 15{,}00{,}000}{5} = \text{Rs. } 3{,}00{,}000$$

(2) *Current Liabilities* :

Current Liabilities to Net Worth = 50%

Current Liabilities = 50% of Rs. 3,00,000 = Rs. 1,50,000

(3) *Total Debt* :

Total Debt to Net Worth = 60%

Total Debt is 60% of Rs.3,00,000 = Rs.1,80,000

(4) *Long-term Debt* :

Long-term Debt = Total Debt – Current Liabilities

= Rs. 1,80,000 – Rs. 1,50,000 = Rs. 30,000

(5) *Current Assets* :

$$\text{Current Ratio} = \frac{\text{Current Assets}}{\text{Current Liabilities}}$$

$$2 = \frac{\text{Current Assets}}{\text{Rs. } 1{,}50{,}000}$$

Current Assets = Rs. 3,00,000

(6) *Stock* :

$$10 = \frac{\text{Rs.}15{,}00{,}000}{\text{Stock}}$$

Stock = Rs. 1,50,000

(7) *Debtors* :

Credit Sales = 60% of Rs. 15,00,000 = Rs. 9,00,000

$$\text{Debtors} = \frac{\text{Credit Sales}}{\text{Debtors Velocity}} = \frac{\text{Rs. } 9{,}00{,}000}{9} = \text{Rs. } 1{,}00{,}000$$

(8) *Fixed Assets* :

$$\text{Fixed Assets to Net Worth Ratio} = \frac{\text{Fixed Assets}}{\text{Net Worth}}$$

$$60 = \frac{\text{Fixed Assets}}{\text{Rs. } 3{,}00{,}000} = \text{Rs.}1{,}80{,}000$$

Illustration 40 With the following ratios and further information given below, prepare a Trading, Profit and Loss Account and Balance Sheet.

Gross Profit Ratio	25%
Net Profit Ratio	20%
Stock Turnover Ratio	10
Net Profit/Capital	1/5
Capital to Total Liabilities	1/2
Fixed Assets/Capital	5/4
Fixed Assets/Total Current Assets	5/7
Fixed Assets	Rs.10,00,000
Closing Stock	Rs. 1,00,000

(*M.Com. Mumbai, Agra, Bhopal*)

Solution :

TRADING AND PROFIT AND LOSS ACCOUNT

	Rs.		*Rs.*
To Opening Stock	20,000	By Sales	8,00,000
To Purchases (Balancing Figure)	6,80,000	By Closing Stock	1,00,000
To Gross Profit	2,00,000		
	9,00,000		9,00,000
To Expenses (Balancing Figure)	40,000	By Gross Profit	2,00,000
To Net Profit	1,60,000		
	2,00,000		2,00,000

BALANCE SHEET As on......

Liabilities	*Rs.*	*Assets*	*Rs.*
Capital	6,40,000	Fixed Assets	10,00,000
Net Profit	1,60,000	Closing Stock	1,00,000
Liabilities	16,00,000	Current Assets	13,00,000
	24,00,000		24,00,000

Workings :

1. *Capital* :

$$\frac{\text{Fixed Assets}}{\text{Capital}} = \frac{5}{4}$$

$$\text{Capital} = \text{Rs. } 10,00,000 \times \frac{4}{5} = \textbf{Rs. 8,00,000}$$

2. *Liabilities* :

$$\text{Capital} = \frac{1}{2} \text{ of Total Liabilities}$$

$$\text{Liabilities} = \text{Rs. } 8,00,000 \times \frac{2}{1} = \textbf{Rs. 16,00,000}$$

3. $\text{Net Profit} = \frac{1}{5} \text{ of Capital} = \text{Rs. } 8,00,000 \times \frac{1}{5} = \textbf{Rs. 1,60,000}$

4. Net Profit = 20% of sales = Rs. 1,60,000

So, $\text{Sales} = \text{Rs. } 1,60,000 \times \frac{100}{20} = \textbf{Rs. 8,00,000}$

5. Gross Profit = 25% of Sales = 25% of Rs. 8,00,000 = **Rs. 2,00,000**

6. *Opening Stock* :

Stock Turnover = 10

Cost of Sales = Rs. 8,00,000 – Rs. 2,00,000 = Rs. 6,00,00

Average Inventory = Rs. 60,000

Opening Stock = Rs. 60,000 × 2 = Rs. 1,20,000 – Rs. 1,00,000 = **Rs. 20,000**

7. *Current Assets* :

Fixed Assets/Total Current Assets = 5/7

$$\text{Current Assets} = \text{Rs.}10,00,000 \times \frac{7}{5} = \text{Rs.}14,00,000$$

Other Current Assets = Current Assets – Stock
= Rs. 14,00,000 – Rs. 1,00,000
= **Rs. 13,00,000**

Illustration 41 You are given the following information pertaining to financial statements of a firm. You are required to prepare Trading and Profit and Loss Account and Balance Sheet :

	Rs.
Net Current Assets	1,00,000
Paid up Capital	3,00,000
Current Ratio	1.8 : 1
Liquid Ratio	1.35 : 1
Fixed Assets to Shareholders' Equity	80%
Gross Profit Ratio	25%
Net Profit to Paid up Capital	20%
Stock Turnover	5 Times
Average Age of Outstanding Customers 36.5 days	

(*M.Com. Indore, Punjab, Lucknow, Delhi*)

Solution :

TRADING AND PROFIT AND LOSS ACCOUNT

	Rs.		*Rs.*
To Cost of Sales	2,81,250	By Sales	3,75,000
To Gross Profit	93,750		
	3,75,000		3,75,000
To Operating Expenses	33,750	By Gross Profit	93,750
To Net Profit	60,000		
	93,750		93,750

BALANCE SHEET AS ON . . . .

	Rs.		*Rs.*
Share Capital	3,00,000	Fixed Assets	4,00,000
Reserves and Surplus	2,00,000	Stock	56,250
Current Liabilities	1,25,000	Debtors	37,500
		Cash	1,31,250
	6,25,000		6,25,000

Workings :

1. *Current Assets* :

Total Current Assets – Total Current Liabilities = Net Current Assets

Current Ratio = 1. 8 : 1

Net Current Assets = 1.8 – 1 = 0.8

0.8 = Rs. 1,00,000

$$1.8\ (\text{Current Assets}) = \frac{\text{Rs.}1,00,000 \times 1.8}{0.8}$$

Current Assets = **Rs. 2,25,000**

2. *Current Liabilities* :

$$= \frac{\text{Net Current Assets} \times 1}{0.8}$$

$$= \frac{\text{Rs.}1,00,000 \times 1}{0.8} = \textbf{Rs. 1,25,000}$$

3. *Liquid Assets* (*Debtors and Cash*)

Liquid Assets = Current Liabilities × Liquid Ratio

= Rs. 1,25,000 × 1.35 = **Rs. 1,68,750**

4. *Closing Stock*:

Stock = Current Liabilities – Liquid Assets

= Rs. 2, 25,000 – Rs. 1,68,750

= **Rs. 56,250**

5. Cost of Sales = Average Stock × Stock Turnover

= Rs. 56,250 × 5 = **Rs. 2,81,250**

6. *Gross Profit* :

Gross Profit Ratio = 25%

Cost of Sales = 100 – 25 = 75%

$$\text{Gross Profit} = \frac{\text{Cost of Sales} \times 25}{75}$$

$$= \text{Rs. } 2,81,250 \times \frac{25}{75} = \textbf{Rs. 93,750}$$

7. Sales = Cost of Sales + Gross Profit

= Rs. 2,81,250 + Rs. 93,750 = **Rs. 3,75,000**

8. Net Profit = 20% of Paid up Capital

= 20% of Rs. 3,00,000

= **Rs. 60,000**

9. Operating Expenses = Gross Profit – Net Profit

= Rs. 93,750 – Rs. 60,000

= **Rs. 33,750**

10. $$\text{Debtors} = \frac{\text{Sales} \times \text{Average Collection Period}}{365}$$

$$= \frac{\text{Rs. } 3,75,000 \times 36.5}{365}$$

= Rs. **37,500**

11. Cash = Liquid Assets – Debtors

= Rs. 1,68,750 – Rs. 37,500

= **Rs. 1,31,250**

12. Fixed Assets 80% of Shareholders' Equity

It means 20% of Shareholders' Equity = Net Current Assets

$$\text{Shareholders' Equity} = \frac{\text{Net Current} \times 100}{20}$$

= Rs. 5,00,000

Fixed Assets = 80% of Rs. 5,00,000

= **Rs. 4,00,000**

13. Reserves and Surplus = Rs. 5,00,000 – Rs. 3,00,000 = **Rs. 2,00,000**

Illustration 42 The financial statements of Good Luck Ltd. for the year 2010, reveal the following information :

Ratio of Current Assets to Current Liabilities	1.75 to 1.0
Liquidity Ratio (Debtors and Bank Balance to Current Liabilities)	1.25 to 1.0
Issued capital in equity shares of Rs.10 each	Rs.1,20,000
Net Current Assets (as over current liabilities)	Rs.60,600
Fixed Assets (net blocks) - Percentage of Shareholders' equity as on the closing date	60%
Gross Profit — Percentage of Turnover	20%
Annual rate of Turnover of stock (based on cost on 31st Dec. 2010	5.26 Times
Average age of outstanding debtors for the year 2010	2 Months
Net Profit (Percentage on issued share capital)	16%

On 31st December 2010, current assets consisted of stock, debtors and bank balances.

You are required to reconstruct, in as much detail as possible:

(*a*) The Balance Sheet as on 31st December 2010, and

(*b*) Trading and Profit and Loss Account for the year ended 31st December, 2010.

(*CA*), (*M.Com. Lucknow, Bhopal Kolkata*)

Solution :

TRADING AND PROFIT AND LOSS ACCOUNT
for the year ended 31st Dec., 2010

	Rs.		*Rs.*
To Cost of Goods sold (Balancing Figure)	2,12,504	By Sales	2,65,630
To Profit & Loss A/c (20% of Sales)	53,126		
	2,65,630		2,65,630
To Selling & Distribution Expenses (Balancing figure)	33,926	By Gross Profit	53,126
To Net Profit 16% of Rs.1,20,000)	19,200		
	53,126		53,126

BALANCE SHEET as on 31st Dec., 2010

Liabilities	*Rs.*	*Assets*	*Rs.*
Share Capital:			
12,000 Equity Shares of Rs.10 each	1,20,000	Fixed Assets	90,900
		Cash	56,728
Profit and Loss A/c (Reserves & Surplus)	31,500	Sundry Debtors	44,272
Current Liabilities	80,800	Stock	40,400
	2,32,300		2,32,300

Workings :

1. *Current Assets and Current Liabilities :*

CA – CL = WC

CA – CL = Rs. 60,600 ...(1)

$$\frac{CA}{CL} = 1.75$$

CA = 1.75 CL = 1 ...(2)

Substract (2) from (1)

We get 0.75 CL = Rs. 60,600

$$CL = \frac{Rs.60,600}{0.75} = Rs.80.800$$

CA = Rs. 80,800 + Rs. 60,600 = Rs. 1,41,400

Current Liabilities = **Rs. 80,800**

Current Assets = **Rs. 1,41,400**

2. *Liquid Assets* :

$$\frac{\text{Liquid Assets}}{CL} = 1.25$$

Liquid Assets = Rs. 80,800 × 1.25 = **Rs. 1,01,000**

3. *Stock* :

Current Assets – Liquid Assets = Stock

Rs. 1,41,400 – Rs. 1,01,000 = **Rs. 40,400**

4. *Fixed Assets* :

Fixed Assets (Net Block) = 60% of Shareholder's Equity

Therefore Current Assets = 40% of Shareholder's Equity

$$\text{Fixed Assets} = \text{Rs. } 60,600 \times \frac{60}{40} = \mathbf{90,900}.$$

5. *Shareholders' Equity* :

Fixed Assets + Net Current Assets

Rs. 90,900 + Rs. 60,600 = **Rs. 1,51,500**

6. *Reserves & Surplus* :

Shareholders' Equity – Issued Share Capital

Rs. 1,51,500 – Rs. 1,20,000 = **Rs. 31,500**

7. *Cost of goods sold* :

$$\text{Stock Turnover} = \frac{\text{Cost of Goods Sold}}{\text{Closing Stock}}$$

$$5.26 = \frac{\text{Cost of Goods Sold}}{\text{Rs. } 40,400}$$

Cost of good sold = Rs. 40,400 × 5.26 = **Rs. 2,12,504**

8. *Debtors* :

$$\text{Debtors Turnover} = \frac{\text{Credit Sales}}{\text{Debtors}}$$

$$6 = \frac{\text{Rs. } 2,65,630}{\text{Debtors}}$$

6 Debtors = Rs. 2,65,630

Debtors = Rs. 44,272

9. Cash = Liquid Assets – Debtors
   Rs.1,01,000 – Rs.44,272 = **Rs. 56,728**

Illustration 43 From the following information, prepare the Balance Sheet of X Company showing the details of working:

Paid up Capital	Rs.50,000
Plant and Machinery	Rs.1,25,000
Total Sales p.a.	Rs.5,00,000
Gross Profit Margin	25%
Annual Credit Sales	80% of Net Sales
Current Ratio	2
Inventory Turnover	4
Fixed Assets Turnover	2
Sales Returns	20% of Sales
Average Collection period	73 days
Bank Credit to trade credit	2
Cash to Inventory	1 : 15
Total debt to Current Liabilities	3

(*CA Final*), (*M.Com. Delhi, Lucknow, Punjab*)

Solution.

BALANCE SHEET OF X CO. as on....

Liabilities		*Rs.*	*Assets*	*Rs.*
Paid up Capital		50,000	Assets:	
Reserves & Surplus		78,000	Fixed Assets:	
Long-term Debt		1,44,000	Plant & Mechinery	1,25,000
Current Liabilities :			Other Fixed Assets	75,000
Bank Credit	48,000		Current Assets :	
Trade Credit	24,000	72,000	Inventory	75,000
			Receivables	64,000
			Cash	5,000
		3,44,000		3,44,000

Workings :

Net Sales = Total Sales – Sales Returns
= Rs. 5,00,000 – Rs. 1,00,000 = **Rs. 4,00,000**

Credit Sales = 80% of Net Sales
= Rs. 4,00,000 × 80% = **Rs. 3,20,000**

Gross Profit = 25% of Net Sales
= 25% of Rs. 4,00,000 = **Rs. 1,00,000**

Cost of Goods Sold = Net Sales – Gross Profit
= Rs. 4,00,000 – Rs. 1,00,000 = **Rs. 3,00,000**

$$\text{Inventory} = \frac{\text{Cost of Goods Sold}}{\text{Inventory Turnover}}$$

$$= \frac{\text{Rs. } 3,00,000}{4} = \textbf{Rs. 75,000}$$

$$\text{Receivables Turnover} = \frac{365}{73} = 5$$

$$\text{Receivables} = \frac{\text{Credit Sales}}{\text{Receivables Turnover}}$$

$$= \frac{\text{Rs. } 3{,}20{,}000}{5} = \textbf{Rs. 64,000}$$

Cash = 1/15 of Inventory

= 1/15 × Rs. 75,000 = **Rs. 5,000**

Total Current Assets = Inventory + Receivable + Cash

= Rs. 75,000 + Rs. 64,000 + Rs. 5,000

= **Rs. 1,44,000**

$$\text{Total Current Liabilities} = \frac{\text{Current Assets}}{2}$$

$$= \frac{\text{Rs. } 1{,}44{,}000}{2} = \textbf{Rs. 72,000}$$

$$\text{Bank Credit} = \frac{2}{3} \times \text{Current Liabilities}$$

$$= \frac{2}{3} \times \text{Rs. } 72{,}000 = \textbf{Rs. 48,000}$$

$$\text{Trade Credit} = \frac{1}{2} \text{ of Bank Credit or } \frac{1}{3} \text{ of Current Liabilities}$$

= **Rs. 24,000**

Total Debt = Current Liabilities × 3

= Rs. 72,000 × 3 = **Rs. 2,16,000**

Long-term Debt = Total Debt – Current Liabilities

= Rs. 2,16,000 – Rs. 72,000 = **Rs. 1,44,000**

$$\text{Fixed Assets} = \frac{1}{2} \text{ of Net Sales} = \frac{1}{2} \text{ of Rs. } 4{,}00{,}000$$

= **Rs. 2,00,000**

Plant and Machinery (given) = **Rs. 1,25,000**

Other Fixed Assets = Fixed Assets – Plant & Machinery

= Rs. 2,00,000 – Rs. 1,25,000 = **Rs. 75,000**

Total Assets = Fixed Assets + Current Assets

= Rs. 2,00,000 + Rs. 1,44,000

= **Rs. 3,44,000**

Net Worth = Total Assets – Total Debt

= Rs. 3,44,000 – Rs. 2,16,000

= **Rs. 1,28,000**

Paid up Capital (given) = **Rs. 50,000**

Reserves & Surplus = Net Worth – Paid up Capital

=Rs. 1,28,000 – Rs. 50,000

= **Rs. 78,000**

Du Pont Chart

The Du Pont Company of US pioneered a system of financial analysis which has received widespread recognition. As a useful tool for financial analysis, it has been adopted by many firms in some form or the other. The earning power, represented by return on capital employed, shows the combined effect of the net profit margin and the capital turnover. A change in any of these ratios will change the firm's earning power. These two ratios are affected by many factors. Any change in these factors will bring a change in these two ratios. The usefulness of the Du Pont type of analysis lies in the fact that it presents the over-all picture of the performance of a firm as also enables the management to identify the factors which have a bearing on profitability. The two components of this ratio, namely, the profit margin and the investment turnover ratio individually do not give an over-all view as the former ignores the profitability of investments while the latter fails to consider the profitability on sales.

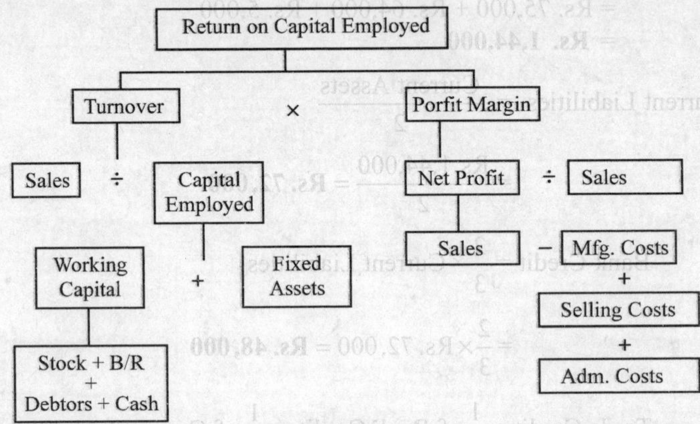

A financial ratio is the principal tool for analysis of financial statements. It helps to ascertain the financial condition of a firm. Financial ratios seem to have predictive ability, particularly in signalling business strengths and weaknesses of a firm. The most important financial ratios may be divided into four types :

(a) LIQUIDITY refers to the ability of a firm to meet its obligations in the short run, usually one year. Liquidity ratios are calculated by establishing relationships between current assets and current liabilities. For examples, Current Ratios, Liquid Ratios, Fund Flow Ratios etc.

(b) FINANCIAL LEVERAGE refers to the use of debt finance. To judge the long-term financial position of a firm, leverage or capital structure ratios are calculated. These ratios indicate the funds provided by owners and creditors. That is, these ratios measure the proportion of outsiders capital in financing the firm's assets and establishing the relationships between borrowed capital and equity capital. For example, Debt-Equity Ratios, Capital-Equity Ratios, Interest Coverage Ratios etc.

(c) TURNOVER RATIOS, also referred to as activity ratios or asset management ratios measure how efficiently the assets are employed by the firm. These ratios are calculated by establishing relationship between sales and assets. For examples, Stock Turnover, Debtors Turnover, Fixed Asset Turnover etc.

(d) PROFITABILITY RATIOS measure the overall performance of Business - *profit margin ratios* and *rate of return ratios*. Profit margin ratios show the relationship between profit and sales, for examples, Gross Profit Margin, Net Profit Margin etc. Rate of Return Ratios reflect the relationship between profit and investment, for examples, Return on Investment, Return on Equity etc.

MISCELLANEOUS

Illustration 44 PQR Pvt. Ltd. was formed on 1st April 2009 for taking over the business of a Partnership firm. The partners were paid the purchase consideration partly by issue of Capital. The Balance as at 31st March 2010 shows the following position :

	Rs.		Rs.
Equity Capital	10,00,000	Goodwill	10,00,000
Debentures	2,50,000	Fixed Assets	5,00,000
Deposits from Director's friends	1,50,000	Stock	50,00,000
Sundry Creditors	80,00,000	Debtors	25,00,000
		Cash	25,000
		Profit & Loss A/c	3,75,000
	94,00,000		94,00,000

The sales for 2009-10 was Rs.75,00,000. The company approaches you for borrowing facilities. Prepare a note setting out your recommendations and the reasoning for the same.

(C.A.I.I.B.)

Solution .

$$\text{(1) Current Ratio} = \frac{\text{Current Assets}}{\text{Current Liabilities}}$$

$$= \frac{75,25,000}{81,50,000} = 0.92$$

From this it is clear that current assets are insufficient to pay off current liabilities.

$$\text{(1) Liquid Ratio} = \frac{\text{Liquid Assets}}{\text{Current Liabilities}}$$

$$= \frac{25,25,000}{81,50,000} = 0.31$$

Current Liabilities cannot be paid off.

$$\text{(3) Debt Collection Period} = \frac{\text{Debtors}}{\text{Sales}} \times 365 = \frac{25,00,000}{75,00,000} \times 365 = 122 \text{ days}$$

It takes a long period in collecting debts.

The firm is running in losses. The losses are about one third of equity share capital. The proposal may be declined.

Illustration 45 A company sells goods on cash as well as credit (though not on deferred instalment terms). The following particulars are extracted from their books of accounts for the calendar year 2010.

Total Gross Sales	2,00,000
Cash Sales (included in above)	40,000
Sales Returns	14,000
Total Debtors for sales on 31.12.2010	18,000
Bills Receivable on 31.12.2010	4,000
Provision for doubtful debts 31.12.2010	2,000
Total Creditors on 31.12.2010	20,000

Calculate the average collection period. *(B.Com., Punjab, C.A.)*

Solution

$$\text{Average Collection Period} = \frac{\text{Debtors + Bills Receivable}}{\text{Net Credit Sales for the year}} \times 365$$

$$= \frac{18,000 + 4,000}{1,46,000^*} \times 365$$

= 55 days

* Net Credit Sales = Total Sales – Cash Sales – Sales Returns
= 2,00,000 – 40,000 – 14,000
= 1,46,000

Illustration 46.

From the following particulars, prepare :

1. Stock Turnover Ratio
2. Fixed Assets Turnover Ratio
3. Debtors Turnover Ratio
4. Creditors Turnover Ratio
5. Debt Collection period and
6. Debt Payment period

	Rs. (figures in '000)
Sales	17,874
Sales Returns	4
Other Income	53
Cost of Sales	15,440
Administration expense	1,843
Depreciation	63
Interest expenses	456
Purchases	15,000
Purchase Returns	5
Debtors	10,000
Bills Receivables	2,000
Creditors	5,000
Bills Payable	3,000
Opening stock	4,000
Closing stock	5,000
Fixed Assets	5,000

(*B.Com. MS, Bharathidasan, M.Com. Delhi, Bhopal*)

Solution :

$$\text{(1) Stock Turnover Ratio} = \frac{\text{Cost of goods sold}}{\text{Average Inventory}}$$

$$= \frac{\text{Rs. } 15,400}{\text{Rs. } 4,500} = \textbf{3.43 Times}$$

$$\left(\text{Average Stock} = \frac{\text{Rs. } 4,000 + \text{Rs. } 5,000}{2} = \text{Rs. } 4,500\right)$$

$$\text{(2) Fixed Assets Turnover Ratio} = \frac{\text{Cost of Sales}}{\text{Fixed Assets}}$$

$$= \frac{\text{Rs. } 15,440}{\text{Rs. } 5,000} = \textbf{3.09 times}$$

$$\text{(3) Debtors Turnover Ratio} = \frac{\text{Credit Sales}}{\text{Average Accounts Receivable}}$$

$$= \frac{17,874 - 4}{2,000 + 10,000} = 1.49 \text{ times}$$

(Accounts Receivable = Debtors + Bills Receivable)

(4) Creditors Turnover Ratio $= \dfrac{\text{Credit Purchases}}{\text{Average Accounts Payable}}$

(Credit Purchase = 15,000 – 5 = 14,995)

$= \dfrac{14{,}995}{8{,}000} = 1.87$ times

(5) Debt Collection Period $= \dfrac{\text{Months in a year}}{\text{Debtors Turnover ratio}}$

$= \dfrac{12}{1.49} = 8.05$ or 8 months

(OR) $= \dfrac{10{,}000 + 2{,}000}{17{,}874 - 4} \times 12$

= 8.05 or 8 months

(6) Debt Payment Period $= \dfrac{\text{Month in a year}}{\text{Creditors Turnover ratio}}$

$= \dfrac{12}{1.87} = 6.4$ months

(or) $= \dfrac{\text{Rs. } 5{,}000 + \text{Rs. } 3{,}000}{14{,}995} \times 12 = 6.4$ months

Illustration 47

Following are the particulars of a company given to you.

(1) Receivable Turnover = 90 days (360 days a year)
(2) Inventory Turnover = 3 Times
(3) Payable Turnover = 3 months
(4) Gross Profit Ratio = 25%

The following are the additional information

(*a*) Gross profit for the year comes to Rs. Rs. 18,000
(*b*) Closing inventory is Rs. 2,000 above the opening stock.
(*c*) Bills Receivable amounted to Rs. 2,500
(*d*) Bills Payable amounted to Rs. 1,000

Find out :

(A) Sales
(B) Debtors
(C) Closing Inventory
(D) Sundry Creditors

(*M.Com. Chennai Delhi*, B. Com. MS, Kolkata)

Solution :

(A) *Sales* :

$$\text{Gross Profit Ratio} = \frac{\text{Gross Profit}}{\text{Sales}} \times 100$$

$$25\% = \frac{\text{Rs. } 18{,}000}{\text{Sales}} \times 100$$

$$\text{Sales} = \frac{\text{Rs. } 18{,}000}{25} \times 100 = \textbf{Rs. 72,000}$$

(B) *Debtors* :

$$90 = \frac{360}{\text{Receivable Turnover Ratio}}$$

$$\text{Receivable Turnover Ratio} = \frac{360}{90} = 4 \text{ Times}$$

$$\text{(or) Receivable Turnover Ratio} = \frac{\text{Credit Sales}}{\text{Average Receivable}}$$

$$4 = \frac{\text{Rs. } 72{,}000}{\text{Average Receivable}}$$

$$4 = \frac{\text{Rs. } 72{,}000}{4} = \text{Rs. } 18{,}000$$

Less : Bills Receivable = 2,500

15,500

(C) *Closing Inventory*

Cost of Sales = Sales – Gross Profit
= Rs. 72,000 – Rs. 18,000
= Rs. 54,000

$$\text{Inventory Turnover Ratio} = \frac{\text{Cost of Sales}}{\text{Average Inventory}}$$

$$3 = \frac{\text{Rs. } 54{,}000}{\text{Average Inventory}}$$

$$\text{Average Inventory} = \frac{\text{Rs. } 54{,}000}{3} = \text{Rs. } 18{,}000$$

$$\text{Average Inventory} = \frac{\text{Opening Inventory} + \text{Closing Inventory}}{2}$$

Assume Opening Inventory = X

$$\text{Rs. } 18{,}000 = \frac{X + X + 2{,}000}{2}$$

Rs. 36,000 = 2X + 2,000

2X = Rs. 36,000 – Rs. 2,000

X = Rs. 17,000

Closing Inventory = Rs. 17,000 + Rs. 2,000 = **Rs. 19,000**

(D) Sundry Creditors

Purchase = Sales + Closing Inventory – (Opening Inventory + Gross Profit)
= Rs. 72,000 + Rs. 19,000 – (Rs. 17,000 + Rs. 18,000)
= Rs. 56,000

$$\text{Payable Turnover (Months)} = \frac{\text{Months in a year}}{\text{Payable Turnover Ratio}}$$

$$3 = \frac{12}{\text{Payable Turnover Ratio}}$$

Payable Turnover Ratio = 12 ÷ 3 = 4 Times

Alternatively :

$$\text{Payable Turnover Ratio} = \frac{\text{Credit Purchase}}{\text{Average Payable}}$$

$$4 = \frac{\text{Rs. 56,000}}{\text{Average Payable}}$$

$$\text{Average Payable} = \frac{\text{Rs. 56,000}}{4} = \text{Rs. 14,000}$$

Less : Bills Payable Rs. 1,000

13,000

Illustration 48.

Balance Sheet of a firm as on 31st December is as follows :

(Figures in '000)

Liabilities	*Rs.*	*Assets*	*Rs.*
Equity Share Capital	200	Fixed Assets	360
9% Preference shares	100	Stock	50
8% Debentures	100	Debtors	110
Profit & Loss A/c	40	Bills Receivables	6
Creditors	90	Bank	4
	530		530

Find out (*a*) Fixed Assets Ratio
(*b*) Capital Gearing Ratio

(*B.Com. Madurai Chennai*)

Solution :

$$(a)\ \text{Fixed Assets Ratio} = \frac{\text{Fixed Assets}}{\text{Long Term Funds}}$$

Fixed Assets (given) = Rs. 360

Long-term Funds (given) = Share Capital + Debentures + P & L A/c
= Rs. 200 + Rs. 100 + Rs. 100 + Rs. 40
= Rs. 440

$$\text{Fixed Assets Ratio} = \frac{360}{440} = 0.82$$

Note : From the above computation it can be ascertained that 82% of the long term funds are sunk into the fixed assets and 18% supplied by them are used for working capital.

$$(b)\ \text{Capital Gearing Ratio} = \frac{\text{Fixed Interest Bearing Funds}}{\text{Equity Share Holders' Funds}}$$

$$= \frac{\text{Rs. 100 + Rs. 100}}{\text{Rs. 200 + Rs. 40}} = \frac{\text{Rs. 200}}{\text{Rs. 240}} = \text{Rs. 0.83}$$

Note : It shows the relation between fixed interest bearing funds and equity shareholders' funds.

Illustration 49 The following are the summarised Profit and Loss Account of Hind Products Ltd. for the year ending 31st December and the Balance Sheet as on that date:

PROFIT AND LOSS ACCOUNT

		Rs.			Rs.
To Opening Stock		99,500	By Sales		8,50,000
To Purchases		5,45,250	By Closing Stock		1,49,000
To Incidental Expenses		14,250			
To Gross Profit		3,40,000			
		9,99,000			9,99,000
To Operating Expenses: Selling and Distribution	30,000		By Gross Profit		3,40,000
			By Non-operating Income:		
Administration	1,50,000		Interest	3,000	
Finance	15,000	1,95,000	Profit on sale of shares	6,000	9,000
To Non-operating Expenses :					
Loss on sale of assets		4,000			
To Net Profit		1,50,000			
		3,49,000			3,49,000

BALANCE SHEET OF HIND PRODUCTS LTD.
as on 31st December

Liabilities	*Rs.*	*Assets*	*Rs.*
Issued Capital		Land and Buildings	1,50,000
2,000 equity		Plant and Machinery	80,000
shares of Rs.100 each	2,00,000	Stock-in-trade	1,49,000
Reserves	90,000	Sundry Debtors	71,000
Current Liabilities	1,30,000	Cash and Bank	
Profit & Loss A/c	60,000	Balance	30,000
	4,80,000		4,80,000

From the above statement you are required to calculate the following ratios and state the purpose they serve :

(1) Gross profit ratio; (2) Net profit ratio; (3) Operating profit ratio; (4) Operating ratio; (5) Current ratio; (6) Acid-Test Ratio. (*B.Com. Madurai*)

Solution :

(1) Gross profit ratio $= \frac{\text{Gross Profit}}{\text{Sales}} \times 100$

$$= \frac{3,40,000}{8,50,000} \times 100 = 40\%$$

(2) Net Profit ratio $= \frac{\text{Net Profit}}{\text{Sales}} \times 100 = \frac{1,50,000}{8,50,000} \times 100 = 17.64\%$

(3) Operating Profit ratio $= \frac{\text{Operating Profit}}{\text{Sales}} \times 100$

$$\frac{1,45,000}{8,50,000} \times 100 = 17.05\%$$

(Operating profit = Net Profit + Non-operating expenses – Non-operating income)
= 1,50,000 + 4,000 – 9,000 = 1,45,000

(4) Operating ratio $= \dfrac{\text{Cost of goods sold + Operating expenses}}{\text{Sales}} \times 100$

$= \dfrac{7,05,000}{8,50,000} \times 100 = 82.95\%$

(5) Current ratio $= \dfrac{\text{Current Assets}}{\text{Current Liabilities}}$

$= \dfrac{1,49,000 + 71,000 + 30,000}{1,30,000} = \dfrac{250,000}{1,30,000} = 1.92 : 1$

(6) Acid test ratio $= \dfrac{71,000 + 30,000}{1,30,000} = 0.77:1$

Illustration 50 From the data, calculate :

(*a*) Gross Profit Ratio
(*b*) Net Profit Ratio
(*c*) Return on Total Assets
(*d*) Inventory Turnover
(*e*) Working Capital Turnover
(*f*) Net Worth to Debt.

Sales	Rs. 25,20,000
Cost of Sales	Rs. 19,20,000
Net Profit	Rs. 3,60,000
Inventory	Rs. 8,00,000
Other Current Assets	Rs. 7,60,000
Fixed Assets	Rs. 14,40,000
Net Worth	Rs. 15,00,000
Debt	Rs. 9,00,000
Current Liabilities	Rs. 6,00,000

[*Company Secretary* (*B.Com. Madurai*)]

Solution :

(*a*) *Gross Profit Ratio* :

Gross Profit = Sales – Cost of Sales
= Rs. 25,20,000 – Rs. 19,20,000
= Rs. 6,00,000

Gross Profit Ratio $= \dfrac{\text{Rs. } 6,00,000}{\text{Rs. } 25,20,000} \times 100 = \mathbf{23.81\%}$

(*b*) *Net Profit ratio* :

$\dfrac{\text{Net Profit}}{\text{Sales}} \times 100$

$\dfrac{\text{Rs. } 3,60,000}{\text{Rs. } 25,20,000} \times 100 = \mathbf{14.29\%}$

(*c*) *Return on Total Assets* :

$\dfrac{\text{Net Profit}}{\text{Total Assets}} \times 100$

Total Assets = Inventories + Other Current Assets + Fixed Assets
= Rs. 8,00,000 + Rs. 7,60,000 + Rs. 14,40,000
= Rs. 30,00,000

$$\text{Return on Total Assets} = \frac{\text{Rs. } 3,60,000}{\text{Rs. } 30,00,000} \times 100 = 12\%$$

(*d*) *Inventory Turnover* :

$$\frac{\text{Cost of Sales}}{\text{Inventory}} = \frac{\text{Rs.} 19,20,000}{\text{Rs.} 8,00,000} = \mathbf{2.4\,Times}$$

(*e*) $\text{Working Capital Turnover} = \frac{\text{Cost of Sales}}{\text{Working Capital}}$

Working Capital = Current Assets – Current Liabilities
= Rs. 8,00,000 + Rs. 7,60,000 – Rs. 6,00,000
= **Rs. 9,60,000**

$$\text{Working Capital Turnover} = \frac{\text{Rs. } 9,20,000}{\text{Rs. } 9,60,000} = \mathbf{2\ Times}$$

(*f*) *Net Worth to Debt Ratio* : $= \frac{\text{Net Worth}}{\text{Debt}} = \frac{\text{Rs.} 15,00,000}{9,00,000} = \mathbf{1.6\ Times}$

Illustration 51 Extracts from financial accounts of X, Y, Z Ltd. are :

	Year I		*Year II*	
	Assets Rs.	*Liabilities Rs.*	*Assets Rs.*	*Liabilities Rs.*
Stock	10,000		20,000	
Debtors	30,000		30,000	
Payment in Advance	2,000		—	
Cash in hand	20,000		15,000	
Sundry Creditors		25,000		30,000
Acceptances		15,000		12,000
Bank Overdraft		—		5,000
	62,000	40,000	65,000	47,000

Sales amounted to Rs.3,50,000 in the first year and Rs.3,00,000 in the second year.

You are required to comment on the solvency position of the concern with the help of accounting ratios. (*C.A. Final*)[*M. Com. Madras*]

Solution :

Short-term Solvency Analysis

(1) $\text{Current Ratio} = \frac{\text{Current Assets}}{\text{Current Liabilities}}$

$$\text{Year I}: \frac{10,000 + 30,000 + 2,000 + 20,000}{25,000 + 15,000} = \frac{62,000}{40,000}$$

$$= 1.55 : 1$$

$$\text{Year II}: \frac{20,000 + 30,000 + 15,000}{30,000 + 12,000 + 5,000} = \frac{65,000}{47,000}$$

$$= 1.38 : 1$$

(2) Liquid or Quick Ratio = $\frac{\text{Liquid Assets}}{\text{Liquid Liabilities}}$

$$\text{Year I}: \frac{30{,}000 + 20{,}000 + 2{,}000}{25{,}000 + 15{,}000} = \frac{52{,}000}{40{,}000}$$

$$= 1.30 : 1$$

$$\text{Year II}: \frac{30{,}000 + 15{,}000}{30{,}000 + 12{,}000 + 5{,}000} = \frac{45{,}000}{47{,}000}$$

$$0.96 : 1$$

(3) Inventory Turnover Ratio = $\frac{\text{Net Sales}}{\text{Average Inventory}}$

$$\text{Year I}: \frac{3{,}50{,}000}{10{,}000} = 35:1$$

$$\text{Year II}: \frac{3{,}00{,}000}{15{,}000} = 20:1$$

(4) Inventory Current Assets Ratio = $\frac{\text{Inventory}}{\text{Total Current Assets}} \times 100$

$$\text{Year I}: \frac{10{,}000}{62{,}000} \times 100 = 16\%$$

$$\text{Year II}: \frac{20{,}000}{65{,}000} \times 100 = 31\%$$

(5) Average Collection period = $\frac{\text{Trade Receivables}}{\text{Net Credit Sales}}$ × No. of Working Days

$$\text{Year I}: \frac{30{,}000}{3{,}50{,}000} \times 365 = 31.3 \text{ days}$$

$$\text{Year II}: \frac{30{,}000}{3{,}00{,}000} \times 365 = 36.5 \text{ days}$$

Long-Term Solvency Analysis

(1) Debt Equity Ratio = $\frac{\text{External Equities}}{\text{Internal Equities}}$

$$\text{Year I}: \frac{25{,}000 + 15{,}000}{62{,}000 - 40{,}000} = \frac{40{,}000}{22{,}000} = 1.82:1$$

$$\text{Year II}: \frac{30{,}000 + 12{,}000 + 5{,}000}{65{,}000 - 47{,}000} = \frac{47{,}000}{18{,}000} = 2.61:1$$

(2) Proprietary Ratio is $= \dfrac{\text{Shareholder's Equities}}{\text{Total Equities}}$

$$\text{Year I}: \frac{22{,}000}{62{,}000} = 0.35:1$$

$$\text{Year II}: \frac{18{,}000}{65{,}00} = 0.28:1$$

Illustration 52 From the data given below compute :

(*a*) Working Capital (*b*) Net Capital Employed
(*c*) Current Ratio (*d*) Acid Test Ratio
(*e*) Debt-equity Ratio (*f*) Fixed Asset Ratio

CROMPTON LTD.
as on 31st December

Liabilities	*Rs.*	*Assets*	*Rs.*
Equity Share Capital	25,000	Fixed Assets	30,000
Preference Share Capital	5,000	Current Assets :	
Reserves and Surplus	4,000	Stores	2,000
Debentures	8,000	Sundry Debtors	1,000
Bank Loan	4,000	Cash	500
Sundry Creditors	1,000	Bank	2,500
Proposed Dividends	1,000	Preliminary Expenses	8,000
Provision for Taxation	2,000	Brokerage on shares	2,000
		Stock	4,000
	50,000		50,000

(*B.Com. Madurai*)

Solution :

(*a*) **Working Capital** : Current Assets – Current Liabilities

Current Assets = Rs. 2,000 + Rs. 1,000 + Rs. 2,500 + Rs. 4,000 + Rs. 500
= Rs. 10,000

Current Liabilities = Rs. 1,000 + Rs. 1,000 + Rs. 2,000
= Rs. 4,000

Working Capital = 10,000 – Rs. 4,000 = **Rs. 6,000**

(*b*) *Net Capital Employed:*

All Assets, excluding fictitious assets - Current Liabilities

Rs. 40,000 – Rs. 4,000

= **Rs. 36,000**

(c) *Current Ratio :*

Current Assets : Current Liabilities

Rs. 10,000 : Rs. 4,000

= **2.5 : 1**

(*d*)*Acid Test Ratio :*

= Liquid Assets : Liquid Liabilities

= Rs. 4,000 : 4,000

= **1 : 1**

(e) *Debt Equity Ratio :*

Debt – Equity Ratio = Outsider's Fund : Shareholder's Fund

= Rs. 8,000 + Rs. 4,000 + Rs. 1,000 + Rs. 1,000 + Rs. 2,000
= Rs. 16,000
= Rs. 25,000 + Rs. 5,000 + Rs. 4,000 = Rs. 34,000

Debt Equity Ratio = Rs. 16,000 : 34,000 = **0.47 : 1**

(*f*) *Fixed Assets Ratio :*

Fixed Assets Ratio :

Fixed Assets Ratio = Fixed Assets : Long-term Funds
= Rs. 30,000 : (Rs. 25,000 + Rs. 5,000 + Rs. 4,000 + Rs. 8,000 + Rs. 4,000)
= 30,000 : Rs 46,000 = **0.65 : 1**

Illustration 53 Calculate the Balance Sheet items given in the undermentioned proforma with the help of following ratios :

Total Assets/Net Worth	=	3.5
Sales/Fixed Assets	=	6
Sales/Current Assets	=	8
Sales/Inventory	=	15
Sales/Debtors	=	18
Current Ratio	=	2.5
Annual Sales	=	Rs.25,00,000

BALANCE SHEET

	Rs.		*Rs.*
Net Worth	—	Fixed Assets	—
Long-term Debt	—	Inventory	—
Current Liabilities	—	Debtors	—
		Liquid Assets	—
Total Liabilities	—	Total Assets	—

(*B.Com. Punjab, Kolkata*)

Solution :

(1) *Fixed Assets :*

$$\frac{\text{Sales}}{\text{Fixed Assets}} = 6$$

$$= \frac{\text{Rs. } 25,00,000}{\text{Fixed Assets}} = 6$$

$$\text{Fixed Assets} = \frac{\text{Rs. } 25,00,000}{6} = \text{Rs. } 4,16,667$$

(2) *Current Assets:*

$$= \frac{\text{Sales}}{\text{Current Assets}} = 8$$

$$= \frac{\text{Rs. } 25,00,000}{\text{Current Assets}} = 8$$

$$\text{Current Assets} = \frac{\text{Rs. } 25,00,000}{8}$$

$$= \text{Rs. } 3,12,500$$

(3) *Debtors :*

$$= \frac{\text{Sales}}{\text{Debtors}} = 18$$

$$= \frac{\text{Rs. } 25{,}00{,}000}{\text{Debtors}} = 18$$

$$\text{Debtors} = \frac{\text{Rs. } 25{,}00{,}000}{18} = \textbf{Rs. 1,38,889}$$

(4) $\text{Inventory} = \frac{\text{Sales}}{\text{Inventory}} = 15$

$$= \frac{\text{Rs. } 25{,}00{,}000}{\text{Inventory}} = 15$$

$$\text{Inventory} = \frac{\text{Rs. } 25{,}00{,}000}{15} = \textbf{Rs. 1,66,667}$$

(5) $\text{Current Liabilities} = \frac{\text{Current Assets}}{\text{Current Liabilities}} = 2.5$

$$= \frac{\text{Rs. } 3{,}12{,}500}{\text{Current Liabilities}} = 2.5$$

$$= \text{Current Liabilities} = \frac{\text{Rs. } 3{,}12{,}500}{2.5} = \textbf{Rs. 1,25,000}$$

(6)Net Worth : $= \frac{\text{Total Assets}}{\text{Net Worth}} = 3.5$

$$\text{Net Worth} = \frac{\text{Rs. } 7{,}29{,}167}{3.5} = \textbf{Rs. 2,08,333}$$

(7) Long-term Debts:

= Total Assets – (Net Worth + Current Liabilities)
= Rs. 7,29,167 – (Rs. 1,78,667 + Rs. 1,25,000)
= Rs. 7,29,167 – Rs. 3,03,667
= Long-term Debts Rs. 4,25,500

BALANCE SHEET as on......

Liabilities	*Rs.*	*Assets*	*Rs.*
Net Worth	1,78,667	Fixed Assets	4,16,667
Long-term Debts	4,25,500	Inventory	1,66,667
Current Liabilities	1,25,000	Debtors	1,38,889
		Liquid Assets	6,944
	7,29,167		7,29,167

Illustration 54 The following are the financial statements of Albeit Company :

BALANCE SHEET
as on 31st December

Liabilities	*Rs.*	*Assets*	*Rs.*
Equity share capital, Rs.10 each	50,000	Plant & Equipment	2,00,000
6% Preference share		Less Depreciation	1,60,000
capital	20,000		40,000
Profit & Loss Account	44,000	Inventory	1,00,000

5 1/4% Mortage loans	80,000	Debtors (Previous year Rs.40,000)	60,000
Bills Payable	30,000	Investments	24,00
Taxes Payable	20,000	Cash	20,000
	2,44,000		2,44,000

PROFIT AND LOSS ACCOUNT
for the year ended 31st December

	Rs.		*Rs.*
The Stock in the beginning	80,000	By Sales	2,40,000
To Purchases	1,20,000	By Stock at the end	1,00,000
To Gross Profit	1,40,000		
	3,40,000		3,40,000
To Operating Expenses :		By Gross Profit	1,40,000
Selling Expenses	30,000		
General and administrative expenses	40,000		
To Net Operating income	70,000		
	1,40,000		1,40,000
To Interest Expense :	4,200	By Net Operating income	70,000
To Income before tax	65,800		
	70,000		70,000
To Income taxes	29,800	By Income before tax	65,800
To Net Income after tax	36,000		
	65,800		65,800

You are required to calculate: (1) Current ratio, (2) Acid test ratio, (3) Debtors turnover, (4) Number of Days uncollectibles (assume a 360-days year), (5) Inventory turnover, (6) Number of times interest earned, (7) Earning per share (equity share), (8) Rate of return on equity shareholders' equity (9) Rate on total assets, and (10) Total debts to shareholder's equity.

Solution :

$$(1)\ \text{Current Ratio} = \frac{\text{Current Assets}}{\text{Current Liabilities}}$$

$$= \frac{\text{Inventory + Debtors + Investment + Cash}}{\text{Bills Payable + Taxes Payable}}$$

$$= \frac{10,00,000 + 60,000 + 24,000 + 20,000}{30,000 + 20,000}$$

$$= \frac{2,04,000}{50,000} = 4,08:1$$

$$(2)\ \text{Acid Test Ratio} = \frac{\text{Quick Assets}}{\text{Current Liabilities}}$$

$$= \frac{\text{Debtors + Investment + Cash}}{\text{Bills Payable + Taxes Payable}}$$

$$= \frac{60,000 + 24,000 + 20,000}{30,000 + 20,000}$$

$$= \frac{1,04,000}{50,000} = 2.08 : 1$$

(3) Debtors Turnover $= \dfrac{\text{Credit Sales}}{\text{Average Debtors}}$

$$= \frac{2,40,000}{1/2\ (60,000 + 40,000)} = \frac{2,40,000}{50,000} = 4.8 : 1$$

(4) Number of days uncollectibles $= \dfrac{\text{360 days in a year}}{\text{Debtors turnover}} = \dfrac{360}{4.8}$ =75 days.

(5) Inventory Turnover $= \dfrac{\text{Cost of Goods Sold}}{\text{Average Inventory}}$

$$= \frac{\text{Opening Stock + Purchases } - \text{Closing Stock}}{\text{1/2(Opening Stock + Closing Stock)}}$$

$$= \frac{80,000 + 1,20,000 - 1,00,000}{1/2(80,000 + 1,00,000)} = \frac{1,00,000}{90,000} = 1.1 : 1$$

(6) Number of time Interest earned $= \dfrac{\text{Income before income tax and interest}}{\text{Interest}}$

$$= \frac{70,000}{4,200} = 16.67 : 1$$

(7) Earning per Share $= \dfrac{\text{Net income (after taxes)} - \text{Preferred Dividend}}{\text{Number of Equity Shares}}$

$$= \frac{36,000 - 1,200}{5,000} = \frac{34,800}{5,000} = \text{Rs. } 6.96$$

(8)Rate of Return on Equity Shareholder's Equity :

$$= \frac{\text{Net income (after taxes)} - \text{Preferred dividend}}{\text{Equity Shares Capital + Retained Earnings}} \times 100$$

$$= \frac{36,000 - 1,200}{50,000 + 44,000} \times 100 = \frac{34,800}{94,000} \times 100 = 37\%$$

(9)Rate of Return on Total Assets

$$= \frac{\text{Net income (after taxes) + Interest}}{\text{Total Assets}} \times 100$$

$$= \frac{36,000 + 4,200}{2,44,000} \times 100 = \frac{40,200}{2,44,000} \times 100 = 16.5\%$$

(10) Total Debts to Shareholders Equity

$$= \frac{\text{Mortage Loans + Bills Payable + Taxes Payable}}{\text{Equity Share Capital + Preference Capital + Retained Earnings}}$$

$$= \frac{80,000 + 30,000 + 20,000}{50,000 + 20,000 + 44,000} = \frac{1,30,000}{1,14,000} = 1.14:1$$

Illustration 55 The following is the Balance Sheet of Raman & Co. Ltd. on 31st March. Comment on its financial stability.

Liabilities	*Rs.*	*Assets*	*Rs.*
Share Capital		Land & Buildings	70,000
1,00,000 Shares of Re.1 each	1,00,000	Plant & Machinery	1,75,000
		Stock-in-trade	1,00,000
Profit & Loss A/c	15,000	Sundry Debtors	50,000
General Reserve	20,000	Bills Receivable	5,000
Development Rebate Reserve	10,000	Cash at Bank	20,000
Bank overdraft (Short-term)	2,00,000		
Sundry Creditors	50,000		
Bills Payable	25,000		
	4,20,000		4,20,000

(*C.A. Final*), (*M. Com. Delhi*)

Solution :

1. $\text{Current Ratio} = \frac{\text{Current Assets}}{\text{Current Liabilities}}$

$$= \frac{1,00,000 + 50,000 + 5,000 + 20,000}{50,000 + 25,000 + 2,00,000} = \frac{1,75,000}{2,75,000} = 0.64$$

2. $\text{Acid Test Ratio} = \frac{\text{Liquid Asset}}{\text{Liabilities}} = \frac{75,000}{2,75,000} = 0.27$

Illustration 56 From the following statements of X Co. for the year ended 31st December, you are required to re-arrange the items in the form of financial statements and calculate the following ratios :

(1) Current Ratio
(2) Liquid Ratio
(3) Operating Ratio
(4) Stock-Turnover Ratio
(5) Turnover to Fixed Assets Ratio
(6) Return on Total Resources
(7) Return on Proprietors' Fund
(8) Net Profit to Capital Employed
(9) Debtors' Velocity
(10) Average Age of Debtors
(11) Creditors' Velocity

BALANCE SHEET
as on 31st December

Liabilities	*Rs.*	*Assets*	*Rs.*
1,00,000 Equity Shares of Rs.5 each	5,00,000	Land & Buildings	3,50,000

General Reserve	3,00,000	Plant & Machinery	2,50,000
Profit & Loss A/c	2,00,000	Stock	3,00,000
Sundry Creditors	2,00,000	Sundry Debtors	2,00,000
		Cash & Bank	1,00,000
	12,00,000		12,00,000

PROFIT & LOSS A/c.

	Rs.		*Rs.*
To Opening Stock	1,00,000	Sales (Credit)	16,00,000
To Purchases (Credit)	8,00,000	By Closing Stock	2,00,000
To Gross Profit	9,00,000		
	18,00,000		18,00,000
To Office & Administration Expenses	2,00,000	By Gross Profit	9,00,000
To Selling & Distributin	1,00,000	By Profit on sale of Assets	25,000
To Other Expenses	25,000		
To Net Profit	6,00,000		
	9,25,000		9,25,000

Solution :

Financial Statements of X Company

BALANCE SHEET as on 31st December

Fixed Asset:	*Rs.*		*Rs.*
Fixed Assets :			
Land & Buildings	3,50,000		
Plant & Machinery	2,50,000		6,00,000
Working Capital :			
Current Assets:			
Stock	3,00,000		
Debtors	2,00,000		
Cash and Bank	1,00,000	6,00,000	
Less :			
Current Liabilities:			
Creditors		2,00,000	4,00,000
			10,00,000
Liabilities :			
Share Capital		5,00,000	
General Reserve		3,00,000	
Profit & Loss A/c		2,00,000	
			10,00,000

PROFIT & LOSS ACCOUNT

Sales	16,00,000
Less: Cost of Sales	7,00,000
(Rs.1,00,000 Plus	
8,00,000	
9,00,000	
Less Rs, 2,00,000	
	9,00,000

Less : Operating Expenses :		
Office & Administration :	2,00,000	
Selling & Distribution	1,00,000	
Other Expenses	25,000	3,25,000
Net Operating Profit		5,75,000
Add : Profit on sale of Fixed Assets		25,000
		6,00,000

(1) *Current Ratio* :

$$\frac{\text{Current Assets}}{\text{Current Liabilities}} = \frac{\text{Rs. 600,000}}{\text{Rs. 2,00,000}} = 3:1$$

(2) *Liquid Ratio* :

$$\frac{\text{Liquid Assets}}{\text{Liquid Liabilites}} = \frac{\text{Rs. 3,00,000}}{\text{Rs.2,00,000}} = 1.5:1$$

(3) *Operating Ratio* :

$$\frac{\text{Cost of Goods Sold + Operating Expenses}}{\text{Sales}}$$

$$\frac{\text{Rs. 7,00,000 + Rs. 3,25,000}}{\text{Rs.16,00,000}} = \frac{\text{Rs.10, 25,000}}{\text{Rs.16,00,000}} = 0.64:1$$

(4) *Stock Turonver Ratio* :

$$\frac{\text{Cost of Goods Sold}}{\text{Average Stock}} = \frac{\text{Rs. 7,00,000}}{\text{Rs. 1,50,000}} = 4.67 \text{ Times}$$

(5) *Turnover to Fixed Assets Ratio* :

$$\frac{\text{Turnover}}{\text{Fixed Assets}} = \frac{Rs.16,00,000}{Rs.6,00,000} = 2.67:1$$

(6) *Return on Total Resources* :

$$\frac{\text{Net Operating Profit}}{\text{Total Assets}} = \frac{\text{Rs. 5,75,000}}{\text{Rs. 12,00,000}} = 0.48 \text{ or } 48\%$$

(7) *Return on Proprietor's Fund:*

$$\frac{\text{Net Operating Profit}}{\text{Proprietors' fund}} = \frac{Rs.5,75,000}{Rs.10,00,000} = 0.57:1$$

(8) *Net Profit to Capital Employed* :

$$\frac{\text{Net Operating Profit}}{\text{Capital Employed}} = \frac{\text{Rs. 5,75,000}}{\text{Rs. 10,00,000}} = 0.57:1$$

(9) *Average Age of Debtors* :

$$\frac{\text{Debtors}}{\text{Credit Sale}} \times 365 = \frac{\text{Rs. 2,00,000}}{\text{Rs.16,00,000}} \times 365 = 46 \text{ Days}$$

(10) *Average Debt Payment Period* :

$$\frac{\text{Creditors}}{\text{Credit Purchase}} \times 365$$

$$\frac{\text{Rs. }2,00,000}{\text{Rs. }8,00,000} \times 365 = 91 \text{ Days}$$

Illustration 57. Following is the summarised Balance Sheet of a concern as at 31st December :

BALANCE SHEET as on 31st December

Liabilities	*Rs.*	*Assets*	*Rs.*
6% Preference Share Capital	1,50,000	Goodwill	20,000
Equity Share Capital	2,50,000	Land & Buildings	2,50,000
General Reserve	20,000	Machinery	1,75,000
Profit and Loss	15,000	Furniture	10,000
5% Debentures	1,00,000	Stock	90,000
Sundry Creditors	28,000	Sundry Debtors	21,000
Bills Payable	12,000	Cash at Bank	5,000
		Preliminary Expenses	4,000
	5,75,000		5,75,000

Other information :

Total sales Rs. 4,00,000 : 20% of which is made on credit. Gross Profit and Net Profit (after tax) for the year ended amounted to Rs. 80,000 and Rs. 20,000 respectively.

Comment on the Financial condition of the concern.

(*M.Com. Calcutta*)

Solution :

(1) *Current Ratio* :

$$\frac{\text{Current Assets}}{\text{Current Liabilites}} = \frac{\text{Rs. }1,16,000}{\text{Rs. }40,000} = 2.9:1$$

(2) *Liquid Ratio* :

$$\frac{\text{Liquid Assets}}{\text{Liquid Liabilities}} = \frac{\text{Rs. }26,000}{\text{Rs. }40,000} = 0.65:1$$

(3) *Proprietary Ratio* :

$$\frac{\text{Proprietors's Equity}}{\text{Total Assets}} = \frac{\text{Rs. }4,11,000}{\text{Rs. }5,51,000} = 0.75:1$$

(4) *Fixed Assets Proprietorship Ratio* :

$$\frac{\text{Fixed Assets}}{\text{Proprietors? Equity}} = \frac{\text{Rs. }4,35,000}{\text{Rs. }4,11,000} = 1.06:1$$

(5) *Debt-Equity Ratio* :

$$\frac{\text{Total Debt}}{\text{Proprietors? Equity}} = \frac{\text{Rs. }1,40,000}{\text{Rs. }4,11,000} = 0.34:1$$

(6) *Capital Gearing Ratio* :

$$\frac{\text{Equity Share Capital}}{\text{Pref. Share Capital + Debentures}} = \frac{\text{Rs. }2,50,000}{\text{Rs. }2,50,000} = 1:1$$

(7) *Gross Profit Ratio* :

$$\frac{\text{Gross Profit}}{\text{Sales}} \times 100 = \frac{\text{Rs. }80,000 \times 100}{\text{Rs. }4,00,000} = 20\%$$

(8) *Net Profit Ratio* :

$$\frac{\text{Net Profit}}{\text{Sales}} \times 100 = \frac{\text{Rs. } 20{,}000}{\text{Rs. } 4{,}00{,}000} \times 100 = 5\%$$

(9) *Stock-Turnover Ratio*:

$$\frac{\text{Cost of Goods Sold}}{\text{Average Stock}} = \frac{\text{Rs. } 3{,}20{,}000}{\text{Rs. } 90{,}000} = 3.6 \text{ Times}$$

(10) *Debtors' Turnover Ratio* :

$$\frac{\text{Debtors}}{\text{Credit Sale}} \times 365 = \frac{\text{Rs. } 21{,}000}{\text{Rs. } 80{,}000} \times 365 = 96 \text{ Days}$$

(11) *Return on Proprietors' Fund* :

$$\frac{\text{Net Profit (after Tax)}}{\text{Proprietors? Fund}} = \frac{\text{Rs. } 20{,}000}{\text{Rs. } 4{,}11{,}000} = 0.05 : 1$$

(12) *Turnover to Fixed Assets Ratio* :

$$\frac{\text{Turnover}}{\text{Fixed Assets}} = \frac{\text{Rs. } 4{,}00{,}000}{\text{Rs. } 4{,}35{,}000} = 0.92 : 1$$

Working :

1. *Current Assets*:

Stock		Rs. 90,000
Debtors		21,000
Cash at Bank		5,000
		1,16,000

2. *Current/Liquid Liabilities* :

Sundry Creditors		Rs. 28,000
Bills Payable		12,000
		40,000

3. *Liquid Assets* :

Sundry Debtors		Rs. 21,000
Cash at Bank		5,000
		26,000

4. *Fixed Assets* :

Land and Buildings		Rs. 2,50,000
Machinery		1,75,000
Furnitures		10,000
		4,35,000

5. *Proprietors' Fund* :

Equity Share Capital		Rs. 2,50,000
Preference Share Capital		1,50,000
General Reserve		20,000
Profit & Loss A/c.		15,000
		4,35,000
Less :		
Goodwill	Rs. 20,000	
Preliminary Expenses	4,000	24,000
		4,11,000

6. *Total Debts/Outside Liabilities :*

5% Debentures	1,00,000
Current Liabilities	40,000
	1,40,000

7. *Shareholders' Equity :*

Proprietors' Equity – Preference Share Capital
= Rs. 4,11,000 – Rs. 1,50,000 = **Rs. 2,61,000**

8. *Total Assets :*

Total Fixed Assets + Total Current Assets
Rs. 4,35,000 – Rs.1,16,000 = **Rs. 5,51,000**

Comments :

1. Liquidity and Solvency Position : Current Ratio is 2.9. It means current assets of Rs.2.90 are available against each rupee of current liability. The position is satisfactory on the basis of current ratio. However, the Liquid Ratio is 0.65 : 1. It means greater part of current assets constitute stock; the stock is slow-moving. Therefore, the liquidity position is not satisfactory.

2. Credit Terms : The collection system is faulty because debtors enjoy a credit facility for 96 days, which is beyond normal period. The performance of Debt Collection Department is poor.

3. Profitability : Gross Profit Ratio is 20% which is a healthy sign. But the Net Profit Ratio is only 5%. It means operating expenses are higher.

4. Investment Structure : Debt-Equity Ratio is 0.34 : 1. It means the firm is not dependent on outside liabilities. The position is satisfactory. Capital Gearing Ratio is also satisfactory. However, the fixed assets to proprietorship ratio reveals that the entire fixed assets were not purchased by the proprietors' equity. It means the firm depends on outside liabilities. It is not desired.

5. Return on Proprietors' Fund : 5% of the sales is net profit and are available for the proprietors. The state of low return is not desirable.

Stock Turnover Ratio and Turnover to fixed assets indicate an unhealthy sign. Fixed assets are not used properly. It is a sign of under trading. The economic condition of the firm is not sound. The firm can increase the rate of return on investment by increasing production.

Illustration 58. You have been asked by the management of a firm to project a Trading and Profit and Loss Account and the Balance Sheet on the basis of the following estimated figures and ratios, for the next financial year.

Ratio of Gross Profit	20%
Stock Turnover Ratio	5 Times
Average Debt Collection Period	3 Months
Creditors	3 Months
Current Ratio	2
Proprietary Ratio (Fixed Assets to Capital Employed)	75%
Capital Gearing Ratio (Pref. Shares & Debentures to Equity)	30%
Net Profit to Issued Equity Capital	10%
General Reserve and Profit and Loss to Issued Equity Capital	25%
Preference Share Capital to Debentures	2
Cost of sales consists of 50% for materials	
Gross Profit Rs.6,25,000	

(*C.A. Final*)

Solution.

PROJECTED TRADING AND PROFIT AND LOSS ACCOUNT

	Rs.		*Rs.*
To Cost of Sales:		Sales	31,25,000
Materials	12,50,000		
Direct Expenses	12,50,000		
To Gross Profit	6,25,000		
	31,25,000		31,25,000
To Indirect Expenses (Balancing Figure)	4,81,500	By Gross Profit	6,25,000
To Net Profit	1,43,500		
	6,25,000		6,25,000

PROJECTED BALANCE SHEET

Liabilities	*Rs.*	*Assets*	*Rs.*
Preference Share Capital	5,12,500	Fixed Assets	19,21,875
Equity Share Capital	14,35,000	Current Assets:	
Debentures	2,56,250	Stock	5,00,000
General Reserve	2,15,250	Debtors	7,81,250
Profit & Loss A/c	1,43,500		
Current Liabilities:			
Overdraft	3,28,125		
Creditors	3,12,500		
	32,03,125		32,03,125

Workings :

(1) *Sales* :

$$\text{Gross Profit Ratio} = \frac{\text{Gross Profit}}{\text{Sales}} \times 100$$

$$\text{(OR)} \quad 20 = \frac{\text{Rs. 6,25,000}}{\text{Sales}} \times 100$$

$$20 \text{ Sales} = \text{Rs. } 6{,}25{,}000 \times 100$$

$$\text{Sales} = \frac{\text{Rs. } 6{,}25{,}000 \times 100}{20}$$

$$= \textbf{Rs. 31,25,000}$$

(2) *Cost of Sales :*

Cost of Sales = Sales – Gross Profit

= Rs. 31,25,000 – Rs. 6,25,000

= **Rs. 25,00,000**

(3) *Materials* :

50% of Cost of Sales = 50% of Rs. 25,00,000 = **Rs. 12,50,000**

(4) *Direct Expenses* :

Direct Expenses = Cost of Sales – Cost of Materials

= Rs. 25,00,000 – Rs. 12,50,000

Rs. 12,50,000

(5) *Stock :*

$$\text{Stock Turnover Ratio} = \frac{\text{Cost of Sales}}{\text{Stock}}$$

$$\text{OR} \quad 5 = \frac{\text{Rs. } 25{,}00{,}000}{\text{Stock}}$$

Stock = Rs. 5,00,000

(6) *Debtors :*

$$\text{Debtors turnover} = \frac{\text{Debtors}}{\text{Credit Sales}} \times 12$$

$$\text{(OR)} \quad 3 = \frac{\text{Debtors}}{\text{Rs. } 31{,}25{,}000} \times 12$$

Debtors = Rs. 7,81,250

(7) *Total Current Assets* = Stock + Debtors
= Rs. 5,00,000 + Rs. 7,81,250
= **Rs. 12,81,250**

(8) *Current Liabilities* :

$$2 = \frac{\text{Current Assets}}{\text{Current Liabilities}}$$

(OR) 2 Current Liabilities = Current Assets

$$\text{Current Liabilities} = \frac{\text{Rs. } 12{,}81{,}250}{2}$$

= **Rs. 6,40,625**

(9) *Creditors :*

$$\text{Creditors Turnover Ratio} = \frac{\text{Creditors}}{\text{Credit Purchases}} \times 12$$

$$3 = \frac{\text{Creditors}}{\text{Rs. } 12{,}50{,}000}$$

Creditors = **Rs. 3,12,500**

(Materials have been purchased on credit)

(10) *Overdraft* :

Overdraft = Current Liabilities – Creditors
= Rs. 6,40,625 – Rs. 3,12,500 = **Rs. 3,28,125**

(11) *Fixed Assets* :

$$\frac{\text{Fixed Assets}}{\text{Capital Employed}} = \frac{75}{100}$$

$$\therefore \quad \frac{\text{Working Capital}}{\text{Capital Employed}} = \frac{25}{100}$$

∴ Working Capital = Current Asset – Current Liabilities
= Rs. 12,81,250 – Rs. 6,40,625
= **Rs. 6,40,625**

Fixed Assets = Rs. 6,40,625 × 3 = **Rs. 19,21,875**

(12) *Capital Employed* :

Capital Employed = Fixed Assets + Current Assets – Current Liabilities

= Rs. 19,21,875 + Rs. 12,81,250 – Rs. 6,40,625

= **Rs. 25,62,500**

(13) *Capital Gearing Ratio*:

$$30\% = \frac{\text{Pref. Share Capital + Debenture}}{\text{Total Capital Employed}}$$

Pref. Share Capital + Debentures

= 30% of Rs. 25.62.500 = **Rs. 7,68,750**

Equity Shareholders' Fund = Capital Fund – (Pref. Share Capital and Debentures)

= Rs. 25,62,500 – Rs. 7,68,750

= **Rs. 17,93,750**

Preference Share Capital = $\text{Rs. } 7{,}68{,}750 \times \frac{2}{3} = \textbf{Rs. 5,12,500}$

Debentures = $\text{Rs. } 7{,}68{,}750 \times \frac{1}{3} = \textbf{Rs. 2,56,250}$

(14) *General Reserve and Profit & Loss* :

25% of Equity Share Capital = $\text{Rs. } 17{,}93{,}750 \times \frac{25}{125} = \textbf{Rs. 3,58,750}$

(Shareholders Fund include General Reserve and Profit)

(15) *Equity Share Capital* :

Equity Shareholders Fund – (Reserve & Profit)

Rs. 17,93,750 – Rs. 3,58,750 = **Rs. 14,35,000**

(16) *Profit* :

10% of Equity Share Capital

10% of Rs. 14,35,000 = **Rs. 1,43,500**

(17) *General Reserve* :

General Reserve and Profit – Profit

Rs. 3,58,750 – Rs. 1,43,500 = **Rs. 2,15,250**

Cautions in using Ratio Analysis

There are certain problems in using ratios. The analyst should be aware of these problems:

1. It is difficult to find out a proper basis of comparison.
2. The differences in the definitions of ratio make the interpretation of ratio difficult.
3. Price level changes make the interpretation of ratios invalid.
4. The comparison of the ratios of two companies becomes difficult and meaningless when they are operating in different situations.
5. The analyst is interested in what happens in future, while the ratios indicate what happened in the past.
6. The ratios at a moment of time suffer from temporary changes.

The following is the summary of the most important financial ratios :

Ratios	Formula
1. Current Ratio	$\frac{\text{Current Assets}}{\text{Current Liabilities}}$

2. Net Working Capital Ratio $\dfrac{\text{Net Working Capital}}{\text{Net Assets}}$

3. Quick Ratio $\dfrac{\text{Quick Assets}}{\text{Liquid Liabilities}}$

4. Cash Position Ratio $\dfrac{\text{Cash + Marketable Securities}}{\text{Liquid Liabilities}}$

5. Proprietary Ratio $\dfrac{\text{Shareholders' Fund}}{\text{Total Asset (or) Total Resources}}$

6. Solvency Ratio $\dfrac{\text{Outside Liabilities}}{\text{Total Assets}}$

7. Fixed Assets to Proprietors' Fund Ratio $\dfrac{\text{Fixed Assets}}{\text{Proprietors' fund}}$

8. Current Assets to Proprietors' Fund Ratio $\dfrac{\text{Current Assets}}{\text{Proprietors' Funds}}$

9. Capital Gearing Ratio $\dfrac{\text{Fixed Interest Bearing Funds}}{\text{Equity Shareholders' Funds}}$

10. Debt-Equity Ratio $\dfrac{\text{External Equities}}{\text{Internal Equities}}$ or $\dfrac{\text{Outsiders Fund}}{\text{Shareholders Fund}}$

11. Fixed Assets to Current Assets $\dfrac{\text{Fixed Assets}}{\text{Current Assets}}$

12. Reserves to Equity Capital Ratio $\dfrac{\text{Revenue Reserve}}{\text{Equity Capital}}$

13. Gross Profit Ratio $\dfrac{\text{Gross Profit}}{\text{Net Sales}} \times 100$

14. Operating Ratio $\dfrac{\text{Cost of Goods Sold + Operating Expenses}}{\text{Net Sales}} \times 100$

15. Material Consumed Ratio $\dfrac{\text{Material Consumed}}{\text{Net Sale}} \times 100$

16. Conversion Cost Ratio $\dfrac{\text{Manufacturing Expenses} - \text{Material Cost}}{\text{Net Sales}} \times 100$

17. Particular Expense Ratio $\dfrac{\text{Particular Expense}}{\text{Net Sales}} \times 100$

18. Net Profit Ratio $\frac{\text{Net Profit}}{\text{Net Sales}} \times 100$

19. Return on Assets $\frac{\text{Net Profit}}{\text{Net Sales}} \times 100$

20. Return on Capital Employed $\frac{\text{Operating Profit}}{\text{Capital Employed}}$

21. Return on Shareholers' Equity $\frac{\text{Net Profit}}{\text{Shareholders' Fund}} \times 100$

22. Stock Turnover Ratio $\frac{\text{Cost of Goods Sold (or) Net Sales}}{\text{Average Inventory}}$

23. Debtors Turnover Ratio $\frac{\text{Credit Sales}}{\text{Average Debtors}}$ (OR) $\frac{\text{Total Sales}}{\text{Closing Debtors}}$

24. Debt Collection Period $\frac{\text{Months (OR) days in a year}}{\text{Debtors Turnover}}$

25. Creditors Turnover Ratio $\frac{\text{Net Credit Purchases}}{\text{Average Accounts Payable}}$

26. Average Payment Period $\frac{\text{Accounts Payable}}{\text{Net Credit Purchase}} \times 365$

27. Working Capital Turnover Ratio $\frac{\text{Cost of Sales}}{\text{Net Working Capital}}$

28. Fixed Assets Turnover $\frac{\text{Cost of Sales}}{\text{Net Fixed Assets}}$

29. Total Capital Turnover $\frac{\text{Cost of Sales}}{\text{Total Capital Employed}}$

30. Capital Turnover $\frac{\text{Cost of Sales}}{\text{Capital Employed}}$

31. Interest Coverage $\frac{\text{EBIT}}{\text{Fixed Interest Charges}}$

32. Dividend Coverage $\frac{\text{NP after Tax \& Interest}}{\text{Preference Dividend}}$

33. Equity Shareholders' Coverage $\frac{\text{Net Profit (after Interest, Tax and Preference Dividend)}}{\text{Equity Dividend}}$

34. Earning per Equity Shares $\frac{\text{Profits available for Equity Shares}}{\text{No. of Equity Shares}}$

35. Dividend Yield $\frac{\text{Dividend Per Share}}{\text{Market Price per Share}}$

36. Price Earning Ratio $\frac{\text{Market Price of a Share}}{\text{Earning per Share}}$

37. Fixed Interest Coverage $\frac{\text{Operating Income}}{\text{Annual Interest Expenses}}$

38. Dividend Per Share $\frac{\text{Dividend Paid to Equity Shareholders}}{\text{No. of Equity Shares}}$

39. Dividend Payout Ratio $\frac{\text{Dividend Per Share}}{\text{Earning Per Share}}$

The above formulae, in an alternative way, is written as follows:

LIST OF IMPORTANT FORMULA

Name of the Ratio	Formula
I Liquidity Ratios	
(a) Current Ratio	$\frac{\text{Current Assets}}{\text{Current Liabilities}}$ = ... : ....
(b) Quick Ratio (or) Acid test Ratio (or Liquid Ratio)	$\frac{\text{Quick Assets}}{\text{Current Liabilities}}$ = ... : .... **Notes :** Quick Assets = Current Assets – Stock – Prepaid Expenses Working capital = Current Assets – Current Liabilities
(c) Absolute Cash Ratio	$\frac{\text{Cash \& Marketable Securities}}{\text{Current Liabilities}}$ = ... : ....
(d) Internal Interval Measure Ratio	$\frac{\text{Quick Assets}}{\text{Average Daily Operating Expenses}}$ = ... : ....
II Solvency Ratios	
(a) Debt-Equity Ratio	$\frac{\text{Long-term Debt}}{\text{Shareholders' Funds}}$ = ... : .... **Note :** Shareholders' Funds can be calculated as under : (i) Equity Share Capital + Preference Share capital + Reserves & Surplus – Miscellaneous Expenditure (ii) Equity Shareholders' Funds + Preference Share Capital (iii) Capital Employed – Long-term Debt (iv) Net Fixed Assets + Investment + Working Capital – Long-term Debts (v) Net Fixed Assets + Investment + Current Assets – Current Liabilities – Long-term Debts (vi) Total Assets – Total Debt
(b) Total Assets to Debt Ratio	$\frac{\text{Long Assets}}{\text{Long-term Debt}}$ = ... : ....

	Note : Total Assets = Net Fixed Assets + Long -term Investments + Current Assets
(c) Proprietary Ratio	$\frac{\text{Equity}}{\text{Total Assets}} \times 100 = ...\%$ **Note :** Equity = Proprietors' Funds = Shareholders' Funds
(d) Capital Gearing Ratio	$\frac{\text{Funds bearing fixed financial payments}}{\text{Equity shareholders' funds}} = ...$
(e) Interest Coverage Ratio	$\frac{\text{Net profit before interest and taxes}}{\text{Interest on Long-term debt}} = ...\text{ Times}$
(f) Preference Dividend Coverage Ratio	$\frac{\text{Net profit after interest and taxes}}{\text{Preference dividend on pref. shares}} = ...\text{ Times}$
(g) Debt-Service Ratio	$\frac{\text{Net profit after interest and taxes}}{\text{Interest} + \frac{\text{Principal portion of instalment}}{1 - \text{Tax rate}}} = ..\text{ Times}$
(h) Debt-Service Coverage Ratio	$\frac{\text{Funds from operations before interest and taxes}}{\text{Interest} + \frac{\text{Principal portion}}{1 - \text{Tax rate}}}$
(i) Debt-Service Coverage Ratio	$\frac{\text{Cash from operations before interest and Taxes}}{\text{Interest} + \frac{\text{Principal portion}}{1 - \text{Tax rate}}}$
III Activity Ratios	
(a) Capital Turnover Raito	$\frac{\text{Net Sales}}{\text{Capital Employed}} = ...\text{ Times}$ Note : (i) Capital employed can be calculated as under: = Shareholders' funds + Long-term debts Or = Net fixed assets + Long-term investment + Net working capital (ii) Non-trading assets should be excluded. (iii) Fictitious assest should be excluded.
(b) Fixed Assets Turnover Ratio	$\frac{\text{Net Sales}}{\text{Net Fixed Assets}} = ...\text{ Times}$ **Notes :** (i) Net Fixed Assets = Gross fixed assests – Depreciation till date (ii) Non-operating fixed assets should be excluded.
(c) Current Assets Turnover Ratio	$\frac{\text{Net Sales}}{\text{Current Assets}} = ...\text{ Times}$

(d) Working Capital Turnover Ratio	$\frac{\text{Net Sales}}{\text{Net Working Capital}}$ = ... Times Note : Working Capital = Current Assets – Current Liabilities
(c) Stock Turnover Ratio	$\frac{\text{Cost of Goods Sold}}{\text{Average Stock}}$ = ... Times **Notes :** (i) Average Stock = $\frac{\text{Opening Stock + Closing Stock}}{2}$ (ii) Cost of Goods Sold = Net Sales – Gross Profit Or = Opening Stock + Purchases + Direct Expenses – Closing Stock
(f) Debtors Turnover Ratio	$\frac{\text{Net Credit Sales}}{\text{Average Debtors}}$ = ... Times **Note :** (i) Average Debtors = $\frac{(\text{Op.Drs + Op. B/R + Cl. Drs. + Cl B/R})}{2}$ (ii) Net Credit Sales = Gross Credit Sales – Sales Returns or = Net Sales – Cash Sales.
(g) Average Debt Collection Period	= $\frac{\text{12 Months/52 Weeks/365Days}}{\text{Debtors Turnover Ratio}}$ = ... Period or = $\frac{\text{Average Debtors}}{\text{Average Monthly/Weekly/Daily Sales}}$ = ... Period **Note :** Average Sales = $\frac{\text{Net Credit Sales}}{\text{12 Months/52Weeks/365Days}}$
(h) Creditors' Turnover Ratio	$\frac{\text{Net Credit Purchases}}{\text{Average Creditors}}$ = ... Times **Note :** (i) Average Creditors = $\frac{(\text{Op. Crs. + Op. B/P + Cl. Drs. + Cl. B/P})}{2}$ (ii) Net Credit Purchases = Gross Credit Purchases – Purchase Returns. or. = Net Purchases – Cash Purchases
(i) Average Debt Payment Period	$\frac{\text{12 Months/52 Weeks/365 Days}}{\text{Creditors Turnover Ratio}}$ = ... Period

(or Creditors' Velocity)	or, $= \frac{\text{Average Creditors}}{\text{Average Monthly/Weekly/Daily Sales}} = ...\text{Period}$ **Note :** $\text{Average Purchases} = \frac{\text{Net Credit Purchases}}{\text{12 Months/52 Weeks/365 Days}}$
IV Profitability Ratios (i) In relation to sales (a) Gross Profit Ratio	$\frac{\text{Gross Profit}}{\text{Net Sales}} \times 100 = ...\%$ **Note :** Gross Profit = Net Sales – Cost of Goods Sold
(b) Operating Ratio	$\frac{\text{Operating Cost}}{\text{Net Sales}} \times 100 = ...\%$ **Note :** Operating Cost = Cost of Golds sold + Operating Expenses
(c) Operating Profit Ratio	$\frac{\text{Operating Profit}}{\text{Net Sales}} \times 100 = ...\%$ **Note :** Operating Profit = Net Sales – Operating Cost
(d) Net Profit Ratio	$\frac{\text{Net Profit}}{\text{Net Sales}} \times 100 = ...\%$ **Note :** Net Profit = Net Sales – Cost of Goods Sold – Operating Expenses – Non-operating Expenses + Non-operating incomes. or, = Gross Profit – Operating Expenses – Non Operating Expenses + Non-operating Incomes or, = Operating Profit – Non-operating Expenses + Non-operating Incomes.
(ii) In relation to investment (a) Return on investment [or Return on Capital Employed]	$\frac{\text{Net Profit Before Interest \& tax}}{\text{Capital Employed}} \times 100 = ...\%$ **Note:** (i) Non-Trading Assets do not form part of Capital Employed (ii) Income from Non-Trading Assets should be excluded from the Net Profit Before Interest & Tax.
(b) Return on Equity [or Return on hare-holders' Funds]	$\frac{\text{Net Profit after Interest \& tax but before preference dividend}}{\text{Shareholders' Funds}} \times 100 = ...\%$ **Note :** Shareholders' Funds = Capital Employed – Long-term Debts or, = Equity Share Capital + Preference Share

	Capital + Reserves & Surplus – Miscellaneous Expenditure or, = Equity Shareholders' Funds + Preference Share Capital
(c) Return on Equity Shareholders' Funds	$\frac{\text{Net Profit after interest \& tax but before preference dividend}}{\text{Equity Shareholders' Funds}} \times 100 = ...\%$ **Note :** Equity Shareholders' Funds = Equity Share Capital + Reserves & Surplus – Miscellaneous Expenditure
(d) Earning per Share	$\frac{\text{Net Profit after interest, Tax \& Pref. Dividend}}{\text{No. of Equity Shares}}$ = ... per share
(e) Dividend per Share	$\frac{\text{Profit disitributed as dividend}}{\text{No. of Equity Shares}} = ...$ per share
(f) Price Earning Ratio	$\frac{\text{Market Price of a Share}}{\text{Earning Per Share}} = ...$ per share
(g) Dividend Payout Ratio	$\frac{\text{Dividend Per Share (DPS)}}{\text{Earning Per Share (ESP)}} \times 100 = ...\%$
(h) Earning Yield	$\frac{\text{Earning Per Share (EPS)}}{\text{Market Price Per Share}} \times 100 = ...\%$
(i) Dividend Yield	$\frac{\text{Dividend Per Share}}{\text{Market Price Per Share}} \times 100 = ...\%$
(j) Market Value/Book Value	$\frac{\text{Market Value Per Share}}{\text{Book Value Per Share}} \times 100 = ...\%$ or, $= \frac{\text{Average/Closing Market Price Per Share}}{\text{Net Worth/No. of Equity Shares}} \times 100$

OBJECTIVE TYPE QUESTIONS

I. State whether the following statements are "True" or "False" :

1. Accounting Ratios facilitate summarisation and simplification of huge mass of data.
2. Debt-Equity Ratio is also known as External-Internal Equity Ratio.
3. Abolute and unconnected figures do convey the desired information.
4. Net profit is the same as operating profit.
5. Accounting ratios are quantitative expressions of cause and effect relationship between figures.
6. There is no difference between structural ratios and trend ratios.
7. The extent of usage of assets of a business in the course of its operations is known as 'turnover'.
8. Current ratio is also known as Liquid ratio.
9. "Acid test" Denotes liquidity.

10. A decreased Stock Turnover Ratio usually indicates expanding business.
11. For Stock Turnover Ratio, average stock is to be calculated.
12. A firm's ability to meet the interest charge and repayment dues on long-term obligations is referred to as its solvency.

Ans. True : 1, 2, 5, 7, 9, 11, 12
False : 3, 4, 6, 8, 10.

II. Choose the correct answer to the following :

1. Return on investment depends upon :
   (a) Gross Profit Ratio
   (b) Operating Profit Ratio
   (c) Net Profit Ratio
   (d) Capital Turnover Ratio
   (e) (b) and (c).
2. Long-term solvency ratio is the same as :
   (a) Current Ratio
   (b) Acid Test Ratio
   (c) Debt-Equity Ratio
3. A ratio can computed by putting together :
   (a) Any two figures
   (b) Any two events
   (c) Any two related figures
4. For the purposes of ratio analysis, the term 'operating profit' means :
   (a) Gross Sales minus cost of goods sold.
   (b) Net Sales minus cost of goods sold.
   (c) Net Profit after interest and taxes.
   (d) Net Profit before interest and taxes.
5. Operating Profit to sales gives us :
   (a) Gross Profit Ratio
   (b) Operating Profit Ratio
   (c) Net Profit Ratio
6. Structural ratios are useful for making :
   (a) Static Analysis
   (b) Dynamic Analysis
   (c) For both types
7. On the basis of source of figures, ratios are classified :
   (a) As Profit & Loss Account Ratios
   (b) As Balance Sheet Ratios
   (c) As combined ratios
   (d) All these ratios.
8. Turnover Ratios help management in :
   (a) Managing Resources
   (b) Managing Debts
   (c) Evaluating Performance.

9. Ratio of 'Net Sales' to 'Net Working Capital' is :
   (a) Working Capital Turnover Ratio
   (b) Profitability Ratio
   (c) Liquidity Ratio
10. On the basis of the purpose of ratios, they are classified into :
   (a) Profitability Ratios
   (b) Turnover Ratios
   (c) Financial Ratios
   (d) All these

Ans : 1. (e) 2. (c) 3. (c) 4. (d)
5. (b) 6. (a) 7. (d) 8. (c)
9. (a) 10. (d)

THEORETICAL QUESTIONS

1. State the purpose and mode of determining the following ratios :
(*i*) Inventory Ratios (*ii*) Debtors Ratio (*iii*) Operating Ratio.

2. State the significance of accounting ratios in the analysis of financial statements.

3. What is meant by Ratio Analysis ? Discuss its objects and limitations.

4. What are turnover ratios ? Discuss their significance.

5. "Ratio analysis is a tool to examine the health of a business with a view to make the financial results more intelligible "

6. What are the limitations of Ratio Analysis ?

7. Describe with illustration :
(*a*) Gross Profit Ratio
(*b*) Net Profit Ratio
(*c*) Working Capital Ratio
(*d*) Current Ratio

8. What do you understand by (*i*) Operating Ratios and (*ii*) Stock turnover. Illustrate.

9. "Accounting Ratios are mere guides and complete reliance on them in decision-making is suicidal". Elucidate.

10. Discuss some of the important ratios usually worked from financial statements showing how they would be useful to higher management ?

PRACTICAL PROBLEMS

1. Determine the value of closing stock from the following details :

Sales	–	Rs. 4,00,000
Gross profit ratio	–	10% on sales
Stock velocity	–	4 times

Closing stock was Rs. 10,000 in excess of opening stock. (*B.Com. MS, Chennai*)

(Ans. Closing Stock : Rs. 95,000)

2. From the information given below, calculate :
(*a*) Current liabilities and (*b*) Inventory

Current ratio	:	2.5
Acid test	:	1.7
Current assets	:	Rs. 2,50,000

(*B. Com. MS, Chennai*)

(Ans. (*a*) Rs. 1,00,000; (*b*) Rs. 80,000)

3. Following are the ratios relating to the Trading activities of a Company :

Receivables turnover 3 months

Gross profit to sales 25%

Gross profit for the year ending 31-12-2010 amounted to Rs. 4,00,000. Bills receivable amount to Rs. 25,000.

Calculate :

(*a*) Sales (*b*) Sundry debtors

(*B. Com. MS, Madurai*)

(Ans. (*a*) Rs. 16,00,000; (*b*) Rs. 3,75,000)

4. From the following details find out

(*a*) Current assets (*b*) Current liabilities

(*c*) Liquid assets and (*d*) Stock

Current ratio : 2.8; Liquid : 1.5; Working capital : Rs. 1,62,000

(*B.Com. MS, Chennai*)

(Ans. (*a*) Rs. 2,52,000; (*b*) Rs. 90,000; (*c*) Rs. 1,35,000; (*d*) Rs. 1,17,000)

5. From the following details find out

(*a*) Current assets (*b*) Current liabilities

(*c*) Liquid assets and (*d*) Stock

Current ratio 3.5; Liquid ratio 2.5; Working capital Rs. 1,00,000

(*B. Com. Madurai, Chennai*)

(Ans. (*a*) Rs. 1,40,000; (*b*) Rs. 40,000; (*c*) Rs. 1,00,000; (*d*) Rs. 40,000)

6. Following are the ratios to the trading activities of a firm :

Debtors velocity	–	3 months
Stock velocity	–	8 months
Gross profit ratio	–	25%

Gross profit for the year amounted to Rs. 2,00,000. Closing stock of the year is Rs. 5,000 above the opening stock.

Find out

(*a*) Sundry debtors and (*b*) Closing stock

(*M. Com. MS, Madurai*)

(Ans. (*a*) Rs. 2,00,000; (*b*) Rs. 4,02,500)

7. From the following details, find out

(*a*) Current assets (*b*) Current liabilities

(*c*) Liquid assets (*d*) Stock

Current ratio : 2.5; Liquid ratio : 1.5; Working capital : Rs. 90,000

(M. Com. Agra, MS, Madurai)

(Ans. (*a*) Rs. 1,50,000; (*b*) Rs. 60,000; (*c*) Rs. 90,000; (*d*) Rs. 60,000)

8. Following are ratios of a Trading Company :

Debtors velocity	3 months
Creditors	2 months
Stock velocity	8 times
Bills payable	Rs. 4,000
Bills receivable	Rs. 10,000
Total sales	Rs. 2,40,000

The closing stock is Rs. 2,000 more than the opening stock. Gross profit on the above sales is Rs. 40,000. There are no cash sales and cash purchases, and the accounting year consists of 360 working days. Find out

(*a*) Sundry debtors (*b*) Sundry creditors
(*c*) Closing stock

(*M. Com. Jabalpur, Andhra, Madurai, MS*)

(**Ans.** (*a*) Rs. 50,000; (*b*) Rs. 29,667; Credit purchases : Rs. 2,02,000; (*c*) Rs. 26,000)

9. Calculate the current assets of a company from the following information :

(*a*) Stock turnover : 5 times
(*b*) Stock at the end is Rs. 5,000 more than stock at the beginning
(*c*) Sales (all credit) : Rs. 2,00,000
(*d*) Gross profit ratio : 20%
(*e*) Current liabilities : Rs. 60,000
(*f*) Quick ratio : 0.75

(*B. Com. Banaras, Poona*)

(**Ans.** Current assets : Rs. 79,500)

10. Determine the value of closing stock from the following details :

Sales : Rs. 6,00,000
Gross profit : 20% on sales
Stock velocity : 3 months

Closing stock was Rs. 10,000 in excess of opening stock.

(*M. Com. Chennai, Madurai, Kolkata*)

(**Ans.** Closing stock : Rs. 1,25,000)

11. The net worth of a firm is Rs. 2,00,000. Other details available are as under :

Current debt to total debt 0.40
Total debt to owners equity 0.60
Fixed assets to owners equity 0.80
Liquid ratio 2 times

Calculate the value of (1) Total current assets (2) Stock (3) Total assets (4) Current

(*M. Com. Madras, Madurai, Punjab*)

(**Ans.** (1) Rs. 1,60,000; (2) Rs. 64,000; (3) Rs. 3,20,000; (4) Rs. 48,000)

12. Following are the ratios relating to the trading activities of a shop

Receivables turnover – 3 months
Inventory turnover – 8 months
Payables turnover – 2 months
Gross profit to sales – 25%

Gross profit for the year ending 31st Dec. amounted to Rs. 4,00,000. Closing inventory of the year is Rs. 1,00,000 above the opening inventory.

Bills receivable – Rs. 25,000; Bills payable – Rs. 10,000. Calculate :

(*a*) Sales (*b*) Debtors
(*c*) Closing inventory (*d*) Sundry creditors

(*M. Com. Bangalore, Kolkata, Delhi*)

(**Ans.** (*a*) Rs. 16,00,000; (*b*) Rs. 3,75,000; (*c*) Rs. 8,50,000; (*d*) Rs. 2,06,667)

13. The ratios relating to a company are given below :

Gross profit – 15%
Stock velocity – 6 months
Debtors velocity – 3 months
Creditors – 3 months

Gross profit for the year ending 31, Dec. amounts to Rs. 60,000. Closing stock is equal to opening stock. Find out (*a*) Sales (*b*) Closing stock (*c*) Sundry debtors (*d*) Sundry Creditors

(*B. Com. Kolkata*)

(**Ans.** (*a*) Rs. 4,00,000; (*b*) Rs. 1,70,000; (*c*) Rs. 1,00,000; (*d*) Rs. 85,000)

14. From the following details, make out a statement of proprietary funds :

(*a*) Long-term loans : Rs. 50,000
(*b*) Working capital : Rs. 80,000
(*c*) Reserves ratio : 1 : 2
(*d*) Current ratio : 2 times
(*e*) Liquid ratio : 1.4 times
(*f*) Fixed assets to proprietors' funds 0.6
(*g*) There are no fictitious or intangible assets.

(*M. Com. Punjab, Delhi, MS*)

(**Ans.** Proprietary funds : Rs. 75,000; Capital : Rs. 50,000; Reserves : Rs. 25,000; Current liabilities : Rs. 80,000; Current assets : Rs. 1,60,000; Fixed assets : Rs. 45,000)

15. From the following given ratios and figures prepare a summarised Balance Sheet of XYZ Co. Ltd., for the year ended 31st Dec. 2010

(*a*) Working capital – Rs. 60,000
(*b*) Reserves and surplus – Rs. 40,000
(*c*) Bank overdraft – Rs. 10,000
(*d*) Asset (fixed) proprietorship ratio – 0.75
(*e*) Current ratio – 2.50
(*f*) Liquid ratio – 1.50

(*B. Com. Agra, Madurai, Chennai*)

(**Ans.** Total Rs. 2,80,000)

16. From the following details prepare statement of proprietary funds with as many details as possible :

(*i*) Stock velocity = 6
(*ii*) Capital turnover ratio = 2
(*iii*) Fixed assets turnover ratio = 4
(*iv*) Gross profit turnover ratio = 20 per cent
(*v*) Debtors velocity = 2 months
(*vi*) Creditors velocity = 73 days

The gross profit was Rs. 60,000. Reserves and surplus amount to Rs. 20,000. Closing stock was Rs. 5,000 in excess of opening stock.

(*M. Com. Chennai, Jabalpur, Bhopal*)

(**Ans.** Proprietary funds: Rs. 1,20,000)

17. Prepare a list of current assets from the following details :

(*i*) Chennai ratio – 2.5
(*ii*) Quick ratio – 1.5
(*iii*) Working capital – Rs. 75,000
(*iv*) Bank overdraft – Rs. 25,000
(*v*) Cash in hand – Rs. 1,000

(*B. Com. MS, Madurai, Kerala, Delhi*)

(**Ans.** Current assets – Total Rs. 1,25,000; Cash in hand : Rs. 1,000; Stock : Rs. 50,000; Other current assets : Rs. 74,000)

18. From the data given below, find out the net asset turnover and rate of return on net assets:

Fixed Assets	Rs. 1,08,000	Return	Rs. 10,000
Current Assets	Rs. 20,000	Sales	Rs. 5,00,000
Current Liabilities	Rs. 28,000		

(**Ans.** Net Asset Turnover Ratio = 5 : 1 Rate of return on Net Assets = 10%)

19. Raj & Co. sell their goods on cash as well as credit (though not on deferred instalment system). The following particulars are extracted from their books of account for the calender year 2010 :

Total gross sales	4,00,000
Cash sales (included in the above)	80,000
Sales Return	28,000
Total Debtors for sales (31.12.2010)	36,000
Bills Receivable (31.12.2010)	8,000
Provision for doubtful debts (31.12.2010)	3,000
Total creditors (31.12.2010)	25,000

Calculate the average collection period (*B. Com. MS*)

(**Ans.** 55 days)

20. From the following you are required to calculate :

(*a*) Debtors Turnover and

(*b*) Average age of Debtors.

	I Year *Rs.*	*II Year* *Rs.*
Net Sales	9,00,000	7,50,000
Debtors (beginning)	86,000	80,000
Debtors (closing)	1,17,000	86,000

(*B.Com. Chennai*)

(**Ans.**	I Yr.	II Yr.
(*a*)	8.9 Times	9 Times
(*b*)	41 Days	41 Days)

21. The following information is taken from a firm :

Sales	33,984
Sales Returns & Allowances	380
Stock at the beginning	1,378
Stock at the end	1,814
Gross Profit for the year	8,068

Calculate (*a*) Pruchase for the year

(*b*) Rate of Stock Turnover

(*c*) Percentage of Gross Profit to Turnover.

(*B. Com. Calicut*)

(**Ans.** (*a*) Rs. 25,972 (*b*) 16 Times (*c*) 24%)

22. Perfect Ltd. gives The following Balance Sheet.

You are required to compute the following ratios :

(*a*) Liquid Ratio (*b*) Debt-Equity Ratio

(c) Solvency Ratio (*d*) Stock-working Capital Ratio.

BALANCE SHEET as on 31st Dec.

	Rs.		*Rs.*
Equity Share Capital	15,00,000	Fixed Assets	14,00,000
Reserves and Surplus	1,00,000	Stock	5,00,000
6% Debentures	3,00,000	Debtors	2,00,000
Overdraft	1,00,000	Cash	1,00,000
Creditors	2,00,000		
	22,00,000		22,00,000

(*B. Com., Mangalore*)

(**Ans.** (*a*) 1.5 : 1 (*b*) 37.5% (*c*) 72.72% (*d*) 100%)

23. From the following information find out

(*i*) Current assets
(*ii*) Current liabilities
(*iii*) Stocks
(*iv*) Fixed assets

(*a*) Current ratio : 2.5
(*b*) Liquid ratio : 1.5
(*c*) Fixed assets/Proprietary funds : 0.75
(*d*) Working capital – Rs. 60,000
(*e*) Reserves and surplus – Rs. 40,000
(*f*) Bank overdraft – Rs. 10,000
(*g*) There is no long-term loan or fictitious asset.

(*B. Com. Chennai*)

(**Ans.** (*i*) Rs. 1,00,000; (*ii*) Rs, 40,000; (*iii*) Rs. 40,000; (*iv*) Rs. 1,80,000)

24. The following figures relate to a firm for the year ended 31st Dec. 2010

TRADING & PROFIT & LOSS ACCOUNT

Dr *Particulars*		*Rs.*	*Particulars*		Cr *Rs.*
To Opening stock		75,000	By Sales	5,20,000	
To Purchases		3,25,000	Less Returns	20,000	5,00,000
To Gross profit		2,00,000	By Closing stock		1,00,000
		6,00,000			6,00,000
Operating expenses :			By Gross profit		2,00,000
Administration	40,000		By Non-operating income:		
Selling & distribution	25,000	65,000	Dividend	9,000	
Non-operating expenses			Profit on sale of shares	11,000	20,000
Loss on sale of assets		5,000			
To Net profit		1,50,000			
		2,20,000			2,20,000

BALANCE SHEET as on 31st Dec. 2010

Liabilities	*Rs.*	*Assets*	*Rs.*
Issued capital : 2,000 equity shares of Rs. 100 each	2,00,000	Land and Building	1,50,000
		Plant and machinery	80,000
		Stock	1,60,000
Reserves	90,000	Debtors	80,000
Current liabilities	1,50,000	Cash and bank	30,000
P & L Account	60,000		
	5,00,000		5,00,000

Calculate :

(*a*) Gross profit ratio
(*b*) Operating ratio
(*c*) Operating profit ratio
(*d*) Net profit ratio
(*e*) Expenses ratios
(*f*) Stock turnover ratio
(*g*) Return on total resources
(*h*) Turnover to fixed assets
(*i*) Turnover to total assets

(*M. Com. Kolkata*)

(**Ans.** (*a*) 40%; (*b*) 73%; (*c*) 27%; (*d*) 30%; (*e*) (1) Administrative expense ratio : 8%

(2) Selling and distribution expense ratio : 5% (3) Non-operating expense ratio : 1% (*f*) 3.43 (*g*) 30%; (*h*) 1.30; (*i*) 1

25. The following are the summarised statements of a firm for the year ended 31 st Dec. 2010 and a Balance Sheet of the company as on that date.

Profit and Loss Account

Dr Particulars	Rs.	Particulars	*Cr* Rs.
To opening stock	19,900	By Sales	1,70,000
To Purchases	1,09,050	By Closing stock	29,800
To Carriage	2,850		
To Gross profit	68,000		
	1,99,800		1,99,800
To Office expenses	30,000	By Gross profit	68,000
To Selling expenses	6,000	By Profit on sale of shares	1,200
To Financial expenses	3,000	By Interest on investments	600
To Loss on sale of an asset	800		
To Net profit	30,000		
	69,800		69,800

BALANCE SHEET

Liabilities	*Rs.*	*Assets*	*Rs.*
Share Capital :		Land and Building	30,000
4,000 shares of Rs. 10 each	40,000	Plant	16,000
Reserves	18,000	Stock	28,000
P & L A/c	12,000	Debtors	14,000
Bank overdraft	6,000	Bills receivable	2,000
Creditors	6,000	Cash	6,000
Outstanding expenses	4,000		
	96,000		96,000

Calculate :

(*a*) Gross profit ratio
(*b*) Debt equity ratio
(*c*) Liquidity ratio
(*d*) Fixed assets turnover
(*e*) Operating net profit ratio

(*M. Com. Agra*)

(**Ans.** (*a*) 40%; (*b*) 0.37; (*c*) 0.85; (*d*) 2.22 (Based on cost of sales) (or) 3.70 (based on sales); (*e*) 18.82%

26. Given below is the summarised Balance Sheet and Profit and loss account of a firm as on 31st December.

(figures in '000)

Liabilities	*Rs.*	*Assets*	*Rs.*
Share Capital	4,000	Land and Buildings	3,000
Reserves	1,800	Plant and Machinery	1,600
Creditors	2,600	Stock	2,960
Profit & Loss A/c	600	Debtors	1,420
6% Debentures	600	Cash	620
	9,600		9,600

PROFIT AND LOSS ACCOUNT

	Rs.		Rs.
To Opening Stock	1,990	By Sales	17,000
To Purchases	10,905	By Closing Stock	2,980
To Direct Expenses	285		
To Gross Profit	6,800		
	19,980		19,980
To Administration Expenses	3,000	By Gross Profit	6,800
To Selling Expenses	600	By Non-operating income	180
To Financial Expenses	300		
To Non-operating Expenses	80		
To Net Profit	3,000		
	6,980		6,980

Prepare the following ratios :

1. Current Ratio
2. Quick Ratio
3. Fixed Assets Ratio
4. Debt Equity Ratio
5. Proprietary Ratio
6. Stock & Turnover Ratio
7. Fixed Assets Turnover Ratio
8. Return on Capital Employed
9. Debtors Turnover Ratio
10. Creditors Turnover Ratio
11. Not Profit Ratio
12. Operating Ratio

(*M. Com. Kolkata, Modified*)

(**Ans.** (1) 1.92 : 1 (2) 0.78 : 1 (3) 0.66 (4) 0.09 (5) 0.67 (6) 4.1 times (7) 3.7 times (8) 45.7% (9) 12 times (10) 4 times (11) 17.6% (12) 81.2%)

27. With the help of the following ratios. Draw the balance sheet of the company for the year 2010.

Current ratio	2.5
Liquidity ratio	1.5
Net working capital	Rs. 3,00,000
Stock turnover ratio (cost of sales/closing stock)	6 times
Gross profit ratio	20%
Debt collection period	2 months
Fixed assets turnover ratio (on cost of sales)	2 times
Fixed assets to shareholders net worth	0.80
Reserves and surplus to capital	0.50

(*M. Com. Agra, Punjab, Chennai, Delhi*)

(**Ans.** Assets – Total : Rs. 11,00,000; Stock : Rs. 2,00,000; Debtors : Rs. 2,50,000; Other current assets : Rs. 50,000; Fixed assets : Rs. 6,00,000; Liabilities – Total : Rs. 11,00,000; Capital : Rs. 5,00,000; Reserves and surplus : Rs. 2,50,000; Current liabilities : Rs. 2,00,000; Long-term loans (Bal. fig. in balance sheet) : Rs. 1,50,000)

28. From the following information, prepare a Balance Sheet. Give the workings also.

(*a*) Working capital – Rs. 75,000
(*b*) Reserves and surplus – Rs. 1,00,000
(*c*) Bank overdraft – Rs. 60,000
(*d*) Current ratio – 1.75
(*e*) Liquid ratio – 1.15
(*f*) Fixed assets to proprietor's fund – 0.75
(*g*) Long-term liabilities – Nil

(*B. Com. M. Com. Delhi, Kolkata*)

(**Ans.** Assets – Total : Rs. 4,00,000; Fixed assets : Rs. 2,25,000; Stock : Rs. 60,000; Other current assets : Rs. 1,15,000; Liabilities – Total : Rs. 4,00,000; Capital : Rs. 2,00,000; Reserves and surplus : Rs. 1,00,000; Bank overdraft : Rs. 60,000; Other current liabilities : Rs. 40,000)

29. Assume that a firm has owners equity of Rs. 1,00,000. The ratios of the firm are :

Current debt to total debt – 0.40
Total debt to owners equity – 0.60
Fixed assets to owners equity – 0.60
Total assets turnover – 2 times
Inventory turnover – 8 times

Complete the following Balance Sheet, given the information above :

Equities	*Rs.*		*Assets*	*Rs.*	
Current debt	–		Cash	–	
Long-term debt	–		Inventory	–	
Total debt		–	Total curent assets		–
Owner's equity		–	Fixed assets		–
Total equity		–	Total assets		–

(*M. Com. Delhi, Allahabad, Jabalpur*)

(**Ans.** Assets – Cash : 60,000; Inventory : Rs. 40,000; Total current assets : Rs. 1,00,000; Fixed assets : Rs. 60,000; Total assets : Rs. 1,60,000; Liabilities – Current debt : Rs. 24,000; Long-term debt : Rs. 36,000; Total debt : Rs. 60,000; Owner's equity : Rs. 1,00,000; Total equity : Rs. 1,60,000)

30. From the following information make out a balance sheet with as many details as possible :

(*a*) Gross profit turnover ratio – 25%
(*b*) Debtors velocity – 3 months
(*c*) Creditors velocity – 2 months
(*d*) Stock velocity – 8 times
(*e*) Capital turnover ratio – 2.5 times
(*f*) Fixed assets turnover ratio – 8 times

Gross profit for the year ended 31st December 2010 was Rs. 80,000. There was no long-term loan or overdraft. Reserves and surplus amounted to Rs. 28,000. Liquid assets were Rs. 97,333.

Closing stock of the year was Rs. 2,000 more than the opening stock. Bills receivable and bills payable were Rs. 5,000 and Rs. 2,000 respectively.

(*M. Com Mumbai, Kolkata, MS*)

(**Ans.** Assets – Total : Rs. 1,68,333; Fixed assets : Rs. 40,000; Debtors : Rs. 75,000; Bills receivable : Rs. 5,000; Stock : Rs. 31,000; Other current assets : Rs. 17,333; Liabilities – Total : Rs. 1,68,333; Capital : Rs. 1,00,000; Reserves and surplus : Rs. 28,000; Bills payable : Rs. 2,000; Creditors : Rs. 38,333)

31. The following data are worked out from the financial statements for the year ended 30-9-2010. You are required to reconstruct Balance Sheet as on 30-9-2010 :

Fixed assets (after 30% depreciation)	–	Rs. 10,50,000
Finished goods/Turnover ratio (on cost of sales)	–	6 (time)
Fixed assets/Turnover ratio (on cost of sales)	–	2 (time)
Gross profit %	–	25%
Net profit (before interest)/Sales	–	8%
Interest cover (Debenture interest at 7%)	–	8
Debt collection period (months)	–	1.5
Materials consumed/Sales	–	30%
Stock of raw materials (months of consumption)	–	3
Current ratio	–	2.4
Quick ratio	–	1
Reserves/capital		0.21

(*M. Com. Delhi, Kolkata*)

(**Ans.** Assets – Total : Rs. 20,10,000; Fixed assets : Rs. 10,50,000; Debtors : Rs. 3,50,000; Stock of raw materials : Rs. 2,10,000; Stock of finished goods : Rs. 3,50,000; Other liquid assets : Rs. 50,000; Liabilities – Capital : Rs. 10,00,000; Reserves : Rs. 2,10,000; Debentures : Rs. 4,00,000; Current Liabilities : Rs. 4,00,000)

32. With the following information relating to HEMWALA Ltd. in respect of the year ended 31-12-2010 prepare a Trading and Profit and Loss Account.

Gross profit ratio	–	25%
Net profit ratio	–	20%
Stock turnover ratio	–	10
Net profit/capital	–	1/5
Fixed assets/capital	–	5/4
Fixed assets	–	Rs. 6,00,000
Closing stock	–	Rs. 48,000

(*M. Com. Delhi, Jabalpur*)

(**Ans.** Sales : 4,80,000; Closing stock : Rs. 48,000; Opening stock : Rs. 24,000; Purchases (Bal. fig.) : Rs. 3,84,000; Gross profit : Rs. 1,20,000; Expenses : Rs. 24,000; Net profit : Rs. 96,000)

33. From the following data, prepare the Balance Sheet of a Company as on 31-12-2010 :

Fixed assets	–	Rs. 6,00,000
Working capital	–	Rs. 4,00,000
Current ratio	–	2 times
Fixed assets to turnover	–	4 times
Gross profit ratio	–	25%
Debtors velocity	–	1.5 months
Creditors velocity	–	2 months
Stock	–	2 months
Net profit	–	5% of turnover
Reserve	–	2/3 of net profits
Capital gearing	–	1 : 1

(*M. Com. Jabalpur, Chennai, Agra*)

(**Ans.** Assets – Total : Rs. 14,00,000; Fixed assets : Rs. 6,00,000; Debtors : Rs. 3,00,000; Stock : Rs. 3,00,000; Other current assets : Rs. 2,00,000; Liabilities – Total : Rs. 14,00,000; Capital: Rs. 4,20,000; Reserves : Rs. 80,000; Long-term borrowings : Rs. 5,00,000; Current liabilities : Rs. 4,00,000)

34. From the following information presented by RAM Co. Ltd. for the year ended 31-12-2010, prepare the Balance Sheet.

Sales to net worth	–	5 times
Current liabilities to net worth	–	50%
Total debt to net worth	–	60%
Fixed assets to net worth	–	60%
Current ratio	–	2 : 1
Sales to stock	–	10 times
Debtors velocity	–	9 times
Annual sales	–	Rs. 15,00,000
(40% of sales were made for cash)		

(*M. Com. Delhi, Chennai, Kerala*)

(**Ans.** Assets – Total : Rs. 4,80,000; Fixed assets ; Rs. 1,80,000; Stock : Rs. 1,50,000; Debtors : Rs. 1,00,000; Other current assets : Rs. 50,000; Liabilities – Total : Rs. 4,80,000; Current Liabilities : Rs. 1,50,000; Long-term debt : Rs. 30,000; Shareholders' not worth (capital and reserves) Rs. 3,00,000)

35. From the following particulars relating to Chand and Co., prepare a Balance Sheet as on 31-12-2010.

Fixed assets turnover ratio	=	2 : 1
Debt collection period	=	2 months
Gross profit	=	25%
Consumption of raw materials	=	40% of cost
Stock of raw materials	=	4 months consumption
Finished goods	=	20% of turnover at cost
Fixed assets to current assets	=	1 : 1
Current ratio	=	2
Long-term loan to current liability	=	1 : 3
Capital to reserves	=	5 : 2
Value of fixed assets	=	Rs. 10,50,000

(*M. Com. Andhra, Mumbai, Bhopal, Agra*)

(**Ans.** Assets – Total : Rs. 21,00,000; Fixed Assets : Rs. 10,50,000; Debtors : Rs. 3,50,000; Stock of raw materials : Rs. 2,10,000; Stock of finished goods : Rs. 3,15,000; Other current assets ; Rs. 1,75,000; Liabilities – Total : Rs. 21,00,000; Share capital : Rs. 10,00,000; Reserves : Rs. 4,00,000; Long-term loans : Rs. 1,75,000; Current liabilities : Rs. 5,25,000)

36. Using the information and the form given below compute the Balance Sheet items for a firm having a sale of Rs. 36 lakhs.

Sales/Total assets	3
Sales/Fixed assets	5
Sales/Current assets	7.5
Sales/Inventories	20
Sales/debtors	15
Current ratio	2
Total assets/Net worth	2.5
Debt/equity	1

BALANCE SHEET

Liabilities	*Rs.*	*Assets*	*Rs.*
Net worth	–	Fixed assets	–
Long-term debt	–	Inventories	–
Current liabilities	–	Debtors	–
		Liquid assets (others)	–

(*M. Com. Chennai, MS, Punjab*)

(**Ans.** Fixed assets : Rs. 7,20,000; Inventories : Rs. 1,80,000; Debtors : Rs. 2,40,000; Other liquid assets : Rs. 60,000; Net worth : Rs. 4,80,000; Long-term debt : Rs. 4,80,000; Current liabilities : Rs. 2,40,000)

37. The following are the summarised Profit and Loss Account and Balance Sheet :

TRADING AND PROFIT AND LOSS ACCOUNT
for the year ended . . . . . .

	Rs.		*Rs.*
To Stock	10,000	By Sales	1,00,000
To Purchases	55,000	By Stock	15,000
To Gross Profit	50,000		
	1,15,000		1,15,000
To Administrative Expenses	15,000	By Gross Profit	50,000
To Interest	3,000		
To Selling Expenses	12,000		
To Net Profit	20,000		
	50,000		50,000

BALANCE SHEET as on . . . . .

Capital	1,00,000	Land & Buildings	50,000
Profit & Loss	20,000	Plant & Machinery	30,000
Creditors	25,000	Stock	15,000
Bills Payable	15,000	Debtors	15,000
		Bills Receivable	12,500
		Cash and Bank	17,500
		Furniture	20,000
	1,60,000		1,60,000

Additional information : Average Debtors Rs, 12,500
Average Credit Purchases Rs. 80,000

Calculate the following Ratios :

(1) Stock Turnover Ratio
(2) Debtors Turnover Ratio
(3) Creditors Turnover Ratio
(4) Sales to working Capital
(5) Sales to Fixed Assets
(6) Sales to Capital Employed
(7) Return on Shareholders' Investment
(8) Current Ratio
(9) Acid Test Ratio
(10) Gross Profit Ratio
(11) Net Profit Ratio
(12) Operating Ratio

(*M. Com. Kolkata Delhi*)

(**Ans.** (1) 4 Times (5) 1 : 1 (9) 1.13 : 1
(2) 8 Times (6) 0.83 : 1 (10) 50%
(3) 1 : 2 (7) $16\frac{2}{3}\%$ (11) 20%
(4) 5 : 1 (8) 1.5 : 1 (12) 77%)

38. From the following details, find out :

(1) Current Assets
(2) Current Liabilities
(3) Liquid Assets
(4) Stock

Given : Current Ratio 2.5
Liquidity Ratio 1.5
Working Capital Rs. 60,000

(*B.Com., Kerala, Madurai*)

(**Ans.** (1) Rs. 1,00,000 ; (2) Rs. 40,000
(3) Rs. 60,000 ; (4) Rs. 40,000)

39. From the following details, prepare statement of proprietary fund with as many details as possible.

(1) Stock Velocity = 6
(2) Capital Turnover Ratio = 2
(3) Fixed Assets Turnover Ratio = 4
(4) Gross Profit Turnover Ratio = 20%
(5) Debtors Velocity = 2 months
(6) Creditors Velocity = 73 days

Gross profit was Rs. 60,000. Reserves and surplus Rs. 20,000. Closing Stock was Rs. 5,000 in excess of opening stock. (*C.A. Final*)

(**Ans.** Proprietors' Fund Rs. 1.20,000 ; Fixed Assets Rs. 60,000
Debtors Rs. 50,000 ; Stock at the end Rs. 42,500
Cash Rs. 16,500 ; Creditors Rs. 49,000
Sales Rs. 3,00,000 ; Purchase Rs. 2,45,000)

40. Debtors Velocity 3 Months
Creditors Velocity 2 Months
Fixed Assets Turnover Ratio 8 times
Gross Profit Turnover Ratio 25%
Gross Profit in the year comes to Rs. 80,000
There is no long-term loan or overdraft
Reserves and Surplus amounted to Rs. 28,000
Liquid Assets are Rs. 97,333
Closing stock is Rs. 2,000 more than the Opening Stock
Bills Receivable and Bills Payable are Rs. 5,000 and Rs. 2,000 respectively.

Find out :

(*a*) Sales
(*b*) Sundry Debtors
(*c*) Closing Stock
(*d*) Sundry Creditors
(*e*) Fixed Assets
(*f*) Proprietors' Fund
(*g*) Make out the Balance Sheet with as many details as possible.

(*M.Com. Jabalpur Delhi*)

(**Ans.** (*a*) Sales Rs. 3,20,000
(*b*) Debtors Rs. 75,000
(*c*) Closing Stock Rs. 31,000

(*d*) Sundry Creditors Rs. 38,333
(*e*) Fixed Assets Rs. 40,000
(*f*) Proprietor's Fund Rs. 1,28,000 (Including Rs. 28,000)
(*g*) Balance Sheet Total Rs. 1.68,333)

41. From the following figures and ratios, make out the Trading and Profit and Loss Account and Balance Sheet :

Share Capital	7,20,000
Working Capital	2,52,000
Bank Overdraft	40,000

There is no fictious assets. In current assets, there are no assets other than Stock, Debtors and Cash. Closing stock is 20% higher than the opening stock.

(*a*) Current Ratio 2.5
(*b*) Quick Ratio 1.5
(*c*) Proprietary Ratio 0.7
(Fixed Assets – Proprietary Fund)
(*d*) Gross Profit Ratio 20%
(*e*) Stock Turnover 4
(*f*) Debtor Turnover 36.5 days
(*g*) Net profit to paid-up Capital 10%

(*B.Com. MS*)

(**Ans.** Opening Stock Rs. 1,40,000 ; Purchases Rs. 6,44,000
Gross Profit Rs. 1,54,000 ; Sales Rs. 7,70,000
Closing Stock Rs. 1,68,000 ; Expense Rs. 82,000
Net Profit Rs. 72,000
Reserves & Surplus Rs. 1,20,000
Cash Rs. 1,75,000
Balance Sheet Total Rs. 10,08,000

42.

Debtors Velocity	3 Months
Creditors Velocity	2 Months
Stock Velocity	8 Times
Bills Payable	Rs. 10,000
Bills Receivable	Rs. 4,000
Total Sales	Rs. 2,40,000

The Closing stock is Rs. 2,000 more than the opening stock. Gross Profit on the above sales Rs. 40,000. There are no cash sales and cash purchased. The accounting year consists of 360 days. Calculate :

(*a*) Sundry Debtors
(*b*) Sundry Creditors
(*c*) Closing Stock

(**Ans.** (*a*) Rs. 56,000; (*b*) Rs. 23,667; (*c*) Rs. 26,000)

(*B.Com. Agra, Bhopal, Punjab*)

43. From the following information, find out :

(*i*) Sales
(*ii*) Closing Stock
(*iii*) Sundry Debtors
(*iv*) Sundry Creditors

Gross Profit Ratio	25%
Debtors Turnover Ratio	4 Months
Stock Turnover Ratio	4 Times
Creditors Turnover Ratio	6 Months

Closing Stock is Rs, 10,000 more than the opening stock. Bills Receivable amount to Rs. 65,000 and Bills Payable to Rs. 80,000. Cost of good sold for the year is RS. 9,00,000.

(B.Com. Madurai)

(**Ans.** (*i*) Sales Rs. 12,00,000
(*ii*) Closing Stock Rs. 2,30,000
(*iii*) Sundry Debtors Rs. 3,35,000
(*iv*) Sundry Creditors Rs. 3,75,000)

44. The following figures relate to the trading activities of a firm for the year ended 30th June :

	Rs.
Sales	15,00,000
Purchases	9,66,750
Opening Stock	2,28,750
Closing Stock	2,95,500
Sales Returns	60,000
Selling & Distribution :	
Salaries	45,900
Advertising	14,100
Travelling	6,000
Non-operating Expenses :	
Loss on sale of Assets	12,000
Administrative Expenses :	
Salaries	81,000
Rent	8,100
Stationery, Postage etc.	7,500
Depreciation	27,000
Other Charges	49,500
Provision for Taxation	1,20,000
Non-operating Income :	
Dividend on Shares	27,000
Profit on sale of Shares	9,000

You are required to :

(*i*) Rearrange the above figures in a form suitable for analysis,

(*ii*) Show the following ratios :

(*a*) Gross profit Ratio

(*b*) Operating Ratio

(*c*) Stock Turnover Ratio

(B.Com. Kerala Mumbai)

(**Ans.** (*i*) 40% (*ii*) 84% (*iii*) 3.43 Times)

45. Calculate proprietary ratio from the following Balance sheet and give your commends :

Liabilities	*Rs.*	*Assets*	*Rs.*
Share Capital	6,00,000	Fixed Assets	16,50,000
Reserves and Surplus	4,50,000	Current Assets	7,50,000
BOD	7,00,000	Investments	3,50,000
Current Liabilities	12,00,000	Preliminary Expenses	1,00,000
		Goodwill	1,00,000
	29,50,000		29,50,000

(*B. Com. Agra*)

(**Ans:** 0.38)

46. From the Following information, prepare projected Trading and Profit and Loss Account and Balance Sheet of a firm relating to the year 2010. Prepare Balance Sheet.

Ratio of Gross Profit	25%
Net Profit to Equity Capital	10%
Stock Turnover Ratio	5 times
Average Debt Collection period	2 times
Creditors Velocity	3 Months
Current Ratio	2
Proprietary Ratio (Fixed Assets to Capital Employed)	80%
Capital Gearing Ratio (Preference Shares and Debentures to Equity	30%
General Reserve & Profit & Loss to issued Equity Capital	25%
Preference share Capital to Debentures	2

Cost of Sales consists of 40% for materials and balance for wages and overheads. Gross Profit Rs. 6,00,000. (*C.A. Final*)

(**Ans.** GP Rs. 6,00,000 NP, Rs. 1,06,400, B/S Total Rs. 22,80,000)

Chapter 4

Fund Flow Statements

Introduction; Meaning of Fund; Meaning of Flow of Fund; Current and Non-current Accounts; Funds Flow Statement; Importance of Fund Flow Statement; Limitations of Fund Flow Statement; Preparation of Fund Flow Statement; Statement of Changes in Working Capital; How to Prepare the above Schedule?; Steps; Alternative Methods to the Above; Fund Flow Statement; Sources and Applications of Funds; Some Practical Hints; Calculation of Funds from Operation; Hidden Information; Objective Type Questions Theoretical Questions; Practical Problems.

Introduction

The 'traditional package' of final accounts and statements, though very significant statements, have as such, a limited role to play in financial analysis. The basic financial statements *i.e.*, the Balance Sheet and Profit and Loss Account or income statement of business reveal the net effect of the various transactions on operational and financial position of the company. The Balance Sheet gives a summary of the assets and liabilities of an undertaking at a particular point of time. It reveals the financial position of the company. The profit and loss reflects the results of the business operations for a period of time. It contains a summary of expenses incurred and the revenue realised in an accounting period.

Every company prepares its Balance Sheet at the end of its accounting year. It reveals the financial position of the company at a certain point of time. It portrays the financial position of the undertaking, the asset side showing the development of resources in various types of properties and the liability side indicating the manner in which these resources were obtained. The Income Statement measures the change in the owners' equity as a result of periodic operating activities. Income Statement and Balance Sheet have a limited role to perform. Income Statement measures flow restricted to transactions that pertaining to productive and commercial activities. The Balance Sheet is merely a static statement. It is a statement of assets and liabilities on a particular date. Balance Sheet does not show the movement of funds. In business concerns, funds flow from different sources and similarly funds are invested in various sources of investment. It is a continuous process. The study and control of this funds-flow process is the main objective of financial management to assess the soundness and the solvency of a firm. The traditional statements—Balance Sheet and Profit and Loss Account of a business tell little about its flow of funds, *i.e.* financing and investing activities over the related period. Hence, the need of another statement to account for periodical increase or decrease of funds of an enterprise. This statement is called Fund Flow Statement. The effectiveness of financial management in generating funds from various sources and using them effectively for generating income without sacrificing the financial health of the entity is reflected in the statement of funds.

Meaning of Fund

Funds Flow Statement is a widely used tool in the hands of financial executives for analysing the financial performance of a concern. Funds keep on moving in a business which itself is based on a going concern concept. In a narrow sense, it means cash only and a funds flow statement prepared on this basis is called as cash flow statement. Such a statement enumerates net effects of the various business transactions on cash and takes into account receipts and disbursements of cash. In a broader sense, the term "fund" refers to money values in whatever form it may exist. Here "funds" means all financial resources in the form of men, materials, money, machinery etc. But in a popular sense, the term "funds", means working capital, *i.e.* the excess of current assets over current liabilities. When the funds move inwards or outwards, they cause a flow or rotation of funds. The word 'fund' here means net working capital.

Working Capital is ordinarily understood as excess of Current Assets over Current Liabilities. Some persons call total Current assets as Gross Working Capital and Current Assets minus Current Liabilities as Net Working Capital or Net Current Assets. In other words, the term Fund stands for Net Working Capital or Net Current Assets or Free Current Assets.

The important components of Current Assets are :

Cash in hand
Cash at Bank
Bills Receivable
Stocks
Debtors
Income earned but not received
Prepaid Expenses etc.

Similarly, the important components of Current Liabilities are :

Creditors
Bills Payable
Expenses O/S
Debts due within a year
Provision for Bad debts etc.

Meaning of Flow of Fund

The term 'Flow' means change. Thus flow of fund means change in fund or change in Working Capital. Flow of fund is said to have taken place when a business transaction makes a change in the amount of fund which existed just before the happening of the transaction. The flow of funds refers to transfer of economic values from one asset to another, from one equity to another, from an asset to an equity or vice versa or a combination of any of these. Fund flow statement essentially study the movements to and from Working Capital Area. Thus at the end of the year we can measure :

(*a*) The inflows into working capital for the whole year as a consequence of raising of capital, raising of loans, sale of fixed assets, sale of investments and operational inflow due to profits. Funds from operation have to be adjusted. Depreciation on fixed assets, amortization of fictitious assets, loss on sale of fixed assets, provisions and reserves are added and gain on sale of fixed assets is to be deducted.

(*b*) Outflows from working capital as a consequence of purchase of fixed assets, payment of dividends, payment of taxes, payment of preference capital and long-term debts, payment of debenture etc.

The term funds flow indicates the inflows and outflows of funds during a particular accounting period, generally a year. The flow exhibits the movements of funds in both the directions—inside the business and outside the business. However, the flow of funds must arise due to external and not internal transactions of the business. For instance, the capitalization of reserves by the issue of bonus shares is an internal transaction. Such transactions are not included in the statement as there is no real addition to the funds of the company. When the term funds is used in the sense of working capital, funds flow will mean inflow and outflow of working capital.

Changes in working capital position of a business unit are significant considerations in the analysis of operating results and financial condition. The sources of working capital, the disposition of working and the composition of the working capital at the end of the period, are all important factors in evaluating past activities and in judging a company's ability to prosper in the future. The flow of funds occurs when a transaction changes on one hand a non-current account, and on the other a current account and vice versa. When a change in a non-current account, for examples, fixed assets, long-term liabilities, reserves and surplus, fictitious assets etc. is followed by a change in another non-current account, it does not amount to flow of funds. This is because of the fact that in such cases neither the working capital increases nor decreases. In the same way, when a change in one current account results in a change in another current account, it does not affect funds. Funds move from non-current to current transactions. In other words, it can be said that only the following transactions may cause the flow of fund.

1. Transactions between current assets and fixed assets.
2. Transactions between current assets and capital & long-term liabilities.
3. Transactions between current liabilities and fixed assets.
4. Transactions between current liabilities and capital & long-term liabilities.

Current and Non-Current Accounts

Current accounts can either be current assets or current liabilities. Current assets are those assets which in the ordinary course of business can be or will be converted into cash within a short period of normally one accounting year. Current liabilities which are intended to be paid in the ordinary course of business within a short period of normally one accounting year out of the current assets or the income of the business. Following is the list of current and non-current accounts :

Current Liabilities	*Current Assets*
1. Bills Payable	1. Cash in hand
2. Sundry Creditors	2. Cash at Bank
3. Expenses Outstanding	3. Bills Receivable
4. Dividends Payable	4. Sundry Debtors
5. Bank Overdraft	5. Short-term loans & Advances
6. Short-term loans	6. Marketable Investments
7. Provision against Current Assets	7. Inventories, such as, Raw Materials, Work in-progress, Finished goods
8. Provision for Taxation etc.	8. Prepaid Expenses
	9. Accrued Incomes etc.

Non-Current or Permanent Liabilities	*Non-Current or Permanent Assets*
1. Equity Share Capital	1. Goodwill
2. Preference Share Capital	2. Land
3. Debentures	3. Building
4. Long-term Loans	4. Plant and Machinery
5. Share Premium	5. Furniture and Fittings
6. Share Forfeited	6. Trade Mark
7. Profit and Loss (Balance of profit)	7. Patent Right
8. Capital Reserve	8. Long-term Investment
9. Capital Redemption Reserve etc.	9. Discounts on Issue of Shares and Debentures
	10. Other Deferred Expenses etc.

Funds Flow Statement

The Fund Flow Statement is a financial statement which reveals the methods by which the business has been financed and how it has used its funds between the opening and closing balance sheet dates. Thus, a fund flow statement is a report on movement of funds explaining wherefrom works capital originates and where into the same goes during an accounting period. This statement consists of two parts—(1) Sources of Funds and (2) Application of Funds. The difference between the two shows the net change in the working capital during the period. It is to be remembered that only those transactions can find place in this statement which affect the net working capital of the firm. The Fund Flow Statement is a supplement to the two principal financial statements. While supplementing the position statement, it describes the sources from which additional fund were derived and the use to which these funds were put. The transactions which increase working capital are sources of funds and the transactions which decrease working capital are application of funds. In the words of Foulke :

> "A Statement of Sources and Application of funds is technical device designed to analyse the changes in the financial condition of a business enterprise between two date."

Fund Flow Statement is called by a variety of names, such as :

Statement of Sources and Application of Funds,
Statement of Funds Supplied and Applied,
Where Got and Where Gone Statement,
Statement of Resources Provided and Applied,
Funds Received and Disbursed Statement,
Fund Movement Statement,
Inflow-Outflow of Fund Statement, etc.

The basic object of this statement is to find out increase or decrease in the working capital during a period by showing sources and uses of working capital.

Fund flow statement is a statement which indicates various means by which the funds have been obtained during a certain period and the ways to which these funds have been used during that period. The term `funds' used here means working capital, *i.e.*, excess of current assets over current liabilities.

Importance of Fund Flow Statement

Funds Flow Statement is a useful tool in the financial manager's analytical kit. The basic purpose of this statement is to indicate where funds came from and where it was used during the certain period. Following are the uses of this which show its importance :

1. Fund Flow Statement determines the financial consequences of business operations. It shows how the funds were obtained and used in the past. Financial manager can take corrective actions.
2. The management can formulate its financial policies— dividend, reserve etc. on the basis of the statement.
3. It serves as a control device, when comparing with budgeted figures. The financial manager can take remedial steps, if there is any deviation.
4. It points out the sound and weak financial position of the enterprise.
5. It points out the causes for changes in working capital.
6. It enables the Bankers, Creditors or financial institutions in assessing the degree of risk involved in granting credit to the business.
7. The management can rearrange the firm's financing more effectively on the basis of the Statement.
8. Various uses of funds can be known and after comparing them with the uses of previous years, improvement or downfall in the firm can be assessed.

9. The statement compared with the budget concerned will show to what extent the resources of the firm were used according to plan and what extent the utilisation was unplanned.
10. It tells whether sources of funds are increasing or decreasing or constant.

Limitations of Fund Flow Statement

1. The Statement lacks originality because it is only rearrangement of data appearing in accounts books.
2. It indicates only the past position and not future.
3. It indicates Fund Flow in a summary form and it does not show various changes which take place continuously.
4. When both the aspects of a transaction are current, they are not considered.
5. When both the aspects of a transaction are non-current, even then they are not included in this statement.
6. It is not an ideal tool for financial analysis.
7. It is not an original statement but simply a rearrangement of data in the financial statements.

Preparation of Fund Flow Statement

Generally speaking, the Fund Flow analysis requires the preparation of two statements.

(*a*) Statement of changes in Working Capital and

(*b*) Fund Flow Statement

(a) Statement of Changes in Working Capital

The working capital does change due to various transactions. The working capital position at the beginning of a period is changed to a different position at the end of that period. A Statement of working capital is prepared to depict the changes in working capital. Working capital represents the excess of Current Assets over Current Liabilities. Since, several items *i.e.* all current assets and current liabilities are the component of working capital, it is necessary to measure the increase or decrease therein, by preparing a Statement or Schedule of changes in Working Capital. This Statement is prepared with current assets and current liabilities as appearing in the Balance Sheets under consideration. The statement shows the changes in individual items of current assets and current liabilities and their effect of working capital. The total increase and the total decrease in the end is compared and the difference of total increase and total decrease shows the net increase or net decrease in the working capital. A form of the Statement is given below :

STATEMENT OR SCHEDULE OF CHANGES IN WORKING CAPITAL

Particulars	*Amount of Previous year*	*Amount of current year*	*Effect on Working Capital*	
			Increase (Dr.)	*Decrease (Cr.)*
	Rs.	*Rs.*	*Rs.*	*Rs.*
Current Assets :				
Cash in hand				
Cash at Bank				
Bills Receivable				
Sundry Debtors				
Temporary Investments				
Stocks/Inventories				
Prepaid Expenses				
Accrued Incomes etc.				
TOTAL CURRENT				

ASSETS or (A)				
Current Liabilities :				
Bills Payable				
Sundry Creditors				
Outstanding Expenses				
Bank Overdraft				
Short-term Advances				
Dividends Payable etc.				
TOTAL CURRENT LIABILITIES or (B)				
WORKING CAPITAL (A—B)				
NET INCREASE/ DECREASE IN WORKING CAPITAL				
TOTAL				

How to Prepare the Above Schedule ?

Remember that :

* The Schedule is prepared with the help of only Current Assets and Current Liabilities.
* The Schedule considers only the Accounts appearing in the Balance Sheets.
* There is no effect of additional information given at the end of problem.

Steps :

1. The amount of every item of Current Asset of the current year is compared with its amount of previous year. If the amount of current asset of the current year is more than its amount of previous year, the *excess* is recorded in debit column.
2. If the amount of current asset of the current year is less than its amount of the previous year, the *deficiency* is recorded in credit column.
3. Make sure that all the accounts relating to current assets appearing in the two Balance Sheets are gone through and differences are properly recorded.
4. If the amount of each current liability of current year is more than its amount of previous year, the *excess* is recorded in the credit column.
5. If the amount of current liability of current year is less than its amount of previous year, the *deficit* is recorded in debit column.
6. Find out totals of all debit amounts and all credit amounts.
7. The above total are compared in the end and the difference shows decrease or increase in the Working Capital.
8. (The difference of total Current Assets and the total Current Liabilities of a year is its Working Capital.) If the Working Capital at the end of the current year is more than the Working Capital at the previous year the excess is called "Increase in Working Capital". If previous year's Working Capital is more than the current year's Working Capital, the excess is called "Decrease in Working Capital".

We can first prepare the "Schedule of changes in Working Capital". It is easy as there is no complications. This facilitate us to know in advance the answer to be disclosed by the Statement of Sources and Applications.

The following rules may be noted :

(*a*) Increase in a current asset item increases working capital.

(*b*) Decrease in current asset item decreases working capital.

(*c*) Increase in current liability item decreases working capital.

(*d*) Decrease in current liability item increases working capital.

The increase or decrease in the Working Capital should be equal to that shown in the Statement of Sources and Applications of Funds.

Illustration 1

Prepare a statement showing the effect of the following transactions on Working Capital.

1. Cash paid to creditors :
2. Cash collected from debtors :
3. Sale of stock at profit for cash :
4. Bills Receivable endorsed to creditors :
5. Issue of fully paid bonus shares :
6. Purchase of stock on credit :
7. Writing off bad debts against provision for doubtful debts :
8. Bill Receivables endorsed to creditors, dishonoured :

Solution :

Statement showing the effect on working capital

Items	**Effect on working capital**	**Reasons**
1.	No effect	Both the current assets and current liabilities are decreased by the same amount.
2.	No effect	It is only conversion of one current assets into another current asset. Neither the current asset nor current liabilities are affected.
3.	Inflow	Current liabilities remain unchanged. Total current assets are increased by the amount of profit.
4.	No effect	Both the current assets and current liabilities are decreased by the same amount.
5.	No effect	Accumulated profits are converted into share capital. Neither current assets nor current liabilities are affected.
6.	No effect	Both the current assets and current liabilities are increased by the same amount.
7.	No effect	Neither the total current assets nor the total current liabilities are affected.
8.	No effect	Both the current assets and current liabilities are increased by the same amount.

Illustration 2

You are given the following Balance Sheets of a Company :

	31st December	
	2009	*2010*
	Rs.	*Rs.*
Assets :		
Cash	3,000	4,700
Accounts Receivable	12,000	11,500
Land	5,000	6,600
Stock	8,000	9,000
	28,000	31,800
Liabilities		
Accounts Payable	7,000	4,500
Capital	20,000	25,000
Retained Earnings	1,000	2,300
	28,000	31,800

Prepare a statement showing the changes in working capital.

Solution :

STATEMENT OF CHANGES IN WORKING CAPITAL

	31st December		*Changes in Working Capital*	
	2009	*2010*	*Increase (Dr.)*	*Decrease (Cr.)*
	Rs.	*Rs.*	*Rs.*	*Rs.*
Current Assets :				
Cash	3,000	4,700	1,700	—
Accounts Receivable	12,000	11,500	—	500
Stock	8,000	9,000	1,000	—
Total (A)	23,000	25,200		
Current Liabilities :				
Accounts Payable	7,000	4,500	2,500	—
Total (B)	7,000	4,500		
WORKING CAPITAL (A) – (B)	16,000	20,700		
INCREASE IN WORKING CAPITAL	4,700	—	—	4,700
Total	20,700	20,700	5,200	5,200

Alternative Methods to the Above

Here we make use of both current assets and current liabilities and non-current assets and non-current liabilities. The schedule is similar to the above but with only one difference of two more columns to record increase or decrease in non-current assets and non-current liabilities. The specimen form is given below : (See Illustration No. 8)

SCHEDULE OF CHANGES IN WORKING CAPITAL

Particulars	*Amount of previous year*	*Amount of the current year*	*Changes in current assets and current liabilities*		*Changes in current and non-current liabilities*	
			Dr.	*Cr.*	*Dr.*	*Cr.*
	Rs.	*Rs.*	*Rs.*	*Rs.*	*Rs.*	*Rs.*
CAPITAL & LIABILITIES						
TOTAL						
ASSETS						
TOTAL						
Net Increase or Decrease in Working Capital						
TOTAL						

> **Note :** It is worth noting that the difference in total of debit amounts and credit amounts of current assets and current liabilities will be the same as that of the balance of the total of debit and credit amounts of non-current assets and liabilities. If current assets and liabilities will show credit balance, then non-current assets and liabilities will show debit balance of the same amount and vice versa.

Illustration 3

The following are the summarised Balance Sheets of Ram Ltd. as at 31st December 2009 and 2010.

BALANCE SHEET

	2009 Rs.	*2010* Rs.		*2009* Rs.	*2010* Rs.
Capital :			Fixed Assets	95,000	1,20,000
Equity Shares	1,00,000	1,00,000	Investments	—	10,000
Preference Shares		50,000	Current Assets :		
General Reserve	30,000	40,000	Stock	40,000	60,000
Profit and Loss	25,000	70,000	Debtors	20,000	40,000
Current Liabilities			B/R	5,000	2,000
Creditors	20,000	10,000	Prepaid Expenses	5,000	18,000
Bills Payable	—	2,000	Cash	20,000	10,000
Overdraft	3,000	—	Advances	10,000	40,000
Taxation Provision	7,000	12,000			
Proposed Dividend	10,000	16,000			
	1,95,000	3,00,000		1,95,000	3,00,000

You are required to prepare a Statement showing the changes in Working Capital.

(*B.Com. MS*)

Solution :

STATEMENT SHOWING CHANGES IN WORKING CAPITAL

	2009	*2010*	*Effect on Working Capital*	
			Increase (Dr.)	*Decrease (Cr.)*
	Rs.	*Rs.*	*Rs.*	*Rs.*
Current Assets :				
Stock	40,000	60,000	20,000	—
Debtors	20,000	40,000	20,000	—
Bills Receivable	5,000	2,000	—	3,000
Prepaid Expenses	5,000	18,000	13,000	
Cash	20,000	10,000	—	10,000
Advances	10,000	40,000	30,000	—
Total	1,00,000	1,70,000		
Current Liabilities				
Creditors	20,000	10,000	10,000	—
Bills Payable	—	2,000	—	2,000
Overdraft	3,000	—	3,000	—
Taxation Provision	7,000	12,000	—	5,000
Proposed Dividend	10,000	16,000		6,000
Total	40,000	40,000	96,000	26,000
Working Capital	60,000	1,30,000	—	—
Net Increase in Working Capital	70,000	—	—	70,000
Total	1,30,000	1,30,000	96,000	96,000

> **Remember :**
> 1. Increase in Current Asset, results in increase in Working Capital.
> 2. Decrease in Current Asset, results in decrease in Working Capital.
> 3. Increase in Current Liability, results in decrease in Working Capital.
> 4. Decrease in Current Liability, results in increase in Working Capital.

Alternatively

STATEMENT SHOWING THE CHANGES IN WORKING CAPITAL

	2009		*2010*	
	Rs.	*Rs.*	*Rs.*	*Rs.*
CURRENT ASSETS :				
Stock	40,000		60,000	
Debtors	20,000		40,000	
Bills Receivable	5,000		2,000	
Prepaid Expenses	5,000		18,000	
Cash	20,000		10,000	
Advances	10,000		40,000	
		1,00,000		1,70,000
Less : CURRENT LIABILITIES :				
Creditors	20,000		10,000	
Bills Payable	—		2,000	

Overdraft	3,000			
Taxation Provision	7,000		12,000	40,000
Proposed Dividend	10,000	40,000	16,000	
WORKING CAPITAL		60,000		1,30,000
INCREASE IN WORKING CAPITAL		70,000		
		1,30,000		1,30,000

Illustration 4

Prepare a Statement of changes in Working Capital from the following Balance Sheets of Ram Seth Company :

BALANCE SHEET as on 31st December

Liabilities	*2009*	*2010*	*Assets*	*2009*	*2010*
	Rs.	*Rs.*		*Rs.*	*Rs.*
Equity Capital	5,00,000	5,00,000	Fixed Assets	6,00,000	7,00,000
Debentures	3,70,000	4,50,000	Long-term Investments	2,00,000	1,00,000
Tax Payable	77,000	43,000	Work-in-progress	80,000	90,000
Creditors	96,000	1,92,000	Stocks	1,50,000	2,25,000
Interest Payable	37,000	45,000	Debtors	70,000	1,40,000
Dividend Payable	50,000	35,000	Cash	30,000	10,000
	11,30,000	12,65,000		11,30,000	12,65,000

(*B.Com. Madurai*)

Solution :

STATEMENT OF CHANGES IN WORKING CAPITAL

Particulars	*2009*	*2010*	*Effect on Working Capital*	
			Increase (+)	*Decrease* (–)
Current Assets :				
Cash	30,000	10,000	—	20,000
Debtors	70,000	1,40,000	70,000	—
Stocks	1,50,000	2,25,000	75,000	—
Work-in-progress	80,000	90,000	10,000	—
	3,30,000	4,65,000		
Current Liabilities :				
Tax Payable	77,000	43,000	34,000	—
Creditors	96,000	1,92,000	—	96,000
Interest Payable	37,000	45,000	—	8,000
Dividend Payable	50,000	35,000	15,000	—
	2,60,000	3,15,000		
Working Capital	70,000	1,50,000		
Net Increase in Working Capital	80,000	—	—	80,000
	1,50,000	1,50,000	2,04,000	2,04,000

Illustration 5

From the following Balance Sheets of the company for the year ended 31st December 2009 and 2010, prepare schedule of changes in working capital and statement showing sources and application of fund :

	31-12-2009 *Rs.*	*31-12-2010* *Rs.*		*31-12-2009* *Rs.*	*31-12-2010* *Rs.*
Share Capital	3,00,000	4,00,000	Plant and Machinery	50,000	60,000
Sundry Creditors	1,00,000	70,000	Furniture and Fixtures	10,000	15,000
Profit and Loss A/c	15,000	30,000	Stocks	85,000	1,05,000
			Debtors	1,60,000	1,50,000
			Cash	1,10,000	1,70,000
	4,15,000	5,00,000		4,15,000	5,00,000

(*B.Com. M.S.*)

Solution :

SCHEDULE OF CHANGES IN WORKING CAPITAL

	2009	*2010*	*Effect on Working Capital*	
	Rs.	*Rs.*	*Increase* *Rs.*	*Decrease* *Rs.*
Current Assets :				
Cash	1,10,000	1,70,000	60,000	
Debtors	1,60,000	150,000	—	10,000
Stock	85,000	1,05,000	20,000	—
	3,55,000	4,25,000		
Current Liabilities :				
Sundry Creditors	1,00,000	70,000	30,000	—
	1,00,000	70,000		
Working Capital	2,55,000	3,55,000		
Net Increase in Working Capital	1,00,000	—	—	1,00,000
	3,55,000	3,55,000	1,10,000	1,10,000

STATEMENT OF SOURCE AND APPLICATION OF FUNDS
for the year ended 2010

Sources	*Rs.*	*Applications*	*Rs.*
Issue of Share Capital	1,00,000	Purchase of Plant and Machinery (Rs. 60,000 – Rs. 50,000)	10,000
Funds from Operations (Rs. 30,000 – Rs. 15,000)	15,000	Purchase of Furniture and Fixtures (Rs. 15,000 – Rs. 10,000)	5,000
		Net Increase in working Capital	1,00,000
	1,15,000		1,15,000

Illustration 6

From the following information relating to A Ltd., prepare Funds Flow Statement :

(Rs. '000)

	2009 Rs.	2010 Rs.		2009 Rs.	2010 Rs.
Share Capital	300	400	Cash	30	90
Reserve	100	50	Accounts Receivable	105	150
Retained Earnings	30	60	Inventories	150	195
Accounts Payable	45	135	Fixed Assets	190	210
	475	645		475	645

Additional information :

(*a*) The company issued bonus shares for Rs. 50,000 and for cash Rs. 50,000.

(*b*) Depreciation written off during the year Rs. 15,000. (*B.Com. M.S.*)

Solution :

SCHEDULE OF CHANGES IN WORKING CAPITAL

	2009 Rs.	2010. Rs.	Changes in Working Capital: Increase Rs.	Decrease Rs.
Current Assets :				
Cash	30,000	90,000	60,000	—
Accounts Receivable	1,05,000	150,000	45,000	—
Inventories	1,50,000	1,95,000	45,000	—
	2,85,000	4,35,000		
Less: Current Liabilities :				
Accounts Payable	45,000	1,35,000	—	90,000
Working Capital	2,40,000	3,00,000		
Increase in Working Capital	60,000	—	—	60,000
	3,00,000	3,00,000	1,50,000	1,50,000

FUND FLOW STATEMENT
for the year ended 31-12-2010

	Rs.		Rs.
Issue of Share	50,000	Purchase of Fixed Assets	35,000
Funds from Operation	45,000	Increase in Working Capital	60,000
	95,000		95,000

Workings :

FIXED ASSETS A/C

	Rs.		Rs.
To Balance b/d	1,90,000	By Adjusted P & L A/c (Depreciation)	15,000
To Cash (Purchase)	35,000	By Balance c/d	2,10,000
	2,25,000		2,25,000

SHARE CAPITAL A/C

	Rs.		Rs.
To Balance c/d	4,00,000	By Balance b/d	3,00,000
		By cash	50,000
		By General Reserves (Bonus Shares)	50,000
	4,00,000		4,00,000

ADJUSTED PROFIT & LOSS A/C

	Rs.		Rs.
To Fixed Assets (Depreciations)	15,000	By Balance b/d	30,000
To Balance c/d	60,000	By Fund from Operation	45,000
	75,000		75,000

Illustration 7

From the following Balance Sheets of a company, prepare a Sources and Uses of Funds Statement for 2010:

	1 January Rs.	*31st December* Rs.
Assets:		
Cash	35,000	75,000
Accounts Receivable	98,000	90,000
Merchandise Inventory	87,000	1,20,000
Long-term Investments	15,000	10,000
Land	20,000	30,000
	2,55,000	3,25,000
Liabilities:		
Equity Accounts Payable	50,000	45,000
Notes Payable (Short-term)	20,000	35,000
Notes Payable (Due Dec. 2011)	—	20,000
Capital Stock	1,25,000	1,50,000
Retained Earnings	60,000	75,000
	2,55,000	3,25,000

(*B.Com. Madras, Madurai*)

Solution :

STATEMENT OF SOURCES AND APPLICATION OF FUNDS

Sources	Rs.	*Application*	Rs.
Capital Stock (Rs. 1,50,000 – 1,25,000)	25,000	Purchase of Land (Rs 30,000 – 20,000)	10,000
Funds from Operations (Rs. 75,000 – 60,000)	15,000	Increase in Working capital	35,000
Sale of Investment (Rs. 15,000 – 10,000)	5,000		
	45,000		45,000

SCHEDULE OF CHANGES IN WORKING CAPITAL

	January Rs.	December Rs.	Changes in Working Capital	
			Increase Rs.	Decrease Rs.
Current Assets :				
Cash	35,000	75,000	40,000	—
Accounts Receivable	98,000	90,000	—	8,000
Merchandise Inventory	87,000	1,20,000	33,000	—
	2,20,000	2,85,000		
Current Liabilities :				
Equity Accounts Payable (Creditors)	50,000	45,000	5,000	—
Notes Payable (Short-term)	20,000	35,000	—	15,000
Notes Payable (Dec. 2011)		20,000	—	20,000
	70,000	1,00,000		
Working Capital	1,50,000	1,85,000		
Increase in working Capital	35,000	—	—	35,000
	1,85,000	1,85,000	78,000	78,000

Illustration 8

From the following Balance Sheets of a Company, you are required to prepare a Schedule of Changes in Working Capital.

BALANCE SHEETS as on 31st December

Liabilities	2009 Rs.	2010 Rs.	Assets	2009 Rs.	2010 Rs.
Share Capital	2,00,000	2,50,000	Land and Buildings	2,00,000	1,90,000
General Reserve	50,000	60,000	Plant and Machinery	1,50,000	1,69,000
Profit and Loss	30,500	30,600	Stocks	1,00,000	74,000
Bank Loan (Short Period)	70,000	—	Debtors	80,000	64,200
Creditors	1,50,000	1,35,200	Cash	500	600
Provision for Taxation	30,000	35,000	Bank	—	8,000
			Goodwill	—	5,000
	5,30,500	5,10,800		5,30,500	5,10,800

(M. Com., Delhi) (B.Com., (Hons) Delhi)

Solution :

SCHEDULE OF CHANGES IN WORKING CAPITAL

Particulars	2009 Rs.	2010 Rs.	Effect on Working Capital	
			Increase (Dr.) Rs.	Decrease (Cr.) Rs.
Current Assets :				
Stock	1,00,000	74,000	—	26,000
Debtors	80,000	64,200		15,800
Cash	500	600	100	—

Bank	—	8,000	8,000	—
	1,80,500	1,46,800		
Current Liabilities :				
Bank Loan	70,000	—	70,000	—
Creditors	1,50,000	1,35,200	14,800	—
	2,20,000	1,35,200		
Working Capital	(–) 39,500	11,600		
Net Increase in Working Capital	51,100			51,100
	11,600	11,600	92,900	92,900

Alternatively :

SCHEDULE OF CHANGES IN WORKING CAPITAL

	2009	*2010*	*Changes in current Asset and Current Liabilities*		*Changes in non-current Assets and non-current Liabilities*	
			Dr.	*Cr.*	*Dr.*	*Cr.*
	Rs.	*Rs.*	*Rs.*	*Rs.*	*Rs.*	*Rs.*
Assets :						
Land and Buildings	2,00,000	1,90,000	—	—	—	10,000
Machinery and Plant	1,50,000	1,69,000	—	—	19,000	—
Stocks	1,00,000	74,000	—	26,000	—	—
Debtors	80,000	64,200	—	15,800	—	—
Cash	500	600	100	—	—	—
Bank	—	8,000	8,000	—	—	—
Goodwill	—	5,000	—	—	5,000	—
	5,30,500	5,10,800				
Share Capital	2,00,000	2,50,000	—	—	—	50,000
General Reserve	50,000	60,000	—	—	—	10,000
Profit and Loss	30,500	30,600	—	—	—	100
Bank Loan	70,000	—	70,000	—	—	—
Creditors	1,50,000	1,35,200	14,800	—	—	—
Provision for Taxation	30,000	35,000	—	—	—	5,000
	5,30,500	5,10,800				
Total			92,900	41,800	24,000	75,100
Net Increase in Working Capital			—	51,100	51,100	
Total			92,900	92,900	75,100	75,100

Non-current Assets : All assets other than current assets come within the category of non-current assets. For examples, Goodwill, Land, Buildings, Plant, Machinery, Patents, Debit balance of P & L A/c. Preliminary Expenses, Discount on Issue of shares or Debentures etc.

Non-current Liabilities : All liabilities other than current liabilities come within the category of non-current liabilities. For example, Share Capital, Debentures, Long-term loans, Share premium, Credit balance of P & L A/c, Capital Reserve etc.

(*b*) Fund Flow Statement

It has been explained earlier in this chapter. This is second but most important part of Fund Flow Statement. After preparing the Statement of Working Capital, the Statement of Sources and Application of Fund is prepared. This statement is prepared with the help of remaining items in the Balance Sheet of the two periods all non-current assets and non-current liabilities and other information given in the problem. That is, it is prepared on the basis of the changes in Fixed Assets, Long-term Liabilities and Share Capital ascertained on the basis of values of these items shown in the Balance Sheets. Of course, additional information, if given, must also be considered. Thus the preparation of this statement involves the ascertainment of increase or decrease in the various items of fixed assets, long-term liabilities and share capital. Those business transactions, which cause an increase in the working capital, are considered as *Source of Fund* and on the same footing business transactions causing a decrease in working capital are known as *Uses of Funds*.

The probable items of sources and uses of fund are tabulated below :

Sources of Funds	*Uses of Funds*
1. Issue of Fresh Shares	1. Redemption of Preference Shares
2. Issue of Debentures	2. Redemption of Debentures
3. New Loans	3. Repayment of Loans
4. Sale of Fixed Assets	4. Purchase of Fixed Assets
5. Non-trading income	5. Loss from Operations
6. Profits from Operation	6. Payment of Dividends etc.

There is no legally prescribed or generally accepted form of Fund Flow Statement. The example of Fund Flow Statement is given below :

Funds flow statement is a statement which indicates various sources from which funds (working capital) have been obtained during a certain period and the uses or applications to which these funds have been put during that period. Generally, this statement is prepared in two formats:

(1) T form or an Account form

(2) Report form

1. FUND FLOW STATEMENT
for the year ended...

	Rs.		
SOURCES OF FUNDS (Inflow)	—	APPLICATION OF FUNDS (Outflow)	
Trading Profit	—	Trading Loss	—
Issue of Share Capital	—	Redemption of Redeemable Preference Shares	—
Issue of Debentures	—	Redemption of Debentures	—
Long-term Borrowings	—	Repayment of Other Long-term Loans	—
Sale of Fixed Assets	—	Purchase of Fixed Assets	—
Non-Trading Incomes	—	Non-Trading Expenditure	—
Total	—	Total	—
Decrease in Working Capital	—	Increase in Working Capital	
Total	—	Total	—

Alternatively :

2. FUND FLOW STATEMENT
for the year ended...

	Rs.	*Rs.*
SOURCES OF FUNDS (Inflow)	—	
Trading Profit	—	
Issue of Share Capital	—	
Issue of Debentures	—	
Long-term Borrowings	—	
Sale of Fixed Assets	—	
Non-Trading Incomes	—	—
Total		
APPLICATION OF FUND :		
Trading Loss	—	
Redemption of Redeemable Preference Shares	—	
Redemption of Debentures	—	
Repayment of other Long-term Loans	—	
Purchase of Fixed Assets		
Non-Trading Expenditure	—	—
Total		
Increase/Decrease in Working Capital		

Note : The change in Working Capital disclosed by the "Statement of changes in Working Capital" will tally with changes disclosed by the Fund Flow Statement.

Distinction between Fund Flow Statement and Balance Sheet

Fund Flow Statement	*Balance Sheet*
1. It is dynamic in nature. It shows the changes in financial position between two dates.	1. It is static in nature. It is prepared at the end of accounting period and portrays the financial position on a particular date.
2. It incorporates items causing changes in working capital.	2. It includes the balance of real and personal accounts and shows the total resources.
3. It is a management tool for financial analysis and helps in decision-making.	3. It reveals the financial position of a business firm and one can examine the soundness of the firm.
4. The preparation of this statement is a post Balance Sheet exercise.	4. It is the end product of all accounting operations for a particular period of time.

SOURCES AND APPLICATIONS OF FUNDS

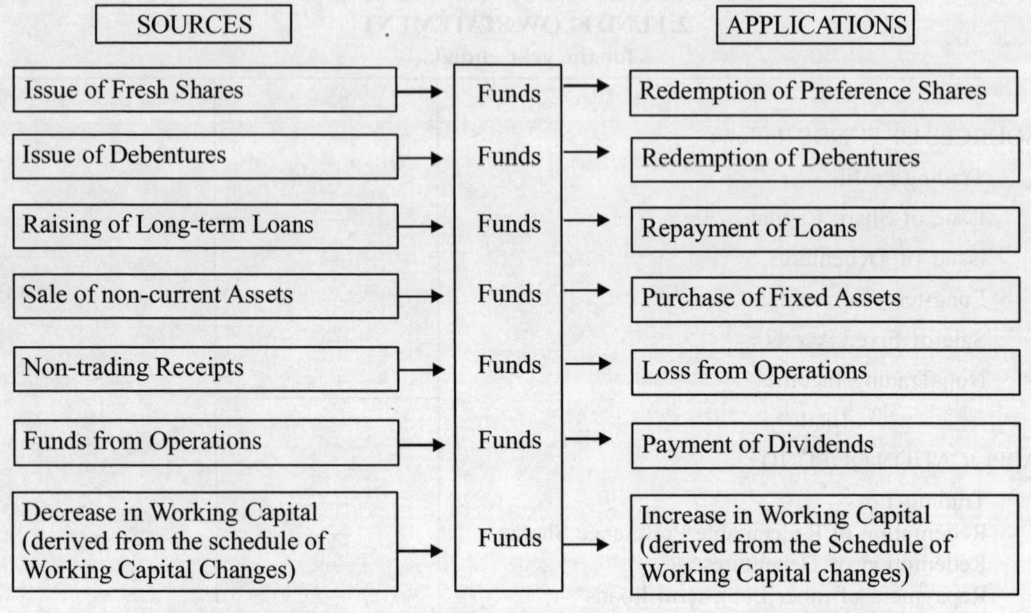

Distinction between Fund Flow Statement and Income Statement

Fund Flow Statement	*Income Statement*
1. There is no prescribed format for preparing a Fund Flow Statement.	1. It is prescribed in a prescribed form.
2. While preparing the statement both capital and revenue items are considered.	2. Only revenue items are considered.
3. Income statement helps the preparation of Funds Flow statement. It is complementary to income statement.	3. Income statement is not prepared from Funds Flow Statement.
4. It highlights the changes in the financial position of a business and indicates the various means by which funds were obtained during a particular period and the ways to which these funds were employed.	4. It does not reveal the inflows and outflows of funds but depict the items of expenses and income arrive at the figure of profit or loss.

Distinction between Fund Flow Statement and Receipt & Payment A/c

Fund Flow Statement	*Receipts & Payments A/c*
1. It contains the movements of cash plus all other items affecting working capital.	1. It contains the summary of only cash transactions.
2. It presents the summary of changes i.e. net changes in working capital.	2. It presents all sources of cash and disbursement of cash during the year are shown.
3. It makes use of all factors affecting working capital i.e. net current assets.	3. It takes notice of only those factors which affect cash.

Illustration 9

From the following Balance Sheets of X Ltd., you are required to prepare a Schedule of Changes in Working Capital and Statement of Flow of Fund :

Assets	*31st Dec. 2009* *Rs.*	*31st Dec. 2010* *Rs.*
Land and Buildings :	50,000	50,000
Plant	24,000	34,000
Stock	9,000	7,000
Debtors	16,500	19,500
Cash at Bank	4,000	9,000
Total :	1,03,500	1,19,500
Capital and Liabilities :		
Capital	80,000	85,000
Profit & Loss	14,500	24,500
Creditors	9,000	5,000
Mortgage		5,000
Total	1,03,500	1,19,500

(*M.Com. Delhi*)

Solution :

SCHEDULE/STATEMENT OF CHANGES IN WORKING CAPITAL

	Balances 31st Dec. 2009 Rs.	*31st Dec. 2010 Rs.*	*Changes in Working Capital* Increase (Dr.) Rs.	Decrease(Cr.) Rs,
Current Assets :				
Stock	9,000	7,000	—	2,000
Debtors	16,500	19,500	3,000	—
Cash at Bank	4,000	9,000	5,000	—
	29,500	35,500		
Current Liabilities :				
Creditors	9,000	5,000	4,000	—
	9,000	5,000		
Working Capital	20,500	30,500		
Net Increase in Working Capital	10,000	—		10,000
	30,500	30,500	12,000	12,000

STATEMENT OF FLOW OF FUNDS OF X LTD.

	Rs.		Rs.
SOURCES OF FUNDS :		APPLICATION OF FUNDS :	
Issue of Shares (Rs. 85,000 – Rs. 80,000)	5,000	Purchase of Plant (Rs. 34,000 – Rs. 24,000)	10,000
Borrowings from Mortgage (Rs. 5,000 – Nil)	5,000	Increase in fund as per Statement of Changes in Working Capital	10,000
Funds from Operation (Rs. 24,500 – Rs. 14,500)	10,000		
	20,000		20,000

Alternatively :

STATEMENT OF FLOW OF FUNDS OF X LTD.

	Rs.	Rs.
SOURCES OF FUNDS :		
Issue of Shares	5,000	
Borrowings from Mortgage	5,000	
Funds from Operation	10,000	
Total :		20,000
APPLICATION OF FUNDS :		
Plant Purchased	10,000	
Total :		10,000
Net increase in Fund as per Statement of Changes in Working Capital		10,000

Illustration 10

For calculating 'Funds from Operations from a given amount of Net Profits earned during a year, how you deal with the following :

1. Decrease in Goodwill
2. Loss on sale of a Machine
3. Increase in General Reserve
4. Decrease in Land Account
5. Decrease in Investment Account
6. Decrease in Debentures
7. Increase in Preliminary Expenses
8. Decrease in Share Capital
9. Increase in Securities Premium Account
10. Interest on Long-term investment.

Solution

Items	Whether to be added to or subtracted from the amount of Net profit earned during the year
1. Decrease in Goodwill	To be added
2. Loss on sale of a Machine	To be added
3. Increase in General Reserve	To be added
4. Decrease in Land A/c	Neither to be added nor to be subtracted
5. Decrease in Investment Account	Neither to be added nor to be subtracted
6. Decrease in Debenture	Neither to be added nor to be subtracted
7. Increase in Preliminary Expenses	Neither to be added nor to be subtracted
8. Decrease in Share Capital	Neither to be added nor to be subtracted
9. Increase in Securities Premium Account	Neither to be added nor to be subtracted
10. Interest on Long-term Investment	To be subtracted

Illustration 11

How you deal the following items while preparing Fund Flow Statements.

1. Increase in Debentures
2. Decrease in Balance of Preliminary Expenses
3. Increase in Balance of Patent
4. Increase in Balance of furniture
5. Increase in General Reserve
6. Proposed Dividend for Current Year
7. Decrease in Balance of Plant
8. Decrease in Preference Share Capital
9. Provision for Tax for Previous Year
10. Increase in Equity Share Capital

Solution

Items	Treatments
1. Increase in Debentures	Sources of fund
2. Decrease in Balance of preliminary Expenses	Add back to current year's profits to find out Funds from Operations.
3. Increase in Balance of Patent	Application of Fund
4. Increase in Balance of Furniture	Application of Fund
5. Increase in General Reserve	Add back to current year's profit to find out Funds from Operations.
6. Proposed Dividend for current year	Add back to current year's profit to find out funds from Operations.
7. Decrease in balance of Plant	Add back to current year's profit to find out Funds from Operations.
8. Decrease in Preference Share Capital	Application of Fund
9. Provision for Tax for Previous Year	Application of Fund
10. Increase in Equity Share Capital	Sources of Fund

SOME PRACTICAL HINTS

Given below are some matters which require special attention while preparing a Statement of Sources and Application of Funds *i.e.*, Fund Flow Statement.

(1) Trading Profit / Fund from Operations

Sales are the major source of cash-inflow and at the same time cost of goods sold and expenses are the main outflow of cash. The difference of these two *i.e.* Sales—(Cost of Goods sold + Expenses) is net profit i.e. net income from operations. However, the profit so calculated is seldom equal to the Funds from Operations because there are many items which are debited or credited in the profit and loss account but which do not affect working capital. Hence, to calculate funds from operations, the following adjustments are to be done :

(a) Items to be Added Back to the Net Profit

(*i*) **Non-Fund Items :** Items which do not increase the current liability or decrease the current asset are non-fund items. They are in brief :

(*a*) **Depreciation and Depletion :** Depreciation and depletion do not affect the working at all. It is usual practice in every business to write off depreciation on fixed assets which is debited to Profit and Loss Account and a corresponding credit is made in the respective asset account. In this way, it is only an accounting entry, having the effect of reducing the book value of fixed asset as well as the profit by the same amount. Thus it affects only the fixed assets. Therefore, to nullify the effect, the amounts of depreciation and depletion already debited to Profit and Loss Account are added back to the profits in order to calculate the amount of funds.

(*b*) **Amortisation of Fictitious and Intangible Assets :** Amortisation of certain fictitious assets in the nature of Deferred Revenue Expenditure like, Preliminary Expenses, Advertising Suspense Account, Discount on Issue of Shares and Debentures, Premium on Redemption of Redeemable Preference Shares or Debentures etc. and write off of certain intangible assets like Goodwill, Trade Marks and Patents are also items which are only accounting entries and do not affect the current assets or current liabilities at all. They are, therefore, added back to the net profit.

(*c*) **Provision for Taxation :** Provision for taxation made out of current year's profit also does not affect the flow of funds. So it must be added back to profit.

(*ii*) **Non-Trading Charges or Losses :** Items which are not trading charges or losses are called non-trading charges or losses. They are :

(*a*) **Appropriation of Retained Earnings :** Transfer of profits to certain reserves, such as, General Reserve, Dividend Equilization Fund, Sinking Fund, Reserve for Contingencies or any other reserves, do not affect the current assets or current liabilities. So, they will be added back to the net profits.

(*b*) **Proposed Dividend on Shares :** It is also an appropriation of profits and not a charge and in no way involves a change in Current Assets or Current Liabilities. So, it is added back to profits.

(*c*) **Loss on Sale of Non-Current Assets :** Loss on sale of fixed assets such as Building, Machinery, Furniture or Investment which has already been debited to Profit and Loss Account, is not a business loss and does not affect the flow of funds. It is therefore, added back to net profit.

(*iii*) **Items to be Deducted from Net Profit :** The non-fund and non-trading revenue receipts or incomes must be deducted from the net profit in order to compute funds from operations. Such items may be as follows :

(*a*) **Dividend Received or Receivable :** Although this transaction increases current assets of the firm but as it is not a trading income, it should be deducted from the net profit.

(*b*) **Retransfer of Excess Provisions :** Where provisions made for Taxation, Depreciation, Doubtful Debts etc. exceed the genuine requirements, the excess amount is transferred back *i.e.* credited back to Profit and Loss Account. But it is simply an accounting entry. It does not create any inflow of fund. Hence it will be deducted from net profit.

(*c*) Profits on sale of Non-Current Assets : Any profits arising out of sale of fixed assets which have already been credited to Profit and Loss Account, must be deducted from the net profit.

(*d*) **Appreciation of Fixed Assets :** The amount of appreciation on revaluation of fixed assets, if credited to Profit and Loss Account, must be deducted from the profit to compute funds from operations.

Calculation of Funds from Operation

There are two methods to find out the amount of Funds from Operation :

1. Statement form and
2. Account form.

STATEMENT FORM : It can be prepared as under :

CALCULATION OF FUNDS FROM OPERATIONS

	Rs.	Rs.
Net Profit for the current year		—
ADD : Non-Fund and Non-Trading Charges already debited to P & L A/c :		
Depreciation and Depletion	—	
Amortization of Fictitious and intangible assets, i.e.		
Preliminary Expenses written off	—	
Discount on Shares written off	—	
Premium on Redemption written off	—	
Goodwill or Patents written off	—	
Appropriation of Retained Earnings	—	
i.e. transfer to General Reserve, —		
Sinking Fund etc.		
Proposed Dividend		
Loss on sale of fixed asset written off	—	
Total :		—
Less : Non-Fund Items and Non-Trading Incomes already credited to P & L A/c :		
Dividend Received/Receivable	—	
Excess Provision written back	—	
Profit on sale of Fixed Asset	—	
Profit on revaluation of Fixed Assets	—	
Total :		—
TRADING PROFIT OR FUND FROM OPERATIONS		

ACCOUNT FORM : Alternatively, an adjusted Profit and Loss account may be written up as follows and the balancing figure thus represents Trading Profit or Fund from Operation.

(See Illustration No. 9)

ADJUSTED PROFIT AND LOSS ACCOUNT

	Rs.		Rs.
To Depreciation	—	By Opening Balance of P & L Appropriation A/c	—
To Preliminary Expenses written off	—	By Dividend Received	—
To Discount on Shares written off	—	By Excess Provision written back	—
To Goodwill written off	—	By TRADING PROFITS OR FUND FROM OPERATION (Balancing figure)	
To Premium on Redemption	—		
To Transfer to Reserves	—		
To Loss on sale of Fixed Assets	—		
To Closing Balance of P & L Appropriation A/c	—		

Illustration 12

A Company's reported current profit is Rs. 70,000 after incorporating the following :

	Rs.		Rs.
Loss on sale of Equipment	10,000	Gain from sale of non-current assets	40,000
Premium on Redemption of Debentures	1,500	Excess provision for Taxation	22,000
Discount on Issue of Debentures	2,000	Dividend income on Investments	4,000
Depreciation on Machinery and Buildings	20,000	Transfer to General Reserve	5,000
Depletion of natural resources	10,000	Preliminary Expenses	1,000
Amortization of Goodwill	30,000	Profit on Revaluation of Investments	2,500
Interim dividend	25,000		

Derive the net inflow of funds from the operations. (*B.Com. Madurai*)

CALCULATION OF FUND FROM OPERATIONS

	Rs.	Rs.
Net Profit for the current year		70,000
Add : Non-Fund or Non-Operating debits :		
Loss on sale of Equipment	10,000	
Discount on issue of Debentures	2,000	
Depreciation on Machinery and Buildings	20,000	
Depletion of Natural Resources	10,000	
Amortization of Goodwill	30,000	
Excess provision for Taxation	22,000	
Transfer to General Reserve	5,000	
Preliminary Expenses	1,000	
Premium on Redemption of Debentures	1,500	
Interim Dividend	25,000	1,26,500
		1,96,500
Less : Non-Fund or Non-Operating Credits :		
Profit on Revaluation	2,500	
Gain from Sale of non-current Assets	40,000	
Dividend Income on Investments	4,000	46,500
Net inflow of funds from Operation :		1,50,000

Alternatively, this figure of Rs. 1,50,000 may be derived by preparing an Adjusted Profit and Loss Account :

ADJUSTED PROFIT AND LOSS ACCOUNT

	Rs.		Rs.
To Loss on sale of Equipment	10,000	By Profit on Revaluation of Investment	2,500
To Discount on Issue of Debentures	2,000	By Gain from sale of Non-Current assets	40,000
To Depreciation on Machinery and Buildings	20,000	By Dividend Income on Investments	4,000
To Depletion of Natural Resources	10,000	By Operating fund (Balancing figure)	1,50,000
To Amortization of Goodwill	30,000		

	Rs.		Rs.
To Excess provision for Taxation	22,000		
To Transfer to General Reserve	5,000		
To Preliminary Expenses	1,000		
To Premium on Redemption of Debentures	1,500		
To Interim Dividend	25,000		
To Closing Balance (Reported Profit)	70,000		
	1,96,500		1,96,500

Illustration 13

Ramco Cements presents the following information and you are required to calculate funds from operations :

PROFIT AND LOSS ACCOUNT

	Rs.		*Rs.*
To Operation Expenses	1,00,000	By Gross Profit	2,00,000
To Depreciation	40,000	By Gain on sale of Plant	20,000
To Loss on sale of Building	10,000		
To Advertisement Suspense account	5,000		
To Discount Allowed	500		
To Discount on Issue of shares written off	500		
To Goodwill written off	12,000		
To Net Profit	52,000		
	2,20,000		2,20,000

(*M.Com. Madurai*)

Solution :

CALCULATION OF FUND FROM OPERATIONS

	Rs.	*Rs.*
Net Profit (given)		52,000
Add : Non-fund or non-operating items which have been debited to Profit & Loss A/c :		
Depreciation	40,000	
Loss on sale of building	10,000	
Advertisement written off	5,000	
Discount written off	500	
Goodwill written off	12,000	67,500
		1,19,500
Less : Non-fund or non-operating items which have been credited to Profit & Loss A/c :		
Gain on Sale of Plant	20,000	20,000
FUNDS FROM OPERATIONS		99,500

Alternatively :

ADJUSTED PROFIT AND LOSS ACCOUNT

	Rs.		Rs.
To Depreciation	40,000	By Opening Balance	—
To Loss on sale of building	10,000	By Gain on sale of Plant	20,000
To Advertisement Suspense A/c	5,000	By Funds from Operations (Balancing figure)	99,500
To Discount written off	500		
To Goodwill written off	12,000		
To Closing Balance	52,000		
	1,19,500		1,19,500

Illustration 14

Calculate the Funds from Operations from the following information as on 31st Dec. 2010.

1. Increase in balance of Profit and Loss account during the year ended on 31st Dec. 2010. Rs. 6,50,000.
2. Gain on sale of building Rs. 35,500.
3. Goodwill appears in the books as on 1.1.2010 at Rs. 1,80,000 of which 10% has been written off during the year.
4. Old machinery worth Rs. 8,000 has been sold during the year for Rs. 6,500.
5. Rs. 1,25,000 have been transferred to General Reserve.
6. Depreciation has been provided during the year on Machinery at 20% on written down value.

NB: The written down value of Machinery as on 31.12.2010 was Rs. 5,20,000.

(*B.Com. MS*)

Solution :

Details	*Rs.*	*Rs.*
Net profit for the year		6,50,000
Add: Depreciation	1,30,000*	
Goodwill written off	18,000	
Loss on sale of Machinery	1,500	
Transfer to General Reserve	1,25,000	(+) 2,74,500
Less: Gain on sale of Buildings		(–) (35,500)
FUND FROM OPERATIONS :		8,89,000

$$* \left(\frac{\text{Rs. } 5{,}20{,}000 \times 100}{80}\right) \times 20\% = \text{Rs. } 1{,}30{,}000$$

$$\text{(OR) Rs. } \frac{5{,}20{,}000}{80} \times 20 = \text{Rs. } 1{,}30{,}000$$

Illustration 15

From the following information, find out funds from operations :

	Jan. 2010 *Rs.*	*Dec.* 2010 *Rs.*
General Reserve	1,000	1,250
Goodwill	500	250
Provision for Depreciation (Plant)	500	600
Preliminary Expenses	300	200
Profit & Loss Appropriation A/c	1,500	2,000

Solution :

CALCULATION OF FUNDS FROM OPERATIONS

	Rs.
Profit & Loss Appropriation A/c (Dec. 2010)	2,000
Add : Items not decreasing funds :	
Transfer to General Reserve	250
Goodwill written off	250
Provision for Depreciation	100
Preliminary Expenses written off	100
	2,700
Less : Profit & Loss Appropriation Account (Jan. 2010)	1,500
FUNDS FROM OPERATIONS	1,200

Alternatively :

ADJUSTED PROFIT & LOSS ACCOUNT

	Rs.		Rs.
To General Reserve	250	By Balance b/d	1,500
To Goodwill written off	250	By Funds from Operations	
To preliminary Expenses written off	100	(Balancing figure)	1,200
To Provision for Depreciation	100		
To Balance c/d (Dec. 2010)	2,000		
	2,700		2,700

Illustration 16

Calculate the Funds from Operations from the following :

Net profit after Tax	Rs. 1,50,000
Provision for Depreciation	Rs. 5,000
Provision for Taxation	Rs. 1,00,000
Refund of Tax	Rs. 1,500
Profit on sale of fixed assets	Rs. 2,000
Loss on sale of Investments	Rs. 5,000
Interest received	Rs. 1,500
Rent received	Rs. 1,000
Dividend received	Rs. 5,000
Discount allowed on Debentures written off	Rs. 1,000
Cost of issue of shares written off	Rs. 500
Preliminary expenses written off	Rs. 800
Goodwill written off	Rs. 1,000
Underwriting commission written off	Rs. 500

Solution :

	Rs.	Rs.
Funds from Operations = Net profit after Tax		1,50,000
Add : Provision for Depreciation	5,000	
Provision for Taxation	1,00,000	

		Rs.	Rs.
	Loss on sale of Investments	5,000	
	Discount allowed on Debentures written off	1,000	
	Cost of issue of Shares written off	500	
	Preliminary expenses written off	800	
	Goodwill written off	1,000	
	Underwriting commission written off	500	(+) 1,13,800
			2,63,800
Less :	Refund of Tax	1,500	
	Profit on sale of fixed assets	2,000	
	Interest received	1,500	
	Rent received	1,000	
	Dividend received	5,000	(–) 11,000
	FUND FROM OPERATION		2,52,800

Illustration 17

From the following details, ascertain 'Funds from Operations'.

Particulars	1.1.2010 *Rs.*	31.12.2010 *Rs.*
P & L A/c Balance at the end	50,000	60,000
General Reserve	30,000	40,000
Goodwill	20,000	12,000
Preliminary expenses	6,000	4,000
Depreciation provision (accumulated)	25,000	40,000
Income from non-trading investments	–	20,000

Preference shares of the face value of Rs. 1,00,000 were redeemed during the year at premium of 10%. The premium on redemption was charged to the Profit and Loss A/c.

(*B. Com. Madurai, Chennai, Bhopal*)

Solution :

ADJUSTED PROFIT & LOSS ACCOUNT for the year 2010

Particulars	*Rs.*	*Particulars*	*Rs.*
To Transfer to general reserve (40,000 – 30,000)	10,000	By Balance b/d	50,000
To Goodwill written off (20,000 – 12,000)	8,000	By Income from non-trading investments	20,000
To Preliminary expenses written off (6,000 – 4,000)	2,000	By Funds from operations (Bal. fig.)	35,000
To Provision for depreciation (40,000 – 25,000)	15,000		
To Prem. on Redem. of Pref. shares	10,000		
To Balance c/d	60,000		
	1,05,000		1,05,000

Note : (1) Transfer to general reserve, goodwill written off, preliminary expenses written off, and provision for depreciation are all 'Paper Transactions' without any effect on current assets or current liabilities.

(2) Income from non trading investments is a 'Non-operating' income. It will be shown as a 'Non-operating source' of funds in the funds flow statement.

Funds from operations can also be ascertained in the following manner.

STATEMENT SHOWING FUNDS FROM OPERATIONS for the year 2010

Particulars	*Rs.*	*Rs.*
P & L A/c Balance as at the end of 2010		60,000
Add: Items which do not decrease funds from operations, but debited to P & L A/c :		
Premium on redemption of Pref. shares	10,000	
Transfer to general reserve (40,000 – 30,000)	10,000	
Goodwill written off (20,000 – 12,000)	8,000	
Preliminary expenses written off (6,000 – 4,000)	2,000	
Depreciation provision (40,000 – 25,000)	15,000	45,000
		1,05,000
Less: Items which do not increase funds from operations, but credited to P & L A/c :		
Income from non trading investments	20,000	
P & L A/c Balance as on 1-1-2010	50,000	70,000
Funds from operations		35,000

Illustration 18

Chrompton Ltd., has provided the following details relating to its working for the year 2010 and you are required to ascertain 'Funds from operations' for the year :

The opening and closing balances of P & L A/c were Rs. 40,000 and Rs. 60,000 respectively. Profit on sale of Motor car Rs. 8,000 was credited to the P & L A/c whereas it was debited with loss on sale of machinery Rs. 20,000. Preliminary expenses written off Rs. 4,000 goodwill written off 10,000 were also debited to the P & L A/c. Transfers and appropriations shown were :

To the general reserve 15,000 to the debenture sinking fund Rs. 10,000 and dividend proposed Rs. 20,000. Depreciaton on fixed assets charged was Rs. 18,000.

(*B. Com. Agra, Delhi, Bhopal*)

Solution :

ADJUSTED PROFIT AND LOSS ACCOUNT for the year 2010

Particulars	*Rs.*	*Particulars*	*Rs.*
To loss on sale of machinery	20,000	By Balance b/d	40,000
To Preliminary expenses written off	4,000	By Profit on sale of Motor car	8,000
To Goodwill written off	10,000	By Funds from operations	
To Transfer to general reserve	15,000	(Bal. fig)	1,09,000
To Transfer to debenture sinking fund	10,000		
To Proposed dividend	20,000		
To Depreciation on fixed assets	18,000		
To Balance c/d	60,000		
	1,57,000		1,57,000

Note : (1) Goodwill and preliminary expenses written off, transfer to general reserve, debenture sinking fund and depreciation are all 'Paper Transactions' without actually affecting funds.

(2) Proposed dividend is treated as a 'Non operating item'. The 'dividend paid' will be shown in the funds flow statement.

(3) Loss on sale of machinery does not involve any out flow of funds, though a part of the past investment is lost at the time of the sale of asset.

(4) Profit on sale of Motor car is not an 'operating income'. It appears as a part of the sale price in the funds flow statement as a 'non operating' source of funds.

Alternative method of ascertaining funds from operations by preparing a 'statement'

STATEMENT SHOWING FUNDS FROM OPERATIONS for the year 2010

Particulars	*Rs.*	*Rs.*
Profit and Loss Account Balance on 31-12-2010		60,000
Add : Loss on sale of machinery	20,000	
Preliminary expenses written off	4,000	
Goodwill written off	10,000	
Transfer to general reserve	15,000	
Tranfer to debenture sinking fund	10,000	
Proposed dividend	20,000	
Depreciation on fixed assets	18,000	97,000
		1,57,000
Less: Profit on sale of Motor Car	8,000	
Profit and Loss Account Balance on 1-1-2010	40,000	48,000
Funds from operations		1,09,000

(2) Analysis of Transactions

The accounts of an undertaking reflect the effect of many different kinds of transactions but for the purpose of funds statement preparation are grouped into three categories :

(a) Transactions Affecting Current Account only :

If both the aspects of a transaction are affecting current account only, no Flow of Fund takes place. Flow of Fund Statement is related with Working Capital and Working Capital is the result of excess of Current Assets over Current Liabilities.

(*i*) Decrease in both C.A. and C.L. by the same amount.

(*ii*) Increase and decrease in C.A. only by the same amount.

(*iii*) Increase in both C.A. and C.L. by the same amount.

(*iv*) Increase and decrease in C.L. only by the same amount.

In order to understand the rules, we take the following examples :

Transactions	*Journal*		*Category of Accounts*	*Flow of Fund*	*Reason*
(i) Cash paid to Creditors	Creditors	Dr.	C.L.	No	Decrease in C.L.
	Bank	Cr.	C.A.		= Decrease in C.A.
(ii) Cash from Debtors	Bank	Dr.	C.A.	No	Decrease in C.A.
	Debtors	Dr.	C.A.		= Increase in C.A.
(iii) Purchased goods on Credit	Purchase	Dr.	C.A.	No	Increase in C.A.
	Creditors	Cr.	C.L.		= Increase in C.L.
(iv) Bills accepted by us	Creditors	Dr.	C.L.	No	Decrease in C.L.
	Bills Payable	Cr.	C.L.		= Increase in C.L.

(b) Transactions Affecting Current and Non-current Accounts

If a transaction is such that one aspect of it affects current account and its other aspect affects non-current account, there will be effect on Working Capital and Fund will flow.

(*i*) Increase in C.A. and non-current liability.
(*ii*) Decrease in non-current liability and C.A.
(*iii*) Increase in non-current asset and decrease in C.A.
(*iv*) Decrease in non-current asset and increase in C.A.

Example :

Transactions	*Journal*		*Category of Accounts*	*Flow of Fund*	*Reason*
(i) Issue of share for cash	Bank Share Cap.	Dr. Cr.	C.A. N.C.L.	Inflow	
(ii) Redeemed Debenture	Debentures Bank	Dr. Cr.	N.C.L. C.A.	Outflow	One account belongs to current category and the other belongs to Non-current category
(iii) Purchase machine for cash	Machine Bank	Dr. Cr.	N.C.A. C.A.	Outflow	
(iv) Sold building for cash	Bank Building	Dr. Cr.	C.A. N.C.A.	Inflow	

(c) Transactions Affecting Non-current Account only

If there is a transaction which affects non-current accounts only, it is not considered for Flow of Fund. That is, when both aspects of a transaction are non-current, no flow of fund takes place.

Example : Machinery purchased by issuing shares.
Journal : Machinery A/c Dr.
To Share Capital A/c

Here Machinery and Share Capital Accounts are non-current accounts, therefore, they do not affect Flow of Fund, which is based on Current Assets and Current Liabilities.

The following chart illustrates the above points :

Debit / Credit	Current Account	Non-Current Account
Current Account	No Impact	Impact
Non-Current Account	Impact	No Impact

(3) Investments

Investments may be held by a trading concern either as a current asset or as fixed asset. If the investments represent surplus funds temporarily invested in marketable securities, they are to be treated as current assets. If on the other hand, investments are of a permanent nature i.e. trade investments or long term investments, they should be treated as fixed assets. The actual sale proceeds, without considering profit or loss on sale should be taken to the Fund Statement as a Source of Fund and the figure of purchase as Application of Fund.

(4) Provision for Tax

It may be treated either as current liability or non-current liability. If it is treated as current liability tax payment is not regarded as an item of application of Fund and provision for tax is not adjusted to Profit or loss for finding out income from operation. If provision for tax is treated as non-current, payment of tax is treated as application of Fund and it is treated for adjustment of profit or loss.

(5) Proposed Dividend

It can be treated as an item of current liability of non-current liability. As current liability, actual payment of this dividend is not treated as application of Fund. If it is treated as non-current, its actual payment treated as application of fund.

(6) Interim Dividend Paid

It will appear as an application in the Funds Statement and on the debit side of Adjusted Profit and Loss Account. No adjustment is necessary for interim dividend paid if Funds from operation are being determined on the basis of 'net profit for the current year before debit for interim dividend.

Hidden Information

Sometimes the information required for Fund Flow Statement is not directly given in the problem. Often student is faced with a situation where he is not able to locate easily transactions taking place in the business. In such circumstances, it is suggested to prepare Accounts. Follow the steps given below :

1. Find out the amount of Working Capital for the two consecutive years from the respective Balance Sheets and determine the schedule of changes in Working Capital which will result in either a decrease or an increase in Working Capital.
2. Open for all other non-current assets and non-current liabilities accounts by taking their respective opening and closing balances.
3. Consider the adjustment given in the problem one by one.
4. Close the acounts one by one which result either as an item of Source of Funds or an item of Application of Funds or close remaining accounts by transferring to Adjusted Profit and Loss Account.

   To make the above discussions clear, the following illustrations are much helpful. They are self-explanatory.

Illustration 19

From the following Balance Sheets of Prem & Company for the year ended on 31st Dec. 2009 and 2010, prepare a statement showing sources and application of funds and schedule of changes in working capital.

Liabilities	*2009*	*2010*	*Assets*	*2009*	*2010*
	Rs.	*Rs.*		*Rs.*	*Rs.*
Share Capital	4,00,000	5,75,000	Plant	75,000	1,00,000
Creditors	1,06,000	70,000	Stocks	1,21,000	1,36,000
Profit & Loss A/c	14,000	31,000	Debtors	1,81,000	1,70,000
			Cash	1,43,000	2,70,000
	5,20,000	6,76,000		5,20,000	6,76,000

(M.Com. Madras)

Solution :

STATEMENT OF SOURCES AND APPLICATION OF FUNDS
for the year ended 31st December 2010

Sources	*Rs.*	*Application*	*Rs.*
Issue of Shares	1,75,000	Plant purchased	25,000
(Rs. 5,75,000 – Rs. 4,00,000)		(Rs. 1,00,000 – Rs. 75,000)	
Funds from Operation (*)	17,000	Increase in Working Capital	1,67,000
	1,92,000		1,92,000

SCHEDULE OF CHANGES IN WORKING CAPITAL

	2009	*2010*	*Changes in Working Capital*	
			Increase	*Decrease*

	Rs.	Rs.	Rs.	Rs.
Current Assets :				
Stocks	1,21,000	1,36,000	15,000	—
Debtors	1,81,000	1,70,000	—	11,000
Cash	1,43,000	2,70,000	1,27,000	—
	4,45,000	5,76,000		
Current Liabilities :				
Creditors	1,06,000	70,000	36,000	—
	1,06,000	70,000		
Working Capital	3,39,000	5,06,000		
Net increase in working capital	1,67,000	—	—	1,67,000
Total	5,06,000	5,06,000	1,78,000	1,78,000

(*) Adjust Profit and Loss Account

	Rs.		Rs.
To Balance c/d	31,000	By Balance b/d	14,000
		By Funds from Operation	17,000
	31,000		31,000

Illustration 20

From the summarised balance sheets of X Ltd., prepare a statement of sources and uses of funds.

Liabilities	31-3-09 Rs.	31-3-10 Rs.	Assets	31-3-09 Rs.	31-3-10 Rs.
Share capital	90,000	90,000	Gross block	1,55,000	1,56,000
Bank loan	1,19,000	2,10,000	Less:		
Current			Depreciation	7,000	10,000
liabilities	46,000	48,000		1,48,000	1,46,000
			Current assets	40,000	1,00,000
			Profit & Loss a/c	67,000	1,02,000
	2,55,000	3,48,000		2,55,000	3,48,000

(*B.Com. MS, Bharathidasan*)

Solution :

SCHEDULE OF CHANGES IN WORKING CAPITAL

Particulars	31-3-09 Rs.	31-3-10 Rs.	Increase Rs.	Decrease Rs.
Current assets	40,000	1,00,000	60,000	
Less : Current liabilities	46,000	48,000		2,000
Working capital	– 6,000	52,000	60,000	2,000
Increase in working capital	58,000			58,000
	52,000	52,000	60,000	60,000

STATEMENT OF SOURCES AND USES OF FUNDS

Sources	Rs.	Uses	Rs.
Bank loan	91,000	Purchase of fixed assets (increase in	

		gross block)	1,000
		Funds lost in operations (1)	32,000
		Increase in working capital	58,000
	91,000		91,000

Workings :

PROVISION FOR DEPRECIATION ACCOUNT

	Rs.		Rs.
		By balance b/d	7,000
To balance c/d	10,000	By Adjusted profit & loss a/c	3,000
	10,000		10,000

(1) ADJUSTED PROFIT AND LOSS ACCOUNT

	Rs.		Rs.
To balance b/d	67,000		
To Provision for depreciation	3,000		
To Funds lost in operations	32,000	By balance c/d	1,02,000
	1,02,000		1,02,000

Illustration 21

From the following balance sheet prepare a funds flow statement for the year ended 30th June 2010 :

BALANCE SHEET as on 30th June

Liabilities	*2009* Rs.	*2010* Rs.	*Assets*	*2009* Rs.	*2010* Rs.
Share capital	2,00,000	2,50,000	Goodwill	70,000	50,000
Debentures	50,000	1,50,000	Machinery	3,10,000	4,40,000
General reserve	70,000	1,20,000	Investments	30,000	80,000
Profit & Loss a/c	50,000	60,000	Discount on issue		
Depreciation	90,000	1,30,000	of debentures	5,000	–
Creditors	75,000	1,10,000	Bank	20,000	30,000
Bank overdraft	10,000	15,000	Debtors	70,000	1,80,000
			Stock	40,000	55,000
	5,45,000	8,35,000		5,45,000	8,35,000

During the year investments costing Rs. 30,000 were sold for Rs. 27,000. A new machine was bought for Rs. 40,000 and the payment was made in fully paid shares. (*B. Com. MS. Madurai*)

Solution :

SCHEDULE OF CHANGES IN WORKING CAPITAL

Particulars	*30th June 2009* Rs.	*30th June 2010* Rs.	*Increase* Rs.	*Decrease* Rs.
Current assets:				
Bank	20,000	30,000	10,000	–
Debtors	70,000	1,80,000	1,10,000	–
Stock	40,000	55,000	15,000	–
	1,30,000	2,65,000		

Less : Current liabilities:				
Creditors	75,000	1,10,000	–	35,000
Bank overdraft	10,000	15,000	–	5,000
	85,000	1,25,000		
Working capital	45,000	1,40,000	1,35,000	40,000
Increasing in working capital	95,000	–	–	95,000
	1,40,000	1,40,000	1,35,000	1,35,000

FUNDS FLOW STATEMENT for the year ended 30th June 2010

Sources	*Rs.*	*Application*	*Rs.*
Issue of shares for cash	10,000	Purchase of investment	80,000
Issue of debentures	1,00,000	Purchase of machinery	90,000
Sale of investment	27,000	Increase in working capital	95,000
Funds from operations	1,28,000		
	2,65,000		2,65,000

Workings :

MACHINERY ACCOUNT (at cost)

	Rs.		*Rs.*
To balance b/d	3,10,000		
To Share capital	40,000		
(Purchase by issue of shares)			
To Bank	90,000	By balance c/d	4,40,000
	4,40,000		4,40,000

PROVISION FOR DEPRECIATION ON MACHINERY

	Rs.		*Rs.*
		By balance b/d	90,000
		By Adjusted Profit	40,000
To balance c/d	1,30,000	& Loss a/c. (Bal. fig)	
	1,30,000		1,30,000

INVESTMENT ACCOUNT

	Rs.		*Rs.*
To balance b/d	30,000	By Bank (sale)	27,000
To Bank (Bal. fig)	80,000	By Adjusted Profit	
(purchase)		& Loss a/c (loss on sale)	3,000
		By balance c/d	80,000
	1,10,000		1,10,000

DISCOUNT ON ISSUE OF DEBENTURES

	Rs.		*Rs.*
To balance b/d	5,000	By adjusted Profit	
		& Loss a/c (written off)	5,000
	5,000		5,000

GOODWILL ACCOUNT

	Rs.		Rs.
To balance b/d	70,000	By Adjusted Profit & Loss a/c (Bal. fig)	20,000
		By balance c/d	50,000
	70,000		70,000

SHARE CAPITAL ACCOUNT

	Rs.		Rs.
		By balance b/d	2,00,000
To balance c/d	2,50,000	By Machinery* (Issue of shares for machinery)	40,000
		By bank	10,000
	2,50,000		2,50,000

GENERAL RESERVE

	Rs.		Rs.
		By balance b/d	70,000
To balance c/d	1,20,000	By Adjusted Profit & Loss a/c (Bal. fig)	50,000
	1,20,000		1,20,000

ADJUSTED PROFIT AND LOSS ACCOUNT

	Rs.		Rs.
To Provision for depreciation on machinery	40,000	By balance b/d	50,000
		By Funds from operations (Bal. fig)	1,28,000
To Investment (loss)	3,000		
To Discount on issue of debentures	5,000		
To Goodwill (written off)	20,000		
To General reserve	50,000		
To balance c/d	60,000		
	1,78,000		1,78,000

Note : * Issue of shares for purchase of machinery is a transaction concerned with non-current items only. The transaction does not affect working capital. Hence, there is no source or application of funds.

Illustration 22

The following are the summarised Balance Sheets of M/s Krishna Ltd. as on 31st December 2009 and 2010.

Capitals & Liabilities	*2009* Rs.	*2010* Rs.	*Assets*	*2009* Rs.	*2010* Rs.
Capitals :					
10% Preference Shares	1,00,000	1,10,000	Fixed Assets :		
Equity Shares	2,20,000	2,50,000	Machinery	2,00,000	2,30,000

Share Premium	20,000	26,000	Buildings	1,50,000	1,76,000
Profit & Loss	1,04,000	1,34,000	Land	18,000	18,000
12% Debentures	70,000	64,000	Current Assets :		
Current Liabilities :			Cash	42,000	32,000
Creditors	38,000	46,000	Debtors	38,000	38,000
Bills Payable	5,000	4,000	Bills		
Provision for Tax	10,000	12,000	Receivable	42,000	62,000
Dividends Payable	7,000	8,000	Stock	84,000	98,000
	5,74,000	6,54,000		5,74,000	6,54,000

You are required to prepare a Statement of Sources and Application of Funds.

(B.Com. Madras, Lucknow, Jabalpur)

Solution :

FUND FLOW STATEMENT
for the year ended 31st December 2010

Sources	*Rs.*	*Applications*	*Rs.*
Funds from Operations (Rs. 1,34,000 – Rs. 1,04,000)	30,000	Purchase of Machinery (Rs. 2,30,000 – Rs. 2,00,000)	30,000
Issue of 10% Preference Shares (Rs. 1,10,000 – Rs. 1,00,000)	10,000	Purchase of Buildings (Rs. 1,76,000 – Rs. 1,50,000)	26,000
Issue of Equity Shares (Rs. 2,50,000 – Rs. 2,20,000)	30,000	Redemption of Debentures (Rs. 70,000 – Rs. 64,000)	6,000
Share Premium (Rs. 26,000 – Rs. 20,000)	6,000	Increase in Working Capital	14,000
	76,000		76,000

STATEMENT OF CHANGES IN WORKING CAPITAL

Particulars	*2009*	*2010*	*Changes in Working Capital*	
			Increase Dr.	*Decrease Cr.*
	Rs.	*Rs.*	*Rs.*	*Rs.*
Current Assets :				
Cash	42,000	32,000	—	10,000
Debtors	38,000	38,000	—	—
Bills Receivable	42,000	62,000	20,000	—
Stock	84,000	98,000	14,000	—
Total : (A)	2,06,000	2,30,000		
Current Liabilities :				
Creditors	38,000	46,000	—	8,000
Bills Payable	5,000	4,000	1,000	—
Provision for Tax	10,000	12,000	—	2,000
Dividend Payable	7,000	8,000	—	1,000
Total : (B)	60,000	70,000		
Working Capital(A) : (B)	1,46,000	1,60,000		
Increase in Working Capital	14,000	—	—	14,000
	1,60,000	1,60,000	35,000	35,000

Illustration 23

Calculate Funds from Operations from the information given below as on 31st March 2010 :

(*a*) Net Profit for the year ended 31st March, 2010 Rs. 6,50,000.

(*b*) Gain on the sale of buildings Rs. 35,500.

(*c*) Goodwill appears in the books at Rs. 1,80,000 out of that 10% has been written off during the year.

(*d*) Old machinery worth Rs. 8,000 has been sold for Rs. 6,500 during the year.

(*e*) Rs. 1,25,000 have been transferred to Reserve Fund.

(*f*) Depreciation has been provided during the year on machinery and furniture at 20% whose total is Rs. 6,50,000. (*B.Com. M.S.*)

Solution :

CALCULATION OF FUNDS FROM OPERATIONS

	Rs.	*Rs.*
Net profit for the year		6,50,000
Add: Non-fund and non-operating items which have been debited to P & L A/c :		
Goodwill written off	18,000	
Loss on sale of machinery (Rs. 8,000 – 6,500)	1,500	
Transfer to Reserve Fund	1,25,000	
Depreciation @ 20% on Rs. 6,50,000	1,30,000	2,74,500
		9,24,500
Less: Non-fund and non operating items which have been credited to P & L A/c :		
Gain on sale of buildings	35,500	35,500
Fund Form Operation		8,89,000

Alternatively :

ADJUSTED PROFIT AND LOSS ACCOUNT

To Goodwill	18,000	By Opening Balance	—
to Loss on sale of machinery	1,500	By Gain on sale of buildings	35,500
To General Reserve	1,25,000	By Funds from operations (Balancing figure)	8,89,000
To Depreciation	1,30,000		
To Closing Balance	6,50,000		
	9,24,500		9,24,500

Illustration 24

From the following Balance Sheets of a Sole trader, prepare a schedule of changes in working capital and a funds flow statement:

Liabilities	*2009* *Rs.*	*2010* *Rs.*	*Assets*	*2009* *Rs.*	*2010* *Rs.*
Capital	63,000	1,00,000	Cash	15,000	20,000
Long-term Loans	50,000	60,000	Debtors	30,000	28,000
Trade Creditors	42,000	39,000	Stock	55,000	72,000
Bank Overdraft	35,000	25,000	Land and Buildings	80,000	1,00,000

O/S Expenses	5,000	6,000	Furniture	15,000	10,000
	1,95,000	2,30,000		1,95,000	2,30,000

(*B.Com. Madras*)

Solution :

SCHEDULE OF CHANGES IN WORKING CAPITAL

	2009 Rs.	2010 Rs.	Effect of Working Capital Increase Rs.	Decrease Rs.
Current Assets:				
Cash	15,000	20,000	5,000	—
Debtors	30,000	28,000	—	2,000
Stock	55,000	72,000	17,000	—
	1,00,000	1,20,000		
Current Liabilities:				
Trade Creditors	42,000	39,000	3,000	—
Bank Over-draft	35,000	25,000	10,000	
O/S Expenses	5,000	6,000	—	1,000
	82,000	70,000		
Working Capital	18,000	50,000		
Net increase in Working Capital	32,000	—	—	32,000
	50,000	50,000	35,000	35,000

FUND FLOW STATEMENT

Sources	Rs.	*Applications*	Rs.
Raising of Long-term Loans (Rs. 60,000–50,000)	10,000	Purchase of Land and Buildings (Rs. 1,00,000 – 80,000)	20,000
Sale of Furniture (Rs. 15,000 – 10,000)	5,000	Net increase in Working Capital	32,000
Funds from Operations (Rs. 1,00,000 – 63,000)	37,000		
	52,000		52,000

N.B. : In the absence of any other information, in case of individual, the difference between the capitals, at the beginning and at the end, is on account of profit or loss.

Illustration 25

From the following Balance Sheets of a concern, prepare a Fund Flow statement:

Liabilities	*2009* Rs.	*2010* Rs.	*Assets*	*2009* Rs.	*2010* Rs.
Share Capital	60,000	65,000	Goodwill	30,000	25,000
Profit & Loss A/c	34,000	26,000	Plant and Machinery	60,000	50,000
Current Liabilities	12,000	3,000	Current Assets	16,000	19,000
	1,06,000	94,000		1,06,000	94,000

Additional information :

(*a*) Depreciation of Rs. 20,000 on plant and machinery was charged to Profit and Loss Account.

(*b*) Dividends of Rs. 12,000 were paid during the year (*B. Com., Madurai*)

Solution :

SCHEDULE OF CHANGES IN WORKING CAPITAL

	2009 Rs.	2010 Rs.	Changes in Working Capital: Increase Rs.	Decrease Rs.
Current Assets	16,000	19,000	3,000	—
Current Liabilities	12,000	3,000	9,000	—
Working Capital	4,000	16,000		
Net increase in Working Capital	12,000	—	—	12,000
	16,000	16,000	12,000	12,000

FUND FLOW STATEMENT

Sources	*Rs.*	*Applications*	*Rs.*
Issue of Share Capital (Rs. 65,000 – 60,000)	5,000	Purchase of Plant and Machinery	10,000
Funds from operations	29,000	Payment of Dividends	12,000
		Net increase in Working Capital	12,000
	34,000		34,000

PLANT AND MACHINERY ACCOUNT

	Rs.		*Rs.*
To Balance b/d	60,000	By Depreciations	20,000
To Cash (Purchase) (Balancing figure)	10,000	By Balance c/d	50,000
	70,000		70,000

ADJUSTED PROFIT AND LOSS ACCOUNT

	Rs.		*Rs.*
To Depreciations	20,000	By Balance b/d	34,000
To Goodwill	5,000	By Funds from Operations	29,000
To Dividends	12,000		
To Balance c/d	26,000		
	63,000		63,000

Illustration 26

The following are the summarised Balance Sheets of X Ltd. as on 31st December, 2009 and 2010.

Liabilities	*31st December 2009* Rs.	*2010* Rs.	*Assets*	*31st December 2009* Rs.	*2010* Rs.
Redeemable Preference Share	—	10,000	Fixed Assets	41,000	40,000
Equity Shares	40,000	40,000	*Less*: Depreciation	11,000	15,000
				30,000	25,000

General Reserve	2,000	2,000	*Current Assets*:		
Profit & Loss Account	1,000	1,200	Debtors	20,000	24,000
			Stock	30,000	35,000
Debentures	6,000	7,000	Prepaid Expenses	300	500
Current Liabilities:					
Creditors	12,000	11,000	Cash	1,200	3,500
Provision for Tax	3,000	4,200			
Proposed Dividend	5,000	5,800			
Bank Overdraft	12,500	6,800			
	81,500	88,000		81,500	88,000

You are required to prepare:

(*a*) A statement showing changes in the working capital, and

(*b*) A statement of sources and application of funds. (*B.Com. Madras, Delhi*)

Solution :

SCHEDULE OF CHANGES IN WORKING CAPITAL

	2009	*2010*	*Changes in Working Capital*	
			Increase	*Decrease*
	Rs.	*Rs.*	*Rs.*	*Rs.*
Current Assets:				
Debtors	20,000	24,000	4,000	—
Stock	30,000	35,000	5,000	—
Prepaid expenses	300	500	200	—
Cash	1,200	3,500	2,300	—
	51,500	63,000		
Current Liabilities:				
Creditors	12,000	11,000	1,000	—
Provision for Tax	3,000	4,200	—	1,200
Proposed Dividend	5,000	5,800	—	800
Bank Overdraft	12,500	6,800	5,700	
	32,500	27,800		
Working Capital	19,000	35,200		
Increase in Working Capital	16,200	—	—	16,200
	35,200	35,200	18,200	18,200

FUND FLOW STATEMENT
for the year ended 31st December, 2010

Sources	*Rs.*	*Applications*	*Rs.*
Redeemable Preference Share	10,000	Increase in Working Capital	16,200
Issue of Debentures	1,000		
Sale of Fixed Assets	1,000		
Fund from Operations	4,200		
	16,200		16,200

Workings :

FIXED ASSETS A/C

	Rs.		Rs.
To Balance b/d	41,000	By Cash (Sales)	1,000
		By Balance c/d	40,000
	41,000		41,000

PROVISION FOR DEPRECIATION A/C

	Rs.		Rs.
To Balance c/d	15,000	By Balance b/d	11,000
		By Adjusted P & L A/c	4,000
	15,000		15,000

ADJUSTED PROFIT & LOSS A/C

	Rs.		Rs.
To Provision for Debentures	4,000	By Balance b/d	1,000
To Balance c/d	1,200	By Funds from Operations	4,200
	5,200		5,200

Illustration 27

From the following Balance Sheets and additional information given, you are required to calculate funds from operations for the year 2010.

	1-1-2010 Rs.	*31-12-2010* Rs.
Share Capital	1,00,000	1,50,000
General reserves	30,000	30,000
Profit and Loss A/c	20,000	22,000
6% Debentures	80,000	80,000
Creditors	65,000	58,000
Provision for Tax	5,000	10,000
	3,00,000	3,50,000
Land and Buildings	1,00,000	95,000
Plant and Machinery	80,000	90,000
Stocks	70,000	1,10,000
Debtors	20,000	25,000
Investments	—	10,000
Cash	10,000	10,000
Goodwill	20,000	10,000
	3,00,000	3,50,000

Additional information :

1. During 2010, dividends of Rs. 15,000 were paid.
2. Depreciation written off Plant and Machinery amounted to Rs. 6,000 and no depreciation has been charged on land and buildings.
3. Provision for tax made during the year Rs. 5,000.
4. Profit on sale of machinery Rs. 2,000. (*B.Com., Madras*)

Solution :

CALCULATION OF FUNDS FROM OPERATIONS

	Rs.	
Closing balance of P & L A/C given		22,000
Add: Non-fund or non-operating items already debited to P & L A/c :		
Depreciation	6,000	
Dividends	15,000	
Provision for Tax*	5,000	
Goodwill**	10,000	36,000
		58,000
Less: Non-fund or non-operating items already credited to P & L A/c:		
Profit on sale of machinery	2,000	
Opening balance of P & L A/c (given)	20,000	22,000
FUNDS FROM OPERATION:		36,000

*Treated as a non-current liability

**Goodwill written off Rs. 20,000 — Rs. 10,000 = 10,000

Alternatively

ADJUSTED PROFIT AND LOSS ACCOUNT

	Rs.		Rs.
To Depreciation	6,000	By Opening Balance	20,000
To Dividends	15,000	By Profit on sale of Machinery	2,000
To provision for tax	5,000	By Funds from operation	36,000
To Goodwill	10,000	(Balancing figure)	
To Closing Balance	22,000		
	58,000		58,000

Illustration 28

The Balance Sheets of National Co. as on 31st December, 2009 and 31st December 2010 are as follows :

Liabilities & Capital	*2009* Rs.	*2010* Rs.	*Assets*	*2009* Rs.	*2010* Rs.
Share Capital	5,00,000	7,00,000	Land and Buildings	80,000	1,20,000
Profit & Loss	1,00,000	1,60,000	Plant and Machinery	5,00,000	8,00,000
General Reserve	50,000	70,000	Stock	1,00,000	75,000
Sundry Creditors	1,53,000	1,90,000	Debtors	1,50,000	1,60,000
Bills Payable	40,000	50,000	Cash	20,000	20,000
Expenses O/S	7,000	5,000			
	8,50,000	11,75,000		8,50,000	11,75,000

Additional Information :

(1) Rs. 50,000 depreciation has been charged on Plant and Machinery during 2010.

(2) A piece of Machinery was sold for Rs. 8,000 during the year 2010. It had cost Rs. 12,000; depreciation of Rs. 7,000 had been provided on it.

Prepare a Schedule of changes in Working Capital and a Statement showing the Sources and Application of Funds for 2010. *(CA)*

Solution :

SCHEDULE OF CHANGES IN WORKING CAPITAL

Items	*2009* *Rs.*	*2010* *Rs.*	*Changes in Working Capital* *Increase Dr.* *Rs.*	*Decrease Cr.* *Rs.*
Current Assets :				
Stock	1,00,000	75,000	—	25,000
Debtors	1,50,000	1,60,000	10,000	—
Cash	20,000	20,000	—	—
	2,70,000	2,55,000	—	—
Current Liabilities :				
Sundry Creditors	1,53,000	1,90,000	—	37,000
Bills Payable	40,000	50,000	—	10,000
Expenses O/S	7,000	5,000	2,000	—
	2,00,000	2,45,000		
Working Capital	70,000	10,000		
Net decrease in Working Capital		60,000	60,000	
	70,000	70,000	72,000	72,000

STATEMENT OF SOURCE AND APPLICATION OF FUNDS
for the year ended 31st December 2010

Sources	*Rs.*	*Applications*	*Rs.*
Funds from Operations (1)	1,27,000	Purchase of Land and Buildings	40,000
Issue of Shares	2,00,000	Purchase of Plant and Machinery (2)	3,55,000
Sale proceeds of Machinery	8,000		
Decrease in Working Capital	60,000		
	3,95,000		3,95,000

Workings :

(1) ADJUSTED PROFIT AND LOSS ACCOUNT

	Rs.		*Rs.*
To Plant & Machinery A/c (Depreciation of 2010)	50,000	By Balance b/d (Opening Balance)	1,00,000
To General Reserve (Transferred during 2010)	20,000	By Profit & Machinery (Profit on sale)	3,000
To Balance c/d	1,60,000	By Funds from Operation (Balancing figure)	1,27,000
	2,30,000		2,30,000

(2) PLANT AND MACHINERY ACCOUNT

	Rs.		*Rs.*
To Balance b/d	5,00,000	By Bank (Sale of Machinery)	8,000
To Profit & Loss A/c (profit on sale)	3,000	By Profit & Loss A/c (Depreciation)	50,000

To Bank A/c (Purchase of Machinery & Plant (Balancing figure)	3,55,000	By Balance c/d	8,00,000
	8,58,000		8,58,000

Illustration 29

From the following Balance Sheets of X Ltd. make out : (*i*) Statement of Changes in Working Capital (*ii*) Fund Flow Statement :

BALANCE SHEETS

Liabilities	*Dec. 2009* *Rs.*	*Dec. 2010* *Rs.*	*Assets*	*Dec. 2009* *Rs.*	*Dec. 2010* *Rs.*
Equity Share Capital	3,00,000	4,00,000	Goodwill	1,15,000	90,000
Redeemable Preference Share Capital	1,50,000	1,00,000	Land & Buildings	2,00,000	1,70,000
			Plant	80,000	2,00,000
General Reserve	40,000	70,000	Debtors	1,60,000	2,00,000
Profit & Loss	30,000	48,000	Stock	77,000	1,09,000
Proposed Dividend	42,000	50,000	Bills Receivable	20,000	30,000
Creditors	55,000	83,000	Cash in hand	15,000	10,000
Bills Payable	20,000	16,000	Cash at Bank	10,000	8,000
Provision for Taxation	40,000	50,000			
	6,77,000	8,17,000		6,77,000	8,17,000

Additional Information :

(1) Depreciation of Rs. 10,000 and Rs. 20,000 have been charged on Plant and Land and Buildings respectively in 2010.

(2) A dividend of Rs. 20,000 has been paid in 2010.

(3) Income-tax of Rs. 35,000 has been paid during 2010. (*B.Com. Hons. Delhi*)

Solution :

STATEMENT OF CHANGES IN WORKING CAPITAL

	2009	*2010*	*Changes in Working Capital* *Increase* *Dr.*	*Decrease* *Cr.*
	Rs.	*Rs.*	*Rs.*	*Rs.*
Current Assets :				
Debtors	1,60,000	2,00,000	40,000	—
Stock	77,000	1,09,000	32,000	—
Bills Receivable	20,000	30,000	10,000	—
Cash in hand	15,000	10,000	—	5,000
Cash at Bank	10,000	8,000	—	2,000
	2,82,000	3,57,000		
Current Liabilities :				
Creditors	55,000	83,000	—	28,000
Bills Payable	20,000	16,000	4,000	
	75,000	99,000		
Working Capital	2,07,000	2,58,000		

Increase in Working Capital	51,000	—	—	51,000
	2,58,000	2,58,000	86,000	86,000

FUND FLOW STATEMENT

Sources of Fund	*Rs.*	*Application of Fund*	*Rs.*
Fund from Operation (c)	1,76,000	Purchase of Plant (a)	1,30,000
Issue of Equity Shares	1,00,000	Redemption of Preference Shares	50,000
Sale of Land and Buildings (b)	10,000	Payment of Dividend	20,000
		Payment of Income Tax	35,000
		Increase in Working Capital	51,000
	2,86,000		2,86,000

Workings :

(a) PLANT ACCOUNT

	Rs.		*Rs.*
To Balance b/d	80,000	By Profit & Loss A/c (Depreciation)	10,000
To Bank (Purchase of Plant) (Balancing figure)	1,30,000	By Balance c/d	2,00,000
	2,10,000		2,10,000

(b) LAND AND BUILDING ACCOUNT

	Rs.		*Rs.*
To Balance b/d	2,00,000	By Profit & Loss A/c (Depreciation)	20,000
		By Bank (Sale of Land & Buildings)	10,000
		By Balance c/d	1,70,000
	2,00,000		2,00,000

(c) ADJUSTED PROFIT AND LOSS ACCOUNT

	Rs.		*Rs.*
To General Reserve	30,000	By Balance b/d	30,000
To Dividend (d)	28,000	By Funds from Operations	1,76,000
To Provision for Taxation(e)	45,000		
To Goodwill	25,000		
To Depreciation :			
Plant	10,000		
Land	20,000		
To Balance c/d	48,000		
	2,06,000		2,06,000

(d) PROPOSED DIVIDEND ACCOUNT

	Rs.		*Rs.*
To Bank A/c	20,000	By Balance b/d	42,000
To Balance c/d	50,000	By Profit & Loss A/c	

		(Balancing figure)	28,000
	70,000		70,000

(e) PROVISION FOR TAXATION ACCOUNT

	Rs.		Rs.
To Bank A/c	35,000	By Balance b/d	40,000
To Balance c/d	50,000	By Profit & Loss A/c	
		(Balancing figure)	45,000
	85,000		85,000

Illustration 30

The following are the summarised Balance Sheets of AB Ltd., on 31-12-2009 and 31-12-2010.

BALANCE SHEETS

Liabilities	*2009* Rs.	*2010* Rs.	*Assets*	*2009* Rs.	*2010* Rs.
Share capital	12,00,000	16,00,000	*Assets :*		
Debentures	4,00,000	6,00,000	Plant & Machinery		
P & L A/c	2,50,000	5,00,000	(at cost)	8,00,000	12,90,000
Creditors	2,30,000	1,80,000	Land & Building		
Provision for :			(at cost)	6,00,000	8,00,000
Bad & Doubtful			Stock	6,00,000	7,00,000
debts	12,000	6,000	Bank	40,000	80,000
Depreciation on			Preliminary exp.	14,000	80,000
land and building	40,000	48,000	Debtors	1,38,000	1,22,000
Depreciation on					
Plant & Machinery	60,000	70,000			
	21,92,000	30,04,000		21,92,000	30,04,000

Additional Information :

(*i*) During the year, a part of the machinery, costing Rs. 1,40,000 (accumulated depreciation thereon Rs. 40,000) was sold for Rs. 1,02,000.

(*ii*) Dividend of Rs. 1,00,000 was paid during the year.

Ascertain :

(1) Changes in working capital for 2010.

(2) Funds Flow Statement for 2010. (*B. Com. Andhra, Jabalpur, Chennai, Delhi*)

Solution :

(1) SCHEDULE OF CHANGES IN WORKING CAPITAL for 2010

Particulars	*2009* Rs.	*2010* Rs.	*Changes in working capital* *Increase* Rs.	*Decrease* Rs.
Current Assets :				
Stock	6,00,000	7,00,000	1,00,000	–
Bank	40,000	80,000	40,000	–
Debtors	1,38,000	1,22,000	–	16,000
Total (A)	7,78,000	9,02,000		
Current Liabilities :				
Creditors	2,30,000	1,80,000	50,000	–

Provision for bad and doubtful debts	12,000	6,000	6,000	–
Total (B)	2,42,000	1,86,000		
Working capital (A – B)	5,36,000	7,16,000		
Increase in working capital	1,80,000	–	–	1,80,000
	7,16,000	7,16,000	1,96,000	1,96,000

Note : Provision for bad and doubtful debts is also treated as a current liability, though it could have been reduced from debtors.

(2) FUNDS FLOW STATEMENT for 2010

Particulars	*Rs.*	*Rs.*
Sources of Funds:		
Issue of shares (16,00,000 – 12,00,000)	4,00,000	
Issue of debentures (6,00,000 – 4,00,000)	2,00,000	
Sale of machinery	1,02,000	
Funds from operations (1)	4,08,000	
Total Sources (A)		11,10,000
Application of funds :		
Purchase of buildings (8,00,000 – 6,00,000)	2,00,000	
Plant purchased (2)	6,30,000	
Divident paid	1,00,000	
Total Applications (B)		9,30,000
Increase in working capital (A – B)		1,80,000

Working :

(1) Adjusted Profit and Loss Account

Particulars	*Rs.*	*Particulars*	*Rs.*
To Depreciataion on :		By Balance b/d	2,50,000
Land & Building (48,000 – 40,000)	8,000	By Profit on sale of Machinery (4)	2,000
Plant & Machinery (3)	50,000		
To Preliminary expenses written off (14,000 – 12,000)	2,000	By Funds from operations (Bal. fig)	4,08,000
To Dividend	1,00,000		
To Balance c/d	5,00,000		
	6,60,000		6,60,000

Note : Dividend provided is paid off. So, it does not appear in the Balance Sheet.

(2) Plant & Machinery Account (at cost)

Particulars	*Rs.*	*Particulars*	*Rs.*
To Balance b/d	8,00,000	By Plant Disposal A/c (sale)	1,40,000
To Bank (Bal. fig.)	6,30,000	By Balance c/d	12,90,000
	14,30,000		14,30,000

(3) PROVISION FOR DEPRECIATION ON PLANT & MACHINERY A/c

Particulars	*Rs.*	*Particulars*	*Rs.*
To Plant Disposal A/c (Depreciaton on machind sold)	40,000	By Balance b/d	60,000
To Balance c/d	70,000	By P & L A/c (Bal. fig.) (current years' depreciation)	50,000
	1,10,000		1,10,000

(4) PLANT DISPOSAL A/c

Particulars	*Rs.*	*Particulars*	*Rs.*
To Plant & Machinery A/c (transfer)	1,40,000	By Provision for Depreciation A/c (Transfer)	40,000
To P & L A/c (profit on sale)	2,000	By Bank (sale)	1,02,000
	1,42,000		1,42,000

Note : Instead of opening plant disposal A/c, the sale and profit on sale and can also be shown in the Plant and Machinery A/c itself.

Illustration 31

Balance Sheets of Harison for the year ended 31st Dec. are given below :

Rs. in thousands

	2009 *Rs.*	*2010* *Rs.*		*2009* *Rs.*	*2010* *Rs.*
Share capital	720	840	Fixed assets	1,200	1,440
General reserve	240	300	*Less* : Accumulated depreciation	240	300
Capital reserve	–	12			
Profit & Loss a/c	120	240	Net fixed assets	960	1,140
7% Debentures	360	240			
Creditors for expenses	12	14.4	Investment at cost	216	216
Creditors for goods	192	300	Inventory cost	240	324
			Sundry debtors less provision	270	294
Proposed dividend	36	42	Bills receivable	48	78
Provision for tax	84	90	Prepayment of expenses	12	14.4
			Mis. expenses	18	12
	1,764	2,078.4		1,764	2,078.4

1. During the year 2010, fixed assets, written down value Rs. 12,000 (Depreciation written off Rs. 36,000) were sold for Rs. 9,600.
2. The proposed dividend of last year was paid in 2010.
3. During the year 2010, investments costing Rs. 96,000 were sold and later in the year, investments of the same cost were purchase.
4. Debentures were redeemed at a premium of 10% in 2010.
5. Liability for taxation for 2009 came to Rs. 66,000.
6. During the year 2010, bad debts Rs. 18,000 were written off against the provision account. Prepare Funds Flow Statement. *(B. Com., Madras)*

Solution :

SCHEDULE OF CHANGES IN WORKING CAPITAL

	2009 Rs.	*2010* Rs.	*Increase* Rs.	*Decrease* Rs.
Current assets :				
Inventories	2,40,000	3,24,000	84,000	–
Debtors	2,70,000	2,94,000	24,000	–
Prepaid expenses	12,000	14,400	2,400	–
Bills receivable	48,000	78,000	30,000	–
	5,70,000	7,10,000		
Less: Current liabilities :				
Creditors for expenses	12,000	14,400	–	2,400
Creditors for goods	1,92,000	3,00,000	–	1,08,000
	2,04,000	3,14,000		
Working capital	3,66,000	3,96,000	1,40,400	1,10,400
Increase in working capital	30,000	–	–	30,000
	3,96,000	3,96,000	1,40,000	1,40,000

FUNDS FLOW STATEMENT

Sources	*Rs.*	*Application*	*Rs.*
Issue of shares	1,20,000	Redemption of debentures	1,32,000
Sale of fixed assets	9,600		
Sale of investments	1,08,000	Fixed assets purchased	2,88,000
Funds from operations	4,10,400	Tax paid	66,000
		Proposed dividend (2009) paid	36,000
		Investment purchased	96,000
		Increase in working capital	30,000
	6,48,000		6,48,000

Workings :

FIXED ASSETS ACCOUNT (at cost)

	Rs.		*Rs.*
To balance b/d	12,00,000	By Provision for depreciation	36,000
To Cash (purchase) (Bal. fig.)	2,88,000	By Cash (sale)	9,600
		By Adjusted Profit and Loss a/c (loss on sale)	2,400
		By balance c/d	14,40,000
	14,88,000		14,88,000

PROVISION FOR DEPRECIATION ACCOUNT

	Rs.		*Rs.*
To Fixed assets (depreciation on asset sold)	36,000	By balance b/d	2,40,000
To balance c/d	3,00,000	By Adjusted Profit & Loss a/c (Bal. fig.)	96,000
	3,36,000		3,36,000

INVESTMENT ACCOUNT

	Rs.		Rs.
To balance b/d	2,16,000	By Cash (sale)	1,08,000
To Cash (purchases)	96,000	(Bal. fig.)	
To Capital reserve (profit on sale)	12,000	By balance c/d	2,16,000
	3,24,000		3,24,000

PROVISION FOR TAXATION ACCOUNT

	Rs.		Rs.
To Cash (tax paid)	66,000	By balance b/d	84,000
To balance c/d	90,000	By Adjusted Profit and Loss a/c (Bal. fig.)	72,000
	1,56,000		1,56,000

PROPOSED DIVIDEND

	Rs.		Rs.
To Cash	36,000	By balance b/d	36,000
To balance c/d	42,000	By Adjusted Profit & Loss a/c (Bal. fig.)	42,000
	78,000		78,000

7% DEBENTURES ACCOUNT

	Rs.		Rs.
To Cash (redemption)	1,32,000	By balance b/d	3,60,000
To balance c/d	2,40,000	By Adjusted Profit and Loss a/c	12,000
	3,72,000	(Bal. fig.)	3,72,000

* Premium on redemption = 10% on Rs. 1,20,000 = Rs. 12,000

ADJUSTED PROFIT AND LOSS ACCOUNT

	Rs.		Rs.
To Fixed assets (loss on sale)	2,400	By balance b/d	1,20,000
To Provision for depreciation	96,000	By Funds from operations (Bal. fig.)	4,10,400
To Provision for taxation	72,000		
To General reserve	60,000		
To Debentures (loss on redemption)	12,000		
To Proposed dividend	42,000		
To Miscellaneous expenses written off	6,000		
To balance c/d	2,40,000		
	5,30,400		5,30,400

Notes : (1) Bad debts is written off against provision account. Hence it is not debited to adjusted P & L A/c.

(2) There is no opening balance of capital reserve. The closing balance represents profit on sale of investments.

Illustration 32

The Balance Sheets of Moon Limited for the year ended 31st December 2009 and 2010 are as follows :

Liabilities	*2009* Rs.	*2010* Rs.	*Assets*	*2009* Rs.	*2010* Rs.
Share capital	80,000	1,20,000	Freehold		
Share premium	8,000	12,000	premises	55,400	1,13,200
General reserve	6,000	9,000	Plant & Machinery	35,600	51,300
Profit & Loss account	19,500	20,800	Furniture & Fixtures	2,400	1,500
5% Debentures	–	26,000			
Income tax			Stock	22,100	26,000
Provision	9,800	10,900	Debtors	36,500	39,100
Creditors	33,500	36,400	Bank	4,800	4,000
	1,56,800	2,35,100		1,56,800	2,35,100

Depreciation written off during the year 2010 was as under :

Plant & Machinery – Rs. 12,800

Furniture & Fixtures – Rs. 400

Prepare a Statement of Sources and Uses of Funds. (*M.C.A., B.Com., Madurai, MS*)

Solution :

SCHEDULE OF CHANGES IN WORKING CAPITAL

Particulars	*2009* Rs.	*2010* Rs.	*Increase* Rs.	*Decrease* Rs.
Current assets :				
Stock	22,100	26,000	3,900	–
Debtors	36,500	39,100	2,600	–
Bank Balance	4,800	4,000	–	800
	63,400	69,100		
Less : Current Liabilities :				
Creditors	33,500	36,400	–	2,900
Income-tax provision	9,800	10,900	–	1,100
	43,300	47,300		
Working capital	20,100	21,800	6,500	4,800
Increase in working capital	1,700	–	–	1,700
	21,800	21,800	6,500	6,500

STATEMENT OF SOURCES AND USES OF FUNDS

Sources	*Rs.*	*Uses*	*Rs.*
Issue of shares	40,000	Purchase of freehold premises	57,800
Share premium	4,000	Purchase of plant and machinery	28,500
Issue of debentures	26,000	Increase in working capital	1,700
Sale of furniture and fixtures	500		
Funds from operations	17,500		
	88,000		88,000

Workings :

PLANT & MACHINERY ACCOUNT

	Rs.		Rs.
To balance b/d	35,600	By Adjusted Profit & Loss a/c	
To Cash (purchase)	28,500	(depreciation)	12,800
(Bal. fig.)		By balance c/d	51,300
	64,100		64,100

FURNITURE AND FIXTURES ACCOUNT

	Rs.		Rs.
To balance b/d	2,400	By Adjusted Profit & Loss a/c	
		(depreciation)	400
		By Cash (sale) (Bal. fig)	500
		By balance c/d	1,500
	2,400		2,400

GENERAL RESERVE ACCOUNT

	Rs.		Rs.
		By balance b/d	6,000
To balance c/d	9,000	By Adjusted Profit & Loss a/c	
		(Bal. fig.)	3,000
	9,000		9,000

ADJUSTED PROFIT & LOSS ACCOUNT

	Rs.		Rs.
To Plant & Machinery		By balance b/d	19,500
(depreciation)	12,800	By Funds from operations	
To Furniture & Fixtures (depn)	400	(Bal. fig.)	17,500
To General reserve	3,000		
To balance c/d	20,800		
	37,000		37,000

Illustration 33

From the following balances as at 31st March, 2009 and 2010, prepare funds flow statement.

Liabilities	*2009* Rs.	*2010* Rs.
Share capital	2,00,000	3,00,000
Share premium	–	10,000
Capital reserve – Profit on redemption of debentures	–	1,000
Profit and Loss account :		
Balance b/f.	40,000	40,000
Profit for the year	–	45,000
5% Debentures	1,00,000	75,000
Sundry creditors	60,000	1,04,000
Taxation account	20,000	5,000
Proposed dividend	10,000	10,000
	4,30,000	5,90,000

Assets		*Rs.*		*Rs.*
Buildings at cost		1,50,000		2,30,000
Plant & Machinery at cost	2,60,000		3,20,000	
Less : Depreciation	85,000		95,000	
		1,75,000		2,25,000
Shares in subsidiary company		20,000		20,000
Stock		45,000		49,000
Sundry debtors		15,000		18,000
Bank		25,000		48,000
		4,30,000		5,90,000

During the year, plant costing Rs. 15,000 (accumulated depreciation thereon Rs. 8,000) was sold for Rs. 5,000, the loss on sale being charged to profit and loss account.

(*B. Com. Sangar, Madras, MS*)

Solution :

SCHEDULE OF CHANGES IN WORKING CAPITAL

Particulars	*31.3.2009* *Rs.*	*31.3.2010* *Rs.*	*Increase* *Rs.*	*Decrease* *Rs.*
Current assets :				
Stock	45,000	49,000	4,000	–
Sundry debtors	15,000	18,000	3,000	–
Bank	25,000	48,000	23,000	–
	85,000	1,15,000		
Less : Current liabilities :				
Sundry Creditors	60,000	1,04,000	–	44,000
Taxation	20,000	5,000	15,000	–
Proposed dividend	10,000	10,000	–	–
	90,000	1,19,000		
Working capital	– 5,000	– 4,000	45,000	44,000
Increase in working capital	+ 1,000			1,000
	– 4,000	– 4,000	45,000	45,000

FUNDS FLOW STATEMENT

Sources	*Rs.*	*Application*	*Rs.*
Issue of shares	1,00,000	Purchase of building	80,000
Share premium	10,000	Purchase of Plant & Machinery	75,000
Sale of Plant & Machinery	5,000	Redemption of debentures	24,000
Funds from operations	65,000	Increase in working capital	1,000
	1,80,000		1,80,000

Working :

DEBENTURES ACCOUNT

	Rs.		*Rs.*
To Cash (Bal. fig.)	24,000	By balance b/d	1,00,000
To Capital reserve (profit on redemption)	1,000		
To balance c/d	75,000		
	1,00,000		1,00,000

PLANT AND MACHINERY ACCOUNT

	Rs.		Rs.
To balance b/d	2,60,000	By Cash (sale)	5,000
To Cash (Bal. fig.)	75,000	By provision for depreciation (depreciation on plant sold)	8,000
		By Adjusted Profit & Loss a/c (loss on sale) (1)	2,000
		By balanced c/d	3,20,000
	3,35,000		3,35,000

PROVISION FOR DEPRECIATION ACCOUNT

	Rs.		Rs.
To Plant & Machinery a/c (depreciation on plant sold)	8,000	By balance b/d	85,000
To balance c/d	95,000	By Adjusted Profit & Loss a/c (current year's provision) (Bal. fig.)	18,000
	1,03,000		1,03,000

1. LOSS ON SALE OF PLANT

	Rs.
Cost of plant sold	15,000
Less : Accumulated depreciation	8,000
Book value	7,000
Sale price	5,000
Loss on sale	2,000

ADJUSTED PROFIT AND LOSS ACCOUNT

	Rs.		Rs.
To Plant & Machinery a/c (Loss on sale)	2,000	By balance b/d	40,000
To Provision for depreciation	18,000	By Funds from operations (Bal. fig.)	65,000
To balance c/d (2)	85,000		
	1,05,000		1,05,000

(2) Closing balance = Opening balance + Current year's profit
= 40,000 + 45,000 = Rs. 85,000

Illustration 34

The following are the summarised balance sheets of a company, as at 31st March, 2009 and 2010.

31.03.2009

Liabilities	Rs.	*Assets*	Rs.
Share capital	4,50,000	Fixed assets	4,00,000
General reserve	3,00,000	Investments	50,000
Profit and Loss a/c	56,000	Stock	2,40,000
Sundry creditors	1,68,000	Sundry debtors	2,10,000
Provision for taxation	75,000	Bank	1,49,000
	10,49,000		10,49,000

31.03.2010

Liabilities	Rs.	Assets	Rs.
Share capital	4,50,000	Fixed assets	3,20,000
General reserve	3,10,000	Investments	60,000
Profit and Loss A/c	68,000	Stock	2,10,000
Mortgage loan	2,70,000	Sundry debtors	4,55,000
Sundry creditors	1,34,000	Bank	1,97,000
Provision for taxation	10,000		
	12,42,000		12,42,000

Additional Information :

1. Investments costing Rs. 8,000 were sold during the year for Rs. 8,500 and further investments were purchased during the year for Rs. 18,000.
2. The net profit for the year was Rs. 62,000 after charging depreciation on fixed assets Rs. 70,000 and provision for taxation Rs. 10,000.
3. During the year part of fixed assets costing Rs. 10,000 was disposed for Rs. 12,000 and the profit is included in the profit and loss account.
4. Dividend paid during the year amounted to 40,000.

Prepare a statement of sources and application of funds for the year ended 31st March, 2010. (*M. Com., Bharathiar Mysore, Jabalpur, Bharathidasan*)

Solution :

SCHEDULE OF CHANGES IN WORKING CAPITAL

Particulars	31.03.2009 Rs.	31.03.2010 Rs.	Increase Rs.	Decrease Rs.
Current assets :				
Stock	2,40,000	2,10,000		30,000
Sundry debtors	2,10,000	4,55,000	2,45,000	–
Bank	1,49,000	1,97,000	48,000	–
	5,99,000	8,62,000		
Less : Current Liability :				
Sundry Creditors	1,68,000	1,34,000	34,000	
Working capital	4,31,000	7,28,000	3,27,000	30,000
Increase in working capital;	2,97,000	–	–	2,97,000
	7,28,000	7,28,000	3,27,000	3,27,000

FUNDS FLOW STATEMENT

Sources	Rs.	Application	Rs.
Sale of fixed assets	12,000	Purchase of investments	18,000
Sale of investments	8,500	Payment of tax	75,000
Mortgage loan rasied	2,70,000	Payment of dividend	40,000
Funds from operations	1,39,500	Increase in working capital	2,97,000
	4,30,000		4,30,000

Working :

FIXED ASSETS ACCOUNT

	Rs.		Rs.
To balance b/d	4,00,000	By Adjusted Profit & Loss a/c (depreciation)	70,000
To Adjusted Profit & Loss a/c (profit on sale)	2,000	By cash (sale)	12,000
		By balance c/d	3,20,000
	4,02,000		4,02,000

INVESTMENT ACCOUNT

	Rs.		Rs.
To balance b/d	50,000	By Cash (sale)	8,500
To Adjusted Profit and Loss a/c (profit on sale)	500		
To Cash (purchase)	18,000	By balance c/d	60,000
	68,500		68,500

PROVISION FOR TAXATION ACCOUNT

	Rs.		Rs.
To Cash (tax paid) (Bal. fig.)	75,000	By balance b/d	75,000
To balance c/d	10,000	By Adjusted Profit and Loss a/c (current year's provision)	10,000
	85,000		85,000

ADJUSTED PROFIT AND LOSS ACCOUNT

	Rs.		Rs.
To Fixed assets (depreciation)	70,000	By balance c/d	56,000
To General reserve	10,000	By Fixed assets (profit on sale)	2,000
To Provision for tax	10,000	By Investments (profit on sale)	500
To dividend	40,000	By Funds from operation (Bal. fig.)	1,39,500
To balance c/d	68,000		
	1,98,500		1,98,000

Illustration 35

From the following Balance Sheet of X Co. Ltd. Prepare a Statement of Changes in Working Capital and the Funds Flow Statement for the year ended 31st March, 2010.

BALANCE SHEETS as on 31st March

Liabilities	*2009* Rs.	*2010* Rs.	*Assets*	*2009* Rs.	*2010* Rs.
Share Capital	3,00,000	3,50,000	Goodwill	1,00,000	80,000
Debentures	1,50,000	2,50,000	Machinery	4,10,000	5,40,000
General Reserve	1,00,000	1,50,000	Investment	30,000	80,000
Profit & Loss	60,000	70,000	Discount on Issue of Debentures	5,000	—
Provision for Depreciation on Machinery	90,000	1,30,000	Cash at Bank	1,20,000	1,30,000
Sundry Creditors	75,000	1,10,000	Sundry Debtor	80,000	1,90,000
Bills Payable	10,000	15,000	Stock	40,000	55,000
	7,85,000	10,75,000		7,85,000	10,75,000

During the year investment costing Rs. 30,000 were sold for Rs. 28,000. A new machine was purchased for Rs. 45,000 and the payment was made in fully paid shares. (*M.Com., Bombay*)

Solution :

STATEMENT OF CHANGES IN WORKING CAPITAL

Items	31st March 2009	31st March 2010	Changes in Working Capital	
			Increase Dr.	Decrease Cr.
	Rs.	Rs.	Rs.	Rs.
Current Assets :				
Cash at Bank	1,20,000	1,30,000	10,000	—
Sundry Debtors	80,000	1,90,000	1,10,000	—
Stock	40,000	55,000	15,000	—
	2.40,000	3,75,000		
Current Liabilities :				
Sundry Creditors	75,000	1,10,000	—	35,000
Bills Payable	10,000	15,000	—	5,000
	85,000	1,25,000		
Working Capital :	1,55,000	2,50,000		
Net Increase in Working Capital	95,000	—		95,000
	2,50,000	2,50,000	1,35,000	1,35,000

FUND FLOW STATEMENT
for the year ended 31st March, 2010

Sources	Rs.	*Applications*	Rs.
Funds from Operations (3)	1,27,000	Purchase of Machinery (1)	85,000
Issue of Share Capital (5)	5,000	Purchase of Investments (2)	80,000
From Debentures (Rs. 2,50,000 — Rs. 1,50,000)	1,00,000	Increase in Working Capital	95,000
Sale of Investments	28,000		
	2,60,000		2,60,00

Workings :

(1) MACHINERY ACCOUNT

	Rs.		Rs.
To Balance b/d	4,10,000	By Balance c/d	5,40,000
To Share Capital A/c	45,000		
To Bank (Purchase of Machinery) (Balancing figure)	85,000		
	5,40,000		5,40,000

(2) INVESTMENT ACCOUNT

	Rs.		Rs.
To Balance b/d	30,000	By Bank (Sale)	28,000
To Bank (Purchase of Investment) (Balancing figure)	80,000	By Profit & Loss (Loss on Sale)	2,000
		By Balance c/d	80,000
	1,10,000		1,10,000

(3) ADJUSTED PROFIT AND LOSS ACCOUNT

	Rs.		Rs.
To General Reserve	50,000	By Balance b/d	60,000
To Provision for Depreciation (4)	40,000	By Funds from Operations	1,27,000
To Goodwill (Rs. 1,00,000 — Rs. 80,000)	20,000		
To Discount on Issue of Debentures	5,000		
To Investment (Loss)	2,000		
To Balance c/d	70,000		
	1,87,000		1,87,000

(4) PROVISION FOR DEPRECIATION ON MACHINERY ACCOUNT

	Rs.		Rs.
To Balance c/d	1,30,000	By Balance b/d	90,000
		By Profit & Loss	40,000
	1,30,000		1,30,000

(5) SHARE CAPITAL ACCOUNT

	Rs.		Rs.
To Balance c/d	3,50,000	By Balance b/d	3,00,000
		By Machinery	45,000
		By Bank	5,000
	3,50,000		3,50,000

Illustration 36

The following are the summarised Balance Sheets of a company as on 31st December 2009 and 2010 :

Liabilities	*31-12-2009* Rs.	*31-12-2010* Rs.
Equity Share Capital	2,00,000	2,40,000
8% Debentures	50,000	—
Share Premium	—	10,000
General Reserve	30,000	50,000
Profit & Loss Account	48,000	68,000
Sundry Creditors	1,30,000	1,50,000
Proposed Dividend	20,000	24,000
Provision for Depreciation:		
Plant & Machinery	1,40,000	1,50,000
Furniture	6,000	4,000
	6,24,000	6,96,000
Assets		
Land and Buildings	1,05,000	1,50,000
Plant and Machinery (at cost)	2,90,000	3,20,000
Furniture (at cost)	9,000	10,000
Inventories	1,30,000	1,05,000
Sundry Debtors	75,000	85,000
Cash	15,000	26,000
	6,24,000	6,96,000

Additional information is as follows :

(1) Furniture which cost Rs. 5,000, written down value Rs. 1,000 was sold during the year 2010 for Rs. 2,000

(2) Plant and Machinery which cost Rs. 20,000 and in respect of which Rs. 13,000 had been written off as depreciation was sold during the year for Rs. 3,000

(3) The dividend of 2009 was paid during 2010

You are required to prepare (*a*) a Statement of changes in working capital during 2010 and (*b*) Funds flow statement for the year 2010. (*M.Com., Madras*)

Solution :

STATEMENT OF CHANGES IN WORKING CAPITAL

	2009	*2010*	*Effect on Working Capital*	
			Increase	*Decrease*
	Rs.	*Rs.*	*Rs.*	*Rs.*
Current Assets :				
Cash	15,000	26,000	11,000	—
Sundry Debtors	75,000	85,000	10,000	—
Inventories	1,30,000	1,05,000	—	25,000
	2,20,000	2,16,000		
Current Liabilities :				
Sundry Creditors	1,30,000	1,50,000	—	20,000
	1,30,000	1,50,000		
Working Capital	90,000	66,000		
Net decrease in Working Capital	—	24,000	24,000	—
	90,000	90,000	45,000	45,000

FUNDS FLOW STATEMENT
for the year ended 31st December 2010

Sources	*Rs.*	*Applications*	*Rs.*
Issue of Share Capital	40,000	Redemption of Debentures	50,000
Share Premium	10,000	Purchase of Land & Buildings	45,000
Sale of Furniture	2,000	Purchase of Plant and Machinery	50,000
Sale of Plant and Machinery	3,000	Purchase of Furniture	6,000
Funds from Operations	92,000	Dividend paid for 2009	20,000
Net decrease in working capital	24,000		
	1,71,000		1,71,000

Workings:

PROVISION FOR DEPRECIATION ON PLANT & MACHINERY

	Rs.		*Rs.*
To Plant & Machinery (on sold machinery)	13,000	By Balance b/d	1,40,000
To Balance c/d	1,50,000	By Adjusted P & L A/c (Depreciation provided during the year) (Balancing figure)	23,000
	1,63,000		1,63,000

PLANT AND MACHINERY ACCOUNT

	Rs.		Rs.
To Balance b/d	2,90,000	By Cash (Sales)	3,000
To Cash (Purchase) (Balancing figure)	50,000	By Provision for Depreciation on Plant and Machinery	13,000
		By Adjusted P & L A/c (Loss on sale)	4,000
		By Balance c/d	3,20,000
	3,40,000		3,40,000

PROVISION FOR DEPRECIATION ON FURNITURE A/C

	Rs.		Rs.
To Furniture A/c (Depreciation on furniture sold)	4,000	By Balance b/d	6,000
To Balance c/d	4,000	By Adjusted P & L A/c (Balancing figure)	2,00
	8,000		8,000

FURNITURE ACCOUNT

	Rs.		Rs.
To Balance b/d	9,000	By Cash (Sales)	2,000
To Adjusted P & L A/c (Profit on sale)	1,000	By provisions for depreciation	4,000
To Cash (Purchase)	6,000	By Balance c/d	10,000
	16,000		16,000

ADJUSTED PROFIT & LOSS ACCOUNT

	Rs.		Rs.
To Transfer to General Reserve	20,000	By Balance b/d	48,000
To Proposed Dividend (2010)	24,000	By Profit on sale of furniture	1,000
To Provision for Depreciation : Plant & Machinery	23,000	By Funds from Operations	92,000
Furniture	2,000		
To Loss on sale of plant	4,000		
To Balance c/d	68,000		
	1,41,000		1,41,000

Illustration 37

The following are the summaries of the Balance Sheets of a Limited company as at 31st December 2009 and 31st December, 2010.

	2009 Rs.	*2010* Rs.
Sundry Creditors	39,500	41,135
Bills Payable	33,780	11,525
Bank Overdraft	59,510	—
Provision for Taxation	40,000	50,000
Reserves	50,000	50,000
Profit and Loss	39,690	41,220

Share Capital	2,00,000	2,60,000
	4,62,480	4,53,880
Cash at Bank	2,500	2,700
Sundry Debtors	85,175	72,625
Sundry Advances	2,315	735
Stock	1,11,040	97,370
Land & Buildings	1,48,500	1,44,250
Plant & Machinery	1,12,950	1,16,200
Goodwill	—	20,000
	4,62,480	4,53,880

The following additional information is obtained from the general ledger :

(1) During the year ended 31st December 2010, an interim dividend of Rs. 26,000 was paid.

(2) The assets of another company were purchased for Rs. 60,000 payable in fully paid shares of the company. These assets consisted of stock Rs. 21,640, machinery Rs. 18,360 and goodwill Rs. 20,000. In addition, sundry purchases of plant were made totalling Rs. 5,650.

(3) Income tax paid during the year amounted to Rs. 25,000.

(4) The net profit for the year before tax was Rs. 62,530.

You are required to prepare a statement showing the sources and applications of funds for the year 2010 and a schedule settling out changes in working capital. (*M.Com., M.S.*)

Solution :

SCHEDULE OF CHANGES IN WORKING CAPITAL

	2009	*2010*	*Changes in Working Capital*	
	Rs.	*Rs.*	*Increase Rs.*	*Decrease Rs.*
Current Assets :				
Cash	2,500	2,700	200	—
Sundry Debtors	85,175	72,625	—	12,550
Sundry Advances	2,315	735	—	1,580
Stock	1,11,040	97,370	—	13,670
	2,01,030	1,73,430		
Current Liabilities :				
Sundry Creditors	39,500	41,135	—	1,635
Bills Payable	33,780	11,525	22,255	
Bank Overdraft	59,510	—	59,510	
	1,32,790	52,660		
Working Capital	68,240	1,20,770		
Net increase in Working Capital	52,530	—	—	52,530
	1,20,770	1,20,770	81,965	81,965

STATEMENT OF SOURCES AND APPLICATION OF FUNDS
for the year ended 2010

Sources	*Rs.*	*Application*	*Rs.*
Issue of Share Capital	21,640	Purchase of Machinery	5,650
Funds from Operations	87,540	Payment of Dividend	26,000
		Payment of Income Tax	25,000
		Net Increase in Working Capital	52,530
	1,09,180		1,09,180

Workings:

SHARE CAPITAL ACCOUNT

	Rs.		Rs.
		By Balance b/d	2,00,000
To Balance c/d	2,60,000	By Stock	21,640
		By Goodwill	20,000
		By Machinery	18,360
	2,60,000		2,60,000

PLANT AND MACHINERY ACCOUNT

	Rs.		Rs.
To Balance b/d	1,12,960	By Adjusted P & L A/c	20,760
To Share Capital (Purchase)	18,360	(Depreciation)	
To Cash (Purchase)	5,650	(Balancing figure)	
		By Balance c/d	1,16,200
	1,36,960		1,36,960

LAND AND BUILDING ACCOUNT

	Rs.		Rs.
To Balance b/d	1,48,500	By Adjusted P & L A/c	4,250
		(Depreciation)	
		(Balancing figure)	
		By Balance c/d	1,44,250
	1,48,500		1,48,500

PROVISION FOR TAXATION A/C

	Rs.		Rs.
To Cash	25,000	By Balance b/d	40,000
To Balance c/d	50,000	By Adjusted P & L A/c	35,000
	75,000		75,000

ADJUSTED PROFIT & LOSS A/C

	Rs.		Rs.
To Depreciation:			
Land & Buildings	4,250	By Balance b/d	39,690
Plant & Machinery	20,760	By Fund from Operations	87,540
To Provision for Taxation	35,000		
To Dividend	26,000		
To Balance c/d	41,220		
	1,27,230		1,27,230

Notes: (1) Although there is an increase in Share Capital amounting to Rs. 60,000, only Rs. 21,640 which has been issued against stock (current asset) has been taken as a source. Issue of shares against machinery and goodwill are transactions concerned with non-current items. They do not affect the flow of funds. They are not taken as source or application.

(2) Net profit for the year before tax (given) Rs. 62,530

Add: Non-fund items already debited to P & L A/c:

Depreciation on Buildings	4,250
Depreciation on Plant & Machinery	20,760
Fund from operations:	87,540

Illustration 38

The following are the summarised Balance Sheets of X Ltd. as at 31st December 2009 and 31st December 2010 :

	2009 Rs.	2010 Rs.		2009 Rs.	2010 Rs.
Share Capital	5,00,000	5,00,000	Land and Buildings (at cost)	2,00,000	2,50,000
Profit & Loss A/c	1,50,000	2,52,000	Plant and Machinery (at cost)	3,50,000	3,60,000
Debentures	2,00,000	2,00,000	Sundry Debtors	1,47,000	1,38,000
Sundry Creditors	1,20,000	1,05,000	Stock	2,50,000	2,74,000
Provision for doubtful Debts	5,000	4,000	Bank	83,000	1,01,000
Provision for Depreciation:			Preliminary Expenses	5,000	4,000
Land & Buildings	30,000	34,000			
Plant and Machinery	30,000	32,000			
	10,35,000	11,27,000		10,35,000	11,27,000

The following additional information is available :

(a) The net profit for the year ending 31st December, 2010 was Rs. 2,52,000 and is arrived at after charging loss on sale of machinery and written off preliminary expenses and adjusting provisions for doubtful debts.

(b) During the year a part of the machinery costing Rs. 7,000 accumulated depreciation thereon being Rs. 1,000 was sold for Rs. 5,000.

(c) Dividend of Rs. 50,000 was paid during the year ended 31st Dec., 2010.

Prepare statements to show the changes in working capital for the year 2010 and the Sources and Application of Funds for 2010. *(M.Com., M.S.)*

Solution :

SCHEDULE OF CHANGES IN WORKING CAPITAL

	2009 Rs.	2010 Rs.	Changes in Working Capital Increase Rs.	Decrease Rs.
Current Assets :				
Sundry Debtors	1,47,000	1,38,000	—	9,000
Stock	2,50,000	2,74,000	24,000	—
Bank	83,000	1,01,000	18,000	—
	4,80,000	5,13,000		
Less: Current Liabilities:				
Sundry Creditors	1,20,000	1,05,000	15,000	—
Provisions for Doubtful Debts	5,000	4,000	1,000	—
	1,25,000	1,09,000		
Working Capital	3,55,000	4,04,000		
Increase in Working Capital	49,000	—		49,000
	4,04,000	4,04,000	58,000	58,000

FUND FLOW STATEMENT
for the year ended 31st December 2010

Sources	*Rs.*	*Application*	*Rs.*
Sale of Plant and Machinery	5,000	Purchase of Land & Buildings	50,000
Fund from Operations	1,61,000	Purchase of Plant & Machinery	17,000
		Dividend Paid	50,000
		Increase in Working Capital	49,000
	1,66,000		1,66,000

Workings:

LAND AND BUILDINGS ACCOUNT

To Balance b/d	2,00,000	By Balance c/d	2,50,000
To Cash (Purchase)	50,000		
	2,50,000		2,50,000

PROVISION FOR DEPRECIATION A/C
(Land & Buildings)

	Rs.		*Rs.*
To Balance c/d	34,000	To Balance b/d	30,000
		By Adjusted Profit and Loss A/c	4,000
	34,000		34,000

PLANT AND MACHINERY ACCOUNT

	Rs.		*Rs.*
To Balance c/d	3,50,000	By Cash (Sales)	5,000
To Cash (Purchase)	17,000	By Provision for Depreciation	1,000
		By Adjusted P & L A/c (Loss)	1,000
		By Balance c/d	3,60,000
	3,67,000		3,67,000

PROVISION FOR DEPRECIATION A/C
(Plant and Machinery)

	Rs.		*Rs.*
To Plant & Machinery	1,000	By Balance b/d	30,000
To Balance c/d	32,000	By Adjusted P & L A/c	3,000
	33,000		33,000

ADJUSTED PROFIT AND LOSS A/C

	Rs.		*Rs.*
To Plant and Machinery (Loss)	1,000	By Balance b/d	1,50,000
To Provision for Depreciation (Land & Buildings)	4,000	By Funds from Operations	1,61,000
To Provision for Depreciation (Plant & Machinery)	3,000		
To Preliminary Expenses	1,000		
To Dividend	50,000		
To Balance c/d	2,52,000		
	3,11,000		3,11,000

Illustration 39

You have been given the following financial statements of A Ltd. as at 31st December 2009 and 31st December 2010:

	31-12-2010 Rs.	*31-12-2009* Rs.
Assets:		
Cash at Bank	45,000	1,30,000
Sundry Debtors	1,40,000	90,700
Stock-in-trade	1,96,000	1,42,500
Fixed assets, less Depreciation	6,00,000	3,60,000
Investments	10,000	11,250
Prepaid Expenses	21,000	14,000
	10,12,000	7,48,450
Liabilities:		
Sundry Creditors	2,98,000	2,51,450
Provision for taxation	1,72,000	65,000
Secured Loans from Bank	—	87,000
Reserve and Surplus	3,12,000	1,48,000
Share capital:		
Ordinary share of Rs. 100 each	2,30,000	1,97,000
	10,12,000	7,48,450

The following further information is available from records :

(1) The position in respect of Reserves and Surplus is as follows :

Balance as on 1st January, 2010	Rs. 1,48,000
Net profit for year	1,98,500
	3,46,500
Less : Dividend	34,500
	3,12,000

(2) On 31st December 2010 the accumulated depreciation on fixed assets was Rs. 1,80,000 and on 31st December 2009 Rs. 1,60,000. Machinery costing Rs. 20,000 which was one-half depreciated was discarded and written off in 2010. Depreciation for the year 2010 amounted to Rs. 30,000.

(3) Investments costing Rs. 5,000 were sold during the year 2010 for Rs. 4,800 and Government Securities of the face value of Rs. 4,000 were purchased during the year for Rs. 3,750.

You are required to prepare :

(a) Statement of Source and Application of Funds, and

(b) Statement showing in details the item-wise increase or decrease in the net working capital.

(*M.Com., Madras*)

Solution :

SCHEDULE OF CHANGES IN WORKING CAPITAL

	2009	*2010*	*Changes in Working Capital*	
			Increase	*Decrease*
	Rs.	*Rs.*	*Rs.*	*Rs.*
Current Assets :				
Cash at Bank	1,30,000	45,000	—	85,000
Sundry Debtors	90,700	1,40,000	49,300	—

Stock	1,42,500	1,96,000	53,500	—
Prepaid Expenses	14,000	21,000	7,000	—
	3,77,200	4,02,000		
Less:				
Current Liabilities:				
Sundry Creditors	2,51,450	2,98,000	—	46,550
Provisions for Taxation	65,000	1,72,000	—	1,07,000
	3,16,450	4,70,000		
Working Capital	60,750	(–) 68,000		
Decrease in Working Capital	—	(+) 1,28,750	1,28,750	
	60,750	60,750	2,38,550	2,38,550

FUND FLOW STATEMENT
for the year ended 31st December, 2010

Sources	*Rs.*	*Application*	*Rs.*
Sale of Investment	4,800	Purchase of Fixed Assets	2,80,000
Issue of Shares	33,000	Purchase of Investment	3,750
Funds from Operations	2,38,700	Dividend Paid	34,500
Decrease in Working Capital	1,28,750	Repayment of Bank Loan	87,000
	4,05,250		4,05,250

Workings :

FIXED ASSET ACCOUNT

To Balance b/d (3,60,000 + 1,60,000)	5,20,000	By Provision for Depreciation	10,000
To Cash (Purchase)	2,80,000	By Adjusted P & L A/c (Loss on Machine discarded)	10,000
		By Balance c/d (6,00,000 + 1,80,000)	7,80,000
	8,00,000		8,00,000

PROVISION FOR DEPRECIATION ACCOUNT

	Rs.		*Rs.*
To Fixed Assets	10,000	By Balance b/d	1,60,000
To Balance c/d	1,80,000	By Adjusted P&L A/c	30,000
	1,90,000		1,90,000

INVESTMENT ACCOUNT

	Rs.		*Rs.*
To Balance b/d	11,250	By Cash (Sales)	4,800
To Cash (Purchase)	3,750	By Adjusted P & L A/c (Loss on Sale)	200
		By Balance c/d	10,000
	15,000		15,000

ADJUSTED PROFIT & LOSS A/C (Reserves and Surplus)

	Rs.		Rs.
To Provision for Depreciation	30,000	By Balance b/d	1,48,000
To Fixed Assets (Loss)	10,000	By Fund from Operations	2,38,700
To Investment (Loss)	200		
To Dividend paid	34,500		
To Balance c/d	3,12,000		
	3,86,700		3,86,700

Illustration 40

Following are the comparative Balance Sheets of Good Luck Co. as at 31st December.

Liabilities	*2009* Rs.	*2010* Rs.	*Assets*	*2009* Rs.	*2010* Rs.
Share Capital	10,00,000	11,00,000	Goodwill	50,000	40,000
Debentures	5,00,000	3,00,000	Land & Buildings	4,20,000	6,60,000
General Reserve	2,00,000	2,00,000			
Profit & Loss	1,10,000	1,90,000	Plant and Machinery	6,00,000	8,00,000
Income Tax Provisions	40,000	1,10,000	Stock	2,50,000	2,10,000
Creditors	50,000	40,000	Debtors	3,00,000	2,40,000
Bills Payable	20,000	30,000	Cash	3,00,000	24,000
Provision for Doubtful Debts	30,000	24,000	Preliminary Expenses	30,000	20,000
	19,50,000	19,94,000		19,50,000	19,94,000

Additional Information :

(*a*) During the year 2010, a part of machinery costing Rs. 7,500 (Accumulated depreciation thereon being Rs. 2,500) was sold for Rs. 3,000.

(*b*) Dividend for Rs. 1,00,000 was paid during the year ended 31st December 2010.

(*c*) Income Tax Rs. 50,000 was paid during the year 2010.

(*d*) Depreciation for the year 2010 was provided as follows :

	Rs.
Land and Buildings	10,000
Plant and Machinery	50,000

You are required to prepare :

(*i*) A schedule of change in Working Capital and

(*ii*) A Statement showing the Sources and Application of Funds. (*CA*)

Solution :

SCHEDULE OF CHANGES IN WORKING CAPITAL

Items	*2009*	*2010*	*Changes in Working Capital* Increase Cr.	Decrease Cr.
Current Assets :	*Rs.*	*Rs.*	*Rs.*	*Rs.*
Closing Stock	2,50,000	2,10,000	—	40,000
Debtors, less Provision	2,70,000	2,16,000	—	54,000
Cash	3,00,000	24,000	—	2,76,000
	8,20,000	4,50,000		

Current Liabilities :				
Creditors	50,000	40,000	10,000	
Bills Payable	20,000	30,000		10,000
	70,000	70,000		
Working Capital	7,50,000	3,80,000		
Net Decrease in Working Capital	—	3,70,000	3,70,000	—
	7,50,000	7,50,000	3,80,000	3,80,000

FUNDS FLOW STATEMENT

Sources	*Rs.*	*Applications*	*Rs.*
Funds from Operations (3)	3,82,000	Payment of Dividend	1,00,000
Sale of Machinery	3,000	Payment of Income Tax	50,000
Issue of Share Capital	1,00,000	Purchase of Land and Buildings (2)	2,50,000
Decrease in Working Capital	3,70,000	Purchase of Plant and Machinery (1)	2,55,000
		Redemption of Debentures	2,00,000
	8,55,000		8,55,000

Working :

(1) PLANT AND MACHINERY ACCOUNT

	Rs.		*Rs.*
To Balance b/d	6,00,000	By Bank (Sales)	3,000
To Bank (Purchase) (Balancing figure)	2,55,000	By Profit & Loss A/c (Loss on Sale)	2,000
		By Profit & Loss A/c (Depreciation)	2,000
		By Profit & Loss A/c (Depreciation)	50,000
		By Balance c/d	8,00,000
	8,55,000		8,55,000

(2) LAND AND BUILDING ACCOUNT

	Rs.		*Rs.*
To Balance b/d	4,20,000	By Profit & Loss A/c (Depreciation)	10,000
To Bank (Purchase) (Balancing figure)	2,50,000	By Balance c/d	6,60,000
	6,70,000		6,70,000

(3) ADJUSTED PROFIT AND LOSS ACCOUNT

	Rs.		*Rs.*
To Depreciation :			
Machinery	50,000	By Balance b/d	1,10,000
Land & Buildings	10,000	By Funds from Operations	3,82,000

To Dividends	1,00,000		
To Income Tax Provision (4)	1,20,000		
To Loss on Sale of Machinery	2,000		
To Goodwill Written Off	10,000		
To Preliminary Expenses Written Off	10,000		
To Balance c/d	1,90,000		
	4,92,000		4,92,000

(4) INCOME TAX PROVISION ACCOUNT

	Rs.		Rs.
To Bank (Payment)	50,000	By Balance b/d	40,000
To Balance c/d	1,10,000	By Profit & Loss A/c (Balancing figure)	1,20,000
	1,60,000		1,60,000

Illustration 41

The Balance Sheets of a Company as on 31st December 2009 and 31st December 2010 are as follows :

Liabilities	*2009* Rs.	*2010* Rs.	*Assets*	*2009* Rs.	*2010* Rs.
Share Capital	2,00,000	2,50,000	Fixed Assets	3,50,000	4,75,000
Retained Earnings	1,60,000	3,00,000	Merchandise Inventory	1,00,000	95,000
Premium on Shares	—	5,000	Accounts Receivable	43,000	50,000
Accumulated Depreciation	80,000	60,000	Prepaid Expenses	4,000	5,000
Debentures	60,000	—	Cash	15,800	10,200
Accounts Payable	37,800	40,200	Commission on Shares	25,000	20,000
	5,37,800	6,55,200		5,37,800	6,55,200

Additional Information :

(1) Net Income for the year Rs. 1,40,000.

(2) An addition to the Fixed Asset was made during the year at a cost of Rs. 1,65,000 and fully depreciated machinery costing Rs. 40,000 was discarded, no salvage being realised.

(3) Depreciation for the year Rs. 20,000.

(4) Income Tax paid was Rs. 40,000.

(5) Interim Dividend paid during the year Rs. 20,000.

You are required to prepare :

(*a*) A Statement of Schedule of Changes in Working Capital.

(*b*) A Statement of Sources and Applications of Funds. (*CA*)

Solution :

STATEMENT OF SCHEDULE OF CHANGES IN WORKING CAPITAL

	2009 Rs.	*2010* Rs.	*Changes in Working Capital* Increase Dr. Rs.	Decrease Cr. Rs.
Current Assets :				
Merchandise Inventory	1,00,000	95,000	—	5,000

Accounts Receivable	43,000	50,000	7,000	—
Prepaid Expenses	4,000	5,000	1,000	—
Cash	15,800	10,200	—	5,600
	1,62,800	1,60,200		
Current Liabilities :				
Accounts Payable	37,800	40,200	—	2,400
	37,800	40,200		
Working Capital	1,25,000	1,20,000		
Net Decrease in Working Capital	—	5,000	5,000	—
	1,25,000	1,25,000	13,000	13,000

STATEMENT OF SOURCES AND APPLICATIONS OF FUNDS

Sources	*Rs.*	*Applications*	*Rs.*
Issue of Shares	50,000	Redemption of Debentures	60,000
Premium on Shares	5,000	Purchase of Fixed Assets	1,65,000
Funds from Operations (A)	2,25,000	Payment of Income Tax	40,000
Decrease in Working Capital	5,000	Payment of Interim Dividend	20,000
	2,85,000		2,85,000

Workings :

(A) RETAINED EARNINGS OR PROFIT AND LOSS ACCOUNT

	Rs.		*Rs.*
To Depreciation	20,000	By Balance b/d	1,60,000
To Income Tax	40,000	By Funds from Operations (Balancing figure)	2,25,000
To Interim Dividend	20,000		
To Commission on Shares Written Off	5,000		
To Balance c/d	3,00,000		
	3,85,000		3,85,000

Illustration 42

Below are given the Balance Sheets as on 31st December 2009 and 31st December 2010 and a Statement of Income and Reconciliation of earnings for 2010 of a firm. The only item in the Buildings and Equipment Account sold during the year was a specialised machine that originally cost Rs. 15,000. The accumulated depreciation on this Machine at the time of sale was Rs. 8,000. The Machine was sold for Rs. 6,000 and full payment was received in cash.

COMPARATIVE BALANCE SHEETS

Liabilities	*2009* *Rs.*	*2010* *Rs.*	*Assets*	*2009* *Rs.*	*2010* *Rs.*
Accounts Payable	58,000	94,000	Cash	74,000	37,000
Notes Payable	28,000	8,000	Accounts Receivable	54,000	47,000
Estimated Income Tax	86,000	12,000	Inventories	3,12,000	2,77,000
Social Security			Prepaid Expenses	6,000	4,000
Taxes Accrued	3,000	5,000	Land	60,000	60,000
Debentures	2,20,000	60,000	Patents	55,000	65,000

Capital	2,50,000	4,60,000	Buildings and Equipments	4,20,000	4,80,000
Retained Earnings	2,31,000	2,11,000	Less : Accumulated	1,05,000	1,20,000
			Depreciation	3,15,000	3,60,000
	8,76,000	8,50,000		8,76,000	8,50,000

STATEMENT OF INCOME AND RECONCILIATIONOF EARNINGS FOR 2010

		Rs.
Net Sales		19,70,000
Less : Cost of goods sold		14,80,000
		4,90,000
Less : Operating expenses (includes depreciation on Buildings and Equipmentof Rs. 23,000 and Patent amortization of Rs. 6,000)		5,00,000
Net Loss from Operation		10,000
Less : Other Revenue		7,000
Net Loss		3,000
Add : Retained earnings of 2009		2,31,000
		2,28,000
Less : Dividend paid	16,000	
Loss on sale of Assets	1,000	17,000
Retained earnings on 31st December 2010 :		Rs. 2,11,000

Prepare a Fund Flow Statement. (*M.Com., Delhi*)

Solution :

FUND FLOW STATEMENT
for the year ended 31st December 2010

Sources	*Rs.*	*Applications*	*Rs.*
Issue of Shares	2,10,000	Patent Acquired (C)	16,000
Sale of Machine	6,000	Purchase of Buildings (D) and Equipment	75,000
Funds from Operations (B)	26,000	Payment of Dividend	16,000
Decrease in Working Capital (A)	99,000	Payment of Income Tax	74,000
		Redemption of Debentures	1,60,000
	3,41,000		3,41,000

Workings :

(A) SCHEDULE OF CHANGE IN WORKING CAPITAL

			Changes in Working Capital	
Particulars	*2009* *Rs.*	*2010* *Rs.*	*Increase (Dr).* *Rs.*	*Decrease (Cr)* *Rs.*
Current Assets :				
Cash	74,000	37,000	—	37,000
Accounts Receivable	54,000	47,000	—	7,000
Inventories	3,12,000	2,77,000	—	35,000
Prepaid Expenses	6,000	4,000	—	2,000
	4,46,000	3,65,000		

Current Liabilities :				
Accounts Payable	58,000	94,000	—	36,000
Notes Payable	28,000	8,000	20,000	
Social Security				
Tax Accrued	3,000	5,000		2,000
	89,000	1,07,000		
Working Capital	3,57,000	2,58,000		
Decrease in Working Capital	—	99,000	99,000	
	3,57,000	3,57,000	1,19,000	1,19,000

(B) ADJUSTED PROFIT AND LOSS ACCOUNT

	Rs.		*Rs.*
To Building & Equipment (Loss)	1,000	By Balance b/d	2,31,000
To Provision for Depreciation	23,000	By Funds from Operations	26,000
To Patents	6,000		
To Dividend Paid	16,000		
To Balance c/d	2,11,000		
	2,57,000		2,57,000

(C) PATENT ACCOUNT

	Rs.		*Rs.*
To Balance b/d	55,000	By Profit & Loss A/c (Amortization)	6,000
To Bank (Purchases)	16,000	By Balance c/d	65,000
(Balancing Figure)	71,000		71,000

(D) BUILDINGS AND EQUIPMENT AMOUNT

	Rs.		*Rs.*
To Balance b/d	4,20,000	By Bank (Sale)	6,000
To Bank (Purchases) (Balancing Figure)	75,000	By Accumulated Depreciation on sold item	8,000
		By Profit & Loss (Loss on Sale)	1,000
		By Balance c/d	4,80,000
	4,95,000		4,95,000

OBJECTIVE TYPE QUESTIONS

State whether the following statements are true or false.

1. A decrease in current liabilities increases working capital.
2. Amortisation of preliminary expenses in use of funds.
3. Payment of dividends is use of funds.
4. Purchase of stock is an application of funds.
5. Working capital is the difference between fixed assets and current liabilites.
6. Cash or credit sales increases the working capital.
7. For Funds flow Statement, provision for taxation will be treated as an item of internal source.

8. Net profit is the same as cash from operations.
9. The funds flow statement summarises the sources of funds and application of funds.
10. The position statement shows assets and liabilities of a firm over a time.
11. Provision for Bad Debts is an item of current liability.
12. Excess of current assets over current liabilities gives us cash on hand.
13. Goodwill is a non-current item.
14. There is movement of funds when a fixed asset is sold for cash.
15. When cash is received from Debtors, there is movement of funds resulting in increase in working capital.
16. Appropriation of profits do affect the flow of funds.
17. When goods purchases on credit, there is no change in the working capital.
18. There is no movement of funds when debentures are issued to the public.
19. Funds from operations mean the same as net profit.
20. The Funds Flow Statement is a statement of changes in financial position of a concern between two Balance Sheet dates.

[**Ans.** True 1, 3, 6, 7, 9, 11, 13, 14, 17, 20.
False 2, 4, 5, 8, 10, 12, 15, 16, 18, 19.]

II Fill in the blanks.

1. Difference between Current Assets and Current Liabilities is known as..........
2. Funds flow refers to changes in .... Capital.
3. Forfeited shares account is a non .... liability.
4. Building sold on credit is .... of funds.
5. Commission outstanding is .... of funds.
6. Preliminary expenses is non .... asset.
7. Funds from operation constitute the chief source of ....
8. Cash or credit sales increases the .... capital.
9. Provision for bad debts is an item of current ....
10. The funds flow statement summarises the sources of .... and .... funds.

[**And :** 1. Working capital ; 2. Working ; 3. Current ; 4. A source ; 5. An application ; 6. Current ; 7. Funds ; 8. Working ; 9. Liability ; 10. Uses, application of.]

III Choose the correct answer to the following.

1. Sale of long-term investments indicates :
   (a) Source of Funds.
   (b) Application of Funds.
   (c) Change in current assets.
2. An increase in the securities premium account is :
   (a) An application of fund.
   (b) A source of fund.
   (c) No flow of fund.
3. Sale of goods on credit results in :
   (a) Increase in working capital.
   (b) Decrease in working capital.
   (c) Increase as well as decrease in working capital.
   (d) None of these.
4. When a fixed asset is sold, the transaction results in increase in working capital because:
   (a) The transaction involves a fixed asset and fixed liability.
   (b) The transaction involves a current asset and non-current asset.
   (c) The transaction results in increase in cash.

5. Increase in a fixed asset due to purchase is :
   (a) Source of funds.
   (b) Use of funds.
   (c) None.
6. Stock in the beginning results in :
   (a) Application of fund.
   (b) Source of fund.
   (c) No flow of fund.
7. Tax paid is
   (a) Application of fund.
   (b) Source of fund.
   (c) No flow of fund.
8. Stock at the end results in the :
   (a) Application of fund.
   (b) Source of fund.
   (c) No flow of fund.
9. Net profit earned plus non-working capital expenses is equal to
   (a) Fund provided by operations.
   (b) Use of funds.
   (c) Sinking fund.
10. Business transaction resulting in the inflow and outflow of funds depict the change that has taken place in :
   (a) Total resources of business.
   (b) Net working capital of business.
   (c) Cash position of business.
   (d) Any of these.

[**Ans.** 1. (a); 2. (b) ; 3. (d) ; 4. (b) ; 5. (b) ; 6. (a) ; 7. (a) ; 8. (b) ; 9 (a) ; 10. (d)]

THEORETICAL QUESTIONS

1. What is a Fund Flow Statement ? How is it prepared ?
2. What are the basic objectives for compiling a Statement of Sources and Applications of Funds ?
3. What do you mean by Funds from Operations ?
4. What is the meaning of Schedule of Changes in Working Capital ?
5. Explain the procedure for preparing a Fund Flow Statement.
6. "Revenue expenditure reduces Working Capital whereas the charging of depreciation does not". Explain.
7. Distinguish between :
   (*a*) Funds Flow Statement and Balance Sheet
   (*b*) Funds Flow Statement and Receipts and Payments Account.

PRACTICAL PROBLEMS

1. From the following two Balance Sheets as on 31st December 2009 and 2010, you are required to prepare the Schedule of Changes in Working Capital and Fund Flow Statement.

	2009	*2010*
	Rs.	*Rs.*
Assets :		
Cash	30,000	47,000
Debtors	1,20,000	1,15,000
Stock	80,000	90,000
Land	50,000	66,000

	2,80,000	3,18,000
Capital & Liabilities :		
Share Capital	2,00,000	2,50,000
Creditors	70,000	45,000
Retained Earnings	10,000	23,000
	2,80,000	3,18,000

(**Ans.** Increase in Working Capital Rs. 47,000. Total of Funds Flow Statement Rs. 63,000)

2. From the following Balance Sheets of a Company, prepare a Statement showing changes in the Working Capital and Statement of Sources and Uses of Funds :

	31st Dec. 2010 *Rs.*	*31st Dec. 2009* *Rs.*
Assets :		
Cash	75,000	35,000
Accounts Receivable	90,000	98,000
Merchandise Inventory	1,20,000	87,000
Long Term Investments	10,000	15,000
Land	30,000	20,000
	3,25,000	2,55,000
Liabilities :		
Accounts Payable	45,000	50,000
Notes Payable (Short-Term)	35,000	20,000
Notes Payable (Due in 2005)	20,000	—
Capital Stock	1,50,000	1,25,000
Retained Earnings	75,000	60,000
	3,25,000	2,55,000

(**Ans.** Increase in Working Capital Rs. 55,000. Total of Fund Flow Statement Rs. 65,000).

3. Balance Sheets of M/s Black and White as on 1st Jan. 2009 and 31st Dec. 2010 were as follows :

Liabilities	*Jan. 2010* *Rs.*	*Dec. 2010* *Rs.*	*Assets*	*Jan. 2010* *Rs.*	*Dec. 2010* *Rs.*
Creditors	40,000	44,000	Cash	10,000	7,000
White's Loan	25,000	—	Debtors	30,000	50,000
Loan from Bank	40,000	50,000	Stock	35,000	25,000
Capital	1,25,000	1,53,000	Machinery	80,000	55,000
			Land	40,000	50,000
			Buildings	35,000	60,000
	2,30,000	2,47,000		2,30,000	2,47,000

During the year machine costing Rs. 10,000 (accumulated Depreciation Rs. 3,000) was sold for Rs. 5,000. The provision for depreciation against machinery as on 1st Jan. 2010 was Rs. 25,000 and on 31st Dec. 2010 Rs. 40,000. Net profit for the year 2010 amounted to Rs. 45,000.

Prepare Fund Flow Statement. (*M.Com. Madurai, MCA Bharathiar*)

(**Ans.** Increase in Working Capital Rs. 3,000. Total of Fund Flow Statement Rs. 80,000. Fund from Operations Rs. 65,000).

4. Calculate funds from operations from the following :

PROFIT AND LOSS ACCOUNT

	Rs.		Rs.
To Rent	10,000	By Gross Profit	9,86,000
To Salary	25,000		
To Depreciation	3,000		
To Discount on Shares	10,000		
To Goodwill written off	5,000		
To Preliminary expenses	6,000		
To Net Profit	9,27,000		
	9,86,000		9,86,000

(*B.Com. MS, Madras, Poona*)

(**Ans.** Funds from operations : Rs. 9,51,000)

5. From the following summarised Balance Sheets of A. Ltd. as on 31st December 2009 and 2010, prepare a Statement showing the Sources and Applications of Funds and the schedule showing the Working Capital for the year ended 31st December 2010.

Liabilities	*2009* Rs.	*2010* Rs.	*Assets*	*2009* Rs.	*2010* Rs.
Share Capital	9,00,000	9,00,000	Fixed Assets	8,00,000	6,40,000
General Reserve	6,00,000	6,20,000	Investments	1,00,000	1,20,000
Profit & Loss	1,12,000	1,36,000	Stock	4,80,000	4,20,000
Creditors	3,36,000	2,68,000	Debtors	4,20,000	9,10,000
Provision for Tax	1,50,000	20,000	Bank	2,98,000	3,94,000
Loan	—	5,40,000			
	20,98,000	24,84,000		20,98,000	24,84,000

Additional Information :

(*i*) Investments costing Rs. 16,000 were sold during the year 2010 for Rs. 17,000.

(*ii*) Provision for taxation made during the year was Rs. 18,000.

(*iii*) During the year, a part of the Fixed Assets costing Rs, 20,000 were sold for Rs. 24,000. The profit was included in the Profit and Loss Account.

(*iv*) Dividend paid during the year amounted to Rs. 80,000. (*B.Com. Agra, Madurai*)

(**Ans.** Increase in Working Capital : Rs. 7,24,000. Total of Fund Flow Statement Rs. 8,40,000. Fund from operation Rs. 2,59,000).

6. Find out Flow of Fund from Operation on the basis of the following :

PROFIT AND LOSS ACCOUNT
for the year ended 31st Dec. 2010

	Rs.		Rs.
To Opening Stock	8,000	By Sales	40,000
To Purchases	12,000	By Closing Stock	5,000
To Wages	5,000		
To Carriage	5,000		
To Gross Profit c/d	15,000		
	45,000		45,000
To Salaries	5,000	By Gross Profit b/d	15,000
To Depreciation on Machinery	100	By Gain on sale of Furniture	150
To Depreciation on Furniture	50		

	Rs.		Rs.
To Preliminary Expenses	100		
To Goodwill	50		
To Loss on sale of machinery	50		
To Net Profit	9,800		
	15,150		15,150
To General Reserve	4,800	By Balance b/d	10,000
To Dividend Equalisation Fund	2,000	By Net Profit of Current Year	9,80
To Proposed Dividend	1,000		
To Interim Dividend	1,000		
To Debenture Redemption Fund	2,000		
To Balance c/d	9,000		
	19,800		19,800

(**Ans.** Flow of Fund from Operation : Rs. 10,000).

7. Following are the summarised Balance Sheets of Amco as on 31st December 2009 and 2010 :

Liabilities	*2009* *Rs.*	*2010* *Rs.*	*Assets*	*2009* *Rs.*	*2010* *Rs.*
Share Capital	2,00,000	2,50,000	Land & Buildings	2,00,000	1,90,000
General Reserve	50,000	60,000	Machinery	1,50,000	1,69,000
Profit & Loss	30,500	30,600	Stock	1,00,000	74,000
Bank Loan (long term)	70,000	—	Debtors	80,000	64,200
Sundry Creditors	1,50,000	1,35,200	Cash	500	600
Provision for Taxation	30,000	35,000	Bank	—	8,000
			Goodwill	—	5,000
	5,30,500	5,10,800		5,30,500	5,10,800

Additional Information :

(*i*) Dividend of Rs. 23,000 was paid.

(*ii*) Assets of another company were purchased for a consideration of Rs. 50,000 payable in shares.

The following assets purchased :

Stock Rs. 20,000

Machinery Rs. 25,000

(*iii*) Machinery was further purchased for Rs. 8,000.

(*iv*) Depreciation written off machinery Rs. 12,000.

(*v*) Income Tax provided during the year Rs. 33,000.

(*vi*) Loss on sale of machine Rs. 200 was written off to General Reserve.

Prepare a Statement of Funds Flow. (*B.Com., Bombay, Madras*)

(**Ans.** Decrease in Working Capital : Rs. 18,900. Fund from Operations : Rs. 88,300. Total of Fund Flow Statement : Rs. 1,129,000).

8. From the following Balance Sheets of X Ltd. on 31st December 2009 and 2010, you are required to prepare :

(*i*) A Schedule of Changes in Working Capital.

(*ii*) A Fund Flow Statement.

Liabilities	*2009* *Rs.*	*2010* *Rs.*	*Assets*	*2009* *Rs.*	*2010* *Rs.*
Share Capital	1,00,000	1,00,000	Goodwill	12,000	12,000
General Reserve	14,000	18,000	Buildings	40,000	36,000

Profit & Loss A/c	16,000	13,000	Plant	37,000	36,000
Sundry Creditors	8,000	5,400	Investments	10,000	11,000
Bills Payable	1,200	800	Stock	30,000	23,400
Provision for Taxation	16,000	18,000	Bills Receivable	2,000	3,200
Provision for Doubtful Debts	400	600	Debtors	18,000	19,000
			Bank	6,600	15,200
	1,55,600	1,55,800		1,55,600	1,55,800

The following information has also been given :

(*i*) Depreciation charged on Plant was Rs. 4,000 and on Buildings Rs, 4,000.

(*ii*) Provision for taxation of Rs. 19,000 was made during the year 2010.

(*iii*) Interim dividend of Rs. 8,000 was paid during the year 2010. (*M.Com. Madras*)

(**Ans.** Increase in Working Capital Rs. 7,000. Total of Fund Flow Statement Rs. 36,000. Fund from Operation Rs,. 36,000).

9. The following are the Balance Sheets of a Company for the last two years :

Liabilities	*2009* *Rs.*	*2010* *Rs.*	*Assets*	*2009* *Rs.*	*2010* *Rs.*
Sundry Creditors	39,500	41,135	Cash at Bank	2,500	2,700
Bills Payable	33,780	11,525	Debtors	85,175	72,625
Bank Overdraft	59,510	—	Advances	2,315	735
Taxation Reserve	40,000	50,000	Stock	1,11,040	97,370
Capital Reserve	50,000	50,000	Land and Buildings	1,48,500	1,44,250
Profit & Loss A/c	39,690	41,220	Plant and Machinery	1,12,950	1,16,200
Share Capital	2,00,000	2,60,000	Goodwill	—	20,000
	4,62,480	4,53,880		4,62,480	4,53,880

The following additional information is obtained from the General Ledger :

(*i*) During the year ended 31st December 2010, an interim dividend of Rs. 26,000 was paid.

(*ii*) The assets of another company were purchased for Rs. 60,000 payable in fully paid shares of the company. The assets consisted of stock Rs. 21,640; machinery Rs. 18,360 and goodwill Rs. 20,000. In addition, sundry purchases of plant were made totalling Rs. 5,650.

(*iii*) Tax liability in respect of 2009 was settled at Rs. 45,000.

(*iv*) The net profit for the year before tax was Rs. 82,530.

You are required to prepare a Statement showing the Sources and Applications of Funds for the year 2010 and a Schedule setting changes in Working Capital. (*CA*)

(**Ans.** Increase in Working Capital Rs. 52,530. Total of Fund Flow Statement Rs. 1,29,180. Funds from Operation Rs. 1,07,540).

10. The following Balance Sheets of X Ltd. for the year 2009 and 2010 are given. You are required to prepare a Fund Flow Statement. ('000 omitted)

(Figures are as on 31st December)

Liabilities	*2009* *Rs.*	*2010* *Rs.*	*Assets*	*2009* *Rs.*	*2010* *Rs.*
Share Capital	150	225	Land	150	150
Share Premium	—	7.5	Plant	156	150
General Reserve	75	90	Furniture	10.5	13.5
Profit & Loss	15	25.5	Investment	90	120
Debenture 6%	105	75	Debtors	45	105

Provision for Depreciation on Plant	75	84	Stock	90	97.5
Provision for Depreciation on Furnitures	7.5	9	Cash	45	67.5
Tax	30	45			
Creditors	129	142.5			
	586.5	703.5		586.5	703.5

Additional Information :

(*i*) Plant purchased for Rs. 6,000 (depreciation value Rs. 3,000) was sold for cash Rs. 1,200 on 30th September 2010.

(*ii*) On 29th June 2010 Furniture was purchased for Rs. 3,000.

(*iii*) Depreciation on Plant at 8% and on Furniture at 12.5% on average cost.

(*iv*) Dividend 22.5% on original Share Capital. (*CAIIB*)

(**Ans.** Increase in Working Capital Rs. 76,500. Total of Fund Flow Statement Rs. 1,73,250. Funds from Operation Rs. 89,550).

11. The Non-current Assets and Equities of Northern Tools Ltd. at the beginning and at the end of the year 2010.

	January	*December*
	Rs.	*Rs.*
Plant and Equipment after Depreciation	1,37,000	2,85,000
Investment in shares of Government	2,64,000	5,80,000
Bonds Payable	5,00,000	1,40,000
Capital Stock	8,00,000	8,00,000
Retained Earnings	4,76,000	8,21,000

You are unable to obtain complete Balance Sheet of Income Statement data for the year, but you obtain the following information :

(*i*) Dividends of Rs. 75,000 were paid.

(*ii*) A gain on the sale of equipment of Rs. 26,000 has been included in net income. The gross plant assets increased by Rs. 1,86,000 even though equipment costing Rs. 58,000 with a net book value of Rs. 38,000 was sold.

Prepare a Statement of Sources and Applications of Funds and the Balance Sheets of January 2010 and December 2010. (*M.Com. Delhi*)

(**Ans.** Decrease in Working Capital Rs. 4,79,000. Funds from Operations Rs. 4,52,000. Fund Flow Statement Total Rs. 9,95,000. Balance Sheet Total Rs. 17,76,000 (January) Balance Sheet Total Rs. 17,61,000 (December).

12. Prepare a Fund Flow Statement of Atlantic Business Corporation for the year 2010 from the following information :

Liabilities	*Jan. 2010*	*Dec. 2010*	*Assets*	*Jan. 2010*	*Dec. 2010*
	Rs.	*Rs.*		*Rs.*	*Rs.*
Current Liabilities	30,000	32,000	Cash & Bank	40,000	44,400
Bonds Payable	22,000	22,000	Accounts Receivable	10,000	20,700
Bonds Payable Discount	(2,000)	(1,800)	Inventories	15,000	15,000
Capital Stock	35,000	43,500	Premises	20,000	16,000
Retained Earnings	15,000	19,500	Plant and Equipment	15,000	17,000
			Accumulated		

				Depreciation	5,000	2,800
			Patent and			
				Trade Mark	1,000	900
	1,00,000	1,15,200			1,00,000	1,15,200

Additional Information :

(1) Income for the period Rs. 10,000.

(2) A building that costs Rs. 4,000 and which had a book value of Rs. 1,000 was sold for Rs. 1,400.

(3) The depreciation charges for the period was Rs. 800.

(4) There was an issue of Capital Stock Rs. 5,000.

(5) Cash dividends of Rs. 2,000 and a Stock dividend of Rs. 3,500 were declared.

(*M.Com. Delhi*)

(**Ans.** Increase in Working Capital Rs. 13,100. Total of Fund Flow Statement Rs. 17,100. Funds from Operations Rs. 10,700).

13. From the following Balance Sheets of Kerox Ltd. prepare Funds Flow Statement for 31st March 2010 :

(Rs. in '000)

	31st March 2009 *Rs.*	*31st March 2010* *Rs.*
Liabilities :		
Equity Share Capital	150	200
9% Redeemable Preference Shares	75	50
Capital Reserve	—	10
General Reserve	20	25
Profit & Loss A/c	15	24
Proposed Dividend	21	25
Sundry Creditors	13	24
Bills Payable	10	8
Liability for Expenses	15	18
Provision for Tax	20	25
	339	409
Assets :		
Goodwill	50	40
Land & Buildings	100	85
Plant	40	100
Investments	10	15
Sundry Debtors	70	85
Stock	39	55
Bills Receivable	10	15
Cash in hand	7	5
Cash at Bank	5	4
Preliminary Expenses	8	5
	339	409

Additional Information :

(*i*) A part of land was sold out in 2010, and the profit was credited to capital Reserve.

(*ii*) A machine has been sold for Rs. 5,000 (written down value of the machine was Rs. 6,000).

Depreciation of Rs. 5,000 was charged on Plant in 2010.

(*iii*) An interim dividend of Rs. 10,000 has been paid in 2010.

(*iv*) An amount of Rs. 1,000 has been received by way of dividend on investment in 2010.

(*MBA Himachal, M.Com., Calcutta*)

(**Ans.** Increase in Working Capital Rs. 21,000. Total of Fund Flow Statement Rs. 1,73,000. Funds from Operations Rs. 92,000).

14. From the following Balance Sheets, make out (*i*) Statement of Changes in Working Capital, (*ii*) Fund Flow Statement.

BALANCE SHEETS OF ALPHA LTD.

Liabilities	*2009* Rs.	*2010* Rs.	*Assets*	*2009* Rs.	*2010* Rs.
Equity Share Capital	3,00,000	4,00,000	Goodwill	1,00,000	80,000
8% Redeemable Preference Share Capital	1,50,000	1,00,000	Land and Buildings	2,00,000	1,70,000
Capital Reserve	10,000	20,000	Plant	80,000	2,00,000
General Reserve	30,000	50,000	Investments	20,000	30,000
Profit & Loss A/c	30,000	48,000	Debtors	1,40,000	1,70,000
Proposed Dividend	42,000	50,000	Stock	77,000	1,09,000
Sundry Creditors	25,000	47,000	Bills Receivable	20,000	30,000
Bills Payable	20,000	16,000	Cash in hand	15,000	10,000
Expenses O/S	30,000	36,000	Cash at Bank	10,000	8,000
Provision for Tax	40,000	50,000	Preliminary Expenses	15,000	10,000
	6,77,000	8,17,000		6,77,000	8,17,000

Notes :

(i) A piece of land had been sold out in 2010 and the profit on sale has been credited to Capital Reserve.

(ii) A machine has been sold for Rs. 10,000. The written down value of the machine was Rs. 12,000. Depreciation of Rs. 10,000 is charged on Plant Account in 2010.

(iii) The investments are trade investments Rs. 3,000 by way of dividend is received including Rs. 1,000 from pre-acquisition profit which has been credited to Investment Account.

(iv) An interim Dividend of Rs. 20,000 has been paid in 2010.

(*M.Com. Meerut, Rajasthan, Bombay*)

(**Ans.** Increase in Working Capital Rs. 31,000. Funds from Operations Rs. 1,43,000. Total of Fund Flow Statement Rs. 2,96,000).

15. The following are the summarised Trial Balance of a Company as at 31st March 2009 and 31st March 2010 :

	31st March 2009		*31st March 2010*	
	Dr. Rs.	*Cr.* Rs.	*Dr.* Rs.	*Cr.* Rs.
Fixed Assets	23,36,960	—	24,60,500	—
Current Assets	9,60,540	—	7,91,800	—
Debenture Discount	30,000	—	25,000	
Issued Capital :				
Equity	—	15,00,000	—	15,00,000
Preference	—	3,00,000	—	4,00,000

USES OF CASH FLOW STATEMENT

A Cash Flow Statement is of primary importance to the financial management. It is an essential tool of short-term financial analysis. Its main uses are as follows :

1. Cash Flow Statement facilitates to prepare sound financial policies. It also helps to evaluate the current cash position.
2. A projected Cash Flow Statement can be prepared in order to know the future cash position of a concern so as to enable a firm to plan and coordinate its financial operations properly.
3. It helps in taking loan from Banks and other financial institutions. The repayment capacity of the firm can be understood by going through the Cash Flow Statement.
4. It helps the management in taking short-term financial decisions.
5. Cash is the soul and heart of the business. Cash is pivot of all business activities. Everyone is cash minded. The aim of business is to gather cash. Business is a source while cash is the end. Therefore, it is very useful.
6. The statement explains the causes for poor cash position in spite of substantial profits in a firm by throwing light on various applications of cash made by the firm.

Difference Between Fund Flow Statement and Cash Flow Statement

1. The Fund Flow Statement shows the causes of changes in net Working Capital whereas the Cash Flow Statement shows the causes for the changes in cash.
2. Cash Flow Statement is started with the opening and closing balances of cash while there are no opening or closing balances in Fund Flow Statement.
3. Cash Flow Statement deals only with cash whereas Fund Flow Statement deals with all the components of Working Capital.
4. Cash Flow Statement is useful for short-term financing while Fund Flow Statement is useful for long-term financing.
5. Cash Flow Statement is based on cash basis of accounting while the Fund Flow Statement is based on accrual basis of accounting.
6. Cash Flow Statement depicts only the changes in cash position, while Fund Flow Statement is concerned with the changes in Working Capital between two Balance Sheet dates.
7. Cash is a part of Working Capital. Improvement in cash position, as indicated by Cash Flow Statement can be taken as an indicator of improved working capital position. But the reverse is not true. That is, sound Fund position may not necessarily mean sound cash position.

Distinction Between Cash Flow Statement and Receipts & Payments A/c

There appears to be many common points in Cash Flow Statement and Receipts and Payments Accounts. Yet, there are differences between the two.

(1) The Cash Flow Statement is prepared to disclose the amount of cash generated from operations and other sources and the amount of outflow, being cash payments during the period. Receipts and Payments Account contains cash receipts (revenue and capital) and cash payments (revenue and capital).

(2) The Cash Flow Statement can be prepared from the Balance Sheets of two dates. The Receipts and Payments Account cannot be prepared so.

Limitation of Cash Flow Statement

Cash Flow Statement is a useful tool of financial analysis. However, it suffers from some limitations, which are as follows :

(1) A Cash Flow Statement only reveals the inflow and outflow of cash. The cash balance disclosed by this statement may not depict the true liquid position. There are controversies over a number of items like cheques, stamps, postal orders etc. to be included in cash.

(2) A Cash Flow Statement cannot be equated with the income statement. An income statement takes into account both cash and non-cash items. Hence Cash Fund does not mean net income of the business.

(3) Working Capital being a wider concept of funds, a funds flow statement presents a more complete picture than cash flow statement.

CASH FLOW STATEMENT (As per AS 3)

In June 1981, the Institute of Chartered Accountants of India issued Accounting Standard 3: Changes in Financial position. This accounting standard dealt with the financial statement that summarised, for the period convered by it, the changes in financial position showing the sources from which funds were obtained by the enterprise and the specific uses to which funds were applied. Funds were defined as cash or cash equivalents or working capital, that is, current assets minus current liabilities. But the flow statements suffered from certain limitations. A Funds Flow Statement showed flows of working capital which included items, like stock of goods and prepaid expenses which did not contribute to the short term ability of the enterprise to pay its debts. Flows were not classified under the heads of operating, financial and investing activities. There was no standard format of the statement. There was the need of a Cash Flow Statement in a standard format classifying flows from different activities. In June 1995 the Securities and Exchange Board of India (SEBI) amended clause 32 of the Listing Agreement requiring every listed company to give prescribed format, showing separately cash flows from operating activities, investing activities and financing activities. In March 1997 the Institute of Chartered Accountants of India issued AS–3 (Revised); Cash Flow Statement. The revised accounting standard supersedes AS–3 : Changes in Financial Position, issued in June 1981. Cash Flow Statement has replaced Statement of Changes in Financial Position.

Meaning of Cash Flow Statement

Cash Flow Statement reports the inflows and outflows of cash and its equivalents of an organisation during a particular period. It reports the cash receipts and payments classified according to the firm's major activities – Operating, Investing and Financing. It shows the net cash inflow or net cash outflow for each activity and for the overall business of the firm. It reports from where cash has come and how it has been utilised. It explains the causes for the change in the cash balance by reconciling the opening balance of the period with the closing balance.

Objectives

Information about the cash flows of an enterprise is useful in providing users of financial statements with a basis to assess the ability of the enterprise to generate cash and cash equivalents and the needs of the enterprise to utilise these cash flows. The economic decisions that are taken by users require an evaluation of the ability of an enterprise to generate cash and cash equivalents and the timing and certainty of their generation.

The statement deals with the provision of information about the historical changes in cash and cash equivalents of an enterprise by means of a cash flow statement which classifies cash flows during the period from operating, investing and financial activities.

Scope

An enterprise should prepare a cash flow statement and should present it for each period for which financial statements are presented.

Users of an enterprise's financial statements are interested in how the enterprise generates and uses and cash and cash equivalents. This is the case regardless of the nature of the enterprise's activities and irrespective of whether cash can be viewed as the product of the enterprise, as may be the case with a financial enterprise. Enterprises need cash for essentially the same reasons, however, different from their principal revenue – producing activities might be. They need cash to conduct their operations, to pay their obligations, and to provide returns to their investors.

Benefits of CFS

Cash Flow Statement has the following benefits, in brief :

1. It is an indicator for the cash flows in the future period. It helps the management in forecasting the future needs and plans.
2. It is an important tool as it helps in efficient management of cash.
3. The cash flow analysis on the basis of major activities i.e. Operating, Investing and Financial, facilitate the management to assess the effectivess of management's financial policies.
4. It reveals the liquidity position of the firm.
5. It provides a better measure for inter period and inter firm comparison.
6. It is very useful in evaluating financial policies and cash position.
7. It highlights the trend of the movement of cash.
8. It enhances the comparability of the reporting of operating performance by different enterprises because it eliminates the effects of using different accounting treatments for the same transactions and events.
9. Cash flow information is useful in assessing the ability of the enterprise to generate cash and cash equivalents and enable the users to develop models to assess and compare the present value of the future cash flows of different enterprises.

Definition

Cash Flow Statement is a statement which shows inflows and outflows of cash and its equivalent in an enterprise during a specified period of time. An enterprise prepares Cash Flow Statement, according to the Revised Accounting Standard – 3, and present it for each period for which financial statements are presented.

The following terms are used in this Statement with the meanings specified:

(*a*) CASH comprises on hand and demand deposits with banks.

(*b*) CASH EQUIVALENTS are short term, highly liquid investments that are readily convertible into known amounts of cash and which are subject to an insignificant risk of changes in value.

(*c*) CASH FLOWS are inflows and outflows of cash and cash equivalents.

CLASSIFICATION OF CASH FLOW STATEMENT

A cash flow statement aims to determine the effects of cash of different type of cash inflows and outflows. In this process, all cash flows are classified into three caegories:

(*a*) Cash flows from Operating Activities

(*b*) Cash flows from Investing Activities

(*c*) Cash flows from Financing Activities.

(a) Cash Flows from Operating Activities

The amount of cash flows arising from operating activities is a key indicator of the extent to which the operations of the enterprise have generated sufficient cash flows to maintain the operating capability of the enterprise, pay dividends, repay loans and make new investments without recourse to external sources of financing. Information about the specific components of historical operating cash flows is useful, in conjunction with other information, in forecasting future operating cash flows.

Cash flows from operating activities are primarily derived from the principal revenue-producing activities of the enterprise. Therefore, they generally result from the transactions and other events, that enter into the determination of net profit or loss. Examples of cash flows from operating activities are:

(1) Cash receipts from the sale of goods and the rendering of services;
(2) Cash receipts from royalties, fees, commissions and other revenue;
(3) Cash payments to suppliers for goods and services;
(4) Cash payments to and on behalf of employees;
(5) Cash receipts and cash payments of an insurance enterprise for premiums and claims, annuities and other policy benefits;
(6) Cash payments or refunds of income taxes unless they can be specifically indentified with financing and investing activities; and
(7) Cash receipts and payments relating to future contracts, option contracts and swap contracts when the contracts are held for dealing or trading purposes.

Some transactions, such as the sale of an item of plant, may give rise to a gain or loss which is included in the determination of net profit or loss. However, the cash flows relating to such transactions are cash flows investing activities.

An enterprise may hold securities and loans for dealing or trading purposes, in which case they are similar to inventory acquired specifically for resale. Therefore, cash flows arising from the purchase and sale of dealing or trading in securities are to be classified as operating activities. Similarly, cash advances and loans made by financial enterprises are usually classified as operating activities since they relate to the main revenue–producing activity of that enterprise.

(b) Cash Flows from Investing Activities

The separate disclosure of cash flows arising from investing activities is important because the cash flows represent the extent to which expenditures have been made for resources intended to generate future income and cash flows. Examples of cashflows arising from investing activities are:

(1) Cash payments to acquire fixed assets, including intangibles. These payments include those relating to capitalised research and development costs and self-constructed fixed assets;
(2) Cash receipts from disposal of fixed assets (including intangibles);
(3) Cash payments to acquire shares, warrants or debt instruments of other enterprises and interest in joint ventures (other than payments for those instruments considered to be cash equivalents and those held for dealing or trading purposes.)
(4) Cash receipts from disposal of shares, warrants or debt instruments of other enterprises and interests in joint ventures (other than receipts from those instruments considered to be cash equivalents and those held for dealing or trading purposes.)
(5) Cash advances and loans made to third parties (other than advances and loans made by a financial enterprise);
(6) Cash receipts from the repayment of advances and loans made to third parties (other than advances and loans of a financial enterprise);
(7) Cash payments for future contracts, forward contracts, option contracts and swap contracts except when the contracts are held for dealing or trading purposes, or the payments are classified as financing activities; and
(8) Cash receipts from future contracts, forward contracts, option contracts and swap contracts except when the contracts are held for dealing or trading purposes, or the receipts are classified as financing activities.

When a contract is accounted for as a hedge of an identifiable position, the cash flows of the contract are classified in the same manner as the cash flows of the position being hedged.

(c) Cash Flows from Financing Activities

The separate disclosure of cash flows arising from financing activities is important because it is useful in predicting claims on future cash flows by providers of funds (both capital and borrowings) to the enterprise. Examples, of cash flows arising from financing activities are:

(1) Cash proceeds from issuing shares or other similar instruments;
(2) Cash proceeds from issuing debentures, loans, notes, bonds, and other short or long-term borrowings and
(3) Cash repayments of amounts borrowed.

Illustration 1

Classify the activities as (a) Operating Activities. (b) Investing Activities and (c) Financial Activities :

1. Issue of Debentures
2. Refund of Income Tax
3. Payment of Interest
4. Sale of Land
5. Cash sales
6. Receipt of dividend
7. Payment of income tax
8. Cash received from Debtors
9. Rent paid
10. Payment of dividend

Solution

1. Financing Activity
2. Operating Activity
3. Financing Activity
4. Investing Activity
5. Operating Activity
6. Financing Activity
7. Operating Activity
8. Operating Activity
9. Operating Activity
10. Financing Activity

Illustration 2

State which of the following would result in inflow or outflow of cash or cash equivalents.

1. Issue of fully paid bonus shares.
2. Cash purchase of stock.
3. Sale or stock for cash at a profit.
4. Bills receivable endorsed to creditors.
5. Issue of shares against purchase of fixed asset.
6. Declaration of final dividend.
7. Cash deposited into Bank.
8. Purchases of mardetable securities for cash.
9. Bills Receivable endorsed to Creditors, dishonoured.
10. Sale of fixed asset (book value Rs. 5,000) at a loss of Rs. 3,000.

Solution :

Items	*Effect on Cash or Cash Equivalent*	
1.	No effect	Cash is not affected
2.	Outflow	Cash is decreased by the amount
3.	Inflow	Cash is increased by the amount of sale
4.	No effect	Cash is not affected
5.	No effect	Cash is not affected
6.	No effect	Cash is not affected
7.	No effect	Cash includes bank : not affected
8.	No effect	Conversion of cash into cash equivalent
9.	No effect	Cash is not affected
10.	Inflow	Cash is increased by Rs. 2,000.

Preparation of the Statement

Cash Flow Statement is prepared with the help of the following :

(1) **Balance sheets** (Opening and Closing) : Balance sheets at the beginning and at end of the accounting period are required to indicate the amount of changes that have taken place in assets, liabilities and capital.

(2) **Income Statement or Profit and Loss account :** It helps to determine the amount of cash provided by or used in operation during the accounting period, after making adjustments for non-cash items, current assets and current liabilities.

(3) **Additional Data :** In addition to the Balance Sheets and Income Statement, additional data are collected to determine how cash has been provided or used. For examples during the period assets might have been purchased and sold, taxes paid, premium paid on redemption of debentures etc.

PRESENTATION OF A CASH FLOW STATEMENT

The Cash Flow Statement should report cash flows during the period classified by operating, Investing and Financing Activities.

An enterprise presents its cash flows from operating, investing and financing activities in a manner which is most appropriate to its business. Classification by activity provides information that allows users to assess the impact of those activities on the financial position of the enterprise and the amount of its cash and cash equivalents. This information may also be used to evaluate the relationships among those activities.

A single transaction may include cash flows that are classified differently. For example, when the instalment paid in respect of a fixed assets acquired on deferred payment basis includes both interest and loan, the interest element is classified under financing activities and the loan element is classified under investing activities.

(a) Reporting Cash Flows from Operating Activities

An enterprise should report cash flows from operating activities using either:

(*a*) the direct method, whereby major classes of gross cash receipts and gross cash payments are disclosed; or

(*b*) the indirect method, whereby net profit or loss is adjusted for the effects of transactions of a non-cash nature, any deferrals or accruals of past or future operating cash receipts or payments, and items of income or expense associated with investing or financing cash flows.

The direct method provides information which may be useful in estimating future cash flows and which is not available under the indirect method and is, therefore, considered more appropriate than the indirect method. Under the direct method, information about major classes of gross cash receipts and gross cash payments may be obtained either:

(*a*) from the accounting records of the enterprise; or

(*b*) by adjusting sales, cost of sales (interest and similar income and interest expense and similar charges for a financial enterprise) and other items in the statement of profit and loss for:

(*i*) changes during the period in inventories and operating receivables and payables;

(*ii*) other non-cash items; and

(*iii*) other items for which the cash effects are investing or financing cash flows.

Under the indirect method, the net cash flows from operating activities is determined by adjusting net profit or loss for the effects of:

(*a*) changes during the period in inventories and operating receivable and payables;

(*b*) non-cash items such as depreciation, provisions, deferred taxes, and unrealised foreign exchange gains and losses; and

(*c*) all other items for which the cash effects are investing or financing cash flows.

Alternatively, the net cash flows from operating activities may be presented under the indirect method by showing the operating revenues and expenses excluding non-cash items disclosed in the statement of profit and loss and the changes during the period in inventories and operating receivables and payables.

(b) Reporting Cash Flows from Investing and Financing Activities

An enterprise should report separately major classes of gross cash receipts and gross cash payments arising from investing and financing activities, except to the extent that cash flows described below are reported on a net basis.

Illustration 3

Extracts from the Balance Sheet of a company i0s given below :

Liabilities	*Jan 2009*	*Dec 2009*	*Assets*	*Jan 2009*	*Dec 2009*
Rs	*Rs*	*Rs.*		*Rs.*	*Rs.*
Profit & Loss Account	50,000	90,000	Goodwill	1,15,000	90,000
			Patents	90,000	1,15,000

How the related items appear in Cash Flow Statement.

Solution :

CASH FLOW STATEMENT FOR THE YEAR ENDED 31st Dec. 2009.

	Rs.
1. **Cash flow from Operating Activities :**	
Closing balance of profit & loss A/c	90,000
Less : Opening balance of profit & losss A/c	(50,000)
Add : Goodwill written off	25,000
Cash from operating Activities	65,000
2. **Cash Flow from Investing Activities:**	
Patents purchased	(25,000)
Cash used in investing Activities	(25,000)

Illustration 4

Extracts from the Balance Sheet of a company is given below :

Liabilities	*Jan. 2009* *Rs.*	*Dec. 2009* *Rs.*	*Assets*	*Jan. 2009* *Rs.*	*Dec. 2009* *Rs.*
Profit & Loss Account	5,00,000	9,00,000	Discount on 15% Debentures	10,000	8,000
15% Debentures	10,00,000	8,00,000			
16% Debentures	8,00,000	10,60,000	Discount on 16% Debentures	8,000	10,000
Unpaid interest on 15% Debentures	—	5,000			

How the above items appear in the Cash Flow Statement.

Solution :

CASH FLOW STATEMENT FOR THE YEAR ENDED 31st Dec. 2009.

		Rs.
1.	**Cash Flow from Operating Activities :**	
	Closing Balance of Profit & Loss Account	9,00,000
	Less : Opening balance of Profit & Loss Account	(5,00,000)
	Add : Discount on issue of 15% Debentures	2,000
	Interest on 15% Debentures	1,50,000
	Interest on 16% Debentures	1,28,000
	Net cash from Operating Activities	6,80,000
2.	**Cash Flow from Financing Activities :**	
	Issue of 16% Debentures (Rs 10,60,000 – Rs. 8,00,000 – Rs. 2,000)	2,58,000
	Redemption of 15% Debentures (Rs. 10,00,000 – Rs. 8,00,000)	(2,00,000)
	Interest paid on 15% Debentures (Rs. 1,50,000 – Rs. 5,000)	(1,45,000)
	Interest on 16% Debentures	(1,28,000)
	Net cash used in Financing Activities	(2,15,000)

Illustration 5

From the following Profit and Loss Account of Ramlal Ltd. calculate Cash generated from "Operating Activities" by Direct Method.

Profit and Loss Account for the Year Ended 31st March 2010.

	Rs.	*Rs.*		*Rs.*
To Opening Stock		1,60,000	By Sale (Cash)	42,50,000
To Purchases (Cash)		31,00,000	By Commission accured	40,000
To Wages	4,40,000		By Dividend received	60,000
Add : Outstanding	60,000	5,00,000	By Profit on sale of plant	2,40,000
To Salaries	2,20,000		(Sale proceeds 22,40,000)	
Add : Outstanding	20,000		— book value Rs. 20,00,000)	
	2,40,000		By Closing Stock	2,20,000
Less : Prepaid	10,000	2,30,000		
To Office Expenses		80,000		
To Selling Expenses		1,20,000		
To Depreciation		1,10,000		

To Income Tax paid	20,000		
To preliminary Expenses			
To Good will written	44,000		
written off	20,000		
To Net profit	4,26,000		
	48,10,000		48,10,000

Solution :

Cash Flow from Operations for the year ended 31st Mar 2010

		Rs.	*Rs.*
(A)	Cash Receipts from Operating Activities :		
	Cash Sales		42,50,000
Less :			
(B)	Cash payments due to operating activities :		
	Purchases	31,00,000	
	Wages	4,40,000	
	Salaries	2,20,000	
	Office Expenses	80,000	
	Selling Expenses	1,20,000	39,60,000
	Cash Flow from operations before Tax		2,90,000
Less :	Income Tax paid		20,000
	Net Cash Inflow from Operations		2,70,000

Notes :

1. Non-cash transactions such as depreciation, Goodwill written off, Preliminary Expenses written off, Commission accrued etc. have been ignored because there is no inflow or outflow of cash.
2. Dividend received, Profit on Sale of Plant are treated cash inflow from 'Investing Activities'.

Illustration 6

(Cash Flows from Operating Activities)

The net income reported on the income statement for the year was Rs. 1,10,000 and depreciation of fixed assets for the year was Rs. 44,000. The balances of the current asset and current liability accounts at the beginning and end of the year are as follows :

	End of the Year	**Beginnig of the Year**
	Rs.	*Rs.*
Cash	1,30,000	1,40,000
Debtors	2,00,000	1,80,000
Inventories	2,90,000	3,00,000
Prepaid Expenses	15,000	16,000
Accounts Payable	1,02,000	1,16,000
Calculate total cash from operating activities		

Solution:

Cash from Operating Activities for the Year

		Rs.	*Rs.*
Net Income			1,10,000
Add :	Depreciation		44,000

Operating profit before working capital changes			1,54,000
Add :	Decrease in Inventories	10,000	
	Decrease in prepaid expenses	1,000	11,000
			1,65,000
Deduct :	Increase in Debtors	20,000	
	Decrease in Accounts Payable	14,000	34,000
Net Cash Flow from Operating Activities			1,31,000

Illustration 7

From the following Profit and Loss A/c and additional information of M/s Dubey Brothers Ltd. compute cash flow from operations.

Profit and Loss Account
for the year ended 31st March, 2010

	Rs.	*Rs.*		*Rs.*
To Opening Stock		1,60,000	By Sale :	
To Purchases			Cash	6,00,000
Cash	2,00,000		Credit	10,00,000
Credit	6,00,000	8,00,000	By Closing Stock	2,08,000
To wages		48,000	By Commission	1,12,000
To Office Expenses		1,76,000	By Royalties	80,000
To Selling Expenses		96,000	By Discount Received	40,000
To Bad debts		16,000		
To Discount Allowed		32,000		
To Depreciation		1,20,000		
To Provision for Tax		2,40,000		
To Net Profit		3,52,000		
		20,40,000		20,40,000

Additional Information	*March 31,2009* Rs.	*March 31, 2010* Rs.
Debtors	1,20,000	1,44,000
Creditors	1,12,000	80,000
O/S Selling Expenses	24,000	32,000
Prepaid Office Expenses	16,000	24,000
Accrued Royalties	96,000	88,000
Advance Commission	72,000	64,000
Provision for Tax	3,20,000	4,80,000

Solution :

Cash Flow from Operations
for the year ended 31st March 2010

	Rs.	Rs.
(A) Receipts from Operations :		
Cash Sales		6,00,000
Cash Received from Debtors (1)		9,76,000

	Cash from Royalties (2)		88,000
	Cash from Commission (3)		1,04,000
			17,68,000
Less:			
(B)	Operating Cash Payments		
	Cash Purchases	2,00,000	
	Cash paid to Creditors (4)	6,32,000	
	Cash Selling Expenses	88,000	
	Cash Office Expenses	1,92,000	11,12,000
	Cash inflow from operations before tax		6,56,000
Less:	Income Tax paid (on operating incomes)		80,000
	Net Cash flow from operations		5,76,000

Workings :

		Rs.
1.	**Cash received from Debtors :**	
	Balance of Debtors (31.3.2009)	1,20,000
	Add : Credit Sales	10,00,000
		11,20,000
	Less : Balance of Debtors (31.3.2010)	1,44,000
	Cash received from Debtors	9,76,000
2.	**Cash received from Royalties :**	
	Royalties accrued (31.3.2009)	96,000
	Add : Royalties, as per P & L A/c	80,000
		1,76,000
	Less : Royalties accrued (31.3.2010)	88,000
	Cash received from Royalties	88,000
3.	**Cash from Commission :**	
	Closing Balance	64,000
	Add : Commission as per P & L A/c	1,12,000
		1,76,000
	Less : Opening balance	72,000
	Cash from Commission	1,04,000
4.	**Cash paid to Creditors :**	
	Opening Balance	1,12,000
	Add : Purchases	6,00,000
		7,12,000
	Less : Closing Balance	80,000
	Cash paid to Creditors	6,32,000

(c) Reporting Cash Flows on a Net Basis

Cash flows arising from the following operating, investing or financing activities may be reported on a net basis:

(*a*) cash receipts and payments on behalf of customers when the cash flows reflect the activities of the customer rather than those of the enterprise; and (*b*) cash receipts and payments for items in which the turnover is quick, the amounts are large, and the maturities are short.

Examples of cash receipts and payments referred to in paragraph (*a*) above are:

(*a*) the acceptance and repayment of demand deposits by a bank;

(*b*) funds help for customers by an investment enterprise; and

(*c*) rents collected on behalf, and paid over to, the owners of properties.

Examples of cash receipts and payments referred to in paragraph (*b*) are advances made for, and the repayments of:

(*a*) principal amounts relating to credit card customers;

(*b*) the purchase and sale investments; and

(*c*) other short-term borrowings, for example, those which have a maturity period of three months or less.

Cash flows arising from each of the following activities of a financial enterprise may be reported on a net basis:

(*a*) cash receipts and payments for the acceptance and repayment of deposits with a fixed maturity date;

(*b*) the placement of deposits with and withdrawal of deposits from other financial enterprises; and

(*c*) cash advances and loans made to customers and the repayment of those advances and loans.

Other Items : In addition to the cash flows described, AS-3 (Revised) also deals with certain other items as shown below:

1. Foreign Currency Cash Flows

Cash flows arising from transactions in a foreign currency should be recorded in an enterprises reporting currency by applying to the foreign currency amount the exchange rate between the reporting currency and the foreign currency at the date of the cash flow : A rate that approximates the actual rate may be used if the result is substantially the same as would arise, if the rates at the date of cash flows were used. The effect of changes in exchange rates on cash and cash equivalents held in a foreign currency should be reported as a separate part of the reconciliation of the changes in cash and cash equivalents during the period.

Cash flows denominated in foreign currency are reported in a manner consistent with Accounting Standard (AS) 11, according for the Effects of Changes in Foreign Exchange Rates. This permits the use of an exchange rate that approximates the actual rate. For example, a weighted average exchange rate for a period may be used for recording foreign currency transactions.

Unrealized gains and losses arising from changes in foreign exchange rates are not cash flows. However, the effect of exchange rate changes on cash and cash equivalents held or due in a foreign currency is reported in the cash flow statement in order to reconcile cash and cash equivalents at the beginning and the end of the period. This amount is presented separately from cash flows from operating, investing and financing activities and include the differences, if any, had those cash flows been reported at the end-of-period exchange rates.

2. Extraordinary Items

The cash flows associated with extraordinary items should be classified as arising from operating, investing or financing activities as appropriate and separately disclosed.

The cash flows associated with extraordinary items are disclosed separately as arising from operating, investing or financing activities in the cash flow statement, to enable users to understand their nature and effect on the present and future cash flows of the enterprise. These disclosures are in addition to the separate disclosures of the nature and amount of extraordinary items required by Accounting Standard (AS) 5, Net Profit or Loss for the Period, Prior Period Items and Changes in Accounting Policies.

3. Interest and Dividends

Cash flows from interest and dividends received and paid should be disclosed each separately. Cash flows arising from interest paid and interest and dividends received in the case of a financial enterprise should be classified as cash flows arising from operating activities. In the case of other enterprises, cash flows arising from interest paid should be classified as cash flows from financing activities while interest and dividends received should be classified as cash flows from investing activities. Dividends paid should be classified as cash flows from financing activities.

The total amount of interest paid during the period is disclosed in the cash flow statement whether it has been recognized as an expense in the statement of profit and loss or capitalized in accordance with Accounting Standard (AS) 10, Accounting for Fixed Assets.

Interest paid, interest and dividends received are usually classified as operating cash flows for a financial enterprise. However, there is no consensus on the classification of these cash flows for other enterprises. Some argue that interest paid, and interest dividends received may be classified as operating cash flows because they enter into the determination of net profit or loss. However, it is more appropriate that interest paid, interest and dividends received are classified as financing cash flows and investing cash flows respectively, because they are cost of obtaining financial resources or returns on investments.

Some argue that dividends paid may be classified as a component of cash flows from operating activities in order to assist users to determine the ability of an enterprise to pay dividends out of operating cash flows. However, it is considered more appropriate that dividends paid should be classified as cash flows from financing activities because they are cost of obtaining financial resources.

4. Taxes on Income

Cash flows arising from taxes on income should be separately disclosed and should be classified as cash flows from operating activities unless they can be specically identified with financing and investing activities.

Taxes on income arise on trasactions that give rise to cash flows that are classfied as operating, investing or financing activities in a cash flow statement. While tax expense may be readily identifiable with investing or financing activities, the related tax cash flows are often impracticable to identify and may arise in a different period from the cash flows of the underlying transactions. Therefore, taxes paid are usually classified as cash flows from operating activities. However, when it is practicable to identify the tax cash flow with an individual transaction that gives rise to cash flows that are classified as investing or financing activities, the tax cash flow is classified as an investing or financing activity as appropriate. When tax cash flow are allocated over more than one class of activity, the total amount of taxes paid is disclosed.

5. Investments in Subsidiaries, Associates and Joint Ventures

When accounting for an investment in an associate or a subsidiary or a joint venture, an investor restricts its reporting in the cash flow statement to the cash flows between itself and the investee/joint venture, for example, cash flows relating to dividends and advances.

6. Acquisitions and Disposals of Subsidiaries and other Business Units

The aggregate cash flows arising from acquisitions and from disposals of subsidiaries or other business unit should be presented separately and classified as investing activities.

An enterprise should disclose, in aggregate, in respect of both acquisition and disposal of subsidiaries or other business units during the period each of the following:

(*a*) the total purchase or disposal consideration; and

(*b*) the portion of the purchase or disposal consideration discharged by means of cash and cash equivalents.

The separate presentation of the cash flow effects of acquisitions and disposals of subsidiaries and other business units as single line items helps to distinguish those cash flows from other cash flows. The cash flows effects of disposals are not deducted from those of acquisition.

7. Non-cash Transactions

Investing and financing transactions that do not require the use of cash or cash equivalents should be excluded from a cash flow statement. Such transactions should be disclosed elsewhere in the financial statements in a way that provides all the relevant information about these investing and financing activities.

Many investing and financing activities do not have a direct impact on current cash flows although they do affect the capital and asset structure of an enterprise. The exclusion of non-cash transactions from the cash flow statement is consistent with the objective of a cash flow statement as these items do into involve cash flows in the current period. Examples of non-cash transactions are :

(*a*) the acquisition of assets by assuming directly related liabilities;

(*b*) the acquisition of an enterprise by means of issue of shares; and

(*c*) the conversion of debt to equity.

8. Components of Cash and Cash Equivalents

An enterprise should disclose the components of cash and cash equivalents and should present a reconciliation of the amounts in its cash flow statement with the equivalent items reported in the balance sheet.

In view of the variety of cash management practices, an enterprise discloses the policy, which it adopts in determining the composition of cash and cash equivalents.

The effect of any change in the policy for determining components of cash and cash equivalents is reported in accordance with Accounting Standard (AS) 5, Net Profit or Loss for the Period, prior period items and changes in Accounting Policies.

Other Disclosures

An enterprise should disclose, together with a commentary by management, the amount of significant cash and cash equivalent balances held by the enterprise that are not available for use by it.

There are various circumstances in which cash and cash equivalents balances held by an enterprise are not available for use by it. Examples include cash and cash equivalent balances held by a branch of the enterprise that operates in a country where exchange controls or other legal restrictions apply as a result of which the balances are not available for use by the enterprise.

Additional information may be relevant to users in understanding the financial position of liquidity of an enterprise. Disclosure of this information, together with a commentary by management, is encouraged and may include :

(*a*) the amount of undrawn borrowing facilitates that may be available for future operating activities and to settle capital commitments, indicating any restrictions on the use of these facilities; and

(*b*) the aggregate amount of cash flows that represent increases in operating capacity separately from those cash flows that are required to maintain operating capacity.

The separate dissclosure of cash flows that represent increase in operating capacity and cash flows that are required to maintain operating capacity is useful in enabling the user to determine whether the enterprise is investing adequately in the maintenance of its operating capacity. An enterprise that does not invest adequately in the maintenance of its operating capacity may be prejudicing future profitability for the sake of current liquidity and distributions to owners.

FORMAT OF CASH FLOW STATEMENT

'AS–3' has not provided any specific format for the preparation of Cash Flow Statement. However, SEBI, which amended clause 32 of the Listing agreement in 1995 requiring all listed companies to prepare a Cash Flow Statement, has provided format for Cash Flow Statement. The following is widely used format of Cash Flow Statement.

CASH FLOW STATEMENT ....(DIRECT METHOD)

	Rs.	*Rs.*
Cash Flows from Operating Activities :		
Cash receipts from customers	xxx	
Less : Cash paid to suppliers and employees	(xxx)	
Cash flows before extraordinary items	xxx	
Less : Income Taxes paid	(xxx)	
Cash flows before extraordinary items	xxx	
Less : Extraordinary items	(xxx)	
Net Cash from Operating activities		xxx
Cash Flows from Investing Activities :		
Purchase of Fixed Assets	(xxx)	
Proceeds from Sale of Fixed Assets	xxx	
Interest received	xxx	
Dividend received	xxx	
Net Cash from Investing Activities		xxx
Cash Flows from Financing Activities :		
Proceeds from Issue of share capital	xxx	
Proceeds from Long-term Borrowings	xxx	
Repayment of Long-term Borrowings	(xxx)	
Interest paid	(xxx)	
Dividend paid	(xxx)	
Net Cash from Financing Activities		xxx
Net Increase/Decrease in Cash and Cash Equivalents		xxx
Add : Cash and Cash Equivalents at the beginning of the period		xxx
Cash and Cash Equivalents at the end of the period		xxx

CASH FLOW STATEMENT FOR .... (INDIRECT METHOD)

	Rs.	*Rs.*
Cash Flows from operating Activities :		
Net Profit before Tax and Extraordinary Items	xxx	
Adjustments for :		
Depreciation	xxx	
Loss on Foreign Exchange	xxx	
Interest Expense	xxx	

Loss on Sale of Fixed Assets	xxx	
Dividend Income	(xxx)	
Interest Income	(xxx)	
Operating profit before working capital changes	xxx	
Adjustments for :		
Sundry Debtors	xxx	
Bills Receivable	xxx	
Inventories	xxx	
Bills Payable	xxx	
Cash generated from operations	xxx	
Less : Income Tax paid	xxx	
Cash flow before extraordinary items	xxx	
Add / Less : Extraordinary Items	xxx	
Net cash from operating activities		xxx
Cash Flows from Investing Activities :		
Purchase of Fixed assets and Investments	(xxx)	
Proceeds from Sale of Fixed Assets and Investments	xxx	
Interest received	xxx	
Dividend received	xxx	
Net cash from investing activities		xxx
Cash flows from Financing Activities		
Proceeds from Issue of Share capital	xxx	
Proceeds from Long-term borrowings	xxx	
Repayment of Long-term borrowings	(xxx)	
Interest Paid	(xxx)	
Dividend Paid	(xxx)	
Net Cash from Financing Activities		xxx
Net Increase / Decrease in Cash and Cash Equivalents		xxx
Add : Cash and Cash Equivalent at the beginning of the period		xxx
Cash and Cash Equivalents at the end of the period		xxx

Cash flows shown in bracket are treated as minus figures while making total.

NB : Indirect method is more popular and usually followed, unless 'Direct Method' is specifically asked.

METHODS OF PRESENTING CASH FLOW STATEMENT

As mentioned earlier, the Cash Flow Statement should report cash flows during the period classified by THREE distinct activities, that is, Operating, Investing and Financing. This type of report provides information which allows the users to assess and examine the impact of those activities on the financial position of the enterprise in terms of its cash and cash equivalents.

(a) Reporting Cash Flows from Operating Activities

An enterprise should report cash flows from operating activities using either of the two methods mentioned below:

(*i*) **Direct Method.** The direct method provides information which may be useful in estimating the future cash flows and which is not available under indirect method. Therefore, direct method is considered more appropriate than indirect method. Under the direct method information about major classes of gross cash receipts and gross cash payments may be obtained either:

(1) from the accounting records of the enterprise;

(2) by adjusting sales, cost of sales (in the case of financial enterprise interest and similar income and interest expense and similar charges) and other items in the statement of Profit and Loss for :

(A) Changes during the period in inventories and operating receivables and payables;

(B) Other non-cash items, and

(C) Other items for which the cash effects are investing or financing cash flows.

(*ii*) **Indirect Method.** Under this method, the net cash flow from operating activities is determined by adjusting net profit or loss for the effects of :

(A) Changes during the period in inventories and operating receivables and payables;

(B) Non-cash items such as depreciation, provisions, deferred taxes and unrealised foreign exchange gains and losses; and

(C) All other items for which cash effects are investing or financing cash flows.

Alternatively, the net cash flow from operating activities may be presented under the indirect method by sharing the operating revenues and expenses excluding non-cash items disclosed in the statement of profit and loss and changes during the period in inventories and operating receivables and payables.

Illustration 8

Following are the summary of Cash Transactions extracted from the books of X Ltd. :

	Rs.		*Rs.*
To Balance b/d (1.1.2010)	35,000	By Payments to Suppliers	20,47,000
To Receipts from Customers	27,83,000	By Payment for Fixed Assets	2,30,000
To Share Capital	3,00,000	By Payments for Overheads	1,15,000
To Fixed Assets (Sales)	1,28,000	By Salaries	69,000
		By Income Tax	2,43,000
		By Dividends Paid	80,000
		By Bank Loan	2,50,000
		By Balance c/d (31.12.2010)	2,12,000
	32,46,000		32,46,000

Prepare a Cash Flow Statement of the Company for the period ended 31st December 2010 in accordance with AS–3 by Direct Method. (*B.Com. MS*)

Solution :

Cash Flow Statement

	Rs.	*Rs.*
1. *Cash Flows from Operating Activities :*		
Receipts from Customers	27,83,000	
Payment to Suppliers	(20,47,000)	
Payment of Salaries	(69,000)	
Payments of Overheads	(1,15,000)	
Payment of Taxes	(2,43,000)	
Net Cash from Operating Activities :		3,09,000
2. *Cash Flows from Investing Activities :*		
Proceeds from Sale of Fixed Assets	1,28,000	
Payments for Fixed Assets	(2,30,000)	

Net Cash from Investing Activities :		(1,02,000)
3. *Cash Flows from Financing Activities :*		
Issue of Shares	3,00,000	
Payment of Dividends	(80,000)	
Repayment of Bank Loan	(2,50,000)	
Net cash from Financing Activities		(30,000)
Net increase in Cash		1,77,000
Cash Balance on 1.1.2010		35,000
Cash Balance at the end 31.12.2010		2,12,000

Illustration 9

The financial position of Ram is given below :

	1.1.2010	31.12.2010		1.1.2010	31.12.2010
Creditors	145	125	Cash	200	150
Capital	3,695	3,075	Debtors	100	65
			Stock	40	65
			Building	500	400
			Plant	3,000	2,500
	3,840	3,200		3,840	3,200

There were no drawings or purchases of assets during the year. Prepare a Statement of Cash Flow from Operating Activities. (*B.Com. Madras*)

Solution :

Statement of Cash Flow from Operating Activities

	Rs.	*Rs.*
Capital (1.1.2010)	3,075	
Less : Capital (31.12.2010)	3,695	
Net Loss		(620)
Add : Non-cash items and appropriations :		
Depreciation : on Buildings	100	
on Plant	500	600
Operating Loss before working Capital Changes		(20)
Add : Decrease in Debtors		15
		(5)
Less : Decrease in Creditors	20	
Increase in Stock	25	(45)
Outflow of cash from Operating Activities :		(50)

Illustration 10

From the following summary of Cash Account of X Ltd., prepare Cash Flow Statement for the year ended 31st March 2010 in accordance with AS–3 using the direct method. The company does not have any cash equivalents.

SUMMARY (CASH ACCOUNT) 31.3.2010

	Rs.		Rs.
To Balance b/d 1.4.2009	50	By Payment to Suppliers	2,000
To Equity Shares	300	By Purchase of Fixed Assets	200
To Receipt from Customers	2,800	By Overhead Expenses	200
To Sale of Fixed Assets	100	By Wages & Salaries	100
		By Taxation	250
		By Dividends	50
		By Repayment of Loan	300
		By Balance c/d (31.8.2010)	150
	3,250		3,250

Solution :

CASH FLOW STATEMENT
for the year ended 31st March 2010

	Rs. ('000)	Rs. ('000)
(A) *Cash Flows from Operating Activities*:		
Cash from customers	2,800	
Cash payment to Suppliers	(2,000)	
Cash paid for overhead expenses	(200)	
Cash paid for salaries	(100)	
Cash generated from Operations	500	
Income Tax paid	(250)	
Net Cash from Operating Activities		250
(B) *Cash Flows from Investing Activities*:		
Purchase of Fixed Assets	(200)	
Cash from Sale of Fixed Assets	100	
Net Cash used in Investing Activities:		(100)
(C) *Cash Flows from Financing Activities*:		
Issue of Equity Shares	300	
Repayment of Loan	(300)	
Payment of Dividends	(50)	
Net Cash used in Financing Activities		(50)
Net increase in Cash & Cash equivalent :		100
Cash and Cash equivalent (1.4.'09)		50
Cash and Cash equivalent (31.3.'10)		150

Illustration 11

The following is the summarised income statement of ABC Ltd. for the year ended 31st March 2010.

Particulars	*Rs.*
Sales (including cash sales Rs. 20,000)	1,60,000
Less : Operating Expenses excluding Depreciation	1,00,000
	60,000

Less :	Depreciation	20,000
	Net Profit before Tax	40,000
Add :	Extraordinary Income – gain on speculation	10,000
		50,000
Less :	Provision for Tax at 40%	20,000
	Net Profit after Tax	30,000

The following additional data is also available for 2009–2010.

(a) Operating expenses include Loss on Sale of Furniture Rs. 4,000.

(b) Tax paid during the year 2008–2009 Rs. 18,000.

(c) Current Assets and Liabilities at the end of 2008–2009 and 2009–2010 were as under :

	31.3.2010	*31.3.2009*
Debtors	16,000	12,000
Stock	13,000	14,000
Creditors	18,000	17,000

You are required to ascertain Net Cash Flow from Operating activities by :

(A) Direct Method

(B) Indirect Method (*B.Com. Madras*)

Solution :

(A) Direct Method :

COMPUTATION OF NET CASH FLOW FROM OPERATING ACTIVITIES

	Particulars	*Rs.*
	Cash receipts from customers (1)	1,56,000
Less :	Cash payments to suppliers and employees (2)	94,000
	Cash generated from operations	62,000
Less :	Income Tax paid	18,000
	Cash flow before extraordinary items	44,000
Add :	Extraordinary income – gain on Speculation	10,000
	Net cash flow from operating activities	54,000

Workings :

1. CASH RECEIPTS FROM CUSTOMERS

	Particulars	*Rs.*
	Credit Sales (1,60,000 – 20,000)	1,40,000
Add :	Opening Debtors	12,000
		1,52,000
Less :	Closing Debtors	16,000
	Cash collecting from Debtors	1,36,000
Add :	Cash Sales	20,000
	Cash receipts from customers	1,56,000

2. CASH PAYMENTS TO SUPPLIERS AND EMPLOYEES

Particulars	Rs.	Rs.
Operating Expenses, as given		1,00,000
Less : Loss on sale of Furniture	4,000	
Less : Decrease in Stock	1,000	
Less : Increase in Creditors	1,000	
		6,000
Cash payment to suppliers and employees		94,000

(B) Indirect Method :

COMPUTATION OF NET CASH FLOW FROM OPERATING ACTIVITIES

Particulars	Rs.	Rs.
Net Profit before Tax and extraordinary items (1)		40,000
Adjustments For :		
Depreciation	20,000	
Loss on Sales of Furniture	4,000	
		24,000
Operating Profit before working capital changes		64,000
Decrease in Stock	1,000	
Increase in Creditors	1,000	
Increase in Debtors	(4,000)	(2,000)
Cash Generated from Operation		62,000
Less : Income Tax Paid		18,000
Cash flow before extraordinary items		44,000
Add : Extraordinary income – Gain on Speculation		10,000
Net Cash Flow from operating activities (1)		54,000

	Rs.
Net Profit after Tax given	30,000
Add : Provision for Tax	20,000
	50,000
Less : Extraordinary Income – gain on speculation	10,000
Net profit before Tax and extraordinary items	40,000

Illustration 12

From the following, calculate cash from operation by Indirect Method.

Profit and Loss Account
for the year ended 31st March, 2010

	Rs.	Rs.		Rs.
To opening stock		2,00,000	By Sales	45,00,000
To Purchses		36,40,000	By Closing Stock	2,40,000
To Wages	2,25,000			
+ Outstanding	25,000	2,50,000		
To Manufacturing Expenses		75,000		
To Gross Profit c/d		5,75,000		

		47,40,000		47,40,000
To Salaries	1,37,500		By Gross Profit b/d	5,75,000
Add Outstanding	62,500	2,00,000	By Rent Received	37,500
To Insurance	30,000		By Commission Accrued	17,500
Less Prepaid	7,500	22,500	By Net Loss	55,000
To Office Expenses		1,17,500		
To Selling Expenses		1,45,000		
To Depreciation		1,25,000		
To Share Issue Expenses w/o		75,000		
		6,85,000		6,85,000

Solution :

Calculatin of Cash From Operating Activities
(Indirect Method)

		Rs.	Rs.
	Net Loss as per Profit and Loss A/c (before tax and extraordinary item)		(55,000)
	Adjustments for Non cash charges and Non-operating items.		
Add	Depreciation	1,25,000	
Add	Share Issue Expenses w/o	75,000	2,00,000
			1,45,000
Less	Rent Received (Non-operating)		(37,500)
	Operating profit before Working Capital Changes		1,07,500
	Adjustment for current assets/liabilities:		
Add	Increase in Current Liabilities		
	Wages O/S	25,000	
	Salaries	62,500	87,500
			1,95,000
Less	Increase in Current Assets		
	Stock	40,000	
	Prepaid Insurance	7,500	
	Accrued Commission	17,500	65,000
	Net cash from operating Activities		1,30,000

Illustration 13

The following details are provided for X Ltd.

INCOME STATEMENT FOR 2010

	Rs.
Revenues	84,000
Cost of goods sold	(48,000)
Depreciation expense	(4,000)
Interest expense	(6,000)
Other expenses	(22,000)
Net income	4,000

Comparative Balance Sheet Data

	2010	2009
Current Assets	*Rs.*	*Rs.*
Cash	20,000	16,000
Debtors (net)	12,000	7,000
Stock in hand	16,000	14,000
Non Current Assets		
Plant and machinery	24,000	20,000
Less : Accumulated Depreciation	(8,000)	(4,000)
Total Assets	64,000	53,000
Liabilities		
Creditors	12,000	14,000
Non-current Note Payable	20,000	20,000
Less: Discount on Note	(1,600)	(2,000)
	30,400	32,000
Owner's Equity		
Equity Share Capital	24,000	14,000
Retained Earnings	9,600	7,000
	33,600	21,000

Prepare statement of cash flows using the indirect Method as per, [AS-3 (Revised)]
Solution :

Cash Flow Statement For the Year Ended 31 December 2010
[AS-3 (Revised)] (Indirect Method)

	Rs.	Rs.
(A) Cash Flows from Operating Activities		
Net Income before tax	4,000	
Adjustments for :		
Depreciation	4,000	
Amortization of discount on note payable	400	
Intereste expense	6,000	
Operating Profit before working capital changes	14,400	
Increase in Debtors	(5,000)	
Increase in Inventories	(2,000)	
Decrease in Creditors	(2,000)	
Net cash provided by operating activities		5,400
(B) Cash Flows from Investing activities		
Purchase of Plant and Machinery	(4,000)	
Net cash used in investing activities		(4,000)
(C) Cash Flows from Financing Activities		
Issues of Share Capital	10,000	
Interest Paid	(6,000)	
Dividends Paid	(1,400)	
Net cash from financing activities		2,600
Net increase in cash and cash equivalents (A + B + C)		4,000
Cash and cash equivalents at the beginning of the period		16,000
Cash and cash equivalents at the end of the period		20,000

Note :

Dividends paid have been calculated as under :

	Rs.
Retained earnings at the beginning	7,000
Add : Net Income	4,000
	11,000
Less: Ratained earnings at the end	9,600
Dividend paid	1,400

Illustration 14

From the following particulars, prepare Cash Flow Statement for the year ended 31st March 2010 using.

(a) Direct Method

(b) Indirect Method

(A) Income Statement For the year ended 31st March, 2010

		Rs.	*Rs.*
	Turnover		12,80,000
Less :	Cost of Goods Sold		8,00,000
			4,80,000
Add :	Other Receipts		
	Insurance Claims for loss of Stock due to fire		20,000
			5,00,000
Less :	Operating Expenses	3,16,000	
	Interest on Debentures	6,000	
	Depreciation	84,000	
	Discount on Debentures w/o	400	4,06,400
	Profit before Tax		93,600
Less :	Provision for Tax		36,800
	Profit after Tax		56,800

(B) The Assest and Liabilities as on 31.3.2009 and 31st March 2010 were as under :

	31.03.2009	*31.03.2010*
	Rs.	*Rs.*
Stock	72,000	88,000
Debtors	16,000	15,200
Bills receivable	12,000	22,000'
Cash and Bank balance	44,800	99,200
Creditors	31,200	38,000
Bills Payable	8,000	6,000
O/S Expenses	12,400	17,600

(C) Additional Information :

(i) Fully paid Equity shares of the face value of Rs. 80,000 were allotted at a premium of @20%.

(ii) Fixed assets were acquired for Rs. 60,000 and the payment was made in 6% convertible debenture at par.

(iii) Income Tax paid during the year amounted to Rs. 38,000.

(iv) Company paid a dividend and corporate dividend tax there on for the year ended 31st

March 2009 amounting to Rs. 44,000.

(v) 9% Debentures for Rs. 1,20,000 were redeemed at a premium of 2%.

Solution :

(A) Cash Flow Statement (Direct Method)

	Rs.	Rs.
Cash Flow from Operating Activities		
(a) Operating Cash Receipts :		
Cash from customers (1)	12,70,800	
(b) Operating cash Payments (2)	11,22,000	
Cash Flow from Operations (a – b)	1,48,800	
Income Tax Paid	(38,000)	
	1,10,800	
	Rs	Rs.
Cash Flow from Extra Ordinary items :		
Add : Claims Received	20,000	
Net Cash Flow from operating activities :		1,30,800
Cash Flow from Financing Activities		
Issue of shares at premium (3)	96,000	
• Redemption of Debentures	(1,22,400)	
• Interest on Debentures	(6,000)	
• Dividend and Corporate dividend Tax	(44,000)	
Net Cash used in financing Activities		(76,400)
Net increase in Cash and Cash Equivalents		54,400
Cash and Cash Equivalents in the beginning		44,800
Cash and Cash equivalents at the end		99,200

	Rs.
1. **ACCOUNTS RECEIVABLE :**	
Debtors + Bills Receivable (31.3.2009) (Rs. 16,000 + Rs. 12,000)	28,000
Add : Sales for the year	12,08,000
	13,08,000
Less : Debtors + Bills Receivable (31.3.2010) (Rs. 15,200 + Rs. 22,000)	37,200
Cash free customers :	12,70,800
2. **Cash paid against Operating Expenses :** (Rs. 12,400 + Rs. 3,16,000 – Rs. 17,600)	3,10,000
Cash paid to Creditors :	8,11,200
	11,22,000
ACCOUNTS PAYABLE :	
Creditors + Bills Payable (31.3.2009) (Rs. 31.200 + Rs. 8,000)	39,200
Add : Purchases*	8,16,000

		8,55,200
Less :	Creditors + Bills Payable (31.3.2010)	
	(Rs. 38,000 + Rs. 6,000)	44,000
	Cash paid to Creditors	8,11,200

*Purchases = Closing Stock + Cost of Goods sold – Opening Stock

(Rs. 88,00 + 8,00,000 + Rs. 72,000 = Rs. 8,16,000)

3. Face value of shares issued	80,000 Add
Premium at 20%	16,000
	96,000

(B) CASH FLOW STATEMENT AS PER AS-3 (REVISED)

(Indirect Method)

	Rs.	Rs.
1. **Cash Flow from Operating Activities :**		
Net Profit before Tax and Extraordinary Item	73,600	
Adjustment for Non Cash and Non Operating Items:		
Depreciation	84,000	
Discount on Issue of Debentures	400	
Interest on Debentures	6,000	
Operating profit before Working Capital Changes	1,64,000	
Adjustment for current items.		
– Increase in Stock	(16,000)	
– Increase in Bills Receivable	(10,000)	
– Decrease in Bills Payable	(2,000)	
+ Decrease in Debtors	800	
+ Increase in Creditors	6,800	
+ Increase in o/s Expenses	5,200	
Cash generated from operation	1,48,800	
Less Income Tax paid	38,000	
Cash flow from operation before Extraordinary item	1,10,800	
Add Insurance Claim for Loss of Stock	20,000	
Net Cash generated from operation		1,30,800
II Cash Flow from Investing Activities		—
III Cash Flow from Financing Activities	—	—
Issue of shares at premium	96,000	
Redemption of Debentures	(1,22,400)	
Interest on Debentures	(6,000)	
Dividend and corprate dividend Tax	(44,000)	
Net cash used in Financing Activities		(76,400)
Net Increase in Cash and Cash Equivalents		54,400
Cash and Cash Equivalents in the beginning		44,800
Cash and Cash Equivalents in the end		99,200

NB : Issue of debenture's against acquisition of land. There in no flow of cash.

Illustration 15

The following are the Balance Sheets and Income Statement of Hari Ltd.

Liabilities	*31.3.2009* Rs.	*31.3.2010* Rs.	*Assets*	*313..2009* Rs.	*31.3.2010* Rs.
Share Capital	1,80,000	2,22,000	Fixed Assets :		
Profit & Loss A/c	75,900	81,900	Land	24,000	48,000
Creditors	1,20,000	1,17,000	Buildings	1,80,000	2,88,000
Outstanding Expenses	12,000	24,000	Current Assets :		
Provision for Tax	6,000	6,600	Cash	30,000	36,000
Depreciation provision			Debtors	84,000	93,000
on Buildings	60,000	66,000	Stock	1,32,000	48,000
			Advances	3,900	4,500
	4,53,900	5,17,500		4,33,900	5,17,500

Cost of Building was Rs. 36,000

Profit and Loss Account
for the year ended 31.3.2010

Particulars	Rs.	*Particulars*	Rs.
To Cost of Sales	9,90,000	By Net Sales	12,60,000
To Wages and Salaries	1,20,000		
To Gross Profit c/d	1,50,000		
	12,60,000		12,60,000
To Operating Expenses	40,000	By Gross Profit b/d	1,50,000
To Depreciation	30,000	By Profit on Sale of Building	6,000
To Provision for Tax	44,000		
To Net Profit c/d	42,000		
	1,56,000		1,56,000
To Proposed dividend	36,000	By Balance b/d	75,900
To Balance carried to		By Net Profit b/d	42,000
Balance Sheet	81,900		
	1,17,900		1,17,900

You are required to prepare a Cash Flow Statement using

(A) Direct Method

(B) Indirect Method (*B.Com. MS*)

Solution :

(A) Direct Method :

Cash Flows Statement of Hari Ltd.
for the year ended 31.3.2010

	Particulars	Rs.	Rs.
I	*Cash flows from operating activities*:		
	Cash receipts from customers (1)	12,51,000	
	Cash paid to Suppliers and Employees (2)	(10,57,600)	
	Cash generated from operations	1,93,400	
	Income Tax paid (3)	(43,400)	
	Net Cash from operating activities		1,50,000

II *Cash flows from Investing activities*:		
Purchase of Land (48,000 – 24,000)	(24,000)	
Purchase of Building (4)	(1,44,000)	
Sale of Building	18,000	
		(1,50,000)
III *Cash flow from Financing Activities*:		
Issue of shares (2,22,000 – 1,80,000)	42,000	
Dividend paid	(36,000)	
Net Cash from Financing Activities		6,000
Net Increase in Cash and Cash equivalents		6,000
Add : Cash and Cash equivalents at the beginning of the year		30,000
Cash and Cash equivalents at the end of the year		36,000

Workings :

(1)

	Rs.	*Rs.*
Cash receipts from customers :	12,60,000	
Sales	84,000	
Add : Opening debtors	13,44,000	
Less : Debtors at the end	93,000	
Cash receipts from customers	12,51,000	

(2)

	Rs.	*Rs.*
Cash paid to suppliers and Employees :		
Cost of Sales		9,90,000
Add : Operating Expenses		40,000
Add : Wages and Salaries		1,20,000
		11,50,000
Add : Opening Creditors	1,20,000	
Closing Stock	48,000	
Closing Advances	4,500	
Closing Outstanding Expenses	12,000	
		1,84,500
		13,34,500
Less : Closing Creditors	1,17,000	
Opening Stock	1,32,000	
Opening Advances	3,900	
Closing Outstanding Expenses	24,000	
		2,76,900
Cash paid to Suppliers and Employees		10,57,600

(3) PROVISION FOR TAX ACCOUNT

Particulars	Rs.	Particulars	Rs.
To Bank (Tax paid) (Bal. fig.)	43,400	By Balance b/d	6,000
To Balance c/d	6,600	By P & L A/c (Provision mode)	44,000
	50,000		50,000

(4) BUILDINGS A/C (AT COST)

Particulars	Rs.	Particulars	Rs.
To Balance b/d	1,80,000	By Depreciation Provision A/c	24,000
To P & L A/c (Profit on Sale)	6,000	(Depreciation on Building Sold)	
To Bank (Purchase)	1,44,000	By Bank (Sale)	18,000
(Bal. fig.)		By Balance c/d	2,88,000
	3,30,000		3,30,000

DEPRECIATION PROVISION ON BUILDINGS A/C

Particulars	Rs.	Particulars	Rs.
To Buildings A/c	24,000	By Balance b/d	60,000
(Depreciation on Building		By P & L A/c (Current year's	30,000
sold) (Bal. fig.)		depreciation)	
To Balance c/d	66,000		
	90,000		90,000

(B) Indirect Method :

CASH FLOW STATEMENT OF HARI LTD.
for the year ending on 31.3.2010

Particulars	Rs.	Rs.
I. *Cash flows from operating activities :*		
Net Profit before Tax and Extraordinary items (42,000 + 44,000)	86,000	
Adjustments for :		
Depreciation	30,000	
Profit on Sale of Building	(6,000)	
Operating Profit before working Capital changes	1,10,000	
Increase in debtors	(9,000)	
Decrease in Stock	84,000	
Increase in Advances	(600)	
Decrease in Creditors	(3,000)	
Increase in outstanding expenses	12,000	
Cash generated from operations	1,93,400	
Income Tax paid (3)	(43,400)	
Net cash from operating activities		1,50,000
II. *Cash flows from Investing activities :*		
Purchase of Land (48,000 – 24,000)	(24,000)	
Purchase of Building (4)	(1,44,000)	
Sale of Building	18,000	

Net Cash used in investing activities		(1,50,000)
III *Cash flows from Financing activities :*		
Issue of Shares (2,22,000 – 1,80,000)	42,000	
Dividend paid	(36,000)	
Net Cash from Financing activities		6,000
Net Increase in Cash and Cash Equivalents		6,000
Add : Cash and Cash equivalents at the beginning of the year		30,000
Cash and Cash equivalents at the end of the year		36,000

Illustration 16

Following are the Balance Sheets of a Ramlal & Sons :

Liabilities	*1.1.2010* *Rs.*	*31.12.2010* *Rs.*	*Assets*	*1.1.2010* *Rs.*	*31.12.2010* *Rs.*
Creditors	36,000	41,000	Cash	4,000	3,600
Loan from partner	–	20,000	Debtors	35,000	38,400
Loan from bank	30,000	25,000	Stock	25,000	22,000
Capital	1,48,000	1,49,000	Land	20,000	30,000
			Building	50,000	55,000
			Machinery	80,000	86,000
	2,14,000	2,35,000		2,14,000	2,35,000

During the year Rs. 26,000 paid as dividends. The provision for depreciation against machinery as on 1.1.2010 was Rs. 27,000 and on 31.12.2010 Rs. 36,000. Prepare a cash flow statement.

(*B.Com. Madras, Bangalore, Poona*)

Solution :

CASH FLOW STATEMENT
for the year ended 31st December 2010

	Rs.	Rs.
(A) *Cash Flows from Operating Activities :*		
Net Profit before tax and extraordinary items	27,000[1]	
Adjustment for Depreciation	9,000	
	36,000	
Increase in Current Liabilities	5,000	
Increase in Debtors	(3,400)	
Decrease in Stock	3,000	
Net Cash from Operating Activities :		40,600
(B) *Cash Flows from Investing Activities :*		
Purchase of Land	(10,000)	
Purchase of Buildings	(5,000)	
Purchase of Machinery	(15,000)	
Net Cash from Investing Activities :		(30,000)
(C) *Cash Flows from Financing Activities :*		
Loan	20,000	
Repayment of Bank Loan	(5,000)	

	Rs.	Rs.
Payment of Dividends	(26,000)	
Net cash from Financing Activities :		(11,000)
Net Cash		(400)
Cash and Cash Equivalent (1.1.2010)		4,000
Cash and Cash equivalent (31.12.2010)		3,600

1. Net Profit before Tax :

Capital (1.1.2010)	Rs. 1,48,000
Capital (31.12.2010)	Rs. 1,49,000
Difference	(–) 1,000
Add : Dividends	26,000
	27,000

Illustration 17

From the following Balance Sheets as on 31st December, prepare Cash Flow Statement :

Balance Sheets

Liabilities	*2010* *Rs.*	*2009* *Rs.*	*Assets*	*2010* *Rs.*	*2009* *Rs.*
Share Capital	1,50,000	1,00,000	Fixed Assets	1,50,000	1,00,000
Profit & Loss A/c	80,000	50,000	Goodwill	40,000	50,000
General Reserve	40,000	30,000	Stock	80,000	30,000
6% Debentures	60,000	50,000	Debtors	80,000	50,000
Creditors	40,000	30,000	Bills Receivable	20,000	30,000
Outstanding exp.	15,000	10,000	Bank	15,000	10,000
	3,85,000	2,70,000		3,85,000	2,70,000

(*B.Com. MS*)

Solution :

CASH FLOW STATEMENT
for the year ended 31st Dec. 2010

Particulars	*Rs.*	*Rs.*
I. *Cash flows from Operating Activities :*		
Net Profit before Tax and Extraordinary items	40,000[1]	
Adjustments for :		
Goodwill written off	10,000	
Operating profit before working capital changes	50,000	
Decrease in Bills Receivable (30,000 – 20,000)	10,000	
Increase in Stock (80,000 – 30,000)	(50,000)	
Increase in Debtors (80,000 – 30,000)	(30,000)	
Increase in Creditors (40,000 – 30,000)	10,000	
Increase in Outstanding Expenses (15,000 – 10,000)	5,000	
Net cash used in operating activities		(5,000)
II. *Cash flows from Investing Activities :*		
Purchase of Fixed Assets	(50,000)	
Net Cash used in investing activities		(50,000)
III. *Cash flows from Financing Activities :*		
Proceeds from issue of shares	50,000	

		Rs.	Rs.
	Proceeds from issue of debentures	10,000	
	Net Cash from Financing Activities		60,000
	Net increase in Cash and Cash equivalents		5,000
Add :	Cash and Cash equivalents at the beginning of the year		10,000
	Cash and Cash equivalents at the end of the year		15,000

1. Profit & Loss A/c (2010) Rs. 80,000 (–)
   Profit & Loss A/c (2009) Rs. 50,000
   30,000 (+)
   Add : Transferred to General Reserve 10,000
   40,000

Illustration 18

Balance Sheets of M/s. Black and White as on 1st January and 31st December 2010 were as follows :

Liabilities	*1.1.2010* *Rs.*	*31.12.2010* *Rs.*	*Assets*	*1.1.2010* *Rs.*	*31.12.2010* *Rs.*
Creditors	40,000	44,000	Cash	10,000	7,000
White's loan	25,000	–	Debtors	30,000	50,000
Loan from bank	40,000	50,000	Stock	35,000	25,000
Capital	1,25,000	1,53,000	Machinery	80,000	55,000
			Land	40,000	50,000
			Buildings	35,000	60,000
	2,30,000	2,47,000		2,30,000	2,47,000

During the year a machine costing Rs. 10,000 (accumulated depreciation Rs. 3,000) was sold for Rs. 5,000. The provision for depreciation against machinery as on 1st Jan. 2010 was Rs. 25,000 and on 31st Dec. 2010 Rs. 40,000. Net profit for the year 2010 amounted to Rs. 45,000. Prepare cash flow statement. (*B.Com., M.Com. Chennai*)

Solution :

Cash Flow Statement of M/s Black and White for the year ending 31.12.2010

Particulars	*Rs.*	*Rs.*
I. *Cash flows from Operating Activities :*		
Net Profit for the year	45,000	
Adjustment for :		
Depreciation on Machinery	18,000[1]	
Loss on Sale of Machinery	2,000[1]	
Operating Profit before working capital changes	65,000	
Decrease in Stock (35,000 – 25,000)	10,000	
Incease in Debtors (50,000 – 30,000)	(20,000)	
Increase in Creditors (44,000 – 40,000)	4,000	
Net Cash from Operating activites		59,000
II. *Cash flows from Investing Activities :*		
Sales of Machinery	5,000	
Purchase of Land (50,000 – 40,000)	(10,000)	

Purchase of Building (60,000 – 35,000)	(25,000)	
Net Cash used in investing activities		(30,000)
III. *Cash flows from Financing Activities :*		
Whites loan repaid	(25,000)	
Drawings	(17,000)[2]	
Loan from Bank (50,000 – 40,000)	10,000	
Net-Cash used in Financing Activities		(32,000)
Net Decrease in Cash and Cash Equivalents		(3,000)
Add : Cash and Cash Equivalents at the beginning of the year		10,000
Cash and Cash Equivalents at the end of the year		7,000

MACHINERY ACCOUNT

	Rs.		*Rs.*
To Balance b/d	80,000	By Sales	5,000
		By Profit & Loss Account (Loss on Sale) (Rs. 10,000 – Rs. 3,000 – Rs. 5,000)	2,000
		By Depreciation (Balancing figure)	18,000
		By Balance c/d	55,000
	80,000		80,000

Calculation of Drawings :

Opening Capital	Rs. 1,25,000
Add : Net Profit	Rs. 45,000
	1,70,000
Less : Closing Capital	1,53,000
Drawings :	17,000

Illustration 19

From the following details relating to the accounts of Parry Ltd. prepare Cash Flow Statement:

	31.3.2010	*31.3.2009*
	Rs.	*Rs.*
Liabilities		
Share Capital	10,00,000	8,00,000
Reserve	2,00,000	1,50,000
Profit and Loss Account	1,00,000	60,000
Debentures	2,00,000	—
Provision for taxation	1,00,000	70,000
Proposed dividend	2,00,000	1,00,000
Sundry Creditors	7,00,000	8,20,000
	25,00,000	20,00,000
Assets		
Plant and Machinery	7,00,000	5,00,000

Land and Building	6,00,000	4,00,000
Investments	1,00,000	—
Sundry Debtors	5,00,000	7,00,000
Stock	4,00,000	2,00,000
Cash on hand/Bank	2,00,000	2,00,000
	25,00,000	20,00,000

(i) Depreciation @ 25% was charged on the opening value of Plant and Mchinery.
(ii) During the year one old machine costing Rs. 50,000 (WDV Rs. 20,000) was sold fro Rs. 35,000.
(iii) Rs. 50,000 was paid towards income tax during the year.
(iv) Building under construction was not subject to any depreciation.

Prepare Cash flow Statement.

Solution :

Cash Flow Statement
For The Year Ended 31 March, 2010

	Rs.	Rs.
(A) Cash Flows from Operating Activities		
Net Profit before Tax and Extra-ordinary, items*	3,20,000	
Adjustment for:		
Transfer to General Reserve	50,000	
Depreciation	1,25,000	
Profit on sale of Plant and Machinery	(15,000)	
Operating Profit before Working Capital changes	**4,80,000**	
Increase in Stock	(2,00,000)	
Decrease in Debtors	2,00,000	
Decrease in Creditors	(1,20,000)	
Cash generated from operation	3,60,000	
Income tax paid	(50,000)	
Net cash provided by operating activities		**3,10,000**
(B) Cash Flows from Investing Activities		
Purchase of fixed assets	(3,45,000)	
Expenses on building	(2,00,000)	
Increase in investments	(1,00,000)	
Sale of old machine	35,000	
Net cash used in investing activities		**(6,10,000)**
(C) Cash Flows from Financing Activities		
Proceeds from issue of shares	2,00,000	
Proceeds from issue of debentures	2,00,000	
Dividend paid	(1,00,000)	
Net cash provided by financing activities		**3,00,000**
Net increase in cash and cash equivalents (A + B + C)		Nil
Cash and Cash equivalents at the beginning of the year		2,00,000
Cash and Cash equivalents at the end of the year		2,00,000

Working Notes

Provision for Taxation Account

	Rs.		Rs.
Bank (paid)	50,000	Balance b/d	70,000
Balance c/d	1,00,000	Profit and Loss Account (Balancing Figure)	80,000
	1,50,000		1,50,000

*Rs. 40,000 + Rs 2,00,000 (Provision for dividend + Rs 80,000 (Provision for Tax.)

Plant and Machinery Account

	Rs.		Rs.
Bank (paid)	5,00,000	Depreciation	1,25,000
Bank (balance Fig.)	3,45,000	Bank (Sale)	20,000
		Balance C/d	7,00,000
	8,45,000	Total	8,45,000

Illustration 20

The summarised Balance Sheets of Kandan Ltd., as on 31.12.2009 and 31.12.2010 are as follows :

Liabilities	*2009* Rs.	*2010* Rs.	*Assets*	*2009* Rs.	*2010* Rs.
Share capital	4,50,000	4,50,000	Fixed Assets	4,00,000	3,20,000
General Reserve	3,00,000	3,10,000	Investments	50,000	60,000
P & L A/c	56,000	68,000	Stock	2,40,000	2,10,000
Creditors	1,68,000	1,34,000	Debtors	2,10,000	4,55,000
Tax Provision	75,000	10,000	Bank	1,49,000	1,97,000
Mortgage Loan	–	2,70,000			
	10,49,000	12,42,000		10,49,000	12,42,000

Additional Details

(1) Investments costing Rs. 8,000 were sold for Rs. 8,500.

(2) Tax provision made during the year was Rs. 9,000.

(3) During the year part of the fixed assets costing Rs. 10,000 was sold for Rs. 12,000 and the profit was included in P & L Account. You are required to prepare cash flow statement for 2010.

Solution :

Cash Flow Statement of Kandan Ltd.
for the year ending 31.12.2010

Particulars	Rs.	Rs.
I. *Cash flows from Operating Activities :*		
Net Profit before tax and extraordinary items	31,000[1]	
Adjustments For :		
Depreciation	70,000[2]	
Profit on Sale of Investments (8,500 – 8,000)	(500)	
Profit on Sale of Fixed Assets (12,000 – 10,000)	(2,000)	

	Operating Profit before Working Capital Changes	98,500	
	Decrease in Stock (2,40,000 – 2,10,000)	30,000	
	Decrease in Creditors (1,68,000 – 1,34,000)	(34,000)	
	Increase in Debtors (4,55,000 – 2,10,000)	(2,45,000)	
	Cash Outflow from Operations	(1,50,500)	
	Income Tax Paid	(74,000)[3]	
	Net Cash used in Operating Activities		(2,24,500)
II	*Cash flows from Investing Activities :*		
	Investments Purchased	(18,000)[4]	
	Sale of Investments	8,500	
	Sale of Fixed assets	12,000	
	Net cash from Investing Activities		2,500
III	*Cash flows from Financing Activities :*		
	Mortgage loan taken		2,70,000
	Net Increase in Cash and Cash Equivalents		48,000
Add :	Cash and Cash Equivalents at the beginning of the year		1,49,000
	Cash and Cash Equivalents at the end of the year		1,97,000

Workings :

(1)

	Closing Balance of P & L A/c	68,000
Less :	Opening Balance of P & L A/c	56,000
		12,000
Add :	Transfer to General Reserve (3,10,000 – 3,00,000)	10,000
Add :	Provision made for Tax	9,000
	Net Profit before Tax	31,000

(2) Fixed Assets Account

	Rs.		*Rs.*
To Balance b/d	4,00,000	By Bank (Sale)	12,000
To Profit & Loss A/c (Rs. 12,000 – Rs. 10,000) (profit)	2,000	By Depreciation (Balancing figure)	70,000
		By Balance c/d	3,20,000
	4,02,000		4,02,000

(3) Provision for Taxation Account

	Rs.		*Rs.*
To Bank (Tax paid) (Balancing figure)	74,000	By Balance b/d	75,000
To Balance c/d	10,000	By Profit & Loss (Provision made)	9,000
	84,000		84,000

(4) Investment Account

	Rs.		*Rs.*
To Balance b/d	50,000	By Bank (Sale)	8,500

To Profit & Loss A/c (Rs. 8,500 – Rs. 8,000)	500	By Balance c/d	60,000
To Bank (Purchase) (Balancing figure)	18,000		
	68,500		68,500

Illustration 21

Following are the Balance Sheets of Fair Deal Co. Ltd.

	31.3.2009	*31.3.2010*
	Rs.	*Rs.*
Cash	10,000	8,000
Short-term Investments	4,000	2,000
Stock	90,000	1,20,000
Debtors	80,000	1,00,000
Prepayments	2,000	3,000
Land and Buildings	1,20,000	1,50,000
Plant and Machinery	1,00,000	2,00,000
	4,06,000	5,83,000
	Rs.	*Rs.*
Sundry Creditors	75,000	65,000
Provision for Depreciation	75,000	1,00,000
Provision for Doubtful Debts	1,000	2,000
Provision for Taxation	15,000	10,000
Long-term Debts	50,000	75,000
Equity Share Capital	1,00,000	2,00,000
Reserves and Surplus	90,000	1,31,000
	4,06,000	5,83,000

Additional information

(*a*) Land was purchased for cash Rs. 30,000.

(*b*) A machine was acquired for cash Rs. 90,000 and long-term debt Rs. 10,000

(*c*) Payment of dividend in cash Rs. 6,000.

(*d*) Equity shares were issued for cash Rs. 1,00,000.

INCOME STATEMENT
for the year ended 31st March, 2010

	Rs.
Sales Revenue	8,00,000
Cost of Goods Sold	6,50,000
Gross Margin	1,50,000
Less : Operating Expenses	50,000
Operating Income	1,00,000
Interest Expense	5,000
Income before Tax	95,000
Law suit compensation	2,000
	97,000

Less : Income Tax	50,000
Net Income	47,000

Prepare Cash Flow Statement for the year ended 31st March, 2010

(*M.Com. Kolkata, Delhi M.K.*)

Solution :

Fair Deal Company Ltd.
CASH FLOW STATEMENT
for the year ended 31st March 2010

		Rs.	*Rs.*
Cash Flow from Operating Activities :			
Net Income before tax and extraordinary item		95,000	
Adjustments for :			
Depreciation	Rs. 25,000		
Interest	5,000		
Provision for doubtful debts	1,000	31,000	
Operating profit before working capital changes		1,26,000	
Increase in Stock	(30,000)		
Increase in Debtors	(20,000)		
Increase in pre-payments	(1,000)		
Decrease in Creditors	(10,000)	(61,000)	
Income Tax Paid		(55,000)	
Cash Flow from Extraordinary Item :			
Law suit compensation		2,000	
Net cash flow from operating activities			12,000
Cash Flow from Investing Activities :			
Purchase of Land		(30,000)	
Purchase of Machine		(90,000)	
Net cash flow from investing activities			(1,20,000)
Cash Flow from Financing Activities :			
Issue of Equity Shares		1,00,000	
Long-term borrowing		15,000	
Dividends paid		(6,000)	
Interest paid		(5,000)	
Net cash flow from financing activities			1,04,000
Net decrease in cash and cash equivalents			(4,000)
Cash and cash equivalents at the beginning			14,000
Cash and cash equivalents at the end			10,000

Illustration 22

Prepare Cash Flow Statement of Suryan Ltd. from the following :

Balance Sheets

Liabilities	*1.1.2010 Rs.*	*31.12.2010 Rs.*	*Assets*	*1.1.2010 Rs.*	*31.12.2010 Rs.*

Share Capital	1,00,000	4,00,000	Goodwill	–	20,000
8% Debentures	–	2,00,000	Machinery	1,25,000	4,75,000
Retained Earnings	60,000	90,000	Stock	20,000	80,000
Creditors	40,000	1,00,000	Debtors	30,000	1,00,000
Bills Payable	20,000	40,000	Cash at Bank	50,000	1,50,000
Provision for Tax	30,000	40,000	Cash in hand	25,000	45,000
	2,50,000	8,70,000		2,50,000	8,70,000

Additional Information :

(*a*) During 2010, the business of a sole trader was purchased by issuing shares for Rs. 2,00,000. The assets acquired from him were: Goodwill Rs. 20,000, Machinery Rs. 1,00,000, Stock Rs. 50,000 and Debtors Rs. 30,000.

(*b*) Provision for tax charged in 2010 was Rs. 35,000.

(*c*) The debentures were issued at a premium of 5% which is included in the retained earnings.

(*d*) Depreciation charged on machinery was Rs. 30,000. (*B.Com. Andhra, M.S.*)

Solution :

Cash Flows Statement of Suryan Ltd., for the year 2010

Particulars	*Rs.*	*Rs.*
I *Cash flows from Operating Activities :*		
Profit before tax and extraordinary items	55,000[1]	
Adjustments For :		
Depreciation on Machinery	30,000	
Operating Profit before Working Capital changes	85,000	
Increase in Creditors (1,00,000 – 40,000)	60,000	
Increase in Bills Payable (40,000 – 20,000)	20,000	
Increase in Stock (Excluding Stock bought by issue of shares) (80,000 – 50,000 – 20,000)	(10,000)	
Increase in Debtors (Excluding debtors acquired by issue of shares) (1,00,000 – 30,000 – 30,000)	(40,000)	
Cash Outflow from Operations	1,15,000	
Income Tax paid	(25,000)[2]	
Net Cash from operating activities		90,000
II *Cash flows from Investing Activities :*		
Machinery Purchased for Cash	(2,80,000)[3]	
		(2,80,000)
III *Cash flows from Financing Activities :*		
Cash Proceeds from issue of shares	1,00,000[4]	
Cash Proceeds from issue of debentures	2,10,000[5]	
Net Cash flows from Financing activities		3,10,000
Net Increase in Cash and Cash and Cash equivalents		1,20,000
Add : Cash and Cash equivalents at the beginning of the year		75,000
Cash and Cash equivalents at the end of the year		1,95,000

Workings :

(1)

		Rs.
	Closing retained earnings	90,000
Less :	Opening retained earnings	60,000
		30,000
Add :	Provision made for Tax	35,000
		65,000
Less :	Premium on issue of Debentures (2,00,000 × 5%)	10,000
	Net Profit before Tax and Extraordinary items	55,000

(2) Provision for Tax Account

	Rs.		*Rs.*
To Bank (Tax paid) (Balancing figure)	25,000	By Balance b/d	30,000
To Balance c/d	40,000	By Profit & Loss (Provision)	35,000
	65,000		65,000

(3) Machinery Account

	Rs.		*Rs.*
To Balance b/d	1,25,000	By Depreciation	30,000
To Bank (Purchase) (Balancing figure	2,80,000	By Balance c/d	4,75.000
To Vendor (Business Purchase	1,00,000		
	5,05,000		5,05,000

(4) Share Capital Account

	Rs.		*Rs.*
To Balance c/d	4,00,000	By Balance b/d	1,00,000
		By Vendor A/c (Business Purchase)	2,00,000
		By Bank (Issue for cash) (Balancing figure)	1,00,000
	4,00,000		4,00,000

(5)

Debenture issue (Face Value)	Rs. 2,00,000
Add : Premium on issue at 5%	10,000
Total Proceeds :	2,10,000

Illustration 23

The following are the summarise of the balance sheets of a limited company as on 31st March 2009 and 2010.

Liabilities	2009 Rs.	2010 Rs.	Assets	2009 Rs.	2010 Rs.
Paid-up share capital	1,00,000	1,00,000	Building	46,800	45,000
General Reserve	38,400	42,000	Plant and machinery	38,280	42,030
Sundry creditors	9,750	6,380	Goodwill	13,000	13,000
Provision for taxation	19,000	21,000	Investments	10,000	11,250
Provision for doubtful			Stock	30,000	28,000
debts	1,000	1,200	Sundry debtors	22,070	22,300
			Cash	8,000	9,000
	1,68,150	1,70,580		1,68,150	1,70,580

After taking the following information into account, prepare a Cash Flow Statement for the year ending 31st March, 2010

(*a*) The profit for 2009-10 was Rs. 8,600. Against this had been charged depreciation Rs. 3,050 and increase in provision for doubtful debts Rs. 200.

(*b*) Income tax Rs. 18,000 was paid during the year charged against the provision and in addition Rs. 20,000 was charged against profit and carried to the provision.

(*c*) An interim dividend of Rs. 5,000 was paid in January, 2010.

(*d*) Additional plant was purchased in September 2009 for Rs. 5,000.

(*e*) Investments (cost Rs. 5,000) were sold in February 2009 for Rs. 4,800 and on 1st March, 2010 another investment was made for Rs. 6,250.

Solution :

CASH FLOW STATEMENT
for the year ended 31-3-2010

	Rs.	Rs.
(A) *Cash Flow from Operating Activities*		
Net Profit before tax and Expenditure items	28,800[1]	
Adjustment for Depreciation	3,050	
Profits from Trading Operations	31,850	
Increase in Provision for D/D	200	
Decrease in Stock	2,000	
Increase in Debtors	(230)	
Decrease in Creditors	(3,370)	
Payment of Tax	(18,000)	
Net Cash Provided by Operating Activities		12,450
(B) *Cash Flows from Financing Activities*		
Sale of Investments	4,800	
Purchase of Investment	(6,250)	
Purchase of Plant	(5,000)	
Payment of Interim Dividend	(5,000)	
		(11,450)
Net Change on Cash & Cash Equivalent		1,000
Cash & Cash Equivalents as on 31.3.2009		8,000
Cash and Cash Equivalents as on 31.3.2010		9,000

Working Notes :

(1) ADJUSTED PROFIT & LOSS ACCOUNT

	Rs.		Rs.
To Provision for Taxation	20,000	By Profits Tax and Extraordinary	28,800
To General Reserve	3,600		
To Loss on Sale of Investment	200		
To Interim Dividend	5,000		
	28,800		28,800

(2) PROVISION FOR TAXATION

	Rs.		Rs.
To Bank A/c	18,000	By Balance b/d	19,000
To Balance c/d	21,000	By Adjusted Profit & Loss A/c	20,000
	39,000		39,000

Illustration : 24

The Balance Sheets of Thirugnanam Ltd., for the years 2009 and 2010 were as follows :

BALANCE SHEETS

Liabilities	*2009* Rs.	*2010* Rs.	*Assets*	*2009* Rs.	*2010* Rs.
Share capital	1,50,000	1,75,000	Buildings	1,10,000	1,50,000
Loan from bank	1,60,000	1,00,000	Plant	2,00,000	1,40,000
Creditors	85,000	93,000	Stock	50,000	45,000
Outstanding exp.	5,000	7,000	Debtors	70,000	80,000
Bills payable	50,000	40,000	Cash	15,000	22,000
Loan from IFC	—	25,000	Prepaid Expenses	5,000	3,000
	4,50,000	4,40,000		4,50,000	4,40,000

Additional Information :

(*a*) Net profit for the year 2010 Rs. 60,000.

(*b*) During the year a plant costing Rs. 25,000.
(accumulating depreciation Rs. 10,000) was sold for Rs. 13,000.

(*c*) The provision for depreciation against plant as on 31-12-2009 was Rs. 50,000 and on 31-12-2010 was Rs. 85,000.

You are required to prepare a cash flow statement.

(*B. Com. Madras, Delhi, Kerala, Bharathiar MS*)

Solution :

CASH FLOW STATEMENT
for the year ended 31st december 2010

	Rs.	Rs.
(A) *Cash Flows from Operating Activities :*		
Net Profit before taxation and extra-ordinary items		60,000
Adjustment for Depreciation	45,000	
Loss on Sale of plant	2,000	47,000
		1,07,000
Decrease in Stock	5,000	
Decrease in Prepaid Expenses	2,000	
Increase in Creditors	8,000	

Increase in O/S Expenses	2,000	
	17,000	
Increase in Debtors	(10,000)	
Decrease in B/P	(10,000)	(3,000)
Net Cash from Operating Activities :		1,04,000
(B) *Cash Flows from Investing Activities :*		
Sale of Plant	13,000	
Purchase of Buildings	(40,000)	(27,000)
(C) *Cash Flows from Fianancing Activities :*		
Drawings	(35,000)	
(Rs. 1,50,000 + Rs. 60,000 – Rs. 1,75,000)		
Repayment of Loan	(60,000)	
Loan from IFC	25,000	(70,000)
Net increase in cash and cash equivalent		7,000
Cash and cash equivalent on 1.1.2010		15,000
Cash and Cash equivalent on 31.12.2010		22,000

Workings :

1. MACHINERY ACCOUNT (AT COST)

	Rs.		*Rs.*
To Balance b/d (2,00,000 + 50,000)	2,50,000	By Cash (sale)	13,000
		By Adjusted Profit and Loss a/c (loss)	2,000
		By Provision for depreciation	10,000
		By Balance c/d (1,40,000 + 85,000)	2,25,000
	2,50,000		2,50,000

2. PROVISION FOR DEPRECIATION AMOUNT

	Rs.		*Rs.*
To Machinery a/c (depn. on machinery sold)	10,000	By Balance b/d	50,000
To Balance c/d	85,000	By Adjusted Profit and Loss a/c (depreciation provided during the year) (Bal. fig.)	45,000
	95,000		95,000

Illustration 25

The Balance Sheets of a firm as on 31st December 2009 and 2010 are given below :

	2009 *Rs.*	*2010* *Rs.*		*2009* *Rs.*	*2010* *Rs.*
Share Capital	1,00,000	1,60,000	Fixed Assets at cost	1,52,000	2,00,000
Retained Earnings	70,250	85,300	Inventory	93,400	89,200
Accumulated Depreciation	60,000	40,000	Debtors	30,800	21,100
12% Debentures	50,000	—	Expenses Prepaid	3,950	3,000
Sundry Creditors	28,000	48,000	Bank	28,100	20,000
	3,08,250	3,33,300		3,08,250	3,33,300

The following additional information for 2010 are also given :

(1) Net Profit Rs. 27,050.

(2) Depreciation charged Rs. 10,000.

(3) Cash dividend declared during the period Rs. 12,000.

(4) An addition to the building was made during the year at a cost of Rs. 78,000 and fully depreciated equipment costing Rs, 30,000 was discarded as no salvage being realised. Prepare a Cash Flow Statement. (*M.Com. Madurai, Bangalore*)

Solution :

CASH FLOW STATEMENT
for the year ended 31st December 2010

	Rs.	Rs.
(A) *Cash Flows from Operating Activities :*		
Net Profit before taxation and Extra ordinary items	27,050	
Adjustment for Depreciation	10,000	
	37.050	
Add : Decrease in Stock	4,200	
Decrease in Debtors	9,700	
Decrease in Prepaid Expenses	950	
Increase in Creditors	20,000	
		71,900
(B) *Cash Flows from Investing Activities :*		
Purchased of Fixed Assets	(Rs. 78,000)	
Redemption of Debentures	(Rs. 50,000)	
		(1,28,000)
		(56,100)
(C) *Cash Flows from Financing Activities :*		
Issue of shares	60,000	
Payment of Dividend	(12,000)	
		48,000
Net decrease in cash and cash equivalents		(8,100)
Cash and Cash equivalent on 31.12.2009		28,100
Cash and Cash equivalent on 31.12.2010		20,000

Workings :

FIXED ASSETS ACCOUNT

	Rs.		Rs.
To Balance b/d	1,52,000	By Accumulated Depreciation	30,000
To Bank	78,000		
		By Balance c/d	2,00,000
	2,30,000		2,30,000

ACCUMULATED DEPRECIATION A/c

	Rs.		Rs.
To Fixed Assets	30,000	By Balance b/d	60,000
To Balance c/d	40,000	By Profit & Loss A/c	10,000
	70,000		70,000

Illustration : 26

The following are the summarised Balance Sheets of a company as on 31st December

	2009 Rs.	2010 Rs.
Liabilities :		
Share Capital	2,00,000	2,50,000
General Reserve	50,000	60,000
Profit & Loss A/c	30,500	30,600
Bank Loan (Long term)	70,000	—
Sundry Creditors	1,50,000	1,35,200
Provision for Taxation	30,000	35,000
	5,30,500	5,10,800
Assets :		
Land & Buildings	2,00,000	1,90,000
Machinery	2,00,000	1,69,000
Stock	1,00,000	74,000
Sundry Debtors	80,000	64,200
Cash	500	600
Bank	—	8,000
Goodwill	—	5,000
	5,30,500	5,10,800

Additional Information :

During the year ended 31st December 2010

(*i*) Dividend of Rs. 23,000 was paid.

(*ii*) The following assets of another company were purchased for a consideration of Rs. 50,000 paid for in shares.

(*a*) Stock Rs. 20,000 and (*b*) Machinery Rs. 25,000

(*iii*) Machinery was further purchased for Rs. 8,000.

(*iv*) Depreciation written off : Machinery Rs. 12,000.

(*v*) Income Tax provided during the year Rs. 33,000.

(*vi*) Loss on Sale of Machinery Rs. 200 was written off to General Reserve.

(*M.Com. Madurai, Raipur, Bangalore*)

Solution :

CASH FLOWS STATEMENT
for the year ended 31st December 2010

	Rs.	Rs.
(A) *Cash Flow Operating Activities*		
Net Income before tax and extraordinary items	66,300	
Adjustment for Depreciation	22,000	
Funds from Trading Operations	88,300	
Decrease in Stock	46,000	
Decrease in Debtors	15,800	
Decrease in Sundry Creditors	(14,800)	
Payment of Tax	(28,000)	
Net Cash provided from operating activities		1,07,300
(B) *Cash Flows from Investing Activities*		
Sale of Machine	1,800	

Purchase of Machinery for Cash	(8,000)	
Net Cash used in investing activities		(6,200)
(C) *Cash Flows from Financing Activities*		
Payment of Bank Loan	(70,000)	
Payment of Dividend	(23,000)	
Net Changes in Cash and Cash Equivalents		(93,000)
Cash and Cash Equivalents as on 31.3.2009		8,100
Cash and Cash Equivalents as on 31.3.2010		500
		8,600

Working Notes :

(1) ADJUSTED PROFIT & LOSS ACCOUNT

	Rs.		*Rs.*
To General Reserve	10,200	By Profit before tax and	
To Profit & Loss	100	extraordinary item	66,300
To Provision for Taxation	33,000		
To Proposed Dividend	23,000		
	66,300		66,300

(2) MACHINERY ACCOUNT

	Rs.		*Rs.*
To Balance b/d	1,50,000	By General Reserve	200
To Share Capital	25,000	By Depreciation	12,000
To Cash	8,000	By Cash (Sale of Machine)	1,800
		By Balance c/d	1,69,000
	1,83,000		1,83,000

(3) PROVISION FOR TAXATION ACCOUNT

	Rs.		*Rs.*
To Bank (Tax paid)	28,000	By Balance b/d	30,000
to Balance c/d	35,000	By Adjusted Profit and Loss A/c	33,000
	63,000		63,000

(4) SHARE CAPITAL ACCOUNT

	Rs.		*Rs.*
		By Balance b/d	2,00,000
		By Stock	20,000
		By Machinery	25,000
To Balance c/d	2,50,000	By Goodwill	5,000
	2,50,000		2,50,000

(5) GENERAL RESERVE

	Rs.		*Rs.*
To Machinery	200	By Balance b/d	50,000
To Balance c/d	60,000	By Profit & Loss A/c	10,200
	66,200		60,200

Illustration : 27

From the following Balance Sheets of Exe Ltd. makeout Cash Flow Statement.

Liabilities	*2009* *Rs.*	*2010* *Rs.*	*Assets*	*2009* *Rs.*	*2010* *Rs.*
Equity Share Capital	3,00,000	4,00,000	Goodwill	1,15,000	90,000
8% redeemable preference Share Capital	1,50,000	1,00,000	Land & Buildings	2,00,000	1,70,000
			Plant	80,000	2,00,000
General Reserve	40,000	70,000	Debtors	1,60,000	2,00,000
Profit & Loss	30,000	48,000	Stock	77,000	1,09,000
Proposed Dividend	42,000	50,000	Bills Receivable	20,000	30,000
Creditors	55,000	83,000	Cash in hand	15,000	10,000
Bills Payable	20,000	16,000	Cash at Bank	10,000	8,000
Provision for Taxation	40,000	50,000			
	6,77,000	8,17,000		6,77,000	8,17,000

Additional Information

(*a*) Depreciation of Rs. 10,000 and Rs. 20,000 have been charged on Plant and Land and Buildings in 2010.

(*b*) An interim dividend of Rs. 20,000 has been paid in 2010.

(*c*) Rs. 35,000 Income tax was paid during 2010. (*M.Com. Madras*)

Solution :

CASH FLOW STATEMENT
for the year ended 31st December 2010

	Rs.	*Rs.*
(A) *Cash Flows from Operating Activities*		
Net Profit before tax and Extraordinary items	1,88,000	
Adjustment for Depreciation	30,000	
Profits from Trading Operations	2,18,000	
Increase in Creditors	28,000	
Increase in Debtors	(40,000)	
Increase in Stock	(32,000)	
Increase in B/R	(10,000)	
Decrease in B/P	(4,000)	
Payment of Tax	(35,000)	
Net cash provided from financial activities		1,25,000
(B) *Cash Flows from Investing Activities*		
Sale of Land & Building	10,000[2]	
Purchase of Plant	(1,30,000)[1]	
Net Cash used in investing activities		(120,000)
(C) *Cash Flows from Financial Activities*		
Issue of Share Capital	1,00,000	
Redemption of Pref. Shares	(50,000)	
Payment of Interim Dividend	(20,000)	
Payment of Dividend	(42,000)	
		(12,000)

Net decrease in Cash and Cash equivalent :	(7,000)
Cash and Cash equivalent as on 31.3.2003 :	25,000
Cash and Cash equivalent as on 31.3.2004 : (10,000 + Rs. 8000)	18,000

(1) PLANT ACCOUNT

	Rs.		Rs.
To Balance b/d	80,000	By P. & L. Account (Dep.)	10,000
To Bank (Purchase of Plant) (Bal. fig.)	1,30,000	By Balance c/d	2,00,000
	2,10,000		2,10,000

(2) LAND AND BUILDING ACCOUNT

	Rs.		Rs.
To Balance b/d	2,00,000	By P. & L. Account (Dep.)	20,000
		By Bank (Sale of Land and Building (Bal. fig.)	10,000
		By Balance c/d	1,70,000
	2,00,000		2,00,000

(3) ADJUSTED PROFIT AND LOSS ACCOUNT

	Rs.		Rs.
To General Reserve	30,000	By Balance b/d	30,000
To Interim Dividend	20,000	By Profits before tax and extraordinary items	1,88,000
To Provision for Taxation (5)	45,000		
To Goodwill	25,000		
To Proposed Dividend (4)	50,000		
To Balance c/d	48,000		
	2,18,000		2,18,000

(4) PROPOSED DIVIDEND ACCOUNT

	Rs.		Rs.
To Bank	42,000	By Balance b/d	42,000
To Balance c/d	50,000	By Profit & Loss A/c (Bal. fig.)	50,000
	92,000		92,000

(5) PROVISION FOR TAXATION ACCOUNT

	Rs.		Rs.
To Bank	35,000	By Bank b/d	40,000
To Balance c/d	50,000	By Profit & Loss Account (bal. fig.)	45,000
	85,000		85,000

Illustration : 28

Form the following summarised financial statements of Abec Ltd. as at 31st March, 2009 and 2010 respectively, prepare a Cash Flow Statement.

Capital & Liabilities	*2009 Rs.*	*2010 Rs.*	*Property & Assets*	*2009 Rs.*	*2010 Rs.*
Paid-up Share Capital	15,00,000	20,00,000	Land	2,30,000	2,30,000
Securities Premium	—	50,000	Buildings (at cost less Depreciation)	6,40,000	6,10,000
General Reserve	6,00,000	7,00,000			
Profit and Loss A/c	3,60,300	4,90,640	Plant and Machinery less Depreciation	18,35,000	22,20,400
Secured Loan	8,60,000	8,60,000			
Proposed Dividend	1,00,000	1,50,000	Investments	50,000	75,600
Sundry Creditors	11,79,700	12,39,360	Investments	8,40,430	9,16,340
			Book Debts (considered good)	9,85,370	13,18,650
			Cash and Bank Balances	19,200	69,010
	46,00,000	54,90,000		46,00,000	54,90,000

During 2009 - 2010 depreciation provided on assets amounted to Buildings Rs. 30,000, Plant and Machinery Rs. 2,40,500.

The final dividend for the year 2008 - 2009 amounting to Rs. 1,00,000 was paid on 8th October, 2009. (*B.Com, Madras*)

Solution :

CASH FLOW STATEMENT
for the year 31st March, 2010

	Rs.	*Rs.*
(A) *Cash Flows from Operating Activities*		
Net profit before tax and Extraordinary items (1)	3,80,340	
Adjustment for Depreciation	2,70,500	
Profits from Trading Operations	6,50,840	
Increase in Creditors	59,660	
Increase in Stock	(75,910)	
Increase in Book Debts	(3,83,280)	
Net Cash Provided by Operating Activities		2.51,310
(B) *Cash Flows from Investing Activities*		
Purchase of Plant & Machinery (3)	(6,25,900)	
Purchase of Investments	(25,600)	
Net Cash used in investing activities		(6,51,500)
(C) *Cash Flows from Financing Activities*		
Issue of Share Capital	5,00,000	
Cash from Securities Premium	50,000	
Payment of Dividend (4)	(1,00,000)	
Net Cash Provided from Financing Activities		4,50,000
Net Cash and Cash equivalents		49,810
Cash and Cash equivalent as on 31.3.2009		19,200
Cash and Cash equivalent as on 31.3.2010		69,010

Workings :

(1) ADJUSTED PROFIT AND LOSS ACCOUNT

	Rs.		Rs.
To Proposed Dividend (4)	1,50,000	By Balance b/d	3,60,300
To General Reserve	1,00,000	By Profit before tax and	
To Balance c/d	4,90,640	Extraordinary Items	3,80,340
	7,40,640		7,40,640

(2) BUILDING ACCOUNT

	Rs.		Rs.
To Balance b/d	6,40,000	By Adj. P. & L. A/c (Dep.)	30,000
		By Balance c/d	6,10,000
	6,40,000		6,40,000

(3) PLANT AND MACHINERY ACCOUNT

	Rs.		Rs.
To Balanced b/d	18,35,000	By Adjusted Profit and Loss A/c	2,40,500
To Bank (Purchase)	6,25,900	By Balance c/d	22,20,400
	24,60,900		24,60,900

(4) PROPOSED DIVIDEND ACCOUNT

	Rs.		Rs.
To Bank (Payment of dividend)	1,00,000	By Balance b/d	1,00,000
To Balance c/d	1,50,000	By Adjusted Profit and Loss	
		Account (Provision)	1,50,000
	2,50,000		2,50,000

QUESTIONS

Objective Type Questions :

I. State whether the following statements are True or False :

1. Cash is the Life-blood of every business.
2. Dividend paid is classified as a financing activity.
3. The Cash Flow Statement is now a part of financial statements.
4. Cash payment for acquisition of fixed assets is an operating activities.
5. Movement of cash into an enterprise and also out of the same enterprise is known as cash 'flows.'
6. The term 'cash' for the purpose of cash flow statement includes only cash as such.
7. Cash receipt from sale of goods is an example of cash flow from operating activities.
8. Amount received or paid for law suits is an example of cash flow from financing activities.
9. Liquidity and short-term solvency of a business depends upon cash.
10. Cash receipt from issue of shares is an investing activity.

(**Ans** : True - 1, 3, 5, 7, 9.

False - 2, 4, 6, 8. 10.)

II. Choose the correct answer to the following :

1. Cash flows from operating activities include :
   (*a*) Cash receipts from sale of goods.
   (*b*) Cash payments for operating machines.
   (*c*) Cash payments for repair of machines.
   (*d*) None of the above.
2. The Cash Flow Statement classifies cash flows from :
   (*a*) Operating activities.
   (*b*) Investing activities.
   (*c*) Financing activities.
   (*d*) All of the above.
3. Cash from operations is equal to :
   (*a*) Net Profit plus decrease in current assets.
   (*b*) Net Profit plus decrease in current liabilities.
   (*c*) Net profit plus increase in fixed assets.
4. Cash flow statement is based upon :
   (*a*) Accrual basis of accounting.
   (*b*) Cash basis of accounting.
   (*c*) (*a*) and (*b*).
5. Increase in the amount of prepaid expenses results in :
   (*a*) Increase in cash.
   (*b*) Decrease in cash.
   (*c*) No change in cash.
6. Increase in the amount of creditors results in :
   (*a*) Decrease in cash.
   (*b*) Increase in cash.
   (*c*) No change in cash.
7. Cash flows from extraordinary items comprise :
   (*a*) Bad debts recovered.
   (*b*) Winning of a lottery.
   (*c*) Winning of a law suit.
   (*d*) All of the above.
8. Which of the following is an item of operating activities?
   (*a*) Claim from an insurance company.
   (*b*) Interest and Dividend received.
   (*c*) Payment of salaries and wages to employees.

(**Ans** : 1. (*a*) ; 2. (*d*) ; 3. (*a*) ; 4. (*b*) ; 5. (*b*) ; 6. (*b*) ; 7. (*d*) ; 8. (*c*).)

THEORETICAL QUESTIONS

1. What is a Cash Flow Statment?
2. What are the objects of Cash Flow Statement?
3. What is the pupose of preparing Cash Flow Statement?
4. Who does Cash Flow Statement differ from Fund Flow Statement?
5. What are the advantages of Cash Flow Statement?

PRACTICAL PROBLEMS

1. (Direct Method)

Prepare a Cash Flow Statement of *XYZ* Co. Ltd. for the ended 31st March, 2010, from the particulars given below :

Credit sales for the year Rs. 80,000 and cash sales Rs, 30,000.

Cash collected from debtors Rs. 40,000.

Purchases of goods are on credit and cost of goods sold is 50% of total sales.

Payments to creditors was Rs. 35,000 and payment of office rent Rs. 8,800. One month's rent Rs. 800 was outstanding.

Depreciation on plant and machinery Rs. 25,000.

The company issued 20,000 Equity Shares of Rs. 10 each.

Plant and Machinery was purchased for Rs. 1,00,000.

Office equipment was purchased for Rs. 5,000 and typewriter was sold for Rs. 6,000.

Payment of dividend Rs. 10,000. Goodwill written off Rs. 10,000. (*B.Com. MS.*)

(**Ans :** Cash flows from Operating Activities : Rs. 26,200

Cash used in Investing Activities : (Rs. 99,000)

Cash flows from Financing Activities : Rs. 1,90,000)

2. (Indirect Method)

Following is the Balance Sheet of *AB* Co. Ltd. as on.

	Rs. 1.1.2010	*Rs.* 31.12.2010
Liabilities :		
Equity Share Capital	3,00,000	3,50,000
Share premium		30,000
General reserve	45,000	65,000
Profit and Loss	30,000	80,000
6% Debentures		70,000
Sundry creditors	85,000	90,700
Provision for taxation	22.500	40,500
Proposed dividend	30,000	35,000
	5,12,500	7,62,000
Assets :		
Land and buildings	2,30,000	3,90,000
Plant and Machinery	85,400	1,40,000
Furniture	5,500	6,500
Stock	82,400	95,700
Sundry debtors	75,000	85,500
Bank Balance	34,200	44,300
	5,12,500	7,62,000

Additional Information :

Depreciation written off during the year :

Land and buildings Rs. 60,000

Plant and Machinery 50,000
Furniture 1,200

You are required to prepare a cash flow statement. (*CS. Inter*)

(**Ans :** Cash flows Operating Activities : Rs. 2,16,900
Cash used in Investing Activities : (Rs. 3,26,800)
Cash used in Financing Activities : (Rs. 1,20,000))

3. The Balance Sheets of *AB* & Co. Ltd. as at the end of 31.3.2009 and 31.3.2010 are given below:

Capital & Liabilities	*2009* *Rs.*	*2010* *Rs.*	*Assets*	*2009* *Rs.*	*2010* *Rs.*
Share Capital	1,00,000	1,50,000	Feehold Land	1,00,000	1,00,000
Securities Premium	—	5,000	Plant at Cost	1,04,000	1,00,000
General Reserve	50,000	60,000	Furniture at Cost	7,000	9,000
Profit & Loss A/c	10,000	17,000	Investment at Cost	60,000	80,000
6% Debentures	70,000	50,000	Debtors	30,000	70,000
Provision for Depreciation			Stock	60,000	65,000
on Plant	50,000	56,000	Cash	30,000	45,000
Provision for Depreciation					
on Furniture	5,000	6,000			
Privision for Taxation	20,000	30,000			
Sundry Creditors	86,000	95,000			
	3,91,000	4,69,000		3,91,000	4,69,000

A plant purchase for Rs. 4,000 (Depreciation Rs. 2,000) was sold for cash Rs. 800 on 30th September, 2009. On 30th June, 2009 an item of furniture was purchased for Rs. 2,000. These were the only transactions concerning fixed assets during 2009. Depreciation on plant was provided at 8% on cost (the sold out item is not taken into consideration) and on furniture at 12.5% on average cost. A dividend of 22.5% on original shares was paid. Rs. 20,000. Debentures were redeemed at a premium of 5%.

You are required to prepare a Cash Flow Statement. (*B.Com. (Hons.) Kolkata, Chennai*)

(**Ans :** Cash flows From Operating Activities : Rs. 24,700
Cash used in Investing Activities : Rs. (21,200)
Cash flows from Financing Activities : Rs. 11,500)

4. The following are the summarised Balance Sheets of M/s Ram Prashad Ltd. as on 31st March :

Capital & Liabilities	*2009* *Rs.*	*2010* *Rs.*	*Assets*	*2009* *Rs.*	*2010* *Rs.*
Capital :			Fixed Assets :		
10% Pref. Share Capital	1,00,000	1,10,000	Machinery	2,00,000	2,30,000
Equity Capital	2,20,000	2,50,000	Building	1,50,000	1,76,000
Reserve & Surplus :			Land	18,000	18,000
Securities Premium	20,000	26,000	Current Assets :		
P.& L. Account	1,04,000	1,34,000	Cash	42,000	32,000
Liabilities (Non-Current):			Debtors	38,000	38,000
12% Debentures	70,000	64,000	B/R	42,000	62,000
Current Liabilities :			Stock in hand	84,000	98,000

Creditors	38,000	46,000			
B/P	5,000	4,000			
Provision for Taxation	10,000	12,000			
Dividends Payable	7,000	8,000			
	5,74,000	6,54,000		5,74,000	6,54,000

You are required to prepare a Cash Flow Statement. (*M.Com. Kolkata*)

(**Ans**: Cash flows from Operating Activities Rs. 6,000.
Cash Used in Investing Activities Rs. (56.000)
Cash flows from Financing Activities Rs. 40,000)

5. From the Balance Sheet of Burn Products Ltd. given below, prepare Cash Flow Statement.

BALANCE SHEET
as on 31st March, 2010 (*Rs. in lakhs*)

Liabilities	*Previous Year*	*Current Year*	*Assets*	*Previous Year*	*Current Year*
	Rs.	*Rs.*		*Rs.*	*Rs.*
Equity Share Capital	8.00	12.00	Freehold Land & Buildings	5.54	11.32
Securities Premium	0.80	1.20	Plant and Machinery	3.56	5.13
General Reserve	0.60	0.90	Furniture and Fittings	0.24	0.15
Profit and Loss A/c	1.95	2.08	Stock	2.21	2.60
5% Debentures	–	2.60	Debtors	3.65	3.91
Income Tax Payable	0.98	1.09	Bank and Cash	0.48	0.40
Creditors	3.35	3.64			
	15.68	23.51		15.68	23.51

Depreciation written off during the year :

Plant and Machinery Rs. 1.28 lakhs
Furniture and Fittings Rs. 0.04 lakh

(**Ans**: Cash flows from Operating Activities Rs. 1.50 lakhs.
Cash used in Investing Activities (Rs. 8.58 lakhs)
Cash flows from Financing Activities Rs. 7.00 lakhs)

6. The Balance Sheets of National Co. Ltd. as on 31st March are as follows :

Capital & Liabilities	*2009*	*2010*	*Assets*	*2009*	*2010*
	Rs.	*Rs.*		*Rs.*	*Rs.*
Share Capital	5,00,000	7,00,000	Land and Buildings	80,000	1,20,000
Profit and Loss Account	1,00,000	1,60,000	Plant and Machinery	5,00,000	8,00,000
General Reserve	50,000	70,000	Stock	1,00,000	75,000
Sundry Creditors	1,53,000	1,90,000	Sundry Debtors	1,50,000	1,60,000
Bills Payable	40,000	50,000	Cash	20,000	20,000
Outstanding Expenses	7,000	5,000			
	8,50,000	11,75,000		8,50,000	11,75,000

Additional Information :

(1) Rs. 50,000 depreciation has been charged on Plant and machinery during the year 2009-10.

(2) A piece of machinery was sold for Rs. 8,000 during the year 2009-10. It had cost Rs. 12,000, depreciation of Rs. 7,000 had been provided on it.

Prepare a Cash Flow Statement for the year 2009-10. (*M.Com. Kolkata, MS*)

(**Ans :** Cash flows from Operating Activities : Rs. 1,87,000
Cash used in Investing Activities : (Rs. 3,87,000)
Cash flows from Financing Activities : Rs. 2,00,000)

7. From the following data of Swadeshi Ltd. prepare the Cash Flow Statement of sources and uses Funds for the year ended 31st December, 2010.

Liabilities	*31-12-09*	*31-12-10*	*Assets*	*31-12-09*	*31-12-10*
Share Capital	30,000	36,000	Goodwill	6,000	5,000
Reserves and Surplus	14,000	19,000	Machinery	25,000	20,000
Debentures	5,000	–	Stock	12,000	18,000
Creditors	11,0000	9,000	Debtors	15,000	19,000
Unclaimed Divided	–	1,000	Cash	2,000	3,000
	60,000	65,000		60,000	65,000

On 1st January, 2010 (*i*) machinery for Rs, 3,000, stock worth Rs. 1,000 and goodwill worth Rs. 2,000 were acquired by issue of shares ; and (*ii*) machinery of the book value of Rs. 6,000 was sold for Rs. 6,500. On 31st December, 2010 the debentures were redeemed for Rs. 4,900 and the shareholders were paid Rs. 2,500 cash dividend.

(**Ans :** Cash flows form Operating Activities : Rs. 900
Cash flows fro Investing Activities : Rs. 6,500
Cash flows used in Financing Activities : (Rs. 6,400))

8. The Balance Sheets of X Ltd. as on 31st March, are given below :

Liabilities	2009 *Rs.*	2010 *Rs.*	*Assets*	2009 *Rs.*	2010 *Rs.*
Share Capital	3,00,000	4,00,000	*Fixed Assets* :		
Capital Reserve	–	10,000	Machinery at cost	5,00,000	6,00,000
General Reserve	50,000	65,000	*Less* : Depreciation	1,50,000	1,70,000
P/L A/c	1,70,000	2,00,000		3,50,000	4,30,000
General Liabilities	1,40,000	1,50,000	Trade Investment	80,000	60,000
Provision for I. Tax	90,000	80,000	*Current Assets* :		
Preferred Dividend	36,000	48,000	Stock	2,00,000	2,63,000
			Debtors	1,06,000	1,50,000
			Bank	30,000	40,000
			Mis. Expenses :		
			Preliminary Expenses	20,000	10,000
	7,86,000	9,53,000		7,86,000	9,53,000

During the year ended 31s March 2010 the company–

(*i*) sold one machine for Rs. 30,000, the cost of which was Rs. 60,000 and depreciation provided on it was Rs. 20,000

(*ii*) sold trade investment at a profit which was credited to capital reserve ; and

(*iii*) decided to write off fixed assets costing Rs. 10,000 (fully depreciated).

(*iv*) Treat Provision of Tax and Proposed Dividend as non-current liabilities.

Prepare Cash Flow Statement for the year ended 31st March, 2010 Show all other workings also.

(**Ans :** Cash flows from Operating Activities : Rs. 56,000 ;
Cash used in Investing Activities : (Rs. 1,10,000)
Cash flows from Financing Activities : Rs. 64,000)

9. From the follwing details relating to the accounts of Grow More Ltd. prepare Cash Flow Statement :

Liabilities	*31-3-2010* *Rs.*	*31-3-2009* *Rs.*	*Assets*	*31-3-2010* *Rs.*	*31-3-2009* *Rs.*
Share Capital	10,00,000	8,00,000	Plant and Machinery	7,00,000	5,00,000
Reserve	2,00,000	1,50,000	Land/Building	6,00,000	4,00,000
Profit and Loss Account	1,00,000	60,000	Investments	1,00,000	–
Debentures	2,00,000	–	Sundry Debtors	5,00,000	7,00,000
Provision for Taxation	1,00,000	70,000	Stock	4,00,000	2,00,000
Proposed Dividend	2,00,000	1,00,000	Cash on Hand/Bank	2,00,000	2,00,000
Sundry Creditors	7,00,000	8,20,000			
	25,00,000	20,00,000		25,00,000	20,00,000

(*i*) Depreciation @ 25% was charged on the opening value of Plant and Machinery.
(*ii*) During the year one old machine costing 50,00-0 (WDV 20,000) was sold for Rs. 35,000.
(*iii*) Rs. 50,000 was paid towards Income Tax during the year.
(*iv*) Building under construction was not suject to any depreciation.

Prepare Cash Flow Statement.

(**Ans :** Cash flows from Operating Activities : Rs. 3,10,000
Cash used in Investing Activities : (Rs. 6,10,000)
Cash flows from Financiing Activities : Rs. 3,00,000)

10. On 1st January 2010, Raman Ltd. wants to implement its programme of expansion but finds that there is shortage of funds. On 1st January 2009, it had a balance in Bank–Rs. 1,80,000.

From the following information, prepare a statement for Board of Directors to show how the overdraft of Rs. 68,750 as at 31st December 2009 has arisen.

Figures as per Balance Sheet as at 31st December each year are as follows:

	Year *2009* *Rs.*	*Year* *2010* *Rs.*
Fixed Assets	7,50,000	11,20,000
Stock & Stores	2,20,000	3,30,000
Sundry Debtors	3,50,000	3,35,000
Bank Balance	1,80,000	68,750 (OD)
Trade Creditors	2,70,000	3,50,000
Share Capital (in shares of Rs. 10 each)	2,50,000	3,00,000
Bills Receivable	2,50,000	3,00,000

The Profit for the year ended 31st December, 2010 before charging depreciation ad taxation amounted to Rs. 2,40,000.

5,000 shares were issued on 1st January, 2010 at a Premium of Rs. 5 per share.

Rs. 1,37,500 were paid in March 2010 by way of Income Tax.

Dividends were paid as follows :

For 2009 (Final) on the capital on 31-12-2009 at 10% less tax at 25%.

For 2010 (Interim) 5%, Free of Tax. Assume that it has been declared after the issue of fresh-shares.

(**Ans :** Cash flows from Operating Activities : Rs. 80,000
Cash used in Investing Activities : (Rs. 3,70,000)
Cash flows from Financing Activities : Rs. 41,250)

11. (Indirect Method)

Given below are the balance sheets of *ABC* Company Ltd., as on 31st march 2009 and 31st March, 2010.

	31.3.2009	*31.3.2010*
	Rs.	*Rs.*
Equity Share capital	2,00,000	3,00,000
Long-term loan	1,00,000	1,00,000
Creditors	1,50,000	2,00,000
Bills payable	2,00,000	3,00,000
Retained earnings	1,80,000	2,00,000
	8,30,000	11,00,000
Cash	60,000	30,000
Stock	1,20,000	1,90,000
Debtors	80,000	1,20,000
Goodwill	2,00,000	1,50,000
Plant and Machinery	1,00,000	2,00,000
Land and Buildings	2,00,000	4,00,000
Furniture	70,000	10,000
	8,30,000	11,00,000

Additional Information :

(*a*) Operating expenses include depreciaton Rs. 80,000 and amortizaton of goodwill Rs. 50,000.

(*b*) A machine has been sold for Rs. 15,000. The written down value of the machine was Rs. 40,000 and Rs. 20,000 depreciation is charged on the same in 2010.

(*c*) Plant and machinery was purchased for cash Rs. 1,40,000 and Land and Buildings for Rs. 2,60,000.

(*d*) Furniture was sold for cash Rs. 60,000.

(*e*) Equity shares were issued for cash Rs. 1,00,000

(*f*) Rs. 80,000 dividend was paid in cash.

(*g*) Net profit for the year 2009-2010 was Rs. 1,00,000.

Prepare a Statement of Cash Flow for the year 2010 under the Indirect Method.

(**Ans :** Cash flows from Operating Activities : Rs. 2,75,000
Cash used in Investing Activities : (Rs. 3,25,000)
Cash flows from Financing Activities : Rs. 20,000)

12. Prepare a Cash flow Statement by Indirect Method of Atlantic Business Corporation from the following :

BALANCE SHEETS
as at Jan. 1 and Dec. 31.2010

Liabilities	*Jan. 1* Rs.	*Dec. 31* Rs.	*Assets*	*Jan. 1* Rs.	*Dec. 31* Rs.
Current Liabilities	30,000	32,000	Cash and Bank Balance	40,000	44,400
Bonds Payable	22,000	22,000	Accounts Receivable	10,000	20,700
Bonds Payable Discount	(2,000)	(1,800)	Inventories	15,000	15,000
Capital Stock	35,000	43,500	Land	4,000	4,000

Retained Earnings	15,000	19,500	Business Premises	20,000	16,000
			Plant & Equipment	15,000	17,000
			Accumulated Dep.	(5,000)	(2,800)
			Patents & Trademarks	1,000	900
	1,00,000	1,15,200		1,00,000	1,15,200

Additional Information :

(*i*) A building that costs Rs. 4,000 and which had a book value of Rs. 1,000 was sold for Rs. 1,400.

(*ii*) The depreciation charge for the period was Rs. 800.

(*iii*) There was a Rs. 5,000 issue of capital stock.

(*iv*) Cash dividend of Rs. 2,000 and a stock dividend of Rs. 3,500 were declared.

(**Ans :** Cash flow from Operating Activities : Rs. 2,000
Cash used in Investing Activities : (Rs. 600)
Cash flows from Financing Activities : Rs. 3,000)

13. From the following Balance Sheets of Excellent Industries Ltd. for the year ended 31st March 2009 and 2010, prepare a Cash Flow Statement, by indirect method :

Liabilities		*31-3-2009*		*31-3-2010*
		Rs.		*Rs.*
Equity Shares of Rs. 10 each		10,00,000		11,50,000
Securities Premium		–		30,000
Profit & Loss Appropriation A/c		3,80,000		3,80,000
Profit for the year		–		5,50,000
6% Debentures		6,00,000		3,00,000
Sundry Creditors		5,55,000		4,00,000
Provision for Taxation		1,20,000		2,20,000
Proposed Dividend		1,50,000		2,20,000
		28,05,000		32,35,000
Assets		*31-3-2009*		*31-3-2010*
		Rs.		*Rs.*
Property		5,00,000		5,50,000
Plant and Machinery	12,00,000		14,50,000	
Less : Depreciation	3,60,000	8,40,000	4,00,000	10,50,000
Share in subsidiary company		4,00,000		4,50,000
Stock in Trade		6,00,000		6,40,000
Debtors		3,60,000		4,00,000
Bank		1,05,000		1,45,000
		2,80,500		32,35,000

The following additional information is available :

(*a*) A machinery costing Rs. 3,00,000 was sold during the year for Rs. 1,80,000. The depreciated value of the equipment was Rs. 1,20,000. The difference between the depreciated value and the amount realised was transferred to profit and loss account.

(*b*) Income Tax paid during the year was Rs. 1,50,000.

Assume that debentures have been partially redeemed at par.

(**Ans :** Cash flows from Operating Activities : Rs. 7,80,000
Cash used in Investing Activities : (Rs. 4,70,000)
Cash used in Financing Activities : (Rs. 2,70,000))

14. Following are the summarised Balance Sheets and Income Statement of X Ltd. for year ending 31st December 2010.

Liabilities	*31.12.2009* *Rs.*	*31.12.2010* *Rs.*
Capital	7,20,000	8,88,000
Profit & Loss	3,03,600	3,27,600
Sundry Creditors	4,80,000	4,68,000
O/S Expenses	48,000	96,000
Income Tax Payable	24,000	26,400
Accumulated Depreciation on Plant	2,40,000	2,64,000
	18,15,600	20,70,000

Assets	*31.12.2009* *Rs.*	*31.12.2010* *Rs.*
Land & Buildings	96,000	1,92,000
Plant	7,20,000	11,52,000
Cash	1,20,000	1,44,000
Debtors	3,36,000	3,72,000
Stock	5,28,000	1,92,000
Advances	15,600	18,000
	18,15,600	20,70,000

NB : Cost of plant sold was Rs. 1,44,000

Income Statement for 2010

			Rs.
	Net Sales		50,40,000
Less :	Cost of Sales	39,60,000	
	Depreciation	1,20,000	
	Salaries & Wages	4,80,000	
	Operating Expenses	1,60,000	
	Provision for Tax	1,76,000	
			48,96,000
			1,44,000
Add :	Profit on Sale of Plant		24,000
	Net Profit		1,68,000
	Retained Earnings		3,03,600
			4,71,6000
Less :	Dividend Paid		1,44,000
			3,27,600

You are required to prepare Cash Flow Statement by Indirect Method. *(B.Com. (Hons) Kolkata)*

(**Ans**: Cash flows form operating Activities : Rs. 6,00,000
Cash used in Investing Activities : (Rs. 6,00,000)
Cash flows from Financing Activities : Rs. 24,000)

Chapter 6

Working Capital Management

Introduction; Concept of Working Capital ; Components of Working Capital; Nature of Working Capital; Kinds of Working Capital; Permanent or Fixed Working Capital; Temporary or Variable Working Capital; Importance of Adequate Working Capital; Dangers of Inadequate Working Capital; Danger of Excessive Working Capital; Determinant of Working Capital; Sources of Working Capital; Financing of Long-term Working Capital; Financing of Short-term Working Capital; Management of Working Capital; Working Capital Forecasting; Trading Concern; Manufacturing Concern; Working Capital Requirement Forecast; Important Working Capital Ratios; Objective Type Questions; Theoretical Questions; Practical Problems.

Introduction

Working Capital may be regarded as the lifeblood of a business. Its effective provision can do much to ensure the success of a business. Its inefficient management can lead not only to loss of profits but also to the downfall of a business. A study of Working Capital is of major importance to internal and external analysis because of its close relationship with the current day-to-day operations of a business. Every business needs funds for two purposes. Long term funds are required to create production facilities through purchase of fixed assets, such as, plants, machineries, land, buildings etc. Investments in these assets represent that part of firm's capital which is blocked on a permanent or fixed basis and is called fixed capital. Funds are also needed for short term purposes for the purchase of raw materials, payment of wages and other day-to-day expenses etc. These funds are known as Working Capital. In other words, Working Capital refers to that part of the firm's capital which is required for financing short-term or current assets, such as, cash, marketable securities, debtors, inventories, Bills Receivable etc. The assets of this type are relatively temporary in nature. Unfortunately, there is much disagreement among financiers, accountants, economists and businessmen as to the exact meaning of the term "Working Capital". However, Working Capital is also known as revolving or circulating capital or short-term capital.

Concept of Working Capital

There are two concepts of Working Capital—Gross concept and Net Concept. The gross working capital, usually referred to as working capital, represents investment in current assets such as marketable securities, inventories and Bills Receivables etc. Current assets are those assets which are normally converted into cash within one year. The term "net working capital" represents the difference between current assets and current liabilities. Current liabilities are those claims of outsiders which are expected to mature for payment within one year and include creditors, bills payable, bank overdraft and expense outstanding. The net working capital can be positive or negative. When current assets exceed current liabilities, the net working capital becomes positive. When current liabilities exceed current assets, the net working capital becomes negative.

As indicated both 'net' and 'gross' concepts of working capital have functional significance. The gross working capital concept is financial or going concern concept and deals with the problems of managing individual current assets in short-term. The net working capital concept is an accounting concept and deals with management of net value of current assets in the long run. Gross and net concept of working capital have their own merits. The net concept of working capital may be suitable only for proprietary form of organizations—sole trader, partnership firm, etc. The gross concept of working capital is suitable to the company form of organization.

At the beginning of a business venture, cash is provided by owners and lenders. A part of this cash is invested in tools, machinery, furniture, equipment, building and other forms of fixed assets which are not to be sold during the normal course of business. The remaining cash is used as working capital to meet the current requirements of a business enterprise, such as the purchase of services, raw materials or merchandise. When a firm's products or finished goods are sold, it has, what is known as cash or receivables. When receivables are collected, cash is available for the planning of services and the purchase of raw materials or merchandise. This flow of cash into production and so on illustrates the circular flow of working capital. The term *circulating capital* is frequently used to denote those assets which are changed with relative rapidity from one form to another. Working Capital is essentially circulating capital. Brown and Howard, who compare the working capital with a river which is always there but whose water level is constantly changing. An accountant defines working capital as the difference between current assets and current liabilities. This is a simplified definition as to how working capital is circulated.

Components of Working Capital

The term working capital refers to the gross working capital and represents the amount of funds invested in current assets. Current assets are those assets which in the ordinary course of business can be converted into cash within a short period of normally one accounting year.

Examples of current assets are :

1. Cash and Bank Balances
2. Short term loans and Advances
3. Bills Receivables
4. Sundry Debtors
5. Inventories such as, Raw materials, Work-in-progress, Finished goods.
6. Prepaid Expenses
7. Accrued Incomes
8. Money receivable within 12 months

In a narrow sense, the term working capital refers to the net working capital. Net working capital is the excess of current assets over current liabilities, or

Net Working Capital = Current Assets – Current Liabilities

Current liabilities are those liabilities which are intended to be paid in the ordinary course of business within a short period of normally one accounting year.

Examples of current liabilities are :

1. Bills Payable
2. Sundry Creditors
3. Accounts Payable
4. Short-term Borrowings
5. Dividends Payable
6. Statutory Liabilities
7. Accrued or Outstanding Expenses
8. Bank Overdraft
9. Provident Fund Dues
10. Any other payment due within 12 months.

Nature of Working Capital

The nature of working capital is described with the help of nature of operation cycle of the firm. The process of cash or operation cycle starts when a firm uses cash to purchase raw materials and pay for other manufacturing costs to produce goods. These goods are carried as inventory for some time till they are sold. When goods are sold, either cash is received or accounts receivable, are created. Accounts Receivables are collected from debtors, this brings cash into firm. Thus, a cash cycle is complete, and a new process of a cash cycle starts over again. These processes are described as circulating nature of current assets. The speed of circulation of working capital or the turnover of current assets is an indicator of the degree of efficiency of the management. The faster the turnover, the higher the degree of efficiency."

Current assets are not only short-lived but also change their form and one type of assets can easily be converted into another, say, cash is converted into Raw Materials, Raw materials into Work-in-progress, Work-in-progress into Finished products, Finished products into Debtors, in case of credit sales or into Cash. That is why they are also defined as circulating assets. The conversion of one item of current asset into another in a manufacturing concern has been depicted below :

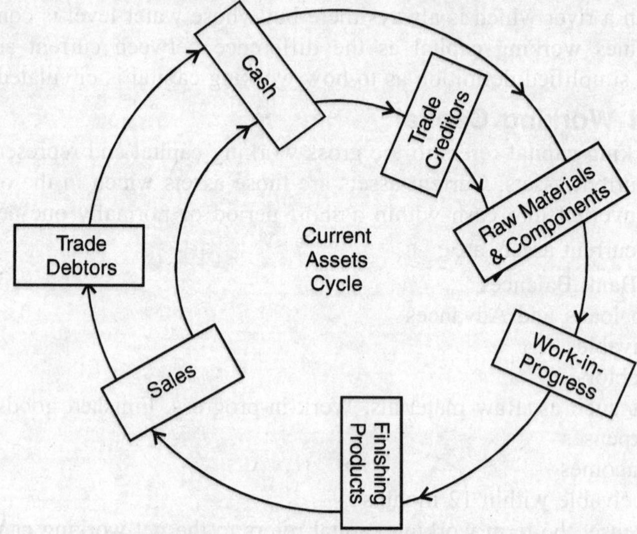

Circulating Nature of Working Capital

The goal of working capital management is to manage the firm's current assets and current liabilities in such a way that a satisfactory level of working capital is maintained. That is so because if the firm cannot maintain a satisfactory level of working capital, it is likely to become insolvent and may even be forced into bankruptcy. The current assets should be large enough to cover its current liabilities in order to ensure a reasonable margin of safety. Each of the current assets must be managed efficiently in order to maintain the liquidity of the firm while not keeping too high a level of any one of them. Each of the short-term sources of financing must be continuously managed to ensure that they are obtained and used in the best possible way. *The interaction between current assets and current liabilities is, therefore, the main theme of the theory of working capital management*.

Kinds of Working Capital

The changes in current assets, in short and long terms, have led to the classification of working capital into two components.

(*a*) Permanent or Fixed Working Capital

This component represents the value of the current assets required on a continuing basis over the entire year, and for several years. Permanent working capital is the minimum amount of current assets which is needed to conduct a business even during the dullest season of the year. This minimum level of current assets is called Permanent or Fixed Working Capital as this part of capital is permanently blocked in current assets. This amount varies from year to year, depending upon the growth of a company and the stage of the business cycle in which it operates. It is the amount of funds required to produce the goods and services which are necessary to satisfy demand at a particular point. It represents the current assets which are required on a continuing basis over the entire year. It is maintained as the medium to carry on operations at any time. Permanent Working Capital has the following characteristics :

(*i*) It is classified on the basis of the time factor ;

(*ii*) It constantly changes from one asset to another and continues to remain in the business process ;

(*iii*) Its size increases with the growth of business operations.

The permanent working capital can further be classified as regular working capital and reserve working capital. Regular working capital is the minimum amount of working capital required to ensure circulation of current assets from cash to inventories, from inventories to receivables and from receivables to cash and so on. Reserve working capital is the excess amount over the requirement for regular working capital which may be provided for contingencies that may arise at unstated periods such as strikes, rise in prices, depression etc.

(*b*) Temporary or Variable Working Capital

This component represents a certain amount of fluctuations in current assets during a short period. These fluctuations are increases or decreases and are generally cyclical in nature. Additional current assets are required at different times during the operating year. Variable working capital is the amount of additional current asset required for a short period. The capital required to meet the seasonal needs of a firm is called seasonal working capital. For example, additional inventory will be required for meeting the demand during the peak selling periods, and receivables increase during the period of high sales. When the peak period is over variable working capital starts decreasing or very little during the normal period. It is temporarily invested in current assets and possesses the following characteristics :

(*i*) It is not always gainfully employed, though it may change from one asset to another, as permanent working capital does.

(*ii*) It is particularly suited to business of a seasonal or cyclical nature.

Importance of Adequate Working Capital

A business firm must maintain an adequate level of working capital in order to run its business smoothly. It is worthy to note that both excessive and inadequate working capital positions are harmful. However, out of the two, inadequacy of working capital is more dangerous for a firm. Excessive working capital results in idle funds on which no profit is earned. Similarly insufficiency of working capital results in interruptions of production. This will lead to inefficiencies, increase in costs and reduction in profits.

Working Capital is just like the heart of business. If it becomes weak, the business can hardly prosper and survive. No business can run successfully without an adequate amount of working capital. The following are a few advantages of adequate working capital in the business:

1. Cash Discount : Adequate working capital enables a firm to avail cash discount facilities offered to it by the suppliers. The amount of cash discount reduces the cost of purchases.

2. Goodwill : Adequate working capital enables a firm to make prompt payment. Making prompt payment is a base to create and maintain goodwill.

3. Ability to face crisis : The provision of adequate working capital facilitates to meet situations of crisis and emergencies. It enables a business to withstand periods of depression smoothly.

4. Credit-worthiness : It enables a firm to operate its business more efficiently because there is no delay in getting loans from banks and others on easy and favourable terms.

5. Regular supply of raw materials : It permits the carrying of inventories at a level that would enable a business to serve satisfactorily the needs of its customers. That is it ensures regular supply of raw materials and continues production.

6. Expansion of Markets : A firm, which have adequate working capital, can create favourable market condition. That is so because purchasing its requirements in bulk when prices are lower and holding its inventories for higher prices. Thus profits are increased.

7. Productivity Increased : Fixed assets of the firm cannot work without adequate working capital. Because the fate of large scale investment in fixed assets is largely determined by the manner in which its current assets are managed.

8. Research Programmes : No research programme, innovation and technical developments are possible to be undertaken without sufficient amount of working capital.

9. High Morale : Adequacy of working capital creates an environment of security, confidence, high morale etc. and creates overall efficiency in business.

10. Liquidity and Solvency : A sound system of working capital enables a concern to pay regular dividends to its investors. This gains confidence in the mind of investors and this situation creates a favourable market to raise additional funds in the future.

Danger of Inadequate Working Capital

When working capital is inadequate, a firm faces the following problems :

1. It may not be able to take advantages of cash discount.
2. It cannot buy its requirements in bulk and unable to utilize the production facilities fully.
3. It may not be able to take advantage of profitable business opportunities.
4. It may fail to pay its dividend because of non-availability of funds.
5. Its low liquidity may lead to low profitability. In the same way, low profitability results in low liquidity.
6. Short-term liabilities cannot be paid because of inadequate working capital. This leads to borrow funds at exorbitant rates of interest.
7. Credit-worthiness of the firm may be damaged because of lack of liquidity. Thus, it will lose its reputation. Thereby, a firm may not be able to get credit facilities.
8. Low liquidity position may lead to liquidation of firm. When a firm is unable to meet its debts at maturity, there is an unsound position.
9. Fixed assets cannot efficiently and effectively be utilised on account of lack of sufficient working capital.

Danger of Excessive Working Capital

When there is too much working capital, it is also dangerous. Excessive working capital raises the following problems :

1. A firm may be tempted to over trade and lose heavily.
2. The situation may lead to unnecessary purchases and accumulation of inventories. This causes more chances of theft, waste, losses etc.
3. There arise an imbalance between liquidity and profitability.
4. Excessive working capital means funds are idle. When funds are idle, no profit is earned. When it is so, the rate of return on its investment goes down.
5. The situation leads to greater production which may not have matching demand.
6. The excess of working capital may lead to carelessness about cost of production.

Determinant of Working Capital

The need for working capital requirement for running day-to-day business activities cannot be over emphasized. The working capital requirement is affected by a number of factors—some of them might be associated with the business concern and some of them might be related to general economic, monetary, business environment etc. It should be, however, noted that these factors affect different enterprises differently. A firm should plan its operations in such a way that it should have neither too much nor too little working capital. The working capital requirement in certain businesses may be negligible while in certain others it may be larger than even the amount of fixed capital. Some of the important determinants of working capital requirements of business enterprises are given below :

1. General Nature of Business

The working capital requirements of an enterprise are basically related to the conduct of the business. Public utility undertakings like Electricity, Water Supply, Railways etc. need very limited working capital because they offer cash sales only and supply services, not products, and as such no funds are tied up in inventories and receivables. But, at the same time, trading firms require large amounts in current assets—inventories, receivables, cash etc. — but have to invest less amount in fixed assets. The manufacturing concerns require sizable working capital alongwith fixed investments as they have to build up inventories. Again, manufacturing concerns face problems of slow turnovers of inventories and receivables, and invest large amounts in working capital.

2. Terms of Sales and Purchases

Credit terms granted by the concerns to its customers as well as credit terms granted by its suppliers also affect the working capital. If the credit terms of purchases are more favourable and those of sales less liberal, less cash will be invested in inventory. With more favourable credit terms, working capital requirements can be reduced. The ratio of cash and credit sales or purchases will also affect the level of working capital. A firm that purchases its requirements on credit and sells its product on cash, requires less amount of working capital. At the same time, a firm buying its requirements for cash and allowing credit to its customers, shall need huge amount of working capital. This is because funds are tied up in Debtors or Bills Receivables.

3. Manufacturing Cycle

The quantum of working capital needed is influenced by the length of manufacturing cycle. Manufacturing process always involves a time-lag between the time when raw materials are fed into the production line and finished products are finally turned out by it. The length of the period of manufacture in turn depends on the nature of product as well as production technology used by a concern. An utmost care should be taken to shorten the period of cycle in order to minimise the working capital requirements.

4. Rapidity of Turnover

If the inventory turnover is high, the working capital requirements will be low. With a better inventory control, a firm is able to reduce its working capital requirements. When a firm has to carry on a large slow moving stock, it needs a larger working capital as against another whose turnover is rapid. A firm should determine the minimum level of stock which it will have to maintain throughout the period of its operation.

5. Business Cycle

Cyclical changes in the economy also influence quantum of working capital. In a period of boom *i.e.* when the business is prosperous, there is a need for larger amount of working capital due to increase in sales, rise in price etc. During the period of depression also a heavy amount of working capital is needed due to the inventories being locked unsold and book debt uncollected.

6. Changes in Technology

Changes in technology may lead to improvements in processing of raw materials, savings in wastage, greater productivity, more speedy production etc.. All these improvements may enable the firm to reduce investments in inventory. Thus changes in technology affect the requirements for working capital. If the firm decides to go for automation, this would reduce the requirements for working capital. If the firm adopts a labour-intensive process, the requirements for working capital will be larger. The shorter the manufacturing process due to use of improved technology, the lower the requirements for working capital. The working capital requirements of a concern increase with the growth and expansion of its business activities. A fast growing concern need larger amount of working capital.

7. Seasonal Variation

The inventory of raw materials, spares and stores depends on the conditions of supply. If the supply is prompt and adequate the firm can manage with small inventory. However, if the supply is unpredictable and scant then the firm, to ensure continuity of production, would have to acquire stocks as and when they are available and carry larger inventory on an average. A similar policy may have to be followed when the raw material is available only seasonally and production operations are carried out round the year.

8. Market Conditions

The degree of competition prevailing in the market place has an important bearing on working capital needs. When competition is keen, a larger inventory of finished goods is required to promptly serve customers who may not be inclined to wait because other manufacturers are ready to meet their needs. Further, generous credit terms may have to be offered to attract customers in a highly competitive market. Thus, working capital needs tend to be high because of greater investment in finished goods inventory and accounts receivable.

9. Seasonality of Operation

Firms which have marked seasonality in their operations usually have highly fluctuating working requirements. To illustrate, consider a firm manufacturing ceiling fans. The sale of ceiling fans reaches a peak during the summer months and drops sharply during the winter period. The working capital need of such a firm is likely to increase considerably in summer months and decrease significantly during the winter period. On the other hand, a firm manufacturing a product lamp, which have fairly even sales round the year, tends to have stable working capital needs.

10. Working Capital Cycle

"The production or manufacturing cycle" refers to the time involved in the manufacture of goods. It covers the time span between the procurement of raw materials and the completion of manufacturing process, *i.e.* leading to finished products. In a manufacturing concern, the working capital cycle starts with the purchase of raw materials and ends with the realisation of cash from the sale of finished products. Generally the working capital cycle involves purchase of raw materials and stores, its conversion into stocks of finished goods through work-in-progress with progressive increment of labour and service costs, conversion of finished goods into sales, debtors, receivables and ultimately realisation of cash. This cycle is repeated again and again.

11. Dividend Policy

Dividend policy has a dominant influence on the working capital position of an enterprise. If a conservative dividend policy is followed by the management, the need for working capital can be met with the retained earnings. When once dividend is declared and the same has to be paid in cash, it consequently drains off large amounts from the pool of working capital.

12. Depreciation Policy

Depreciation charges do not involve any cash outflow. Depreciation affects the tax liability and retention of profits. It is allowable expenditure in calculating net profits. Higher depreciation will mean lower disposable profits and therefore, a smaller dividend payment. Thus cash will be preserved.

The level of working capital is determined by a wide variety of factors which are partly internal to the firm and partly external to it. Efficient working capital management requires efficient planning and a constant review of the needs for an appropriate working capital strategy.

SOURCES OF WORKING CAPITAL

The financial manager is always interested in obtaining the working capital at the right time, at a reasonable cost and at the best possible favourable terms. In any concern, a part of the working capital investments are permanent investments in fixed assets. Because, there is always a minimum level of current assets which are continuously required by the enterprise to carry out its day-to-day business operations. The minimum level cannot be expected to reduce at any time. This minimum level of current assets gives rise to permanent working capital, which is permanently blocked in current assets. The following is a snapshot of various sources of working capital available to a firm.

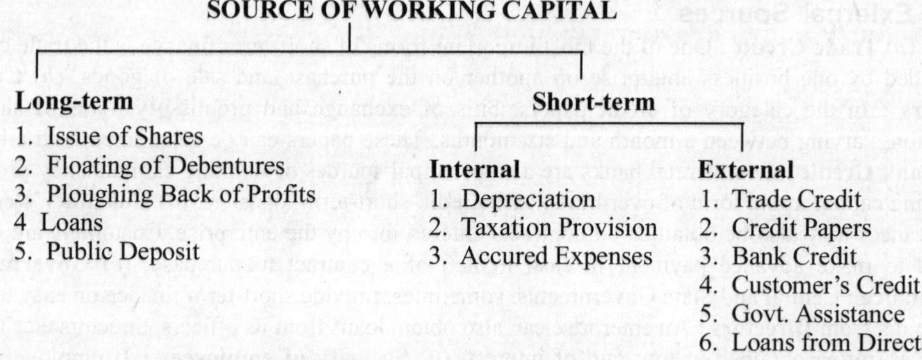

Financing of Long-term Working Capital

Long-term working capital should be provided in such a manner that the enterprise may have its uninterrupted use for a long time. It can be conveniently financed by the following sources :

1. Issue of Shares

Issue of shares is the most important source for raising the permanent working capital. Shares are of two types—Equity Shares and Preference Shares. Maximum amount of permanent capital should be raised by the issue of shares.

2. Floating of Debentures

A debenture is an instrument issued by the company acknowledging its debt to its holder. It is also an important source of long term working capital. The firm issuing debentures also enjoy a number of benefits, such as trading on equity, retention of control, tax benefits etc.

3. Ploughing Back of Profits

It means the reinvestment by a concern of its surplus earnings in its business. That is, a part of the earned profits may be ploughed back by the firm, in meeting their working capital needs. It is an internal source of finance and is most suitable.

4. Long-term Loans

Financial institutions such as Commercial Banks, Life Insurance Corporation of India, Industrial Finance Corporation of India, State Financial Corporations, Industrial Development Bank of India etc. provide all types of loans—long-term, medium-term and short-term loans. This type of finance is ordinarily repayable in instalments.

5. Accepting Public Deposits

Public deposits are the fixed deposits accepted by a business enterprise directly from public. Public deposits as a source of finance have a large number of advantages such as simple and convenient source of finance. taxation benefits, inexpensive sources of finance etc.

Financing of short-term working capital

The category of funds covers the need of working capital for financing day-to-day business requirements. They are of two types—Internal source and External source.

(A) Internal Sources

(*a*) **Depreciation Funds :** Depreciation reserve provides a good source of funds for working capital. (*b*) **Provision for Taxation :** The provision for taxation can also be used by the concern as a source of working capital during intermitant periods. (*c*) **Accrued Expenses :** The firm can postpone the payment of expenses for short periods. This constitute as a source of working capital.

(B) External Sources

(*a*) **Trade Credit :** One of the most important forms of short-term finance is the trade credit extended by one business enterprise on another on the purchase and sale of goods. (*b*) **Credit Papers :** In the category of credit papers, bills of exchange and promissory notes of shorter duration, varying between a month and six months. These papers can be discounted with a bank. (*c*) **Bank Credit :** Commercial banks are also principal sources of working capital. They provide working capital in the form of overdrafts, cash credit, short-term loans etc. (*d*) **Customer's credit :** Advances may also be obtained on contracts entered into by the enterprise. Customers are often asked to make advance payment in cash in lieu of a contract to purchase. (*e*) **Government Assistance :** Central and State Governments, sometimes, provide short-term finance on easy terms. (*f*) **Loans from Directors :** An enterprise can also obtain loans from its officers, directors etc. These loans are often obtained at low rate of interest. (*g*) **Security of employees :** If employees are required to make deposits with their employer companies, such deposits are available for short-term working capital.

Management of Working Capital

Working Capital management is an integral part of overall corporate management. To a financial manager, a working capital sphere throws a welcome challenge and opportunity. Working capital, in general practice, refers to the excess of current assets over current liabilities. Management of working capital, therefore, is concerned with the problems that arise in attempting to manage the current assets, current liabilities and the inter-relationship that exist between them. Both inadequate as well as excessive working capital position are bad for a concern. Inadequacy of working capital may lead the firm to insolvency and excessive working capital implies idle funds, which earn no profits for the business. The twin objectives of working capital management are profitability and liquidity. Investment in current as well as long-term assets have to be undertaken so as to offer the most satisfactory returns to shareholders. The goal of liquidity is to ensure that a company satisfies financial obligations and continues as a going concern. Profitability and liquidity frequently conflict with each other. Attempts to produce maximum profitability out of various elements of working capital do create severe liquidity problems. At the same time, over concentration on liquidity does dilute profits. A sound working capital management policy is one which ensures higher profitability, proper liquidity and sound structural health of the organisation. The management of working capital has the following problems :

1. Estimating the working capital requirments.
2. To decide the optimal level of investment in various current assets.
3. To decide optimal mix of short-term funds in relation to long- term capital.
4. To locate the appropriate means of short-term financing.

"We need to know when to look for working capital funds, how to use them and how to measure, plan and control them". Thus the financial manager has to perform the following two basic functions :

1. Forecasting the working capital requirements.
2. Financing of working capital needs.

Working Capital Forecasting

The most ticklish problem that is faced by a businessman is the determination of the amount of working capital required at a particular level of business operation. Working capital is the life-blood of a business. No businessman can successfully run without an adequate amount of working capital. A working capital forecast is prepared for this purpose involving some calculations after taking into consideration all the aspects of business activity.

Trading Concern

The estimated requirement of working capital for the budgeted period can be determined on the basis of data contained in the Balance sheet of previous year. The current assets and current liabilities are to be adjusted in relation to the budget period and the working capital requirement can easily be determined by deducting the estimated total value of current liabilities from the estimated total value of current assets. This is clear from the following illustration :

Illustration 1. From the following information of X Ltd., a trading concern, you are asked to ascertain the estimated additional requirement of working capital :

BALANCE SHEETS AS ON....

Fixed Assets :	*Rs.*		*Rs.*
Land and Buildings	2,000		
Plant,Machinery etc.	1,000		
			3,000
Working Capital :			
Current Assets:			
Stock	4,000		
Debtors	3,000		
Cash and Bank	1,000	8,000	
Less : Current Liabilities			
Creditors	2,000		
Taxation	600		
Overdraft	1,400		
O/S Liabilities	1,000	5,000	3,000
			6,000

Additional information :

(*a*) It is estimated that the company will be able to increase sales by 25% in the following year.

(*b*) Maximum limit of overdraft facility granted is Rs. 1,500.

(*c*) Credit period allowed to customers and the level of stock will remain unaltered.

Solution :

Requirement of Additional Working Capital

	Current year level (as per B/S) *Rs.*	*Estimated Increase* *Rs.*	*Estimated Requirement* *Rs.*
CURRENT ASSETS :			
Stock	4,000	1,000	5,000
Debtors	3,000	750	3,750
Cash and Bank	1,000	250	1,250
Total (A)	8,000	2,000	10,000
CURRENT LIABILITIES :			
Creditors	2,000	500	2,500
Taxation	600	150	750
Overdraft	1,400	100	1,500
O/S Liabilities	1,000	250	1,250
Total (B)	5,000	1,000	6,000
WORKING CAPITAL (A) – (B)	3,000		4,000

Requirement of Additional
Working Capital = **Rs. 1,000** (Rs. 4,000 – Rs. 3,000)

Where the Balance Sheet of the earlier period is not available, the amount of current assets and current liabilities for the budget period should be ascertained on the basis of the given data and deduct the current liabilities from current assets in order to get the estimated requirement of working capital. The following illustration will clear the point.

Illustration 2. A firm is engaged in large scale consumer retailing. From the following information, you are required to forecast their working capital requirement :

Projected Annual Sales = Rs. 65,00,000
Percentage of Net Profit on Cost of Sales – 25%
Average credit period allowed to Debtors – 10 weeks
Average credit period allowed by Creditors – 4 weeks
Average stock carrying (in terms of sales requirement) – 8 weeks
Add 10% to computed figures to allow for contingencies.

(*B. Com., M. Com., Calcutta*)

Solution :

Projected Annual Sales = Rs. 65,00,000

Projected Annual Sales per week = $\frac{\text{Rs. } 65,00,000}{52}$		Rs. 1,25,000
Less : Net Profit thereom (25% on cost or 20% on sales)		Rs. 25,000
Projected Cost per week		Rs. 1,00,000
WORKING CAPITAL REQUIREMENT FORECAST		
Current Assets :	*Rs.*	*Rs.*
Stock (8 weeks) Rs. 1,00,000 × 8		8,00,000
Debtors (10 weeks) Rs. 1,00,000 × 10	10,00,000	
Add : Profit @25% on Cost	2,50,000	12,50,000
		20,50,000

Less : Current Liabilities :	
Creditors (4 weeks) Rs. 1,00,000 × 4	4,00,000
Working Capital Computed :	16,50,000
Add : 10% for contingencies	1,65,000
Total Requirement of Working Capital :	18,15,000

Manufacturing Concern

The following items are taken into consideration at the time of ascertaining the requirement of working capital for a manufacturing concern.

1. Total quantity of units to be produced throughout the year.
2. Total costs incurred on materials, wages and overheads.
3. Information about the length of time for which raw materials are to remain in store before they are issued for production. (The longer the period, the more will be the requirement of working capital).
4. Information about the length of production cycle. (The longer the period, the larger will be the requirement of working capital)
5. Information about the length of sales cycle. That is, the period during which finished products will remain in the warehouse. (The longer the period of stay, the more will be the requirement of working capital)
6. Information about the average of credit allowed to debtors. (The longer the period allowed to customers, the more will be the requirement of working capital).
7. Information about the average of credit allowed by suppliers. (The longer the period allowed by creditors, the less will be the requirement of working capital).
8. Information about the business expenses.
9. Information about the lag in payment of wages and overheads. (The longer the period, the less will be the requirement of working capital).

Forecast of working capital is compiled on the basis of estimate only. Therefore, in order to provide for contingencies, a provision (percentage basis) may be added as a margin of safety. This provision helps in cushioning all uncertainties involved in making the estimates.

Illustration 3. From the following particulars prepare a statement showing working capital needed to finance a level of activity of 12,000 units of output per annum.

Analysis of selling price per unit

	Rs.
Raw Materials	5
Labour	3
Overhead	2
Total Cost	10
Profit	2
Selling Price	12

Additional Information :

(*a*) Raw materials are to remain in store on an average – one month.

(*b*) Materials are in process, on an average – 2 months

(*c*) Finished goods are in stock on an average – 3 months

(*d*) Credit allowed to Debtors is 4 months

(*e*) Credit allowed by suppliers is 2 months.

It may be assumed that production and overheads accrue evenly throughout the year.

(*B.Com. Madurai*)

Solution :

Sales for the year = 12,000 × Rs. 12 = Rs. 1,44,000

Sales per month = Rs. 1,44,000 ÷ 12 = Rs. 12,000

Amount to be blocked :

In materials $\text{Rs.}12,000 \times \frac{5}{12} = \text{Rs.}5,000$

In Labour $\text{Rs.}12,000 \times \frac{3}{12} = \text{Rs.}3,000$

In Overheads $\text{Rs.}12,000 \times \frac{2}{12} = \text{Rs.}2,000$

Alternatively :

Monthly production 12,000 ÷ 12 = 1,000 units

Average cost of production per month :

Materials 1,000 × Rs. 5 = Rs. 5,000

Labour 1,000 × Rs. 3 = Rs. 3,000

Overheads 1,000 × Rs. 2 = Rs. 2,000

WORKING CAPITAL REQUIREMENT FORECAST

Current Assets :			
1. Stock of Raw Materials (1 month)			
Raw Materials	Rs. 5,000 × 1	5,000	5,000
2. Work-in-progress (2 months)			
Raw Materials	Rs. 5,000 × 2	10,000	
Labour	Rs. 3,000 × 2	6,000	
Overheads	Rs. 2,000 × 2	4,000	20,000
3. Stock of Finished Goods (3 months)			
Raw Materials	Rs. 5,000 [illegible]	15,000	
Labour	Rs. 3,000 × 3	9,000	
Overhead	Rs. 2,000 × 3	6,000	30,000
4. Debtors (4 months)			
Raw Materials	Rs. 5,000 × 4	20,000	
Labour	Rs. 3,000 × 4	12,000	
Overhead	Rs. 2,000 × 4	8,000	
		40,000	
Profit (1/5th of cost)		8,000	48,000
			1,03,000
Less :			
Current Liabilities :			
1. Creditors (2 months)	Rs. 5,000 × 2	10,000	10,000
Requirement of Working Capital			93,000

Alternative approach (in a columnar form)

WORKING CAPITAL REQUIREMENT FORECAST

Particulars	*Periods in months*	*Total* *Rs.*	*Raw Material* *Rs.*	*Work-in-progress* *Rs.*	*Finished Goods* *Rs.*	*Debtors* *Rs.*	*Creditors* *Rs.*
1. Materials :							
In Stores	1		5,000				

In Process	2			10,000			
In FinishedGoods	3				15,000		
With Debtors	4					20,000	
	10						10,000
Less : Credit from Creditors	2						
	8	40,000					
2. Wages :							
In Process	2			6,000			
In Finished Goods	3				9,000		
With Debtors	4					12,000	
	9	27,000					
3. Overheads :							
In Process	2			4,000			
In Finished Goods	3				6,000		
With Debtors	4					8,000	
	9	18,000					
4. Profit :							
Credit to Debtors	4					8,000	
Total		93,000	5,000	20,000	30,000	48,000	10,000

Total Working Capital Requirement is **Rs. 93,000.**

The traditional 'Balance Sheet Approach' to project Working Capital requirement of a firm is now sought to be replaced by a modern approach which does by the name of 'Operating Cycle Approach' or Cash Working Capital Approach' to Working Capital requirement. Unlike the conventional approach, consistent with the definition, this approach views Working Capital as a function of the volume of operating expenses. This approach suggests that actual level of Working Capital requirement of a firm in a period can be appropriately determined with reference to the length of Net Operating Cycle and the operating expenses needed for the period. The net duration of operating cycle is equal to the number of days involved in the different stages of operation commencing from purchase of raw materials and ending up with the collection of sale proceeds from Debtors against which the number of days credit allowed by suppliers are to be adjusted. The number of operating cycle in a period is determined by dividing the number of days in the same by the length of Net Operating Cycle. Once the number of operating cycle has been determined, the actual Working Capital requirement is then arrived at by dividing the total operating expenses for the period by the number of operating cycle in that period.

Illustration 4. From the following information, prepare a statement showing the working capital requirements :

		Rs. 2,60,000 p.a.
Budgeted Sales (Rs. 10 per unit)		
Analysis of one type of sales :		
Raw Materials	0.30	
Direct Labour	0.40	
Overheads	0.20	
Total Cost :	0.90	
Profit	0.10	
	Re. 1.00	

It is estimated that :

1. Raw materials are carried in stock for three weeks and finished goods for two weeks.
2. Factory processing will take three weeks.
3. Suppliers will give full five weeks' credit.
4. Customers will require eight weeks' credit.

It may be assumed that production and overheads accrue evenly throughout the year.

(*M.Com. Madurai*)

Solution :

WORKING CAPITAL REQUIREMENT

		Rs.
(A)	Total current assets to be maintained :	
	Stock of Raw Materials[1]	4,500
	Work-in-progress[2]	9,000
	Stock of Finished Goods[3]	9,000
	Debtors[4]	40,000
		62,500
(B)	Current Liabilities to be created :	
	Trade Creditors[5]	7,500
	Working Capital Required : (A) – (B)	55,000

Workings :

(1) Stock of Raw Materials :

Budgeted Sales Rs. 2,60,000

Selling Price per unit = Rs. 10

Number of units = Rs. 2,60,000 ÷ 10 = 26,000 units

Cost of Raw Materials = 26,000 × 0.30 × 10 = Rs. 78,000

Stock of Raw Materials = $\text{Rs.}78,000 \times \frac{3}{52} = \textbf{Rs.4,500}$

(2) Work-in-progress

Since wages and overheads have accrued evenly, only half of their amounts shall be included in the cost of work-in-progress.

Cost of Sales :		Rs.
Raw Materials	26,000 × 0.30 × 10	78,000
Direct Labour	26,000 × 0.40 × 10	1,04,000
Overheads	26,000 × 0.20 × 10	52,000
		2,34,000
Raw Materials :	$78,000 \times \frac{3}{52}$	4,500
Direct Labour :	$1,04,000 \times \frac{3}{52} \times \frac{1}{2}$	3,000
Overheads :	$52,000 \times \frac{3}{52} \times \frac{1}{2}$	1,500
		9,000

3. Stock of Finished Stocks :

$$\text{Rs.}2,34,000 \times \frac{2}{52} = \textbf{Rs.9,000}$$

4. Debtors at sales value :

Total Sales per year (assumed to be credit) Rs. 2,60,000

8 weeks credit sales $\text{Rs.}260,000 \times \frac{8}{52} = \textbf{Rs. 40,000}$

5. Creditors :

Credit purchase (cost of materials) p.a. = Rs. 78,000

So, 5 weeks credit purchase (creditor) = $\text{Rs.}78,000 \times \frac{5}{52} = \textbf{Rs.7,500}$

Illustration 5. From the following information, you are required to estimate the net working capital :

	Cost per unit *Rs.*
Raw Materials	400
Direct Labour	150
Overheads (excluding depreciation)	300
Total Cost	850

Additional Information :

Selling price	1,000 per unit
Output	52,000 units
Raw Material in stock	Average 4 weeks
Work-in-progress (assumed 50% completion stage with full material consumption	Average 2 weeks
Finished goods in stock	Average 4 weeks
Credit allowed by suppliers	Average 4 weeks
Credit allowed to Debtors	Average 8 weeks
Cash at Bank is expected to be :	Rs. 50,000

Assume that production is sustained at an even pace during the 52 weeks of the year. All sales are on credit basis. (*ICWA Final*)

Solution :

WORKING CAPITAL REQUIREMENT FORECAST

1. Stock of Raw Materials (4 weeks)			
Raw Materials	Rs. 4,00,000 × 4		16,00,000
2. Work-in-progress : (2 weeks)			
Raw Materials	4,00,000 × 2	8,00,000	
Labour	Rs. 1,50,000 × 1	1,50,000	
Overheads	Rs. 3,00,000 × 1	3,00,000	12,50,000
3. Stock of Finished Goods (4 weeks)			
Raw Materials	Rs. 4,00,000 × 4	16,00,000	
Labour	Rs. 1,50,000 × 4	6,00,000	
Overheads	Rs. 3,00,000 × 4	12,00,000	34,00,000
4. Debtors (8 weeks)			
Raw Materials	Rs. 4,00,000 × 8	32,00,000	
Labour	Rs. 1,50,000 × 8	12,00,000	
Overheads	Rs. 3,00,000 × 8	24,00,000	68,00,000

5. Cash expected		50,000
		1,31,00,000
Less : Current Liabilities :		
Creditors (4 weeks)		
Raw Materials :	$Rs. 52,000 \times 400 \times \frac{4}{52}$	16,00,000
Net Working Capital Required :		1,15,00,000

Workings :

Sales for the year : 52,000 × Rs. 1,000 = Rs. 5,20,00,000

Sales per week = Rs. 5,20,00,000 ÷ 52 = Rs. 10,00,000

Amounts to be blocked :

In Materials = $Rs. 10,00,000 \times \frac{400}{1,000} = Rs. 4,00,000$

In Labour = $Rs. 10,00,000 \times \frac{150}{1,000} = Rs. 1,50,000$

In Overheads $Rs. 10,00,000 \times \frac{300}{1,000} = Rs. 3,00,000$

Note : Profit has been ignored and debtors have been taken at cost. The profit has been ignored because this may or may not be used as a source of working capital.

Illustration 6. A proforma cost sheet of a company provides the following particulars :

Elements of cost	*Amount per unit*
	Rs.
Raw Materials	80
Direct Labour	30
Overheads	60
	170
Total Cost Profit	30
Selling Price	200

The following further particulars are available :

Raw materials are in stock on average one month. Materials are in process, on average, half a month. Finished goods are in stock on average one month.

Credit allowed by suppliers is one month.

Credit allowed to debtors is two months.

Lag in payment of wages is $1\frac{1}{2}$ weeks.

Lag in payment of overhead expenses one month.

One-fourth of the output is sold against cash.

Cash on hand and at bank is expected to be Rs. 25,000.

You are required to prepare a statement showing the working capital needed to finance a level of activity of 1,04,000 units of production.

You may assume that production is carried on evenly throughout the year, wages and overheads accrue similarly and a time period of 4 weeks is equivalent to a month.

(*CA Final, M.Com. Calcutta*)

Solution.

STATEMENT OF WORKING CAPITAL REQUIREMENT

Current Assets		Rs.	Rs.
1. *Stock of Materials* (4 weeks)			
Raw Materials	Rs. 1,60,000 × 4		6,40,000
2. *Work-in-progress* (2 weeks)			
Raw Materials	Rs. 1,60,000 × 2	3,20,000	
Direct Labour :	Rs. 60,000 × 2	1,20,000	
Overheads :	Rs. 1,20,000 × 2	2,40,000	6,80,000
3. *Stock of Finished goods* (4 weeks)			
Raw Materials	Rs. 1,60,000 × 4	6,40,000	
Direct Labour	Rs. 60,000 × 4	2,40,000	
Overheads	Rs. 1,20,000 × 4	4,80,000	13,60,000
4. *Sundry Debtors* : (8 weeks)			
Raw Materials	$Rs. 1,60,000 \times \frac{3}{4} \times 8$	9,60,000	
Direct Labour	$Rs. 60,000 \times \frac{3}{4} \times 8$	3,60,000	
Overheads :	$Rs. 1,20,000 \times \frac{3}{4} \times 8$	7,20,000	20,40,000
5. *Cash on hand at Bank*			25,000
			47,45,000
Less : Current Liabilities :			
Sundry Creditors	Rs. 1,60,000 × 4	6,40,000	
O/S Wages	$Rs.\ 60,000 \times 1\frac{1}{2}$ weeks	90,000	
O/S Overhead :	Rs. 1,20,000 × 4	4,80,000	12,10,000
			35,35,000

Note : (*i*) It has been assumed that direct labour and overheads are in process, on average, half a month.

(*ii*) Profit has been ignored and debtors have been taken at cost.

Workings :

Sales for the year = 1,04,000 × Rs. 200 = Rs. 2,08,00,000

Sales per week = Rs. 2,08,00,000 ÷ 52 = Rs. 4,00,000

Amounts to be blocked, per week :

$$\text{In Materials} = Rs. 4,00,000 \times \frac{80}{200} = Rs. 1,60,000$$

$$\text{In Labour} = Rs. 4,00,000 \times \frac{30}{200} = Rs. 60,000$$

$$\text{In Overhead} = Rs. 4,00,000 \times \frac{60}{200} = Rs. 1,20,000$$

Illustration 7. You are required to prepare for the Board of Directors of a Ltd. Company, a statement showing the working Capital needed to finance a level of activity of 5200 units of output. You are given the following information:

Elements of Cost	Amount per unit
	Rs.
Raw materials	8
Direct Labour	2
Overheads	6
Total Cost	16
Profit	4
Selling Price	20

Raw materials are in stock on average one month.
Materials are in process on average half a month.
Finished goods are in stock on average 6 weeks.
Credit allowed by creditors is one month.
Credit allowed to debtors is two months.

Lag in payment of wages $1\frac{1}{2}$ weeks.

Cash in hand and at Bank is expected to be Rs. 7,300. You are informed that production is carried on evenly during the year and wages and overheads accrue similarly.

(*M.Com. Kolkata, Madurai M.S.*)

Solution:

Sales for the year: 5,200 × Rs. 20 = Rs. 1,04,000

$$\text{Sales per week} = \frac{\text{Rs. } 1,04,000}{52} = \text{Rs. } 2,000$$

Amounts to be blocked in:

$$\text{Materials : Rs. } 2,000 \times \frac{8}{20} = \text{Rs. 800 per week}$$

$$\text{Labour: Rs. } 2,000 \times \frac{2}{20} = \text{Rs. 200 per week}$$

$$\text{Overhead : Rs. } 2,000 \times \frac{6}{20} = \text{Rs. 600 per week}$$

Working Capital Requirement Forecast

Current Assets	*Rs.*	*Rs.*
1. Stock of Raw Materials (4 weeks)		
Raw Materials	800 × 4	3,200
2. Work-in-progress (2 weeks)		
Raw Materials	800 × 2 = 1,600	
Labour	200 × 1 = 200	
Overheads	600 × 1 = 600	2,400
3. Stock of finished goods (6 weeks)		
Raw Materials	800 × 6 = 4,800	
Labour	200 × 6 = 1,200	
Overheads	600 × 6 = 3,600	9,600
4. Debtors (8 weeks)		
Raw Materials	800 × 8 = 6,400	
Labour	200 × 8 = 1,600	
Overheads	600 × 8 = 4,800	
	12,800	

	Profit: Credit to Debtors (25% on cost)	3,200	16,000
	Less: Current Liabilities:		31,200
1.	Creditors (4 weeks)		
	Raw Materials	$800 \times 4 = 3{,}200$	
2.	Lag in payment of wages ($1\frac{1}{2}$ weeks)		
	Labour	$200 \times 1\frac{1}{2} = 300$	3,500
	Net Working Capital		27,700
	Add: Cash as per estimate		7,300
	Estimated requirement of working capital		35,000

Alternatively:

Working Capital Requirement Forecast

Particulars	*Periods in weeks*	*Total Rs.*	*Raw Materials Rs.*	*Work-in-progress Rs.*	*Finished goods Rs.*	*Debtors Rs.*	*Creditors Rs.*
1. Materials:							
In stock	4		3,200				
In work-in progress	2			1,600			
In Finished goods	6				4,800		
With Debtors	8					6,400	
	20						3,200
Less: Credit from Creditors	4						
	16	12,800					
2. Wages:							
In work-in-progress	1			200			
In Finished goods	6				1,200		
With Debtors	8					1,600	
	15						
Less: Credit from employees	$1\frac{1}{2}$						300
	$13\frac{1}{2}$	2,700					
3. *Overheads*:							
In work-in-progress	1			600			
In Finished goods	6				3,600		
With Debtors	8	9,000				4,800	
4. *Profit*:	15						
Credit to Debtors	8	3,200				3,200	
		27,700	3,200	2,400	9,600	16,000	3,500

Requirement	Rs. 27,700
Add: Cash as per estimate	7,300
Total requirement of working capita	35,000

Illustration 8. Lucky Ltd., a trading company, provides the following information: Annual sales during the year Rs. 1,20,000

Analysis of Sales:

Materials	60%
Expenses	15%
Profit	25%

Average credit allowed to Debtors $-2\frac{1}{2}$ months

Average credit period allowed by creditors $-1\frac{1}{2}$ months.

Raw materials are to remain in store on average –1 month

Processing period on average – 2 months

Finished goods remain in warehouse on average – 3 months

Bank overdraft Rs. 90,000.

10% of the total working capital (including contingencies) is to be kept in hand for contingencies.

You are required to determine the working capital requirement of Lucky Ltd. on the basis of above information. (*M.Com. Kolkata, Bombay*)

Solution:

$$\text{Sales per Month} = \text{Rs.}\frac{1,20,000}{12} = \text{Rs.}10,000$$

Amount to be blocked in Materials and Expenses per Month are:-

Materials = Rs. 10,000 × 60% = Rs. 6,000

Expenses = Rs. 10,000 × 15% = Rs. 1,500

Working Capital Requirement Forecast

			Rs.
Current Assets:			
1.	Stock of Raw materials (1 Month):		6,000
	Raw Materials	Rs. 6,000 × 1 = 6000	
2.	Work-in-progress: (2 Months)		
	Raw Materials	Rs. 6,000 × 2 = Rs. 12,000	
	Expenses	Rs. 1,500 2 = Rs. 3,000	15,000
3.	Stock of Finished Goods (3 Months)		
	Raw Materials	Rs. 6,000 × 3 = Rs. 18,000	
	Expenses	Rs. 1,500 × 3 = Rs. 4,500	22,500
4.	Debtors $\left(2\frac{1}{2}\text{Months}\right)$		
	Raw Materials	$\text{Rs.}6,000\times2\frac{1}{2}$ = Rs. 15,000	
	Expenses:	$\text{Rs.}1,500\times2\frac{1}{2}$ = Rs. 3,750	
		18,750	
	Profit: Credit to Debtors (1/3rd of cost)	6,250	25,000
	Less: Current Liabilities		68,500
	1. Creditors $\left(1\frac{1}{2}\text{ months}\right)$		
	Raw Materials	$\text{Rs. }6000\times1\frac{1}{2}$	9,000
			59,500
	Add: Cash required for contingencies		6,611

$\left(\frac{1}{9}\text{ of the above}\right)$	
Total estimated working capital	66,111
Less: Bank Overdraft	90,000
Requirement of working capital (Negative)	23,889

Illustration 9. From the following information presented by a manufacturing company, prepare a working capital requirement forecast statement for the coming year.

Expected monthly sales of 32,000 units at Rs. 10 per unit.

The anticipated ratios of cost to selling price are:

Raw Materials	40%
Labour	30%

Budgeted Overhead Rs. 16,000 per week.

Planned stock include Raw Materials for Rs. 96,000 and 16,000 units of finished goods.

Materials will stay in process for 2 weeks.

Credit allowed to debtors is 5 weeks.

Credit allowed by creditors is 1 month.

Lag in payment of overhead is 2 weeks.

Wages will be paid at the beginning of the week following the week of work.

Cash in hand in expected to be 10% of the Net Working Capital.

Assume that production is carried on evenly throughout the year and overhead accrue similarly and time period of a 4 weeks is equivalent to a month. (*M.Com. Kolkata*)

Solution :

Elements of Cost:	Per unit
Materials (Rs. 10 × 40%)	4
Labour (Rs. 10 × 30%)	3
Overhead $\left(\frac{\text{Rs. }16{,}000}{8{,}000}\right)$	2
Total Cost	9
Cash Profit	1
Selling Price	10

Weekly production $= \frac{32{,}000}{4} = 8{,}000$ units

Cost = 8000 × Rs. 4 = Rs. 32,000

So, time lag in store $= \frac{\text{Rs.}96{,}000}{\text{Rs.}32{,}000} = 3$ weeks

Average staying period of finished goods in store $= \frac{16{,}000}{8{,}000} = 2$ weeks

Average cost of labour per week = 8,000 × Rs. 3 = Rs. 24,000

Average cost of overhead per week = 8,000 × Rs. 2 = Rs. 16,000

Average profit per week = 8,000 × Rs. 1 = Rs. 8,000

Working Capital Requirement Forecast

Particulars	*Period in weeks*	*Total*	*Raw Materials*	*Work-in-progress*	*Finished goods*	*Debtors*	*Creditors*
		Rs.	*Rs.*	*Rs.*	*Rs.*	*Rs.*	*Rs.*
1. Materials:							
In Store	3		96,000				

In work-in-progress	2			64,000			
In Finished goods	2				64,000		
With Debtors	8					1,60,000	
	12						1,28,000
Less: Credit from Creditors	4	2,56,000					
	8						
2. Wages:							
In work-in-Progress	1			24,000			
In finished goods	2				48,000		
With Debtors	5					1,20,000	
	8	1,92,000					
3. Overhead:							
In work-in-progress	1			16,000			
In finished goods	2				32,000		
With Debtors	5					80,000	
	8						
Less: Credit from creditors	2						32,000
	6	96,000					
4. Profit: Credit to Debtors	5	40,000				40,000	
		5,84,000	96,000	1,04,000	1,44,000	4,00,000	1,60,000

Estimated requirement of working capital as per the statement: Rs.5,84,000

Add: Expected cash in hand @ 10% of total requirement 64,889

$$\left(Rs.5,84,000 \times \frac{1}{9}\right)$$

Total requirement of working capital 6,48,889

Illustration 10. The annual capacity of a manufacturing company is to produce 10,000 units. But owing to scarcity of resources the normal level of activity has been 60%.

From the information given below, calculate the working capital requirement on an estimated basis to sustain the normal activity level.

(1) Elements of cost — Per unit Rs.

	Per unit Rs.
Direct Material	4
Direct Labour	3
Overheads 100% of Direct Labour	

(2) Profit per unit: 1/6 of selling price

(3) Other particulars:

(*a*) Raw materials storages period – 2 months
(*b*)Processing time –3 months
(*c*)Finished goods in store –1 month
(*d*) Credit to Debtors –2 months
(*e*) Credit from Creditors –1 month
(*f*) Lag in wage payment –1 month

It may be assumed that production and overhead accrue evenly throughout the year.

(*M.Com. Bombay, Madurai, M.S.*)

Solution:

Production 60% of 10,000 units, *i.e.* 6000 units

Element of Cost:

	per unit Rs.
Direct Materials	4
Direct Labour	3
Overhead (100% of Direct Labour)	3
Total Cost	10
Profit (1/6 of sales)	2
Selling Price	12

Sales for the year = 6,000 × Rs. 12 = Rs. 72,000

$$\text{Sales per month} = \frac{\text{Rs.}72,000}{12} = \text{Rs.}6,000$$

Amount to be blocked in Materials, Labour and Overheads per month are:

$$\text{Materials} \quad \text{Rs.}\,6,000 \times \frac{4}{12} = \text{Rs.}2,000$$

$$\text{Labour} \quad \text{Rs.}\,6,000 \times \frac{3}{12} = \text{Rs.}1,500$$

$$\text{Overhead} \quad \text{Rs.}\,6,000 \times \frac{3}{12} = \text{Rs.}1,500$$

Working Capital Requirement Forecast

Particulars	*Periods in months*	*Total Rs.*	*Raw Materials Rs.*	*Work-in-progress Rs.*	*Finished goods Rs.*	*Debtors Rs.*	*Creditors Rs*
1. Raw Materials							
In stock	2		4,000				
In work-in progress	3			6,000			
In Finished goods	1				2,000		
With Debtors	2					4,000	
	8						2,000
Less: Credit from Creditors	1						
	7	14,000					
2. Wages:							
In work-in-progress	$1\frac{1}{2}$			2,250			
In Finished goods	1				1,500		
With Debtors	2					3,000	
	$4\frac{1}{2}$						
Less: Credit from employees	1						1,500
	$3\frac{1}{2}$	5,250					
3. Overheads:							

In work-in-progress	$1\frac{1}{2}$			2,250			
In Finished goods	1				1,500		
With Debtors	2					3,000	
	$4\frac{1}{2}$	6,750					
4. Profit: Credit to Debtors	2	2,000				2,000	
		28,000	4,000	10,500	5,000	12,000	3,500

Estimated requirement of working capital = Rs. 28,000.

Illustration 11. X and Company desirous to purchase a business and has consulted you and one point on which you are asked to advise them is the average amount of working capital which will be required in the first year's working.

You are given the following estimates and are instructed to add 10% to your computed figure to allow for contingencies :

	Figures for the year Rs.
(*a*) Amount blocked up for stocks :	
Stocks of finished product	5,000
Stocks of stores, materials etc.	8,000
(*b*) Average credit given :	
Inland Sales — 6 weeks credit	3,12,000
Export Sales — $1\frac{1}{2}$ weeks credit	78,000
(*c*) Lag in payment of wages and other outgoings :	
Wages — $1\frac{1}{2}$ weeks	2,60,000
Stocks of materials etc. — $1\frac{1}{2}$ months	48,000
Rent, Royalties etc. — 6 months	10,000
Clerical Staff — $\frac{1}{2}$ months	62,400
Manager — $\frac{1}{2}$ month	4,800
Miscellaneous Expenses — $1\frac{1}{2}$ months	48,000
(*d*) Payment in Advance :	
Sundry Expenses (Paid quarterly in advance)	8,000
(*e*) Undrawn profit on the average throughout the year	11,000

Set up your calculation for the average amount of working capital required.

(*M.Com. Madurai*)

Solution :

STATEMENT AVERAGE WORKING CAPITAL REQUIREMENT

	Rs.	Rs.
Current Assets :		
Inventories :		
Stock of Finished products	5,000	
Stock of Stores, Materials etc.	8,000	13,000
Book Debts :		
Inland Sales : 6 weeks credit of yearly sale of Rs. 3,12,000 $\left(\text{Rs. }3{,}12{,}000 \times \frac{6}{52}\right)$	36,000	
Export Sales : $1\frac{1}{2}$ weeks sale of Rs. 78,000 p.a.	2,250	38,250
Advance payment of Expenses : $\frac{\text{Rs.}8{,}000}{4}$		2,000
Investment in Current Assets		53,250
Less : Current Liabilities :		
Lag in Payments :		
Wages[(1)]	7,500	
Stores, Materials etc.[(2)]	6,000	
Rent, Royalities etc.[(3)]	5,000	
Clerical staff[(4)]	2,600	
Manager[(5)]	200	
Miscellaneous Expenses[(6)]	6,000	27,300
		25,950
Add : 10% for Contingencies		2,595
Average Working Capital Requirement		28,545

Workings :

1. $\text{Rs.}\frac{2{,}60{,}000 \times 3}{52 \times 2} = \text{Rs.}7{,}500$

2. $\text{Rs.}48{,}000 \times \frac{1\frac{1}{2}}{12} = \text{Rs. }6{,}000$

3. $\text{Rs.}10{,}000 \times \frac{6}{12} = \text{Rs.}5{,}000$

4. $\text{Rs.}62{,}400 \times \frac{\frac{1}{2}}{12} = \text{Rs.}2{,}600$

5. $\text{Rs.}4{,}800 \times \frac{\frac{1}{2}}{12} = \text{Rs.}200$

6. $\text{Rs.}4{,}800 \times \frac{1\frac{1}{2}}{12} = \text{Rs.}6{,}000.$

Note : Undrawn profit has been ignored in the working capital computation because (*i*) for the purpose of determining working capital provided by net profit, it is necessary to adjust the net profit for income tax, dividends etc. And the net profit may be used for other purposes like purchase of fixed asset, repayment of long-term loan etc.

Illustration 12. On Ist January of the year, the Managing Director of Company wanted to know the amount of working capital that will be required during the year.

From the following information prepare the forecast of working capital requirements.

Production in the last year was 60,000 units. The same will be the production this year.

Estimated ratios of different costs to selling prices are :

Raw Materials	—	60%
Direct Wages	—	10%
Overheads	—	20%

Raw materials will remain in store, on an average, for 2 months, before issued for production.

Each unit will be in production-process for one month, the raw materials being fed into pipeline immediately. The labour and overhead costs will occur evenly during the period.

Finished goods stay in the warehouse, awaiting despatch to customers, for approximately 3 months.

Credit allowed by creditors is 2 months from the date of delivery of raw materials.

Credit allowed to debtors is 3 months from the date of despatch.

There are regular production and sales cycles.

Wages are paid on Ist day of a month. The company keeps normally Rs. 20,000 as cash in kind.

Selling price is Rs. 5 per unit. (*M.Com. Kolkata*)

Solution :

WORKING CAPITAL REQUIREMENT

	Rs.	*Rs.*
Current Assets :		
Raw Materials(1)	30,000	
Finished Products(2)	67,500	
Work-in-progress(3)	18,750	
Debtors(4)	75,000	
Cash	20,000	2,11,250
Current Liabilities :		
Creditors(5)	30,000	
Outstanding Expenses(6)	2,500	32,500
Working Capital Requirement		1,78,750

Workings :

1. Investment in Raw Materials :

Sales = 60,000 × Rs. 5 = Rs. 3,00,000

Annual Investments in Raw Materials = Rs. 3,00,000 × 60%
= Rs. 1,80,000

$$\text{Average Investment} = \text{Rs.}\frac{1,80,000}{12\,\text{months}} = \text{Rs.}\,15,000$$

Investment for Raw Materials = Rs. 15,000 × 2 months
= **Rs. 30,000**

2. Investment in Finished Products :

Cost of Sales (as percentage) = 60 + 10 + 20 = 90%

$$\text{Annual Investment} = \text{Rs.}\,3,00,000 \times \frac{90}{100} = Rs.\,2,70,000$$

$$\text{Average Investment} = \text{Rs.}\frac{2,70,000}{12\text{ Months}} = \text{Rs.}\,22,500$$

Investment in Finished products = Rs. 22,500 × 3 = **Rs. 67,500**

3. Investment in Work-in-progress :

Cost of Raw Materials (1 Month) = Rs. 15,000

Labour : = 15 days

Total Labour Cost = 10% of Rs. 3,00,000

= Rs. 30,000

Average Labour Cost $= \frac{\text{Rs. } 30,000}{12}$

= Rs. 2500

For 15 days $= \text{Rs. } 2500 \times \frac{1}{2} = 1,250$

Overhead Cost (15 days)

Total Overhead = 20% of Rs. 3,00,000

= Rs. 60,000

Average $= \frac{\text{Rs.} 60,000}{12} = \text{Rs. } 5,000$

For 15 days $= \text{Rs. } 5000 \times \frac{1}{2} = 2,500$

(Rs. 15,000 + 1250 + 2500) = 18,750

4. Investment in Debtors :

Sales per month : $\frac{\text{Rs. } 3,00,000}{12} = \text{Rs. } 25,000$

Investment in Debtors = Rs. 25,000 × 3 = Rs. 75,000

5. Financing from Creditors :

Sales per month = Rs. 25,000

Cost of Raw Materials $= \text{Rs. } 25,000 \times \frac{60}{100} = \text{Rs.} 15,000$

Financing from Creditors = Rs. 15,000 × 2 Months

= **Rs. 30,000**

6. Outstanding Expenses :

Total wages : $\text{Rs. } 3,00,000 \times \frac{10}{100}$

= Rs. 30,000

Average wage $= \frac{\text{Rs. } 30,000}{12}$

= **Rs. 2500**

Illustration 13. From the information given below, you are required to prepare a projected Profit and Loss Account, Balance Sheet and an estimate of working capital requirements :

		Rs.
(*a*)	Issued Share Capital	2,00,000
	8% Bonds	75,000
	Fixed Assets at cost	2,00,000
(*b*)	The expected ratios of cost to selling price :	
	Raw Materials	40%
	Labour	30%
	Overheads	20%
	Profit	10%

(*c*) Raw materials are kept in store for average of 2 months.

(*d*) Finished goods remain in stock for an average period of one month.

(*e*) Work-in-progress (100% complete in regard to materials and 50% for labour and overheads) will approximately be to half a month's production.

(*f*) Credit allowed to customers is two months and given by suppliers is one month.

(*g*) Production during the previous year was 40,000 units and it is planned to maintain the same in the current year also.

(*h*) Selling price is Rs. 9 per unit.

(*i*) Calculation of debtors may be made at selling price. (*M.Com. Madurai*)

Solution :

PROJECTED PROFIT AND LOSS ACCOUNT

	Rs.		*Rs.*
To Cost of Goods sold :			
Raw Materials[4]	1,44,000	By Sales[1]	3,60,000
Labour	1,08,000		
Overheads	72,000		
To Gross Profit	36,000		
	3,60,000		3,60,000
To Interest on Bonds	6,000	By Gross Profit	36,000
To Net Profit	30,000		
	36,000		36,000

PROJECTED BALANCE SHEET

Liabilities	*Rs.*	*Assets*	*Rs.*
Share Capital	2,00,000	Fixed Assets (at cost)	2,00,000
8% Bonds	75,000	Current Assets :	
Profit & Loss	30,000	Inventories :	
Creditors[4]	12,000	Raw Materials[2]	24,000
Bank Overdraft (Balancing figure)	3,750	Finished Goods[2]	27,000
		Work-in-progress[2]	9,750
		Debtors[3]	60,000
	3,20,750		3,20,750

Working Capital = Current Assets – Current Liabilities

Current Assets = Rs. 24,000 + Rs. 27,000 + 9,750 + Rs. 60,000
= Rs. 1,20,750

Current Liabilities = Rs. 12,000 + Rs. 3,750 = Rs. 15,750

So, Working Capital = Rs. 1,20,750 – Rs. 15,750 = **Rs. 1,05,000**

Workings :

1. Calculation of Sales :

Total Sales = 40,000 × Rs. 9 = **Rs. 3,60,000**

2. Calculation of amounts blocked in inventories :

(*a*) Stock of Materials = $\text{Rs. } 3,60,000 \times \frac{40}{100} \times \frac{2}{12}$ = **Rs. 24,000** (*b*) Stock of Finished goods at cost :

(Materials + Labour + Overheads)

$$\text{Rs.}3,60,000 \times \frac{90}{100} \times \frac{1}{12} = \textbf{Rs. 27,000}$$

(c) Work-in-progress :

$$\text{Raw Materials : Rs. }3,60,000 \times \frac{40}{100} \times \frac{1}{2} \times \frac{1}{12} = \text{Rs. }6,000$$

$$\text{Labour : Rs. }3,60,000 \times \frac{30}{100} \times \frac{1}{2} \times \frac{1}{12} \times \frac{50}{100} = \text{Rs. }2,250$$

$$\text{Overheads : Rs. }3,60,000 \times \frac{20}{100} \times \frac{1}{2} \times \frac{1}{12} \times \frac{50}{100} = \text{Rs. }1,500$$

$$\underline{\text{Rs. }9,750}$$

3. Debtors at selling price :

$$\text{Rs. }3,60,000 \times \frac{2}{12} = \textbf{Rs. 60,000}$$

4. Creditors :

$$\text{Total Purchase} = \text{Rs. }3,60,000 \times \frac{40}{100} = \textbf{Rs. 1,44,000}$$

$$\text{Creditors} = \text{Rs. }1,44,000 \times \frac{1}{12} = \textbf{Rs. 12,000}$$

Illustration 14. Gujrat Ltd. is a newly set up enterprise. With the help of the following particulars, determine the magnitude of working capital :

1. Various elements of cost bear the following relationship to the selling price *i.e.* Rs. 200 per unit)

Materials	40%
Labour	30%
Overhead	10%

2. Production in 2010 is estimated to be 6,000 units.
3. Materials are expected to remain in the stores for an average period of one month.
4. Finished goods are likely to stay in warehouse for two months on average.
5. Each unit of production will be in process for half a month on average.
6. 50% of the sales will be on credit. Customers are allowed two months credit.
7. Credit period allowed by the suppliers is one month.
8. The lag in payment to labour is one month. 50% of the overhead consists of salaries of non-production staff.
9. Allow 20% to your computed figures for contingencies.
10. Assume that sales and production follow a constant pattern.

(*M.Com. Bombay*)

Solution :

WORKING CAPITAL FORECAST

	Rs.	*Rs.*
(*a*) Current Assets :		
(1) Stock of Raw Materials[(1)]	40,000	
(2) Stock of Finished goods[(2)]	1,60,000	
(3) Stock of work-in-progress[(3)]	40,000	

	(4) Debtors (at cost)[4]	80,000	3,20,000
(b)	Current Liabilities :		
	(1) Creditors[5]	40,000	
	(2) O/S Wages[6]	30,000	
	(3) O/S Salaries[7]	5,000	75,000
			2,45,000
	Add : 20% for contingencies :		49,000
	Working Capital Required		2,94,000

Workings :

1. Stock of Raw Materials :

$$\text{Cost of Raw Materials} = 6000 \times \text{Rs.}200 \times \frac{40}{100} = \text{Rs. } 4,80,000$$

$$\text{Average Cost per month} = \frac{\text{Rs. } 4,80,000}{12 \text{ months}} = \textbf{Rs. 40,000}$$

2. Stock of Finished goods :

$$\text{Cost} = 6000 \times \text{Rs. } 200 \times \frac{80}{100} = \text{Rs. } 9,60,000$$

$$\text{Average Stock} = \frac{\text{Rs. } 9,60,000}{12} = \textbf{Rs.}\ 80,000$$

Two months Stock = Rs. 80,000 × 2 = **Rs. 1,60,000**

3. Stock in Work-in-progress :

$$\text{Cost : } 6,000 \times \text{Rs. } 200 \times \frac{80}{100} = \text{Rs. } 9,60,000 \text{ p.a.}$$

$$\frac{1}{2} \text{ month Stock} = \text{Rs. } 9,60,000 \times \frac{1}{12} \times \frac{1}{2} = \textbf{Rs. 40,000}$$

4. Debtors (at cost) :

Cost of Total Sales = 6000 × Rs. 160 = Rs. 9,60,000

Cost of Credit Sales = 50% of Rs. 9,60,000 = Rs. 4,80,000

$$\text{Two months Credit Sales} = \frac{\text{Rs. } 4,80,000 \times 2}{12} = \textbf{Rs. 80,000}$$

5. Creditors :

Total Credit Purchases = Rs. 80 × 6000 = Rs. 4,80,000

$$\therefore \quad \text{Creditors (one month)} = \frac{\text{Rs. } 4,80,000 \times 1}{12} = \textbf{Rs. 40,000}$$

6. Outstanding Wages :

Total Wages = 6000 × Rs. 60 = Rs. 3,60,000

$$\text{One month's wages} = \text{Rs. } 3,60,000 \times \frac{1}{12} = \textbf{Rs. 30,000}$$

7. Outstanding Salaries :

$$\text{Total Salaries : } 6,000 \times \text{Rs. } 20 \times \frac{50}{100} = \text{Rs. } 60,000$$

$$\text{One month Salary : } \text{Rs. } 60,000 \times \frac{1}{12} = \textbf{Rs. 5,000}$$

Illustration 15. On 1st January, the Board of Directors of XYZ Co. Ltd. wishes to know the amount of working capital that will be required to meet the programme they have planned for the year. From the following information prepare a working capital requirement forecast and forecast Profit and Loss Account and Balance Sheet.

Issued Share Capital :

10,000 Equity Shares of Rs. 20 each fully paid — Rs. 2,00,000
8% Debentures — Rs. 1,00,000
Fixed assets on I[st] January valued at — Rs. 1,10,000
Estimated production 48,000 units per annum.

The expected ratios of cost to selling price are :

Materials 50%
Direct wages and overhead 20%

Raw materials are expected to remain in stock for an average of $1\frac{1}{2}$ months before issue to production.

Processing time 2 months.

Finished goods will stay in the warehouse awaiting despatch to customers : 2 months

Credit to debtors : $2\frac{1}{2}$ months
Credit from creditors : 1 month
Time lag in Wage payment : $\frac{1}{2}$ month
Lag in payment of all expenses : 1 month

Selling price is Rs. 10 per unit.
There is a regular production and sales cycle.
Ignore depreciation. (*M.Com. Kolkata*)

STATEMENT OF WORKING CAPITAL REQUIREMENT

Particulars	*Period*	*Total* *Rs.*	*Raw Materials* *Rs.*	*Work-in-progress* *Rs.*	*Finished goods* *Rs.*	*Debtors*	*Creditors*
1. Raw Materials							
In Store	$1\frac{1}{2}$		30,000				
In Work-in Progress	2			40,000			
In Finished goods	2				40,000		
With Debtors	$2\frac{1}{2}$					50,000	
	8						
Less : Credit from Creditors	1	1,40,000					20,000
	7						
2. Wages and Overheads							
In Work-in-progress	1			8,000			
In Finished goods	2				16,000		

With Debtors	$2\frac{1}{2}$					20,000	
	$5\frac{1}{2}$						
Less : Credit	$1\frac{1}{2}$						12,000
from creditors & employees	4	32,000					
3. Profit :	$2\frac{1}{2}$	30,000				30,000	
Credit to Debtors		2,02,000	30,000	48,000	56,000	1,00,000	32,000

Sales for the year : $48,000 \times \text{Rs.}10 = \text{Rs. } 4,80,000$

Sales per month : $\dfrac{\text{Rs. } 4,80,000}{12} = \text{Rs. } 40,000$

Amount to be blocked :

In Materials $= 50\% \text{ of Rs. } 40,000 = \text{Rs. } 20,000$

In wages and overhead $= \text{Rs. } 40,000 \times \dfrac{20}{100} = \text{Rs. } 8,000$

PROJECTED PROFIT AND LOSS ACCOUNT
for the year ended . . .

To Materials Consumed (50% of Rs. 4,80,000)	2,40,000	By Cost of goods Manufactured	3,36,000
To Wages Overheads (20% of Rs. 4,80,000)	96,000		
	3,36,000		3,36,000
To Cost of goods Manufactured	3,36,000	By Sales	4,80,000
To Gross Profit	1,44,000		
	4,80,000		4,80,000
To Debenture Interest	8,000	By Gross Profit	1,44,000
To Net Profit	1,36,000		
	1,44,000		1,44,000

PROJECTED BALANCE SHEET
as on......................

Liabilities	*Rs.*	*Assets*	*Rs.*
Share Capital :		Fixed Assets :	1,10,000
10,000 Equity shares of Rs. 20 each	2,00,000	Working Capital :	
Profit and Loss	1,36,000	Stock : Raw Materials	30,000
8% Debentures	1,00,000	Work-in-progress	48,000
Creditors	20,000	Finished Goods	56,000
O/S item	12,000	Debtors	1,00,000
		Cash (Balancing figure)	1,24,000
	4,68,000		4,68,000

Important Working Capital Ratios

As pointed out earlier, the working capital magnitude of a concern should neither be too inadequate nor too exessive as compared to its requirement. Maintaining adequate working capital ensures the improvement of profitability. The finance manager always tries to maintain an adequate working capital at every time so as to carry on the operations successfully and maximize the return on investment. When we make a deep examination of various components of working capital with an objective to ensure its adequacy or otherwise, it is known as "analysis of working capital". There are several tools of financial analysis of working capital and ratio analysis is the most common among them. Ratio analysis can be used by financial executives to check upon the efficiency with which working capital is being used in the enterprise. The following are the important ratios to measure the efficiency of working capital.

1. Current Ratio
2. Quick Ratio
3. Cash Ratio
4. Creditors Turnover Ratio
5. Debtors Turnover Ratio
6. Working Capital Turnover
7. Average Collection Period
8. Average Payment Period.
9. Inventory to Working Capital etc.

All these ratios have been explained in the Chapter 3.

Objective Type Questions

A. State whether the following statements are true of false :

(1) Gross working capital refers to the captal invested in the total assets of an enterprise.

(2) Net working capital is the excess of current liabilities over current assets.

(3) Every business concern should have excessive working capital.

(4) Longer the process period of manufacture, larger is the amount of working capital needed.

(5) The fixed proportion of working capital should be generally financed from the fixed capital sources.

(6) Commercial banks provide loans for working capital.

(Ans: (1) False (2) False (3) False (4) True (5) True (6) True

B. Fill in the blanks :

(1) Net working capital is the excess of .... over ....

(2) Working capital is also known as........................ or ....

(3) The gross working capital is a .... concern concept.

(4) The rate of return on investments .... with the shortage or working capital.

(5) Greater the size of a business unit .... will be the requirements of working capital.

(Ans: (1) Current assests : current liabilities (2) Revolving circulating : (3) Going : (4) Falls (5) largers.

THEORETICAL QUESTIONS

1. Define the term Working Capital. What factors would you take into consideration in estimating the Working capital needs of a concern."

2. Explain the constituents of working capital cycle.
3. What is working capital ? On the formation of a new business, what considerations are taken into account in estimating the amount of working capital needed ?
4. What are the advantages of adequate working capital ?
5. Describe the need and determinants of working capital in a business.
6. Explain various factors influencing working capital.
7. What do you understand by working capital management ? Discuss the principles of working capital management.
8. Give a lucid account of the various sources of working capital available for a firm.
9. How would you differentiate between current assets and current liabilities.
10. State the significance of permanent working capital.
11. What is 'Operating cycle' of working capital.

PRACTICAL PROBLEMS

1. X Ltd. wishes to purchase a business and seeks your advice about the average working capital requirements in first year's trading. The following data are available and you are told to add 10% to allow for contingencies.

		Per annum Rs.
(*a*) Average amount locked up in stocks of :		
Work-in-progress and Finished goods		10,000
Materials and stores		16,000
(*b*) Average credit allowed to :		
Local sales	2 weeks	1,56,000
Export sales	6 weeks	6,24,000
(*c*) Time lag in payment for :		
Purchases	4 weeks	1,92,000
Wages	2 weeks	5,20,000

Calculate the average amount of working capital required. (**Ans.** Rs. 76,153)

2. A proforma cost sheet of a company provides the following particulars:

Elements of cost

Raw materials	40%
Labour	10%
Overheads	30%

The following further particulars are available :

(*a*) Raw materials are to remain in stores on an average : 6 weeks
(*b*) Processing time is : 4 weeks — — —
(*c*) Finished goods are required to be in stock on an average period of : 8 weeks
(*d*) Credit period allowed to debtors, on average : 10 weeks
(*e*) Lag in payment of wages : 2 weeks
(*f*) Credit period allowed by creditors : 4 weeks
(*g*) Selling price is Rs. 50 per unit.

You are required to prepare an estimate of working capital requirements adding 10% margin for contingencies for a level of activity of 1,30,000 units of production.

(*M.Com. Madurai*)

(Ans. Rs. 25,02,500)

3. The Board of Directors of the Progressive Engineering Company Ltd. requires you to prepare a statement showing the working capital requirements forecast for a level of activity of 1,56,000 units of production for the year.

The following information is available :

	Cost per unit
	Rs.
Raw Materials	90
Direct Labour	40
Overheads	75
Total Cost	205
Profit	60
Selling Price	265

(*i*) Raw materials are in stock on an average for one month.
(*ii*) Materials are in process on an average for 2 weeks.
(*iii*) Finished goods are in stock on an average for one month.
(*iv*) Credit allowed by suppliers is one month.
(*v*) Time lag in payment for debtors 2 months.
(*vi*) Lag in payment of wages $1\frac{1}{2}$ weeks.
(*vii*) Lag in payment of overhead is one month. All sales are on credit.

Cash in hand and at Bank are expected to be Rs. 60,000. It is assumed that production is carried on evenly throughout the year. Wages and overheads accrued evenly and a period of 4 weeks is equivalent to a month (*M.Com. Madras*)

(**Ans.** Rs. 75,90,000)

4. The following information has been submitted by a borrower :

(*i*) Expected level of production 1,20,000 units
(*ii*) Raw materials to remain in stock on an average 2 months
(*iii*) Processing period for each unit of product 1 month
(*iv*) Finished goods remain in stock on an average 3 months
(*v*) Credit allowed to the customers from the date of despatch 3 months
(*vi*) Expected ratios of cost to selling price :
(*a*) Raw material : 60%
(*b*) Direct wages : 10%
(*c*) Overheads : 20%
(*vii*) Selling price per unit Rs. 10
(*viii*) Expected margin on sale 10%

You are required to estimate the working capital requirements of the borrower.

(*B.Com. Chennai*)

(**Ans.** Rs. 7,50,000)

5. Calculate working capital from the following particulars :

	Rs.
1. Annual Expenses :	
Wages	52,000
Stores and material	9,600
Office Salaries	12,480
Rent	2,000
Other Expenses	9,600
2. Average amount of stock to be maintained :	
Stock of finished goods	1,000

Stock of materials and stores	1,600
Expenses paid in advance :	
Quarterly advance	1,600 p.a.
3. Annual Sales :	
Home market	62,400
Foreign market	15,600
4. Lag in payment of expenses :	
Wages	$1\frac{1}{2}$ weeks
Stores and material	$1\frac{1}{2}$ months
Office salaries	$\frac{1}{2}$ month
Rent	6 months
Other Expenses	$1\frac{1}{2}$ month
5. Credit allowed to customers :	
Home market	6 weeks
Foreign market	$1\frac{1}{2}$ weeks

(*M.Com. Rajasthan, Madras*)

(**Ans.** Rs. 5,230)

6. Prepare a working capital forecast from the following information :

	Rs.
Issued Share Capital	4,00,000
6% Debentures	1,50,000

The fixed assets are valued at 3 lakhs. Production during the previous year is one lakh units. The same level of activity is intended during the current year.

The expected ratios of cost to selling price are :

Raw Materials	50%
Direct Wages	10%
Overheads	25%

The raw materials ordinarily remain in stores for 2 months before production. Every unit of production remains on process for 2 months. Finished goods remain in the warehouse for 4 months. Credit allowed by creditors is 3 months from the date of delivery of raw materials and credit given to debtors is 3 months from the date of despatch.

Selling price is Rs. 6 per unit. Both production and sales are in a regular cycle.

(*B.Com. Madurai*)

(**Ans.** Rs. 3,57,500).

7. The Board of Directors of a Company request you to prepare a statement showing the working capital requirements for a level of activity of 1,56,000 units of production.

The following information is available for your calculations :

(A)	*Per unit*
	Rs.
Raw Materials	90
Direct Labour	40

Overheads	75
Total Cost	205
Profit	60
Selling Price	265

(B)

(1) Raw materials are in stock, on average one month.
(2) Materials are in process, on average 2 weeks.
(3) Finished goods are in stock, on average one month.
(4) Credit allowed by suppliers, one month.
(5) Time lag in payment from debtors, 2 months.
(6) Lag in payment of wages, $1\frac{1}{2}$ weeks.
(7) Lag in payment of overheads is one month.

20% of the output is sold against cash. Cash in hand and at Bank is expected to be Rs. 60,000. It is to be assumed that production is carried on evenly throughout the year, wages and overheads accrue similarly and a time period of 4 weeks is equivalent to a month. *(CA Final)*

(Ans. Rs. 66,06,000)

8. Manufacturing Company sells goods in the home market and earns a gross profit of 25% on sales. Its annual figures are as follows :

	Rs.
Sales	3,00,000
Materials used	1,08,000
Wages	96,000
Manufacturing Expenses	1,20,000
Administrative and Other Expenses	30,000
Selling and Distribution Expenses	18,000
Depreciation	12,000
Income tax payable in four instalments of which one falls in the next financial year	60,000

Additional information is as follows :

(1) Credit given by suppliers of materials is 2 months.
(2) Credit allowed to customers is one month.
(3) Wages are paid half month in arrear.
(4) Manufacturing and administrative expenses are paid one month in arrear.
(5) Selling and distribution expenses are paid quarterly in advance.
(6) The company wishes to keep one month stock of raw material and also of finished goods.
(7) The company believes in keeping cash of Rs. 50,000 including the overdraft limit of Rs. 20,000 not yet utilised by the company.

You are required to prepare a statement showing the working capital requirement of the company adding 10% margin for contingencies.

(M.Com. Chennai)

(Ans. Rs. 53,900)

9. A proforma cost sheet of a company provides the following particulars:

Elements of Cost

Materials	40%
Direct Labour	20%
Overheads	20%

The following further particulars are available :

(*a*) It is proposed to maintain a level of activity of 2,00,000 units.

(*b*) Selling price is Rs. 12 per unit.

(*c*) Raw materials are expected to remain in store for an average period of one month,

(*d*) Materials will be in process, on average, half a month.

(*e*) Finished goods are required to be in stock for an average period of one month.

(*f*) Credit allowed to debtors is two months.

(*g*) Credit allowed by suppliers is one months.

You may assume that sales and production follow a consistent pattern.

You are required to prepare a statement of working capital requirements, a forecast Profit and Loss Account and Balance Sheet of the company assuming that :

	Rs.
Share Capital	15,00,000
8% Debentures	2,00,000
Fixed Assets	13,00,000

(*M.Com. Chennai*)

(**Ans.** Net Working Capital needed : Rs. 5,60,000.

Cost of goods sold : Rs. 19,20,000.

Gross Profit : Rs. 4,80,000.

Net Profit : Rs.4,64,000.

Balance Sheet Total : Rs. 22,44,000).

10. The management of a Company has called for a statement showing the working capital needed to finance a level of activity of 3,00,000 units of output for the year. The cost structure for the company's product, for the above mentioned level, is detailed below :

	Cost per unit *Rs.*
Raw Materials	20
Direct Labour	5
Overheads	15
Total Cost	40
Profit	10
Selling Price	50

(*a*) Past experience indicates that raw materials are held in stock, on an average for two months.

(*b*) Work-in-progress (100% complete in regard to materials and 50% for labour and overheads) will approximately be to half a month's production.

(*c*) Finished goods remain in warehouse, on an average for a month.

(*d*) Suppliers of materials extend a month's credit.

(*e*) Two months credit is allowed to debtors, calculation of debtors may be made at selling price.

(*f*) A minimum cash balance of Rs. 25,000 is expected to be maintained.

(*g*) The production pattern is assumed to be even during the year.

Prepare the statement of working capital requirements. (*M.Com. Chennai*)

(**Ans.** Rs. 44 ,00,000)

11. A proforma cost sheet of a manufacturing company provides the following particulars :

Element of Cost	*Per unit* *Rs.*
Raw Materials	8
Direct Labour	3
Overheads	6
	17

The following further particulars are available :

Selling Price	Rs. 20 per unit
Level of Activity	1,04,000 units p.a.
Raw materials in stock	On an average 4 weeks
Processing time	On an average 2 weeks
Finished goods in Store	On an average 4 weeks.
Credit period :	
(*a*) Customers	On an average 8 weeks
(*b*) Suppliers	On an average 4 weeks
Lag in payment :	
(*a*) Wages	On an average $1\frac{1}{2}$ weeks
(*b*) Overheads	On an average 2 weeks

75% of the output is sold on credit basis. Cash in hand and at Bank is expected to be Rs. 5,000.

You are required to prepare a statement showing the working capital requirement to finance a level of activity of 1,04,000 units of production per annum. You may assume that all wages and overheads accrue evenly and are completely introduced for half of the processing time, *i.e.* one week. (*ICWA Final*)

(**Ans.** Rs. 3,98,000)

Chapter 7

Marginal Costing

Definition of Marginal Cost and Marginal Costing; Main Features of Marginal Costing ; Advantages; Disadvantages; Absorption Costing and Marginal Costing; Cost-Volume-Profit Analysis; Marginal Cost Equations ; Contribution; Break-Even Analysis; Profit Volume Ratio; Margin of Safety; Break-Even Chart; Significance of B.E.C. at Various Levels of Activity; Assumptions of Break-Even Chart; Construction of Break-Even Chart; Advantages of Break-Even Analysis and Chart; Limitation of B.E.C.; Forms of Break-Even Chart; Angle of Incidence; Problem of Key or Limiting Factor; Application of Marginal Costing Techniques Cost Control; Fixation of Selling Price; Closure of a Department or Discontinuing a Product; Selection of a Profitable Product Mix ; Profit Planning; Decision to Make or Buy; Decision to Accept a Bulk Offer or Foreign Market Order; Introduction of a New Product; Choice of Technique; Evaluation of Performance; Decision Making; Maintaining a Desired Level of Profit; Level of Activity Planning; Alternative Methods of Production; Introduction of New Product or Product Line; Miscellaneous; Objective Type Questions; Theoretical Questions; Practical Problems.

Marginal costing is not a method of cost ascertainment like job costing or contract costing. Marginal costing is a technique of costing, which may be used with other methods of costing, *viz.*, job or process. For decision-making, it is more helpful to the management. The other names for marginal costing are direct costing, differential costing, incremental costing and comparative costing.

In marginal costing, only variable items of costs are taken into account. These variable costs will change in direct relation to the change in the volume of production or change in the production by one unit. As such, variable costs are called product costs and are charged to production. Fixed costs are not allocated to cost unit ; and these are charged directly to profit and loss account during the period and are called as period costs or capacity costs.

Definition of Marginal Cost and Marginal Costing

Marginal cost means the same thing as variable cost. The term is not a new one. The accountants' concept of marginal cost differs from economists' concept of marginal cost. Economists define marginal cost as the additional cost of producing one additional unit. This shall include an element of fixed cost also. Moreover, the economists' marginal cost per unit cannot be uniform with the additional production since the law of diminishing or increasing returns is applicable ; whereas the accountants' marginal cost shall be constant per unit of output with the additional production.

The Institute of Cost and Works Accountants of India defined marginal cost as, "the amount at any given volume of output by which aggregate costs are changed, if the volume of output is increased or decreased by one unit". Here a unit may be a single article, a batch of articles, an order, a stage of production capacity, a process or a department. To ascertain the marginal cost, we need the following elements of cost :

(*a*) Direct materials
(*b*) Direct labour
(*c*) Other direct expenses, and
(*d*) Total variable overheads.

That is, Marginal Cost = Prime Cost + Total variable overheads.

or

Marginal Cost = Total Cost – Fixed Cost

Marginal costing is defined by the ICWA as, "the ascertainment by differentiating between fixed costs, and variable costs, of marginal costs and of the effect on profit of changes in volume of type of output". According to Dr. Joseph, "Marginal costing is a technique of determining the amount of change in the aggregate costs due to an increase of one unit over the existing level of production. As such, it arises from the production of additional increments of output."

Batty defines Marginal Costing as "a technique of cost accounting which pays special attention to the behavior of costs with changes in the volume of output".

Example :

	Rs.
Variable cost 8,000 @ Rs. 50	40,000
Fixed Cost	10,000
Total Cost	50,000

If production is increased by one unit, the following expenditure will be necessary :

	Rs.
Variable Cost 8,001 × Rs. 5	40,005
Fixed Cost	10,000
Total Cost	50,005
Less : Total Cost of 8,000 units	50,000
Marginal Cost of one unit :	5

$$\text{Marginal Cost} = \frac{\text{Increase in total cost}}{\text{Increase in total units}}$$

It may be remembered that marginal cost takes into account only variable cost and excludes the fixed cost.

The following example will clarify the above point.

Unit	*Total Cost*	*Fixed Cost*	*Variable Cost*	*Marginal Cost*
1	400	200	200	200
2	600	200		200
3	800	200		200

In the above example, marginal cost is Rs. 200 per unit. (Total cost – Fixed cost = Variable cost). The marginal cost of 3 units is Rs. 600 (Rs. 200 × 3). It is added to fixed cost, Rs. 200. Then the total cost is Rs. 800.

The definition of fixed cost given by the I.C.M.A., London, is "a cost which accrues in relation to the passage of time and which, within certain output or turnover limits, tends to be unaffected by fluctuations in volume of output or turnover. Examples are rent, rates, insurance and executive and salaries".

Fixed cost is one which tends to be unaffected by variation in volume of output. Fixed cost does not change with the increase or decrease in production with a certain range. Period cost is another name for fixed cost, as it is related to periods.

Variable cost is one which tends to vary directly with the volume of output. Variable cost changes with the increase or decrease in production. In direct costing variable cost is known as direct.

Main Features of Marginal Costing

1. Marginal costing is a technique or working of costing, which is used in conjunction with other methods of costing (process or job).
2. Fixed and variable costs are kept separate at every stage. Semi- variable costs are also separated into fixed and variable.
3. As fixed costs are period costs, they are excluded from product cost or cost of production or cost of sales. Only variable costs are considered as the cost of the product.
4. When evaluation of finished goods and work-in-progress are taken into account, they will be only variable costs.
5. As fixed costs are period costs, they are charged to profit and loss account during the period in which they are incurred. They are not carried forward to the next year's income.
6. Marginal income or marginal contribution is known as the income or the profit.
7. The difference between the contribution and fixed costs is the net profit or loss.
8. Fixed costs remain constant irrespective of level of activity.
9. Sales price and variable cost per unit remain the same.
10. Cost-volume-profit relationship is fully employed to reveal the state of profitability at various levels of activity.

Advantages

1. **Constant in nature.** Variable costs fluctuate from time to time, but in the long run, marginal costs are stable. Marginal costs remain the same, irrespective of the volume of production.

2. **Effective cost control.** It divides cost into fixed and variable. Fixed cost is excluded from product. As such, management can control marginal cost effectively.

3. **Treatment of overheads simplified.** It reduces the degree of over or under-recovery of overheads due to the separation of fixed overheads from production cost.

4. **Uniform and realistic valuation.** As the fixed overhead costs are excluded from product cost, the valuation of work-in-progress and finished goods becomes more realistic.

5. **Helpful to management.** It enables the management to start a new line of production which is advantageous. It is helpful in determining which is profitable—whether to buy or manufacture a product. The management can take decision regarding pricing and tendering.

6. **Helps in production planning.** It shows the amount of profit at every level of output with the help of cost volume profit relationship. Here the break-even chart is made use of.

7. **Better results.** When used with standard costing, it gives better results.

8. **Fixation of selling price.** The differentiation between fixed costs and variable costs is very helpful in determining the selling price of the products or services. Sometimes, different prices are charged for the same article in different markets to meet varying degrees of competition.

9. **Helpful in budgetary control.** The classification of expenses is very helpful in budgeting and flexible budget for various levels of activities.

10. **Preparing tenders.** Many business enterprises have to compete in the market in quoting the lowest price. Total variable cost, when separately calculated, becomes the 'floor price'. Any price above this floor price may be quoted to increase the total contribution.

11. **"Make or Buy" decision.** Sometimes a decision has to be made whether to manufacture a component or a product or to buy it readymade from the market. The decision to purchase it would be taken if the price paid recovers some of the fixed expenses.

12. **Better presentation.** The statements and graphs prepared under marginal costing are better understood by management executives. The break-even analysis presents the behaviour of cost, sales, contribution etc. in terms of charts and graphs. And, thus the results can easily be grasped.

Disadvantages

1. **Difficulty to analyse overhead.** Separation of costs into fixed and variable is a difficult problem. In marginal costing, semi-variable or semi-fixed costs are not considered.

2. **Time element ignored.** Fixed costs and variable costs are different in the short run ; but in the long run, all costs are variable. In the long run all costs change at varying levels of operation. When new plants and equipments are introduced, fixed costs and variable costs will vary.

3. **Unrealistic assumption.** Assumption of sale price will remain the same at different levels of operation. In real life, they may change and give unrealistic results.

4. **Difficulty in the fixation of price.** Under marginal costing, selling price is fixed on the basis of contribution. In case of cost plus contract, it is very difficult to fix price.

5. **Complete information not given.** It does not explain the reason for increase in production or sales.

6. **Significance lost.** In capital-intensive industries, fixed cost occupy major portions in the total cost. But marginal costs cover only variable costs. As such, it loses its significance in capital industries.

7. **Problem of variable overheads.** Marginal costing overcomes the problem of over and under-absorption of fixed overheads. Yet there is the problem in the case of variable overheads.

8. **Sales-oriented.** Successful business has to go in a balanced way in respect of selling production functions. But marginal costing is criticised on account of its attaching over-importance to selling function. Thus it is said to be sales-oriented. Production function is given less importance.

9. **Unreliable stock valuation.** Under marginal costing stock of work-in-progress and finished stock is valued at variable cost only. No portion of fixed cost is added to the value of stocks. Profit determined, under this method, is depressed.

10. **Claim for loss of stock.** Insurance claim for loss or damage of stock on the basis of such a valuation will be unfavourable to business.

11. **Automation.** Now-a-days increasing automation is leading to increase in fixed costs. If such increasing fixed costs are ignored, the costing system cannot be effective and dependable.

Marginal costing, if applied alone, will not be much in use, unless it is combined with other techniques like standard costing and budgetary control.

Absorption Costing and Marginal Costing

Absorption costing is the practice of charging all costs, both fixed and variable to operations, process or products. In marginal costing, only variable costs are charged to production.

The Institute of Cost and Management Accountants (U.K.) defines it as, "the practice of charging all costs, both variable and fixed to operations, processes or products." This explains why this technique is also called full costing. Administrative, selling and distribution overheads as much form part of total cost as prime cost and factory burden.

The following example illustrates the difference between the two techniques.

Illustration 1. The monthly cost figures for production in a manufacturing company are :

Variable Cost	Rs. 1,20,000
Fixed Costs	35,000

Total Cost : 1,55,000

Normally monthly sales figure is Rs. 2,00,000.

Actual sales figures for three separate months are :

I Month	II Month	III Month
Rs.	Rs.	Rs.
2,00,000	1,65,000	2,35,000

Under a system of marginal costing stock are valued as :

	I Month	II Month	III Month
	Rs.	Rs.	Rs.
Opening Stock	84,000	84,000	1,05,000
Closing Stock	84,000	1,05,000	84,000

If the marginal costing technique were not used stocks would be valued as follows :

	I Month	II Month	III Month
	Rs.	Rs.	Rs.
Opening Stock	1,08,500	1,08,500	1,35,625
Closing Stock	1,08,500	1,35,625	1,08,500

Prepare two Tabulation, side-by-side, to summarise these results for each of the three months, basing one tabulation on marginal cost theory and the other tabulation alongside on absorption cost theory. (*ICWA*)

Solution :

	Marginal Costing			*Absorption*		
	Months			*Months*		
	1	*2*	*3*	*1*	*2*	*3*
	Rs.	*Rs.*	*Rs.*	*Rs.*	*Rs.*	*Rs.*
Opening Stock	84,000	84,000	1,05,000	1,08,500	1,08,500	1,35,625
Variable Cost	1,20,000	1,20,000	1,20,000	1,20,000	1,20,000	1,20,000
Fixed Cost	—	—	—	35,000	35,000	35,000
Total	2,04,000	2,04,000	2,25,000	2,63,500	2,63,500	2,90,625
Less : Closing Stock	84,000	1,05,000	84,000	1,08,500	1,35,625	1,08,500
Cost of Sales :	1,20,000	99,000	1,41,000	1,55,000	1,27,875	1,82,125
Sales	2,00,000	1,65,000	2,35,000	2,00,000	1,65,000	2,35,000
Contribution	80,000	66,000	94,000	45,000	37,125	52,875
Less : Fixed Cost	35,000	35,000	35,000	Shown above		
Profit :	45,000	31,000	59,000	45,000	37,125	52,875
Margin % on Sales	40%	40%	40%	22.5%	22.5%	22.5%
Profit on Sales	22.5%	18.8%	25%	22.5%	22.5%	22.5%

Differences between absorption costing and marginal costing.

Absorption Costing	*Marginal Costing*
1. All costs—fixed and variable are charged to product.	1. Only variable costs are charged to products ; fixed costs are transferred to Profit & Loss Account.
2. Profit = Sales – Cost of goods sold	2. Contribution margin = S – VC. Profit = Contribution – F.C.
3. It does not reveal the cost volume profit relationship.	3. Cost Volume profit relationship is an important part of marginal costing.

4. Closing inventories are valued at full cost. Absorption costing reveals more profit since the inclusion of fixed costs in inventories.	4. Closing inventories are valued at variable cost. Marginal costing reveals less profit, when compared to absorption cost.
5. Costs are included in the products, this leads to over or under-absorption	5. Fixed costs are not included in the product ; so it will not lead to the problem of under-absorption.

Cost-Volume-Profit Analysis

As the term itself suggests, the cost-volume-profit (CVP) analysis is the analysis of three variables, *viz*., cost, volume and profit. In CVP analysis, an attempt is made to measure variations of costs and profit with volume. Profit as a variable is the reflection of a number of internal and external conditions which exert influence on sales revenue and costs.

The cost volume profit analysis helps or assists the management in profit planning. In order to increase the profit, a concern must increase the output. When the output is at maximum, within the installed capacity, it adds to the contribution. In the words of Heiser, "The most significant single factor in profit planning of the average business is the relationship between the volume of business, costs and profit." Thereby, cost volume profit analysis is the relationship among cost, volume and profit. When volume of output increases, unit cost of production decreases, and vice versa; because the fixed cost remains unaffected. When the output increases, the fixed cost per unit decreases. Therefore, profit will be more, when sales price remains constant. Generally, costs may not change in direct proportion to the volume. Thus, a small change in the volume will affect the profit.

The management is always interested in knowing that which product or product mix is most profitable, what effect a change in the volume of output will have on the cost of production and profit etc. All these problems are solved with the help of the cost-volume-profit-analysis.

To know the cost volume profit relationship, a study of the following is essential.

1. Marginal cost formulae ;
2. Break-even analysis ;
3. Profit volume ratio ;
4. Profit graph ;
5. Key factor ; and
6. Sales mix. etc.

Marginal Cost Equations

Sales = Variable Cost + Fixed Cost ± Profit or loss

Sales – Variable Cost = Fixed Cost ± Profit or loss

Sales – Variable Cost = Contribution

Contribution = Fixed Cost + Profit

From the above equation, we can understand that in order to earn profit, the contribution must be more than the fixed cost. To avoid any loss, the contribution must be equal to fixed cost.

Contribution

Contribution is the difference between sales and marginal cost of sales. Contribution enables to meet fixed costs and adds to the profit. Contribution is also known as gross margin. Fixed costs are covered by the contribution ; and the balance amount is an addition to the net profit.

Marginal Cost = Prime Cost + Variable overhead

Contribution = Sales – Marginal Cost
Contribution = Sales – Variable Cost
Contribution = Fixed Cost ± Profit or Loss
Profit = Contribution – Fixed Cost
Sales – Variable Cost = Fixed Cost + Profit
(or) $C = S - V$
C = F + P
S – V = F + P
C = Contribution ; S = Sales ; V = Variable Cost
P = Profit ; F = Fixed Cost.

Illustration 2. From the following information, find out the amount of profit earned during the year using marginal costing technique :

Fixed Cost Rs. 5,00,000
Variable Cost Rs. 10 per unit
Selling Price Rs. 15 per unit
Output level 1,50,000 units. (*B.Com. Calicut*)

Solution :

Contribution = Selling Price – Marginal Cost
= Rs. 22,50,000 – 15,00,000
= (1,50,000 × 15) – (1,50,000 × 10)
= Rs. 7,50,000

Contribution = Fixed Cost + Profit
Rs. 7,50,000 = 5,00,000 + Profit
Rs. 7,50,000 – 5,00,000 = Profit
Profit = Rs. 2,50,000

This equation is known as Marginal Cost Equation. If the three factors of the equation are known, it is easy to find the fourth factor. This equation is useful for the ascertainment of break-even point, profit volume ratio and margin of safety.

Break-Even Analysis

The break-even point and break-even chart are two by-products of break-even analysis. In a narrow sense, it is concerned with the break-even point and in a broad sense, it is concerned with break-even chart. Break-even analysis is also known as cost volume profit analysis. The analysis is a tool of financial analysis whereby the impact on profit of the changes in volume, price, costs and mix can be estimated with reasonable accuracy. Break-even point is equilibrium point or balancing point of no-profit no-loss. This is a point at which loss ceases and profit begins. This is a point where income is exactly equal to expenditure.

Break-Even Point. Break-even point is a point where the total sales are equal to total cost. In this point there is no profit or loss in the volume of sales. The formula to calculate break-even point is :

$$\text{B.E.P. (in units)} = \frac{\text{Total fixed cost}}{\text{Contribution per unit}}$$

or

$$= \frac{\text{Fixed cost}}{\text{Selling price per unit} - \text{Variable cost per unit}}$$

Illustration 3. From the following particulars calculate the break-even point :

Variable cost per unit	Rs. 12	
Fixed expenses	Rs. 60,000	
Selling price per unit	Rs. 18	(*B.Com. Calicut*)

Solution :

$$\text{B.E.P. (in units)} = \frac{\text{Fixed Cost}}{\text{Contribution per unit}}$$

(Selling Price – Variable Cost = Contribution)

(Rs. 18 – Rs. 12 = 6)

Rs. 60,000 ÷ Rs. 6 = 10,000 Units

B.E.P. Sales = 10,000 × Rs. 18 = **Rs. 1,80,000**

Illustration 4. A company estimates that next year it will earn a profit of Rs. 50,000. The budgeted fixed costs and sales are Rs. 2,50,000 and Rs. 9,93,000 respectively. Find out the break-even point for the company.

Solution :

$$\text{B.E.P. (in units)} = \frac{\text{F} \times \text{S}}{\text{Contribution}}$$

Contribution = S – V = F + P

F + P = Rs. 2,50,000 + Rs. 50,000 = Rs. 3,00,000

$$\text{B.E.P Sales} = \frac{2{,}50{,}000 \times 9{,}93{,}000}{3{,}00{,}000}$$

= **Rs. 8,27,500**

Illustration 5. From the following particulars, find out the selling price per unit if B.E.P. is to be brought down to 9,000 units.

Variable cost per unit Rs. 75

Fixed expenses Rs. 2,70,000

Selling price per unit Rs. 100. (*B.Com. Calicut*)

Solution :

Let us assume that the contribution per unit at B.E. sales of 9,000 units is *x*.

$$\text{B.E.P} = \frac{\text{Fixed Cost}}{\text{Contribution per unit}}$$

Contribution per unit is not known. Therefore

$$9{,}000 \text{ units} = \frac{2{,}70{,}000}{x}$$

$$9{,}000\, x = 2{,}70{,}000$$

$$x = 30.$$

Contribution is Rs. 30 per unit, in place of Rs. 25. Therefore, the selling price should have been Rs. 105, *i.e.*, Rs. 75 + Rs. 30.

Illustration 6. From the following data, calculate break-even point expressed in terms of units and also the new B.E.P., if selling price is reduced by 10%.

Fixed expenses :

	Rs.
Depreciation	1,00,000
Salaries	1,00,000

Variable expenses :

Materials	Rs. 3 per unit
Labour	Rs. 2 per unit
Selling price	Rs. 10 per unit

(*B. Com.* (*Pass*) *Delhi*)

Solution :

$$\text{B.E.P.} = \frac{\text{Fixed Cost}}{\text{Contribution per unit}}$$

$$= \frac{2,00,000}{5} = \mathbf{40,000} \text{ units}$$

When the selling price is reduced by 10%, selling price becomes Rs. 10 – 1 = Rs. 9 per unit. So, Contribution = Rs. 9 – Rs. 5 = Rs. 4.

$$\text{B.E.P.} = \frac{\text{Fixed Cost}}{\text{Contribution per unit}}$$

$$= \frac{2,00,000}{4} = \mathbf{50,000\ units}$$

Profit Volume Ratio

Profit volume ratio, which is popularly known as P/V Ratio, expresses the relationship of contribution to sales. Another name for this ratio is contribution-sales ratio or marginal-income ratio or variable-profit ratio. The ratio, expressed as a percentage, indicated the relative profitability of different products.

The formula for computing the P/V ratio is given below :

$$\text{P/V Ratio} = \frac{\text{Contribution}}{\text{Sales}} \text{ (or) } \frac{C}{S}$$

or $$= \frac{\text{Fixed Cost + Profit}}{\text{Sales}} \text{ (or) } \frac{F+P}{S}$$

or $$= \frac{\text{Sales} - \text{Variable Cost}}{\text{Sales}} \text{ (or) } \frac{S-V}{S}$$

It can also be expressed in percentage. Normally, this ratio is expressed in percentage. When we know the P/V ratio, B.E.P. can be calculated, by using the formula :

$$\text{B.E.P. (Sales volume)} = \frac{\text{Fixed Cost}}{\text{P/V Ratio}} \text{ (or) } \frac{F}{\text{P/V Ratio}}$$

The profit of a business can be increased by improving P/V ratio. As such management will make efforts to improve the ratio. A higher ratio means a greater profitability and vice versa. So management will increase the P/V ratio :

(*a*) by increasing sales price per unit

(*b*) by decreasing variable costs

(*c*) by increasing the production of products which is having a high P/V ratio and vice versa.

P/V ratio is very important in decision-making. It can be used for the calculation of B.E.P. and in problems regarding profit sales relationship.

1. $\text{B.E.P} = \frac{\text{Fixed Cost}}{\text{P/V ratio}} = \frac{F}{\text{P/V ratio}}$
2. Fixed Cost = B.E.P. × P/V ratio
3. Sales required in units to maintain a desired profit

$$\frac{\text{F.C.} + \text{Desired profit}}{\text{P/V ratio}} = \frac{\text{F + P}}{\text{P/V ratio}}$$

$$= \frac{\text{Required contribution}}{\text{New contribution per unit}}$$

4. Contribution = Sales × P/V ratio
5. Variable Costs = Sales (1 – P/V ratio)
6. $\text{P/V Ratio} = \frac{\text{Change in Profit}}{\text{Change in Sales}}$

Illustration 7.

Marginal cost Rs. 2,400
Selling Price Rs. 3,000
Calculate P/V Ratio,

Solution :

$$\text{P/VRatio} = \frac{\text{Contribution}}{\text{Sales}} \times 100 = \frac{\text{Rs.}3,000 - \text{Rs.}2,400}{\text{Rs.}3,000} \times 100$$

$$= \frac{\text{Rs.}600}{\text{Rs.}3,000} \times 100 = \mathbf{20\%}$$

Illustration 8. The sales turnover and profits during two periods are as under :

Period I : Sales Rs. 20 lakhs ; Profit Rs. 2 lakhs
Period II : Sales Rs. 30 lakhs ; Profit Rs. 4 lakhs
Calculate P/V Ratio. *(B. Com., Osmania)*

Solution :

$$\text{P/V Ratio} = \frac{\text{Change in profit}}{\text{Change in sales}} \times 100 = \frac{\text{Rs. } 4{,}00{,}000 - 2{,}00{,}000 \times 100}{\text{Rs. } 30{,}00{,}000 - \text{Rs. } 20{,}00{,}000}$$

$$= \frac{2,00,000}{10,00,000} \times 100 = \mathbf{20\%}$$

Illustration 9. The following data are obtained from the records of a company :

	First Year	Second Year
	Rs.	Rs.
Sales	80,000	90,000
Profit	10,000	14,000

Calculate the break-even point. *(B.Com., Calicut)*

Solution :

$$\text{B.E.P. (Sales)} = \frac{\text{Fixed Cost}}{\text{P/VRatio}}$$

$$\text{P/V Ratio} = \frac{\text{Change in profit}}{\text{Change in sales}} \times 100 = \frac{4,000}{10,000} \times 100 = 40\%$$

Fixed Cost = Contribution – Profit

$$\text{Fixed Cost} = 80,000 \times \frac{40}{100} - \text{Rs.}10,000$$

= 32,000 – 10,000 = Rs. 22,000

$$\text{B.E.P. (Sales)} = \frac{22,000 \times 100}{40} = \mathbf{Rs.\ 55,000.}$$

Illustration 10. You are required to calculate the break-even point in the following case :

The fixed cost for the year is Rs. 80,000; variable cost per unit for the single product being made is Rs. 4.

Estimated sales for the period are valued at Rs. 2,00,000. The number of units involved coincides with the expected volume of output. Each unit sells at Rs. 20.

Calculate break-even point by applying important formulae. *(C.A. Final)*

Solution :

	Per unit	*Total*
	Rs.	Rs.
Sales	20	2,00,000
Variable Cost	4	40,000
Contribution	16	1,60,000
Fixed Cost		80,000
Profit		80,000

(1) Sales at B.E.P.

(*a*) $$\text{B.E.P.} = \frac{F \times S}{S - V} = \frac{80,000 \times 2,00,000}{2,00,000 - 40,000} = \textbf{Rs. 1,00,000}$$

(or)

(*b*) $$\text{B.E.P.} = \frac{F}{1 - \frac{V}{S}} = \frac{80,000}{1 - \frac{40,000}{2,00,000}} = \frac{80,000}{1 - \frac{1}{5}} = 80,000 \times \frac{5}{4} = \textbf{Rs.1,00,000}$$

(or)

(*c*) $$\text{B.E.P.} = \frac{F}{\text{P/V Ratio}}$$

(or)

We have to find out P/V Ratio

$$\text{P/V Ratio} = \frac{\text{Contribution}}{\text{Sales}} = \frac{1,60,000}{2,00,000} = 80\%$$

Sales × 80% = 80,000 *i.e.,* F.

$$\therefore \quad \text{Sales} = \frac{80,000 \times 100}{80} = \textbf{Rs. 1,00,000}$$

(or)

(*d*) $$\text{B.E.P.} = \frac{F}{\text{C\% (Contribution \% on sales)}}$$

$$= \frac{80,000 \times 100}{80} = \textbf{Rs. 1,00,000}$$

(2) Break-even point in units :

(*a*) $$\frac{\text{B.E. Sales}}{\text{S.P.}} = \frac{1,00,000}{20} = \textbf{5,000 units}$$

(or)

(*b*) $$\frac{F}{SP - V} = \frac{80,000}{20 - 4} = \frac{80,000}{16} = \textbf{5,000 units}$$

(or)

(c) $$\frac{F}{C} = \frac{80,000}{16} = \textbf{5,000 units}$$

Margin of Safety

Margin of Safety is an important concept in Marginal Costing approach. Total sales minus the sales at break-even point is known as the Margin of Safety (M/S). That is, Margin of Safety is the excess of normal or actual sales over sales at break-even point. In other words, sales over and above break-even sales are known as Margin of Safety. The Margin of Safety refers to the amount by which sales revenue can fall before a loss is incurred.That is, it is the difference between the actual sales and sales at the break-even point. Break-even point can be compared to a Red Signal Point. If the Margin of Safety is large, it is a sign of soundness of the business and vice versa. The Margin of Safety serves as a guide, is a reliable indicator of the business strength and soundness. Margin of safety can be expressed in absolute sales amount or in percentage.

High Margin of Safety indicates the soundness of a business because even with substantial fall in sale or fall in production, some profit shall be made. Small margin of safety on the other hand is an indicator of the weak position of the business and even a small reduction in sale or production will adversely affect the profit position of the business.

Margin of safety can be increased by :

(*a*) Decreasing the fixed cost ;
(*b*) Decreasing the variable cost ;
(*c*) Increasing the selling price ;
(*d*) Increasing output and sales ;
(*e*) Changing to a product mix that improves P/V Ratio.

Margin of Safety : Actual Sales – Sales at BEP

$$(\text{OR}) = \frac{\text{Profit}}{\text{P/V Ratio}}$$

$$(\text{OR}) = \frac{\text{Profit}}{\text{Contribution}}$$

$$\text{As a percentage} = \frac{\text{Margin of Safety}}{\text{Total Sales}} \times 100$$

Illustration 11. From the following details find out (*a*) Profit Volume Ratio, (*b*) B.E.P., (*c*) Margin of Safety.

	Rs.
Sales	1,00,000
Total Costs	80,000
Fixed Costs	20,000
Net Profit	20,000

Solution :

(*a*) $$\text{P/V Ratio} = \frac{\text{Sales} - \text{Variable expenses}}{\text{Sales}} \times 100$$

$$= \frac{1,00,000 - 60,000}{1,00,000} \times 100 = 40\%$$

(*b*) $$\text{B.E.P.} = \frac{\text{Fixed Cost}}{\text{P/V Ratio}}$$

$$= \frac{20,000}{40\%} \text{ (or) } \frac{20,000 \times 100}{40}$$

= Rs. 50,000

(c) $\text{Margin of Safety} = \dfrac{\text{Profit}}{\text{P/V Ratio}}$

$= \dfrac{20{,}000}{40\%}$

$= \dfrac{20{,}000 \times 100}{40}$

$=$ **Rs. 50,000.**

(or) Margin of Safety = Actual Sales – Sales at BEP

= 1,00,000 – 50,000 = **Rs. 50,000**

Illustration 12. The following information was obtained from a Company in a certain year :

Sales	Rs. 1,00,000
Variable Costs	Rs. 60,000
Fixed Costs	Rs. 30,000

Find the P/V Ratio, break-even point and margin of safety. (*B. Com., Bombay*)

Solution :

$$\text{P/V Ratio} = \frac{S-V}{S} \times 100 = \frac{1{,}00{,}000 - 60{,}000}{1{,}00{,}000} \times 100 = \mathbf{40\%}$$

$$\text{Break-Even Point} = \frac{F}{\text{P/V Ratio}} = \frac{30{,}000}{40\%} = \textbf{Rs. 75,000}$$

$$\text{Margin of safety} = \frac{\text{Profit}}{\text{P/V Ratio}} = \frac{10{,}000}{40\%} = \textbf{Rs. 25,000}$$

(OR) Sales – Break-Even Sales = Rs. 1,00,000 – Rs. 75,000 = **Rs. 25,000**

Illustration 13. The following information is obtained from a Company for January :

	Rs.
Sales	20,000
Variable Costs	10,000
Fixed Costs	6,000

(*a*) Find P/V Ratio, Break-Even Point and Margin of Safety at this level, and the effect of;

(*i*) 20% decrease in fixed costs ;

(*ii*) 10% increase in fixed costs ;

(*iii*) 10% decrease in variable costs ;

(*iv*) 10% increase in selling price ;

(*v*) 10% increase in selling price together with an increase of fixed overheads by Rs. 1,200 ;

(*vi*) 10% decrease in sales price ;

(*vii*) 10% decrease in sales price accompanied by 10% decrease in variable costs.

(*B. Com., Madurai, modified*)

Solution :

$\text{P/V} = \dfrac{\text{Contribution} \times 100}{\text{Sales}}$		
$\text{(OR)} = \dfrac{\text{Sales} - \text{variable cost}}{\text{Sales}} \times 100$	$\text{BEP} = \dfrac{\text{Fixed Cost}}{\text{P/V Ratio}}$	$\text{MS} = \dfrac{\text{Profit}}{\text{P/V Ratio}}$

(*a*) $\frac{\text{Rs.}20{,}000 - \text{Rs.}10{,}000}{\text{Rs.}20{,}000} \times 100 = 50\%$	$\frac{\text{Rs.}6{,}000}{50\%} = \text{Rs.}12{,}000$	$\frac{\text{Rs.}4{,}000}{50\%} = \text{Rs.}8{,}000$ (OR)(Rs. 20,000 – Rs. 12,000)
(*b*) (*i*) 50%	$\frac{\text{Rs.}4{,}800}{50\%} = \text{Rs.}9{,}600$	$\frac{\text{Rs.}5{,}200}{50\%} = \text{Rs.}10{,}400$ (OR) (Rs. 20,000 – Rs. 9,600)
(*ii*) 50%	$\frac{\text{Rs.}6{,}600}{50\%} = \text{Rs.}13{,}200$	$\frac{\text{Rs.}3{,}400}{50\%} = \text{Rs.}6{,}800$ (OR) (Rs. 20,000 – Rs. 13,200)
(*iii*) $\frac{\text{Rs.}20{,}000 - \text{Rs.}9{,}000 \times 100}{\text{Rs.}20{,}000} = 55\%$	$\frac{\text{Rs.}6{,}000}{55\%} = \text{Rs.}10{,}909$	$\frac{\text{Rs.}5{,}000}{55\%} = \text{Rs.}9{,}091$ (OR) (Rs. 20,000 – Rs. 10,909)
(*iv*) $\frac{\text{Rs.}22{,}000 - \text{Rs.}10{,}000 \times 100}{\text{Rs.}22{,}000} = 54.55\%$	$\frac{\text{Rs.}6{,}000}{54.545\%} = \text{Rs.}11{,}000$	$\frac{\text{Rs.}6{,}000}{54.55\%} = \text{Rs.}11{,}000$ (OR) (Rs. 22,000 – Rs. 11,000)
(*v*) $\frac{\text{Rs.}22{,}000 - \text{Rs.}10{,}000 \times 100}{\text{Rs.}22{,}000} = 54.545\%$	$\frac{\text{Rs.}7{,}200}{54.545\%} = \text{Rs.}13{,}200$	$\frac{\text{Rs.}4{,}800}{54.545\%} = \text{Rs.}8{,}800$ (OR) (Rs. 22,000 – Rs. 13,200)
(*vi*) $\frac{\text{Rs.}18{,}000 - \text{Rs.}10{,}000 \times 100}{\text{Rs.}18{,}000} = 44.44\%$	$\frac{\text{Rs.}6{,}000}{44.44\%} = \text{Rs.}13{,}500$	$\frac{\text{Rs.}2{,}000}{44.44\%} = \text{Rs.}4{,}500$ (OR) (Rs. 18,000 – Rs. 13,500)
(*vii*) $\frac{\text{Rs.}18{,}000 - \text{Rs.}9{,}000 \times 100}{\text{Rs.}18{,}000} = 50\%$	$\frac{\text{Rs.}6{,}000}{50\%} = \text{Rs.}12{,}000$	$\frac{\text{Rs.}3{,}000}{50\%} = \text{Rs.}6{,}000$ (OR) (Rs. 18,000 – Rs. 12,000)

Break-Even Chart

The technique of break-even analysis can be made easy with the help of graph or mathematical formula. Graphical representation of break-even point (or cost volume-profit) is known as the break-even chart. Dr. Vance is of the opinion that "it is a graph showing the amounts of fixed variable costs and the sales revenue at different volumes of operation. It shows at what volume the firm first covers all costs with revenue of break-even." B.E.C. shows the profitability or otherwise of an undertaking at various levels of activity, and indicates the point at which neither profit nor loss is made. Break-even point is known as "no profit, no loss point". So the chart is also known as break-even chart. At this point, the total costs are recovered and profit begins.

Significance of B.E.C. at various levels of activity :

1. It will show the variable costs, fixed costs and total costs.
2. Sales unit or value can be known.
3. Profit or loss can be known.
4. Margin of safety can be known.
5. Angle of incidence or the intersection of sales line with costs line can also be known.

Thus, it is very useful for managerial decision.

Assumptions of Break-even Chart

1. Fixed costs remain the same and do not change with level of activity.
2. Costs are divided into fixed and variable costs. Variable costs change according to the volume of production.
3. Variable cost vary with the volume of output but price of variable costs such as wage rate, price of materials, supplies, will be unchanged.
4. Selling price remains the same at different levels of activity.
5. There is no change in the product mix.
6. There is no change in the level of efficiency.
7. Policies of management do not change.
8. No change in the manufacturing process is due to non-static operating efficiency.
9. As the number of units produced and sold are the same, there is no closing or opening stock.

Construction of Break-Even Chart

1. On the graph the 'X' axis (horizontal axis) shows the volume of production and the 'Y' axis (Vertical axis) shows the cost and sales. A graph has two sides which are known as "axes". The horizontal side at the bottom of the graph is the X-axis. The left hand vertical side is the Y-axis. On the Y-axis, costs and revenues are exhibited. On the X-axis one or more of production quantity, capacity in percentage form, sales volume etc. are shown.
2. Draw both axes on the suitable graph paper on the basis of appropriate scale.
3. Insert production quantity on X-axis and costs and sales revenues on Y-axis.
4. Draw the fixed cost line on the graph. Even at zero production, the fixed costs remain the same. At zero production, the fixed costs will be the loss.
5. The total cost line is drawn above the fixed cost line. For this purpose, the variable cost is added to the fixed cost to arrive at the total cost and drawn at each and every scale of production.
6. Sales revenue line is drawn commencing at zero and finishing at the last point.
7. Then the sales line cuts the total cost line *i.e.*, sales equals the total cost. This is known as Break-Even Point. If dotted line is drawn from BEP to X-axis, it indicates BEP (Units) and if it is drawn towards Y-axis, it indicates BEP (Value).
8. The difference between the sales line and total cost line is marked as profit and it is to the right of BEP. The angle at which sales line cuts the total cost line is the angle of incidence.
9. The position to the left of the BEP on the graph indicates the loss which goes upto the total amount of fixed costs which is the maximum loss at the zero production.
10. Then the graph will indicate the BEP, profit or loss at different level of output, margin of safety, contribution and the relationship between the marginal cost, fixed cost and total cost.

Illustration 14. From the following information, prepare the break-even chart.

Fixed Cost Rs. 2,000

Variable Cost Re. 0.50 per unit

Sales Re. 1 per unit

Units produced and sold 2,000; 4,000; 6,000; 8,000 and 10,000.

Solution :

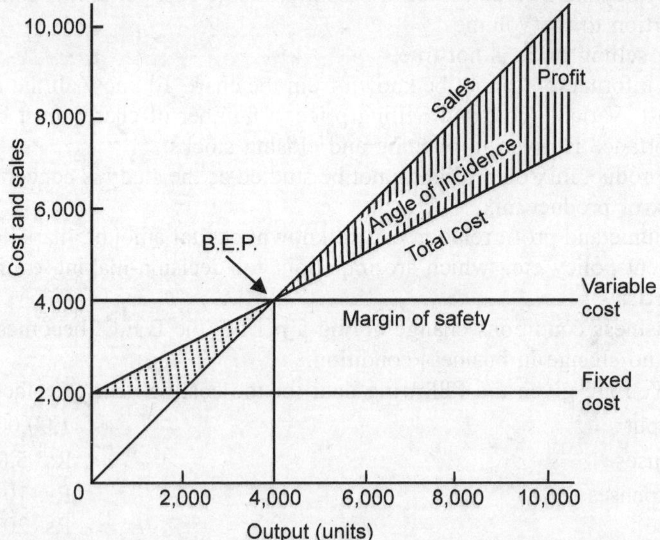

X-axis also shows the units for production and percentage of capacity and output.

The above chart is prepared from the following information ;

Fixed Cost Rs. 2,000, Variable Cost Re. 0.50, Sales Re. 1 per unit.

Units produced and sold, 2,000; 4,000; 6,000; 8,000 and 10,000.

Fixed cost is drawn parallel to the 'X' axis (Rs. 2,000) as it remains the same. Variable costs are drawn above the fixed cost line, as they vary with the volume of production. It is the total cost which is drawn above the fixed cost.

Sale line is drawn by joining the different levels of activity with the sale value or by joining sale value (2,000; 4,000; 6,000; etc.). It is inclined at 45° to the X-axis.

The margin of safety is the distance between the B.E.P. and the total output produced or sold. In the above chart the margin of safety is 6,000.

Margin of safety = Actual sales – B.E. sales = 10,000 – 4,000 or 60%. If the distance is larger, it shows better safety, and profit can afford to increase and *vice versa.*

Angle of incidence is the angle where the sales line intersects the total cost line; *i.e.*, Rs. 4,000. It is the B.E.P. If the angle is larger, the profit will be larger and *vice versa.*

Advantages of Break-Even Analysis and Chart

1. Total cost, variable cost and fixed cost can be determined.
2. B.E. output or sales value can be determined.
3. Cost, volume and profit relationship can be studied, and they are very useful to the managerial decision-making.
4. Inter-firm comparison is possible.
5. It is useful for forecasting plans and profits.
6. The best products mix can be selected.
7. Total profits can be calculated.
8. Profitability of different levels of activity, various products or profit, *i.e.*, plans can be known.
9. It is helpful for cost control.

Limitations of B.E.C.

B.E.C. is constructed under some unrealistic assumptions :

1. Exact and accurate classification of cost into fixed and variable is not possible. Fixed

costs vary beyond a certain level of output. Variable cost per unit is constant and it varies in proportion to the volume.

2. Constant selling price is not true.
3. Detailed information cannot be known from the chart. To know all the information about Fixed cost, Variable cost and Selling price, a number of charts must be drawn.
4. No importance is given to opening and closing stocks.
5. Various product mix on profits cannot be studied as the study is concerned with only one sales mix or product mix.
6. Cost, volume and profit relation can be known; capital amount, market aspects, effect of government policy etc., which are important for decision-making cannot be considered from B.E.C.
7. If the business conditions change during a period, the B.E.C. becomes out of date as it assumes no change in business condition.

Illustration 15. You are given the following data for the costing year of a factory.

Budget Output	1,00,000 Units
Fixed Expenses	Rs. 5,00,000
Variable Expenses	Rs. 10 per unit
Selling Price	Rs. 20 per unit

Draw a break-even chart showing the break-even point. If the selling price is reduced to Rs. 18 per unit, what will be the new break-even point. *(B. Com., Jabalpur)*

Solution :

$$\text{B.E.P.} = \frac{\text{F.C.}}{\text{S} - \text{V}}$$

$$= \frac{\text{Rs.}5,00,000}{10} = \mathbf{50,000\ Units}$$

B.E.S. = 50,000 × Rs. 20 = **Rs. 10,00,000**

If selling price is reduced to Rs. 18, then the contribution will be Rs. 8.

$\therefore$ The new $\quad \text{B.E.P.} = \dfrac{5,00,000}{8} = \mathbf{62,500\ Units}$

B.E.S. = 62,500 × Rs. 18 = **Rs. 11,25,000.**

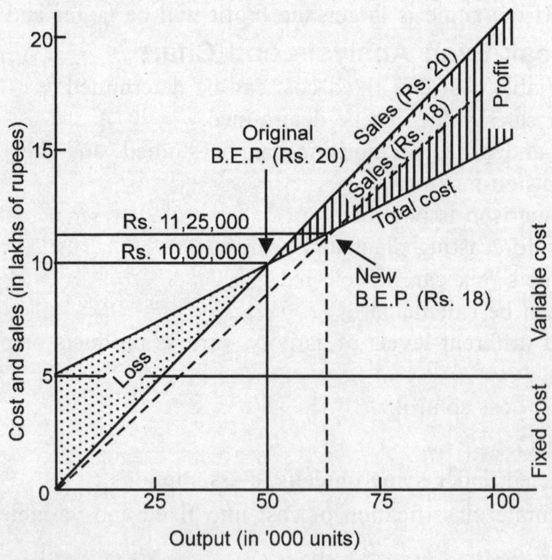

Forms of Break-Even Chart

There are different ways of constructing a break-even chart. Charts which depict cost-volume-profit data are visual aids which serve to dramatise the effect of changes in cost, volume and profit. Like other charts, they impress effectively and tell their stories at a glance. There are numerous ways in which break-even charts are prepared depending upon the purpose which they are meant to serve and the details which they are required to exhibit. The forms of break-even charts, which are of importance, have been explained next :

(*a*) **Simple Break-Even Chart.** This is a traditional break-even chart. This chart is used to predict profit or loss to be obtained from a certain level of sales or production. It is a combination of fixed cost line, variable cost line and the sales line. The following example illustrates.

Illustration 16. The following figures relate to a particular year working at 100% capacity level in a manufacturing concern :

Fixed Overheads	Rs. 1,20,000
Variable Overheads	2,00,000
Direct Wages	1,50,000
Direct Materials	4,10,000
Sales	10,00,000

Represent the above figures on the Break-even chart and determine from the chart the break-even point : verify your results by calculations. (*B.Com., Delhi*)

Solution :

	Rs.
Sales	10,00,000
Less : Variable Cost	7,60,000
Contribution	2,40,000
Fixed Cost	1,20,000
Profit	1,20,000

$$\text{P/V Ratio} = \frac{\text{Contribution}}{\text{Sales}} \times 100 = \frac{\text{Rs. } 2,40,000}{10,00,000} \times 100 = 24\%$$

$$\text{B.E.P.} = \frac{\text{Fixed Cost}}{\text{P/V Ratio}} = \frac{\text{Rs. } 1,20,000}{24} \times 100 = \textbf{Rs. 5,00,000}$$

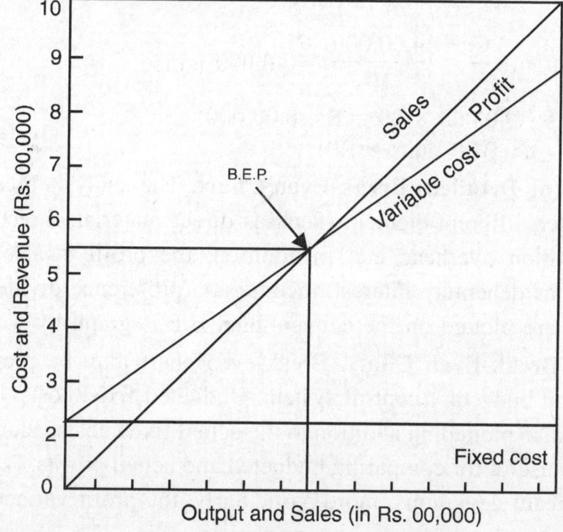

(*b*) **Contribution Break Even Chart.** In the case of simple break even chart variable cost line is shown above the fixed cost line. Some times fixed costs can be shown above the variable costs. In such a case the chart is known as *contribution break even chart.* The speiciality of this chart is that contribution is indicated clearly in the chart by way of difference between variable cost line and sales line.

Illustration 17.

You are given the following data for the coming year of a factory :

Budgeted Output	80,000 units
Fixed Expenses	Rs. 4,00,000
Variable Expenses	Rs. 10 per unit
Selling Price	Rs. 20 per unit

Draw contribution break even chart. (*I.C.W.A.*)

Solution :

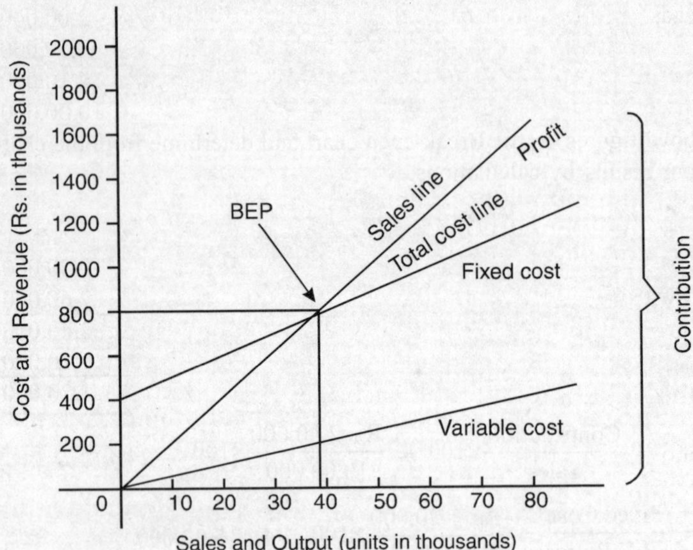

C = S – V = Rs. 20 – 10 = Rs. 10

$$\text{BEP} = \frac{\text{FC}}{\text{C}} = \frac{4,00,000}{10} = 40,000 \text{ units}$$

BEP units = 40,000 × 20 = Rs. 8,00,000
(BEP units × SP)

(*c*) **Analysis (or Detailed) Break-Even Chart.** The analysis break-even chart analyses the variables costs under different elements such as direct material, direct labour, factory overhead, selling and distribution overhead etc. In addition, the profit is also sub-divided into various appropriation such as debenture interest, income tax, preference dividends, equity dividends and reserves. All these are plotted on the conventional B.E.P. graph by way of analysis.

(*d*) **Control Break-Even Chart.** Break-even chart may be prepared in conjunction with standard costing and budgetary control system. Budgeted fixed costs, budgeted variable cost and budgeted sales are also plotted, in addition to the actual fixed costs, actual variable costs and actual sales. This graph is useful for comparing budgeted and actual profits, B.E.P. and sales. It facilitates to study the significant deviations, more particularly, the profit variance.

Illustration 18.

From the following data, draw control break-even chart and analyse the same.

(*a*) Budgeted Costs : Fixed Costs Rs. 45,000
Variable Costs Rs. 36,000
Sales Rs. 1,20,000

(*b*) Actual Costs : Fixed Costs Rs. 45,000
Variable Costs Rs. 48,600
Sales Rs. 1,35,000

(M. Com, Bangalore)

Solution :

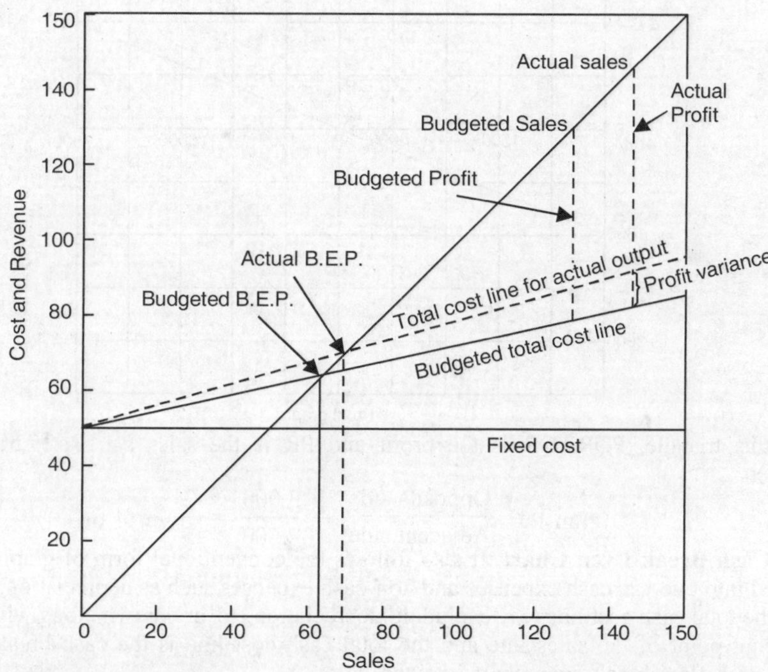

(*e*) **Profit–Volume Chart.** It is a simplified and improved form of break-even graph. It is a pictorial representation of cost-volume-profit relationship. All basic data, required for BE chart, are required for the construction of the profit volume graph. In this chart, the horizontal axis represents the sales volume and the vertical axis shows profit or loss. The vertical slope line above the horizontal line represents the profit and below the horizontal line shows loss. The diagonal line presents the total marginal contribution of the business. The horizontal line at zero profit level represents the break-even point where there are no profits or losses. The profit can be determined at any given point of sale with the help of this profit-volume chart.

Illustration 19.

Draw the profit-volume graph and find out P/V ratio with the following information :

Output	3,000 units
Volume of Sales	Rs. 7,500
Variable Cost	Rs. 1,500
Fixed Cost	Rs. 1,500

Solution :

From the profit-volume graph, we can find the profit is Rs. 1,500. The fixed cost is Rs. 1,500. PQ intersects sale line at point P, which is the break-even point *i.e.*, Rs. 3,750. The P/V ratio can easily be found out with the help of this graph as follows :

$$\text{Sales at B.E.P.} = \frac{F \times S}{S - V} = \frac{1{,}500 \times 7{,}500}{7{,}500 - 4{,}500} = \text{Rs. } 3{,}750$$

$$\text{Margin of safety} = \text{Rs. } 7{,}500 - \text{Rs. } 3{,}750 = \text{Rs. } 3{,}750$$

$$\text{P/V Ratio} = \frac{S - V}{S} \quad \frac{7{,}500 - 4{,}500}{7{,}500} = \frac{2}{5} \text{ or } .4 \text{ or } 40\%$$

Profit graph

In this triangle, PQR, QR is the profit and PR is the sales *i.e.*, Rs. 7,500 – Rs. 3,750 = Rs. 3,750

$$\text{Tan P} = \frac{\text{Opposite side}}{\text{Adjacent side}} = \frac{3{,}000}{7{,}500} = \frac{2}{5} \text{ or } .4 \text{ or } 40\%$$

(*f*) **Cash Break-Even Chart.** It also follows the conventional form of graph. The expenses are divided into two *viz.* cash expenses and non-cash expenses such as depreciation. The cash fixed cost and the total cash cost lines *i.e.* excluding depreciation etc. are drawn along with the sales line. The meeting point of the sales line and the total cash cost line is the cash break-even point. A model of cash flow break-even chart is given below :

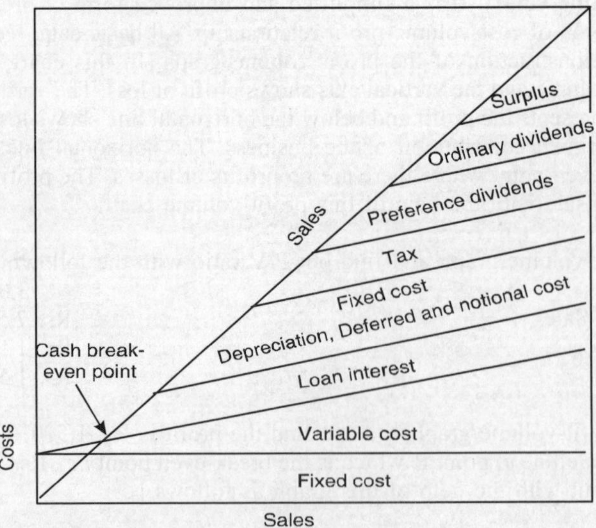

Angle of Incidence

The angle, to the right of B.E.P., is formed, by intersecting the sales line and the total cost line. It indicates the profit-earning capacity. The angle may be large or small. A greater angle of incidence means that the profits are made at high rate and vice versa. Generally, a large or wider angle of incidence together with a high margin of safety indicate the most favourable situations.

Problem of Key or Limiting Factor. Firms would try to produce such commodities which fetch a higher contribution or the highest contribution. This assumption is based on the possibility of selling out the products at the maximum. Sometimes, it may happen that the firm may not be able to push out all the products manufactured. And sometimes, the firm can sell all the products it manufactures, but production may be limited, due to shortage of materials, labour, plant-capacity, capital, demand etc. The key factor or limiting factor is that factor which puts a limit on the production and profit of the firm. These factors are also known as principal factors or critical factors. When there is no limiting factor, the production can be on the basis of the highest P/V ratio. When two or more limiting factors are in operation, they will be seriously considered to determine the profitability.

$$\text{Profitability} = \frac{\text{Contribution}}{\text{Key factor}} \text{ (materials or labour or capital etc.)}$$

Illustration 20. The following information in respect of product A and product B of a firm is given :

	Product A	*Product B*
Sales Price	Rs. 75	Rs. 48
Direct material	Rs. 30	Rs. 30
Direct labour hours (Re. 0.50 per hour)	15 hours	2 hours
Variable Overhead—100% of direct wages		
Fixed Overhead Rs. 3,000		

Present the above information to show the profitability of products during labour shortage.

Solution :

Contribution Statement

	A Rs.		*B* Rs.	
Sales		75		48
Less: Marginal Cost :				
Direct Materials	30		30	
Direct Wages	7.5		1	
Variable Overhead	7.5	45	1	32
Contribution : (per unit)		30		16
Profitability : $\frac{\text{Contribution}}{\text{Labour hours}}$		$\frac{30}{\text{15 hours}}$ = Rs. 2 per hour		$\frac{16}{2}$ = Rs. 8 per hour

Therefore, product B is more profitable than A during labour shortage.

Illustration 21. In a factory producing two different kinds of articles, the limiting factor is the availability of labour. From the following information from the factory for 2010, show which product is more profitable.

	Product A Cost per unit Rs.	*Product B* Cost per unit Rs.
Materials	5.00	5.00
Labour :		
6 hrs @ 0.50	3.00	
3 hrs. @ 0.50		1.50
Overheads :		
Fixed 50% of labour	1.50	0.75
Variable	150	1.50
Total Cost	11.00	8.75
Selling Price	14.00	11.00
Profit	3.00	2.25
Total production for the month	500 units	600 units

Maximum capacity per month, 4,800 hours. Also give proof in support of your answer.

(*B. Com. Madurai*)

Solution :

MARGINAL COST STATEMENT

	Product A Per unit Rs.	*Product A* Total Rs.	*Product B* Per unit Rs.	*Product B* Total Rs.
Production in Units		500 units		600 units
Selling Price	14.00	7,000	11.00	6,600
Less : Marginal Cost :				
Materials 5.00 5.00				
Labour 3.00 1.50				
Overheads 1.50 1.50	9.50	4,750	8.00	4,800
Contribution	4.50	2,250	3.00	1,800
Less : Fixed Cost	1.50	750	0.75	450
Profit	3.00	1,500	2.25	1,350

Contribution per unit of limited factor.

$$\frac{\text{Contribution}}{\text{Key Factor}} = \frac{\text{Rs.}4.50}{6 \text{ hours}} \qquad \frac{\text{Rs.}3.00}{3 \text{ hours}}$$

$$= \text{Re. } 0.75 \qquad = \text{Re. } 1$$

On the basis of contribution, Product A is more profitable. And on the basis of net profit, Product A is more profitable. On the basis of limiting factor, Product B is more profitable, as contribution is greater.

Application of Marginal Costing Techniques

Marginal Costing is an extremely valuable technique with the management. The cost-volume-profit relationship has served as a key to locked storehouse of solutions to many situations. It enables the management to tackle many problems which are faced in the practical business. "All the introduction of marginal cost principles does is to give the management a fresh, and perhaps a refreshing, insight into the progress of their business." Now, we explain the application of the techniques of marginal costing in certain important spheres :

Marginal Costing helps the management in decision-making in respect of the following vital areas :

1. Cost Control
2. Fixation of Selling Price
3. Closure of a Department or Discontinuing a Product
4. Selection of a Profitable Product Mix
5. Profit Planning
6. Decision to make or buy
7. Decision to accept a bulk order
8. Introduction of a new product
9. Choice of technique
10. Evaluation of performance
11. Decision making
12. Maintaining a desired level of profit
13. Level of activity planning
14. Alternative methods of production
15. Introduction of product line

1. Cost Control. The two types of costs—variable and fixed—are controllable and non-controllable respectively. The variable cost is controlled by production department and the fixed cost is controlled by the management.

2. Fixation of Selling Price. Product pricing is a very important function of management. One of the purposes of cost accounting is the ascertainment of cost for fixation of selling price. Marginal cost of a product represents the minimum price for that product and any sale below the marginal cost would entail a loss of cash. There are cyclic periods in business—boom, depression, recession etc. During normal circumstances, price is based on full cost. The theory is that only those products should be produced or sold which make the largest contribution towards the recovery of fixed costs. The selling price fixation is also done under different circumstances. Some important circumstances are as follows :

(a) Fixing Selling Price

Illustration 22. P/V ratio is 60% and the marginal cost of the product is Rs. 50. What will be the selling price ?

Solution :

$$\text{Selling Price} = \frac{\text{Variable Cost}}{(100 - \text{P/V Ratio})} = \frac{\text{Rs.}50}{(100 - 60\%)} = \frac{50 \times 100}{40} = \textbf{Rs.125.00}$$

$$\text{Verification : P/V Ratio} = \frac{\text{Contribution}}{\text{Sales}} \times 100 = \frac{\text{S}-\text{V}}{\text{S}} \times 100$$

$$= \frac{\text{Rs.}125 - 50}{125} \times 100 = \frac{75}{125} \times 100 = \textbf{60\%}$$

(b) Reducing Selling Price

Illustration 23. From the following data, calculate :

1. P/V Ratio
2. Profit when sales are Rs. 20,000
3. New break even point if selling price is reduced by 20%

Fixed Expenses	Rs. 4,000
Break-Even Point	Rs. 10,000

(*B.Com., (Hons.), Delhi*)

Solution :

(*i*) $\text{Break-Even Sales} = \dfrac{\text{Fixed Expenses}}{\text{P/V Ratio}}$

$$\text{P/V Ratio} = \frac{\text{Fixed Expenses}}{\text{Break-Even Sales}} = \frac{4,000}{10,000} \times 100 = 40\%$$

(*ii*) When sales are Rs. 20,000, the profit is
= Sales × P/V Ratio – Fixed Expenses
= 20,000 × 40% – 4,000 = Rs. 8,000 – Rs. 4,000 = Rs. 4,000

(*iii*) If selling price is reduced by 20%, the new break-even point would be Rs. 80 (say Rs. 100 – Rs. 20).
Variable Cost per unit = 100 – 40% = Rs. 60

$$\text{New P/V Ratio} = \frac{80-60}{80} \times 100 = 25\%$$

$$\therefore \text{ New Break-Even Point} = \frac{4,000 \times 100}{25} = \textbf{Rs. 16,000.}$$

Illustration 24. A company has a P/V ratio of 40%. By what percentage must sales be increased to offset :

(*a*) 10% reduction in selling price
(*b*) 20% reduction in selling price (*B.Com., Hons. Delhi*)

Solution :

If sales are 100 units @ Re. 1 per unit then :

Sales	Rs. 100
Contribution	Rs. 40
Variable Cost	Rs. 60

(*a*) If selling price is reduced by 10%

Sales	Rs. 90
Contribution	Rs. 30
Variable Cost	Rs. 60

Volume of sales to maintain the same contribution will be equal to :

$$= \frac{\text{Contribution}}{\text{New Contribution}} \times \text{New Sales} = \frac{40}{30} \times 90 = \textbf{Rs. 120}$$

Thus if the selling price is reduced by 10%, the volume of sales will have to be increased by 20%.

(*b*) If selling price is reduced by 20%

New Sales	Rs. 80
New Contribution	Rs. 20
Variable Cost	Rs. 60

In order to maintain the same contribution, the volume of sales should be :

$$\frac{40}{20} \times 80 = \textbf{Rs. 160}$$

Thus if selling price is reduced by 20%, the sales will have to be increased by 60%.

Illustration 25. A company produces and sells 100 units of A per month at Rs. 20. Marginal cost per unit is Rs. 12.00 and fixed costs are Rs. 300 per month. It is proposed to reduce the selling price by 20%. Find the additional sales required to earn the same profit as before.

(*B. Com., Osmania*)

Solution :

Present Profit :

	Rs.
Sale Price of 100 units @ Rs. 20	2,000
Less : Marginal Cost of 100 units 100 × Rs. 12	1,200
Contribution	800
Less : Fixed Cost	300
Net Profit	500

At reduced price, to earn the same amount of profit, the sales required is :

$$= \frac{\text{Fixed Cost} + \text{Desired Profit}}{\text{Contribution}} = \frac{300 + 500}{16 - 12} = 200 \text{ units}$$

100 units (sold at present)

Additional units = **100**

Check :

Sales = 200 × Rs. 16	= 3,200
Less : Variable : (200 × 12)	= 2,400
Contribution	800
Less : Fixed Cost	300
Net Profit	500

(*c*) **Selling at or Below Marginal Cost.** When we sell a commodity at marginal cost, only variable cost is recovered. Generally, the price of a product is fixed to cover variable cost as well as fixed cost, in addition to a desired profit. Fixing the selling price below the marginal cost, invites loss of some of variable cost. The products may be sold below the marginal cost in the following cases, when :

1. A competitor is to be driven out of market.
2. To popularise the product.
3. Labour engaged cannot be retrenched.
4. The goods are of perishable nature.
5. To keep the plant in running condition.
6. There is a cut throat competition.
7. To use the materials, which is about to perish.
8. The product is used as a loss leader for the sale of another product.
9. Not to close down the firm.
10. Fear of market which may go out of hand.
11. To prevent the loss of future orders.
12. To capture the foreign market.

3. Closure of a Department or Discontinuing a Product. Marginal costing technique shows the contribution of each product to fixed costs and profit. If a department or a product contributes the least amount, then the department can be closed or its production can be discontinued. It means the product which gives a higher amount of contribution may be chosen and the rest should be discontinued.

Illustration 26. The records of Ram Ltd., which has three departments give the following figures :

	Department A	*Department B*	*Department C*	*Total*
	Rs.	*Rs.*	*Rs.*	*Rs.*
Sales	12,000	18,000	20,000	50,000
Marginal Cost	13,000	6,000	15,000	34,000

Fixed Cost	1,000	4,000	10,000	15,000
Total Cost :	14,000	10,000	25,000	49,000
Profit/Loss	– 2,000	+ 8,000	– 5,000	+ 1,000

The management wants to discontinue product C immediately as it gives the maximum loss. How would you advise the management ?

Solution :

Marginal cost statement

	A	*B*	*C*	*Total*
	Rs.	Rs.	Rs.	Rs.
Sales	12,000	18,000	20,000	50,000
Less : Marginal Cost	13,000	6,000	15,000	34,000
Contribution	– 1,000	12,000	5,000	16,000
Fixed Cost				15,000
Profit				1,000

Here department A gives negative contribution, and as such it can be given up. Department C gives a contribution of Rs. 5,000. If department C is closed, then it may lead to further loss. Therefore, C will be continued.

4. Selection of a Profitable Product Mix. In a multiproduct concern, a problem is faced by the management as to which product mix or sales mix will give the maximum profit. The product mix which gives the maximum profit must be selected. Product mix is the ratio in which various products are produced and sold. The marginal costing technique helps the management in taking decisions regarding changing the ratio of product mix which gives maximum contribution or in dropping unprofitable product line. The product which has comparatively less contribution, may be reduced or discontinued.

Illustration 27. Present the following information to show to the management : (*a*) the marginal product cost and the contribution per unit; (*b*) the total contribution and profits resulting from each of the following sales mixtures :

	Product	*Per unit*
Direct Materials	A	Rs. 10
	B	Rs. 9
Direct Wages	A	Rs. 3
	B	Rs. 2

Fixed Expenses Rs. 800.

Variable Expenses are allocated to products as 100% of direct wages.

Sales Price A Rs. 20
B Rs. 15

Sales mixtures :

(*i*) 1,000 units of product A and 2,000 units of B

(*ii*) 1,500 units of product A and 1,500 units of B

(*iii*) 2,000 units of product A and 1,000 units of B. (*M.Com. Madurai*)

Solution :

(*a*) **Marginal Cost Statement**

	A	*B*
	Rs.	*Rs.*
Direct Materials	10	9
Direct Wages	3	2
Variable Overheads (100%)	3	2

Marginal Cost	16	13
Sales Price	20	15
Contribution	4	2

(*b*) **Product mix choice**

	(*i*) *Rs.*	(*ii*) *Rs.*	(*iii*) *Rs.*
Total sales	(1000 × 20 + (2000 × 15) = 50,000	1500 × 20 + 1500 × 15) = 52,500	(2000 × 20 + 1000 × 15) = 55,000
Less : Marginal Cost	(1,000 × 16 + 2,000 × 13) = 42,000	(1,500 × 16 + 1,500 × 13) = 43,500	(2,000 × 16 + 1,000 × 13) = 45,000
Contribution	8,000	9,000	10,000
Less : Fixed Costs	800	800	800
Profit	7,200	8,200	9,200

Therefore sales mixture (*iii*) will give the highest profit ; and as such, mixture (*iii*) can be adopted.

5. **Profit Planning.** Profit planning is a plan for future operation or planning budget to attain the given objective or to attain the maximum profit. The volume of sale required to maintain a desired profit can be known from the formula :

$$\text{Desired Profit} = \frac{\text{F.C.} + \text{Desired profit}}{\text{P/V Ratio}}$$

$$\text{Or} \quad = \frac{\text{Required Contribution}}{\text{New Contribution in units}}$$

Illustration 28. The Delhi Mixy Co, manufactured and sold 1,000 mixies last year at a price of Rs. 800 each. The cost structure of a mixy is as follows :

	Rs.
Materials	200
Labour	100
Variable Cost	50
Marginal Cost	350
Factory Overhead (fixed)	200
Total Cost	550
Profit	250
Sale Price	800

Due to heavy competition, price has to be reduced to Rs. 750 for the coming year. Assuming no change in costs, state the number of mixies that would have to be sold at the new price to ensure the same amount of total profits as that of the last year. (*B.Com. MS*)

Solution :

Profit for 1000 mixies = 1,000 × 250 = Rs. 2,50,000

Contribution at the price of Rs. 750 = 750 – 350 = Rs. 400

$$\text{P/V Ratio} = \frac{\text{Contribution per unit}}{\text{Sales price per unit}} = \frac{400}{750}$$

Sales required at Rs. 750 per mixy to earn a profit of Rs. 2,50,000 =

$$\frac{\text{Fixed Cost + Profit}}{\text{P/V Ratio}} = \frac{2,00,000 + 2,50,000}{400/750} = \text{Rs. } 8,43,750$$

$$\text{Sales in units} = \frac{8,43,750}{750} = 1,125 \text{ mixies}$$

or $$\frac{\text{F.C. + Profit}}{\text{Contribution per unit}} = \frac{20,000 + 2,50,000}{400} = \mathbf{1,125, mixies}$$

Verification :

Sales = 1,125 × Rs. 750 =	Rs. 8,43,750
Less : Variable Cost = 1,125 0+ 350	Rs. 3,93,750
	Rs. 4,50,000
Less : Fixed Cost	Rs. 2,00,000
Profit :	Rs. 2,50,000

6. **Decision to make or buy.** A firm may make some products, parts or tools or sometimes it may buy the same thing from outside. The management must decide which is more profitable to the firm. If the marginal cost of the product is lower than the price of buying from outside, then the firm can make the product.

Illustration 29. A radio manufacturing company finds that while it costs Rs. 6.25 to make each component X 2730, the same is available in the market at Rs. 4.85 each, with an assurance of continued supply. The breakdown of cost is :

Materials	Rs. 2.75 each
Labour	Rs. 1.75 each
Other Variables	Rs. 0.50 each
Depreciation and other Dixed Cost	Rs. 1.25 each
	6.25

Should you make or buy ? (*I.C.W.A*)

Solution :

Variable cost of manufacturing is Rs. 5; (Rs. 6.25 – 1.25) but the market price is Rs. 4.85. If the fixed cost of Rs. 1.25 is also added, it is not profitable to make the component. Because there is a profit of Rs. 0.15 even in variable cost, it is profitable to procure from outside.

7. Decision to accept a bulk order or foreign market order. Large scale purchasers may demand products at less than the market price. A decision has to be taken now whether to accept the order or to reject it. By reducing the normal price, the volume of output and the sales can be increased. If the price is below the total cost, rejection of the order is aimed at. In marginal costing, the offer may be accepted, if the quoted price is above marginal cost, because of the reason that existing business contribution can recover the fixed costs and the margin of profits. In such cases, the contribution made by foreign market or bulk orders will be an addition to the profit. But the price should not be less than the marginal cost. However, it should not affect the normal market price.

Illustration 30. Due to industrial depression, a plant is running at present, at 50% of its capacity. The following details are available.

	Cost of production per unit
Direct Materials	Rs. 2
Direct Labour	Rs. 1
Variable Overhead	Rs. 3
Fixed Overhead	Rs. 2

	Rs. 8
Production per month	20,000 units
Total cost of production	Rs. 1,60,000
Sales Price	Rs. 1,40,000
Loss :	Rs. 20,000

An exporter offers to buy 5,000 units per month at the rate of Rs. 6.50 per unit and the company hesitates to accept the offer for fear of increasing its already operating losses.

Advise whether the company should accept or decline this offer. (*B.Com., Rajasthan*)

Solution :

	Existing (20,000 units) *Rs.*	*Offer (5,000 units)* *Rs.*	*Total* *Rs.,*
Sales	1,40,000	32,500	1,72,500
Variable cost :			
Materials	40,000	10,000	50,000
Labour	20,000	5,000	25,000
Variable Overhead	60,000	15,000	75,000
Total Variable Overhead	1,20,000	30,000,	1,50,000
Contribution	20,000	2,500	22,500
Less : Fixed Cost	40,000	—	40,000
Profit/Loss	– 20,000	2,500	– 17,500

The firm must accept the offer, because the amount of loss stands reduced from Rs. 20,000 to Rs. 17,500.

8. Introduction of a New Product. A producing firm may add additional products with the available facility. The new product is sold in the market at a reasonable price, in order to sell it in large quantities. It may become popular. If favourable, the sales can be increased ; thus the total cost comes down and contributes some amount towards fixed costs and profits.

Illustration 31. A decision is to be taken by the management of a company relating to the possible introduction of a new product. There can be three models of this product, aimed at different sections of the consumer market. The relevant figures are as follows :

	Model I *Rs.*	*Model II* *Rs.*	*Model III* *Rs.*
Variable Cost (per unit)			
Materials	1.54	1.22	0.86
Labour	1.06	0.95	0.58
Variable Overheads	0.40	0.33	0.31
	3.00	2.50	1.75
Selling price (per unit)	4.25	3.50	2.50
Expected Sales Volume per month	800 units	2,000 units	4,000 units
Capital Expenditure before production can commence (financed by bank at 5% p.a.)	*Rs.* 800	*Rs.* 3,000	*Rs.* 4,000
Fixed Overheads per month attributable to new model including depreciation on capital expenditure	280	850	1,100

You are required to prepare a statement of relative profitability and determine for each model the percentage of net profit to selling price at the expected sales volume. Also state, keeping into consideration all factors, the production of which model should be commenced by the company ? (*M.Com. Agra*)

Solution :

PROFITABILITY STATEMENT

	Model I (800 units) Rs.		*Model II (2,000 units)* Rs.		*Model III (4,000 units)* Rs.	
	Per unit	*Total*	*Per unit*	*Total*	*Per unit*	*Total*
Sales	4.25	3,400	3.50	7,000	2.50	10,000
Less : Variable Cost	3.00	2,400	2.50	5,000	1.75	7,000
Contribution	1.25	1,000	1.00	2,000	0.75	3,000
Less : Fixed Overheads excluding interest	0.35	280	0.425	850	0.275	1,100
Net Profit	0.90	720	0.575	1,150	0.480	1,900
% of net profit on Selling price		21.2%		6.4%		19%
Contribution %		29.4%		28.6%		30%

The management is advised to commence production of Model III, as the contribution percentage is the highest and the percentage of net profit to selling price is also satisfactory.

9. **Choice of Technique.** Every management wishes to manufacture the products at the most economical way. For this, the managerial costing is a good guide as to the products at different stages of production, that is to say whether the management has to adopt hand operated system or semi-automatic system or complete automatic system. When operations are done by hand, fixed cost will be lower than the fixed cost incurred by machines and in complete automatic system fixed costs are more than variable cost.

Illustration 32. A firm has to instal a machine for production of a part. Two machines X and Y are being considered. Their particulars are as follows :

	Machine X	*Machine Y*
Cost	Rs. 10,000	Rs. 20,000
Annual capacity	2,000 units	5,000 units
Economic life	10 years	10 years
Salvage value	Nil	Nil
Material per unit	3.00	3.00
Production cost per unit other than depreciation	5.00	4.50
Part of existing overheads per annum	Rs. 1,000	1,000

Interest is at 9% p.a. The part is available in the market @ Rs. 9 per unit and can be sold at a net price of Rs. 8.50. The firm requires 3,000 units. Show which of the machines will be most economical ? (*M. Com Saugar*)

Solution :

COST STATEMENT

	Machine X Rs.	*Machine Y* Rs.
Annual Costs :		
Materials	6,000	15,000
Production costs	10,000	22,500

Depreciation	1,000	2,000
Cost of production	17,000	39,500
Interest on investment at 9%	900	1,800
	17,900	41,300
Add cost of 1,000 units to be purchased @ Rs. 9 to meet out the firm's total requirement.	9,000	—
Less sale value of 2,000 units which will be in surplus and will be sold @ Rs. 8.50	—	17,000
	26,900,	24,300

The above figures show that Machine Y is more economical because the net cost of 3,000 units is lower on Machine Y as compared to Machine X.

10. **Evaluation of Performance.** Marginal costing helps the management in measuring the performance efficiencies of a department or a product line or sales division. The department or the product or division which gives the highest P/V ratio will be the most profitable one or that is having the highest performance efficiency.

Illustration 33. Given fixed cost Rs. 8,000; Profit earned Rs. 2,000; and Break-even sales Rs. 40,000, find the actual sales. *(B.Com., Calicut)*

Solution :

Let the actual sales be x.

$$\text{Break-Even Sales} = \frac{\text{Fixed Cost}}{\text{Contribution}} \times \text{Sales}$$

$$\text{Rs.}40{,}000 = \frac{8{,}000\,x}{8{,}000 + 2{,}000}$$

$$\text{Rs.}40{,}000 = \frac{\text{Rs.}8{,}000x}{\text{Rs.}8{,}000 + \text{Rs.}2{,}000}$$

i.e. $$\text{Rs. } 40{,}000 = \frac{8{,}000\,x}{10{,}000}$$

$$\text{Rs. } 40{,}000 = 0.8\,x$$

$$x = \frac{Rs.\,40{,}000}{0.8} = \textbf{Rs. 50,000}$$

Illustration 34. From the following data, find break-even point.

	Rs.
Selling price per unit	10
Trade discount	5%
Direct material cost per unit	3
Direct labour cost per unit	2
Fixed Overheads	10,000

Variable Overheads 100% on direct labour cost.

If sales are (*a*) 10% and (*b*) 15% above the Break-Even Volume, determine the net profits. *(M.Com. Bombay)*

Solution :

	Rs.
Selling Price	10
Less : Trade discount	0.50
	9.50
Less : V.C. (3 + 2 + 2)	7.00
Contribution	2.50

$$\text{B.E.P} = \frac{F}{C} = \frac{10,000}{2.50} = 4,000 \text{ units}$$

(*a*) B.E.P. = 4,000
Add : 10% = 400
4,400 units

	Rs.
Contribution from 4,400 units @ Rs. 2.50	11,000
Less : Fixed Cost	10,000
Profit	1,000

(*b*) B.E. units = 4,000
Add : 15% 600
4,600

	Rs.
Contribution from 4,600 units @ Rs. 2.50	11,500
Less : Fixed Cost	10,000
Profit	1,500

11. Decision Making. Price must not be less than total cost under normal conditions. Marginal costing acts as a price fixer and a high margin will contribute to the fixed cost and profit. But this principle cannot be followed at all times. Prices should be equal to marginal cost plus a reasonable amount, which depends upon demand and supply, competition, policy of pricing etc. If the price is equal to marginal cost, then there is a loss equal to fixed costs. Sometimes, the businessman has to face loss when, (*a*) there is cut-throat competition, (*b*) there is the fear of future market, (*c*) the goods are of perishable nature, (*d*) the employees cannot be removed, (*e*) a new product is introduced in the market, (*f*) competitors cannot be driven out etc.

Illustration 35. From the following data, calculate the break-even point :

	Rs.
Selling Price per unit	20
Direct Material Cost per unit	8
Direct labour cost per unit	2
Direct expenses per unit	2
Overheads per unit	3
Fixed Overheads (total)	20,000

If sales are 20%, above the break-even point, determine the net profit.

(*M.Com., Calcutta*)

Solution :

$$\text{B.E.P.} = \frac{P}{S - V}$$

$$= \frac{20,000}{20 - 15} = \frac{20,000}{5} = 4,000 \text{ units.}$$

$$Add : 20\% \quad \frac{800}{4,800 \text{ units}}$$

Therefore, total contribution 4,800 × Rs.5 = 24,000

less : fixed cost	20,000
Profit	Rs. 4,000

Verification

Sales (4,800 units × Rs. 20)	96,000
Less : V.C. (4,800 Units × Rs. 15)	72,000
Contribution	Rs. 24,000
Less : Fixed Cost	Rs. 20,000
Profit	Rs. 4,000

12. Maintaining a desired level of profit. An industry has to cut prices of its products from time to time on account of competition, government regulations and other compelling reasons. The contribution per unit on account of such cutting is reduced while the industry is interested in maintaining a minimum level of its profits. Marginal costing technique can ascertain how many units have to be sold to maintain the same level of profits. Charles points out "when desired profits are agreed upon, their attainability may be quickly appraised by computing the number of units that must be sold to secure the wanted profits. The computation is easily made by dividing the fixed costs plus desired profits by the contribution margin per unit".

Sales required to earn a desired Profit,

$$= \frac{\text{Fixed Cost} + \text{Profit}}{\text{P/V Ratio}} \quad \text{(OR)} \quad S = \frac{F + P}{\text{P/V Ratio}}$$

$$= \frac{\text{Contribution}}{\text{P/V Ratio}} \quad \text{(OR} \quad S = \frac{C}{\text{P/V Ratio}}$$

$$\text{Sales in Units} = \frac{\text{Fixed Cost} + \text{Profit}}{\text{Contribution per unit}} \quad \text{(OR)} \quad S(\text{units}) = \frac{F + P}{C \text{ per unit}}$$

Illustration 36. Sales 10,000 units @ R. 25 per unit

Variable Cost Rs. 15 per unit

Fixed Costs Rs. 1,00,000

Find out the sales for earning a profit of Rs. 50,000

Solution :

Sales to earn a profit of Rs. 50,000

$$= \frac{(\text{Fixed Cost} + \text{Profit}) \text{ Sales}}{\text{Sales} - \text{Variable Cost}}$$

$$= \frac{(\text{Rs.}1,00,000 + \text{Rs.}50,000) \times \text{Rs.}2,50,000}{2,50,000 - 1,50,000}$$

$$= \frac{\text{Rs.}1,50,000 \times \text{Rs.}2,50,000}{\text{Rs.}1,00,000} = \textbf{Rs.3,75,000.}$$

Illustration 37. You are given the following data for the year 2010 of the company.

Variable Cost	Rs. 6,00,000
Fixed Cost	Rs. 3,00,000
Net Profit	Rs. 1,00,000
Sales	Rs. 10,00,000

Find (*a*) P/V ratio (*b*) B.E.P. (*c*) profit when sales amounted to Rs. 12,00,000 (*d*) Sales required to earn a profit of Rs. 2,00,000. (*B.Com. Madurai*)

Solution :

Marginal Cost Statement

Sales	Rs. 10,00,000
Less : Variable Cost	Rs. 6,00,000
Contribution	Rs. 4,00,000
Less : Fixed Cost	Rs. 3,00,000
Profit	Rs. 1,00,000

(*a*) Profit-Volume Ratio $= \dfrac{\text{Marginal Contribution} \times 100}{\text{Sales}}$

$$\frac{4,00,000}{10,00,000} \times 100 = 40\%$$

(*b*) Break-Even Point $= \dfrac{\text{Fixed Cost}}{\text{P/V Ratio}} = \dfrac{3,00,000 \times 100}{40}$

= **Rs. 7,50,000**

(*c*) Sales Rs. 12,00,000
P/V Ratio 40%
40% of 12,00,000 = **Rs. 4,80,000**
Contribution = F + P
4,80,000 = 3,00,000 + Profit
Profit = 4,80,000 – 3,00,000 = **Rs. 1,80,000**

(*d*) Sales required to earn a profit of Rs. 2,00,000

$$\frac{\text{Fixed Cost + Desired Profit}}{\text{P/V Ratio}} = \frac{3,00,000 + 2,00,000}{40\%}$$

$$= \frac{5,00,000 \times 100}{40}$$

= **Rs. 12,50,000**

Illustration 38. The Reliable Battery Co. furnishes you the following information :

	First half	*Second half*
Sale	Rs. 8,10,000	Rs. 10,28,000
Profit earned	21,800	64,800

From the above you are required to compute the following assuming that the fixed cost remains the same in both the periods.

(1) P/V Ratio
(2) Fixed Cost
(3) The amount of profit or loss where sales are Rs. 6,48,000.
(4) The amount of sales required to earn a profit of Rs. 1,08,000. (*C.A. Inter*)

Solution :

	Sales	*Profit*
(1) Second half	Rs. 10,26,000	Rs. 64,800
First half	8,10,000	21,600
Change	2,16,000	43,200

$$\text{P/V Ratio} = \frac{\text{Change in Contribution}}{\text{Change in Sales}} = \frac{43,200}{2,16,000} \times 100 = \mathbf{20\%}$$

(2) Fixed Cost :

Contribution = Fixed Cost + Profit

Fixed Cost = Contribution – Profit

= 20% of 8,10,000 – 21,600 = 1,40,400

(OR) = 20% of 10,26,000 – 64,800 = 140,400

(3)Profit/Loss at sales of Rs. 6,48,000 :

Contribution, = 20% of 6,48,000 =	1,29,600
Less : Fixed Cost =	1,40,400
Loss	10,800

(4)Sales required to earn a profit of Rs. 1,08,000 :

$$\text{Sales} = \frac{\text{Fixed Cost} + \text{Desired Profit}}{\text{P/V Ratio}}$$

$$= \frac{1,40,400 + 1,08,000}{20\%}$$

$$= \frac{1,40,400 + 1,08,000 \times 100}{20}$$

= Rs. 12,42,000

Illustration 39. The sales turnover and profit during the two periods were as follows :

Period No. 1, Sales Rs. 20,00,000, Profit 2,00,000

Period No. 2, Sales Rs. 30,00,000, Profit Rs. 4,00,000

Calculate : P/V Ratio and the sales required to earn a profit of Rs. 5,00,000.

(B.Com. Andhra, Osmania)

Solution :

	Period No.1	*Period No. 2*	*Increase*
Sales	Rs. 20,00,000	Rs. 30,00,000	Rs. 10,00,000
Profit	Rs. 2,00,000	Rs 4,00,000	Rs. 2,00,000

Contribution on increased sales of Rs. 10,00,000 is Rs. 2,00,000

$$\text{P/V Ratio} = \frac{\text{Contribution}}{\text{Sales Value}} = \frac{2}{10} \times 100 = \mathbf{20\%}$$

Contribution of period No. 1 = 20% of 20 lakhs = 4,00,000

Profit of period No. 1 = Rs. 2,00,000

Fixed cost = Rs. 2,00,000

$$\text{Required Sales Values} = \frac{\text{Fixed Cost} + \text{Required Profit}}{\text{P/V Ratio}}$$

$$= \frac{\text{Rs. } 2,00,000 + 5,00,000}{20\%}$$

= Rs. 35,00,000

Illustration 40. From the following find out :

(*i*) Profit-Volume Ratio

(*ii*) Break-Even Point

(*iii*) Sales for 40% P/V Ratio

(*iv*) Margin of safety from the sales Rs. 3,00,000

(*v*) Net profit from the sales of Rs. 3,00,000

(*vi*) Required sales for the net profit of Rs. 70,000

(*vii*) Required sales for the net profit of Rs. 70,000 after tax, the corporate income tax rate being 60%

(*viii*) Additional sales required to cover an increase of Rs. 3,000 p.a. in the sales manager's salary.

Position of the Company for the year 2010

	Rs.
Sales	2,00,000
Variable Overheads	1,50,000
Contribution	50,000
Fixed Overheads	15,000
Net Profit	35,000

Solution :

(*i*) $\text{P/V Ratio}: \frac{S-V}{S} \times 100 = \frac{2,00,000 - 1,50,000}{2,00,000} \times 100 = \mathbf{25\%}$

(*ii*) $\text{Break-Even Point}: \frac{F}{\text{P/V Ratio}} = \frac{15,000}{25\%} = \mathbf{Rs.\ 60,000}$

(*iii*) $\text{Sales} = \frac{\text{Total Contribution}}{\text{New P/V Ratio}} = \frac{50,000}{40\%} = \mathbf{Rs.\ 1,25,000}$

(*iv*) $\text{Margin of Safety}: \frac{\text{Profit}}{\text{P/V Ratio}} = \frac{60,000}{25\%} = \mathbf{Rs.\ 2,40,000}$

(OR) Sales – B.E. Sales = 3,00,000 – 60,000 = **Rs. 2,40,000**

(*v*) Net profit from sales of Rs. 3,00,000 = S (P/V Ratio) – F

= 3,00,000 × (25%) – 15,000 = **Rs. 60,000**

(OR) = P/V Ratio × Margin Safety

= 25% × 2,40,000 = Rs. 60,000

(*vi*) Required sales for the net profit of Rs. 70,000 = $\frac{\text{F + Profit}}{\text{P/V Ratio}}$

$$= \frac{15,000 + 70,000}{25\%} = \mathbf{RS.\ 3,40,000}$$

(*vii*) $$\text{Sales} = \frac{F + \{\text{N.P. } (1/1 - t)\}}{\text{P/V Ratio}}$$

$$= \frac{15,000 + \left\{70,000\left(\frac{1}{1-0.6}\right)\right\}}{25\%} = \mathbf{Rs.\ 7,60,000}$$

(*viii*) Additional sales required to cover an increase of Rs. 3,000

$$S = \frac{\text{Increased Amount}}{\text{P/V Ratio}} = \frac{3{,}000}{25\%} = \textbf{Rs. 12,000}$$

Illustration 41. A company budgets for a production of 1,50,000 units. The variable cost per unit is Rs. 14 and fixed cost is Rs. 2 per unit. The company fixes its selling price to fetch a profit of 15% of cost.

(*a*) What is break-even point ?

(*b*) What is profit-volume ratio ?

(*c*) If it reduces its selling price by 5%, how does the revised selling price affect the break-even and P/V Ratio ?

(*d*) If a profit increase of 10% is desired more than the budget, what should be the sale at the reduced price ? (*C.A. Inter*)

Solution :

Variable Cost	Rs. 14
Fixed Cost	Rs. 2
	16

Selling Price = 16 + 15% of Rs. 16 = 16 + 2.40 = **Rs. 18.40**

Contribution = Sales – Variable Cost = 18.40 – 14 = **Rs. 4.40**

(*a*) $$\text{BEP} = \frac{F}{C} = \frac{3{,}00{,}000}{4.40} = \textbf{68,182 units}$$

(*b*) $$\text{P/V Ratio} = \frac{\text{Contribution}}{\text{Sales}} \times 100 = \frac{4.40}{18.40} \times 100 = 23.91\%$$

(*c*) Revised selling price:

Rs. 18.40 – 5% = 18.40 – 0.92 = **Rs. 17.48**

Contribution = Rs. 17.48 – Rs. 14 = Rs. 3.48

$$\text{BEP} = \frac{F}{C} = \text{Rs.}\ \frac{3{,}00{,}000}{3.48} = \textbf{86,207 units}$$

$$\text{P/V Ratio} = \frac{C}{S} \times 100 = \frac{3.48}{17.48} \times 100 = 19.9\%$$

(*d*) Budgeted Profit = 1,50,000 units @ Rs. 2.40 =Rs. 3,60,000

Add 10%	36,000
Desired Profit	3,96,000

$$\text{Sales required} = \frac{\text{Fixed Cost + Profit}}{\text{Contribution at Reduced price}}$$

$$= \frac{\text{Rs. } 3{,}00{,}000 + \text{Rs. } 3{,}96{,}000}{\text{Rs. } 3.48}$$

= **2,00,000 units**

(OR) = 2,00,000 × Rs. 17.48 = **Rs. 34,96,000**

13. Level of activity planning. Where different levels of production and/or selling activities are being considered and the management has to decide the optimum level of activity, the marginal costing technique helps the management. What level of activity is optimum for a business to adopt, is an important problem faced by businesses.

Illustration 42. A factory engaged in manufacturing plastic buckets is working at 40% capacity and produces 10,000 buckets per annum.

The present cost break up for one bucket is as under :

Materials	Rs. 10
Labour cost	Rs. 3
Overheads	Rs. 5 (60% fixed)

The selling price is Rs. 20 per bucket.

If it is decided to work the factory at 50% capacity, the selling price falls by 3%. At 90% capacity the selling price falls by 5% accompanied by a similar fall in the prices of material.

You are required to calculate the profit at 50% and 90% capacities and also the break-even points for the same capacity productions. (*C.A. Inter*)

Solution :

Statement showing profit and break-even point at different capacity levels

Capacity level Production (units)	50% 12,500		90% 22,500	
	Per unit Rs.	*Total Rs.*	*Per unit Rs.*	*Total Rs.*
(*a*) Sales	19.40	2,42,500	19.00	4,27,500
Variable Cost Material	10.00	1,25,000	9.50	2,13,750
Wages	3.00	37,500	3.00	67,500
Variable Overhead	2.00	25,000	2.00	45,000
(*b*) Total Variable Cost	15.00	1,87,500	14.50	3,26,250
(c) Contribution (S – V) or (a – b)	4.40	55,000	4.50	1,01,250
Less : Fixed Cost		30,000		30,000
Net Profit		25,000		71,250

Break-even point at 50%, 90%

$$\text{Units} = \frac{\text{Fixed Cost}}{\text{Contribution per unit}}$$

$$= \frac{30,000}{4.40} = 6818; \qquad \frac{30,000}{4.50} = 6667$$

Sales value = **Rs. 1,32,269** = **1,26,673**

14. Alternative methods of production. Marginal costing techniques are also used in comparing the alternative methods of manufacture *i.e.* machine work or hand work, whether one machine is to be employed instead of another etc. Many a time, management has to choose a course of action from among so many alternatives, the changes in the marginal contribution under each of the proposed methods are worked out and the method which gives the greatest contribution is obviously adopted keeping in view the limiting factor if any.

Illustration 43. The variable cost of the power drill manufactured by Home Tools Limited is Rs. 4 and selling price Rs. 10. The Company expects its net profit for the year just ending to be Rs. 2,75,000 after charging fixed costs amounting to Rs. 85,000.

The company's production capacity is not fully utilised and market research suggests three alternative strategies for the forthcoming year, *viz.*

Strategy	*Reduce selling price by*	*Sales volume expected to increase by*
1	5%	10%
2	7%	20%
3	10%	25%

(*a*) Assuming the same cost structure as the current year, evaluate the alternative strategies available to the company and state which is the most profitable one. (*CA*)

Solution :

	Rs.
Selling Price Per Unit	10
Less :Variable Cost	4
Contribution per unit	6
Net Profit	Rs. 2,75,000
Add : Fixed Cost	85,000
Total Contribution:	3,60,000

Units to be sold = Rs. 3,60,000 ÷ Rs. 6 = 60,000 units

(*a*) Alternative strategies

Strategy *Rs.*	*Selling price per unit* *Rs.*	*Contribution per unit* *Rs.*	*Estimated Sales units* *Rs.*	*Total Contribution* *Rs.*
1	9.50	5.50	66,000	3,63,000
2	9.30	5.30	72,000	3,81,600
3	9.00	5.00	75,000	3,75,000

Therefore, Strategy 2 is the most profitable.

Illustration 44. Product A can be produced either by Machine X or Machine Y. Machine X can produce 200 units of A per hour and Machine Y 300 units per hour. Total Machine hours available during the year are 2,500. Taking into account the following data determine the profitable method of manufacture :

	Per unit of Product A	
	Machine X *Rs.*	*Machine Y* *Rs.*
Marginal Cost	10	12
Selling Price	18	18
Fixed Cost	4	4

(*B.Com. Madurai*)

Solution :

	Machine X *Rs.*	*Machine Y* *Rs.*
Selling Price per unit	18	18
Less : Marginal Cost	10	12
Contribution per unit	8	6
Output per hour	200	300
Contribution per hour	1,600	1,800
Machine hour per year	2,500	2,500
Annual Contribution	**Rs. 40,00,000**	**Rs. 45,00,000**

Therefore, production by Machine Y is profitable.

15. Introduction of new product or product line. The technique to assess the profitability of line extension products is the incremental contribution estimates. The same technique of contribution analysis would be followed in assessing the profitability of a new product line. Sales forecast would result from a market survey and market research. This is clear from the following example.

Illustration 45. A ball pen manufacturer has developed a new ball pen with unique features. His design development executive has suggested three possible retail prices *viz.* Rs. 15 for super star; Rs. 10 for deluxe and Rs. 7.50 for economy model. His marketing manager says that the wholesalers and retailers have to be given at least 30% discount.

The estimated fixed cost would be around Rs. 70,000 and variable cost per unit would be Rs. 3.50.

(*a*) Calculate break-even point for each model of ball pen.

(*b*) How much should the manufacturer sell in order to make a profit of Rs. 21,000 ? Work out for each model of ball pen.

Solution :

STATEMENT OF CONTRIBUTION PER UNIT

Particulars	*Super Star Rs.*	*Deluxe Rs.*	*Economy Model Rs.*
Selling Price per unit	15.00	10.00	7.50
Less : Discount at 30%	4.50	3.00	2.25
Net Sales per unit	10.50	7.00	5.25
Variable Cost per unit	3.50	3.50	3.50
Contribution per unit	7.00	3.50	1.75

(*a*) Break-even point (in units) $= \dfrac{\text{Fixed Cost}}{\text{Contribution per unit}}$

$$= \frac{70{,}000}{7} \quad \frac{70{,}000}{3.50} \quad \frac{70{,}000}{1.75}$$

= **10,000 units** **20,000 units** **40,000 units**

(*b*) Sales (in units) $= \dfrac{\text{Fixed Cost + Profit}}{\text{Contribution per unit}}$

$$= \frac{70{,}000 + 21{,}000}{7} \quad \frac{91{,}000}{3.50} \quad \frac{91{,}000}{1{,}75}$$

= **13,000 units** **26,000 units** **52,000 units**

Illustration 46.

Discuss the influence of Fixed Cost, Variable Cost, Selling price and sales volume on P/V Ratio, B.E.P. and Profit. (*CS*)

Solution :

The effect of changes are shown below :

	Effect on		
Change	P/V Ratio	B.E.P.	Profit
A. Increase in Fixed Cost	No effect	Higher	Lower
B. Decrease in Fixed Cost	No effect	Lower	Higher
C. Increase in Variable Cost	Decrease	Higher	Lower
D. Decrease in Variable Cost	Improve	Lower	Higher
E. Increase in Selling Price	Improve	Lower	Higher
F. Decrease in Selling Price	Decrease	Higher	Lower
G. Increase in Sales Volume	No effect	No effect	Higher
H. Decrease in Sales Volume	No effect	No effect	Lower

Illustration 47.

The Asian Industries specialise in the manufacture of small capacity motors. The cost structure of a motor is under :

Material	Rs. 50
Labour	Rs. 80
Variable Overheads	75% of Labour cost

Fixed Overheads of the company amount to Rs. 2.40 lakhs per year.

Sale price of the motor is Rs. 230 each.

(*a*) Determine the number of motors that have to be manufactured and sold in a year in order to break-even.

(*b*) How many motors have to be made and sold to make a profit of Rs. 1 lakh per year?

(*c*) If the sale price is reduced by Rs. 15, how many motors have to be sold to break-even.

(*ICWA*)

Solution :

Calculation of Contribution

(*a*) Sale Price per unit (motor)		Rs. 230
Less : Marginal Cost per motor :		
Material	Rs. 50	
Labour	Rs. 80	
Variable Overhead (75% of Rs. 80)	Rs. 60	Rs. 190
Contribution per unit		Rs. 40

Fixed Overhead per year = Rs. 2,40,000

$$\text{B.E.P. (units)} = \frac{\text{Fixed Cost}}{\text{Contribution per unit}}$$

$$= \frac{2,40,000}{40} = \textbf{6,000 motors}$$

(*b*)
$$\text{Sales (units)} = \frac{\text{Fixed Cost + Profit}}{\text{Contribution per unit}}$$

$$= \frac{2,40,000 + 1,00,000}{40}$$

$$= \textbf{8,500 motors}$$

	Rs.
(*c*) Revised Selling Price = 230 – 15	= 215
Marginal Cost	= 190
Revised Contribution per motors	25

$$\text{B.E.P. (units)} = \frac{2,40,000}{25}$$

$$= \textbf{9,600 motors}$$

Illustration 48. A company is considering expansion. Fixed costs amount to Rs. 4,20,000 and are expected to increase by Rs. 1,25,000 when plant expansion is completed. The present plant capacity is 80,000 units a year. Capacity will increase by 50% with the expansion. Variable costs, currently Rs. 6.80 per unit, are expected to go down by Re. 0.40 per unit with the expansion. The current selling price is Rs. 16 per unit and is expected to remain the same under each alternative.

What are the break-even points under either alternative? Which alternative is better and why.

(*B. Com. Mumbai*)

Solution :

1. *Current Break even point*

Present capacity 80,000 units a year

Contribution = Selling price per unit – Variable cost per unit

= Rs. 16 – Rs. 6.8 = Rs. 9.2

$$\text{P/V Ratio} = \frac{\text{Contribution}}{\text{Sales}} \times 100$$

$$= \frac{\text{Rs. } 9.2}{\text{Rs. } 16} \times 100 = 57.5\%$$

$$\text{Break-even point (in units)} = \frac{\text{Fixed Expenses}}{\text{Contribution per unit}}$$

$$= \frac{4{,}20{,}000}{9.2} = 45{,}652.173 \text{ (or) } = \mathbf{45{,}652 \text{ units}}$$

$$\text{Break-even point (in rupees)} = \frac{\text{Fixed expenses}}{\text{P/V ratio}} = \frac{4{,}20{,}000}{57.5\%} = \text{Rs. } \mathbf{7{,}30{,}435}$$

2. **Break-even point after expansion**

Expanded capacity 1,20,000 units

New Variable Cost = Rs. 6.80 – Rs. 0.40 = Rs. 6.40

New Fixed Cost = 4,20,000 + 1,25,000 = Rs. 5,45,000

Contribution = 16 – 6.40 = 9.60

$$\text{P/V Ratio} = \frac{\text{Contribution}}{\text{Sales}} \times 100 = \frac{9.6}{16} \times 100 = 60\%$$

$$\text{New Break-even point (in units)} = \frac{\text{Fixed Expenses}}{\text{Contribution per unit}} = \frac{5{,}45{,}000}{9.6}$$

= 56,770.833 = 56,771 units

$$\text{New Break-even point (in rupees)} = \frac{\text{Fixed Expenses}}{\text{P/V Ratio}} = \frac{5{,}45{,}000}{60\%}$$

= Rs. **9,08,333**

Conclusion

	Current position	*Position* After expansion
Total contribution at	80,000 × 9.2	1,20,000 × 9.6
Installed capacity	Rs. 7,36,000	Rs. 11,52,000
Less : Fixed cost	Rs. 4,20,000	Rs. 5,45,000
Profit at full capacity	Rs. 3,16,000	Rs. 6,07,000

There is improvement in the P/V Ratio after expansion; 57.5% to 60%. The position will be better as the profit can be almost doubled when capacity increases.

Illustration 49. The selling price of a particular product is Rs. 100 and the marginal cost is Rs. 65. During the month of April, 800 units were produced of which 500 were sold. There was no opening stock at the commencement of the month. Fixed costs amounted to Rs. 18,000. Provide a statement using (*a*) Marginal costing (*b*) Absorption costing, showing the closing stock valuation and the profit earned under each principle. (*B. Com Madras, MS*)

Solution :

Income Statement (Absorption costing)

Particulars	*Amount* Rs.	*Amount* Rs.
Sales 500 × 100		50,000
Less : Cost of goods sold :		
Marginal Cost 800 × 65	52,000	
Fixed Cost	18,000	
Cost of production	70,000	
Less : Closing Stock $70{,}000 \times \frac{300}{800}$	26,250	
Cost of Sales		43,750
Profit		6,250

Income Statement (Marginal costing)

Particulars	*Amount* Rs.	*Amount* Rs.
Sales 500 × 100		50,000
Less : Marginal Cost 800 × 65	52,000	
Less : Closing Stock = $52{,}000 \times \frac{300}{800}$	19,500	32,500
Contribution		17,500
Less : Fixed Cost		18,000
Loss		– 500

Closing Stock : It is valued at cost of production (Absorption Costing)

It is valued at marginal cost (Marginal Cost)

Illustration 50. From the particulars given below calculate :

(*a*) Break-even point

(*b*) Profit or Loss when sales are Rs. 12,000 and

(*c*) Sales required to earn a profit of Rs. 5,000

	Sales Rs.	*Profit/Loss* (–) Rs.
Period 1	10,000	– 500
2	14,000	1,500

(*B. Com. Bhopal, Ujjain, Madras*)

Solution.

P/V Ratio $= \frac{\text{Change in profit}}{\text{Change in sales}} \times 100$

Change in profit = 1,500 + 500 = Rs. 2,000

Change in sales = 14,000 – 10,000 = Rs. 4,000

∴ P/V Ratio $= \frac{2{,}000}{4{,}000} \times 100 = 50\%$

Note : Loss in period 1 and profit in period 2 should be added to get change in profit.

Fixed expenses = Contribution – Profit

Contribution = Sales × P/V Ratio

Using sales of period 2 $= 14{,}000 \times \frac{50}{100} =$ Rs. 7,000

Fixed expenses = 7,000 – 1,500 = Rs. 5,500

(*a*) Break even point (in rupees) $= \frac{\text{Fixed expenses}}{\text{P/V Ratio}}$

$= \frac{5{,}500}{50\%} =$ **Rs. 11,000**

(*b*) Profit or Loss when sales are Rs. 12,000

Contribution = Sales × P/V Ratio

$= 12{,}000 \times \frac{50}{100} =$ Rs. 6,000

Profit = Contribution – Fixed Cost

= 6,000 – 5,500 = Rs. 500

(*c*) Sales required to earn profit of Rs. 5,000

Required sales $= \frac{\text{Required Profit + Fixed Expenses}}{\text{P/V Ratio}}$

$= \frac{5{,}000 + 5{,}500}{50\%} =$ **Rs. 21,000**

Illustration 51. The following figures are extracted from the books of Vijay Ltd. for the years 2009 and 2010 whose capacity is 10,000 irons p.a.

	Per unit
Direct Material	3.50
Direct Labour	0.50
Fixed Overhead	2.00
Selling Price	8.00

Production in 2009 was 10,000 units and in 2010 also it was 10,000 units. Sales was 8,000 units in 2009 and 12,000 units in 2010.

Prepare cost statements assuming that the company uses :

(*a*) Absorption costing (*b*) Marginal costing. (*M. Com. Osmania*)

Solution :

(*a*) **Income Statement (under Absorption costing)**

Particulars	*2009*			*2010*		
	Units	*Per unit Rs.*	*Total Rs.*	*Units*	*Per unit Rs.*	*Total Rs.*
Direct Material	10,000	3.5	35,000	10,000	3.5	35,000
Direct Labour	–	0.5	5,000	–	0.5	5,000
Prime Cost	10,000	4.0	40,000	10,000	4.0	40,000
Add : Fixed Overhead		2.0	20,000		2.0	20,000
Cost of production	10,000	6.0	60,000	10,000	6.0	60,000
Add : Opening Stock	–	–	–	2,000	6.0	12,000
	10,000	6	60,000	12,000	6.0	72,000

Less : Closing Stock	2,000	6	12,000	–	–	–
Cost of Sales	8,000	6	48,000	12,000	6.0	72,000
Add : Profit	–	2	16,000	–	2.0	24,000
Sales	8,000	8	64,000	12,000	8.0	96,000

(*b*) **Income Statement (under Marginal costing)**

Particulars	*2009*			*2010*		
	Units	*Per unit Rs.*	*Total Rs.*	*Units*	*Per unit Rs.*	*Total Rs.*
Sales (A)	8,000	8	64,000	12,000	8	96,000
Variable Costs :						
Direct Material	10,000	3.5	35,000	10,000	3.5	35,000
Direct Labour		0.5	5,000		0.5	5,000
	10,000	4.0	40,000	10,000	4.0	40,000
Add : Opening Stock	–	–	–	2,000	4.0	8,000
	10,000	4	40,000	12,000	4	48,000
Less : Closing Stock	2,000	4	8,000	–	–	–
Variable Cost of Sales (B)	8,000	4	32,000	12,000	4	48,000
Contribution (A – B)		4	32,000		4	48,000
Less : Fixed Cost			20,000			20,000
Profit			12,000			28,000

Illustration 52. A company had incurred fixed expenses of Rs. 4,50,000 per half year with sales of Rs. 15,00,000 and earned a profit of Rs. 3,00,000 during the first half year. In the second half, it suffered a loss of Rs. 1,50,000.

Calculate :

(*i*) The profit-volume ratio, break-even point and margin of safety for the first half year.

(*ii*) Expected sales-volume for the second half year assuming that selling price and fixed expenses remained unchanged during the second half year.

(*iii*) The break-even point and margin of safety for the whole year. (*CA Inter*)

Solution :

(*i*) For the first half year :

Contribution = Fixed Cost + Profit

= 4,50,000 + 3,00,000

= Rs. 7,50,000

P/V Ratio $= \frac{\text{Contribution}}{\text{Sales}} \times 100$

$= \frac{7,50,000}{15,00,000} \times 100 = 50\%$

B.E.P. $= \frac{\text{Fixed Cost}}{\text{P/V Ratio}} = \frac{4,50,000}{50\%}$

= Rs. 9,00,000

Margin of Safey = Sales – B.E.P.

= 15,00,000 – 9,00,000

= **Rs. 6,00,000**

(*ii*) For the second half year :

$$\text{Sales} = \frac{\text{Fixed Cost} - \text{Loss}}{\text{P/V Ratio}}$$

$$= \frac{4,50,000 - 1,50,000}{50\%}$$

$$= \frac{3,00,000}{50\%} = \textbf{Rs. 6,00,000}$$

(*iii*) Fixed expenses for the whole year = Rs. 9,00,000

$$\text{B.E.P.} = \frac{\text{Fixed Cost}}{\text{P/V Ratio}} = \frac{9,00,000}{50\%}$$

$$= \textbf{Rs. 18,00,000}$$

	Rs.
Sales : During first half year	15,00,000
During second half year	6,00,000
Sales for the whole year	21,00,000

Margin of Safety = Total Sales – B.E.P.

= 21,00,000 – 18,00,000

= **Rs. 3,00,000**

Illustration 53. Any change in fixed costs, variable costs or selling price has the effect of shifting the B.E.P. although the impact of each such change on the B.E.P. and the profit is different. Illustrate this with the help of the figure given below assuming a 10% increase individually in each of the three elements stated above. Also show how the profit figure is affected if all the elements increase collectively, each by 10%.

Sales (30,000 units)		Rs. 1,20,000
Variable Cost	Rs. 40,000	
Fixed Cost	Rs. 50,000	90,000
		30,000

(*ICWA*)

Solution :

Existing Position :

$$\text{P/V Ratio} = \frac{\text{Contribution}}{\text{Sales}} = \frac{1,20,000 - 40,000}{1,20,000}$$

$$= \frac{2}{3} \quad \text{or} \quad 66\frac{2}{3}\%$$

$$\text{B.E.P. (value)} = \frac{\text{Fixed Cost}}{\text{P/V Ratio}} = \frac{50,000}{2/3} = \text{Rs. } 75,000$$

$$\text{B.E.P. (units)} = \frac{\text{B.E.P. sales}}{\text{Selling price per unit}} = \frac{75,000}{4}$$

$$= \textbf{18,750 units}$$

Effect on B.E.P. under each of the following conditions :

(*a*) Increase in Fixed Cost by 10% : F.C = 50,000 + 10%

$$\text{B.E.P.} = \frac{\text{Fixed Cost}}{\text{P/V Ratio}} = \frac{50,000}{\frac{2}{3}\%} = \textbf{Rs. 82,500}$$

$$\text{B.E.P. (units)} = \frac{\text{Rs. } 82,500}{4} = \textbf{Rs. 20,625 units}$$

(*b*) Increase in Variable Cost by 10% : V.C. = 40,000 + 10%

P/V Ratio $= \dfrac{\text{Contribution}}{\text{Sales}} = \dfrac{1,20,000 - 44,000}{1,20,000}$

$= 63\frac{1}{3}\%$

B.E.P. $= \dfrac{\text{F.C.}}{\text{P/V Ratio}} = \dfrac{50,000}{63\frac{1}{3}\%} = \textbf{Rs. 78,952}$

B.E.P. (units) $= \dfrac{78,952}{4} = \textbf{19,738 units}$

(*c*) Increase in Selling Price by 10% : 1,20,000 + 10%

P/V Ratio $= \dfrac{\text{Contribution}}{\text{Sales}} \times 100$

$= \dfrac{(1,20,000 + 10\% - 40,000)}{1,32,000} \times 100$

$= \dfrac{92,000}{1,32,000} \times 100 = 69.7\%$

B.E.P. $= \dfrac{\text{Fixed Cost}}{\text{P/V Ratio}} = \dfrac{50,000}{69.7\%} = \text{Rs. } 71,736$

B.E.P. (units) $= \dfrac{71,736}{4.40} = \textbf{16,304 units}$

Effect on B.E.P. if all the element increase collectively each by 10%

		Rs.
Sales		1,32,000
	Less : Variable Cost	44,000
	Contribution	88,000
	Less : Fixed Cost	55,000
	Profit	33,000

P/V Ratio $= \dfrac{\text{Contribution}}{\text{Sales}} = \dfrac{88,000}{1,32,000} = 66\frac{2}{3}\%$

B.E.P. $= \dfrac{\text{Fixed Cost}}{\text{P/V Ratio}} = \dfrac{55,000}{66\frac{2}{3}\%} = \textbf{Rs. 82,500}$

B.E.P. (units) $= \dfrac{82,500}{4.40} = \textbf{18,750 units}$

Illustration 54. The P/V Ratio of a firm dealing in precision instruments is 50% and margin of safety is 40%.

You are required to work-out break-even point and the net profit if the sales volume is Rs. 50,00,000. If 25% of variable cost is labour cost, what will be the effect on BEP and profit when labour efficiency decreases by 5%. (*M. Com. Bombay, Delhi, Madras*)

Solution :

1. Calculation of Break-even point

Margin of safety is 40% of sales

$$= 50,00,000 \times \frac{40}{100} = \text{Rs. } 20,00,000$$

Break-even sales = Sales – Margin of safety
= 50,00,000 – 20,00,000
= Rs. 30,00,000

Calculation of fixed cost :

$$\text{Break-even sales} = \frac{\text{Fixed cost}}{\text{P/V Ratio}}$$

Fixed Cost = (Break-Even Sales × P/V Ratio)
= Rs. 30,00,000 × 50% = Rs. 15,00,000

2. Calculation of Profit

Contribution = Sales × P/V Ratio

$$= 50,00,000 \times \frac{50}{100} = \text{Rs. } 25,00,000$$

Net profit = Contribution – Fixed Cost
= 25,00,000 – 15,00,000
= Rs. 10,00,000

3. Effect of decrease in labour efficiency by 5%

Variable Cost = Sales – Contribution
= 50,00,000 – 25,00,000 = Rs. 25,00,000

$$\text{Labour Cost} = 25,00,000 \times \frac{25}{100} = \text{Rs. } 6,25,000$$

New Labour Cost when Labour efficiency decreases by 5%

$$= 6,25,000 \times \frac{100}{95} = \text{Rs. } 6,57,895$$

Increase in Labour Cost = 6,57,895 – 6,25,000
= Rs. 32,895

∴ New Variable Cost = 25,00,000 + 32,895
= Rs. 25,32,895

Contribution = 50,00,000 – 25,32,895
= Rs. 24,67,105

Profit = Contribution – Fixed Cost
= 24,67,105 – 15,00,000 = Rs. 9,67,105

$$\text{New P/V Ratio} = \frac{24,67,105}{50,00,000} \times 100 = 49.34\%$$

$$\text{New B.E.P} = \frac{\text{Fixed Cost}}{\text{P/V Ratio}}$$

$$= \frac{15,00,000}{49.34} \times 100$$

= Rs. 30,40,130

Note : If for 100 units labour cost is Rs. 100, 5% decrease in efficiency makes the labour to produce only 95 units in the same time.

∴ Cost of 95 units = Rs. 100

Cost of 100 units $= 100 \times \frac{100}{95} = 105.2635$

$\therefore$ Original labour cost has to be multiplied with $\frac{100}{95}$ to get new labour cost.

Illustration 55.

The following details relate to product X :

	Rs.	Rs.
Selling Price		1,200
Costs :		
Materials	600	
Labour	150	
Variable Overheads	50	
Fixed Overheads	100	900
Profit		300

During the forthcoming year it is expected that material costs will increase by 10%, wages by $33\frac{1}{3}$%, and other variable costs by 20%. You are required to calculate the percentage increase in selling price of X which will maintain the firm's contribution/sales ratio.

(M. Com. Banaras, Delhi, Madras)

Solution :

Statement showing Contribution and Sales

	Current year Per unit Rs.		Forthcoming year Per unit Rs.
Materials	600	600 + 60	660
Labour	150	150 + 50	200
Variable Overheads	50	50 + 10	60
Total Variable cost	800		920
Contribution at $\frac{1}{3}$ on sale or $\frac{1}{2}$ on Variable Cost	400		460
Selling Price	1,200		1,380
Increase in selling price over previous year		1,380 – 1,200 = 180	
Percentage increase in selling price		$\frac{180}{1,200} \times 100 = 15\%$	

Working notes : (1) Old material cost Rs. 600

Increase at 10% $= 600 \times \frac{10}{100} = 60$

(2) Old Labour Cost $= 150$

Increase at $33\frac{1}{3}\% = 150 \times \frac{1}{3} = 50$

(3) Increase in variable overheads at 20% = Rs. 50 × Rs. 20% = Rs. 10

(4) Contribution to sales ratio:

Current year Rs. 400 ÷ Rs. 1,200 = 33%

Forthcoming year 1/3 on sale or $\frac{1}{2}$ on Variable Cost = Rs. 920 × $\frac{1}{2}$ = Rs. 460

Illustration 56.

The following figures are extracted from the books of a manufacturing concern for the year 2009 – 2010.

	Rs.
Direct Materials	2,05,000
Direct Labour	75,000
Fixed Overheads	60,000
Variable Overheads	1,00,000
Sales	5,00,000

Calculate the break-even point. What will be the effect on B.E.P. of an increase of 10% in :
(*a*) Fixed Expenses and (*b*) Variable Expenses? (*CS*)

Solution :

Calculation of P/V Ratio

	Rs.
Direct Materials	2,05,000
Direct Labour	75,000
Variable Overheads	1,00,000
Variable Cost	3,80,000
Sales	5,00,000
Contribution	1,20,000

$$\text{P/V Ratio} = \frac{\text{Contribution}}{\text{Sales}} \times 100 = \frac{1,20,000}{5,00,000} \times 100 = 24\%$$

$$\text{B.E.P. (Value)} = \frac{\text{Fixed Cost}}{\text{P/V Ratio}} = \frac{60,000}{24\%}$$

= **Rs. 2,50,000**

Effect on B.E.P. :

(*i*) If Fixed Expenses increase by 10% *i.e.* 60,000 + 10% = **Rs. 66,000**

$$\text{B.E.P.} = \frac{66,000}{24\%} = \text{Rs. } 2,75,000$$

(*ii*) If Variable Expenses increase by 10% :

	Rs.
Variable Expenses = 3,80,000 + 10%	= 4,18,000
Sales	= 5,00,000
Contribution	= **82,000**

$$\text{Revised P/V Ratio} = \frac{82,000}{5,00,000} \times 100$$

= 16.4%

$$\text{B.E.P.} = \frac{60,000}{16.4\%} = \textbf{Rs. 3,65,854}$$

Illustration 57. X Ltd. manufactures and sells four types of products under the brand names of A, B, C and D. The sales mix. in value comprises $33\frac{1}{3}\%$, $41\frac{2}{3}\%$, $16\frac{2}{3}\%$ and $8\frac{1}{3}\%$ of products A, B, C and D respectively. The total budgeted sales (100%) are Rs. 60,000 per month.

Operating costs are :

Variable Cost :

Product A	60% of selling price
B	68% of selling price
C	80% of selling price
D	40% of selling price

Fixed Cost : Rs. 14,700 per month

Calculate the break-even point for the products on an overall basis and also the B.E. Sales of individual products. Show the proof for your answer. (*M. Com. Madras*)

Solution :

P/V Ratio for invidual products = 100 – % of variable cost to sales

A = 40% (100 – 60)
B = 32% (100 – 68)
C = 20% (100 – 80)
D = 60% (100 – 40%)

Calculation of composite P/V Ratio

(1) Products	*(2)* Sales	*(3)* % to total sales	*(4)* P/V Ratio	*(Col 3 × Col 4)* Composite P/V Ratio
A	20,000	$33\frac{1}{3}\%$	40%	13.33%
B	25,000	$41\frac{2}{3}\%$	32%	13.33%
C	10,000	$16\frac{2}{3}\%$	20%	3.33%
D	5,000	$8\frac{1}{3}\%$	60%	5.00%
	60,000			34.99 or 35

$$\text{Composite BEP in Rs.} = \frac{\text{Total Fixed Cost}}{\text{Composite P/V Ratio}}$$

$$= \frac{\text{Rs. } 14{,}700}{35\%} = \text{Rs. } 42{,}000$$

Proof of validity of composite B.E.P.

Break-even sales of :	*Contribution*	*Rs.*
A Rs. 42,000 × $33\frac{1}{3}\%$ = Rs. 14,000	14,000 × 40%	5,600
B Rs. 42,000 × $41\frac{2}{3}\%$ = Rs. 7,500	17,500 × 32%	5,600
C Rs. 42,000 × $16\frac{2}{3}\%$ = Rs. 7,000	7,000 × 20%	1,400
D Rs. 42,000 × $8\frac{1}{3}\%$ = Rs. 3,500	13,500 × 60%	2,100
	Total contribution	14,700
	Total Fixed Cost	14,700
	Profit/Loss	Nil

Illustration 58. A toy manufacturer earns an average net profit of Rs. 3 per piece in a selling price of Rs. 15 by producing and selling 60,000 pieces at 60% of the potential capacity. Composition of his cost of sales is :

Direct materials	:	Rs. 4
Direct Wages	:	Re. 1
Works Overhead	:	Rs. 6 [50% fixed]
Sales Overhead	:	Re. 1 [25% varying]

During the current year, he intends to produce the same number but anticipates that :

(*i*) his fixed charge will go up by 10%
(*ii*) rates of direct labour will increase by 20%
(*iii*) rates of direct material will increase by 5%
(*iv*) selling price cannot be increased.

Under these circumstances he obtains an order for a further 20% of his capacity. What minimum price will you recommend for accepting the order to ensure the manufacturer an overall profit of Rs. 1,80,500? *(M. Com. Delhi, Agra, Madras, MS)*

Solution :

Marginal Cost and Contribution statement

Particulars	*Per unit* *Rs.*	*Total (60,000 units)* *Rs.*
Sales	15.00	9,00,000
Variable costs : Direct Material	4.00	2,40,000
Direct Wages	1.00	60,000
Works Overhead (6 × 50%)	3.00	1,80,000
Sales Overhead (1 × 25%)	0.25	15,000
Total Variable Cost	8.25	4,95,000
Contribution (Sales – Variable Cost)	6.75	4,05,000
Fixed Cost : Works Overhead (6 × 50%)	3.00	1,80,000
Sales Overhead (1 × 75%)	0.75	45,000
Total Fixed Cost	3.75	2,25,000
Profit (Contribution – Fixed Cost)	3.00	1,80,000

1. *Calculation of cost and profit of current year, with increased costs, on 60,000 units :*

		Rs.
Direct Materials :	Rs. 4.20[1] × 60,000 =	2,52,000
Direct Wages :	Rs. 1.20[2] × 60,000 =	72,000
Variable Works Overhead	3 × 60,000 =	1,80,000
Variable Sales Overhead	0.25 × 60,000 =	15,000
Total Variable Cost		5,19,000
Add : Fixed Cost[3]		2,47,500
Total Cost	(Rs. 1,80,000 + Rs. 45, 000) + 10% there of)	7,66,500
Sales	60,000 × 15	9,00,000
Profit		1,33,500

2. *Calculation of required profit from new order*

	Rs.
Overall profit required	1,80,500
Less : Profit expected from current output	1,33,500
Profit required from new order	47,000

Note : (1) Rs. 4 + 5% thereof = Rs. 4.20

(2) Rs. 1 + 20% thereof = Rs. 1.20

(3) (Rs. 1,80,000 + Rs. 45,000) + 10% thereof.

3. *Calculation of minimum price to be charged for the new order*

60% of potential capacity	=	60,000 units
New order at 20% of capacity = 60,000 × $\frac{20}{60}$		20,000 units
Variable Costs (4.20 + 1.20 + 3 + 0.25) × 20,000 or 8.65 × 20,000 =		1,73,000
Add : Required profit from new order		47,000
Sales value of new order		2,20,000

$$\text{Selling Price per unit} = \frac{2,20,000}{20,000} = \text{Rs. 11 per unit}$$

MISCELLANEOUS

Illustration 59. From the following information relating to Quick Standard Ltd., you are required to find out

(*a*) Contribution.

(*b*) B.E.P in units,

(*c*) Margin of safety, and

(*d*) Profit.

Total Fixed Costs Rs. 4,500

Total Variable Costs Rs. 7,500

Total Sales Rs. 15,000

Units Sold 5,000.

(*e*) Also calculate the volume of sales to earn a profit of Rs. 6,000.

(*B.Com., ACS Madras*)

Solution :

(*a*) Sales – Variable Cost = Contribution ; Rs. 15,000 – Rs. 7,500

$$\text{Contribution per unit} = \frac{7,500}{5,000} = \textbf{Rs. 1.50}$$

(*b*) $\text{B.E.P in units} = \frac{F}{C} \text{ per unit} = \frac{4,500}{1.5} = \textbf{3,000 units}$

(*c*) Margin of Safety

$$\text{P/V Ratio} = \frac{C}{S} \times 100 = \frac{7,500}{15,000} \times 100 = 50\%$$

$$\text{B.E.P Sales} = \frac{F}{\text{P/V Ratio}} = \frac{4,500}{50\%} = \text{Rs. } 9,000$$

Margin of Safety = Total Sales – B.E.P Sales = Rs. 15,000 – Rs. 9,000 = **Rs. 6,000**

(*d*) Profit = Total Sales – Total Cost = 15,000 – (7,500 + 4,500) = 15,000 – 12,000 = **Rs. 3,000**

(*e*) Sales to earn a profit of Rs. 6,000

$$\frac{F + \text{Desired Profit}}{\text{P/V Ratio}} = \frac{4,500 + 6,000}{50\%} = \textbf{Rs. 21,000}$$

Illustration 60. A multipurpose Co. Furnishes you the following data relating to a year :

	I half *Rs.*	*II half* *Rs.*
Sales	45,000	50,000
Total Cost	40,000	43,000

Assuming that there is no change in prices and variable costs and that the fixed expenses are incurred equally in two half years, calculate :

(1) P/V Ratio (2) Fixed expenses

(3) B.E. Sales (4) Percentage of Margin of Safety. (*C.A. Inter*)

Solution:

	Sales	*Total cost*	*Profit*
II half	50,000	43,000	7,000
I half	45,000	40,000	5,000
Difference =	5,000	3,000	2,000

(1) $\text{P/V Ratio} = \dfrac{\text{Change in Profit}}{\text{Change in Sales}} \times 100 = \dfrac{2,000}{5,000} \times 100 = \mathbf{40\%}$

(2) Total Sales = 95,000

Contribution = 40% of Rs. 95,000 = Rs. 38,000

Less : Profit Rs. 12,000

Fixed Cost Rs. 26,000

(3) $\text{B.E. Sales} = \dfrac{\text{F}}{\text{P/V Ratio}} = \dfrac{26,000}{40\%} = \textbf{Rs. 65,000}$

(4) Margin of Safety = 95,000 – 65, 000 = Rs. 30,000

$$\% \text{ of Margin of Safety} = \frac{\text{Total Sales} - \text{B.E. Sales}}{\text{Total Sales}} \times 100$$

$$= \frac{95,000 - 65,000}{95,000} \times 100 = \mathbf{31.58\%}$$

Illustration 61. The break-down of cost per unit at an activity 10,000 units is as follows:

	Rs.
Raw Materials	10
Direct Expenses	8
Chargeable Expenses	2
Variable Overheads	4
Fixed Overheads	6
Total Cost per unit	30
Selling Price	32
Profit per unit	2

How many units must be sold to break-even? (*ICWA, B.Com. M.S.*)

Solution:

		Rs.	Rs.
Selling Price			32
Less :	Variable costs:		
	Raw Materials	10	
	Direct Expenses	8	
	Chargeable Expenses	2	
	Variable Overheads	4	24
	Contributions		8
Less :	Fixed Cost		6
	Profit		2

$$B.E.P = \frac{F}{C} = \frac{Rs.6 \times 10,000}{Rs.8}$$

$$= \frac{Rs.60,000}{8} = \textbf{7,500 units}$$

Illustration 62. Calculate the BEP in units and in rupees and also arrive at margin of safety ratio from the following information:

	Rs.	*Rs.*
Estimated Sales (1,00,000 units)		20,00,000
Less: Variable Costs	12,00,000	
Fixed Cost	4,00,000	16,00,000
Profit		4,00,000

(*B.Com. Madras*)

Solution:

$$\text{Selling Price per unit} = \frac{Rs.20,00,000}{1,00,000} = Rs.20$$

$$\text{Variable Cost per unit} = \frac{Rs.12,00,000}{1,00,000} = Rs.12$$

$$C = S - V = Rs.20 - Rs.\ 12 = Rs.\ 8$$

$$P/V\ Ratio = \frac{C}{S} = \frac{Rs.8}{Rs.20} \times 100 = \textbf{40\%}$$

$$B.E.P\ (\text{in units}) = \frac{F}{C} = \frac{Rs.4,00,000}{Rs.8} = \textbf{50,000 units}$$

$$B.E.P\ (\text{in Value}) = \frac{F}{P/V\ Ratio} = \frac{Rs.4,00,000}{40\%} = \textbf{Rs. 10,00,000}$$

$$\text{Margin of Safety Ratio} = \frac{\text{Total Sales} - \text{B.E.P Sales}}{\text{Total Sales}}$$

$$= \frac{Rs.\ 20,00,000 - Rs.10,00,000}{Rs.20,00,000} = \frac{1}{2} = \textbf{0.5 : 1} \text{ or } 50\%$$

Illustration 63. X Ltd. makes products of particular type. The budgets for a year are as follows:

	Units	*Rs.*
Sales	13,750	2,75,000
Costs	*Variable*	*Fixed*
	Rs.	Rs.
Direct Materials	55,000	
Direct Labour	41,250	70,000
Overhead:		
Production	27,500	—
Administration	—	51,000
	1,23,750	1,21,000

You are required to calculate:

(1) the contribution per unit.

(2) the contribution margin ratio,

(3) the break-even point in both units and sales

(4) the margin of safety ratio. (*M.Com. Madras*)

Solution:

(1) Contribution:

Sales	Rs. 2,75,000
Less: Variable Costs	Rs. 1,23,750
Contribution	Rs. 1,51,250

Contribution per unit $\frac{\text{Rs. } 1,51,250}{13,750}$ = **Rs. 11**

(2) Contribution Margin Ratio : $\frac{C}{S} \times 100$

$= \frac{\text{Rs. } 1,51,250}{\text{Rs. } 2,75,000} \times 100 = \mathbf{55\%}$

(3) B.E.P (in units) $= \frac{F}{C}$

$= \frac{\text{Rs. } 1,21,000}{\text{Rs. } 11} = \mathbf{11,000 \text{ units}}$

B.E.P (in sales value) $= \frac{F}{\text{P/V Ratio}}$

$= \frac{\text{Rs. } 1,21,000}{55\%} = \mathbf{Rs.\ 2,20,000}$

(4) Margin of Safety Ratio $= \frac{\text{Total Sales} - \text{B.E.P Sales}}{\text{Total Sales}}$

$= \frac{\text{Rs. } 2,75,000 - \text{Rs. } 2,20,000}{\text{Rs. } 2,75,000} = \frac{\mathbf{1}}{\mathbf{5}}$ **or 20%.**

Illustration 64. From the following information, calculate:

(*a*) P/V Ratio

(*b*) Break-even point

(*c*) Margin of Safety

	Rs.
Total Sales	3,60,000
Selling Price per unit	100
Variable Cost per unit	50
Fixed Cost	1,00,000

(*d*) If the selling price is reduced to Rs. 90, by how much is the margin of safety reduced? (*B.Com. Madurai*)

Solution:

(*a*) $P/V \text{ Ratio} = \frac{\text{Contribution}}{\text{Sales}} = \frac{\text{Sales} - \text{Variable Cost}}{\text{Sales}}$

$$= \frac{\text{Rs. }3,60,000 - \text{Rs.}1,80,000}{\text{Rs. }3,60,000} = \mathbf{50\%}$$

(*b*) $\text{Break-Even Point} = \frac{\text{Fixed Cost}}{\text{P/V Ratio}}$

$$= \frac{\text{Rs. }1,00,000}{50\%}$$

= **Rs. 2,00,000**

(*c*) Margin of Safety = Actual Sales – BEP Sales

Rs. 3,60,000 – Rs. 2,00,000

= **Rs. 1,60,000**

(*d*) If selling price is reduced to Rs. 90,

$$\text{Sales} = \frac{\text{Rs.}3,60,000 \times 90}{100} = \mathbf{Rs.\ 3,24,000}$$

$$\text{B.E.P} = \frac{\text{Fixed Cost}}{\text{Contribution per unit}}$$

$$= \frac{\text{Rs. }1,00,000}{\text{Rs. }90 - \text{Rs.}50}$$

$$= \frac{\text{Rs. }1,00,000}{\text{Rs. }40}\ \mathbf{2500\ units}$$

B.E.P (in value) = 2500 units × Rs. 90

= Rs. 2,25,000

Reduced Margin of safety = NEW B.E.P – OLD B.E.P

= Rs. 2,25,000 – Rs. 2,00,000

= **Rs. 25,000**

Illustration 65. You are given the following information in respect of a company :

	Rs.
(*i*) Fixed Cost	13,000
(*ii*) Variable Cost	14,000
(*iii*) Total Cost	27,000
(*iv*) Net Profit	3,000
(*v*) Net Sales	30,000

(*a*) Find out the break-even point.
(*b*) Forecast the profit for sales volume Rs. 50,000.
(*c*) Estimate the volume of sales turnover to make a net profit of Rs. 10,000.

(*A.C.S. Final*)

Solution :

Contribution = 30,000 – 14,000 = Rs. 16,000

$$P/V \text{ Ratio} = \frac{\text{S} - \text{V}}{\text{S}} \times 100 \text{ or } \frac{\text{C}}{\text{S}} \times 100 = \frac{16,000}{30,000} \times 100 = \mathbf{53\frac{1}{3}\%}$$

(*a*) $\text{B.E.P.} = \frac{\text{F}}{\text{P/V Ratio}} = \frac{13,000}{53\frac{1}{3}\%} = \mathbf{Rs.\ 24,375}$

(*b*) Profit $= (\text{S} \times \text{P/V Ratio}) - \text{F} = \left(50{,}000 \times 53\frac{1}{3}\%\right) - 13{,}000$

= 26,667 – 13,000 = **Rs. 13,667.**

(c) Sales $= \frac{\text{F + P}}{\text{P/V Ratio}} = \frac{13{,}000 + 10{,}000}{53\frac{1}{3}\%} = \textbf{Rs. 43,125}$

Illustration 66. Calculate the break-even point from the following figures :

	Rs.
Sales	3,00,000
Fixed Expenses	75,000
Direct Materials	1,00,000
Direct Labour	60,000
Direct Expenses	40,000

(*B.Com., Kerala*)

Solution :

$$\text{Break-Even Sale} = \frac{\text{Fixed Cost} \times \text{Sales}}{\text{Sales} - \text{Variable Cost}}$$

(Variable Cost = 1,00,000 + 60,000 + 40,000 = Rs. 2,00,000)

$$= \frac{75{,}000 \times 3{,}00{,}000}{3{,}00{,}000 - 2{,}00{,}000} = \textbf{Rs. 2,25,000}$$

Alternatively

$$\text{B.E.S} = \frac{F}{1 - \frac{V}{S}}$$

$$1 - \frac{V}{S} = 1 - \frac{2{,}00{,}000}{3{,}00{,}000}$$

$$= \frac{75{,}000}{1{,}00{,}000/3{,}00{,}000}$$

$$= \frac{75{,}000 \times 3{,}00{,}000}{1{,}00{,}000} = \textbf{Rs. 2,25,000}$$

Verification

For a sale of Rs. 3,00,000, variable cost is Rs. 2,00,000. Therefore, for a sale of Rs. 2,25,000, variable cost should be

$$\frac{2{,}00{,}000}{3{,}00{,}000} \times 2{,}25{,}000 = \text{Rs. } 1{,}50{,}000$$

Sales	Rs. 2,25,000
(—) Variable cost	1,50,000
	75,000
(—) Fixed Cost	75,000
Profit	Nil

Illustration 67. A company has a P/V Ratio of 40%. By what percentage sales be increased or decreased to offset :

(*a*) 10% reduction in selling price, and

(*b*) 10% increase in selling price. (*B.Com. (Hons.), Delhi*)

Solution :

Let present units sold be 100 @ Re. 1 per unit.

	Rs.
Present total sales	100
Present Variable cost	60
Pesent Contribution	40

(*a*) If the Selling Price is reduced by 10%

Selling Price per unit	0.90
Variable Cost per unit	0.60
Contribution per unit	0.30

In order to maintain the same contribution the volume of sales should be

$$\frac{\text{Present total contribution}}{\text{New contribution per unit}} \times \text{New selling price per unit}$$

$$= \frac{40}{0.30} \times 0.90 = \textbf{Rs. 120}$$

Thus, volume of sales will have to be increased by 20% from the existing level if the selling price is reduced by 10%.

(*b*) If the selling price is increased by 10%

	Rs.
Selling Price per unit	1.10
Variable Cost per unit	0.60
Contribution per unit	0.50

In order to maintain the same contribution, the volume of sales should be

$$\frac{40}{0.50} \times 1.10 = \textbf{Rs. 88}$$

The sales volume will have to be decreased by 12% over the existing level, if selling price is increased by 10%

Illustration 68. From the following information, calculate the break-even point and turnover required to earn a profit of Rs. 36,000.

Fixed Overheads	Rs. 1,80,000
Variable Cost per unit	Rs. 2
Selling Price	Rs. 20

If the company is earning a profit of Rs. 36,000, express the margin of safety available to it. (*C.A. Inter*)

Solution :

(*a*) Break-even point :

	Rs.
Selling Price per unit	20
Variable Cost per unit	2
Contribution per unit	18

Fixed Overhead Rs. 1,80,000

$$\text{B.E.P} = \frac{\text{F}}{\text{C.per unit}} = \frac{1,80,000}{18} = \textbf{10,000 units}$$

or Sales = Rs. 2,00,000

(*b*) Turnover required to earn a profit of Rs. 36,000.

$$= \frac{\text{F + Desired Profit}}{\text{C. per unit}} = \frac{\text{Rs.1,80,000 + Rs. 36,000}}{18}$$

= 12,000 units or sales = Rs. 2,40,000

(c) Margin of Safety :

	Units	*Rs.*
Actual Sales	12,000	2,40,000
Sales at B.E.P	10,000	2,00,000
Margin of Safety	2,000	40,000

Margin of safety may also be calculated as follows :

$$\text{Margin of Safety} = \frac{\text{Net Profit}}{\text{P/V Ratio}} = \frac{36,000}{90\%} = 36,000 \times \frac{100}{90} = \textbf{Rs. 40,000}$$

Illustration 69. You are given the following data for the coming year of a factory :

Budgeted output	80,000 units
Fixed Expenses	Rs. 4,00,000
Variable Expenses per unit	Rs 10
Selling Price per unit	Rs. 20

(*a*) Draw a break-even chart showing the break-even point. If the selling price is reduced to Rs. 18 per unit, what will be the new break-even point ?

(*b*) Draw contribution break-even chart. (*I.C.W.A. Inter*)

Solution :

$$\text{Original P/V Ratio} = \frac{S-V}{S} \times 100 = \frac{20-10}{20} \times 100 = 50\%$$

$$\text{New P/V Ratio} = \frac{18-10}{18} \times 100 = 44.44\%$$

$$\text{B.E.P (Original)} = \frac{F}{\text{P/V Ratio}} = \frac{4,00,000}{50\%} = \textbf{Rs. 8,00,000.} \quad \text{or } \textbf{40,000 units.}$$

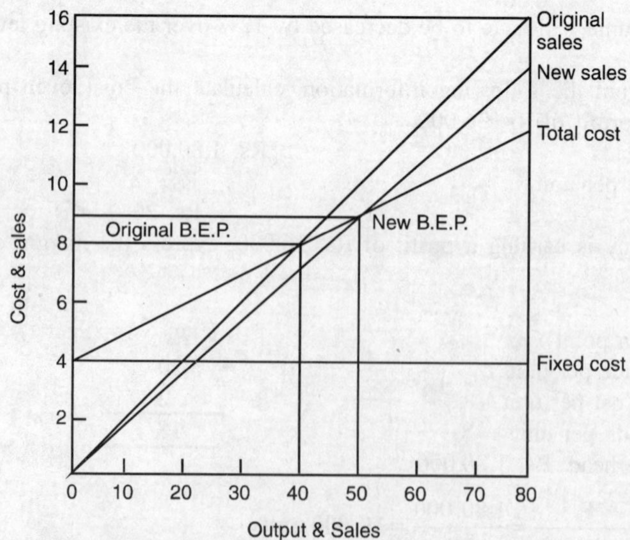

$$\text{B.E.P (New)} = \frac{4,00,000}{44.44\%} = \text{Rs. } 9,00,000$$

or **50,000 units**.

Illustration 70. Calculate :

(*i*) The amount of fixed expenses,

(*ii*) The number of units of break-even,

(*iii*) The number of units to earn a profit of Rs. 40,000

The selling price can be assumed of Rs. 100.

The company sold in two successive periods 7,000 units and 9,000 units and has incurred a loss of Rs. 10,000 and earned Rs. 10,000 as profit respectively. (*I.C.W.A.*)

Solution :

	Sales	*Profit/Loss*
I	9,000	Rs. + 10,000
II	7,000	Rs. – 10,000
	2,000	Rs. 20,000 (Change)

	Rs.	*Rs.*
(*i*) Contribution	7,000 × 10 = 70,000	9,000 × 10 = 90,000
Profit/Loss	– 10,000	+ 10,000
Fixed Cost	80,000	80,000

(Contribution = Fixed Cost + Profit)

(*ii*) $$\text{Contribution} = \frac{20,000}{2,000} = \text{Rs. } 10 \text{ per unit}$$

$$\text{B.E.P} = \frac{FC}{C} = \frac{80,000}{10} = \textbf{8,000 units}$$

(*iii*) The No. of units to earn a profit of Rs. 40,000

$$\frac{\text{F + Desired profit}}{\text{C per unit}} = \frac{80,000 + 40,000}{10} = \textbf{12,000 units}$$

Illustration 71. An analysis of Sultan Manufacturing Co. led to the following information :

Cost Element	Variable Cost (*% of sales*)	Fixed Cost *Rs.*
Direct Material	32.8	—
Direct Labour	28.4	—
Factory Overheads	12.6	1,89,900
Distribution Overheads	4.1	58.400
General Administration Overheads	1.1	66,700

Budgeted sales are Rs. 18,50,000. You are required to determine:

(*a*) the break-even sales volume,

(*b*) the profit at the budgeted sales volume.

(*c*) the profit if actual sales:

(*i*) drop by 10%

(*ii*) increase by 5% from budgeted sales. (*B.Com., Delhi*)

Solution :

Total Variable Cost as % of sales = 32.8 + 28.4 + 12.6 + 4.1 + 1.1

= 79 %

$$\text{P/V Ratio} = \frac{\text{Sales} - \text{Variable Cost}}{100} = \frac{100-79}{100} = 21\%$$

Total Fixed Cost = 1,89,900 + 58,400 + 66,700 = Rs. 3,15,000.

(*a*) $\text{B.E.S.} = \frac{\text{F}}{\text{P/V Ratio}} = \frac{3,15,000 \times 100}{21} = \textbf{Rs. 15,00,000.}$

(*b*) Profit = Sales × P/V Ratio – Fixed Cost
= 18,50,000 × 21% – 3,15,000
= 3,88,500 – 3,15,000
= **Rs. 73,500.**

(*c*) Profit when actual sales :

(*i*) drop by 10%

Actual sales = Rs. 18,50,000 – 10% (or) Rs. 1,85,000
= Rs. 16,65,000

Profit = Rs. 16,65,000 × 21% – Rs. 3,15,000
= Rs. 3,49,650 – Rs. 3,15,000
= **Rs. 34,650.**

(*ii*) Increase by 5%

Actual Sales = Rs. 18,50,000 + Rs. 92,500
= Rs. 19,42,500

Profit = Rs. 19,42,500 × 21% – Rs. 3,15,000
= Rs. 4,07,925 – Rs. 3,15,000
= **Rs. 92,925.**

Illustration 72. From the following data you are required to calculate break-even point and net sales value at this point :

	Rs.
Direct Material Cost per unit	8
Direct Labour Cost per unit	5
Fixed Overheads	24,000
Variable Overheads @ 60% on Direct labour :	
Selling Price per unit	25
Trade discount	4%

If sales are 15% and 20% above the break-even volume, determine the net profits.

(*C.A. Inter*)

Solution :

Statement of Contribution per unit

		Rs.
(*a*)	Selling Price per unit	25
	Trade discount	1
(*b*)	Net Realisation per unit	24
(*c*)	Marginal Cost :	
	Direct Material	8
	Direct Labour	5
	Variable overhead	
	60% on Direct Labour *i.e.* $\frac{60}{100} \times 5$	3
	Total	16
	Contribution per unit (24 – 16)	8

$$\text{B.E.P. (in units)} = \frac{\text{F}}{\text{C. per unit}} = \frac{24,000}{8} = \textbf{3,000 units}$$

Net Sales Value at this point :

Sales Value = 3,000 × 25	75,000
Less : Trade Discount 4%	3,000
Net Sales Value	72,000

Net profit if sales are 15% above B.E.P :

Sales at B.E.P = 3,000 units

15% above $= \frac{450 \text{ units}}{3,450 \text{ units}}$

Sales Value = 3,450 × 25 = Rs. 86,250

P/V Ratio $= \frac{C}{S} \times 100 = \frac{8}{25} \times 100 = 32\%$

Profit $= (S \times P/V \text{ Ratio}) - F$

= (86,250 × 32%) – 24,000

= 27,600 – 24,000 = **Rs. 3,600**

Net profit if sales are 20% above B.E.P :

Sale at B.E.P = 3,000 units

20% above = 600 units

Total = 3,600 units

Sales Value = 3,600 × 25 = Rs. 90,000

Profit = (S × P/V Ratio) – F

= (90,000 × 32%) – 24,000

= 28,800 – 24,000

= **Rs. 4,800**

Illustration 73. From the following information relating to Quick Standard Ltd., you are required to find out— (*a*) Contribution, (*b*) Break-even point in units; (*c*) Margin of safety, (*d*) Profit.

Total Fixed Costs	Rs. 4,500
Total Variable Costs	Rs. 7,500
Total Sales	Rs. 15,000
Units Sold	5,000 (units)

Also calculate the volume of sales to earn profit of Rs. 6,000. (*C.S.*)

Solution : (*a*)

Contribution Statement

	Output and Sales = 5,000 units	
	Total	*Per unit*
	Rs.	*Rs.*
Sales	15,000	3.00
Less : Variable Cost	7,500	1.50
Contribution	7,500	1.50

(*b*) Break-even point in units

B.E.P. (in units) $= \dfrac{\text{F}}{\text{C. per unit}} = \dfrac{4,500}{1.50} = \mathbf{3,000\ units}$

Break-even point of sales value = 3000 × 3 = **Rs. 9,000**

(c) Margin of Safety = Actual Sales – Sales at BEP

= Rs. 15,000 – Rs. 9,000 = Rs. 6,000

In percentage $= \dfrac{6,000}{15,000} \times 100 = \mathbf{40\%}$

(*d*) Profit = Sales – (F + V)

= Rs. 15,000 – (Rs. 4,500 + Rs. 7,500)

or = Rs. 15,000 – Rs. 12,000 = **Rs. 3,000**

Contribution – Fixed Cost

= 7,500 – 4,500 = Rs. 3,000

Volume of Sales to earn a profit of **Rs. 6,000**

Volume of Sales $= \dfrac{\text{F + Desired Profit}}{\text{P/V Ratio*}}$

$= \dfrac{\text{Rs. } 45,00 + \text{Rs. } 6,000}{50\%}$

$= \dfrac{\text{Rs. } 10,500 \times 100}{50} = \mathbf{Rs.\ 21,000}$

Illustration 74. Raj Corpn. Ltd. has prepared the following budget estimates for the year.

Sales units	15,000
Fixed Expenses	Rs. 34,000
Sales Value	Rs. 1,50,000
Variable Costs	Rs. 6 per unit.

You are required to :

(*i*) Find the P/V ratio, break-even point and margin of safety.

(*ii*) Calculate the revised P/V ratio, break-even point and margin of safety in each of the following cases :

(*a*) Decrease of 10% in selling price;

(*b*) Increase of 10% variable costs;

(*c*) Increase of sales volume by 2000 units;

(*d*) Increase of Rs. 6,000 in fixed costs. (*C.A. Inter*)

Solution :

	Rs.
(*i*) Selling Price per unit $= \dfrac{1,50,000}{15,000}$	10
Variable Cost per unit	6
Contribution per unit	4

* P/V Ratio $= \dfrac{\text{Contribution}}{\text{Sales}} \times 100 = \dfrac{\text{Rs. } 7,500}{\text{Rs. } 15,000} \times 100 = 50\%$

$$\text{P/V Ratio} = \frac{S-V}{S}\times 100 = \frac{10-6}{10}\times 100 = 40\%$$

$$\text{B.E.P. unit} = \frac{F}{\text{C.per unit}} = \frac{34,000}{4} = \textbf{8,500 units}$$

B.E.P. sales = 8,500 × 10 = **Rs. 85, 000**

$$\text{(or)} \quad = \frac{F}{\text{P/V Ratio}} = \frac{34,000}{40\%} = \textbf{Rs. 85,000}$$

Margin of Safety = Total Sales – B.E.P. Sales = 1,50,000 – 85,000 = **Rs. 65,000**

(*ii*) *Particulars*	*P/V Ratio*	*B.E.P. (Value)*	*Margin of Safety*
		Rs.	*Rs.*
(*a*) Decrease of 10% in S.P. *i.e.* Rs. 9 per unit	$\frac{9-6}{9}\times 100$ $= -33\frac{1}{3}\%$	$\frac{34,000}{33\frac{1}{3}\%}$ = 1,02,000	9 × 15,000 – 1,35,000 – 1,02,000 = 33,000
(*b*) Increase of 10% in V.C. *i.e.* Rs. 6.60	$\frac{10-6.60}{10}\times 100$ = 34%	$\frac{34,000}{34\%} = 1,00,000$	1,50,000 – 1,00,000 = 50,000
(*c*) Increase of sales volume by 2,000 units	No change *i.e.* 40%	No change *i.e.* 85,000	170,000 – 85,000 = 85,000
(*d*) Increase of Rs. 6,000 in F.C.	No change *i.e.* 40%	$\frac{40,000}{40\%} = 1,00,000$	1,50,000 – 1,00,000 = 50,000

Illustration 75. In a year, the position of Y Ltd., was as follows :

	Rs.
Sales	1,20,000
Variable Overheads	96,000
Gross Profit	24,000
Fixed Overhead	16,000
Net Profit	8,000

Find out :

(*a*) P/V Ratio
(*b*) B.E.P.
(*c*) Net profit from the sales of Rs. 1,30,000
(*d*) Required sales for a net profit Rs. 10,000.

(*B. Com Madurai, Mysore, Nagpur, Agra*)

Solution :

$$(a)\ \text{P/V Ratio} = \frac{S-V}{S}\times 100$$

$$= \frac{1,20,000-96,000}{1,20,000}\times 100 = \textbf{20\%}$$

$$(b)\ \text{B.E.P.} = \frac{F\times S}{C} = \frac{F}{\text{P/V Ratio}}$$

$$= \frac{16{,}000 \times 120{,}000}{24{,}000} = \textbf{Rs. 80,000} \quad \text{(or)} \quad \frac{16{,}000}{20} \times 100 = \textbf{Rs. 80,000}$$

(*c*) Contribution $= \text{P/V Ratio} \times \text{S} = \frac{20}{100} \times 1{,}30{,}000$

= Rs. 26,000.

Net Profit = C – F = 26,000 – 16,000 = **Rs. 10.000**

(*d*) C = F + Profit = 16,000 + 10,000 = **Rs. 26,000**

$$\text{S} = \frac{\text{C}}{\text{P/V Ratio}} = \frac{26{,}000}{20\%} = \textbf{Rs. 1,30,000}$$

$$\text{(or)} \quad \frac{(\text{F}+\text{P}) \times \text{S}}{\text{S}-\text{V}} = \frac{26{,}000 \times 1{,}20{,}000}{1{,}20{,}000 - 96{,}000} = \textbf{Rs. 1,30,000}$$

$$\text{(or)} \quad \frac{\text{F}+\text{P}}{1-\text{V/S}} = \frac{16{,}000 + 10{,}000}{1 - \frac{96{,}000}{1{,}20{,}000}} = \frac{26{,}000}{24{,}000/1{,}20{,}000}$$

$$= \frac{26{,}000 \times 1{,}20{,}000}{24{,}000} = \textbf{Rs. 1,30,000}$$

Illustration 76. The particulars of two plants producing an identical product with the same selling price are as under :

	Plant A	*Plant B*
Capacity utilisation	70%	60%
	(Rs. Lakhs)	(Rs. Lakhs)
Sales	150	90
Variable Cost	105	75
Fixed Cost	30	20

It has been decided to merge Plant B with Plant A. The additional fixed expenses involved in the merger amount to Rs. 2 lakhs.

(1)Find the break-even point of plant 'A' and Plant 'B' before merger and the break-even point of the merger plant.

(2)Find the capacity utilization of the integrated plant required to earn a profit of Rs. 18 lakhs.

(*C.A. Inter*)

Solution :

(1) Statement of Break-even Point

Particulars	*Plant A*	*Plant B*	*Merger Plant*
	Rs.	*Rs.*	*Rs.*
Sales	150	90	240
Variable Costs	105	75	180
Contribution	45	15	60
Fixed Cost	30	20	52
			(30 + 20 + 2)

$$\text{P/V ratio} = \frac{\text{C}}{\text{S}} \times 100 : \frac{45}{150} \times 100 : \frac{15}{90} \times 100 : \frac{60}{240} \times 100$$

$$= 30\% \qquad = 16.7\% \qquad = 25\%$$

$$\text{B.E.P} = \frac{F}{\text{P/V Ratio}} \quad \frac{30}{30\%} \quad \frac{20}{16.7\%} \quad \frac{52}{25\%}$$

= **100 lakhs** = **120 lakhs** = **208 lakhs**

Sales of integrated plant :

$$\frac{F+P}{\text{P/V Ratio}} = \frac{52+18}{25\%} = \frac{70}{25\%} = \textbf{280 lakhs}$$

Plant A 100% capacity sales would be $150 \times \frac{100}{70} = 214.29$ lakhs

Plant B 100% capacity sales would be $\frac{90 \times 100}{60} = 150$ lakhs

100% capacity of integrated plant = 214.29 + 150 = 364.29 lakhs

Capacity : sales of 280 lakhs $= \frac{280 \times 100}{364.29} = \textbf{76.86\%}$

Thus 76.86% capacity must be utilised to earn a profit of Rs. 18 lakhs.

Illustration 77. Following information has been made available from the cost records of a Company, manufacturing spare parts :

	Per Unit
	Rs.
Direct Materials :	
X	8
Y	6
Direct Wages :	
X	24 hours @ 25 Paise per hour
Y	16 hours @ 25 Paise per hour
Variable Overheads	150% of Wages
Fixed Overheads	Rs. 750
Selling Price of X	Rs. 25
Selling Price of Y	Rs. 20

The directors want to be acquainted with the desirability of adopting any one of the following alternative sales mixes in the budget for the next period.

(*a*) 250 units of X and 250 units of Y

(*b*) 400 units of Y only

(*c*) 400 units of X and 100 units of Y

(*d*) 150 units of X and 350 units of Y

State which of the alternative sales mixes you would recommend to the management.

(*B.Com. Madurai*)

Solution :

Marginal Cost Statement (Per Unit)

	X	Y
	Rs.	Rs.
Direct Matrials	8	6
Direct Wages	6	4
Variable Overheads	9	6
Marginal Cost	23	16
Contribution	2	4
Selling Price	25	20

Alternative of Sales Mixes

		Rs.
(*a*) 250 units of X and 250 units of Y: Rs.		
Contribution : Product X : 250 × Rs. 2 = 500		
Product Y : 250 × Rs. 4 = 1,000		1,500
Less : Fixed Overheads		750
Profit		750
(*b*) 400 units of Product Y only :		
Contribution : Product Y: 400 × Rs. 4		1,600
Less : Fixed Overheads		750
Profit		850
(*c*) 400 units of Product X and 350 units of Product Y:		
Contribution : Product X 400 × Rs. 2 = 800		
Product Y 100 × Rs. 4 = 400		1,200
Less : Fixed overheads		750
Profit		450
(*d*) 150 units of X and 350 units of Y:		
Contribution : Product X 150 × Rs. 2 = 300		
Product Y 350 × Rs. 4 = 1,400		1,700
Less : Fixed Overheads		750
Profit		950

The alternative (*d*) is the most profitable since it gives the maximum profit of Rs. 950.

Illustration 78. A manufacturer with an overall (interchangeable among the products) capacity of one lakh machine hours has been so far producing a standard mix of 15,000 units of Product A, 10,000 units of Products B and C each. On experience the total expenditure exclusive of his fixed changes is found to be Rs. 2.09 lakhs and the cost ratio among the products approximates 1: 1.5: 1.75 respectively per unit. The fixed charges comes to Rs. 2 per unit. When the unit selling prices are Rs. 6.25 for A, 7.50 for B and Rs. 10.50 for C he incurs a loss.

He desires to change the product mix as under :

	Mix 1	*Mix 2*	*Mix 3*
A	18,000	15,000	22,000
B	12,000	6,000	8,000
C	7,000	13,000	8,000

As a Cost Accountant what mix will you recommend ? (*I.C.W.A. Final; C.A. Final*)

Solution :

Product	*No. of units*	*Weightage*	*Total Equivalent units*
A	15,000	× 1	= 15,000
B	10,000	× 1.5	= 15,000
C	10,000	× 1.75	= 17,500
Total	35,000		47,500

$$\text{Variable cost per equivalent unit} = \frac{2,09,000}{47,500} = \text{Rs. } 4.40$$

Variable cost

		Per unit *Rs.*	No. of units	Total *Rs.*
A	4.40 × 1	= 4.40	× 15,000	= 66,000
B	4.40 × 1.5	= 6.60	× 10,000	= 66,000
C	4.40 × 1.75	= 7.70	× 10,000	= 77,000

Total	35,000	2,09,000

Statement of contribution per unit

Particulars	A	B	C
	Rs.	Rs.	Rs.
Sales price per unit	6.25	7.50	10.50
Less : Variable cost per unit	4.40	6.60	7.70
Contribution per unit	1.85	0.90	2.80

Statement of Comparative Profitability

	Mix 1	*Mix 2*	*Mix 3*
Contribution from :	Rs.	Rs.	Rs.
Product A	33,300(*a*)	27,750(*d*)	40,700(*g*)
Product B	10,800(*b*)	5,400(*e*)	7,200(*h*)
Product C	19,600(*c*)	36,400(*f*)	22,400(*i*)
Total Contribution	63,700	69,550	70,300
Less : Fixed charges			
35,000 × Rs. 2	70,000	70,000	70,000
Profit (+)/Loss (–)	(–) 6,300	(–) 450	(+) 300

Mix 3 is recommended, as it is profitable.

$$\left.\begin{array}{ll}(a) & 18,000 \times \text{Rs.}1.85 = \text{Rs.}\,33,300\\ (b) & 12,000 \times \text{Rs.}\,0.90 = \text{Rs.}\,10,800\\ (c) & 7,000 \times \text{Rs.}\,2.80 = \text{Rs.}\,19,600\end{array}\right\}\ \text{Rs.}\,63,700$$

$$\left.\begin{array}{ll}(d) & 15,000 \times \text{Rs.}1.85 = \text{Rs.}\,27,750\\ (e) & 6,000 \times \text{Rs.}\,0.90 = \text{Rs.}\,5,400\\ (f) & 13,000 \times \text{Rs.}\,2.80 = \text{Rs.}\,36,400\end{array}\right\}\ \text{Rs.}\,69,550$$

$$\left.\begin{array}{ll}(g) & 22,000 \times \text{Rs.}1.85 = \text{Rs.}\,40,700\\ (h) & 8,000 \times \text{Rs.}\,0.90 = \text{Rs.}\,7,200\\ (i) & 8,000 \times \text{Rs.}\,2.80 = \text{Rs.}\,22,400\end{array}\right\}\ \text{Rs.}\,70,300$$

Formula—Marginal Costing

1. Marginal Cost = Prime Cost + Variable Overheads
   (or) = Total Cost – Fixed Cost
2. Contribution = Sales – Marginal Cost C = S – MC
3. Contribution = Fixed Cost ± Profit/Loss C = FC ± P/L
4. Contribution = Sales × P/V Ratio C = S × P/V Ratio
5. $\text{Sales} = \dfrac{\text{Contribution}}{\text{P/V Ratio}}$ $S = \dfrac{C}{\text{P/V Ratio}}$
6. Profit = Sales × P/V Ratio – Fixed Costs P = S × P/V Ratio – FC

Profit-Volume Ratio :

7. $\text{P/V Ratio} = \dfrac{\text{Contribution}}{\text{Sales}} \times 100$ $\qquad \text{P/V Ratio} = \dfrac{C}{S} \times 100$

(OR) $= \dfrac{\text{Sales} - \text{Variable Cost}}{\text{Sales}} \times 100$ $\qquad \text{P/V Ratio} = \dfrac{S - VC}{S} \times 100$

(OR) $= \dfrac{\text{Fixed Cost} + \text{Profit}}{\text{Sales}} \times 100$ $\qquad \text{P/V Ratio} = \dfrac{F + P}{S} \times 100$

(OR) $= \dfrac{\text{Profit}}{\text{Margin of Safety Ratio}}$ $\qquad \text{P/V Ratio} = \dfrac{P}{\text{M/S Ratio}}$

(OR) $= \dfrac{\text{Change in Contribution}}{\text{Change in Sales}}$

(OR) $= \dfrac{\text{Change in Profits}}{\text{Change in Sales}}$

8. $\text{Sales} = \dfrac{\text{Contribution}}{\text{P/V Ratio}}$ $\qquad \text{Sales} = \dfrac{C}{\text{P/V Ratio}}$

9. Variable Cost

$= \text{Sales (100\% – P/V Ratio)}$ $\qquad VC = S\ (100\% - \text{P/V Ratio})$

10. B.E.P Sales (in Units)

$= \dfrac{\text{Fixed Cost}}{\text{Contribution per Unit}}$ $\qquad \text{B.E.P} = \dfrac{FC}{C \text{ per unit}}$

11. B.E.P Sales (in Rupees)

$= \dfrac{\text{Fixed Cost} \times \text{Sales}}{\text{Sales} - \text{Variable Cost}}$ $\qquad \text{B.E.P} = \dfrac{F \times S}{S - VC}$

(OR) $= \dfrac{\text{Fixed Cost}}{\text{P/V Ratio}}$ $\qquad$ (OR) $= \dfrac{FC}{\text{P/V Ratio}}$

12. Margin of Safety

$= \text{Total Sales} - \text{B.E.P Sales}$ $\qquad M/S = S - \text{B.E.P Sales}$

13. Margin of Safety Ratio

$= \dfrac{\text{Total Sales} - \text{B.E.P Sales}}{\text{Total Sales}}$

$\text{M/S Ratio} = \dfrac{S - \text{B.E.P Sales}}{S}$

14. Sales required to earn a desired profit:

$\text{Sales (in Rupees)} = \dfrac{\text{Fixed Cost} + \text{Desired Profit}}{\text{P/V Ratio}}$

$\text{Sales (in Units)} = \dfrac{\text{Fixed Cost} + \text{Profit} \times \text{Sales}}{\text{Contribution per Unit}}$

15. Sales in units required to maintain the present level of profit:

$= \dfrac{\text{Total Contribution Required}}{\text{New Contribution per unit}}$

16. $\text{Profitability} = \dfrac{\text{Contribution}}{\text{Key Factor}}$

Profit = (Sales × P/V Ratio) – Fixed Cost
Profit = P/V Ratio × M/S Ratio × Sales

Objective Type Questions

A. Choose the correct answer to the following :

(a) Contribution margin is also known as :
   (i) Mariginal Income.
   (ii) Gross Profit.
   (iii) Net

(b) Period cost means :
   (i) Variable cost.
   (ii) Fixed Cost.
   (iii) Prime Cost.

(c) The costing method in which fixed factory overheads are added to inventory is :
   (i) Direct Costing
   (ii) Marginal Costing
   (iii) Absorption Costing

(d) When fixed cost is Rs. 10,000 and P/V reatio is 50% the break-even point will be :
   (i) Rs. 20,000
   (ii) Rs. 40,000
   (iii) Rs. 50,000'

(e) When P/V Ratio is 40% and sales value is Rs. 10,000 the variable costs will be :
   (i) Rs. 4,000
   (ii) Rs. 6,000
   (iii) Rs. 10,000

(f) When margin of safety is 20% and P/V ratio is 60% the profit will be :
   (i) 30%
   (ii) 33.3%
   (iii) 12%

(g) When sales are Rs. 2,00,000 fixed cost Rs. 30,000 P/V Ratio 40% the amount of profit will be:
   (i) Rs. 50,000
   (ii) Rs. 80,000
   (iii) Rs. 12,000

(Ans. (a) Marginal Income; (b) Fixed cost ; (c) Absorption Costing ; (d) Rs. 20,000 (e) Rs. 6,000 ; (f) 12% ; (g) Rs. 50,000.

B. State whether each of the following statements is true or false :

1. The technique of marginal costing can be used in conjunction with standard costing or budgetary control.
2. The fixed costs are included in the valuation of work-in-progress and finished goods stocks in case of marginal costing.
3. Semi-variable costs form a part of product cost in marginal costing.

4. Absorption costing is not as suitable for decision-making as marginal costing.
5. Direct costing and marginal costing techniques are same in all cases.
6. Break-even chart depicts cost-volume profit relationship.
7. The angle formed at the intersection of the sales line and the total cost line is called "angle of incidence."
8. A high margin of safety shows that the actual sales are more than break-even sales.
9. Increase in selling price will have no effect on margin of safety.
10. Profit-Volume Ratio indicates the relationship between profit and sales

(Ans: (1) True : (2) False (3) False ; (4) True ; (5) False ; (6) True ; (7) True ; (8) True; (9) False; (10) False)

C. Fill in the blanks :

1. The technique of Marginal Costing in based on classification of costs into .... and .... costs.
2. Contribution is the difference between sales and ....
3. In Marginal Costing stock of finished goods is valued at .... cost.
4. Direct costing is based on classification of costs into .... and .... costs.
5. Both fixed and variable costs are charged to products in case of .... costing.
6. At break-even point, total cost is equal to ....
7. The break-even piont .... when selling price is increased.
8. The break-even point inceased when fixed cost is..................
9. The fixed costs and profit added together will make......................
10. The excess of actual sales over break-even sales is termed as.................

(Ans: (1) Fixed, Variable; (2) Variable Cost; (3) Marginal (4) Direct, Indirect; (5) Absorption ; (6) Total sales (7) Decreases ; (8) Increased; (9) Contribution; (10) Margin of Safety.

THEORETICAL QUESTIONS

1. Define marginal costing. How does marginal costing differs from total cost ? (*B.Com., Madras*)
2. Explain : Key factor, P/V ratio and Margin of safety.
3. Explain the break-even analysis in the profit planning. (*B.Com., Madras*)
4. What are the uses of break-even analysis ? (*B.Com., Delhi*)
5. How is marginal costing useful in the decision-making of a firm ? (*B.Com., Karnataka*)
6. What are the advantages of break-even point ? (*B.Com. Karnataka*)
7. Discuss the importance of the following in relation to marginal costing : (*a*) Break-even point (*b*) Margin of safety (*c*) Contribution (*d*) P/V Ratio. (*B.Com., Meerut*)
8. What is meant by Cost-volume-profit analysis ? Explain its importance. (*B.Com., Nagarjuna*)
9. What is marginal cost? (*B. Com MS*)
10. What are the limitations of Break-even chart? (*B. Com. Kerala*)
11. Briefly explain the different kinds of Break-even charts. (*B. Com. Agra*)
12. What is "Angle of Incidence"? Explain its significance. (*B. Com. Poona*)
13. Mention the assumptions underlying a Break-even chart. (*B. Com. Madurai*)
14. Explain the different kinds of Break-even charts. (*B. Com. Punjab*)
15. What are the salient features of Marginal Cost? (*B. Com. Madras*)

PRACTICAL PROBLEMS

16. Calculate the P/V ratio and Break-even point from the following particulars :

	Rs.
Sales	5,00,000
Fixed Cost	1,00,000
Profit	1,50,000

[**Ans :** *50% 2,00,000*] (*B.Com., Madurai*).

17. In a trading concern there was increase in profit from Rs. 10,000 to 16,000 when sales increased by Rs. 50,000. The fixed expenses were Rs. 24,000. Ascertain the break-even sales. [**Ans:** *Rs. 2,00,000*] (*B.Com., Calicut*)

18. From the following information, calculate the break-even point and turnover required to earn a profit of Rs. 30,000.

Fixed Overheads	Rs. 21,000
Variable Costs	Rs. 2 per unit
Selling Price	Rs. 5 per unit

If the company is earning a profit of Rs. 30,000, express the margin of safety available to it. [**Ans :** *Rs. 50,000 or 10,000 units*] (*C.A., Final*)

19. The Profit/volume ratio of X Ltd. is 50% and the margin of safety is 40%. You are required to calculate the net profit if sales volume is Rs. 10,00,000.

[**Ans : Rs. 2,00,000**] (*B. Com., Calicut*)

20. Find the profit from the following data :

	Rs.
Sales	80,000
Marginal Cost	60,000
Break-even Point	60,000 Sales

[**Ans :** *Profit Rs. 5,000*] (*S.A.S. Commercial*)

21. From the following information find out the amount of profit earned during the year using the marginal costing technique :

Fixed Cost	Rs. 5,00,000
Variable Cost	Rs. 10 per unit
Selling Price	Rs. 15 per unit
Output level	1,50,000 unit

(**Ans :** *Profit Rs. 2,50,000*) (*B. Com., Calicut*)

22. From the following particulars, calculate the sales required to earn a profit of Rs. 1,20,000.

	Rs.
Sales	6,00,000
Variable Costs	3,75,000
Fixed Costs	1,80,000

(**Ans :** *Rs. 8,00,000*) (*B.Com. Calicut*)

23. The sales turnover and profit during the two years were as follows :

	Sales	*Profit*
First year	Rs. 2 lakhs	Rs. 20,000
Second year	3 lakhs	40,000

(*a*) P/V Ratio
(*b*) Fixed Cost
(*c*) Break-even Point

[**Ans :** (*a*) *20%* (*b*) *Rs. 20,000* (*c*) *Rs. 1,00,000*] (*B. Com., Calicut*)

24. From the following data relating to a company, calculate :
(*i*) The break-even sales; and
(*ii*) Sales required to earn a profit of Rs. 6,000 per period.

Period	*Total* *Rs.*	*Total Cost* *Rs.*
1	42,500	38,700
2	39,200	36,852

[**Ans :** (*i*) *Rs. 33,864*; (*ii*) *Rs. 47,500*] (*C.A. Final*)

25. The following figures relate to one year's working at 100 per cent capacity level in a manufacturing business :

	Rs.
Fixed Overhead	1,20,000
Variable Overhead	2,00,000
Direct Wages	1,50,000
Sales	10,00,000
Direct Materials	4,10,000

Calculate the Break-even Point
[**Ans :** *Rs. 5,00,000*] (*B.Com., Madurai, 1980; B.Com., Meerut*)

26. The sales turnover and profit during two periods were as follows :
Period No. 1 Sales Rs. 20 lakhs, Profit Rs. 2 lakhs
Period No. 2 Sales Rs. 30 lakhs, Profit Rs. 4 lakhs.
Calculate
(*i*) P/V Ratio, and
(*ii*) The sales Rquired to earn a profit of Rs. 5 lakhs.
(**Ans :** (*i*) 20% (*ii*) *Rs. 35,00,000*) (*B.Com., Andhra, Osmania*)

27. From the following data, calculate the margin of safety :

Sales	Rs. 10,00,000
Fixed Expenses	Rs. 3,00,000
Profit	Rs. 2,00,000

[**Ans :** *Rs. 4,00,000*] (*M.Com., Madurai*)

28. From the following data calculate (*i*) P/V Ratio, (*ii*) profit when sales are Rs. 20,000 and (*iii*) The new break-even point, if the selling price is reduced by 20%.

Fixed Expenses	Rs. 4,000
Break-even Point	Rs. 10,000

[**Ans :** *40%, Rs. 4,000 Rs. 20,000*] (*B. Com., (Hons.) Delhi*)

29. The Bombay Radio Co. manufactured and sold 10,000 radios last year at a price of Rs. 500 each. The cost structure per radio is as follows :

	Rs.
Materials	100
Labour	50
Variable Overheads	25
Marginal Cost	175
Fixed Overheads	200
Total cost	375
Profit	125
Sales Price:	500

Due to heavy competition prices have to be reduced to Rs. 425 for the coming year. Assuming no change in costs, state the number of radios that would have to be sold at the new price to ensure the same amount of total profits as in the last year.
(*M.Com. Bombay, B.Com. Madurai*)

(**Ans** : *Profit needed = Rs. 12,50,000*
Number of radios to be sold : 13,000 radios)

30. The cost data in a factory is as follows :

Variable Cost	Rs 40 per unit.
Fixed Expenses	Rs 12,000
Selling Price	Rs 100 per unit

What is the profit when the sale is at 500 units ?
[**Ans** : *Rs. 18,000*] (*B.Com., Calicut*)

31. Sales of a product amount to 200 units per month at Rs. 10 per unit. Fixed overhead is Rs. 400 per month and variable cost Rs. 6 per unit. There is a proposal to reduce prices by 10%. Calculate present and future P/V ratio, and how many units must be sold to earn the present total profit ? (*ICWA India*)
(**Ans** : *Present P/V Ratio : 40% Future P/V Ratio : 33 1/3% Desired Units : 267 units*)

32. (a) A company has fixed expenses of Rs. 90,000 with sales at Rs. 3,00,000 and a profit of Rs. 60,000. Calculate the profit/volume ratio. If in the next period the company suffered a loss of Rs. 30,000, calculate the sales volume.
(b) What is the margin of safety for a profit of Rs. 60,000 in (a) above.
(**Ans** : (*a*) *P/V Ratio* : *50%, Sales volume Rs. 1,20,000*)
(*b*) *Margin of safety Rs. 1,20,000*)

33. From the following information, calculate the break-even point and turnover required to earn a profit of Rs. 36,000.

Fixed Overhead	Rs. 1,80,000
Variable Cost	Rs. 2 per unit
Selling Price	Rs. 20 per unit

If the company is earning a profit of Rs. 36,000 express the margin of safety available to it. (*C.A. Inter*)
(**Ans** : *Required turnover : 12,000 units Margin of safety : 2,000 units or Rs. 40,000*)

34. From the following data calculate
(*i*) B.E.P expressed in amount of sale in rupees,
(*ii*) Number of units that must be sold to earn a profit of Rs. 60,000 per year.

Sale Price	Rs. 20 per unit
Variable Manufacturing Expense	Rs. 11 per unit
Variable Selling Cost	Rs. 3 per unit
Fixed Factory Overheads	Rs 5,40,000 p.a.
Fixed Selling Costs	Rs. 2,52,000 p.a.

[**Ans** : (*i*) *Rs. 26,40,000* (*ii*) *1,42,000 units*] (*I.C.W.A.*)

35. The following are obtained from records of a factory :-

	Rs.	*Rs.*
Sales 4,000 units @ Rs. 25 each		1,00,000
Materials consumed	40,000	
Labour charges	20,000	
Variable Overheads	12,000	
	72,000	
Fixed Overhead Expenses	18,000	90,000
Profit		10,000

It is proposed to reduce the selling price by 20%. What extra units should be sold to obtain the same amount of profit as above ?
(**Ans** : *Extra Units* : *10,000 Units*) (*B.Com., Punjab*)

36. Raj Corporation Ltd. has prepared the following budget estimates for the year 2010 :

Sales Units	15,000
Fixed Expenses	Rs. 34,000
Sales Value	Rs. 1,50,000
Variable Costs	Rs. 6 per unit

You are required to :

(*i*) Find the P/V ratio, break-even point and margin of safety.

(*ii*) Calculate the revised P/V ratio, break-even point and margin of safety in each of the following cases :

(*a*) Decrease of 10% in selling price.

(*b*) Increase of 10% in variable costs.

(*c*) Increase of sales volume by 2,000 units

(*d*) Increase of Rs. 6,000 in fixed costs. (*CA Inter*)

(**Ans :** *P/V Ratio*

	P/V Ratio	*B.E.P*	*M.S*
		Rs.	*Rs.*
(*i*)	40%	*Rs. 85,000 or 8,500 units*	*Rs. 65,000*
(*ii*) (*a*)	*33.33%*	*Rs. 1,02,000*	*Rs. 33,000*
(*b*)	*34%*	*Rs. 1,00,000*	*Rs. 50,000*
(*c*)	*40%*	*Rs. 85,000*	*Rs. 85,000*
(*d*)	*40%*	*Rs. 1,00,000*	*Rs. 50,000*

37. The following data relate to a manufacturing company :

Plant capacity : 4,00,000 units per annum

Present utilisation : 40%

Actuals for the year 2000 were :

Selling Price	Rs. 50 per unit
Materials Cost	Rs. 20 per unit
Variable Manufactuing Costs	Rs. 15 per unit
Fixed Costs	Rs. 27 lakhs

In order to improve capacity utilisation the following proposals are considered :

Reduce Selling Price by 10%

Spend additional Rs. 3 lakhs on Sales Promotion

How many units should be made and sold in order to earn a profit of Rs. 5 lakhs per year ?

(**Ans.** *3,50,000 units to be sold*) (*C.A. Inter*)

38. Company A and company B, both under the same management, make and sell the same type of product. Their budgeted profit and loss accounts for January-June are as under :

	Company A		*Company B*	
	Rs.	Rs.	Rs.	Rs.
Sales		3,00,000		3,00,000
Less : Variable Cost	2,40,000		2,00,000	
Fixed Cost	30,000	2,70,000	70,000	2,70,000
		30,000		30,000

You are required to :

(*i*) Calculate the break-even point for each company

(*ii*) Calculate the sales volume at which each of the two companies will make a profit of Rs. 10,000. (*ICWA Inter*)

(**Ans :**	*Company A*	*Company B*
P/V Ratio	20%	33 1/3%
B.E.P	Rs. 1,50,000	Rs. 2,10,000
Sales Volume	Rs. 2,00,000	Rs. 2,40,000)

39. Kerala Products Ltd., produces 1,00,000 units of an article and sells them at the rate of Rs. 50 per unit. The marginal cost per unit is 60% of the selling price and the total fixed costs of the company are Rs. 10,00,000.

Draw a Break-even chart showing (*a*) B.E.P., (*b*) Margin of Safety; (*c*) Angle of incidence.

(**Ans :** (*a*) *Rs.* 25,00,000 (*b*) 25,00,000) (*B. Com., Kerala*)

40. Calculate 'Margin of Safety' from the following data :

	Rupa & Co.	*Ratna & Co.*
Sales	Rs. 1,00,000	Rs. 1,00,000
Cost	80,000	80,000
Fixed : Rupa & Co.	Rs. 30,000	
Ratna & Co.	50,000	
Variable :		
Rupa & Co.	50,000	
Ratna & Co.	30,000	
Profit	20,000	20,000

(*C.A. Final*)

(**Ans :**	*Rupa & Co.*	*Ratna & Co.*
P/V Ratio	50%	70%
B.E.S	Rs. 60,000	Rs. 71,429
MS	Rs. 40,000	Rs. 28,571)

41. Examination of cost accounting records of Elora Engineering Works Ltd., revealed that the company operated with a margin of safety ratio of 25% and a profit volume ratio of 40%. Fixed costs for the year were Rs. 5,04,000. You are required to compute the following using the above information :

(*a*) Break-even sales volume

(*b*) Sales volume for the year

(*c*) Total variable cost of sales for the year

(*d*) Profit for the year.

[**Ans :** (*a*) *12,60,000* (b) *Rs. 16,80,000* (*c*) *Rs. 10,08,000*, (*d*) *Rs. 1,68,000*]

(*M.Com., Gujarat*)

42. The operating results of a company for the last two years are as follows :

	Sales	*Profit*
2009	Rs. 2,70,000	Rs. 6,000
2010	Rs. 3,00,000	Rs. 15,000

You are required to calculate the break-even point.

[**Ans :** Rs. 2,50,000] (*M. Com., Kerala*)

43 The "Containers and Cases Private Limited" produces and markets industrial containers and packing cases. Due to competition the company propose to reduce the selling price. If the present level of profits is to be maintained, indicate the number of units to be sold if the proposed reduction in selling price is : (*a*) 5% (*b*) 10% and (*c*) 15%.

The following additional information is available :

	Rs.	*Rs.*
Present sales turnover (30,000 units)		3,00,000
Variable Cost (30,000 units)	1,80,000	
Fixed Cost	70,000	2,50,000
Net Profit		50,000

(*C.A. Final*)

(**Ans :** *Number of units to be sold : 30,000 at present price*
Number of units to be sold : 34,286 at 5% reduced price
Number of units to be sold : 40,000 units at 10% reduced price
Number of units to be sold : 48,000 units at 15 % reduced price)

44. From the following data, which product would you recommend to be manufactured in a factory, time being the key factor ?

	Per unit of Product A	*Per unit of Product B*
	Rs.	*Rs.*
Direct Material	24	14
Direct Labour (Re. 1 per hr.)	2	3
Variable Overhead (Rs. 2 per hr.)	4	6
Selling Price	100	113
Standard time to produce	2 hrs.	3 hrs.

[**Ans :** *Product A is profitable*] (*I.C.W.A. Inter*)

45. The following figures are extracted from the books of a manufacturing concern for the year :

	Rs.
Direct Materials	2,05,000
Direct Labour	75,000
Fixed Overheads	60,000
Variable overheads	1,00,000
Sales	5,00,000

Calculate the Break-even point and find out the impact of (*a*) 10% increase in fixed costs and (*b*) 3% decrease in variable costs on the break-even point.

[**Ans :** *Rs. 2,50,000* (*a*) *Rs. 2,75,000* (*b*) *Rs. 2,28,310*] (*M.Com., Madurai*)

46. You are given :

Margin of Safety : Rs. 10,000 which represents 40% of Sales, P/V Ratio : 50%. Find out
(*a*) Break-even Sales,
(*b*) Fixed Costs,
(*c*) Total Sales and Profit.

[**Ans :** (*a*) *15,000* (*b*) *7,500* (*c*) *5,000*]

47. For production of 1,000 units, the following costs are incurred :

	Rs.
Direct Materials	48,000
Direct Labour	32,500
Variable on Cost	4,500

The unit selling price is Rs. 105 and the gross profit per unit is Rs. 15. Ascertain the fixed oncosts.

[**Ans :** *Rs. 5,000*] (*B.Com., Madurai*)

48. Alcos Ltd. Manufacturers and sells four types of products under the brand names, A, B, C and D. The sales mix in value comprises of $33\frac{1}{3}\%$, $41\frac{1}{3}\%$, $16\frac{1}{3}\%$ and $18\frac{1}{3}\%$ of A, B, C and D respectively. The total budgeted sales (100%) are Rs. 60,000 per month. The opening costs are:

Variable Costs :

Product	A	60% of the Selling Price
	B	68% of the Selling Price
	C	80% of the Selling Price
	D	40% of the Selling Price

The Fixed Cost is Rs. 14,700 per month.

Calculate the break-even point for the products on an overall basis.

It has been proposed to change the sales mix as follows, the total sales per month remaining at Rs. 60,000:

Product	A	25%
	B	40%
	C	30%
	D	5%

Assuming that the proposal is implemented, calculate the break-even point.

[*Ans : Rs. 42,000*] (*B.Com., Calcutta*)

49. The price structure of a cycle made by the Cycle Co. Ltd., is as follows :

	Per Cycle Rs.
Material	60
Labour	20
Variable Overheads	20
	100
Fixed Overheads	50
Profit	50
Selling Price	200

This is based on the manufacture of one lakh cycles per annum.

The Company expects that due to competition they will have to reduce selling prices, but they want to keep the total profits intact. What level of production will have to be reached *i.e.* how many cycles will have to be made to get the same amount of profit, if :

(*a*) The selling price is reduced by 10% ?

(*b*) The selling price is reduced by 20% ?

(**Ans :** (*a*) *1,25,000 cycles* (*b*) *1,66,667 cycles* (*I.C.W.A., Inter*)

50. You are given the following information in respect of a company :

		Rs.
(*i*) Fixed Cost	—	13,000
(*ii*) Variable Cost	—	14,000
(*iii*) Total Cost	—	27,000
(*iv*) Net Profit	—	3,000
(*v*) Net Sales	—	30,000

(*a*) Find out the Break-even point.

(*b*) Forecast the profit for sales volume Rs. 50,000

(c) Estimate the volume of sales turnover to make a net profit of Rs. 10,000. (*ACS*)

(**Ans :** (*a*) B.E.P : *Rs. 24,375*
(b) Profit Rs. 13,667
(c) Sales required : Rs. 43,125)

51. From the following particulars find out the selling price per unit if the break-even point is to be brought down to 9,000 units.

	Rs.
Variable Cost per unit	75
Fixed Expenses	2,88,000
Selling Price per unit	100

(**Ans :** *Rs. 107 per unit*] (*B.Com., Kerala*)

52. Find out the break-even point from the following information :
(*a*) Fixed Cost Rs. 20,000; Variable Cost Rs. 2 per unit and Sales Price Rs. 4 per unit.
(*b*) Sales Rs. 6,000; Variable Cost Rs. 3,600 and Fixed Cost Rs. 2,000.
(*c*) Sales Rs. 4,000; Variable Cost Rs. 2,400 and Profit Rs. 400.

(**Ans :** (*a*) 10,000 units (*B.Com. Calicut*)
(b) Rs. 5,000
(c) Rs. 3,500)

53. A factory manufacturing machines has the capacity to produce 500 machines p.a. The marginal cost of each machine is Rs. 200 and each machine is sold for Rs. 250. Fixed Overheads are Rs. 12,000 p.a. Calculate the break-even points for output and sales and show what profit will result if output is 90% capacity ? (*B.Com., Madras*)

(**Ans :** *B.E.P : 240 machines*
B.E.P : Sales: Rs. 60,000
Profit Rs. 10,500)

54. The following information relating to a company is given to you :

	Rs.
Sales	4,00,000
Fixed Cost	1,80,000
Variable Cost	2,50,000

Ascertain how much the value of sales must be increased for the company to break even.
(**Ans :** *Value of sales to be increased by Rs. 80,000*) (*B.Com., Calicut*)

55. Margin of safety ratio is 20%
P/V Ratio is 60%
Fixed Cost = Rs. 30,000
Find out : (*a*) B.E.P sales
(*b*) Actual total sales for the year
(*c*) Variable cost for the year
(*d*) Profit for the year (*B.Com., Madurai*)

(**Ans :** (*a*) *Rs. 50,000*
(b) Rs. 62,500
(c) Rs. 7,500
(d) Rs. 25,000)

56. From the following data, calculate break-even point expressed in terms of units and also the new break-even point, if selling price is redued by 10% :

Fixed Expenses :

Depreciation	Rs. 1,00,000
Salaries	Rs. 1,00,000

Variable Expenses :

Materials	Rs. 3 per unit
Labour	Rs. 2 per unit
Selling Price	Rs. 10 per unit

(Ans : *40,000 units* *(B.Com., Delhi)*

50,000 units, if selling price is reduced by 10%)

57. The following information, relating to a company, is given to you.

	Rs.
Sales	4,00,000
Fixed Cost	1,80,000
Variable Cost	2,50,000

Ascertain how much value of sales must be inceased for the company to break-even.

(Ans : *Sales to be increased to Rs. 4,80,000*) *(B.Com., Calicut)*

58. That Cost Sheet of a Radiogram set is as follows :

	Rs.
Materials	330
Labour	390
Variable Expenses	240
Fixed Expenses	180
Total Cost	1,140
Profit	360
Selling Price	1,500

The number of sets now made and sold are = 50,000.

Calculate

(*a*) Break-even point, and

(*b*) No. of sets that should be produced and sold when selling price is reduced by Rs. 60 so as to break-even.

(Ans : (*a*) *Rs. 2,50,00,500* *(B.Com., Bangalore)*

(*b*) *18,750 units*)

59. From the following information relating to a firm, you are required to find out :

(*a*) Contribution

(*b*) Break-even point in units

(*c*) Margin of Safety

(*d*) Profit :

Total fixed Costs	Rs. 4,500
Total variable Costs	Rs. 7,500
Total Sales	Rs. 15,000
Units Sold	5,000 units

Also calculate the volume of sales to earn profit of Rs. 6,000.

(Ans : (*a*) *Contribution Rs. 1.50 per unit and total 7,500*

(*b*) *Rs. 9,000*

(*c*) *Rs. 6,000 or 40%*

(*d*) *Rs. 3,000*)

60. The following information is obtained from A Co. Ltd., in a certain year :

	Rs.
Sales (1,00,000 Units)	1,00,000
Variable Cost	60,000
Fixed Cost	30,000

(*a*) Find P/V Ratio, Break-even point, and Margin of Safety at this level.

(*b*) Calculate the effect of—

(*i*) 20% increase in Selling Price;

(*ii*) 10% decrease in Selling Price;

(*iii*) 5 % decrease in Sales Volume;

(*iv*) 10% decrease in Fixed Costs;

(*v*) 10% decrease in Variable Costs;

(*vi*) 20% increase in Sales Price accompained by an increase of Fixed Overhead by Rs. 10,000.

(*vii*) 20% increase in Sales Price accompanied by 10% decrease in Variable Costs and 10% increase in Fixed Costs. (*B. Com., Delhi*)

(Ans :		*P/V Ratio*	*B.E.P*	*M.S*
(*a*)		*40%*	*Rs. 75,000*	*Rs. 25,000*
(*b*)	(*i*)	*50%*	*Rs. 60,000*	*Rs. 60,000*
	(*ii*)	*33 1/3%*	*Rs. 90,000*	*Nil*
	(*iii*)	*40%*	*Rs. 75,000*	*Rs. 20,000*
	(*iv*)	*40%*	*Rs. 67,500*	*Rs. 32,500*
	(*v*)	*46%*	*Rs. 65,217*	*Rs. 34,783*
	(*vi*)	*50%*	*Rs. 80,000*	*Rs. 40,000*
	(*vii*)	*55%*	*Rs. 60,000*	*Rs. 60,000)*

61. From the information given below, comment on the performance of departments X, Y and Z.

	Total Rs.	Dept.'X'Rs.	Dept. 'Y' Rs.	Dept. 'Z' Rs.
Sales	90,000	20,000	40,000	30,000
Variable Cost of Sales	62,000	12,000	30,000	20,000
Total Cost of Sales	82,000	14,000	36,000	32,000
Net Profit (Loss)	8,000	6,000	4,000	(2,000)

(**Ans :** *P/V Ratios : 40% (X) It gives maximum profit*) (*I.C.W.A., Final*)
25% (Y)
33 1/3% (Z)

62. The following production/sales mix is capable of achievement in a factory :

(*i*) 2,000 units of product 'A' and 2,000 units of product 'C'

(*ii*) 4,000 units of product 'B'

(*iii*) 1,000 units of product 'A', 2,000 units of product 'B' and 1,600 units of product 'C'.

Cost per unit is as follows :

	A	B	C
Direct Materials	Rs. 20	Rs. 16	Rs. 40
Direct Wages	Rs. 8	10	20

Fixed Cost is Rs. 20,000 and variable overheads per unit of A, B and C are Rs. 2, 4 and Rs. 8 respectively. Selling prices of A, B and C are Rs. 36, Rs. 40 and Rs. 100

per unit respectively. Determine the marginal contribution per unit of A, B and C and the profit resulting from product mixes (*i*), (*ii*) and (*iii*). (*ICWA. Inter*)

(**Ans :** *Profit : Rs. 6, Rs. 10 and Rs. 32*
Total profit Rs. 56,000, Rs. 20,000 and Rs. 57,200)

63. You are required to calculate the break-even point in the following case :

The Fixed Costs for the year are Rs. 80,000; Variable Cost per unit for the single product being made is Rs. 4.

Estimated sales for the period are valued at Rs. 2,00,000. The number of units involved coincides with the expected volume of output. Each unit sells at Rs. 20.

Calculate break-even point (B.E.P) by applying important formulae.

(**Ans :** *Rs. 5,000 units or Rs. 1,00,000*) (*C.A. Final*)

64. From the following data you are required to calculate :

(*i*) the marginal cost of products M and N and the contribution per unit;

(*ii*) the contributions of profits resulting from each of the suggested sales mixtures and the best combinations thereof.

	Rs. per unit	
	Product M	*Product N*
Direct Materials	21.00	17.00
Direct Wages	6.00	4.00
Sales Price	41.00	29.00

Fixed Expenses (Total) Rs. 1,600

Variable Expenses—100% on direct wages per product.

Suggested Sales Mixtures :

	No. of units	
	M	*N*
(*a*)	200	400
(*b*)	300	300
(*c*)	400	200

(**Ans :** *Profit : Rs. 1,600; Rs. 2,000 and Rs. 2,400* (*ICWA Inter*)
Sales Mix C is the best)

65. From the following data, you are required to calculate the Break-even point and net sales value at this point :

Selling Price per unit Rs. 25
Direct Material Cost per unit Rs. 8
Direct Labour Cost per unit Rs 5
Fixed Overheads Rs. 24,000
Variable Overheads @ 60% on Direct Labour
Trade discount 4%.

If sales are 15% and 20% above the Break-even volume, determine the net profits. (*CA Inter*)

(**Ans :** *B.E.P : 3,000 units; Sales Value Rs. 72,000 (Less Trade discount)*
Profit Rs. 3,600 at 15% above BEP
Profit Rs. 4,800 at 20% above BEP)

66. The following two suggestion are under consideration:

(*a*) 10 per cent reduction in price to yield an increase in sales volume from 6,600 to 7,900 units.

(*b*) 10 percent increase in price with decrease in volume of sales from 6,600 to 5,700 units.

The following particulars are given :

	Rs.
Current Unit Price	1,000
Unit Variable Cost	500
Fixed Cost	30 Lakhs

Prepare a statement comparing gross revenue, profit contribution and P/V Ratio of the two alternatives with present results. Which suggestion would you recommend ?

(*I.C.W.A., Final*)

(**Ans :** *P/V Ratio : Present Position : 50%*
P/V Ratio : Proposal (*a*) *40%*
P/V Ratio : Proposal (*b*) *54%. it is more profitable*)

67. The annual sales budget of a company is :

	STATE A	*STATE B*	*STATE C*
	Rs.	*Rs.*	*Rs.*
Net Sales	4,00,000	6,00,000	10,00,000
Variable Selling Cost	1,00,000	2,00,000	2,50,000

The cost of goods sold excluding selling costs is 50% of the net sales.

If the break-even points of the three States A, B and C are 50%, 60% and 70% respectively of the net sales budgeted, ascertain the total fixed selling expense of the company and the profit or loss made in each state. (*M. Com., Karnataka*)

(**Ans :** *Fixed Selling Expenses : Rs. 50,000* (*State A*)
Rs. 60,000 (*State B*)
Rs. 1,75,000 (*State C*)
Profit : Rs. 50,000 (*State A*); *Rs. 40,000* (*State B*); *Rs. 75,000* (*State C*)

68. The Novelties Ltd is not keen on making special efforts to push the sales of product B, one of three main products it deals in, since product B is not considered to be as profitable as the other two. The selling price and cost of the three products are :

			Direct Labour		
Product	*Selling Price*	*Direct Material*	*Dept. X*	*Dept. Y*	*Dept. Z*
	Rs.	*Rs.*	*Rs.*	*Rs.*	*Rs.*
A	340	50	40	10	10
B	290	30	10	40	10
C	320	40	10	10	40

Overhead rates for each department per rupee of direct labour are as follows :

	Dept. X	*Dept. Y*	*Dept. Z*
	Rs.	*Rs.*	*Rs.*
Variable Overhead	1.20	0.40	1.00
Fixed Overhead	1.20	2.00	1.40
Total	2.40	2.40	2.40

What will be your advice about the profitability of product B ? Give reasons.

(**Ans :** *Product* *A* *B* *C*
Profit Rs. 86 Rs. 56 Rs. 76 *Thus product B*
Contribution Rs. 168 Rs. 162 Rs. 164 *should be encouraged*)

69. There are two plants manufacturing the same products under one corporate management which has decided to merge them. The following particulars are available regarding the two plants :

	Plant I	Plant II
Capacity operation	100%	60%
Sales	Rs. 6,00,000	Rs. 2,40,000
Variable Costs	Rs. 4,40,000	Rs. 1,80,000
Fixed Cost	Rs. 80,000	Rs. 40,000

You are required to calculate for the consideration of the Board of Directors :

(*a*) What would be the capacity of the merged plant to be operated for the purpose of break-even ?

(*b*) What would be the profitability on working at 75% of the capacity ?

(**Ans :** (*a*) *Rs. 4,61,538* (*b*) *46.15%, 10%*) (*M.Com.*)

70. The trading results of Raja & Co. for the last two quarters are :

The quarter ended	*Sales*	*Profit*
June	Rs. 25,000	Rs. 5,000
September	Rs. 37,500	Rs. 10,000

Calculate

(*a*) Profit-Volume Ratio

(*b*) Fixed Costs

(*c*) Break-even Sales Volume

(*d*) Sales to earn a profit of Rs. 7,500

(*e*) Profit when sales are Rs. 20,000

(**Ans :** (*a*) *40%;* (*b*) *Rs. 5,000* (*c*) *Rs. 12,500* (*d*) *Rs. 31,250;* (*e*) *Rs. 3,000*)

71. A. Calculate the Break-Even point from the following :

(*a*) Sales Price Rs. 10 per unit

(*b*) Variable Cost Rs. 6 per unit

(c) Fixed Overheads Rs. 20,000

B. Calculate the revised Break-Even point if :

(*i*) Sale Price is increased to Rs. 11 per unit

(*ii*) Sale Price is reduced to Rs. 9 per unit“

(*iii*) Variable Cost increased to Rs. 7 per unit

(*iv*) Variable Cost reduced to Rs. 5 per unit

(*v*) Fixed Overheads rised to Rs. 25,000

(*vi*) Fixed Overheads fall to Rs. 15,000

(**Ans :** (*a*) *5,000 units ;* (*b*) (*i*) *4,000 units;* (*ii*) *6,667 units* (*iii*) *6,667 units* (*iv*) *4,000 units* (*v*) *6,250 units* (*vi*) *3,750 units.*)

72. A factory produces 1,000 articles for home consumption at the following costs :

	Rs.	*Rs.*
Materials		40,000
Wages		36,000
Factory Overheads :		
Fixed	12,000	
Variable	20,000	32,000
Administration Overheads Fixed		18,000
Selling & Distribution Overheads :		
Fixed	10,000	
Variable	16,000	26,000
Total		1,52,000

The home market can consume only 1,000 articles at a selling price of Rs. 155 per article; it can consume on more articles. The foreign market for this product can, however, consume additional 4,000 articles if the price is reduced to Rs. 125.

Is the foreign market worth trying ? *(M.Com., Calcutta)*

(**Ans :** *Contribution Rs. 13 per unit and total contribution Rs. 52,000. The foreign market is worth trying*)

73. Ambitious Enterprises is currently working at 50% capacity and produces 10,000 units. At 60% working, raw material cost increases by 2% and selling price falls by 2 per cent. At 80 per cent working, raw material cost increases by 5 per cent and selling price falls by 5 per cent

At 50% capacity working, the product costs Rs. 180 per unit and is sold at Rs. 200 per unit.

The unit cost of Rs. 180 is made up as follows :

	Rs.
Material	100
Wages	30
Factory Overheads	30 (40% fixed)
Administration Overheads	20 (50% fixed)

Prepare a marginal cost statement showing the estimated profit of the business when it is operated at 60% and 80% capacity. *(B.Com Hon., Delhi)*

(**Ans :** *Profit per unit = Rs. 17.67 ; Total profit = Rs. 2,12,000 at 60% Capacity. Profit per unit = Rs. 13.75 ; Total profit = Rs. 2,12,000 at 80% capacity*)

74. There are two similar plants under the same management. The management desires to merge these two plants. The following particulars are available :

	Factory *I*	Factory *II*
Capacity operation	100 per cent	60 per cent
Sales	Rs 300 lacs	Rs. 120 lacs
Variable Costs	Rs. 220 lacs	Rs. 90 lacs
Fixed Costs	Rs. 40 lacs	Rs. 20 lacs

You are required to calculate (*a*) what would be the capacity of merged plant to be operated for the purpose of Break-even, and (*b*) what would be the profitability on working at 75% of merged capacity.

(**Ans :** *P/V Ratios : 26.7% (Plants I) : 25% (Plant II); 26% merged plant percentage of profit to sales : 10%*)

75. A company manufactures a machine which has a variable cost structure as follows :

	Rs.
Materials	40
Labour	10
Overhead	4
Selling Price	90

Sales during the current year are expected to be Rs. 13,50,000 and Fixed Overhead Rs. 1,40,000.

Under a wage agreement, an increase of 10% is payable to all direct workers from the beginning for the forthcoming year, while material costs are expected to increase by 7.5%, variable overhead costs by 5% and fixed overhead costs 3%.

You are required to calculate :

(*a*) The new selling price if the current profit/volume ratio is to be maintained; and (*b*) The quantity to be sold during the forthcoming year to yield the same amount of profit as the current year assuming the selling price to remain at Rs. 90.

(*C.A. Inter*)

(**Ans :** (*a*) *P/V Ratio : 40%, New Selling Price Rs. 97.00*
(*b*) *Contribution required : Rs. 5,44,200 or 17,113 Machines*)

76. Production costs of Original Enterprises Ltd., are as follows :

	Level of Activity		
	60%	70%	80%
Output (in units)	1,200	1,400	1,600
Costs (in Rs.)			
Direct Materials	24,000	28,000	32,000
Direct Labour	7,200	8,400	9,600
Factory Overheads	12,800	13,600	14,400
Works Cost	44,000	50,000	56,000

A proposal to increase production to 90% level of activity is under consideration of management. The proposal is not expected to involve any increase in fixed factory overheads.

Prepare a statement showing the prime cost, total marginal cost and total factory cost at 90% level of activity. (*B.Com. Hons. Delhi*)

(**Ans :** *At 90% Activity: Prime Cost is Rs. 46,800; Marginal Cost Rs. 54,000, Factory Cost Rs. 62,000*)

77. The Super Cooperative Stores in Delhi owns and operates twelve super markets in Delhi. You are given the following budget of firm for the year 2010.

	Rs.
Sales	5,00,000
Fixed Expenses	82,000
Variable Expenses	4,00,000

(*a*) Find the P/V Ratio, Break-even point and margin of safety at this level.

(*b*) Compute the effect on the expected profit for each of the following deviations from budgeted data.

(*i*) 10% increase in total Contribution Margin
(*ii*) 10% decrease in total Contribution Margin
(*iii*) 5% increase in Fixed Costs
(*iv*) 5% decrease in Fixed Costs
(*v*) 8% increase in Sales Volume
(*vi*) 8% decrease in Sales Volume
(*vii*) 10% increase in Fixed Costs and 10% increase in Sales Volume and
(*viii*) 5% increase in Fixed Costs and 5% decrease in variable costs.

(**Ans :**	*P/V Ratio*	*B.E.PRs.*	*Margin of Safety*
	%	*Rs.*	*Rs.*
(*a*)	*20%*	*4,10,000*	*90,000*
(*b*) (*i*)	*21.57%*	*3,80,158*	*1,29,842*
(*ii*)	*18,4%*	*4,46,663*	*43,377*
(*iii*)	*20%*	*4,30,500*	*69,500*

(iv)	*20%*	*3,89,500*	*1,10,500*
(v)	25.9%	3,16,602	2,23,398
(vi)	*13%*	*6,30,769*	*Nil*
(vii)	*27.7%*	*3,30,766*	*2,19,234*
(viii)	*24%*	*3,58,750*	*1,41,250)*

78. A company has a capacity of producing 1,00,000 units of a certain product in a month. The sales department reports that the following schedule of sales prices is possible :

Volume of Production	*Selling Price per unit*
%	*Price*
60	90
70	80
80	75
90	67
100	61

The Variable Cost of manufacture between these levels is 15 paise per unit and Fixed Cost Rs. 40,000.

(*a*) Prepare a statement showing incremental revenue and differential cost at each stage. At which volume of production will the profit be maximum ?

(*b*) If there is bulk offer at 50 paise per unit for the balance capacity over the maximum profit-volume for export and price quoted will not affect the internal sale, will you advise accepting this bid and why ? *(I.C.W.A., Inter)*

(**Ans :** (*a*) *Profit is maximum at 80% level of production*
(*b*) *Additional profit of Rs. 7,000. The Company can accept*)

79. From the following information relating to Quick Stds. Ltd. you are required to find out :

(*a*) Contribution,
(*b*) Break-even point in units,
(*c*) Margin of Safety,
(*d*) Profit :

	Rs
Total Fixed Costs	4,500
Total Variable Costs	7,500
Total Sales	15,000
Units Sold	5,000 (units)

(*e*) Also calculate the volume of sales to earn a profit of Rs. 6,000. *(A.C.S. Final)*

(**Ans :** (*a*) *Rs. 7,500;* (*b*) *3,000 units* (*c*) *Rs. 6,000* (*d*) *Rs. 3,000* (*e*) *Rs. 6,000)*

80. Following information is given :

Fixed Costs	Rs. 18,000	Sales	5,000 units
Break-even units	3,000	Selling Price per units Rs.	20

Calculate :

(*a*) Profit/Volume Ratio.
(*b*) Margin of Safety.
(*c*) Profit if sales are Rs. 1,30,000
(*d*) Additional units to be sold increasing the present profit by Rs. 5,400.

(M. Com., Kanpur)

(**Ans :** (*a*) *30%;* (*b*) *Rs. 40,000* (*c*) *Rs. 21,000* (*d*) *900 units)*

81. The following figures relate to a company manufacturing a varied range of products :

	Total Sales	Total Cost
	Rs.	Rs.
Year ended 31st Dec., 2010	39,00,000	34,80,000
Year ended 31st Dec., 2011	43,00,000	37,60,000

Assuming stability in prices, with variable costs carefully controlled to reflect predetermined relationships and an unvarying figure for fixed costs, calculate : (*a*) P/V Ratio, to reflect the rates of growth for profit and for sales; and (*b*) any other cost figures to be deducted from the data. (*C.A. Inter*)

(**Ans :** *(a) P/V Ratios : 30% (2010) and 30% (2011)*
(b) MS : Rs. 14,00,000 (2010) and %, Rs. 18,00,000 (2011).

82. The sales of a company in the first half of 2010, amounted to Rs. 2,70,000 and profit earned was Rs. 7,200. The sales in the second half registered an increase and amounted to Rs. 3,42,000. The profit earned was Rs. 20,700 in that half year. Assuming no change in fixed costs, calculate :

(*i*) P/V Ratio
(*ii*) The amount of profit when sales are Rs. 2,16,000
(*iii*) The amount of sales required to earn a profit of Rs. 36,000 (*B.Com., Delhi*)

(**Ans :** *(i) 18.75%, (ii) Loss : Rs. 2,925 and (iii) Rs. 4,23,600*)

83. You are given the following information :

Selling Price	Rs. 10 per unit
Variable Cost	Rs. 6 per unit
Fixed Cost	Rs. 10,000

Present production and sales 5,000 units.

The directors of the company propose to reduce the selling price by 20%. Find out the additional number of units that should be sold to maintain the profit at present. (*B. Com., Rajasthan*)

(**Ans :** *Present profit Rs. 10,000, additional number of units 5,000*)

84. In 2010, the position of a firm was as follows :

	Rs.
Sales	2,40,000
Variable Costs	1,92,000
Gross Profit	48,000
Fixed Cost	32,000
Net Profit	16,000

Find out : (*i*) P/V Ratio
(*ii*) B.E.P
(*iii*) Net Profit from the sale of Rs. 2,60,000

(**Ans :** *(i) 20% (ii) Rs. 1,60,000 (iii) Rs. 20,000*) (*B.Com. Madras*)

85. The following miscellaneous information regarding the operations of 2010 has been made available from the records of a firm :

	Rs.
Sales	1,00,000
Direct Materials used	40,000
Direct Labour	15,000
Fixed manufacturing Overheads	20,000
Fixed Selling and Administration Expenses	10,000
Gross Profit	20,000
Net Loss	5,000

There are no beginning or ending inventories.

It is required to calculate :

(*a*) Variable selling and administration expenses

(*b*) Contribution margin in rupees

(*c*) Variable factory overhead

(*d*) Break-even point sales in rupees

(*e*) Factory cost of goods sold. (*B. Com. Hons. Delhi*)

(**Ans :** *(a) Rs. 15,000; (b) Rs. 25,000: (c) Rs. 5,000 (d) Rs. 37,500 (e) Rs. 80,000*)

86. The Reliable Battery Co. Furnishes you the following information :

	Year 2010	
	First half	*Second half*
Sales	Rs 8,10,000	10,26,000
Profit earned	Rs. 21,600	64,800

From the above you are required to compute the following assuming that fixed cost remains the same in both the periods.

1. P/V Ratio
2. Fixed Cost
3. The amount of Profit or Loss when sales are Rs. 6,48,000.
4. The amount of sales required to earn a profit of Rs. 1,08,000. (*C.A. Inter*)

(**Ans :** *(1) 20%; (2) Rs. 1,40,400; (3) Loss : Rs. 10,800 (4) Rs. 12,42,000*)

87. The sales turnover and profit during two years were as follows :

Year	*Sales*	*Profit*
Rs.	*Rs.*	
2009	1,50,000	20,000
2010	1,70,000	25,000

You are required to calculate :

(*i*) P/V Ratio

(*ii*) Break-even point

(*iii*) The sales required to earn a profit of Rs. 40,000

(*iv*) Profit when sales are Rs. 2,50,000

(*v*) Margin of Safety at a profit of Rs. 50,000

(*vi*) Variable Costs of the two periods. (*B.Com., M.Com., Madurai*)

(**Ans :** *(i) 25%; (ii) Rs. 70,000; (iii) Rs. 2,30,000 (iv) Rs. 45,000 (v) Rs. 2,00,000 (vi) Rs. 1,27,500*)

88. You are given the following data for the coming year of a factory : Budgeted output 80,000 units

Fixed Expenses	Rs. 4,00,000
Variable Expenses per unit	Rs. 10
Selling Price per unit	Rs. 20

(*a*) Find out the Break-even point.

(*b*) If the Selling Price is reduced to Rs. 15, find out the new Break-even point. (*B.Com., Osmania*)

[**Ans :** *(a) 40,000 units or Rs. 8,00,000; (b) 80,000 units or Rs., 12,00,000*]

89. S. Ltd. furnishes you the following information relating to the half year ended 30th June:

	Rs.
Fixed Expenses	45,000
Sales Value	1,50,000
Profit	30,000

During the second half of the year, the company has projected a loss of Rs. 10,000. Calculate :

(*a*) The Break-even point and Margin of Safety for six months ending 30th June.

(*b*) Expected sales volume for second half of the year assuming that the P/V Ratio and Fixed Expenses remain constant in the scond half year also.

(*c*) The Break-even point and Margin of Safety for the whole year. (*C.A. Inter*)

(**Ans :** *(a) Rs. 60,000 (b) Rs. 70,000; (c) BEP = Rs. 1,80,000, Rs. 40,000*)

90. The following suggestions are under consideration :

(*a*) 10% reduction in price to yield an increase in sales volume from 6,600 to 7,400 units.

(*b*) 10% increase in price with decrease in volume of sales from 7,600 to 6,700 units.

The following particulars are given :

Current unit price	Rs. 1,000
Unit variable Cost	Rs. 500
Fixed Cost	Rs. 30,00,000

Prepare a statement comparing gross revenue, profit, contribution and P/V Ratio of the two alternatives with present results. Which suggestion would you recommend ?

(**Ans :** *Proposal (b) can be accepted and P/V Ratio is 54.5%*) (*ICWA*)

91. During a year, a manufacturing company has produced and sold three products *viz.* product A —20,000 units, B—14,000 units and C—10,000 units. The following further information is also available.

	Per Unit		
	A	*B*	*C*
Marginal Cost (Rs.)	10	18	16
Time taken (hours)	2.5	3	2.5
List Price	20	30	40

Fixed Cost (total) Rs. 2,00,000

The list prices of the products are subject to a uniform trade discount of 10%. Due to shortage of labour the available working hours for the next year are estimated to be only 90,000.

Suggest a suitable sales-mix for the next year.

(*a*) When there is enough demand for all the products;

(*b*) When the potential demand is 18,000 units for A, 10,000 units for B and 12,000 units for C. (*M.Com., Calcutta*)

92. The following particulars are extracted from the records of a company:

	Product A	*Product B*
Sales per unit	Rs. 100	Rs. 120
Consumption of Material	2 kg.	3 kg.
Material Cost	Rs. 10	Rs. 15
Direct Wages Cost	Rs. 15	Rs. 10
Direct Expenses	Rs. 5	Rs .6
Machine hours used	3	2
Overhead Expenses :		
Fixed	Rs. 5	Rs. 10
Variable	Rs. 15	Rs. 20

Direct Wage per hour Rs. 5. Commend on the profitability of each product (both use the same new materials) when :

(*i*) Total sales potential in units is limited ;
(*ii*) Total sales potential in value is limited ;
(*iii*) Raw material is in short supply ; and
(*iv*) Production capacity (in terms of machine hours) is the limiting factor.

Assuming raw material as the key factor, availability of which is 10,000 kg. and maximum sales potential of each product being 3,500 units, find out the product mix which will yield the maximum profit.

[**Ans :** *Product A is more profitable.*] (*ICWA Inter*)

Chapter 8

Standard Costing-I

Introduction; Definition; Estimated Costing Vs. Standard Costing; Standard Cost Vs. Budgetary Control; Similarity between Standard Cost and Budget; Advantages of Standard Costing; Limitations of Standard Costing; Applicability of Standard Costing; Setting the Standard; Determination of Standard Costs; Revision of Standards; Standard Cost Card; Objective Type Questions; Theoretical Questions.

Introduction

One of the most important functions of management accounting is to facilitate managerial control. The major aspect of managerial control is cost control. The efficiency of management, among other things, depends upon the effective control of costs. For controlling costs, management should not only know actual cost – the cost actually incurred but also pre-determined costs – the cost which should have been incurred. Standard costs are the widely used form of pre-determined costs. The system of standard costing is the most efficient way of controlling costs.

Historical cost systems are principally associated with recording of historical, or as they are commonly called, actual cost. Historical costing is the ascertainment of costs after they have been incurred. No doubt, information on actual costs is useful in determining the cost of production per unit; but from the point of view of decision-making and costs control, actual costs are not useful to management. Actual costs are meaningful only when they are compared with pre-determined costs.

Historical costs have the following limitations:

1. Historical costs do not provide any means of evaluating and comparing performances. Therefore, historical costs are ineffective in cost control.
2. Historical costs do not provide reliable guides to management in the tasks of budgeting, planning and decision-making. Costs incurred in the past reflect a situation in a previous period. The conditions prevailing in one period are unlikely to repeat in another period.
3. Historical costs are not helpful in cost reduction since they contain no standard or goals towards which employee can work.

Historical Costing or actual costing is a system where costs are ascertained after they are incurred. It is a postmortem of the costs. Historical Costing does not help in finding mistakes and inefficiencies, which all lead to variation in profit. Due to these disadvantages and limitations of historical costing, the standard costing technique was introduced in U.S.A. and in U.K. In India also standard costing is used widely and recognised greatly.

Standard cost seeks to establish the cost of a product, operations or process under standard operating conditions. The aim of standard cost is to eliminate the influence of abnormal changes in prices. It is used as a guide for future decision and action over a period of time. Standard

Costing is an effective management tool for planning, decision-making, coordination and control of business. The object of standard cost is to ascertain the quotation and determination of price policy. It is a technique of cost control.

Definition

Standard. According to Prof. Eric L. Kohler, "Standard is a desired attainable objective, a performance, a goal, a model". Standard may be used to a predetermined rate or a predetermined amount or a predetermined cost.

Standard Cost. Standard costs are predetermined cost or forecast estimate of cost. I.C.M.A. Terminology defines Standard Cost as, "a predetermined cost, which is calculated from management standards of efficient operations and, the relevant necessary expenditure. It may be used as a basis for price-fixing and for cost control through variance analysis". The other names for standard costs are predetermined costs, budgeted costs, projected costs, model costs, measured costs, specification costs etc. Standard Cost is a predetermined estimate of cost to manufacture a single unit or a number of units of a product during a future period. Actual costs are compared with these standard costs.

Standard Costing is defined by I.C.M.A. Terminology as, "The preparation and use of standard costs, their comparison with actual costs and the analysis of variances to their causes and points of incidence".

"Standard Costing is a method of ascertaining the costs whereby statistics are prepared to show (*a*) the standard cost (*b*) the actual cost (*c*) the difference between these costs, which is termed the variance" says Wheldon. Thus the technique of standard cost study comprises of :

1. Pre-determination of standard costs :
2. Use of standard costs;
3. Comparison of actual cost with the standard costs;
4. Find out and analyse reasons for variances;
5. Reporting to management for proper action to maximise efficiency.

Estimated Costing versus Standard Costing

Both Standard Costing and Estimated Costing are predetermined costs. But the object of standard costing differs. The differences between these two costs are :

Estimated Cost	*Standard Cost*
1. It is used as statistical data and leads to a lot of guess work.	It is scientifically used and it is a regular system of account based upon estimation and time studies.
2. Its object is to ascertain "What the costs will be".	Its object is to ascertain "what the costs should be".
3. It gives importance to cost ascertainment for fixing sale price.	It is used for effective cost control and to take proper action to maximise efficiency.
4. It is used for a specific use; *i.e.,* fixing sale price.	It is a continuous process of costing and takes into account all the manufacturing processes.
5. It can be used where costing is in operation.	It can be used where standard costing is in operation.
6. It is not accurate. It is an approximation based on past experience.	As it is based on scientific analysis it is more accurate than the estimated cost.

Historical Cost versus Standard Cost

Historical Cost	*Standard Cost*
1. It is an after-production-recorded cost.	It is a predetermined cost.
2. It is actually, incurred cost.	It is an ideal cost.
3. As it relates to the past it is not useful for cost control.	It is a future cost. It can be used for cost control.
4. It is used to ascertain the profit or the loss incurred during a period.	It is used for the measurement of operational efficiency of the enterprises.

Standard Cost versus Budgetary Control

Both standard costing and budgetary control aim at the objective of maximum efficiency and managerial control. Standard cost and budgetary control have the comparing actual performance with the predetermined standards, analysing and reporting of variances.

Without standard cost figure, preparation of budget or a real budgetary control system cannot be achieved.

Similarity between Standard Cost and Budget

1. Both aim at the determination of cost in advance.
2. For both of them predetermined standards are fixed.
3. In both of them actual costs are compared with standard costs.
4. Both require periodic cost reports.
5. Both aim at the maximum efficiencies and managerial costs. But they differ in scope and technique.

Budgetary Control and Standard Costing Compared

Budgetary Control	*Standard Costing*
1. It is extensive in its application, as it deals with the operation of department or business as a whole.	It is intensive as it is applied to manufacturing of a product or providing a service.
2. Budgets are prepared for sales, production, cash etc.	It is determined by classifying recording and allocating expenses to cost unit.
3. It is a part of financial account, a projection of all financial accounts.	It is a part of cost account, a projection of all cost accounts.
4. Control is exercised by taking into account budgets and actuals. Variances are not revealed through accounts.	Variances are revealed through different accounts.
5. Budgeting can be applied in parts.	It cannot be applied in parts.
6. It is more expensive and broad in nature, as it relates to production, sales, finance etc.	It is not expensive because it relates to only elements of cost.
7. Budgets can be operated with standards.	This system cannot be operated without budgets.

Advantages of Standard Costing

1. It helps the management in formulating price and production policy.

2. It is a yardstick of performance. Standard costs are compared with actual costs, and the differences are analysed and effective cost control is taken. Thus reduction of cost is possible by increasing the profits.

3. It reduces avoidable wastages and losses.

4. It facilitates to reduce clerical and accounting cost and managerial time.

5. It creates cost consciousness among the personnel, because the variance analysis fixes responsibility for favourable or unfavourable performances.

6. Executives become more responsible, as it shows clearly who is responsible for the cost centres.

7. By the variance analysis and reporting, "the principle of management by exception" is facilitated. Management must concentrate their attention on variations only.

8. It aids in budgetary control and in decision-making.

9. Opening stock and closing stock are valued at the standard price. This helps in the preparation of Profit and Loss Account for a short period—say a week, a month etc.

10. It facilitates timely cost reports to management and a forward looking mentality is encouraged at all levels of the management. It is a basis for the implementation of an incentive system for the employees.

Standard costs form a basis for future planning, preparation of tenders, fixation of price etc. Otherwise, or in the absence of standard cost, decision will be based on actual cost. The prices of material, labour etc, may change from time to time. There must be a fixed cost structure based on normal standard efficiency. Thus it helps the management in formulating price and production policy.

When standards have been fixed, the section-heads safely delegate the responsibility to the workers. The standard of activity can be measured through the costing reports.

Introduction of standard cost facilitates timely reporting. The management gives attention to the variances and takes corrective steps. The costing reports, based on standard cost, reveal the overall result of the manufacturing side.

Limitations of Standard Costing

1. It is costly, as the setting of standards needs high technical skill.

2. Keeping of up-to-date standard is a problem. Periodic revision of standard is a costly thing.

3. Inefficient staff is incapable of operating this system.

4. Since it is difficult to set correct standards, it is difficult to ascertain correct variance.

5. Industries, which are subject to frequent changes in technological process or the quality of material or the character of labour, need a constant revision of standard. But revision of standard is more expensive.

6. For small concerns, standard costing is expensive.

7. It is difficult to apply this method where production takes more than one accounting period. Standard costing may not be effective in industries which deal in non-standardised products or jobs according to customer's requirements.

Applicability of Standard Costing

Standard Costing is a control device. It is not a separate method of product costing. Any activity of recurring nature is susceptible for setting standards. The standard-cost process is mostly used to control the operating tasks. Manufacturing activities are routine and frequent and therefore easy for establishing standards.

Industries where standardised and uniform work of repetitive nature is done, are suitable for introduction of standard costing. Standard costing system is of little use or no use where work vary from job to job or contract to contract.

Setting the Standard

While setting standard cost for operations, process or products, the following preliminaries must be gone through :

1. There must be Standard Committee, similar to Budget Committee, in which Purchase Manager, Personnel Manager, and Production Manager are represented. The Cost Accountant coordinates the functions of the Standard Committee.
2. Study the existing costing system, cost records and forms in use. If necessary, review the existing system.
3. A technical survey of the existing methods of production should be undertaken so that accurate and reliable standards can be established.
4. Determine the type of standard to be used.
5. Fix standard for each element of cost.
6. Determine standard costs for each product.
7. Fix the responsibility for setting standards.
8. Classify the accounts properly so that variances may be accounted for in the manner desired.
9. Comparison of actual costs with pre-determined standards to ascertain the deviations.
10. Action to be taken by management to ensure that adverse variances are not repeated.

Determination of Standard Costs

The following preliminary steps are to be considered before setting standards :

(*a*) Establishment of cost centre

(*b*) Classification and codification of accounts

(*c*) Types of standards

(*d*) Setting the standards.

(*a*)**Establishment of Cost Centre.** It is the first step which is essential before setting of standards. By definition "A cost centre is a location, person or item of equipment (or group of these) for which costs may be ascertained and used for the purpose of cost control." A personal cost centre relates to a person and an impersonal cost centre relates to a location or equipment. By determining the cost centre, the standards are prepared and the variances are analysed. For fixing responsibility and defining the lines of authority, cost centre is necessary.

(*b*) **Classification and Codification of Accounts.** Accounts are classified not only for the purpose of collection and analysis, but also according to different items of expenses under suitable accounting heading. Each accounting heading may be given codes and symbols. Coding is useful for speedy collection, analysis of cost information and mechanical devices.

(*c*) **Types of Standards.**The different types of standards are given below :

(*i*) **Basic Standard.** It is a fixed or bogey standard for use unaltered for an indefinite period for forward planning. According to I.C.M.A. London, it is "an underlying standard from which a current standard can be developed." From this basic standard, changes in current standard and actual standard can be measured. But it is not helpful for cost control and cost ascertainment.

(*ii*) **Current Standard.** It is a short-term standard, as it is revised at regular intervals. I.C.M.A. London refers to it as "a standard which is established for use over a short period of time and is related to current conditions." This standard is realistic and helpful to business, as it is related to current conditions of the budgeted period. It is useful for cost control. But it increases clerical costs. For studying long-term trend of costs, it is not useful.

(*iii*) **Normal Standard.** It is an average standard, and is based on normal condition which prevail over a long period of a trade cycle. I.C.M.A. defines it as "the average standard which, it is anticipated, can be attained over a future period of time, preferably long enough to cover one trade-cycle." An average of current standard or expected standard set for different periods or years, can work as normal standard. It is used for planning and decision making during the period of trade cycle to which it is related. It is very difficult to apply in practice.

(*iv*) **Ideal Standard.** It is set up under ideal conditions. I.C.M.A. defines it as "the standard which can be attained under the most favourable condition possible" This standard is fixed and needs a high degree of efficiency, best possible conditions of management and performance. Existing conditions and conditions capable of achievement should be taken into consideration. It is difficult to attain this ideal standard. As such, it is having little practical value.

(*v*) **Expected Standard.** It is a practical standard. I.C.M.A. defines it as, "the standard which, it is anticipated, can be attained during a future specified budget period." for setting this standard, due weightage is given for all the expected conditions. As such, it is more realistic than the ideal standard. It fulfils all the features of a good standard, *i.e.*, it is consistent, provides incentive to improve performance, is capable of attainment and get better results.

(*d*) **Setting the Standards.** After choosing the standard, the setting of standard is vested with the standard committee. It is similar to the budget committee. It consists of (*i*) the Production Manager (*ii*) the Purchasing Manager (*iii*) the Personnel Manager (*iv*) the Production Engineer (*v*) the Sales Manager (*vi*) the Cost Accountant and other functional heads.

The Cost Accountant is more important than the others, and he has to supply the necessary cost figures and co-ordinate the activity committee. He must ensure that the setting standards are accurate.

Standard cost is determined for each element of the following costs.

(*i*) **Direct Material Cost.**Standard material cost is equal to the standard quantity multiplied by the standard price. The setting of standard costs for direct materials involves:

(*a*) Fixation of standard material quantities and

(*b*) Standard material prices.

(*a*) **Standard Material Quantity.**The production department consisting of production engineers, designers, chemists and work-study practitioners develops standard quantities of direct materials. For each product or part or the process, mechanical calculation or mechanical analysis is made. Standard may be passed on technical data or past performance data. Normal wastage allowance is made high; this allowance will conceal inefficiencies in usage, and a low allowance will lead to adverse or unfavourable variance. As such, the allowance for normal wastage or loss must be fixed very carefully. Similarly, where different kinds of materials are used as a mix for a process, standard material mix is determined to produce the desired quality product.

(*b*) **Standard Material Price.** The setting of a material standard price is not an easy matter. Material price varies from time to time. Setting of material standard price is done by the cost accountant and the purchase manager. The current standard is the desirable and effective standard for fixing the price. Normally one year is the period for fixation of standard price. If there are more fluctuations in material prices, then revision of standard price is necessary. Before fixing the standard, the following points must be considered :

Prices of materials in stock

Price quoted by suppliers

Trade and cash discounts received

Future prices based upon statistical data

Materials price already contracted.

(*ii*) **Setting Standard for Direct Labour.**The standard labour cost is equal to the standard time for each operation multiplied by the standard wage rate. Setting of standard cost of direct labour involves :

(*a*) Fixation of standard time

(*b*) Fixation of standard rate.

(*a*) **Fixation of Standard Time.** Standard time is fixed by time or motion study or past records or test runs or estimates. Labour time is fixed by the work study engineer. While fixing standard time, normal ideal is allowed for fatigue, normal delays or other contingencies.

(*b*)**Fixation of Standard Rate.** With the help of the personnel manager, the accountant determines the standard rate. Fixation of standard rate is influenced by (*i*) Union's influence (*ii*) Demand for labour (*iii*) Policy to be followed. Fixation of standard rate will also depend on the method of wage payment, like time wage system or piece rate system. In the former system wages are paid according to the standard hour or per day. In the latter system wages are paid according to standard piece rate.

(*iii*) **Setting Standard for Overhead**

1. Determination of standard overhead costs
2. Estimation of production
3. Computation of standard overhead rate are the problems of the fixation of standard overhead cost.

Overheads are divided into fixed, variable and semi-variable. Standard overhead rate is determined for these on the basis of past records and future trend of prices. It is calculated for a unit or for an hour.

Standard Variable Overhead Rate =

$$\frac{\text{Standard Variable Overhead for the budget period}}{\text{Budgeted production units or budgeted hours for the budgeted period (or some other base)}}$$

Standard fixed overhead rate =

$$\frac{\text{Standard Overheads for the budget period}}{\text{Budgeted production units or budgeted hours for the budgeted period (or some other base)}}$$

Standardisation of overhead costs can be done with reference to a particular level of activity.

Standard Hour. Physical units are kilogram, tonne, gallon, dozen etc. Production is expressed in these units. All products cannot be expressed in one unit. Time is a common factor for all the products. Standard hour can be used to measure all the types of work. Thus standard hour is a unit of work and not a unit of time.

Standard hour is the quantity of output, or an amount of work, performed in one hour. I.C.M.A. London defines it as, "a hypothetical hour which represents the amount of work which should be performed in one hour under standard conditions". It is useful in ascertaining overhead variances. When there are many products, it can be used for calculation of production cost for a period.

Revision of Standards

Standard cost may be established for a period—indefinite period. There are no definite rules for the selection of a particular period. If the standards are fixed for a short period, it is expensive and frequent revision of standards will impair the utility and purpose for which standard is set. At the same time, if the standard is set for a longer period, it may not be useful particularly in the days of high inflation and large fluctuations of rates in case of materials and labour. Standard cost is the resultant effect of a number of factors that vary from time to time in different situations, both internal and external. Standard may become unrealistic with the changing conditions, needs revision. Without revision, the standards becomes outmoded. If the changes are of a temporary or minor nature, it is not advisable to revise the standards. Current standards are reviewed every year at the beginning of the accounting period under the following circumstances :

1 Errors in setting the standards.
2 Changes in price level of materials, labour and overheads.
3. Change in method of production.
4. Change in designs or specifications.
5. Technological advances etc.

Apart from the above, basic standards are revised in the course of time under the following circumstances, when :

1. There are permanent changes in the method of production —designs and specifications.
2. Plant capacity is changed.
3. There is a large variation between the standard and the actual.

Standard Cost Card

When all the standard costs have been determined, a Standard Cost Card is prepared for each product or service. The process of setting standards for materials, labour and overheads results in the establishment of the standard cost for the product. Such a cost card shows for a specified unit of production, quantity, quality and price of each type of materials to be used, the time and the rate of pay of each type of labour, the various operations the product would pass through, the recovery of overhead and the total cost. The build-up of the standard cost of each item is recorded in Standard Cost Card. These details serve as a basis to measure the efficiency against which actual quantities and costs are compared. The type of standard cost card varies with the requirements of individual firm, hence no uniform format can be prescribed.

Objective Type Questions

A. Choose the correct answer to the following :

(1) Standard costs are :
   (a) Ideal costs.
   (b) Normal costs.
   (c) Reasonably attainable costs.

(2) The type of costing which is most suitable for cost control purpose is :
   (a) Standard costing
   (b) Post costing
   (c) Continous costing.

(3) Budgetary control and standard costing are :
   (a) Interdependent on each other.
   (b) Independent of each other.
   (c) Interrelated with each other.

(4) One of the objective of standard costing is to :
   (a) Promote performance
   (b) Control and reduce costs.
   (c) Simplify production operation.

(5) The type of standard that is best suited from cost control point of view :
   (a) Ideal standard.
   (b) Expected standard.
   (c) Normal standard.

(6) Standard costing involves in the :
   (a) Fixation of estimated cost.
   (b) Determination of standard cost.
   (c) Setting of budgeted costs.

(7) The difference between actual cost and standard cost is known as :
   (a) Variance.
   (b) Profit.
   (c) Differential cost.

(8) Standard costing helps in :
   (a) Measuring efficiency
   (b) Reducing losses.
   (c) Controlling prices.

(9) Standard cost cannot be used :
   (a) Where management is inefficient.
   (b) Workers are slow.
   (c) Where non-standard products are manufactured.

(10) Basic standard is established for a :
   (a) Short period
   (b) Current period.
   (c) Indefinite period.

(Ans. (1) (c) ; (2) (a) ; (3) (c) ; (4) (b) ; (5) (b) ;
(6) (b) ; (7) (a) ; (8) (a) ; (9) (c) ; (10) (c) ;

B. State whether the following statements are ture or false :

1. Standard costing aids managment in planning and control.
2. Standard costing and process costing cannot be used simultaneously in the same industry.
3. Standard costing and budgetary control are not interdependent.
4. Standard costing does not help the manager is decision making.
5. Standard costing may not be suitable in small concerns.
6. Standard costs once fixed cannot be changed.
7. Standard costs are computed after the product is manufactured.
8. Standard costing and estimated costing mean one and the same thing.
9. Standard costing is a technique which aims at controlling.
10. Standard costs are pre-determined.

(Ans: 1. True ; 2. False ; 3. True ; 4. False ; 5. True ;
2. False ; 7. False ; 8. False ; 9. True ; 10. True.

THEORETICAL QUESTIONS

1. What is Standard Costing ? State its advantages.
2. What do you mean by Historical Costing ?
3. Distinguish between Budgetary Control and Standard Costing.
4. Explain the steps in the Fixation of Standard costs.
5. Distinguish between Estimated Costs and Standard Costs.

6. Explain the different types of Standards Applicable under Standard Costing.
7. What are the merits of Standard Costing?
8. Explain the limitations of Standard Costing.
9. What do you understand by "Standard hour"?
10. Explain the preliminary step for establishing a system of standard costing.

Chapter 9

Standard Costing-II

Introduction; Variances; Favourable Variance; Unfavourable Variances; Controllable Variances; Uncontrollable Variances; Uses; Analysis of Variances; Computation of Variances; Material Cost Variance; Relationship; Labour Variances Favourable Factors; Unfavourable Factors; Overhead Variances; Variable Overhead Variances; Fixed Overhead Variances; Classification of Volume Variances; Relationship; Sales Variances; Value Method; Profit or Margin Method; Disposal of Variances; Objective Type Questions; Theory Questions; Practical Problems.

Introduction

The most significant contribution of standard costing to the science and art of management is the presentation of 'variances'. As a matter of fact, without determination and analysis of variances, standard costing is meaningless. The term 'Variances' has been derived from the verb 'To vary' meaning to differ. In cost accounting, variance means deviation of the actual cost from the standard cost. In standard costing, standard costs are pre-determined and refer to the amounts which ought to be incurred. These become the yardsticks against which actual costs can be compared.

Variance

Variance analysis is the process of analysing variances by sub-dividing the total variance in such a way that management can assign responsibility for off-standard performance. It, thus, involves the measurement of the deviation of actual performance from the intended performance. That is, variance analysis is a tool to measure performances and based on the principle of management by exception. In variance analysis, the attention of management is drawn not only to the monetary value of unfavourable and favourable managerial performance but also to the responsibility and causes for the same.

After the standard costs have been fixed, the next stage in the operation of standard costing is to ascertain the actual cost of each element and compare them with the standard already set. Computation and analysis of variances is the main objective of standard costing. The deviation of actual from the standard is called 'variance'. The difference between the actual cost and the standard cost is known as the 'cost variance'.

Favourable and Unfavourable Variances

Variances may be favourable (positive or credit) or unfavourable (or negative or adverse or debit) depending upon whether the actual resulting cost is less or more than the standard cost.

Favourable Variance : When the actual cost incurred is less than the standard cost, the deviation is known as favourable variance. The effect of the favourable variance increases the profit. Again, favourable variance would result when the actual cost is lower than the standard cost. It is also known as positive or credit variance and viewed only as savings.

Unfavourable Variance :When the actual cost incurred is more than the standard cost, there is a variance, known as unfavourable or adverse variance. Unfavourable variance refers to deviation to the loss of the business. It is also known as negative or debit variance and viewed as additional costs or losses.

When the profit is greater than the standard profit, it is known as favourable variance. When the profit is less than the standard profit, it is known as unfavourable variance. This favourable variance is a sign or efficiency of the organisation and the unfavourbale variance is a sign of inefficiency of the organisation.

Controllable and Uncontrollable Variances

Variances may be controllable or uncontrollable, depending upon the controllability of the factors causing variances.

Controllable Variance : A variance is said to be controllable if it can be identified as the primary responsibility of a specified person or department. That is, it refers to a deviation caused by such factors which could be influenced by the executive action. For example, excess usage of materials, excess time taken by a worker, etc. are examples for controllable variance. When compared to the standard cost it becomes controllable because the responsibility can be fixed on the in-charge or foreman of the department.

Uncontrollable Variance : When variance is due to the factors beyond the control of the concerned person (or department), it is said to be uncontrollable. Cost variance is due to outside factors, for example, the wage rate increased on account of strike, Government restrictions, change in market price etc. No person or department can be held responsible for uncontrollable variances. Here revision of standards is required to remove such variances in future.

The size of controllable variance reflects the degree of efficiency of the person or department concerned. Actually, it is the controllable variance with which the management is concerned because it is here where corrective action is required. That is, the management gives attention to the controllable variances and it is known as management by exception. Variances can be expressed in absolute (in money) or in relative terms (on percentage).

Uses

Again, it is important to note that the mere finding out of the variances is not sufficient, but their analysis and finding the causes for variance is the ultimate aim to control costs. Thus, the variances are analysed for their causes.

The variance analysis are important tools of cost control and cost reduction and they generate an atmosphere of cost consciousness in the organisation. In short, the uses of variances are :

1. Comparison of actual with standard cost which reveals the efficiency or inefficiency of performance. The inefficiency or unfavourable variance is analysed and immediate action is taken. Thus variance is like a barometer.
2. It is a tool of cost control and cost reduction.
3. It helps the management to apply the principle of management by exception.
4. It helps the management to maximise the profits by analysing the variances into controllable and uncontrollable; the controllable variances are further analysed so as to bring a cost reduction, indirectly more profit.
5. Future planning and programmes are based on the variance analysis, because standard costing and variance analysis need a complete study of the organisation. Thus, the factors of profits can be known and future plan made.

6. Within the organisation, a cost consciousness is created alongwith the team spirit. The variance analysis and fact finding further boost the profits of the organisation.

Analysis of Variances

It must be remembered that the main purpose of standard costing is the computation and analysis of variances. A variance is the difference between the actual costs and standard costs. Calculation of variances indicates to management whether costs are under control or not. A variance may be favourable or unfavourable (adverse). When the actual cost is less than the standard cost, it is known as Favourable or Credit Variance. When the actual cost is more than the standard cost, the same is known as Unfavourable or Debit Variance. Generally, a favourable variance implies that the costs are under control and performance is efficient. When the variance has been calculated, it needs proper management attention. Variance should be analysed. Significant variance should be reported to the appropriate levels of management for corrective actions. Mere calculation of variance does not imply control. Control of costs lies in the corrective actions taken by the management on the basis of variance analysis. The analysis of variance helps to locate and to pin-point responsibilities. According to Brown and Howard, "Standard costing is a technique of cost accounting which compares the standard cost of each product or service with actual cost to determine the efficiency of the operation so that any remedial action may be taken immediately". According to W.W. Bigg "Standard costing discloses the cost of deviations from the standard and classifies these as to their causes so that management is immediately informed of the sphere of operations in which remedial action is necessary."

Computation of Variances

The computation and analysis of variance are the objectives of standard costing. The causes of variance are necessary to find remedial measures; and therefore a detailed study of variance analysis is essential. Variances can be found out with respect to all the elements of cost, i,e., direct material, direct labour and overheads. In other words, the total cost variance is split into its component parts on the basis of elements, and each element is further subdivided to locate the responsibility of variance. The following are the common variances, which are calculated by the management. Sub-divisions of variances really give detailed information to the management in order to control the cost.

1. Material Cost variances
2. Labour or Wage Variances
3. Overhead Cost Variances (*a*)Variable (*b*) Fixed.
4. Sales Variances.

I. MATERIAL COST VARIANCES

The following are the variance in the case of materials :

Materials Variances (Diagrammatice representation).

MATERIAL COST VARIANCE (OR) MCV

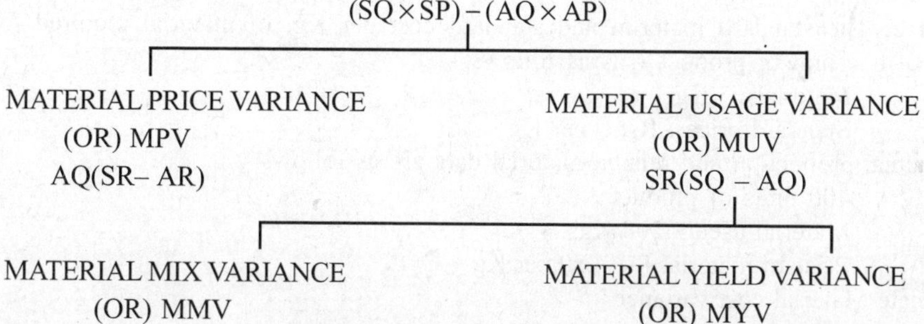

SR (SQ – AQ) OR SR (RSQ – AQ) SR(AY– SY)
MCV = MPV + MUV
MUV = MMV + MYV
MCV = MPV + MMV + MYV

(*a*) *Direct Material Cost Variance*. It is the difference between the standard cost of direct materials specified for the output achieved and the actual cost of direct materials used. The standard cost of materials is computed by multiplying the standard price with the standard quantity for actual output; and the actual cost is computed by multiplying the actual price with the actual quantity.

Materials form a very high percentage of total cost. Thus, it is important to study its variances. Materials Cost Variance is also called Total Variance. The formula is :

Direct Material Cost Variance

(OR)

$$\text{Materials Cost Variance} = \left(\begin{matrix}\text{Standard Cost of}\\ \text{Materials}\end{matrix} - \begin{matrix}\text{Actual Cost of}\\ \text{Materials used}\end{matrix}\right)$$

(OR) (OR)

$$(\text{MCV}) = \left(\begin{matrix}\text{Standard Cost of}\\ \text{Actual Output}\end{matrix} - \text{Actual Cost}\right)$$

(OR)

$$= \left(\begin{matrix}\text{Standard Quantity}\\ \text{for Actual Output}\end{matrix} \times \begin{matrix}\text{Standard}\\ \text{Price}\end{matrix}\right) - \left(\begin{matrix}\text{Actual}\\ \text{Quantity}\end{matrix} \times \begin{matrix}\text{Actual}\\ \text{Price}\end{matrix}\right)$$

(OR)

$$= (SQ \times SP) - (AQ \times AP)$$

If the standard cost is more than the actual cost, the variance will be favourable and on the other hand if the actual cost is more than the standard cost, the variance will be unfavourable or adverse.

Illustration 1. The standard cost of material for manufacturing a unit of a particular product is estimated as follows :

16 kg. of raw materials @ Re. 1 per kg.

On completion of the unit, it was found that 20 kg. of raw material costing Rs.1.50 per kg. has been consumed.

Compute material variances (*C.S.*)

Solution :

We calculate only Material Cost Variance :

MCV = (SQ × SP) – (AQ × AP)
= (16 × Re.1) – (20 × Rs. 1.50)
= Rs. 16 – Rs. 30 = **Rs. 14 (Adverse)**

Note: Since no information is given regarding standard yield and actual yield, it is assumed that both are equal.

Illustration 2. The standard material and standard cost per Kg. of material required for the production of one unit of product A is as follows:

Material : 5 Kg.
Standard price : Rs. 5 per Kg.

The actual production and related material data are as follows:

400 units of product A
Material used 2,200 Kgs.
Price of material Rs. 4.50 per Kg.

Calculate Material cost variance.

Solution:

Material cost variance = (SQ × SP) – (AQ × AP)

SQ refers to standard quantity for actual production

Standard quantity for actual production of 400 units = 400 × 5 = 2,000 Kgs.

MCV = (2,000 × Rs. 5) – (2,200 × Rs. 4.50)

= Rs. 10,000 – Rs. 9,900 = **Rs. 100 (F)**

Note: Here standard yield and actual yield are different. Hence we have to calculate first standard quantity for actual yield.

(*b*) *Material Price Variance.* This is the responsibility of the Purchase Manager. Material price variance is that portion of the direct material cost variance which is the difference between the standard price specified and the actual price paid for the direct materials used. The formula is :

Direct material price variance = (Actual quantity consumed × Standard price) – (Actual quantity consumed × Actual price)

or

Actual quantity consumed (Standard Rate – Actual Rate)

MPV = AQ (SR – AR)

A favourable variance arises if the actual price is less than the standard price and vice versa.

The reasons for direct material price variances are :

1. Fluctuations in market price
2. Non-availability of standard quality
3. Using cheaper materials or substitute
4. Inefficiency in buying
5. High cost of transportation and carriage of goods
6. Loss of discount and fraud in purchases
7. Changes in price policies
8. Emergency purchase leading to higher price
9. Government interferences leading to rise in prices
10. Incorrect setting of standard
11. Untimely purchase
12. Loss in transit, in excess of normal loss
13. Unexpected additional cost
14. Failure to enter into forward contract.

Illustration 3. The standard cost of material for manufacturing a unit of a particular product is estimated as follows:

20 Kg. of raw materials @ Rs. 2 per kg.

On completion of the unit, it was found that 25 Kg. of raw material costing Rs. 3 per kg. has been consumed.

Solution :

MPV = AQ (SR – AR)

= 25 (Rs.2 – Rs. 3)

= 25 × (Re. – 1)

= – 25 or **Rs. 25** (adverse)

(*c*) *Direct Material Usage (Quantity) Variance.* It is the deviation caused by the standards due to the difference in quantity used. It is calculated by multiplying the difference between the standard quantity specified and the actual quantity used by the standard price.

Thus material usage variance is "that portion of the direct materials cost variance which is the difference between the standard quantity specified for the production achieved, whether completed or not, and the actual quantity used, both valued at standard prices."

Material Usage or Quantity Variance

= Standard Rate (Standard Quantity – Actual Quantity)

(OR)

MUV = SR (SQ – AQ)

The reasons for usage variance are :

1. Careless handling of materials;
2. Wastage, scrap, spoilage etc. due to inefficient production method or unskilled employees;
3. Changes in design or specifications of product;
4. Use of inferior materials;
5. Defective equipments and tools;
6. Non-standard material used;
7. Accounting errors;
8. Setting of improper standards;
9. Improper inspection;
10. Non-standard substitutes used;
11. Theft of materials;
12. Difference between actual yield from materials and standard yield.
13. Lack of proper tools and machines.

Illustration 4. From the following data calculate material usage variance.

Standard	20 kg. at Rs. 5.50 per kg.
Actual	25 kg. at Rs. 6 per kg.

Solution :

MUV = SR (SQ – AQ)
= Rs. 5.50 (20 – 25)
= Rs. 5.50(–5)
= Rs. – 27.50 or Rs. **27.50** (Adverse)

Direct material usage variance may further be classified into Material mix (Mixture) variance and either Material yield variance or Material revised usage variance.

(*d*) *Direct Material Mix Variance.* I.C.M.A. defines it as "that portion of direct material usage variance which is the difference between the actual quantities of ingredients used in a mixture at standard price and the total quantity of ingredients used at the weighted average price per unit of ingredient as shown by the standard cost sheet". When two or more materials are used in the manufacture of a product, the difference between the standard composition and the actual composition of material mix is the Material mix variance. The variance arises due to the change in the ratio of material and the standard ratio. The formula is :

Direct material mix variance = Standard Rate (Standard mix – Actual mix)

(*i*) When actual weight of mix and standard weight of mix are the same.

DMMV = Standard Rate (Standard quantity – Actual quantity)

or SR (SQ – AQ)

Standard is revised due to the shortage of a particular type of material.

The formula is :

MMV = Standard Rate (Revised standard quantity–Actual quantity)

Revised standard quantity

$$= \frac{\text{Total weight of actual mix}}{\text{Total weight of Standard mix}} \times \text{Standard quantity}$$

(*ii*)When the actual weight of mix and standard weight of mix differ from each other, the formula to find new standard mix is,

$$\frac{\text{Total weight of actual mix}}{\text{Total weight of standard mix}}$$

After finding out this revised standard mix it is multiplied by the revised standard cost of standard mix and then the standard cost of actual mix is subtracted from the result.

(*or*)

$$\left[\frac{\text{Total weight of actual mix}}{\text{Total weight of Standard mix}} \times \text{Revised std. cost of std. mix}\right] - \text{Std. cost of actual mix}$$

Revised usage variance or sub-usage variance =

Standard Rate (Standard quantity – Revised Standard quantity)

Materials mix variance arises when standard mix of the materials is different from the actual mix ratio. If the ratio of standard mix and actual mix is the same, though the quantities may differ, there will be no mix variance.

Illustration 5. Calculate the materials mix variance from the following:

Material	Standard	Actual
A	90 units at Rs. 12 each	100 units at Rs. 12 each
B	60 units at Rs. 15 each	50 units at Rs. 16 each

(*B.Com., Calicut*)

Solution :

Material	*Standard*			*Actual*		
	Qty.	*Rate*	*Amount*	*Qty.*	*Rate*	*Amount*
	Rs.	Rs.	Rs.	Rs.	Rs.	Rs.
A	90	12	1,080	100	12	1,200
B	60	15	900	50	16	800
	150		1,980	150		2,000

MMV = SR (SQ – AQ)

Material A : MMV = Rs. 12 (90 – 100)
= Rs. 12 × – 10
= Rs. 120 (A)

Material B : MMV = Rs. 15 (60 – 50)
= Rs. 15 × 10
= Rs. 150 (F)

Total MMV = Rs. 120 (A) + Rs. 150 (F)
= Rs. 30 (F)

Note: Here the total actual weight of mix and the total standard weight of mix are the same. Under such situations, revised standard quantity is equal to the standard quantity.

Illustration 6. From the data given below, calculate the material price variance, the material usage variance and material mixture variance.

Consumption per 100 units of product

Material	*Standard*	*Actual*
A	40 units @ Rs. 50 per unit	50 units @ Rs. 50 per unit
B	60 units @ Rs. 40 per unit	60 units @ Rs. 45 per unit

(I.C.W.A)

Solution :

Material	*Standard*			*Actual*		
	Qty.	*Rate*	*Amount*	*Qty.*	*Rate*	*Amount*
	Rs.	Rs.	Rs.	Rs.	Rs.	Rs.
A	40	50	2,000	50	50	2,500
B	60	40	2,400	60	45	2,700
	100		4,400	110		5,200

1. *Material Price Variance :*

(*or*) MPV = Actual Quantity (Standard Rate – Actual Rate)

Material A : 50 (Rs. 50 – Rs. 50) = Nil

B : 60 (Rs. 40 – Rs. 45) = Rs. 300 (A)

2. *Material Usage Variance :*

(*or*) MUV = Standard Rate (Standard Quantity–Actual Qty.)

Material A : Rs. 50(40 – 50) = Rs. 500 (Adverse)

Material B : Rs. 40(60 – 60) = Nil

500 (A)

3. *Material Mix Variance :*

Here, the actual weight of mix and standard weight of mix differ from each other. Therefore,

MMV = Standard Rate (Revised Standard Quantity–Actual Quantity)

Here, the revised standard quantity formula :

$$\frac{\text{Total weight of Actual mix}}{\text{Total weight of Standard mix}} \times \text{Standard Quantity}$$

RSQ for material $A = \frac{110}{100} \times 40 = 44$ units

$B = \frac{110}{100} \times 60 = 66$ units

Then,

MMV = Standard Rate (Revised Standard Quantity – Actual Quantity)

= SR(RSQ – AQ)

Material A : 50(44 – 50) = Rs. 300 (Adverse)

B : 40 (66 – 60) = Rs. 240 (Favourable)

Rs. 60 (Adverse)

Revised material usage variance = Standard Rate (Standard Qty.–Revised Std. Qty.)

Material A : Rs. 50 (40 – 44) = 200 (Adverse)

B : Rs. 40 (60 – 66) = 240 (Adverse)

Rs. 440 (A)

Material Cost Variance :

Material : MCV = (SQ × SP) – (AQ × AP)

A : = (40 × 50) – (50 × 50) = 500 (A)

B : = (60 × 40) – (60 × 45) = 300 (A)

Rs. 800 (A)

Verification :

MCV = MPV + MUV

Rs. 800 (A) = Rs. 300 (A) + Rs. 500 (A)

MUV = RUV + MMV

Rs. 500 (A) = Rs. 440 (A) + Rs. 60 (A)

(e) Direct Material Yield Variance. It is that portion of the direct material usage variance which is due to the difference between the standard yield specified and the actual yield obtained. The variance arise is due to abnormal contingencies like spoilage, chemical reaction etc. Since the variance is a measure of the waste or loss in the production, it can be known as material loss or waste variance.

ICMA, London, it is defined as "the difference between the standard yield of the actual material input and the actual yield, both valued at the standard material cost of the product". In case actual yield is more than the standard yield, the materials yield variance is favourable and, if the actual yield is less than the standard yield, the variance is unfavourable or adverse.

(See Illustration 12)

(*i*) When Actual Mix and Standard Mix are the same the formula is :

MYV = Standard Yield Rate (Standard Yield – Actual Yield)

(Or) = Standard Revised Rate (Actual Loss – Standard Loss)

$$\text{Here Standard Yield Rate} = \frac{\text{Standard cost of Standard Mix}}{\text{Net Standard Output}}$$

Net Standard Output = Gross Output – Standard Loss

(*ii*) When the Actual Mix and the Standard Mix differ from each other, the formula is :

$$\text{Standard Rate} = \frac{\text{Standard cost of Revised Standard Mix}}{\text{Net Standard Output}}$$

Material Yield Variance

$$= \text{Standard Rate}\left(\begin{matrix}\text{Actual Standard}\\ \text{Yield}\end{matrix} - \begin{matrix}\text{Revised Standard}\\ \text{Yield}\end{matrix}\right)$$

Relationship

(*a*) Material Cost Variance = Material Price Variance + Material Usage Variance

(*b*) Material Usage Variance = Material Mix Variance + Material Yield Variance

(*c*) Material Cost Variance = Material Price Variance

+ Material mix Variance + Material sub-usage Variance

(*d*) Material sub-usage Variance = Material Usage Variance – Material Mix Variance

Illustration 7. A manufacturing concern, which has adopted standard costing, furnished the following information :

Standard

Material for 70 kg finished products : 100 kg.

Price of materials : Re. 1 per kg.

Actual

Output : 2,10,000 kg.
Material used : 2,80,000 kg.
Cost of material : Rs. 2,52,000.

Calculate

(*a*) Material Usage Variance (*b*) Material Price Variance (*c*) Material Cost Variance

(*B.Com., Calicut, Kerala*)

Solution :

1. Standard quantity :

For 70 kg standard output

Standard quantity of material =100 kg.

∴ 2,10,000 kg. of finished products

$$= \frac{2,10,000 \times 10}{70} = 3,00,000 \text{ kg}$$

2. Actual price per kg. $\frac{\text{Rs.}2,52,000}{2,80,000} = \text{Re.}0.90$

(*a*) Material Usage Variance = Standard Rate (Standard Quantity for actual output – Actual quantity)

= SR (SQ – AQ)
= Re. 1 (3,00,000 × 2,80,000)
= Re. 1 × 20,000
= Rs. 20,000 (Favourable)

(*b*) Material Price Variance = Actual quantity (Standard Price – Actual Price)

= AQ (SR – AR)
= 2,80,000 (Re. 1 – Re. 0.90)
= 2,80,000 × Re. 0.10
= **Rs. 28,000 (Favourable)**

(*c*) Material Cost Variance =

Standard Quantity for actual output × Standard Rate) – (Actual Quantity × Actual Rate)

= (SQ × SR) – (AQ × AR)
= (3,00,000 × 1) – (2,80,000 × 0.90)
= Rs. 3,00,000 – Rs. 2.52,000
= **Rs. 48,000 (Favourable)**

Verification :

MCV = MPV × MUV

Rs. 48,000 (F) = Rs. 28,000 (F) + Rs. 20,000 (F)

Illustration 8. From the following particulars compute (*a*) Material Cost Variance, (*b*) Materials Price Variance and (*c*) Material Usage Variance :

Quantity of materials purchase	3,000 units
Value of materials purchased	Rs. 9,000
Standard quantity of materials required per tonne of output	30 units
Standard rate of material	Rs. 2.50 Per unit
Opening stock of material	Nil

Closing stock of material 500 units
Output during the period 80 tonnes

(*B.Com. (Hons.), Delhi*)

Solution :

Materials consumed = 3,000 – 500
= 2,500 units

$$\text{Actual Rate of material} = \frac{\text{Rs.}9,000}{3,000} = \text{Rs. 3 per unit}$$

Standard quantity for actual output = 30 × 80 = 2,400 units

Material Cost Variance = Standard Cost – Actual Cost

(*or*) = (Standard Rate × Standard quantity) – (Actual Rate × Actual quantity)

$= (\text{Rs. } 2.50 \times 24,00) - (\text{Rs. } 3 \times 2,500)$

$= \text{Rs.}6,000 - \text{Rs.}7,500 =$ **Rs. 1,500 (Adverse)**

Material Price Variance = Actual quantity/(Standard Price – Actual Price)
= 2,500/(Rs. – Rs. 3)=2,500(–Re. 0.50) = **Rs. 1,250 (Adverse)**

Material Usage Variance = Standard Price × (Std. qty – Actual quantity)

$= \text{Rs. } 2.50 \times (2,400 - 2,500)$

$= \text{Rs.}2.50\ (-100)$

= Rs. 250 (Adverse)

Verification :

MCV = *MPV* + *MUV*

Rs. 1500(*A*) = Rs. 1250 (*A*) + Rs. 250(*A*)

Illustration 9. From the following particulars calculate —

(*a*) Total Material Cost Variance;
(*b*) Material Price Variance;
(*c*) Material Usage Variance.

	Standard		*Actual*	
Materials	*Units*	*Price (Rs)*	*Units*	*Price (Rs)*
A	2,020	2	2,160	2.40
B	820	3	760	3.60
C	700	4	760	3.80

(*B.Com., Delhi*)

Solution :

(*a*) Material Cost Variance :

Std. Unit Cost × Std. Quantity – Actual Unit Cost × Actual Quantity or SC – AC.

Standard Cost of Material	*Actual Cost of Material*
Material A: 2,020 units @ Rs.2 = 4,040	2,160 units @ Rs. 2.40 = 5,184
Material B: 820 Units @ Rs. 3 = 2,460	760 units @ Rs. 3.60 = 2,736
Material C: 700 units @ Rs. 4 = 2,800	760 units @ Rs. 3.80 = 2,888
Total Cost 9,300	10808

∴ Material Cost Variance = SC – AC = Rs. 9,300 – Rs. 10,808 = Rs. 1,508 (*A*) (*b*) Material Price Variance : AQ (SR – AR)

Material A	2,160 (Rs. 2 – Rs. 2.40)	= Rs. 864 (A)
Material B	760 (Rs. 3 – 3.60)	= Rs. 456 (A)
Material C	760 (Rs. 4 – 3.80)	= Rs. 152 (F)
Total Material Price Variance		= Rs. 1,168 (A)

(*c*) Material Usage Variance :

SR (SQ – AQ)

Material A	Rs. 2(2,020 – 2,160)	= Rs. 280 (A)
Material B	Rs. 3(820 – 760)	= Rs. 180 (F)
Material C	Rs. 4(700 – 760)	= Rs. 240 (A)
Total Material Usuage Variance		= Rs. 340 (A)

Verification :

MCV = MPV + MUV = Rs. 1508(A) = Rs. 1,168 (A) + Rs. 340 (A)

Illustration 10. A furniture manufacturer uses sunmica tops for tables, from the following information find out price variance, usage variance and cost variance.

Standard quantity of sunmica per table	4 sq. ft.
Standard price per sq. ft of sunmica	Rs. 5.00
Actual production of tables	1,000
Sunmica actually used	4,300 sq.ft.
Actual purchase price of sunmica per sq. ft 5.50	

(*Punjab B. Com.*)

Solution :

Material Price Variance :

MPV = Actual quantity (Standard Price – Actual Price)

= 4,300 (5.00 – 5.50)

= 4,300 (– Re. 0.50) = Rs. – 2.150 = **Rs. 2,150 (Adverse)**

Material Usage Variance :

MCV = Standard Price (Standard quantity – Actual quantity)

= Rs. 5(4 × 1,000) – (4,300) = 5(4,000 – 4,300)

= Rs. 5(–300) = – Rs. 1500 = **Rs. 1,500 (Adverse)**

Material Cost Variance :

MCV = Standard Cost of Material – Actual Cost of Material

or = (Std. quantity × Standard price) – (Actual quantity × Actual price)

= (4,000 × Rs. 5) – (4,300 × Rs. 5.50)

= 20,000 – 23,650 = Rs. – 3650

= **Rs. 3,650 (Adverse)**

Verification :

Material Cost Variance = Material Price Variance + Usage Variance

= Rs. 3,650(A) = Rs. 2,150 (A) + Rs. 1,500 (A)

Illustration 11. Standard mix for production of "X".

Material A : 60 tonnes @ Rs. 5 per tonne

Material B : 40 tonnes @ Rs. 10 per tonne

Actual mixture being :

Material A : 80 tonnes @ Rs. 4 per tonne

Material B : 70 tonnes @ Rs. 8 per tonne

Calculate

(*a*) Material price variance

(*b*) Material sub-usage variance and

(*c*) Material mix variance. (*B. Com., Madurai*)

Solution :

(*a*) Material price variance = Actual quantity × (Std. price – Actual price)

Material A = 80 (5 – 4) = Rs. 80 favourable

Material B = 70 (10 – 8) = Rs. 140 favourable

MPV = 80 + 140 = **Rs. 220 (favourable)**

(b) Revised std.quantity = $\dfrac{\text{Total weight of actual mix}}{\text{Total weight ofstd. mix}} \times \text{Standard quantity}$

RSQ for material $A = \dfrac{150}{100} \times 60 = 90$ tonnes

RSQ for material $B = \dfrac{150}{100} \times 40 = 60$ tonnes

Material sub-usage (Revised usage) variance =

Standard price (Std. quantity – Revised standard quantity)

RUV for material A = 5(60 – 90) = – 150 = Rs. 150 (adverse)

RUV for material B = 10(40 – 60) = – 200 = Rs. 200 (adverse)

MRV = 150 + 200 = **Rs. 350 (adverse)**

(*c*) Material mix variance = Standard Rate × (Revised std. qty – Actual qty.)

MMV for material A = Rs. 5(90 – 80) = Rs. 50 (favourable)

MMV for material B = Rs. 10 (60 – 70) = Rs. 100 (adverse)

MMV = 50 – 100 = – 50 = **Rs. 50 (adverse)**

Illustration 12. The standard mix of product is :

X 600 units at 15 paise per unit

Y 800 units at 20 paise per unit

Z 1,000 units at 25 paise per unit

The consumption was :

X 640 units at 20 paise per unit

Y 960 units at 15 paise per unit

Z 840 units at 30 paise per unit

Calculate the material variances. (*B.Com.*)

Solution :

Standard cost of std. materials

X 600 × Re. 0.15 = Rs. 90

Y 800 × Re. 0.20 = Rs. 160

$\dfrac{Z\ 1{,}000 \times \text{Re. } 0.25}{\mathbf{2{,}400}} = \dfrac{\text{Rs. } 250}{\mathbf{Rs.\ 500}}$

Actual cost of actual materials

X 640 × Re. 0.20 = Rs. 128

Y 960 × Re. 0.15 = Rs. 144

$\dfrac{Z\ 840 \times \text{Re. } 0.30}{\mathbf{2{,}440}} = \dfrac{\text{Rs. } 252}{\mathbf{Rs.\ 524}}$

Revised Quantity

$$X \frac{2,440}{2,400} \times 600 = 610 \text{ units}$$

$$Y \frac{2,440}{2,400} \times 800 = 813 \text{ units}$$

$$Z \frac{2,440}{2,400} \times 1000 = 1017 \text{ units}$$

(*a*) Material Cost Variance :

SC – AC = 500 – 524 = Rs. 24(A)

(*b*) Material Price Variance : AQ (SP – AP)

X 640 (0.15 – 0.20) = Rs. 32 (A)
Y 960 (0.20 – 0.15) = Rs. 48 (F)
Z 840 (0.25 – 0.30) = Rs. 42(A)
MPV = **Rs. 26 (A)**

(*c*) Material Usage Variance = SP (SQ – AQ)

X Re. 0.15 (600 – 640) = Rs. 6(A)
Y Re. 0.20 (800 – 960) = Rs. 32(A)
Z Re. 0.25 (1,000 – 840) = Rs. 40 (F)
MUV = **Rs. 2(F)**

(*d*) Material Mix Variance = SP (RSQ – AQ)

X 0.15 (610 – 640) = Rs. 4.50 (A)
Y 0.20 (813 – 960) = Rs. 29.40 (A)
Z 0.25 (1,017 – 840) = Rs. 44.25 (F)
MMV = Rs. 10.35 (F)

Illustration 13. From the following information, calculate the material mix variance.

Material	*Standard*	*Actual*
A	200 units @ Rs. 12	160 units @ Rs. 13
B	100 units @ Rs. 10	140 units @ Rs. 10

Due to shortage of material A, it was decided to reduce consumption of A by 15% and increase that of material B by 30%. (*B. Com. Madurai*)

Solution:

Material Mix Variance : SP (RSQ – AQ)

$$\text{Revised Standard Quantity} = \frac{\text{Total weight of Actual Mix}}{\text{Total weight of Std. Mix}} \times \text{SQ}$$

$$\text{Material } A = \frac{300}{300} \times 200 = 200 \text{ units}$$

Less: Reduction of consumption of A by 15% 30
170 units

$$\text{Material } B = \frac{300}{300} \times 100 = 100 \text{ units}$$

Add: Increase of Material B by 30% = 30 units
130 units

Material Mix Variance:

Material A = 12 (170 – 160) = Rs. 120 (F)
Material B = 10 (130 – 140) = Rs. 100 (A)
Total Material Mix Variance = Rs. 20 (F)

Illustration 14. From the following information, compute material variances:

	Standard			*Actual*		
	Quantity (kg.)	*Unit price Rs.*	*Total Rs.*	*Quantity (kg.)*	*Unit price Rs.*	*Total Rs.*
Material A	100	20	200	50	30	150
Material B	200	30	600	100	60	600
Material C	200	60	1200	150	50	750

(*B. Com. M. Com. Madras*)

Solution:

Material Cost Variance : (SQ × SP) – (AQ × AP)

Material A = (100 × 20) – (50 × 30) = Rs. 500 (F)
Material B = (200 × 30) – (100 × 60) = Nil
Material C = (200 × 60) – (150 × 50) = Rs. 4,500 (F)
Total Material Cost Variance = Rs. 5,000 (F)

Material Price Variance : AQ (SP – AP)

Material A = 50 (20 – 30) = Rs. 500 (A)
Material B = 100 (30 – 60) = Rs. 3,000 (A)
Material C = 150 (60 – 50) = Rs. 1,500 (F)
Total Material Price Variance = Rs. 2,000 (A)

Material Usage Variance : SP (SQ – AQ)

Material A = 20 (100 – 50) = Rs. 1000 (F)
Material B = 30 (200 – 100) = Rs. 3000 (F)
Material C = 60 (200 – 150) = Rs. 3000 (F)
Total Material Usage Variance = Rs. 7,000 (F)

Material Mix Variance : SP (RSQ – AQ)

$$\text{Revised Standard Quantity} = \frac{\text{Total weight of actual Mix}}{\text{Total weight of std. Mix}} \times \text{Std. Quantity}$$

$$\text{Material A} = \frac{300}{500} \times 100 = 60$$

$$\text{Material B} = \frac{300}{500} \times 200 = 120$$

$$\text{Material C} = \frac{300}{500} \times 200 = 120$$

Material Mix Variance:

Material A = 20 (60 – 50) = Rs. 200 (F)
Material B = 30 (120 – 100) = Rs. 600 (F)
Material C = 60 (120 – 150) = Rs. 1800 (A)

Total Material Mix Variance = Rs. 1000 (A)

Material Sub-Usage Variance : SP (SQ – RSQ)

Material A = 20(100 – 60) = Rs. 800 (F)

Material B = 30(200 – 120) = Rs. 2,400 (F)

Material C = 60(200 –120) = Rs. 4,800 (F)

Total Material Sub-Usage Variance = Rs. 8000 (F)

Verification:

MCV = MVP + MUV

Rs. 5000 (F) = Rs. 2000 (A) + Rs. 7,000 (F)

MUV = MMV + M.Sub.U.V.

Rs. 7000 (F) = Rs. 1000 (A) + Rs. 8000 (F)

Illustration 15. The standard quantity and standard price of raw material required for one unit of product A are given below:

	Quantity	Standard Price
Material X	2 Kgs.	Rs. 3 per Kg.
Material Y	4 Kgs.	Rs. 2 per Kg.

The actual production and relevant data are as follows:

Output 500 units of product A

	Total Quantity for 500 units	Total Cost
Material X	1,200 Kgs.	Rs. 3,900
Material Y	1,800 Kgs.	Rs. 4,500

Calculate Material Cost, Price and Usage Variances. (*B. Com. M.S.*)

Solution:

Material Cost Variance: MCV = (SQ × SP) – (AQ AP)

Standard Quantity refers to Standard Quantity for actual Production.

For one unit of Product A, Material X = 2kgs.

For 500 units of Product A, Material X = 2 × 500 = 1,000 kgs.

For one unit of Product A, Material Y = 4 kgs.

For 500 units of Product A, Material Y = 4 × 500 = 2000 kgs.

MCV : Material X = (1000 × 3) – (3900) = Rs. 900 (A)

Material Y = (2000 × 2) – (4500) = Rs. 500 (A)

Total Material Cost Variance = Rs. 1400 (A)

Material Price Variance = AQ (SP – AP)

Material X = 1,200 (3 – 3.25) = Rs. 300 (A)

Material Y = 1,800 (2 – 2.50) = Rs. 900 (A)

Total Material Price Variance = Rs. 1200 (A)

Material Usage Variance = SP (SQ – AQ)

Material X = 3 (1,000 – 1,200) = Rs. 600 (A)

Material Y = 2 (2,000 Ä 1,800) = Rs. 400 (F)

Total Material Usage Variance = Rs. 200 (A)

Verification:

MCV = MPV + MUV

Rs. 1400 (A) = Rs. 1200 (A) + Rs. 200 (A)

Illustration 16.

Material	*Standard*			*Actual*		
	Qty. Kg.	*Price Rs.*	*Total Rs.*	*Qty. Rs.*	*Price Rs.*	*Total Rs.*
A	500	6	3,000	400	6	2,400
B	400	3.75	1,500	500	3.60	1,800
C	300	3	900	400	2.80	1,120
	1,200			1,300		
Less: 10% Normal Loss	120			220		
	1,080		5,400	1,080		5,320

(*M. Com. Madurai, Madras*)

CALCULATE MATERIAL VARIANCES

Solution:

1. Material Cost Variance = (SQ × SP) – (AQ × AP)
   Material A = (500 × Rs. 6) – (400 × Rs. 6)
   = 3000 – 2400 = Rs. 600 (F)
   Material B = (400 × Rs. 3.75) – (500 × Rs. 3.60)
   = 1500 – 1800 = Rs. 300 (A)
   Material C = (300 × Rs. 3) – (400 × Rs. 2.80)
   = 900 – 1120 = Rs. 220 (A)
   Total Material Cost Variance = Rs. 80 (F)
2. Material Price Variance : AQ (SP – AP)
   Material A = 400 (6 – 6) = Nil
   Material B = 500 (3.75 – 3.60) = 75 (F)
   Material C = 400 (3 – 2.80) = 80 (F)
   Total Material Price Variance = Rs. 155 (F)
3. Material Usage Variance = SP (SQ – AQ)
   Material A = 6 (400 – 500) = 600 (F)
   Material B = 3.75 (400 – 500) = 375 (A)
   Material C = 3 (300 – 400) = Rs. 300 (A)
   Total Material Usage Variance = Rs. 75 (A)
4. Material Mix Variance = SP (RSQ – AQ)

$$RSQ = \frac{\text{Total Actual Quantity}}{\text{Total Standard Quantity}} \times \text{Standard Quantity}$$

Material A $= \frac{1300}{1200} \times 500 = 541.67\ kg.$

Material B $= \frac{1300}{1200} \times 400 = 433.33\ kg.$

Material C $= \frac{1300}{1200} \times 300 = 325.00\ kg.$

Material Mix Variance:
Material A = 6 (541.67 – 400) = 850 (F)

Material B = 3.75 (433.33 – 500) = 250 (A)
Material C = 3 (325 – 400) = 225 (A)
Total Material Mix Variance = Rs. 375 (F)

5. Material Yield Variance:
Average Standard Price per unit = (Standard Loss on Actual Output – Actual Loss)
Standard loss on an input of 1200 kg = 120

Standard loss on the actual input of 1300 kg = $\frac{120}{1200} \times 1300 = 130\ kg$

Average Standard Price per unit = $\frac{\text{Total Standard Cost}}{\text{Standard Output}} = \frac{5400}{1080} = \text{Rs. } 5$

Material Yield Variance = 5 (130 – 220) = **Rs. 450 (A)**

Verification:

MCV = MPV + MUV

Rs. 80 (F) = Rs. 155 (F) + Rs. 75 (A)

MUV = MMV + MYV

Rs. 75 (A) = Rs. 375 (F) + Rs. 450 (A)

Illustration 17. The standard material cost for 100 kg of chemical D is made up of :

Chemical A – 30 kg. @ Rs. 4 per kg.
Chemical B – 40 kg. @ Rs. 5 per kg.
Chemical C – 80 kg. @ Rs. 6 per kg.

In a batch, 500 kg of Chemical D were produced from a mix of

Chemical A – 140 kg. at a cost of Rs. 588
Chemical B – 220 kg. at a cost of Rs. 1,056
Chemical C – 440 kg. at a cost of Rs. 2,860

How do the yield, mix and the price factor contribute to the variance in the actual per 100 kg of Chemical D over the standard cost ? *(B. Com., Calicut, Bangalore, I.C.W.A.)*

Solution :

MCV Rs.
Rs. 100.80(A)

MPV (Rs. 40.80)(A) MUV(Rs. 60)(A)

MMV(Rs. 6.67)(A) MYV (Rs. 53.33)(A)

We have to find out the variances only for 100 kg of output. Therefore, the data required is calculated as follows :

Chemical A : Rate $= \frac{588}{140} = \text{Rs. } 4.20 \text{ per kg}$

Chemical B : Rate $= \frac{1,056}{220} = \text{Rs. } 4.80 \text{ per kg.}$

Chemical C : Rate $= \frac{2,860}{440} = Rs. 6.50 \text{ per kg}$

Chemical D (500 kg) the Chemical A is 140 kg.

∴ 100 kg. of Chemical D, the required :

Chemical A is $\frac{140 \times 100}{500} = 28$ kg.

Chemical B is $\frac{220 \times 100}{500} = 44$ kg.

Chemical C is $\frac{440 \times 100}{500} = 88$ kg.

(*a*) Material Cost Variance :

(SQ × SP) – (AQ × AP)

Chemical A = (30 × Rs. 4) – (28 × Rs. 4.20) = Rs. 2.40 (F)
Chemical B = (40 × Rs. 5) – (44 × Rs. 4.80) = Rs. 11.20 (A)
Chemical C = (80 × Rs. 6) – (88 × Rs. 6.50) = Rs. 92.00 (A)
Total MCV = Rs. 100.80 (A)

(*b*) Material Price Variance :

AQ(SP – AP)

Chemical A = 28 (4 – 4.20) = Rs. 5.60 (A)
Chemical B = 44 (5 – 4.80) = Rs. 8.80 (F)
Chemical C = 88 (6 – 6.50) = Rs. 44.00 (A)
Total MPV = Rs. 40.80 (A)

(c) Material Usage Variance :

SP (SQ – AQ)

Chemical A : 4(30 – 28) = Rs. 8 (F)
Chemical B : 5(40 – 44) = Rs. 20 (A)
Chemical C : 6(80 – 88) = Rs. 48 (A)
Total MUV = Rs. 60 (A)

(*d*) Material Mix Variance :

SP(RSQ – AQ)

The actual quantity of 160 kg to be apportioned in the standard proportion, i.e., 30 : 40 : 80

For Chemical A $= \frac{160 \times 30}{150} = 32$ kg.

Chemical B $= \frac{160 \times 40}{150} = 42\frac{2}{3}$ kg.

Chemical C $= \frac{160 \times 80}{150} = 85\frac{1}{3}$ kg.

MMV = SP(RSQ – AQ)

For Chemical A : 4(32 – 28) = Rs. 16.00 (F)

Chemical B : $5\left(42\frac{2}{3} - 44\right) = Rs. 6.67(A)$

Chemical C : $6\left(85\frac{1}{3} - 88\right) = Rs. 16.00\,(A)$

Total MMV = Rs. 6.67 (A)

(e) *Material Yield Variance* :

$$\text{Average standard price} = \frac{\text{Total standard price}}{\text{Standard output}} = \frac{800}{100} = \text{Rs. } 8$$

Total std. Price = 30 kg × Rs. 4 + 40 kg × Rs. 5 + 80 kg × Rs. 6 = Rs. 800
150 kg. mix will produce 100 kg.

$$\therefore \text{ 160 kg. of mix will produce } = \frac{100 \times 160}{150} = 106\frac{2}{3} \text{ kg}$$

MYV = Average standard price (Actual Production – Standard Production)

$$= \text{Rs. } 8\left(100 \text{ kgs.} - 106\frac{2}{3} \text{ kgs}\right) = \text{Rs. } 8\left(6\frac{2}{3}\right) = \text{Rs. } 53.33 \text{(A)}$$

Illustration 18. Vinak Ltd. produces an article by blending two basic raw materials. It operates a standard costing system and the following standards have been set for new materials.

Material	*Standard Mix*	*Standard price per kg.*
A	40%	Rs. 4.00
B	60%	Rs. 3.00

The standard loss in processing is 15%

During April the company produced 1700 kgs. of finished output. The position of stocks and purchases for the month of April is as under:

Material	*Stock on 1st April*	*Stock on 30th April*	*Purchased during April*	
	kgs	*kgs*	*kgs.*	*Cost Rs.*
A	35	5	800	3400
B	40	50	1200	3000

Calculate the following variances :

1. Material Price Variances.
2. Material Usage Variances.
3. Material Yield Variances.
4. Material Mix Variances.
5. Total Material Cost Variances. (*C.A. Inter*)

Solution :

Finished output 1,700 kgs. Standard Loss in processing 15%

Therefore input is $1,700 \times \frac{100}{85} = 2000$ kgs.

For an input of 2,000 kgs., the Standard Cost will be as follows :

A 40% of 2,000 = 800 kgs. at Rs. 4.00 = Rs. 3,200

$$\text{B 60\% of 2,000} = \frac{1,200 \text{ kgs.}}{2,000 \text{ kgs.}} \text{ at Rs. 3} = \frac{\text{Rs. } 3,600}{\text{Rs. } 6,800}$$

$$\text{Loss 15\%} \quad \frac{300 \text{ kgs.}}{1,700 \text{ kgs.}} \qquad \frac{-}{\text{Rs. } 6,800}$$

$$\text{Standard Yield Rate} = \frac{6,800}{1,700} = \text{Rs. 4 per kg}$$

Actual cost :

		Rs.
A 35 + 800 – 5 = 830 kgs. Consumed	35 × 4 (assumed)	= 140
	795 × 4.25 (Purchase price)	= 3,378.75

		3,518.75
B 40 + 1,200 – 50 = 1190 kgs. Consumed 40 × 3 (assumed)		= 120.00
1150 × 2.50 (Purchase price)		= 2,875.00
Total	2,020	2,995.00
Less : Loss	320	–
Finished output	1,700	6,513.75

Material Price Variance : AQ (SR – AR) *or* (AQ × SR) – (AQ × AR)

A = 830 × 4 = 3,320 – 3,518.75 = Rs. 198.75 (A)

B = 1,190 × 3 = 3,570 – 2,995 = Rs. 575.00 (F)

Rs. 376.25 (F)

1. Material Usage Variance : SR (SQ – AQ)

A = 4(800 – 830) = 120 (A)

B = 3(1,200 – 1,190) = 30 (F)

Rs. 90 (A)

2. Material Yield Variance : SYR × (AY – SY)

= 4 (1,700 – 1,717) = **68(A)**

[* SY For 2,000 kgs. input SY = 1,700

$$\text{For 2,020 kgs. input SY} = \frac{2020}{2,000} \times 1,700 = 1,717 \text{ kgs.}]$$

3. Material Mix Variance: SR(RSQ – AQ)

$$\text{RSQ} = \frac{\text{Total weight of actual Mix}}{\text{Total weight of Std. Mix}} \times \text{SQ}$$

$$A = 800 \times \frac{2020}{2,000} = 808$$

$$B = 1,200 \times \frac{2,020}{2,000} = \text{Rs. } 1,212$$

MMV A = 4(808 – 830) = 88(A)

B = 3(1,212 – 1,190) = 66 (F)

Rs. 22 (A)

Material Cost Variance = SC – AC = 6,800 – 6,513.75 = **Rs. 286.25 (F)**

Verification:

MCV = MPV + MUV

286.25 (F) = 376.25 (F) + 90(A)

MCV = MPV + MYV + MMV

286.25(F) = 376.25 (F) + 68(A) + 22(A)

Illustration 19. The standard cost of a certain drug is :

40% of Material X at Rs. 20 per lb.

60% of Material Y at Rs. 30 per lb.

Standard loss expected in production is 10%. In a certain period 90 lbs of Material X at Rs. 18 per lb and 110 lbs of material Y at Rs. 34 per lb were used. Good production realised was 182 lbs.

Calculate the different material variances.

(*B. Com., Madurai*)

Solution :

1. M.P.V. = AQ(SP – AP)

	Rs.
Material A : 90(20 – 18)	= 180 (F)
Material B : 110(30 – 34)	= 440 (A)
	Rs. 260 (A)

2. M.U.V = SP (SQ for actual output – AQ)

Material A : 20 (80.88 – 90)	= 182. 4 (A)
Material B : 30 (121.33 – 110)	= 339.9 (F)
	Rs. 157.5 (F)

Note : If 90 is output, standard material of A = 40

If 182 is output, standard material of $A = \frac{40}{90} \times 182 = 80.88$

If 182 is output, standard material of $B = \frac{60}{90} \times 182 = 121.33$

3. M.C.V. = (SP × SQ) – (AP × AQ)

A : (20 × 80.88) – (18 × 90)	= 2.4 (A)
B : (30 × 121.33) – (34 × 110)	= 100.1 (A)
	Rs. 102.5(A)

Check : MCV = MPV + MUV

102.5 (A) = 260 (A) + 157.5 (F)

MMV = SP (SQ – AQ)

A : 20(80 – 90) = 200 (A)

B : 30(120 – 110) = 300(F)

Rs. 100 (F)

$$\text{MYV=Average SP}\left(\begin{array}{ccc}\text{Actual Loss on} & - & \text{Standard Loss on}\\ \text{Actual Output} & & \text{Actual Output}\end{array}\right)$$

$$\text{Average SP of Standard Mix} = \frac{80 \times 20 + 120 \times 30}{200 - 10\%} = \text{Rs. } 28.8$$

MYV = 28.8(18 – 20) = Rs. 57.6 or Rs. 57.5 (F)

Because actual loss is less

Check : MUV = MMV + MYV

Rs. 157.5(F) = Rs. 100 (F) + Rs. 57.5 (F)

Illustration 20.

From the following information of a product, calculate :

1. Material Cost Variance,
2. Material Price Variance,
3. Material Usage Variance,
4. Material Mix Variance and
5. Material sub-usage Variance.

Material	Standard Quantity Kg.	Standard Price Rs.	Actual Quantity Kg.	Actual Price Rs.
X	20	5	24	4.00
Y	16	4	14	4.50
Z	12	3	10	3.25
	48		48	

(*M. Com. Madras, Agra, Panjab*)

Solution :

1. Material Cost Variance :

Material : MCV = (SQ × SP) – (AQ × AP)

X = (20 × 5) – (24 × 4) = 100 – 96 = Rs. 4 (F)
Y = (16 × 4) – (14 × 4.5) = 64 – 63 = Re. 1 (F)
Z = (12 × 3) – (10 × 3.25) = 36 – 32.5 = Rs. 3.5 (F)
Rs. 8.5 (F)

2. Material Price Variance : AQ (SR – AR)

X = 24(5 – 4) = Rs. 24 (F)
Y = 14(4 – 4.5) = Rs. 7 (A)
Z = 10(3 – 3.25) = Rs. 2.5 (A)
Rs. 14.5 (F)

3. Material Usage Variance : SR (SQ – AQ)

X = 5(20 – 24) = Rs. 20 (A)
Y = 4(16 – 14) = Rs. 8 (F)
Z = 3(12 – 10) = Rs. 6 (F)
Rs. 6 (A)

4. Material Mix Variance : SP (SQ – AQ)

X = 5(20 – 24) = Rs. 20 (A)
Y = 4(16 – 14) = Rs. 8 (F)
Z = 3(12 – 10) = Rs. 6 (F)
Rs. 6 (A)

5. Material sub-usage Variance = Std. Price (Std. Qty – Revised Std. Qty)

The total actual weight of mix and the total standard weight of mix are the same. Under such situations, material sub-usage variance is nil.

MCV = MPV + MUV
Rs. 8.5 (F) = 14.5 (F) + Rs. 6 (A)
MUV = MMV + M sub. uv
Rs. 6 (A) = Rs. 6 (A) + Nil

Illustration 21.

From the following data compute the Material Cost Variances :

Name of Material	*Standard*		*Actual*	
	Units	*Price*	*Units* *Rs.*	*Price* *Rs.*
Zee	3,500	10	3,700	12
Wee	1,500	21	1,650	20
Tee	1,000	33	1,250	36

(*ICWA*)

Solution :

Name of Material	*Standard Cost*			*Actual Cost*		
	Units	*Rate* *Rs.*	*Amount* *Rs.*	*Unit*	*Rate* *Rs.*	*Amount* *Rs.*
Zee	3,500	10	35,000	3,700	12	44,000
Wee	1,500	21	31,500	1,650	20	33,000
Tee	1,000	33	33,000	1,250	36	45,000
Total	6,000		99,500	6,600		1,22,400

Material Cost Variance MCV = SC – AC

= 99,500 – 1,22,400 = Rs. 22,900 (A)

Material Price Variance MPV = AQ (SR – AR)

Zee = 3,700 (10 – 12) = Rs. 7,400 (A)
Wee = 1,650 (21 – 20) = Rs. 1,650 (F)
Tee = 1,250 (33 – 36) = Rs. 3,750 (A)

Rs. 9,500 (A)

Material Usage Variance : MUV = SR (SQ – AQ)

Zee = 10 (3,500 – 3,700) = Rs. 2,000 (A)
Wee = 21 (1,500 – 1,650) = Rs. 3,150 (A)
Tee = 33 (1,000 – 1,250) = Rs. 8,250 (A)

Rs. 13,400 (A)

$$\text{Revised Standard Quantity} = \frac{\text{Total Weight of Actual Mix}}{\text{Total Weight of Standard Mix}} \times \text{Std. Quantity}$$

$$\text{Zee} = \frac{6,600}{6,000} \times 3,500 = 3,850 \text{ units}$$

$$\text{Wee} = \frac{6,600}{6,000} \times 1,500 = 1,650 \text{ units}$$

$$\text{Tee} = \frac{6,600}{6,000} \times 1,000 = 1,100 \text{ units}$$

Material Mix Variance : MMV = SR (RSQ – AQ)

units

Zee = 10 (3,850 – 3,700) = 1,500 (F)
Wee = 21 (1,650 – 1,650) = Nil
Tee = 33 (1,100 – 1,250) = 4,950 (A)

3,450 (A)

Verification:

MCV = MPV + MUV

Rs. 22,900 (A) = Rs. 9,500 (A) + Rs. 13,400 (A)

Illustration 22.

The Standard mix of product A2 is as follows :

Kgs.	*Material*	*Price per Kg. (Rs.)*
45	X	6.00
25	Y	4.50
30	Z	9.50

The Standard loss in production is 10% of input. There is no scrap value. Actual production for a month was 7,425 Kgs. of A2 from 80 mixes. Actual consumption and purchases of material during the month were.

Kgs.	*Material*	*Price per Kg. (Rs.)*
4,200	X	6.50
1,700	Y	4.25
2,600	Z	9.75

You are required to calculate the following variances for presentation to the management :

(*a*) Material Cost Variance

(*b*) Material Price Variance

(*c*) Material Mix Variance

(*d*) Material Yield Variance. (*CS Inter*)

Solution :

Standard Cost				*Actual Cost*			
Material	*Kg.*	*Price Rs.*	*Amount Rs.*	*Material*	*Kg.*	*Price Rs.*	*Amount Rs.*
X	80 × 45 = 3,600	6.00	21,600	X	4,200	6.50	27,300
Y	80 × 25 = 2,000	4.50	9,000	Y	1,700	4.25	7,225
Z	80 × 30 = 2,400	9.50	22,800	Z	2,600	9.75	25,350
Input	8,000		53,400		8,500		59,875
Loss 10%	800		–	Loss	1,075		–
Output	7,200		53,400	Output	7,425		59,875

$$\text{Standard Cost} = \frac{53,400}{7,200} = \text{Rs. } 7.4167 \text{ per Kg.}$$

Standard Cost of Actual Production = 7,425 × 7.4167 = Rs. 55,069

$$\text{Revised Standard Quantity : RSQ} \times \frac{\text{Total Weight of Actual Mix}}{\text{Total Weight of Standard Mix}}$$

Kgs.

$$X = 3,600 \times \frac{8,500}{8,000} = 3,825$$

$$Y = 2,000 \times \frac{8,500}{8,000} = 2,125$$

$$Z = 2,400 \times \frac{8,500}{8,000} = 2,550$$

8,500

(*i*) Material Cost Variance : MCV= SC for Actual Production – AC

= Rs. 55,069 – Rs. 59,875 = Rs. 4,806 (A)

(*ii*) Material Price Variance : MPV = AQ (SR – AR)

	Rs.
X = 4,200 (Rs. 6.00 – Rs. 6.50) =	2,100 (A)
Y = 1,700 (Rs. 4.50 – Rs. 4.25) =	425 (F)
Z = 2,600 (Rs. 9.50 – Rs. 9.75) =	650 (A)
	2,325 (A)

(*iii*) Material Mix Variance : MMV = SR (RSQ – AQ)

	Rs.
X = Rs. 6.00 (3,825 – 4,200)	= 2,250 (A)
Y = Rs. 4.50 (2,125 – 1,700)	= 1,912.50 (F)
Z = Rs. 9.50 (2,550 – 2,600)	= 475 (A)
	812.50 (A)

(*iv*) Material Yield Variance : MYV = SC (AY – SY)

For 8,000 Input Yield = 7,200

For 8,500 Input yield = $\frac{8,500}{8,000} \times 7,200$ = 7,650 Kgs.

MYV = 7.4167 (7,425 – 7,650) = Rs. 1,668.50 (A) (Approx)

Verification:

MCV = MPV + MMV + MYV

Rs. 4,806 (A) = Rs. 2,325 (A) + Rs. 812.50 (A) + Rs. 1,668.50 (A)

II. LABOUR VARIANCES

Labour variances arise because of (*i*) difference in actual rates and standard rates of labour and (*ii*) the variation in actual time taken by workers and the standard time allotted to them for performing a job. These are computed on the same pattern as those of material variances. Labour variances can be very easily calculated by applying the same techniques as used in calculation of material variances. One can find out the various formulae for Direct Labour Variances by simply putting the word "time" in place of "Quantity" in the formula meant for Direct Material Variances. The various labour variances can be analysed as follows:

(A) Labour Cost Variance
(B) Labour Rate Variance
(C) Labour Time or Efficiency Variance
(D) Labour Idle Time Variance
(E) Labour Mix Variance or Gang Composition Variance

The second important element of cost is labour. The management keeps a close watch on the labour cost in order to keep the cost of production low. The various labour variances are:

When one type of labour is employed :

LABOUR COST VARIANCE
(ST × SR) – (AT × AR)

Rate Variance	Either
AT(SR – AR)	Total Efficiency Variance SR (ST – AT) *or* *Yield Variance*

Total efficiency variance may be sub-divided into two :

TOTAL EFFICIENCY VARIANCE
SR(ST – AT)

Idle time	*either*
(SR × IT)	Efficiency Variance SR(ST – AT) AT means less idle time (*or*) Yield Variance

When different grades of labour are employed :

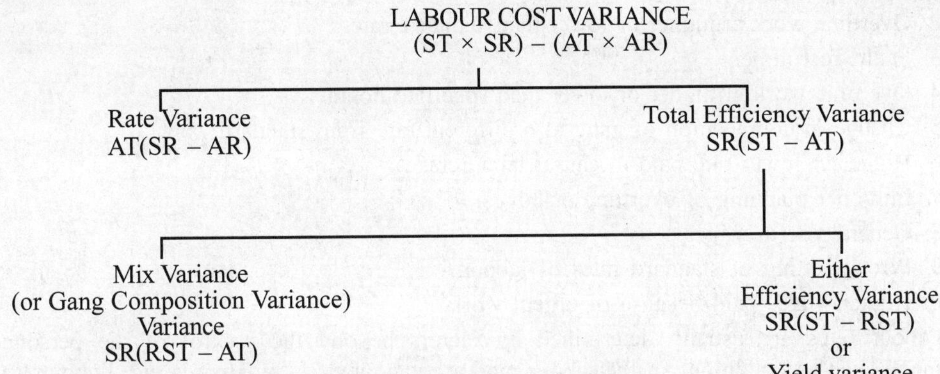

Total efficiency may be sub-divided into three, when idle time variance is also to be calculated :

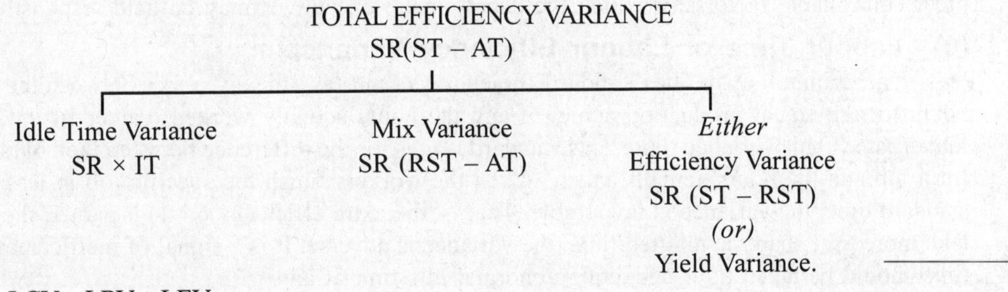

LCV = LRV + LEV
LEV = LMV + LYV + LITV

(a) Labour Cost Variance or Labour Wage Variance

This variance represents the difference between the standard labour costs and the actual labour costs. That is, it is the difference between standard direct wages specified for the activity achieved and the actual direct wages paid. Labour costs may be considered wages including pay, allowances and other expenses on labour. As per the terminology of ICMA, London, this variance is defined as "the difference between the standard direct labour cost and the actual direct labour cost incurred for the production achieved".

If the standard cost is higher, the variation is favourable and vice versa. This variance can be calculated with the help of the following formula :

Labour Cost Variance = Standard Cost of Labour – Actual Cost of Labour)
= (Standard Time × Standard Rate) – (Actual Time × Actual Rate)
= (ST × SR) – (AT × AR)

(b) Labour or Wage Rate Variance

This variance is the direct result of the wages paid at a rate different from the standard rate. That is, it is the difference between the standard rate of pay specified and the actual rate paid. According to ICMA, London, the variance is "the difference between the standard and the actual direct labour rate per hour for the total hours worked." The calculation of variances is similar to the material price variance. If the standard rate is higher, the variance is favourable and vice versa.

Labour Rate = Actual Time (Standard Wage Rate × Actual Wage Rate Variance)
= AT (SR – AR)

The reasons for wage rate variance :

1. Changes in basic wage rates.

2. Overtime work at higher or lower than standard rate.
3. Faulty recruitment.
4. Overtime work at higher or lower than specified hours.
5. Change in composition of gang at a different rate from standard.
6. Higher or lower rate paid to causal labourers.
7. Improper planning of overtime or bonus.
8. General rise in wages.
9. Wrong setting of standard rates of labour.
10. Higher wages paid because of urgent work.

Labour rates are usually determined by factors beyond the control of the personnel department, such as conditions in the labour market, wage awards by Boards etc. Labour Rate Variances are, therefore, mostly uncontrollable except for the portion which arises due to employment of wrong grade of labour, use of different mode of payment, overtime work or such other controllable factors for which the departmental executives may be held responsible.

(c) Labour Time or Labour Efficiency Variance

The terminology defines Labour Efficiency Variance as "the difference between the standard hours for the actual production achieved and the hours actually worked, valued at the standard labour rate." This variance represents standard wages for the difference between the hours allowed for a job and the hours actually taken. When the workers finish the specific job in less than the standard time, the variance is favourable. That is, the extra efficiency on their part. If the workers take more time than the allotted time, the variance is adverse. It is a signal of inefficiency. Actual time should be taken after deducting abnormal idle time if any.

Labour Efficiency Variance = Standard Rate (Standard Time – Actual Time)

= SR (ST – AT)

The variance may be favourable or unfavourable because of the following reasons :

Favourable Factors

1. Strict supervision
2. Use of good quality materials
3. Low labour turnover rate
4. High morale of workers
5. Proper working condition
6. Improved tools and machines
7. Good incentives
8. Workers' co-operation
9. Right man at right work
10. Employment of skilled workers.

Unfavourable Factors

1. Improper training to employees
2. Inadequate supervision
3. Low employee morale
4. More idle time than normal
5. Incorrect instruction
6. Engaging new or unskilled workers
7. Workers' dissatisfaction

8. Defective machinery
9. High labour turnover rate
10. Bad working condition
11. Failure of power supply
12. Use of sub-standard materials
13. Delay due to waiting for materials
14. Fixation of incorrect standard
15. Lack of co-operation

(*d*) Idle Time Variance

This type of variance arises because of the time during which the labour remains idle due to abnormal reasons, *i.e.,* power failure, strikes, machine breakdown, shortage of materials etc.

The standards are fixed carefully. Even then idle time occurs because of unforeseen reasons. This abnormal idle time must be shown separately. If not separated, the idle time will affect the efficiency of employees when such time loss is beyond their control.

This will always be an adverse variance.

Labour Idle Time Variance = Abnormal Idle Time × Standard Hourly Rate

(e) Labour Mix Variance or Gang Composition Variance

It results from employing different grades of labour from the standard fixed in advance. It is the difference between the standard composition of workers and the actual gang of workers.

It is a part of labour efficiency variance. This variance corresponds to material mix variance. This variance enables the management to study the labour cost variance occurred because of the changes in the composition of labour force.

This variance is quite similar in concept and formula to Material Mix Variance. The rates of pay of the different categories of workers—skilled, semi-skilled and unskilled, are different. Hence, any change made in composition of the workers will naturally cause variance. How much is the variance due to the change, is indicated by Labour Mix Variance.

There are two situations of the changes in the composition of workers. Accordingly, there are two versions of the formulae. In Material Mix Variance also, there were two formulae and similar is the position here.

(*i*) When the total hours *i.e.* time of the standard composition and actual composition of workers do not differ, the formula is :

$$\text{Labour Mix Variance} = (\text{Standard Cost of Standard Mix}) - (\text{Standard Cost of Actual Mix})$$

(*ii*) When the total hours *i.e.* time of the standard composition and actual composition of workers differ, the formula is :

$$\text{Labour Mix Variance} = \left[\frac{\text{Total Time of Actual Mix}}{\text{Total time of Standard Mix}} \times \text{Standard Cost of Standard Mix}\right] - (\text{Standard Cost of Actual Mix})$$

If, on account of short availability of some category of workers, the standard composition is itself revised, then Labour Mix Variance will be calculated by taking Revised Standard Mix in place of Standard Mix.

Wages Revision Variance

Trade Union movement is quite strong. Trade Unions struggle for a raise in remuneration on account of price-rise, increase in rate of productivity etc. Many times it may happen due to settlement with the workers' union, the management has to make an upward revision of wage rates during the year, after the standard rates have been fixed. Wages Revision Variance shows the impact on the wage bill on account of the wages revision. Standard labour cost for actual output is calculated at pre-revision rates as also at post-revision rates. Both are standard rates — the original and revised. The difference between the two cost figures is the Wage Revision Variance.

Formula :

$$\text{Wage Revision Variance} = \begin{bmatrix}\text{Standard Labour cost of}\\ \text{Actual Output at pre-}\\ \text{revision Standard Rate}\end{bmatrix} - \begin{bmatrix}\text{Standard Labour Cost of}\\ \text{Actual Output at Post-}\\ \text{revision Rate}\end{bmatrix}$$

OR

$$= \begin{bmatrix}\text{Original}\\ \text{Rate of pay}\end{bmatrix} \times \begin{matrix}\text{Standard}\\ \text{Time}\end{matrix}\Bigg] - \begin{bmatrix}\text{Revised Standard}\\ \text{Rate of Pay}\end{bmatrix} \times \text{Standard Time}\Bigg]$$

OR

$$= \text{Standard Time}\left(\begin{matrix}\text{Original Standard}\\ \text{Rate of Pay}\end{matrix} - \text{Revised Standard Rate of Pay}\right)$$

(*f*) Labour Yield Variance

It is just like Material Yield Variance. It is the difference between the standard labour output and actual output or yield. It is calculated as below :

$$\text{Labour Yield Variance} = \begin{matrix}\text{Standard Cost}\\ \text{per unit}\end{matrix}\left(\begin{matrix}\text{Standard Production}\\ \text{of Actual Mix}\end{matrix} - \text{Actual Production}\right)$$

If the actual production is more than standard production, it would result in a favourable variance and vice versa.

Relationship

(*a*) Labour cost variance = Labour rate variance + Labour efficiency variance

(*b*) Labour efficiency variance = Labour mix variance + Idle time variance

(*c*) Labour efficiency variance = Labour yield variance + Idle time variance

(*d*) Efficiency variance = Labour mix variance + Yield variance + Idle time variance

Illustration 23. With the help of following information calculate

(*a*) Labour cost variance

(*b*) Labour rate variance

(*c*) Labour efficiency variance

Standard hours : 40 @ Rs. 3 per hour

Actual hours : 50 @ Rs. 4 per hour (*B. Com., Rajasthan*)

Solution :

(*a*) Labour Cost Variance = (Std. time × Std. rate) – (Actual time × Actual rate)
= (40 × Rs. 3) – (50 × Rs. 4)
= Rs. 120 – 200 = Rs. – 80
= **Rs. 80 (Adverse)**

(*b*) Labour Rate Variance = Actual Time (Std. rate – Actual rate)
= 50 (Rs. 3 – Rs. 4) = Rs. – 50
= **Rs. 50(Adverse)**

(*c*) Labour Efficiency Variance = Std. Rate (Std. time – Actual time)
= Rs. 3 (40 – 50) = Rs. – 30
= **Rs. 30 (Adverse)**

Verification:

Labour Cost Variance Labour Rate Variance + Labour Efficiency Variance
Rs. 80 (A) = Rs. 50(A) + Rs. 30(A)

Illustration 24. The following information relates to the manufacturing process of a company :

Number of employees	200
Weekly hours worked	40
Standard wage rate	50 P. per hour
Standard output	250 units per hour

During the first week of February four employees were paid at 45 P. per hours and two employees at 55 P. per hour, the rest were paid at standard rates. Idle time is one hour per employee. Actual output was 10,250 articles. Calculate labour variances.

Solution :

(*i*) Actual Cost of Labour :

		Rs.
4 employees × 40 hours × 45 P.	=	72
2 employees × 40 hours × 55 P.	=	44
194 employees × 40 hours × 50 P.	=	3,880
		3,996

(*ii*) Actual hours = 200 × 40 = 8,000 hours
Idle time is 1 hour per employee.
So actual hours = 8,000 – 200 = 7,800

(*iii*) Standard Gang Hour $= \dfrac{\text{Actual output}}{\text{Standard output per gang hour}}$

$= \dfrac{10{,}250}{250} = 41$ hours

Standard hours = Standard Gang hour × No. of workers
= 41 × 200 = 8,200 hours

(*iv*) Standard Cost of Labour = Standard time × Standard Rate
$= 8{,}200 \text{ hours} \times 50\text{P.} = \text{Rs. } 4{,}100$

(*a*) Labour Cost Variance = Standard Cost of Labour – Actual Cost of Labour
= Rs. 4,100 – Rs. 3,996
= **Rs. 104** (Favourable)

(*b*) Labour Rate Variance = AT (SR – AR)
(*i*) 4 × 40(50P – 45P) = 160 × 5P.
= Rs. 8 (Favourable)
(*ii*) 2 × 40(50P – 55P) = 80(– 5P)
= **Rs. 4** (Adverse)
Therefore LRV = Rs. 8 – Rs. 4 = Rs. 4 (Favourable)

(*c*) Labour Efficiency Variance = SR (ST – AT)
= 50 P(8,200 – 7,800)
= **Rs. 200** (Favourable)

(*d*) Idle Time Variance = Idle hours × Std. hourly rate
= 200 × 50 P.
= **Rs. 100 (Adverse)**

Verification:

LCV = LRV + LEV + ITV
Rs. 104 (F) = Rs. 4(F) + Rs. 200(F) + Rs. 100(A)
Rs. 104 (F) = Rs. 104(F)

Illustration 25. Find out different Labour Variances.

Standard	Actual
Output : 1,000 units	1,200 units
Rate of payment : Rs. 6 per unit	Wages paid with bonus : Rs. 8,000
Time taken : 50 hours	40 hours.

Solution :

$$\text{Standard Rate} = \frac{1,000 \times 6}{50 \text{ hrs}} = \text{Rs. } 120 \text{ per hour}$$

$$\text{Actual Rate} = \text{Rs. } \frac{8000}{40} = \text{Rs. } 200 \text{ per hour}$$

Standard hours for 1,200 units actually produced

$$50 \text{ hrs.} \times \frac{1,200}{1,000} = 60 \text{ hrs.}$$

1. Labour Cost Variance :
(ST × SR) – (AT × AR)
(60 Hrs × Rs. 120) – (40 Hrs × Rs. 200) = 7,200 – 8,000
= **Rs. 800(A)**
2. Labour Rate Variance : AT(SR – AR) = 40 Hrs. (Rs. 120 – Rs. 200) = **Rs. 3,200 (A)**
3. Labour Efficiency Variance : SR (ST – AT) = Rs. 120 (60 – 40) = **Rs. 2,400 (F)**

Verification:

LCV = LRV × LEV
Rs. 800 (A) = Rs. 3,200(A) + Rs. 2,400(F)

Illustration 26. The labour budget of a Company for a week is as follows :

20 skilled men @ 50 paise per hour for 40 hours	= 400
40 unskilled men @ 30 paise per hour for 40 hours	= 480
	880

The actual labour force was used as follows :

30 skilled men @ 50 paise per hour for 40 hours	= 600
30 unskilled men @ 35 paise per hour for 40 hours	= 420
	1,020

Analysis labour variances.

Solution :

Labour rate variance	= AH(SR – AR)	
(*a*) Skilled men	= 1,200(Re. 0.50 – Re. 0.50)	= 0
(*b*) Unskilled men	= 1,200 (Re.0.30 – Re. 0.35)	= Rs. 60(A)
Labour Mix variance	= SR(SH – AH)	
(a) Skilled men	= Re. 0.50(800 – 1200)	= Rs. 200 (A)

(b) Unskilled men = Re. 0.30(1600 – 1200) = Rs. 120 (F)

Total Labour variances : Rs. 140 (A)

Total Labour Cost Variance = Std. labour cost – Actual cost

= Rs.880 – Rs.1020 = Rs.140 (A)

Illustration 27. Using the following information, calculate the labour variance :

Direct wages	:	Rs. 3,000
Standard hours produced	:	1,600
Standard rate per hour	:	1.50

Actual hours paid 1,500 hours, out of which hours not worked (abnormal idle time) are 50.

Solution :

(*a*) *Labour Cost Variance*

= (Std. time × Std. rate) – (Actual time × Actual rate)

= (1,600 × Rs. 1.50) – (1,500 × Rs. 2)

= Rs. 2,400 – Rs. 3,000

= **Rs. 600 (Adverse)**

(*b*) *Labour Rate Variance*

= Actual time (Std. rate – Actual rate)

= 1,500 (Rs. 1.50 – 2.00)

= 1500 (– Re. .50) = – Rs. 750

= **Rs. 750 (Adverse)**

(*c*) *Labour Efficiency Variance*

= Std. rate (Std. time – Actual time)

Actual time = Actual hour paid – Abnormal idle time

= 1,500 – 50 = 1,450

LEV = Rs. 1.50(1,600 – 1,450)

= Rs. 1.50 × 150

= **Rs. 225 (Favourable)**

(*d*) *Idle Time Variance*

= Idle time × Standard hourly rate

= 50 × Rs. 1.50

= **Rs. 75 (A)**

Verification:

LCV = LRV + LEV + ITV

Rs. 600(A) = Rs. 750(A) + Rs. 225 (F) + Rs. 75(A)

Rs. 600(A) = Rs. 600(A)

Illustration 28. Calculate, (1) Labour Cost Variance,

(2) Labour Rate Variance

(3) Labour Efficiency Variance

The details are given below:

	Deptt. A	*Deptt. B*
Actual Direct Wages	Rs. 80,000	Rs. 72,000
Standard hours produced	10,000	8,000
Standard Rate per hour	Rs. 8	Rs. 10
Actual hours worked	12,000	7,000

(*B. Com. MS, Agra, Nagarjuna*)

Solution :

1. Labour Cost Variance = (Std. Time × Std. Rate) – (Actual Time × Actual Rate)

Deptt. A = (10,000 × Rs. 8) – (Rs. 80,000)
= Rs. 80,000 – Rs. 80,000 = 0

Deptt. B = (8,000 × Rs. 10) – (Rs. 72,000)
= Rs. 80,000 – Rs. 72,000 = Rs. 8,000 (F)

Labour Cost Variance = Rs. 8,000 (F)

2. Labour Rate Variance = Actual Time (Std. Rate – Actual Rate)

Deptt. A = (12,000 × Rs. 8) – Rs. 80,000
= Rs. 96,000 – Rs. 80,000 = Rs. 16,000 (F)

Deptt. B = (7,000 × Rs. 10) – (Rs. 72,000)
= Rs. 70,000 – 72,000 = Rs. 2,000 (A)

= Rs. 14,000 (F)

3. Labour Efficiency Variance = Std. Rate (Std. Time – Actual Time)

Deptt. A = Rs. 8 (10,000 – 12,000)
= Rs. 8 × 2,000 = Rs. 16,000 (A)

Deptt. B = Rs. 10 (8,000 – 7,000)
= Rs. 10 × 1,000 = Rs. 10,000 (F)

Rs. 6,000 (A)

Verification:

Labour Cost Variance = Labour Rate Variance + Labour Efficiency Variance

Rs. 8,000 (F) = Rs. 14,000 (F) + Rs. 6,000 (A)

NB : Actual Time × Actual Rate = Actual Direct Wages, which are given in the problem.

Illustration 29. Calculate labour variances from the following data :

A factory worked for 6,000 labour hours during a week;
200 hours were wasted due to power failure;
The works done by workers were 6,400 standard hours;
The Standard Rate per hour was Rs. 15.
The Actual Wage Rate was Rs. 20 per hour. (*M. Com. Madras, Poona, Nagpur*)

Solution :

Labour Cost Variance : (ST × SR) – (AT × AR)
= (6,400 × 15) – (20 × 6,000)
= 96,000 – 1,20,000 = **Rs. 24,000 (A)**

Labour Rate Variance = AT (SR – AR)
= 6,000 (15 – 20) = **Rs. 30,000 (A)**

Labour Efficiency Variance : SR (ST – AT)

Actual Time worked = Actual Time – Idle Time
= 6,000 – 200 = 5,800

LEV = 15(6,400 – 5,800) = **Rs. 9,000 (F)**

Labour Idle Time Variance = SR × Idle Time
= 15 × 200 = **Rs. 3,000 (A)**

Verification:

LCV = LRV + LEV + ITV

Rs. 24,000 (A) = Rs. 30,000 (A) + Rs. 9,000 (F) + Rs. 3,000 (F)

Illustration 30. Using the following information, calculate labour cost variance, labour rate variance, labour efficiency and idle time variance :

Standard hours : 5,000

Standard wage rate : Rs. 4 per hour.

Actual hours : 6,000

Actual wage rate : Rs. 3.50 per hour.

Time lost on account of machinery breakdown : 300 hours. (*B. Com., Calicut*)

Solution :

(*a*) *Labour Cost Variance* :

= (SH for Actual Production × SR) – (AH × AR)

= (5,000 × Rs. 4) – (6,000 × Rs. 3.50) = (Rs.20,000) – Rs. 21.000) = **Rs. 1,000 (A)**

(*b*) *Labour Rate Variance* :

= AH (SR – AR)

= 6,000 (Rs. 4 – Rs. 3.50)

= **Rs. 3,000 (F)**

(*c*) *Labour Efficiency Variance :*

= SR (SH for Actual Production – AH)

= Rs. 4(5,000 – 6,000) = **Rs. 4,000 (A)**

(*d*) *Idle Time Variance :*

= (Abnormal Idle Time × SR)

= (300 × Rs. 4) = **Rs. 1200 (A)**

Verification:

LCV = LRV + LEV

Rs. 1,000(A) = Rs. 3,000 (F) + Rs. 4,000 (A)

Illustration 31. Standard labour hours and rate for production of Article A are given below :

	Hrs.	*Rate* *Rs.*	*Total* *Rs.*
Skilled worker	5	1.50 per hour	7.50
Unskilled worker	8	0.50 per hour	4.00
Semi-skilled worker	4	0.75 per hour	3.00
			14.50

Actual data		*Rate per hour* *Rs*	*Total.* *Rs.*
Articles produced	1,000 units		
Skilled worker	4,500 hrs.	2.00	9,000
Unskilled worker	10,000 hrs	0.45	4,500
Semi-skilled worker	4,200 hrs.	0.75	3,150
			16,650

Calculate :

(*a*) Labour Cost Variance

(*b*) Labour Rate Variance

(*c*) Labour Efficiency Variance

(*d*) Labour Mix Variance. (*M. Com. Madurai*)

Solution :

(a) *Labour Cost Variance* : (SH for Actual Production × SR) – (AH × AR)

Standard Hours for Actual Production = Actual Units × SH.

Skilled Worker = 1,000 × 5 = 5,000 Hrs.

Unskilled Worker = 1,000 × 8 = 8,000 Hrs.

Semi-skiled Worker = 1,000 × 4 = 4,000 Hrs.

Labour Cost Variance :

Skilled Worker = (5,000 × Rs. 1.50) – (4,500 × 2)
= Rs. 7,500 – Rs. 9,000 = **Rs. 1,500 (A)**

Unskilled Worker = (8,000 × Rs. 0.50) – (10,000 × 0.45)
= 4,000 – 4,500 = **Rs. 5,00(A)**

Semi-skilled Worker = (4,000 × Rs. 0.75) – 4,200 × Rs. 0.75)
= 3,000 – 3,150 = **Rs. 150(A)**

Total Labour Cost Variance = **Rs. 2150(A)**

(*b*) *Labour Price Variance* : AH(SR – AR)

Skilled Worker = 4,500(1.50 – 2) = Rs. 2250(A)

Unskilled Worker = 1000(0.50 – 0.45) = **Rs. 500(F)**

Semi-skilled Worker = 4,200(0.75 – 0.75 = Nil

Total Labour Price Variance = **Rs. 1,750(A)**

(*c*) *Labour Mix Variance* :

$$= SR\left(\begin{array}{c}\text{Revised Std. Mix of}\\ \text{Actual hours worked}\end{array}\right) - \text{Actual Mix}$$

$$\text{Revised Std. Mix of Actual hours worked} = \frac{\text{Std. Mix}}{\text{Total Std. Hours}} \times \text{Total Actual Hrs.}$$

$$\text{Skilled Worker} = \frac{5,000}{17,000} \times 18,700 = 5,500 \text{ Hrs}$$

$$\text{Unskilled Worker} = \frac{8,000}{17,000} \times 18,700 = 8,800 \text{ Hrs.}$$

$$\text{Semi-Skilled Worker} = \frac{4,000}{17,000} \times 18,700 = 4,400 \text{ Hrs.}$$

Labour Mix Variance :

Skilled Workers = 1.50(5,500 – 4,500) = Rs. 1,500 (F)

Unskilled Workers = 0.50(8,800 – 10,000) = Rs. 600(A)

Semi-skilled Workers = 0.75(4,400 – 4,200) = **Rs. 150(F)**

Total Labour Mix Variance = **Rs. 1050 (F)**

(*d*) *Labour Efficiency Variance* : = SR (SH for Actual Production – Revised Std. Hrs)

Skilled Worker = 1.50(5,000 – 5,500) = Rs. 750(A)

Unskilled Worker = 0.50(8,000 – 8,800) = Rs. 400(A)

Semi-skilled Worker = 0.75(4,000 – 4,400) = Rs. 300(A)

Total Labour Efficiency Variance = **Rs. 1,450(A)**

Verification:

L.C.V. = L.R.V. + L.M.V. + M.E.V.

Rs. 2,150(A) = Rs. 1,750(A) + Rs. 1050(F) + Rs. 1,450(A)

Illustration 32. Calculate the variances from the following information according to originating causes:

Standard Direct Cost per unit:

Material Cost : 5 Kgs.	= Rs. 50
Labour Cost : 20 hours	= Rs. 10
	Rs. 60

For the production of 500 units, material consumption amounted to Rs. 25,650 against 2,700 Kgs. Wage payment was Rs. 6,050 for 11,000 hours including 20 hours idle time due to machine breakdown. (*M. Com. Bombay, Madras*)

Solution:

1. *Material Variance:*

(*a*) Material Cost Variance : (SC – AC)

(Standard Cost = 500 units × 5 Kgs. Rs. 10 per Kg.

= Rs. 25,000

Actual Cost = 25,650 given)

MCV = Rs. 25,000 – 25,650 = **Rs. 650 (A)**

(*b*) Material Price Variance = AQ (SR – AR) or

(SR × AQ) – (AR × AQ)

= (10 × 2700) – (25650) = **Rs. 1350 (F)**

(*c*) Material Quantity Variance : SR (SQ – AQ)

= 10 (2500 – 2700) = **Rs. 2000 (A)**

2. *Labour Variance:*

(*a*) Labour Cost Variance :

Standard Cost of Labour – Actual Cost of Labour.

Standard Cost of Labour = (500 units × 20 hours × 0.50) = Rs. 5000

LCV = (5,000 – 6050) = Rs. 1050 (A)

(*b*) Labour Rate Variance : AT (SR – AR) or

(SR × AT) – (AR × AT)

(0.50 × 11,000) – (6,050) = **Rs. 550 (A)**

Labour Efficiency Variance = SR (ST – AT)

= 0.50 (10,000 – 10,980)= Rs. 490 (A)

Idle Time Variance = Idle Time × Standard hourly rate.

20 × 0.50 = Rs. 10(A).

Verification:

MCV = MPV + MQV

Rs. 650 (A) = Rs. 1350 (F) + Rs. 2000 (A)

LCV = LRV + LEV + ITV

Rs. 1050 (A) = Rs. 550 (A) + Rs. 490 (A) + Rs. 10 (A)

Illustration 33. X Ltd. furnish you the following particulars:

Product X requires 20 hours per unit

Standard Rate per hour is Rs. 2

Units produced : 4,000

Hours taken 76,000 (including 200 hours for power failure) at Rs. 2.10 per hour.

Calculate:

(*a*) Direct Labour Cost Variances;

(*b*) Direct Labour Rate Variances;

(*c*) Direct Labour Efficiency Variance; and

(*d*) Direct Labour Idle Time Variance. (*M. Com. Madras*)

Solution:

Labour Cost Variance: (SC – AC) or (ST × SR) – (AT × AR)

$$= (4000 \times 2 \times 20) - (76000 \times 2.10)$$

= 1,60,000 – 1,59,600 = **Rs. 400 (F)**

Labour Rate Variance = Actual Time (Std. Rate – Actual Rate)

= 76000 (2 – 2.10) = **Rs. 7600 (A)**

Labour Efficiency Variance : Std. Rate (Std. Time – Actual Time)

= 2 (80,000 – 75,800) = **Rs. 8400 (F)**

Labour Idle Time Variance : Idle Time × Std. Rate = 200 × 2 = Rs. 400 (A)

Verification:

LCV = LRV + LEV + ITV

Rs. 400 (F) = Rs. 7600 (A) + Rs. 8400 (F) + Rs. 400 (A)

Illustration 34. A group of workers normally consists of 30 men, 15 women and 10 boys. They are paid a standard hourly rates as under:

Men	Re. 0.80
Women	Re. 0.60
Boys	Re. 0.40

In a normal working week of 40 hours, the group is expected to produce 2,000 units of output.

During the week ended 31st December, the group consisted of 40 men, 10 women and 5 boys. The actual wages paid were @ Re. 0.70, Re. 0.65 and Re. 0.30 respectively. 4 hours were lost due to abnormal idle time and 1,600 units were produced.

Calculate:

(*a*) Wage Variance,

(*b*) Wage Rate Variance,

(*c*) Labour Efficiency Variance,

(*d*) Group Composition Variance, (i.e. Labour Mix Variance)

(*e*) Labour Idle Time Variance. (*CA. M. Com. Delhi, Madras*)

Solution:

(1) Actual Cost = Actual Hours × Actual Rate

	Hours		*Rs.*
40 × 40 =	1600	Hours × 0.70 =	1,120
10 × 40 =	400	Hours × 0.65 =	260
5 × 40 =	200	Hours × 0.30 =	60
	2,200		1440

(2) Standard Cost of Gang Labour :

Group	*No.*	*Rate* *Rs.*	*Amount* *Rs.*
Men	30	0.80	24
Women	15	0.60	9
Boys	10	0.40	4
			37

$$\text{Standard group hours required} = \frac{\text{Actual Output}}{\text{Std. Output per group}}$$

$$= \frac{1600}{\frac{2000}{40}} = 32$$

Standard Cost = Std. Cost per group × Std. group hours required

= 37 × 32 = Rs. 1,184

(3) Standard Hours for Actual Production

	Std. Composition	Total group hours for actual production	Total Std. hours required
Men	30	32	= 960
Women	15	32	= 480
Boys	10	32	= 320

(4) Actual Hours used = Total Actual Hours – Idle Time

= 2,200 – 220 = 1,980

Calculation of Variances:

(*a*) Wage Variance: (SC – AC) = (1184 – 1440) = Rs. 256 (A)

(*b*) Wage Rate Variance = AH (SR – AR)

Men = 1600 (0.80 – 0.70) = Rs. 160 (F)

Women = 400 (0.60 – 0.65) = Rs. 20 (A)

Boys = 200 (0.40 – 0.30) = Rs. 20 (F)

Total Wage Rate Variance = **Rs. 160 (F)**

(*c*) Labour Efficiency Variance = Std. Hourly Rate (Std. Hours for Actual Production – Actual Hours)

Men = Re. 0.80 (960 – 1600) = Rs. 512 (A)

Women = Re. 0.60 (480 – 400) = Rs. 48 (F)

Boys = Re. 0.40 (320 – 200) = Rs. 48 (F)

Rs. 416 (A)

(*d*) Labour Composition (Mix) Variance = Std. Cost of Std. Mix – Std. Cost of Actual Mix

Note:

	Std. Cost of Std. Mix	Std. Cost of Actual Mix
Men :	$\frac{30}{55} \times 1980 \times \text{Re. } 0.80 = \text{Rs. } 864$	40 × 36 × 0.80 = Rs. 1152
Women :	$\frac{15}{55} \times 1980 \times \text{Re. } 0.60 = \text{Rs. } 324$	10 × 36 × 0.60 = Rs. 216
Boys :	$\frac{10}{55} \times 1980 \times \text{Re. } 0.40 = \text{Rs. } 144$	5 × 36 × 0.40 = Rs. 72

LMV = Men = (Rs. 864 – 1152) = Rs. 288 (A)

Women = (Rs. 324 – 216) = Rs. 108 (F)

Boys = (Rs. 144 – 72) = Rs. 72 (F)

Total Labour Mix Variance **108 (A)**

(*e*) Idle Time Variance = Idle Time × Std. Rate

Men = 40 × 4 × 0.80 = Rs. 128 (A)

Women = 10 × 4 × 0.60 = Rs. 24 (A)

Boys = 5 × 4 × 0.40 = Rs. 8 (A)

160 (A)

III. OVERHEAD VARIANCE

Total Overhead Cost Variance

$$\text{Recovered Overheads} = \frac{\text{Standard Overheads}}{\text{Standard Output}} \times \text{Actual Output}$$

It is the difference between Standard Overheads for actual output *i.e.* Recovered Overheads and Actual Overheads. It is the total of both fixed and variable overhead variances. The variable overheads are those costs which tend to vary directly in proportion with changes in the volume of productive activity. In contrast to variable overheads, fixed overheads consist of costs which are not subject to change with the change in the volume of productive activity. The variances under overheads are analysed in two heads, *viz*, Variable Overheads and Fixed Overheads :

$$\text{Overheads Cost Variance} = \left(\begin{array}{l}\text{Standard Total Overheads}\\ \text{for Actual Output}\end{array}\right) - \begin{array}{c}\text{Actual Total}\\ \text{Overheads}\end{array}$$

OR

$$(\text{Total Variance}) = \left(\text{Actual Output} \times \text{Standard Overheads}) - \begin{array}{r}\text{Actual}\\ \text{Total Overheads}\end{array}\right)$$

Overhead variance is "the difference between the standard cost of overhead absorbed in the actual output achieved and the actual overhead cost". The term overhead includes indirect material, indirect labour and indirect expenses and the variances relate to factory, office or selling and distribution overheads. Overhead variances are divided into two broad categories; (*i*) Variable overhead variances and (*ii*) Fixed overhead variances. To compute overhead variances, the following terms must be understood :

(*a*) Standard overheads rate per unit $= \dfrac{\text{Budgeted overhead}}{\text{Budgeted output}}$

(*b*) Standard overheads rate per hour $= \dfrac{\text{Budgeted overhead}}{\text{Budgeted hours}}$

(*c*) Standard hours for actual output $= \dfrac{\text{Budgeted hours}}{\text{Budgeted output}} \times \text{Actual output}$

(*d*) Standard output for actual time $= \dfrac{\text{Budgeted output}}{\text{Budgeted hours}} \times \text{Actual hours}$

(*e*) Recovered or Absorbed overheads = Standard rate per unit × Actual output

or

Standard rate per hour × Standard hours for actual output

(*f*) Budgeted overheads = Standard rate per unit × Budgeted output

or

Standard rate per hour × Budgeted hours

(*g*) Standard overheads = Standard rate per unit × Standard output for actual time

or

Standard rate per hour × Actual hours

(*h*) Actual overheads = Actual rate per unit × Actual output

or

Actual rate per hour × Actual hours.

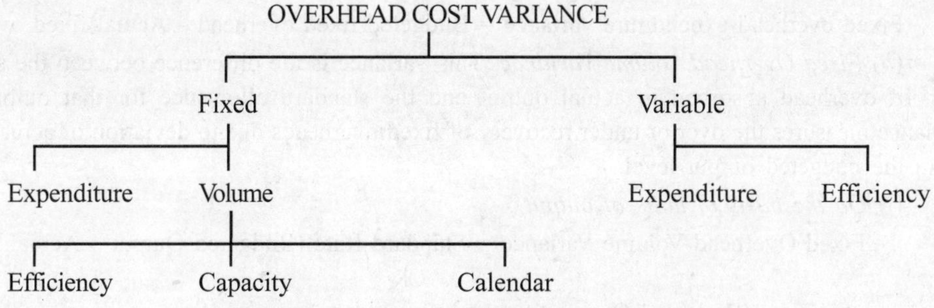

(A) VARIABLE OVERHEAD VARIANCE

Variable cost varies in proportion to the level of output, while the cost is fixed per unit. As such the standard cost per unit of these overheads remains the same irrespective of the level of output attained. As the volume does not affect the variable cost per unit or per hour, the only factor leading to difference is price. The variance will result because of the change in the expenditure incurred.

(*i*) *Variable Overhead Expenditure Variance* :

It is the difference between actual variable overhead expenditure incurred and the standard variable overheads set in for a particular period.

$$\text{Variable Overhead Expenditure Variance} = \left[\begin{array}{l}\text{Actual} \\ \text{Hours} \\ \text{Worked}\end{array} \times \begin{array}{l}\text{Standard Variable} \\ \text{Overhead Rate} \\ \text{per hour}\end{array}\right] - \begin{array}{c}\text{Actual Variable} \\ \text{Overheads}\end{array}$$

(*ii*) *Variable Overhead Efficiency Variance* :

It shows the effect of change in labour efficiency on variable overheads recovery.

Formula :

Variable Overhead Efficiency Variance = Standard Rate (Standard Quantity – Actual Quantity)

Standard Overhead Rate = (Standard Time for Actual Output – Actual Time)

(*iii*) *Variable Overhead Cost Variance*

It is divided into two : Overhead Expenditure Variance and Overhead Efficiency Variance. That is,

Formula :

Variable Overhead Cost Variance

= Variable Overhead Expenditure Variance + Variable Overhead Efficiency Variance

OR

= (Standard variable Overhead) – (Actual Variable Overhead)

(B) FIXED OVERHEAD VARIANCE

Fixed overhead variance depends on (*a*) fixed expenses incurred and (*b*) the volume of production obtained. The volume of production depends upon (*i*) efficiency (*ii*) the days for which the factory runs in a week (calendar variance) (*iii*) capacity of plant for production.

FOV = Actual Output (Fixed Overhead Rate – Actual Fixed Overheads)

(*a*) *Fixed Overhead Expenditure Variance*. (Budgeted or cost variance). It is that portion of the fixed overhead which is incurred during a particular period due to the difference between the budgeted fixed overheads and the actual fixed overheads.

Fixed overhead expenditure variance = Budgeted fixed overhead – Actual fixed overhead.

(*b*) *Fixed Overhead Volume Variance*. This variance is the difference between the standard cost of overhead absorbed in actual output and the standard allowance for that output. This variance measures the over or under recovery of fixed overheads due to deviation of actual output from the budgeted output level.

(*i*) *On the basis of units of output* :

Fixed Overhead Volume Variance = Standard Rate (Budgeted Output – Actual Output)

OR

= (Budgeted Cost – Standard Cost)

OR

= (Actual Output times × Standard Rate) – Budgeted fixed overheads

(*ii*) *On the basis of standard hours* :

Fixed Overhead Volume Variance = Standard Rate per Hour (Budgeted Hours – Standard Hours)

Standard Hours = Actual Output ÷ Standard Output per hour

CLASSIFICATION OF VOLUME VARIANCES

(*i*) *Fixed Overhead Efficiency Variance* :

This variance is closely related to labour efficiency variance. If the workers have been efficient, the production will be above standard as such overheads will be over-recovered. The portion of the overhead variation, which is due to the differences between the budgeted efficiency of production and the actual efficiency attained, is the efficiency variance.

Efficiency variance = Standard Rate (Actual Production – Std. Production)

(or)

= Standard Rate (Actual Quantity – Std. Quantity)

(*ii*) *Fixed Overheads Calendar Variance* :

It is the difference between the number of working days anticipated in the budget period and actual working days in the budget period. This may be the result of unexpected public holiday being declared, as such the work in the unit is stopped.

$$\text{Fixed Overhead Calendar Variance} = \begin{pmatrix}\text{Standard Rate}\\ \text{Per Hour (Day)}\end{pmatrix} \times \begin{pmatrix}\text{Excess or Deficit Hours}\\ \text{or days worked}\end{pmatrix}$$

(*iii*) *Fixed Overhead Capacity Variance* :

The variance which is related to the over and under-utilisation of plant or equipment is known as capacity variance. This variance arises because of the working above or below standard capacity. Strikes, idle time, lock-out etc. leads to under-utilisation, and extra shifts, overtime etc. lead to over-utilisation.

Capacity Variance = Standard Rate (Revised Budgeted Units – Budgeted Units)

(OR) = Standard Rate(Revised Budgeted Hours – Budgeted Hours)

Relationship

Total Overhead Cost Variance = Variable Overhead Cost Variance + Fixed Overhead Cost variance

Variable overhead cost vriance = Expenditure Variance + Volume Variance

Fixed Overhead Variance = Expenditure Variance + Volume Variance

Volume Variance = Capacity Variance + Calendar Variance + Efficiency Variance.

Illustration 35. From the following data, calculate overhead variances.

	Budgeted	*Actual*
Output	15,000 units	16,000 units
Number of working days	25	28
Fixed Overheads	Rs. 30,000	Rs. 30,500
Variable Overhead	Rs. 45,000	Rs. 47,000

There was an increase of 5% in capacity.

Solution :

$$\text{Std. Rate} = \frac{\text{Standard Overheads}}{\text{Standard Output}}$$

Fixed $\frac{30,000}{15,000}$ = Rs. 2.00 *Variable* $\frac{45,000}{15,000}$ = Rs. 3.00

(*a*) Variable Overhead Expenditure Variance:

= Actual Units × Std. Rate – Actual Variable Overhead Cost

= (16,000 × Rs. 3) – 47,000 = **Rs. 1,000 (F)**

(*b*) Fixed Overhead Expenditure Variance :

= Actual units × Std. rate – Actual fixed overhead cost

= 16,000 × Rs. 2 – 30,500

= **Rs. 1,500 (F)**

(*c*) Total Overhead Cost Variance = VOEV + FOV

= Rs. 1,000 (F) + 1,500 (F)

= **Rs. 2,500 (F)**

(*d*) Volume Variance = Actual Units × Std. Rate – Budgeted Fixed Overheads

= 16,000 × 2 – 30,000

= **Rs. 2,000 (F)**

(*e*) Expenditure Variance = Budgeted Fixed Overheads – Actual Fixed Overheads

= Rs. 30,000 – Rs. 30,500

= **Rs. 500 (A)**

(*f*) Capacity Variance = Std. Rate (Revised Budgeted Units – Budgeted Units)

Revised budgeted units = budgeted units + increase in capacity

$$= 15,000 + \left(\frac{5}{100} \times 15,000\right)$$

= Rs. 15,750

Capacity Variance = Rs. 2 (15,750 – 15,000)

= **Rs. 1,500 (F)**

(*g*) Calendar Variance = Increase or decrease in production due to more or less working days × Std. Rate per unit with the increase in capacity.

The Std. Production = 15.750

∴ For 3 days (28 – 25) production

$$= \frac{15,750}{25} \times 3 = 1890 \text{ units}$$

∴ C.V. = 1,890 × Rs. 2 = **Rs. 3,780 (F)**

(*h*) Efficiency Variance = Std. Rate (Actual Production – Std. Production)

Std. Production = 15,000 units (Budgeted)

= 750 units (Capacity increased)

$$= \frac{1,890}{17,640} \text{ units (3 days increased)}$$

∴ E.V. = Rs. 2(16,000 – 17,640) = **Rs. 3,280 (A)**

Verification:

Fixed Overhead Variance = Fixed Efficiency Variance + Fixed Volume Variance

Rs. 1,500 (F) = Rs. 500(A) + Rs. 2,000 (F)

Volume Variance = Capacity Variance + Calandar Variance + Efficiency Variance

Rs. 2,000 (F) = Rs. 1,500 (F) + Rs. 3,780 (F) + Rs. 3,280 (A)

Illustration 36. Vinak Ltd. has furnished you the following information for the month of August.

	Budget	*Actual*
Output (Units)	30,000	32,500
Hours	30,000	33,000
Fixed overhead	Rs. 45,000	50,000
Variable overhead	Rs. 60,000	68,000
Working days	25	26

Calculate the Variances. (*I.C.M.A. Inter., C.A. Inter*)

Solution :

$$\text{Standard time per unit} = \frac{\text{Budgeted hours}}{\text{Budgeted units}} = \frac{30,000}{30,000} = 1 \text{ hour}$$

$$\text{Total standard overhead rate per hour} = \frac{\text{Budgeted overheads}}{\text{Budgeted hours}} = \frac{1,05,000}{30,000} = \text{Rs. } 3.50 \text{ per hour}$$

Standard fixed overhead rate per hour

$$= \frac{\text{Budgeted fixed overhead}}{\text{Budgeted hour}} = \frac{45,000}{30,000} = \text{Rs. } 1.50$$

Standard variable overhead rate per hour

$$= \frac{\text{Budgeted variable overhead}}{\text{Budgeted hour}} = \frac{60,000}{30,000} = \text{Rs. } 2$$

Overhead cost variance = Recovered overheads – Actual overheads

Recovered overheads = Actual output × Standard rate per unit

= 32,500 × Rs. 3.50 = **Rs. 1,13,750**

Overhead cost variance = Rs. 1,13,750 – Rs. 1,18,000

= **Rs. 4,250** (Adverse)

Variable overhead cost variance = Recovered overheads – Actual overheads

= 32,500 hrs. × Rs. 2 – Rs. 68,000

= **Rs. 3,000** (Adverse)

Fixed overhead cost variance = Recovered overheads – actual overheads
= 32,500 hrs. × Rs. 1.50 – Rs. 50,000
= Rs. 48,750 – Rs. 50,000
Rs. 1,250 (Adverse)

Expenditure variance = Budgeted overheads – Actual overheads
= Rs. 45,000 – Rs. 50,000
= Rs. 5,000 (A)

Volume variance = Recovered overheads – Budgeted overheads
= 32,500 hrs × Rs. 1.50 – Rs. 45,000
= Rs. 48,750 – Rs. 45,000
= **Rs. 3,750 (F)**

Efficiency variance = Recovered overheads – Standard overheads

or

Standard rate(Standard hours for actual output – Actual hours)
= Rs. 1.50(32,500 – 33,000)
= **Rs. 750 (A)**

Capacity variance = Standard overheads – Budgeted overheads

or

= Std. rate (Actual hrs – budgeted hrs)
= Rs. 1.50(33,000 – 30,000) = **Rs. 4,500 (F)**

Calendar variance = Extra/Deficit hours worked × Standard Rate.

One extra day has been worked.

∴ The total number of extra hours worked

$$= \frac{30,000}{25} = 1,200 = 1,200 \times 1.50 = \textbf{Rs. 1,800 (F)}$$

Verification:

OCV = FOCV + VOCV
Rs. 4,250 (A) = Rs. 1,250 (A) + Rs. 3,000 (A)
FOCV = FOEV + FOVV
Rs. 1,250(A) = Rs. 5,000 (A) + Rs. 3,750(F)
FOVV = FOCAV + FOEV.
Rs. 3,750 (F) = Rs. 4,500(F) + Rs. 750(A)

Illustration 37. S.V. Ltd has furnished you the following data :-

	Budget	*Actual July*
No. of working days	25	27
Production in units	20,000	22,000
Fixed Overheads Rs.	30,000	31,000

Budgeted fixed overhead rate is Rs. 1.00 per hour. In July, the actual hours worked were 31,500.

Calculate the following Variances :-

1. Efficiency Variance;
2. Capacity Variance;
3. Calendar Variance;
4. Volume Variance;

5. Expenditure Variance;
6. Total Overhead Variance. (*C.A. Inter*)

Solution :

$$\text{Budgeted Hours} = \frac{\text{Rs. } 30,000}{\text{Rs. } 1} = 30,000 \text{ hours}$$

Budgeted Production = 20,000 units

$$\text{Standard time per unit} = \frac{30,000 \text{ Hours}}{20,000 \text{ units}} = 1.5 \text{ Hours}$$

$$\text{Standard rate} = \frac{\text{Rs. } 30,000}{20,000 \text{ units}} = \text{Rs. } 1.50$$

(1) Efficiency Variance :

$$= \text{Std Overhead rate per hour} \times \left(\begin{matrix}\text{Std hours for} \\ \text{actual output}\end{matrix} - \begin{matrix}\text{Actual hours} \\ \text{worked}\end{matrix}\right)$$

= Rs. 1.00 (33,000 – 31,500) = **Rs. 1,500 (F)**
(22,000 units @ 1.5 hours = 33,000 hours)

(2) Capacity Variance

$$= \begin{matrix}\text{Std. Rate} \\ \text{per hour}\end{matrix} \times \left(\begin{matrix}\text{Actual hours} \\ \text{worked}\end{matrix} - \begin{matrix}\text{Budgeted hours for} \\ \text{27 days}\end{matrix}\right)$$

= Rs. 1.00 (31,500 – 32,400) = **Rs. 900 (A)**

$$\left(\frac{30,000}{25} \times 27 = 32,400 \text{ hours}\right)$$

(3) Calendar Variance : SR (Budgeted hours – Actual hours)
= Rs. 1 (30,000 – 32,400) = **Rs. 2,400 (F)**

(4) Volume Variance : SR (Actual output – Std. output)
= Rs. 1.50(22,000 – 20,000) = **Rs. 3,000 (F)**

(5) Expenditure Variance :
Budgeted Overheads – Actual Overheads
30,000 – 31,000 = **Rs. 1,000 (A)**

(6) Total Overhead Variance :
Std. overheads for actual output – Actual overhead
Rs. 33,000 – 31,000 = **Rs. 2000 (F)**

Verification:

I Total Overhead Variance = Expenditure Variance + Volume Variance
Rs. 2,000 (F) = Rs. 1,000 (A) + Rs. 3,000 (F)

II Total Overhead Variance = Expenditure Variance + Efficiency Variance
+ Capacity Variance + Calendar Variance

Rs. 2,000 (F) = Rs. 1,000 (A) + Rs. 1,500 (F) + Rs. 900 (A) + Rs. 2,400 (F)

Illustration 38. The following information was obtained from the records of a manufacturing firm using standard costing system.

	Standard	*Actual*
Production	4,000 units	3,800 units

Working days	20	21
Fixed Overheads	Rs. 40,000	Rs. 39,000
Variable Overhead	Rs. 12,000	Rs. 12,000

You are required to calculate:

(1) Variable Overhead Variance

(2) Fixed Overhead Variance

(*a*) Expenditure Variance

(*b*) Volume Variance

(*c*) Efficiency Variance

(*d*) Calendar Variance (*M. Com. M.S.*)

Solution:

Standard Fixed Overhead Rate (per unit) $\frac{\text{Rs.}40,000}{4,000} = \text{Rs.}10$

Std. Variable Overhead Rate (per unit) $= \frac{\text{Rs.}12,000}{4,000} = \text{Rs.}3$

Standard Production per day $= \frac{4,000}{20} = 200$ units

Standard Fixed Overhead per day = 200 units × Rs. 10 = Rs. 2,000

(1) *Variable Overhead Variance*:

(Actual Output × Std. Variable Overhead Rate) – Actual Variable Overhead

(3,800 × Rs. 3) – Rs. 12,000

Rs. 11,400 – Rs. 12,000 = Rs. 600 (A)

(2) *Fixed Overhead Variance*:

Actual Output × Std. Fixed Overhead Rate – Actual Fixed Overhead

(3,800 × Rs. 10) – Rs. 39,000

Rs. 38,000 – Rs. 39,000 = Rs. 1000 (A)

(*a*) *Expenditure Variance*:

Budgeted Fixed Overhead – Actual Fixed Overhead

Rs. 40,000 – Rs. 39,000 = Rs. 1,000 (F)

(*b*) *Volume Variance*:

Std. Fixed Overhead Rate (Actual output – Budgeted Output)

Rs. 10 (3,800 – 4,000) = Rs. 2,000 (A)

(*c*) *Efficiency Variance*:

Std. Fixed Overhead Rate (Actual Production – Std. Production in actual days)

Rs. 10 (3,800 units – 4,200 units) Rs. 4,000 (A)

(*d*) *Calendar Variance:*

Std. Fixed Overhead per day (Actual days – Budgeted days)

Rs. 2,000 (21 – 20) = Rs. 2,000 (F)

Illustration 39. A factory has estimated its overhads for the next year at Rs. 48,000. The factory works 300 days in a year. It works for 8 hours a day. The total budgeted production for the year is 24,000 units.

Actual data for the month of April are given as under:

Actual overheads	: Rs. 4,250
Actual output	: 2,100 units
Idle time	: 4 hours

Calculate:
1. Overhead Cost Variance
2. Overhead Expenditure Variance
3. Overhead Efficiency Variance
4. Idle Time Variance (*M. Com. M.S.*)

Solution:

Standard Overhead Rate per unit $= \frac{48,000}{24,000} = \text{Rs. } 2$

Standard Overhead Rate per hour $= \frac{48,000}{300 \times 8} = \text{Rs. } 20.$

Overhead Cost Variance = (Actual Output × Standard Overheads Rate) – Actual Total Overheads
= (2,100 × 2) – 4250 = **Rs. 50 (A)**

Overhead Expenditure Variance = Budgeted Overheads – Actual Overheads
= 4000 – 4250 = **Rs. 250 (A)**

Overhead Efficiency Variance = Std. Overheads for actual hours worked – Std. Overheads for actual production.
= (20 × 196) – (2 × 2100)
= 3920 – 4200 = **Rs. 280 (F)**

Idle Time Variance = Idle Time × Std. Overhead Rate per hour
4 × 20 = **Rs. 80 (A)**

IV. SALES VARIANCE

Standard costing is considered to be a system of cost variances. Costs affect profits of the business. But sales determine the volume of profit or loss. It is therefore very instructive for the management to calculate sales variances. Business houses generally compute sales variance alongwith cost variances, to have full advantage of Budgetary Control and Standard Costing. Normally, if the selling price goes high, the volume of sales shall be lower than the standard. It may result in a favourable variance as to price and unfavourable variance as to quantity. The variances may be on account of controllable as well as non-controllable factors. Changes in market conditions, demand by customers etc. are, of course, beyond the control of management. But certain factors like non-accessibility to the buyers, lack of advertisement, submission of high priced tenders, etc. are controllable and an effort can be made to check the adverse variance.

The variances indicate the difference between actual value of sales and budgeted or standard value of sales. When the actual sales are more than the standard or budgeted sales, the variance will be favourable and vice versa. The sales variances are calculated under the two methods :

1. Value Method
2. Sales Margin or Profit Method

(1) VALUE METHOD

The value method is used to denote variances arising out of changes in sales price, sales quantity, sales mix etc.

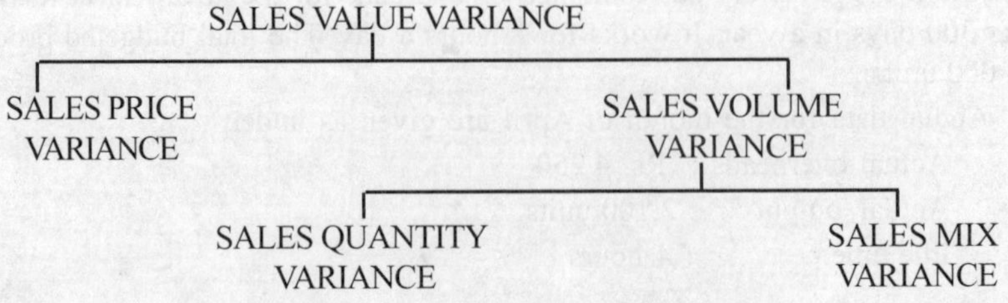

(*a*) **Sales Value Variance.** It represent the difference between the actual sales and the budgeted sales. If actual sales are more than the budgeted sales, the variance is favourable. If actual sales happen to be less than the budgeted figure, the variance is unfavourable or adverse.

Sales value variance = Actual sales – Budgeted sales

(*b*) **Sales Price Variance.** This is the variance arising out of difference between actual price and the standard price of sales.

Sales price variance = actual sales – Standard sales
(or Actual quantity sold (Actual price – Standard price)

(*c*) **Sales Volume Variance.** It can be calculated like material usage variance. It represents that portion of value variance which is caused by the difference in actual quantity sold and standard quantity of sales.

Formula :

Sales volume variance = Standard sale price (Actual quantity sold – Standard quantity)

(*d*) **Sales Mix Variance.** Some business concerns may sell more than one product, and the sales of each type of product are budgeted in a certain ratio. But the sales may not be in the same ratio. It is a part of Sales Volume Variance. It arises due to the changes made in standard mix of different articles sold.

Formula :

Sales Mix Variance = (Standard value of Actual mix – Standard value of revised Standard mix)

Standard value of revised mix

$$= \frac{\text{Total quantity of actual sales mix}}{\text{Total quantity of standard sales mix}} \times \text{Standard quantity}$$

(*e*) **Sales Quantity Variance.** It is a part of sales volume variance. It represents the difference between the sales volume variance and the sales mix variance arising on account of difference in the quantity sold.

Formula :

Sales quantity variance = Standard selling price (Revised standard sales quantity – Standard budgeted sales quantity)

Illustration 40. From the budgeted and actual sales for July in respect of three products given below, you are required to calculate sales variances :

	Budgeted		*Actual*	
	Units	*Sale Price Rs.*	*Units*	*Sale Price Rs.*
Product				
X	5,000	5.00	5,000	5.00
Y	4,000	6.00	6,000	6.25
Z	3,000	7.00	4,000	6.75
	12,000		15,000	

(*M. Com. Madurai, B.Sc. Bharathidasan*)

Solution :

(1) Sales Value Variance = (AQ × AP) – (SQ × SP)

Product X = (5,000 × Rs. 5) – (5,000 × Rs. 5)
= Rs. 25,000 – Rs. 25,000 = **Nil**

Product Y = (6,000 × Rs. 6.25) – (4,000 × Rs. 6)

= Rs. 37,500 × Rs. 24,000 = **Rs. 13,500 (F)**

Product Z = (4,000 × Rs. 6.75) – (3,000 × Rs. 7)

= Rs. 27,000 – Rs. 21,000 = **Rs. 6,000 (F)**

Total Sales Value Variance : Rs. 19,500 (F)

(2) Sales Price Variance = AQ (AP – SP)

Product X : 5,000 (Rs. 5 – Rs. 5) = Nil

Product Y : 6,000 (Rs. 6.25 – Rs. 6) = Rs. 1,500 (F)

Product Z : 4,000 (Rs. 6.75 – Rs. 7) = Rs. 1,000 (A)

Total Sales Value Variance : **Rs. 500 (F)**

(3) Sales Mix Variance :

SP (Actual Sales – Revised Standard Mix of Actual Sales)

$$\text{Revised Standard Mix} = \frac{\text{Actual Mix}}{\text{Standard Mix}} \times \text{Standard Quantity}$$

Revised Standard :

$$\text{Product X} = \frac{15,000}{12,000} \times 5,000 = 6,250 \text{ Units}$$

$$\text{Product Y} = \frac{15,000}{12,000} \times 4,000 = 5,000 \text{ Units}$$

$$\text{Product Z} = \frac{15,000}{12,000} \times 3,000 = 3,750 \text{ Units}$$

Sales Mix Variance :

Product X = Rs. 5(5,000 – 6,250) = Rs. 6,250(A)

Product Y = Rs. 6(6,000 – 5,000) = Rs. 6,000 (F)

Product Z = Rs. 7(4,000 – 3,750) = Rs. 1,750 (F)

Total Sales Mix Variance 1,500 (F)

(4) Sales Sub-volume Variance :

SP(Revised Standard Mix – Standard Mix)

Product X = Rs. 5(6,250 – 5,000) = Rs. 6,250 (F)

Product Y = Rs. 6(5,000 – 4,000) = Rs. 6,000 (F)

Product Z = Rs. 7(3,750 – 3,000) = Rs. 5,250 (F)

Total Sub-volume Variance : 17,500 (F)

Verification :

S.V.V. = S.P.V. + S.M.V. + S.S.V.V.

Rs. 19,500 (F) = Rs. 500 (F) + Rs. 1,500 (F) + Rs. 17,500 (F)

Rs. 19,500 (F) = Rs. 19,500 (F)

(2) PROFIT OR MARGIN METHOD

This is "the difference between the standard margin appropriate to the quantity of sales budgeted for a period and the margin between the standard cost and the actual selling price of sales effected." The margin means the profit on the sales. This variance arises because of the difference between total budgeted profit and total actual profit. Variances based on profits are the following :

(*a*) Total Sales Margin Variance = Total Actual Margin – Total Budgeted Margin

(*or*)

(Actual Margin per unit × Actual Quantity Sold) – (Budgeted Margin per unit × Budgeted Quantity of Sales)

(*b*) Sales Margin Price Variance = Actual Quantity Sold (Actual Sales price per unit – Standard Sales price per unit)

(*or*)

= Actual Profit – Standard Profit

(*or*)

= Actual Margin (Standard Rate of Margin per unit × Actual Units Sold)

(c) Sales Margin Volume Variance = Standard Margin per unit (Actual Quantity Sold – Standard Quantity of Sales)

(*d*) Sales Margin Mix Variance = (Revised Standard Profit – Standard Profit)

(*e*) Sales Margin Quantity or (Sub-volume) Variance = (Budgeted Profit – Revised Standard Profit)

Illustration 41. From the following information calculate sales margin variances :

Budgeted sales				*Actual sales*		
Product	*Qty. (units)*	*Sales price per unit Rs.*	*Std. cost per unit Rs.*	*Product*	*Qty. (units)*	*Sales price per unit Rs.*
A	600	20	12	A	800	24
B	400	15	9	B	600	12
	1,000				1,400	

Solution :

Standard margin on standard mix

	Units	*Rate Rs.*	*Amount Rs.*
A	600	8	4,800
B	400	6	2,400
	1,000		7,200

(*a*) Std. margin per unit of std. mix = $\frac{7,200}{1.000}$ = Rs. 7.20

Standard margin on actual mix

	Units	*Rate Rs.*	*Amount Rs.*
A	800	8	6,400
B	600	6	3,600
	1,400		10,000

(*b*) Std. margin per unit of actual mix = $\frac{10,000}{1,400}$ = Rs. 7.143

Actual margin on actual mix

	Units	*Rate Rs.*	*Amount Rs.*
A	800	12	9,600
B	600	3	1,800
	1,400		11,400

1. Total sales margin variance = Total actual margin – Total budgeted margin
   Rs. 11,400 – Rs. 7,200 = Rs. 4,200 (F)
2. Sales margin price variance = Actual quantity of sales (Actual price – Std. price)
   A = 800(24 – 20) = Rs. 3,200 (F)
   B = 600(12 – 15) = Rs. 1,800 (A)
   1,400 (F)
3. Sales margin volume variance =
   Standard margin per unit (Actual sales – Budgeted sales)
   A : 8(800 – 600) = 1,600 (F)
   B : 6(600 – 400) = 1,200 (F)
   2,800 (F)

(*i*) Sales margin mix variance = Standard margin (Standard Proportion of mix – Actual mix)

Standard proportion of Mix	*Mix variance*
$A = 600 \times \frac{1,400}{1,000} = 840$	8(800 – 840) = 320 (A)
$B = 400 \times \frac{1,400}{1,000} = 560$	6(600 – 560) = 240(F)
	80 (A)

(*ii*) Sales margin quantity variance =

Total Std. margin rate (Total Actual Quantity – Total Std. Quantity)

= Rs. 7.20 (1,400 – 1,000)

= **2,880 (F)**

Illustration 42. PH Ltd. furnishes the following information relating to budgeted sales and actual sales for April.

	Product	*Sales qty. (units)*	*Selling price per unit*
			Rs.
Budgeted sales	A	1,200	15
	B	800	20
	C	2,000	40
Actual sales	A	880	18
	B	880	20
	C	2,640	38

Calculate the following Variances :

(*i*) Sales Quantity Variance

(*ii*) Sales Mix Variance

(*iii*) Sales Price Variance

(*iv*) Total Sales Variance. (*C.A. Inter*)

Solution :

Product	Quantity	Budget rate	Amount	Quantity	Actual rate	Amount
		Rs.	Rs.		Rs.	Rs.
A	1,200	15	18,000	880	18	15,840
B	800	20	16,000	880	20	17,600
C	2,000	40	80,000	2,640	38	1,00,320
	4,000		1,14,000	4,400		1,33,760

(*i*) Sales Quantity Variance

= Standard rate (Actual quantity – Budgeted quantity)

A = 15 (880 – 1200) = Rs. 4,800 (A)

B = 20 (880 – 800) = Rs. 1,600 (F)

C = 40 (2,640 – 2,000) = Rs. 25,600 (F)

Total **Rs. 22,400** (Favourable)

(*ii*) Sales Mix Variance = Standard Rate (Actual quantity – Revised standard quantity)

$$\text{Revised Standard Quantity} = \frac{\text{Actual mix}}{\text{Standard mix}} \times \text{Standard quantity}$$

$$A = \frac{4,400}{4,000} \times 1,200 = 1,320$$

$$B = \frac{4,400}{4,000} \times 800 = 880$$

$$C = \frac{4,400}{4,000} \times 2,000 = 2,200$$

A = 15 (880 – 1320) = 15 × 440 = 6,600(A)

B = 20 (880 – 880) = 20 × 0 = Nil

C = 40 (2,640 – 2,200) = 40 × 440 = 17,600 (F)

Total Rs. 11,000 (favourable)

(*iii*) Sales Price Variance = Actual quantity (Actual Rate – Standard Rate)

A = 880 × (18 – 15) = Rs. 2,640 (F)

B = 880 × (20 – 20) = Nil

C = 2,640 × (38 – 40) = Rs. 5,280 (A)

Total = Rs. 2,640 (Adverse)

(*iv*) Total Sales Variance = Actual Sales – Budgeted Sales

= Rs. 1,33,760 – Rs. 1,14,000

= **Rs. 19,760** (Favourable)

Verification:

Total Sales Variance Sales Price Variance + Sales Quantity Variance

Rs. 19,760(F) = Rs. 2,640(A) + Rs. 22,400 (F)

Illustration 43. From the following particulars, calculate (*a*) Sales Value Variance, (*b*) Sales Price Variance, (*c*) Sales Volume Variance.

The budgeted and actual sales for a period in respect of two products are :

Product	Budgeted quantity		Actual quantity	
	Units	Price	Units	Price
A	1,000	Rs. 20	1,300	Rs. 21
B	2,000	Rs. 15	2,300	Rs. 14
	3,000		3,600	

(*B. Com., Madurai*)

Solution :

(*a*) Sales Value Variance = Actual Value of Sales – Standard Value of Sales
= (1,300 × 21 + 2,300 × 14) – (1,000 × 20 + 2,000 × 15)
= Rs. 59,500 – Rs. 50,000
= **Rs. 9,500 (favourable)**

(*b*) Sales Price Variance = Actual unit sold (Actual Price – Standard Price)
Product A = 1,300(21 – 20) = Rs. 1,300 (favourable)
Product B = 2,300(14 – 15) = Rs. 2,300 (adverse)
SPV = **Rs. 1,000 (A)**

(*c*) Sales Volume Variance = Std. Price (actual qty. of sales – Std. quantity of sales)
Product A = 20(1,300 – 1,000)
= Rs. 6,000 (favourable)
Product B = 15(2,300 – 2,000)
= **Rs. 4500 (favourable)**
SSV = Rs. 6,000 (F) + Rs. 4,500(F) = **Rs. 10,500 (F)**

Verification:

Sales value variance = SPV + SVV
Rs. 9,500(F) = Rs. 1,000(A) + Rs. 10,500(F)

Illustration 44. From the following data, calculate :

(*a*) Sales price variance,
(*b*) Sales volume variance, and
(*c*) Sales mix variance.

Product	*Standard*		*Actual*	
	Units	*Price perUnit* Rs.	*Units*	*Price perUnit* Rs.
A	1,500	30	2,000	29
B	1,000	50	700	50

(*B. Com. Madurai*)

Solution :

(*a*) Sales price variance : = Actual quantity of sales (Actual Price – Standard Price)

Product A	= 2,000 (Rs. 29 – Rs. 30)	= Rs. 2,000 (A)
Product B	= 700 (Rs. 50 – Rs. 50)	= Rs. Nil
		Rs. 2,000 (A)

(*b*) Sales Volume Variance :

SP (AQ – SQ)

Product A	= Rs. 30(2,000 – 1,500)	= Rs. 15,000 (F)
Product B	= Rs. 50(700 –1,000)	= Rs. 15,000 (A)
		Nil

(*c*) Sales Mix Variance :

SP (Actual production – Revised Std. Mix. of actual sales)

Revised Standard Mix : $= \frac{\text{Actual Mix}}{\text{Standard Mix}} \times$ Standard Quantity

Product A $= \frac{2,700}{2,500} \times 1,500 = 1620$ Units

Product B $= \frac{2,700}{2,500} \times 1,000 = 1080$ units

Sales Mix Variance :

Product A = Rs. 30(2,000 – 1,620 = Rs. 11,400 (F)

Product B = Rs. 50(700 – 1,080) = Rs. 19,000 (A)

Total Sales mix variance = Rs. 7,600 (A)

Illustration 45. For the month, the budgeted and actual figures for sales in a company were as under :

Product	*Budgeted*			*Actual*		
	Qty	*Price* Rs.	*Value* Rs.	*Qty*	*Price* Rs.	*Value* Rs.
I	20	2	40	15	2	30
II	10	1	10	15	1.5	22.50
III	5	3	15	10	2.50	25
IV	10	3.50	35	10	3	30
	45		100	50		107.50

The budgeted costs for the different products were:

I Rs. 1.50

II Rs. 0.80

III Rs. 2.00

IV Rs. 3.00

Calculate the sales variances, based on turnover : (*M.Com. M.S.*)

Solution :

1. Standard Value of Actual Sales

Product	*Qty*	*Price* *Rs.*	*Value* *Rs.*
I	15	2	30
II	15	1	15
III	10	3	30
IV	10	3.50	35
Total	50		110

2. Revised Standard Sales = $\frac{\text{Actual Mix}}{\text{Standard Mix}} \times \text{Standard Quantity}$

$$= \frac{50}{45} \times 100 = \textbf{Rs. 111}$$

1. Sales Value Variance = Actual Sales – Standard Sales

= Rs. 107.50 – Rs. 100 = Rs. 7.50 (F)

2. Sales Price Variance = AQ (AP – SP)

I — 15 (Rs. 2 – Rs. 2) = 0

II — 15 (Rs. 1.50 – Rs. 1) = 7.50 (F)

III — 10 (Rs. 2.50 – Rs. 3) = 5.00 (A)

IV — 10 (Rs. 3 – Rs. 3.50) = 5.00 (A)

2.50 (A)

3. Sales Volume Variance = SP (AQ — SQ)

I — Rs. 2(15 – 20) = Rs. 10 (A)

II — Rs. 1(15 – 10) = Rs. 5 (F)

III — Rs. 3 (10 – 5) = Rs. 15 (F)
IV — Rs. 3.50 (10 – 10) = 0

Rs. 10 (F)

4. Sales Quantity Variance = RSS – SS
= Rs. 111 – Rs. 100 = **Rs. 11 (F)**
5. Sales Mix Variance = Std. value of AS – RSS
= Rs. 110 – Rs. 111 = **Re. 1 (F)**

Verification:

Sales Value Variance = Sales Price Variance + Sales Volume Variance
Rs. 7,50 (F) = Rs. 2.50 (A) + Rs. 10 (F)
Sales Volume Variance = Sales Quantity Variance + Sales Mix Variance
Rs. 10(F) = Rs. 11 (F) + Re. 1 (A)

Illustration 46. From the following data calculate sales variances:

Product	*Standard*		*Actual*	
	Quantity	*Price Per Unit Rs.*	*Quantity*	*Price Per Unit Rs.*
X	200	15	220	12.5
Y	120	20	100	22.5
Z	80	10	120	15.0

(*B. Com. Madurai*)

Solution:

Sales Value Variance = Actual Sales – Standard Sales (or) (AP × AQ) – (SP – SQ)
(or) (SP × SQ) (AP × AQ)
X — Rs. 2750 – Rs. 3000 = Rs. 250 (A)
Y — Rs. 2250 – Rs. 2400 = Rs. 150 (A)
Z — Rs. 1800 – Rs. 800 = Rs. 1,000 (F)
Rs. 600 (F)

Sales Volume Variance = SP (AQ – SQ)
X — Rs. 15 (220 – 200) = Rs. 300 (F)
Y — Rs. 20 (100 – 120) = Rs. 400 (A)
Z — Rs. 10 (120 – 80) = Rs. 400 (F)
Rs. 300 (F)

Sales Price Variance: AQ (AP – SP)
X — 220 (12.5 – 15) = 550 (A)
Y — 100 (22.5 – 20) = 250 (F)
Z — 120 (15 – 10) = 600 (F)
300 (F)

Check: Sales Value Variance = SPV + SVV
Rs. 600 (F) = Rs. 300 (F) + Rs. 300 (F)

Sales Mix Variance: SP (AQ – RSQ)
X — Rs. 15 (220 – 220) = 0
Y — Rs. 20 (100 – 132) = Rs. 640 (A)
Z — Rs. 10 (120 – 88) = Rs. 320 (F)
320 (A)

Sales Quantity Variance: SP (RSQ – SQ)

X — Rs. 15 (220 – 200) = Rs. 300 (F)
Y — Rs. 20 (132 –120) = Rs. 240 (F)
Z — Rs. 10 (88 – 80) = Rs. 80 (F)
Rs. 620 (F)

Note: Revised Standard Quantity

RSQ = Standard proportion of actual quantity

$$X = 440 \times \frac{5}{10} = 220 \text{ units}$$

$$Y = 440 \times \frac{3}{10} = 132 \text{ units}$$

$$Z = 440 \times \frac{2}{10} = 88 \text{ units}$$

Check:

Volume Variance = Mix Variance + Quantity Variance
Rs. 300 (F) = Rs. 320 (A) + 620 (F)

Disposition of Variances

Variance is the difference between the standard and actual performance. As cost levels change from month to month, the changes are shown as variances from standard. These variances, properly recorded and analysed, are important tools for management control. Variances denote the deviation from the standard. Variances are of two types – credit or favourable variances and debit or unfavourable variances. After analysing the variances, they should be reported to the management. A favourable variance is generally known as an index of efficiency. But it is not always correct. Because a favourable variance may be due to obsolete standard. In order to make the variance a control instrument, the management should investigate the causes of variances and take necessary corrective measures. There is no uniformity of opinion regarding the disposal of variances. Thus, the method which will be followed depends on the accountant's attitude and the practice that is followed by the firm. However, the following methods are usually applied:

1. Transfer to current year's income statement

According to this method, the unfavourable variances are debited to Profit and Loss Account whereas favourable variances are credited to Profit and Loss Account, at the end of accounting period. The stock of finished goods, work-in-progress and cost of sales are shown at standard cost.

2. Allocation of variances to stock etc.

According to this method, cost variances are allocated among finished goods, work-in-progress and cost of sales on the basis of units or value. Thus, the work-in-progress, finished stock etc. are shown at actual cost.

3. Transfer of variances to reserve account

The variances, whether favourable or unfavourable, are transferred to a Reserve Account, are set-off. If the variances are favourable, they are shown on liability side of Balance Sheet. If variances are unfavourable, they are shown on asset side of Balance Sheet. For instance variance losses will be carried forward until there happen a corresponding variance gain.

If the variance arises either due to the incorrect standard or uncontrollable condition, the same should be allocated to the work-in-progress, finished stock and cost of sales. But if the variances arise from an uncontrollable situation, the same should be transferred to Profit and Loss Account accordingly.

Illustration 47.

From the following information, calculate sales margin variances.

Product	*Budgeted Sales*			*Actual Sales*	
	Quantity (Units)	Sale price per unit Rs.	Standard Cost per unit Rs.	Quantity (Units)	Sales Price per unit Rs.
X	900	20	15	1,200	24
Y	600	15	10	900	12
	1,500			2,100	

(*B. Com. MS*)

Solution :

Total Sales Margin Variance : Actual Profit – Budgeted Profit

= (Actual Quantity × Actual profit per unit)

= (1,200 × 9) + (900 × 2) – (900 × 5) + (600 × 5)

= Rs. 12,600 – Rs. 7,500 = Rs. 5,100 (F)

Total Sales Margin Price Variance : AQ (Actual profit per unit – S. profit per unit)

Rs.

Product X = 1,200 (9 – 5) = 4,800 (F)

Product Y = 900 (2 – 5) = 2,700 (A)

2,100 (F)

Total Sales Margin Volume Variance : Std. Profit per unit (AQ – BQ)

Rs.

Product X = 5 (1,200 – 900) = 1,500 (F)

Product Y = 5 (900 – 600) = 1,500 (F)

3,000 (F)

Total Sales Margin Mix Variance : Std. profit per unit (Actual Mix – Std. Proportion of Mix)

Std. Proportion of Mix.

$$\text{Product X} = 800 \times \frac{2,100}{1,500} = 1,260 \text{ units}$$

$$\text{Product Y} = 600 \times \frac{2,100}{1,500} = 840 \text{ units}$$

TSMMV :

Rs.

Product X = Rs. 5 (1,200 – 1,260) = 300 (A)

Product Y = Rs. 5 (900 – 840) = 300 (F)

Nil

Total Sales Margin Quantity Mix : Std. profit per unit (Revised Std. profit – Budgeted profit)

= 5 (1,260 + 840) – 5 (900 + 600)

= 10,500 – 7,500 = Rs. 3,000 (F)

Workings :

Actual profit = Actual Selling Price per unit – Actual Cost per unit

X = Actual Profit per unit = 24 – 15 = Rs. 9

Y = Actual Profit per unit = 12 – 12 = Rs. 2

Budgeted Profit = Sales Price per unit – Std. Cost per unit

X = Rs. 20 – Rs. 15 = Rs. 5

Y = Rs. 15 – Rs. 10 = Rs. 5

Illustration 48. The following information is available from the records of a factory:

	Budget *Rs.*	*Actual* *Rs.*
Fixed Overheads for June	10,000	12,000
Production in June (Units)	2,000	2,100
Standard time per unit (hours)	10	–
Actual hours worked in June	–	22,000

Compute :

1. Fixed Overheads Cost Variance
2. Expenditure Variance
3. Volume Variance
4. Capacity Variance
5. Efficiency Variance (*CA Inter*)

Solution :

1. Budgeted Quantity (BQ) = 2,000 units
2. Actual Quantity (AQ) = 2,100 Units
3. $\text{Standard Quantity} = \dfrac{\text{Actual hours worked}}{\text{Standard Time per unit}} = \dfrac{22,000}{10} = 2,200 \text{ units}$

$$\text{Standard Rate} = \frac{\text{BFO}}{\text{BQ}} = \frac{\text{Rs. } 10,000}{2,000 \text{ units}} = \text{Rs. } 5 \text{ per unit}$$

4. Budgeted Fixed Overhead (BFO) = Rs. 10,000
5. Actual Fixed Overhead (AFO) = Rs. 12,000
6. Standard Fixed Overhead (SFO) = 2,100 × 5 = Rs. 10,500

(*i*) Fixed Overhead Cost Variance :

FOCV = SFO – AFO

= 10,500 – 12,000 = Rs. 1,500 (A)

(*ii*) Fixed Overhead Expenditure Variance :

FOFV = BFO – AFO

= 10,000 – 12,000 = Rs. 2,000 (A)

(*iii*) Fixed Overhead Volume Variance :

FOVV = SR (AQ – BQ)

= 5 (2,100 – 2,000) = Rs. 500 (F)

(*iv*) Fixed Overhead Capacity Variance :

FO Cap. V = SR (SQ – BQ)

= 5(2,200 – 2,000) = Rs. 1,000 (F)

(*v*) Fixed Overhead Efficiency Variance :

FO Eff. V = SR (AQ – SQ)]

= 5 (2,100 – 2,200) = Rs. 500 (A)

Verification:

FOCV = FO Exp. V + FOVV

Rs. 1,500 (A) = Rs. 2,000 (A) + Rs. 500 (F)

FOVV = FO Cap. V + FO Eff. V

Rs. 500 (F) = Rs. 1,000 (F) + Rs. 500 (A)

Illustration 49.

(*a*) The budget for a period indicates :

Works Overhead Fixed	Rs. 50,000
Works Overhead Variable	Rs. 1,50,000
Normal Activity	100%

During the period the actual activity was only 70% of the normal load for a total expenditure of Rs. 1,50,000. What are the budget and volume variances?

(*b*) Determine the budget and capacity variances from the following data :

Estimated Factory Overhead	Rs. 25,000
Estimated Direct Labour Hours	Rs. 5,000
Actual Overhead Expenses	Rs. 26,500
Applied Overhead Expenses	Rs. 22,500

(*ICWA*)

Solution :

(*a*) Overhead recovered on actual activity of 70% (Budgeted Overhead)

	Rs.
Works Overhead – Fixed 70% of 50,000	35,000
Works Overhead – Variable 70% of 1,50,000	1,05,000
Total Recovered	**1,40,000**
Actual Expenditure	1,50,000
Budget for actual activity :	
Works Overhead – Fixed	50,000
Works Ovehead – Variable (70% of 1,50,000)	1,05,000
	1,55,000

Expenditure (Budget) Variance :

Budgeted Fixed Overhead – Actual Fixed Overhead

1,55,000 – 1,50,000 = Rs. 5,000 (F)

Volume Variance = Recovered Overhead – Budgeted Overhead

1,40,000 – 1,55,000 = Rs. 15,000 (A)

(*b*) $\text{Estimated Hourly rate of recovery} = \dfrac{\text{Estimated Factory Overhead}}{\text{Estimated Direct Labour Hour}}$

$= \dfrac{\text{Rs. } 25{,}000}{5{,}000 \text{ L.H}} = \text{Rs. } 5 \text{ per L.H.}$

$\text{Actual Hours Worked} = \dfrac{\text{Applied Overhead Expenses}}{\text{Rate per Labour Hour}}$

$= \dfrac{22{,}500}{5} = 4{,}500 \text{ L.H.}$

Capacity Variance SR (BH – AH)

= 5.00 (5,000 – 4,500) = Rs. 2,500 (A)

Expenditure Variance or Budget Variance : BFO – AFO

= Rs. 25,000 – Rs. 26,500 = Rs. 1,500 (A)

Illustration 50. A Cost Accountant of a company was given the following information regarding the overheads for February.

(*a*) Overheads Cost Variance : Rs. 1,400 Adverse

(*b*) Overheads Volume Variance : Rs. 1,000 Adverse

(*c*) Budgeted hours for February : Rs. 1,200 hours

(*d*) Budgeted overheads for February : Rs. 6,000

(*e*) Actual rate of recovery of overheads : Rs. 8 per hour.

You are required to assist him in computing the following for February.

1. Overhead Expenditure Variance
2. Actual Overhead Incurred
3. Actual hours for Actual Production
4. Overheads Capacity Variance
5. Overheads Efficiency Variance
6. Standard hours for Actual Production (*CA Inter*)

Solution :

1. Overhead Expenditure Variance :

OEXV = Overhead Cost Variance – Overhead Volume Variance

= Rs. 1,400 (A) – Rs. 1,000 (A) = **Rs. 400 (A)**

2. Actual Overhead Incured :

= Budgeted Overhead + Overhead Expenditure Variance

= Rs. 6,000 + Rs. 400 = **Rs. 6,400**

3. Actual Hours for Actual Production :

$$= \frac{\text{Actual Overhead Incurred}}{\text{Actual Rate of Recovery of Overhead per Hour}}$$

$$= \frac{6,400}{8} = \textbf{800 Hours}$$

4. Overhead Capacity Variance :

OCAV = SR (AH – BH)

= 5 (800 – 1,200) = **Rs. 2,000 (A)**

$$\left(SR = \frac{\text{Budgeted Overhead}}{\text{Budgeted Hours}} = \frac{6,000}{1,200} = \text{Rs. 5 per Hour} \right)$$

5. Overhead Efficiency Variance :

Overhead Volume Variance = Overhead Capacity Variance + Overhead Efficiency Variance

∴ Overhead Efficiency Variance = Overhead Volume Variance – Overhead Capacity Variance

= Rs. 1,000 (A) – Rs. 2,000 (A)

= Rs. 1,000 – (– Rs. 2,000)

= – Rs. 1,000 + Rs. 2,000

= **Rs. 1,000 (F)**

6. Standard Hours for Actual Production :

Volume Variance = SR per hour (SH for Actual Production – Budgeted Hours)

Rs. 1,000 (A) = Rs. 5 (SH – 1,200 Hours)

$$\text{SH} - 1200 \text{ Hours} = \frac{\text{Rs. } 1{,}000 \text{ (A)}}{\text{Rs. } 5}$$

SH – 1200 Hours = – 200 Hours

SH for Actual production = 1200 Hours – 200 Hours

= 1000 Hours

Verification:

1. OCV = OEx. V + OVV

Rs. 1,400 (A) = Rs. 400 (A) + Rs. 1,000 (A)

2. OVV = OCa. V + OEf.V

Rs. 1,000 (A) = Rs. 2,000 (A) + Rs. 1,000 (F)

Illustration 51. The following information is available from the records of factory :

	Budget	*Actual*
Fixed Overhead for March	Rs. 2,00,000	Rs. 2,40,000
Production in March (Units)	40,000	42,000
Actual hours worked	–	4,40,000
Standard time in hours	4,00,000	–

Calculate all Fixed Overhead Variances.

(*M. Com. Poona, Osmania*)

Solution :

(*a*) Calculation of Standard Fixed Overhead :

Recovered Fixed Overhead = Actual Output × Budgeted Rate per unit

Budgeted Rate per unit = = Rs. 5 per unit

∴ Recovered Fixed Overhead = 42,000 × 5 = Rs. 2,10,000

(*b*) Standard Fixed Overhead : Actual hours worked × Budgeted Rate per unit

$$\text{Budgeted Rate per howr} = \frac{\text{Budgeted Overhead}}{\text{Budgeted hours}}$$

$$= \frac{2{,}00{,}000}{4{,}00{,}000} = \text{Re. } 0.50 \text{ per hour}$$

∴ Standard Fixed Overhad = 4,40,000 × 0.50 = Rs. 2,20,000

1. Fixed Overhead Cost Variance = Recovered Fixed Overhead – Actual Fixed Overhead
= 2,10,000 – 2,40,000= Rs. 30,000 (F)
2. Fixed Overhead Expenditure Variance = Budgeted Fixed Overhead – Actual Fixed Overhead
= 2,00,000 – 2,40,000 = Rs. 40,000 (F)
3. Fixed Overhead Volume Variance = Recovered Fixed Overhead – Budgeted Fixed Overhead
= 2,10,000 – 2,00,000 = Rs. 10,000 (F)
4. Fixed Overhead Capacity Variance = Standard Fixed Overhead – Budgeted Fixed Ovehead
= 2,20,000 – 2,00,000 = Rs. 20,000 (F)
5. Fixed Overhead Efficiency Variance = Recovered Fixed Overhead – Standard Fixed Overhead
= Rs. 2,10,000 – 2,20,000 = Rs. 10,000 (A)

Illustration 52. The standard rate per labour hour in a factory was Rs. 50. Due to an agreement with labour, the rate is increased by 20% from 1st Jan. During January, 10,000 labour hours were worked but the work done was equivalent to 8,000 hours only. The actual labour cost for the month was Rs. 6,00,000.

Calculate the revision variance and also other labour cost variance.

(*B. Com. MS, Bangalore, Saugar*)

Solution :

1. Revision Variance = Original Std. Cost of Actual Output – Revised Std. Cost of Actual Output

   Revised Std. Cost = Rs. 50 + 20% of Rs. 50 = Rs. 60

   Actual output is equivalent to 8000 hours

   Revision Variance = (SR × ST) – (RSR × ST)

   = (50 × 8000) – (60 × 8000) = Rs. 80,000 (A)

2. Labour Cost Variance : (ST × SR) – (AT × AR)

   (Std. Rate × Std. Time for Actual Output) – Actual Rate × Actual Time

   = (60 × 8,000) – (6,00,000) = 4,80,000 – 6,00,000

   = Rs. 1,20,000 (A)

3. Labour Rate Variance : AT (SR – AR)

   = 10,000 × 60 – 6,00,000

   = 6,00,000 – 6,00,000 = Nil.

4. Labour Efficiency Variance = SR (ST for Actual output – AT)

   = 60 (8,000 – 10,000) = Rs. 1,20,000 (A)

Verification:

L.C.V. = LRV + LEV.

Rs. 1,20,000 (A) = Nil + 1,20,000 (A)

NB : Actual Rate × Actual Time = Actual Labour Cost *i.e.* Rs. 6,00,000 (given in the problem)

Illustration 53. A limited company uses standard costing system and their results for the month January are as follows :

Budgeted Total Overhead	: Rs. 50,000 (Fixed : Rs. 30,000 Variable Rs. 20,000)
Budgeted Hours	: 20,000
Budgeted Output	: 2 units per hour
Actual Overhead	: Rs. 52,000 (Rs. Fixed Rs. 30,500 Variable Rs. 21,500)
Actual Hours	: 16,000
Actual output in units	: 30,000

Compute Overhead Variances. (*M. Com. Delhi, Kolkata*)

Solution :

1. Budgeted Rate per hour $= \frac{\text{Budgeted Overhead}}{\text{Budgeted Hours}}$

   Variable Overhead $= \frac{20,000}{20,000}$ = Rs. 1 per hour

   Fixed Overhead $= \frac{30,000}{20,000}$ = Rs. 1.5 per hour

2. Budgeted Rate per unit $= \frac{\text{Budgeted Overhead}}{\text{Budgeted Output}}$

$$\text{Total Overhead Rate per unit} = \frac{50,000}{20,000 \times 2} = \text{Rs. } 1.25$$

$$\text{Fixed Overhead Rate per unit} = \frac{30,000}{40,000} = \text{Re. } 0.75 \text{ per unit}$$

$$\text{Variable Rate per unit} = \frac{20,000}{40,000} = \text{Re. } 0.50 \text{ per unit}$$

3. Recovered Overhead = Actual Output × Budgeted Rate per unit
   Recovered Total Overhead = 30,000 × 1.25 = Rs. 37,500
   Recovered Fixed Overhead = 30,000 × 0.75 = Rs. 22,500
   Recovered Variable Overhead = 30,000 × 0.50 = Rs. 15,000
4. Standard Overhead = Actual Hours × Budgeted Rate per hour
   Standard Fixed Overhead = 16,000 × 1.5 = Rs. 24,000
   Standard Variable Overhead = 16,000 × 1 = Rs. 16,000

(*a*) Total Overhead Cost Variance = Recovered Total Overhead – Actual Total Overhead
= Rs. 37,500 – 52,000 = Rs. 14,500 (A)

(*b*) Variable Overhead Cost Variance = Recovered Variable Overhead – Actual Variable Overhead
= 15,000 – 21,500 = Rs. 6,500 (A)

(*c*) Variable Expenditure Variance = Std. Variable Overhead – Actual Variable Overhead
= 16,000 – 21,500 = Rs. 5,500 (A)

(*d*) Variable Overhead Efficiency Variance = Recovered Variable Overhead – Std. Variable Overhead
= 15,000 – 16,000 = Rs. 1,000 (A)

(*e*) Fixed Overhead Cost Variance = Recovered Fixed Overhead – Actual Fixed Overhead
= 22,500 – 30,500 = Rs. 8,000 (A)

(*f*) Fixed Overhead Expenditure Variance = Budgeted Fixed Overhead – Actual Fixed Overhead
= 30,000 – 30,500 = Rs. 500 (A)

(*g*) Fixed Overhead Volume Variance = Recovered Fixed Overhead – Budgeted Fixed Overhead
= 22,500 – 30,000 = Rs. 7,500 (A)

(*h*) Fixed Overhead Capacity Variance = Std. Fixed Overhead – Budgeted Fixed Overhead
= 24,000 – 30,000 = Rs. 6,000 (A)

(*i*) Fixed Overhead Efficiency Variance = Recovered Fixed Overhead – Std. Fixed Overhead
= 22,500 – 24,000 = Rs. 1,500 (A)

Verification:

Total VOCV = VOEx. V + VO Eff. V
Rs. 6,500 (A) = Rs. 5,500 + 1,000 (A)
FOCV = FOEx. V + FOVV
Rs. 8,000 (A) = Rs. 500 (A) + Rs. 7,500 (A)
FOVV = FOCap. V + FOEff. V
Rs. 7,500 (A) = Rs. 6,000 (A) + Rs. 1,500 (A)
Total Overhead Cost Variance = VOCV + FOCV
Rs. 14,500 (A) = Rs. 6,500 (A) + Rs. 8,000 (A)

MISCELLANEOUS

Illustration 54. From the following, you are required to calculate :

(*a*) Material price variance
(*b*) Material usage variance
(*c*) Material cost variance

Quantity of material purchased : 3,000 units
Value of material purchased : Rs 9,000
Standard quantity of material required for one tonne of finished product : 25 units
Standard rate of material : Rs. 2 per unit
Opening stock of material : Nil
Closing stock of material : 500 units
Finished product during the period : 80 tons (*I.C.W.A. Inter*)

Solution :

Actual Price = Rs. 9,000 ÷ 3,000 = Rs. 3 per unit.
Standard Quantity = 80 × 25 = 2,000 units
Actual Quantity used = 3,000 – 500 = 2,500

(*a*) Material Price Variance : AQ (SP – AP)
= 2,500 (Rs. 2 – Rs. 3)
= **Rs. 2,500 (A)**

(*b*) Material Usage Variance : SP(SQ) – AQ)
= Rs. 2(2,000 – 2,500)
= **Rs. 1,000 (A)**

(*c*) Material Cost Variance : (SQ × SP) – (AQ × AP)
= (2,000 × Rs. 2) – (2,500 × Rs. 3)
= 4,000 – 7,500
= **Rs. 3,500 (A)**

Verification:

MCV = MPV + MUV
Rs. 3,500 (A) = Rs. 2,500(A) + Rs. 1,000 (A)

Illustration 55. The standard cost card shows the following details relating to the materials needed to produce 1 kg. of groundnut oil :

Quantity of groundnut 3 kg.
Price of groundnut Rs. 2.28 per kg.

Actual production data :

Production during a week 1,000 kgs.
Quantity used 3,500 kgs.
Price of groundnut Rs. 3 per kg.

Calculate :

(*a*) Material Cost Variance
(*b*) Material Price Variance
(*c*) Material Usage Variance.

Solution :

(a) Material Cost Variance : (SQ × SP) – (AQ – AP)
= (3,000 × Rs. 2.28) – (3,500 × Rs. 3)

= Rs. 6,840 – Rs. 10,500

= **Rs. 3,660 (A)**

(*b*) Material Price Variance : AQ(SP – AP)

= 3,500(Rs. 2.28 – Rs. 3)

= 3,500 × – 0.72

= **Rs. 2,520 (A)**

(c) Material Usage Variance : SP(SQ – AQ)

= Rs. 2.28(3,000 – 3,500)

= **Rs. 1,140 (A)**

Verification:

MCV = MPV + MUV

Rs. 3,660 (A) = Rs. 2,520 (A) + Rs. 1,140 (A)

Illustration 56. From the following data for May for a factory, calculate :

(*a*) Material Cost Variance
(*b*) Material Price Variance
(*c*) Material Usage Variance
(*d*) Material Mixture Variance
(*e*) Material Yield Variance.

Items of Material	*Standard*	*Rate*	*Actual*	*Rate*
X	8,000 kg.	1.05	7,500 Kg.	1.20
Y	3,000 Kg.	2.15	3,300 Kg.	2.30
Z	2,000 Kg.	3.30	2,400 Kg.	3.50

(*I.C.W.A. Inter*)

Solution :

Items of Material	*Standard*			*Actual*		
	Qty Kg.	Rate Rs.	Amount Rs.	Qty. Kg.	Rate Rs.	Amount Rs.
X	8,000	1.05	8,400	7,500	1.20	9,000
Y	3,000	2.15	6,450	3,300	2.30	7,590
Z	2,000	3.30	6,600	2,400	3.50	8,400
Total	13,000		21,450	13,200		24,990

(*a*) Marginal Cost Variance :

(SC – AC) = Rs. 21,450 – Rs. 24,990 = Rs. 3,540 (A)

(*b*) Material Price Variance : AQ(SP – AP)

X = 7,500 (Rs. 1.05 – Rs. 1.20) = 1,125 (A)

Y = 3,300 (Rs. 2.15 – Rs. 2.30) = Rs. 495 (A)

Z = 2,400 (Rs. 3.30 – Rs. 3.50) = Rs. 480 (A)

Rs. 2,100 (A)

(c) Material Usage Variance : SP(SQ – AQ)

X = Rs. 1.05(8,000 – 7,500) = Rs. 525 (F)

Y = Rs. 2.15(3,000 – 3,300) = Rs. 645 (A)

Z = Rs. 3.30 (2,000 – 2,400) = Rs. 1,320 (A)

Rs. 1,440 (A)

(*d*) Material Mix Variance : SP(RSQ – AQ)

$$RSQ = \frac{\text{Total weight of Actual mix}}{\text{Total weight of Std. mix}} \times \text{Std. quantity}$$

$$X = \frac{13{,}200}{13{,}000} \times 8{,}000 = 8123.08$$

$$Y = \frac{13{,}200}{13{,}000} \times 3{,}000 = 3{,}046.15$$

$$Z = \frac{13{,}200}{13{,}000} \times 2{,}000 = 2{,}030.8$$

MMV : X : Rs. 1.05(8,123.08 – 7,500) = Rs. 654.23 (F)
Y : Rs. 2.15(3,046.15 – 3,300) = Rs. 545.78 (A)
Z : Rs. 3.30(2,030.8 – 2,400) = Rs. 1,218.36 (A)
Rs. 1,109.91 or Rs. 1,110 (A)

(*e*) Material Yield Variance:

To calculate material yield variance, actual yield and standard yield must be given. In this problem these two are not given. Hence, material yield variance cannot be calculated.

Verification:

MCV = MPV + MUV

Rs. 3540 (A) = Rs. 2100 (A) + Rs. 1440 (A)

Illustration 57.

Item	*Budget*	*Actual*
No. of working days	20	22
Man-hours per day	8,000	8,400
Output per man-hour in unit	1	0.90
Overhead Cost	Rs. 1,60,000	1,68,000

Calculate :

(*i*) Overhead Cost Variance.
(*ii*) Overhead Efficiency Variance.
(*iii*) Overhead Capacity Variance.
(*iv*) Overhead Calendar Variance. (*C.A. Inter*)

Solution :

Budgeted Man-hours = 8,000 × 20 = 1,60,000 hours.
Budgeted Output = 1,60,000 × 1 = 1,60,000 units.
Actual Man-hours = 8,400 × 22 = 1,84,800 hours.
Actual output = 1,84,800 × 0.90 = 1,66,320

Standard Overhead Rate per unit :

$$\frac{\text{Budgeted Overheads}}{\text{Budgeted Output}} = \frac{1{,}60{,}000}{1{,}60{,}000} = \text{Re. 1 per unit}$$

Standard Overhead Rate per hour :

$$\frac{\text{Budgeted Overheads}}{\text{Budgeted Output}} = \frac{1{,}60{,}000}{1{,}60{,}000} = \text{Re. 1 per hr.}$$

Overhead Cost Variance = Recovered Overheads – Actual Overheads

1,66,320 × Re. 1 – 1,68,000 = **Rs. 1,680(A)**

Overhead Expenditure = Budgeted Overheads – Actual Overheads

= 1,60,000 – 1,68,000 = **Rs. 8,000 (A)**

Overhead Volume Variance = Recovered Overheads – Budgeted Overheads

= Rs. 1,66,320 – Rs. 1,60,000 = **Rs. 6,320 (F)**

Overhead Capacity Variance = Std. Overhead Rate per hour (Actual hrs. – Budgeted hrs.)

Re. 1(1,84,800 – 1,60,000) = **Rs. 24,800 (F)**

Overhead Efficiency Variance = Std. Overhead per hour (Std. hrs. for actual output – Actual hours)

Re. 1(1,66320 – 1,84,800) = **18,480 (A)**

Calendar Variance = Std. Rate per hour (Possible hours – Budgeted Hours)

= Re. 1(22 × 8,000 – 1,60,000)

= Rs. (1,76,000 – Rs. 1,60,000)

= **Rs. 16,000 (F)**

Revised Capacity Variance = Std. rate per hour (Actual hours – Possible hours)

= Re. 1(1,84,800 – 1,76,000)

= **Rs. 8,800 (F)**

Verification:

Overhead Cost Variance = Exp. Variance + VV

Rs. 1680 (A) = Rs. 8,000 (A) + Rs. 6,320 (F)

Overhead VV = CV + EV

Rs. 6,320 (F) = Rs. 24,800 (F) + Rs. 18,480 (A)

OCV = CV + R. Capacity Variance

Rs. 24,800 (F) = Rs. 16,000 (F) + Rs. 8,800 (F)

Illustration 58. In department A, the following data is submitted for the week ended 31st Oct.

Standard output for 40 hours per week = 1400 units
Standard fixed overhead = Rs. 1400
Actual output = 1200 units
Actual hours worked = 32 hours
Actual fixed overhead = Rs. 1500
Prepare a statement of variances. *(C.A. Inter)*

Solution :

$$\text{Standard Overhead Rate per unit} = \frac{\text{Standard Fixed Overhead}}{\text{Standard Output}}$$

$$= \frac{1,400}{1,400} = \text{Re. 1 per unit}$$

$$\text{Standard Fixed Overhead Rate per hour} = \frac{\text{Standard Fixed Overhead}}{\text{Standard Hour}}$$

$$= \frac{1,400}{40 \text{ hours}} = \text{Rs. 35 per hour}$$

$$\text{Standard Output per hour} = \frac{\text{Standard Output}}{\text{Standard hours}}$$

$$=\frac{1,400}{40}=35 \text{ units}$$

Statement of Fixed Overhead Variances.

Fixed Overhead Cost Variance = (Recovered Overheads – Actual Overheads)

= Rs. 1,200 × 1 – Rs. 1,500) = **Rs. 300 (A)**

Fixed Overhead Expenditure Variance : (Budgeted Overhead – Actual Overheads)

= Rs. 1,400 – Rs. 1,500

= **Rs. 100 (A)**

Fixed Overhead Volume Variance :

Recovered Overheads – Budgeted Overheads

= Rs. 1200 – Rs. 1400 = **Rs. 200 (A)**

Fixed Overhead Capacity Variance :

Std. Rate per hour (Std. Hours for actual production – Actual hours)

$$= \text{Rs. } 35\left(\frac{\text{Rs. } 1,200}{35} - \text{Rs. } 32\right) = \textbf{Rs. 80 (F)}$$

Verification:

FOCV = FOEXV + FOVV

Rs. 300(A) = Rs. 100 (A) + Rs. 200 (A)

FOVV = FOCV + FOEFV

Rs. 200 (A) = Rs. 280 (A) + Rs. 80 (F)

Illustration 59. The Standard Cost Card for one unit of a product shows the following costs for material and labour.

Material 4 pieces @ Rs. 5.00

Labour 10 hours @ Rs. 1.50

5,700 units of the product were manufactured during the month of March 1986 with the following material and labour costs :

Material 23,000 pieces @ Rs. 4.95

Labour 56,800 hours @ Rs. 1.52

Calculate appropriate material and labour variances. (*B. Com.,* (*Hons.*), *Delhi*)

Solution :

Material Cost Variance : (SC – AC)

= (5,700 × 4 × Rs. 5) – (23,000 × Rs. 4.95)

= Rs. 1,14,000 – Rs. 1,13,850 = **Rs. 150 (F)**

Material Price Variance : AQ (SP – AP)

= 2,3000 (Rs. 5 – Rs. 4.95) = **Rs. 1,150 (F)**

Material Usage Variance : SP (SQ – AQ)

= Rs. 5(5,700 × 4 – 23,000)

= Rs. 5(22,800 – 23,000) = **Rs. 1000 (A)**

Labour Cost Variance : Standard Cost of labour – Actual cost of labour

= 5,700 × 10 × Rs. 1.50 – 56,800 × Rs. 1.52

= Rs. 85,500 – Rs. 86,336 = **Rs. 836(A)**

Labour Rate Variance : AT (SR – AR)

= 56,800 (Rs. 1.50 – Rs. 1.52) = **Rs. 1,136 (A)**

Labour Efficiency Variance : SR (ST – AT)

= Rs. 1.50(5,700 × 10 – 56,800) = **Rs. 300 (F)**

Verification:

MCV = MPV + MUV

Rs. 150(F) = Rs. 1,150(F) + Rs. 1,000 (A)

LCV = LRV + LEV

Rs. 836 (A) = Rs. 1,136 (A) + Rs. 300 (F)

Illustration 60. The standard labour component and the actual labour component engaged in a week for a job are as under.

	Skilled Workers	*Semi-skilled Workers*	*Unskilled Workers*
(*a*) Standard number of workers in the gang	32	12	6
(*b*) Standard wage rate per hour (Rs.)	3	2	1
(*c*) Actual number of workers employed in the gang during the week	28	18	4
(*d*) Actual wage rate per hour (Rs.)	4	3	2

During the 40-hour working week, the gang produced 1,800 standard labour hours of work. Calculate the different labour variances.

Solution :

Category of workers	*Standard*			*Actual*		
	Hrs	*Rate Rs.*	*Amount Rs.*	*Hrs.*	*Rate Rs.*	*Amount Rs.*
Skilled	1,280	3	3,840	1,120	4	4,480
Semi-skilled	480	2	960	720	3	2,160
Unskilled	240	1	240	160	2	320
	2,000		5,040			6,960

Labour Cost Variance : SC – AC

$$\text{Standard Cost of Actual Output} = \frac{5,040}{2,000} \times 1,800 = \text{Rs. } 4,536$$

$$\text{LCV} = 4,536 - 6,960 = \text{Rs. } 2,424\ (\text{A})$$

Labour Rate Variance : AT(SR – AR)

Skilled = 1,120 (Rs. 3 – Rs. 4) = Rs. 1,120 (A)

Semi-skilled = 720 (Rs.2 – Rs. 3) = Rs. 720 (A)

Unskilled = 160 (Re. 1 – Rs. 2) = Rs. 160 (A)

2,000 (A)

Labour Efficiency Variance : SR(ST – AT)

Standard Time for Actual Output :

$$\text{Skilled} = \frac{1,800}{2,000} \times 1,280 = 1,152 \text{ hrs.}$$

$$\text{Semi-skilled} = \frac{1,800}{2,000} \times 480 = 432 \text{ hrs}$$

$$\text{Unskilled} = \frac{1,800}{2,000} \times 240 = 216 \text{ hrs.}$$

LEV :

Skilled = Rs. 3(1,152 – 1,120), = Rs. 96 (F)
Semi-skilled = Rs. 2 (432 – 720) = Rs. 576 (A)
Unskilled = Rs. 1(216 – 160) = Rs, 56 (F)
Total = Rs. 424 (A)

Labour Mix Variance : SR(RST – AT)

$$\text{Revised Standard Times} = \frac{\text{Actual Mix}}{\text{Standard Mix}} \times \text{Std, Time}$$

As the Standard Mix and Actual Mix are the same, the Standard Time will also be the Revised Standard Time.

Skilled = Rs. 3(1,280 – 1,120) = Rs. 480 (F)
Semi-skilled = Rs. 2 (480 – 720) = Rs. 480 (A)
Unskilled = Rs. 1(240 – 160) = Rs. 80 (F)
Total = Rs. 80 (F)

Labour Yield Variance : SR (SY – AY)

Standard Rate per hour of Standard work

$$= \frac{\text{Total Standard Cost}}{\text{Total Standard hours of work}} = \frac{5,040}{2,000} = \text{Rs. } 2.52$$

LYV = 2.52(2,000 – 1,800) = Rs. 504 (A)

Verification:

LCV = LRV + LEV
Rs. 2,424 (A) = Rs. 2,000 (A) + Rs. 424 (A)
LEV = LMV + LYV
Rs. 424 (A) = Rs. 80 (F) + Rs. 504 (A)

Illustration 61. The budgeted sales for one month and the actual results achieved are as under :

Product	*Qty. Nos.*	*Budget Rate Rs.*	*Amount Rs.*	*Qty. Nos.*	*Actual Rate Rs.*	*Amount Rs.*
A	1,000	100	1,00,000	1,200	125	1,50,000
B	700	200	1,40,000	800	150	1,20,000
C	500	500	1,50,000	600	300	1,80,000
D	300	500	1,50,000	400	600	2,40,000
	2,500		5,40,000	3,000		6,90,000

Calculate in respect of each product, the sales variances. (*I.C.W.A. Final*)

Solution :

Sales Value Variance : Actual Sales – Budgeted Sales
= Rs. 6,90, 000 – Rs. 5,40,000
= Rs. 1,50,000 (F)

Sales Price Variance : AQ(AR – SR)

A = 1,200 (Rs. 125 – Rs. 100) = Rs. 30,000 (F)
B = 800 (Rs. 150 – Rs. 200) = Rs. 40,000 (A)
C = 600 (Rs. 300 – Rs. 300) = Nil
D = 400 (Rs. 600 – Rs. 500= Rs. 40,000 (F)
Total = Rs. 30,000 (F)

Sales Volume Variance : SR(AQ – BQ)

A = Rs. 100(1,200 – Rs. 1,000)	= Rs. 20,000 (F)
B = Rs. 200 (800 – 700)	= Rs. 20,000 (F)
C = Rs. 300 (600 – 500)	= Rs. 30,000 (F)
D = Rs. 500 (400 – 300)	= Rs. 50,000 (F)
Total	Rs. 1,20,000 (F)

Sales Mix Variance : SR(AQ – RSQ)

$$RSQ = \frac{\text{Total Actual Mix of Sales}}{\text{Total Standard Mix of Sales}} \times SQ$$

$$A = \frac{3,000}{2,500} \times 1,000 = 1,200 \text{ units}$$

$$B = \frac{3,000}{2,500} \times 700 = 840 \text{ units}$$

$$C = \frac{3,000}{2,500} \times 500 = 600 \text{ units}$$

$$D = \frac{3,000}{2,500} \times 300 = 360 \text{ units}$$

SMV :		
	A = Rs. 100 (1,200 – 1,200)	= Nil
	B = Rs. 200 (800 – 840)	= Rs. 8,000 (A)
	C = Rs. 300 (600 – 600)	= Nil
	D = Rs. 500 (400 – 360)	= Rs. 20,000 (F)
	Total	Rs. 12,000 (F)

Verification:

Sales Value Variance = Sales Price Variance + Volume Variance

Rs. 1,50,000 (F) = Rs. 30,000 (F) + Rs. 1,20,000 (F)

FORMULAE MATERIAL VARIANCES

Material Cost Variance = [Standard Cost of Materials – Actual Cost of Materials]

(OR)

(MCV) = [Standard Quantity × Standard Price] – [Actual Quantity × Actual Price]

= (SQ × SP) – (AQ × AP)

Material Price Variance : = Actual Quantity (Standard Rate – Actual Rate)

(OR) (MPV) = AQ(SR – AR)

Material Usage Variance : = Standard Rate (Standard Quantity – Actual Quantity)

(OR) (MUV) = SR (SQ – AQ)

Material Mix Variance

(*a*) When actual weight of mix is equal to Std. Mix :

= Standard Rate (Standard Quantity – Actual Quantity

= SR (SQ – AQ)

(*b*) When Actual Weight of mix differs from Std. Mix:

= SR (RSQ – AQ)

$$RSQ = \frac{\text{Total Weight Actual Mix}}{\text{Total Weight Std. Mix}} \times \text{Standard Quantity}$$

Material Yield Variance = Standard Yield Rate (Standard Yield – Actual Yield)

SYR (SY – AY)

When Actual Mix differ from Standard Mix:

= SYR (ASY – RSY)

ASY = Actual Standard Yield

RSY = Revised Standard Yield

LABOUR VARIANCES

Labour Cost Variance = Standard Cost of Labour – Actual Cost of Labour

(OR) = (ST × SR) – (AT × AR)

Labour Rate Variance (OR) (LRV) = Actual Time (Standard Rate of pay – Actual Rate of pay)

(OR) = AT (SR – AR)

Labour Efficiency Variance (OR) (LEV) = Standard Rate (Standard Time – Actual Time)

(OR) = SR (ST – AT)

Labour Idle Time Variance = Standard Rate of pay × abnormal Idle Time

Labour Mix Variance (OR) (LMV) When the standard composition of labour force and total time expended is equal to the standard time:

LMV = Standard Cost of Standard Mix – Standard Cost of Actual Mix

(OR) = (Standard Rate of pay × Standard Time) – (Standard Rate of pay × Actual Time)

(OR) = (SR × ST) – (SR × AT)

When the actual time of labour differs from the standard time of labour:

LMV = SR (RST – AT)

RST (Revised Standard Time)

$$= \frac{\text{Total Time of Actual Mix}}{\text{Total Time of Std. Mix}} \times \text{Standard Cost of Actual Mix}$$

Labour Yield Variance (LYV)

= Standard Cost per unit (Standard production of Actual Mix – Actual Production)

OVERHEAD VARIANCES

1. Total Variable Overhead Variance = Std. Variable Overhead – Actual Variable Overhead

= Actual Output × Std. Variable Rate – Actual Variable Overhead

= Std. hours for Actual output × Std. Variable Overhead Rate per hour – Actual Variable

2. Variable Expenditure Variance = Budgeted Overhead – Actual Overhead

= Actual Output × Std. Variable Overhead – Actual Overheads

= Actual hours worked × Std. Overhead rate per hour Actual Overhead

3. Variable Overhead Efficiency Variance = Std. Overhead Rate(Std. Time for Actual Output – Actual time)

4. Fixed Overhead Variance : = Actual Output × Std. Fixed Overhead Rate – Actual Fixed Overheads.

(*a*) Expenditure Variance = Budgeted Fixed Overheads – Actual Fixed Overheads

(*b*) Volume Variance = Actual Output × Std. Rate – Budgeted Fixed Overheads
= Std. Rate (Actual Output – Budgeted Output)

(*c*) Capacity Variance = Std. Rate (Revised Budgeted Units – Budgeted Units)
= Std. Rate (Revised Budgeted Hours – Budgeted Hours)

(*d*) Calendar Variance = Std. Rate per hour (per day) × Excess or Deficit hour worked (per day)

(*e*) Efficiency Variance = Std. Rate (Actual Production – Std. Production)
= Std. Rate per hour (Std. Hours produced – Actual Hours)

Verification:

Total Overhead Cost Variance = Variable Overhead Cost Variance + Fixed Overhead Cost Variance

Variable Overhead Cost Variance = Expenditure Variance + Volume Variance

Fixed Overhead Variance = Expenditure Variance + Volume Variance

Volume Variance = Capacity Variance + Calendar Variance + Efficiency Variance

SALES VALUE METHOD

1. Sales Variance = Actual sales – Std. sales
2. Sales Price Variance = Actual Quantity Sold (Actual Price – Std. Price)
3. Sales Volume Variance = Std. Price (Actual Quantity – Std. Qty)
4. Sales Mix Variance = (Std. Value of Actual Mix) – (Std. Value of Revised Std. Mix)
5. Sales Quantity (Sub-volume Variance) = Std. Selling Price (Revised Std. Sale) Qty. – Budgeted Sales Qty.)

Verification:

S.V. = S.P.V. + S.Q.V.
S.Q.V. = S.M.V. + S.Q.V.

Sales Margin Variance (Profit Method)

1. Total Sales Margin Variance = Actual Sales – Budgeted Sales

$$= \left(\text{Actual Qty of sales} \times \text{Actual Profit per Unit}\right) - \left(\text{Bud. Qty of sales} \times \text{Bud. Profit per unit}\right)$$

2. Sales Margin Price Variance = AQ of sales (Actual selling price per unit – Std. Selling price per unit)
3. Sales Margin Volume Variance
= Std. Rate Profit (Actual Qty. of sales – Std. Qty. of sales)
4. Sales Margin Mix Variance = Revised Std. Profit – Standard Profit
5. Sales Margin Qty. Variance = Budgeted Profit – Revised Std. Profit.

Verification:

S.M.V. = S.M.P.V. + S.M.Vo.V
S.M.Vo.V = S.M.M.V. + S.M.Q.V

Objective Type Questions

A. Choose the correct answer to the following :

(i) Overhead cost variance is the difference between :

(a) Recovered overheads and actual overhead.

(b) Budgeted overheads and actual overheads.

(c) Budgeted overheads and standard overheads.

(ii) Overheads expenditure variance is the difference between :

(a) Recovered overheads and budgeted overheads.

(b) Budgeted overheads and actual overheads.

(c) Standard overheads and actual overheads.

(iii) Sales value variance is the difference between :

(a) Standard sales and actual sales.

(b) Budgeted sales and actual sales.

(c) Budgeted sales and standard sales.

(iv) The difference between actual cost and standard cost is known as :

(a) Variance

(b) Profit

(c) Differential cost

(v) Standard costing helps in :

(a) Measuring officiency.

(b) Reducing losses.

(c) Controlling prices.

(Ans: (i) (a) ; (ii) (b) ; (iii) (b) ; (iv) (a) ; (v) (a)

B. State whether the following statements are ture or false :

1. Variances can be classified into controllable and uncontrollable categories
2. All price variance are uncontrollable.
3. A cost variance is said to be favourable if the standard cost is more than the actual cost.
4. Material yeild variance is favourable if the standard output is more than the actual output.
5. Material yield variance is a sub-variance of material usage variance.
6. Standard sales and budgeted sales are synonymous terms.
7. Recovered overheads and absorbed overheads moon one and the same thing.
8. Purchase department should be held responsible for material price variance.
9. The selling department is responsible for factory overhead volume variance.
10. Material mix variance is a sub-variance of material price variance.

(Ans: 1. True; 2. False; 3. True; 4. False; 5. True
6. False; 7. True; 8. True; 9. False; 10. False.

THEORETICAL QUESTIONS

1. What is meant by standard costing ? State its main objectives. *(C.A. Inter)*
2. What is standard cost and standard costing ? State the advantages of standard costing. *(B. Com., Mysore)*
3. Differentiate between standard cost and estimate cost. *(B. Com., Madurai)*
4. Discuss the relationship of budgetary control and standard costing. *(I.C.W.A.)*

5. What are the several types of standards and what are the assumptions as to the factors on which these standards are based ? (*B. Com., Madurai*)
6. "Setting of standards is the most important mission of standard cost system. These should be set with the greatest care and sound judgement". Discuss the statement and show how standards are fixed for different elements of cost. (*I.C.W.A.*)
7. What is 'Variance'? Indicate its significance to the management. (*B. Com., Gurunanak*)
8. Describe the managerial use of variance analysis.
9. Define and explain briefly the following terms :
   (*a*) Material price variance
   (*b*) Material usage variance
   (*c*) Material mix variance
   (*d*) Material yield variance (*I.C.W.A.*)
10. Define and explain briefly the following terms :
    (*a*) Wage rate variance.
    (*b*) Labour efficiency variance
    (*c*) Labour mix variance
    (*d*) Labour idle time variance
11. Define and explain briefly the following terms :
    (*a*) Variable overhead expenditure variance
    (*b*) Variable overhead efficiency variance
    (*c*) Fixed overhead volume variance
    (*d*) Fixed overhead capacity variance
    (*e*) Fixed overhead calendar variance.

PRACTICAL PROBLEMS

Material Cost Variances

12. From the following data, calculate the material price variance and state whether it is favourable or unfavourable :

    Standard : 10 kg. at Rs. 5 per kg.

    Actual : 12 kg. at Rs. 6 per kg.

    [**Ans.** *Rs. 12 adverse*] (*B.Com., Calicut*)
13. From the data given below, calculate the material price variance, the material usage variance and material mix variance.

Raw material	*Standard*	*Actual*
A	40 units @ Rs. 50 per unit	50 units @ Rs. 50 per units
B	60 units @ Rs. 40 per unit	60 units @ Rs. 45 per units

(*I.C.W.A.*)

[**Ans:** *MPV = Rs. 300 (A), MUV = Rs. 500 (A), MMV = Rs. 60 (A)*]

14. Mixers Ltd. is engaged in producing a standard mix using 60 kgs of chemical X and 40 kgs. of chemical Y. The standard loss of production is 30%. The standard price of X is Rs. 5 per kg. and of Y is Rs. 10 per kg.

    The Actual mixture and yield were as follows :

    X 80 kgs. @ Rs. 4.50 per kg.
    Y 70 kgs. @ Rs. 8.00 per kg.
    Actual yield 115 kgs.

Calculate material variances.

[**Ans :** *MCV : Rs. 230 (F)* (*C.S.*)
MPV : Rs. 180 (F)
MYV : Rs. 100 (F)
MMV : Rs. 50 (A)]

15. The standard estimate for materials for manufacture of 1,000 units of a commodity is 400 kgs. at Rs. 2.50 per kg.
When 2,000 units of the commodity are manufactured, it is found that 820 kgs. of materials are consumed @ Rs. 2.60 per kg.
Calculate the material variances. (*B. Com., Madurai*)
[**Ans :** *MCV = Rs. 132 (A), MPV = Rs. 82 (A), MUV = Rs. 50 (A)*]

16. From the following data, calculate material usage variance :
Standard : 10 kg. at Rs. 4 per kg.
Actual : 12 kg. at Rs. 4.50 per kg.
[**Ans :** *MCV : Rs. 14 (A) MUV : Rs. 8 (A)*] (*B. Com., Madurai*)

17. The standard cost of material for manufacturing a unit of a particular product X is estimated as follows :
16 kgs. of raw material @ Rs. 1.00 per kg.
On completion of the unit, it was found that 20 kgs of raw material costing Rs. 1.50 per kg. has been consumed.
Compute material variances. (*B. Com., Madurai*)
[**Ans :** *MPV : Rs. 10 (A)*
MUV : Rs. 4.00 (A)
MCV : Rs. 14 (A)]

18. Gemini industries provide the following information from their records : For making 10 kg. of GEMCO, the standard requirement is :

	Quantity kg.	*Rate per kg. Rs.*
Material A	8	6.00
Material B	4	4.00

During April, 100 kgs. of GEMCO were produced. The actual consumption of material is as under:

	Quantity Kg.	*Rate per kg.*
Material A	750	7.00
Material B	500	8.00

Calculate :
(*a*) Material Cost Variance
(*b*) Material Price Variance
(*c*) Material Usage Variance (*C.A. Inter*)
[**Ans :** *MPV : Rs. 1,250 (A)*
MCV : Rs. 1,350(A)
MUV : Rs. 100 (A)]

19. Given that the cost standard for materials consumption are 40 kgs. at Rs. 10 per kg, compute the variances when actuals are :
(*a*) 48 kgs. at Rs. 10 per kg.
(*b*) 40 kgs. at Rs. 12 per kg.
(*c*) 48 kgs. at Rs. 12 per kg.
(*d*) 36 kgs. for a total of Rs. 360. (*C.A. Inter*)

[**Ans :**	*MCV*	*MUV*	*MPV*
	(*a*) Rs. 80(A)	Rs. 80(A)	Nil
	(*b*) Rs. 80(A)	Nil	Rs. 80 (A)
	(*c*) Rs. 176(A)	Rs. 80(A)	Rs. 96 (A)
	(*d*) Rs. 40(F)	Rs. 40(F)	Nil]

20. From the following particulars compute (*a*) Material Cost Variance (*b*) Material Price Variance, and (*c*) Material Usage Variance.

Quantity of materials purchased	3,000 units
Value of materials purchased	Rs. 9,000
Std. qty. of materials required per tonne of output	30 units
Standard Rate of Materials	Rs. 2.50 per unit
Opening Stock of Materials	Nil
Closing stock of materials	500 units
Output during the period	80 tonnes

[**Ans :** (*a*) *Rs. 1500 (A); (b) Rs. 1250 (A);* (*c*) *Rs. 250(A)*] (*B. Com., Hons. Delhi*)

21. The standard cost card shows the following details relating to the materials needed to produce one kilogram of groundnut oil.

Quantity of groundnut required	3 kg.
Price of groundnut	Rs. 2.50 per kg
Actual production data :	
Production during the week	1,000 kg.
Quantity used	3,500 kg.
Price of groundnut per kg.	Rs. 3

Calculate :

(*a*) Material Cost Variance

(*b*) Material Price Variance

(c) Material Usage Variance (*B. Com., Calicut, Madurai*)

[**Ans :** *MCV : Rs. 3,000* (A) *MPV : Rs. 1,750* (A) *MUV : Rs. 1,250*(A)]

22. A manufacturing concern which has adopted standard costing furnishes the following information :

Standard :

Finished product 100 kg.	Materials 70 kgs.
Price of materials	Re. 1 per kg.

Actual :

Output	2,10,000 kg.
Material Used	2,80,000 kg.
Cost of Materials	Rs. 2,52,000

Calculate

(*a*) Materials Usage Variance

(*b*) Materials Price Variance

(*c*) Materials Cost Variance (*C.A. Inter, B. Com., Kerala, Calicut*)

[**Ans :** *Rs 20,000 (F), Rs. 28,000 (F), Rs. 48,000 (F)*]

23. Following are the particulars in respect of a product where two types of materials A and B are used :

Material input	*Standard*		*Actual*	
	Tonnes	*Rate*	*Tonnes*	*Rate*
A	120	10.00	140	9.50
B	80	7.50	60	9.00
	200		200	
Less : Loss	20		18	
Net production	180		182	

You are required to calculate :

(*a*) Material Price Variance.

(*b*) Material Mix Variance, and

(*c*) Material Yield Variance (*M. Com., Madras, 1980*)

[**Ans :** *(a) Rs. 20 (A); (b) Rs. 50 (A);(c) Rs. 20 (F)*]

24. The standard material cost for 100 kg of chemical D is made up of :
Chemical A : 30 kgs. @ Rs. 4.00 per kg.
Chemical B : 40 kgs. @ Rs. 5.00 per kg.
Chemical C : 80 kgs. @ Rs. 6.00 per kg
In a batch of 500 kgs. of chemical D were produced from a mix of :
Chemical A : 140 kgs. at a cost of Rs. 588
Chemical B : 220 kgs. at a cost of Rs. 1,056
Chemical C : 440 kgs. at a cost of Rs. 2,860
How do the yield, mix and the price factors contribute to the variance in the actual cost per 100 kgs. of chemical D over the standard cost ?

(*C.A., I.C.W.A., B. Com., Calicut*)

[**Ans :** *MPV = Rs. 40.80 (A); MMV = Rs. 6.67 (A);*
MYV = Rs. 53.33 (A)]

25. The standard material cost to produce a tonne of chemical X is :
300 kg. of material A @ Rs. 10 per kg.
400 kg. of material B @ Rs. 5 per kg.
500 kgs. of material C @ Rs. 6 per kg.
During a period 100 tonnes of mixture X were produced from the usage of :
35. tonnes of material A at a cost of Rs. 9,000 per tonne
42 tonnes of material B at a cost of Rs. 6,000 per tonne
53 tonnes of material C at a cost of Rs. 7,000 per tonne
Calculate price usage and mix variances. (*B. Com., (Hons.), Delhi*)
[**Ans :** *MCV = RS. 1,38,000 (A) ; MPV = Rs. 60,000 (A) ;*
MUV = Rs. 78,000 (A); MMV = Rs. 11,333 (A);
MYN = Rs. 66,667 (A)]

26. XY Ltd., manufacturers of product P, uses a standard cost system. Standard product and cost specifications for 1,000 kg. of product P are as follows :

Ingredients	*Qty. kg.*	*Price per kg.*	*Cost*
A	800	2.50	2,000
B	200	4.00	800
C	200	1.00	200

Input	1,200	3,000
		@ *Rs.*2.50 per kg.
Output	1,000	3,000
		@Rs. 3 per kg.

Material records indicate :

	Consumption in Jan.
A	1,57,000 kg at Rs. 2.40 per kg.
B	38,000 kg. at Rs. 4.20 per kg.
C	36,000 kg. at Rs. 1.10 per kg.

Actual finished production for the month of January is 2,00,000 kg. Calculate, MPV, MMV and MYV (*I.C.W.A.*)

[**Ans** : *MPV : Rs. 4,500 (F)*
MMV : Rs. 3,000 (A)
MYV : Rs. 22,500 (F)]

27. From the following data, calculate materials yield variance :

Standard Mix	*Actual Mix*
Material A–200 units at Rs. 12	160 units at Rs. 13
Material B–100 units at Rs. 10	140 units at Rs. 10
Standard loss allowed is 10% of input	Actual output is 275 units

(*B. Com., Madurai*)

[**Ans** *: MYV : Rs. 62.95 (A)*]

28. From the following information calculate the Materials Mixture Variance

Materials	*Standard Quantity*	*Actual Quantity*	*Standard Price per unit*	*Actual Price per unit*
A	100	150	Rs. 5	Rs. 5.50
B	200	250	Rs. 6	Rs. 6.00
C	300	400	Rs. 4	Rs. 3.50

Due to shortage of B, it was decided to reduce consumption of B by 5% and increase that of A by 10%. (*B. Com., Madurai*)

[**Ans :** *MMV : Rs. 3.33 (F)*]

29.

Material	*Standard*			*Actual*		
	Qty.	*Price*	*Total*	*Qty.*	*Price*	*Total*
	Kg.	Rs.	Rs.	Kg.	Rs.	Rs.
A	500	6	3,000	400	6	2,400
B	400	3.75	1,500	500	3.60	1,800
C	300	3.00	900	400	2.80	1,120
	1,200			1,300		
Less 10% normal loss	120		Actual loss	220		
	1,080		Rs. 5,400	1,080		Rs. 5,320

Calculate (*i*) Material Cost Variance

(*ii*) Material Price Variance

(*iii*) Material Mix Variance

(*iv*) Material Yield Variance

(v) Total Material Usage Variance.

[**Ans :** *MVC : Rs. 80 (F)*
MPV : Rs. 155 (F)
MMV : Rs. 375 (F)
MYV : Rs. 450 (A)
Total MUV : Rs. 75 (A)

30. From the following particulars, calculate the following Material Variances and give their relationships.

1. Material Cost Variance
2. Material Usage Variance
3. Material Price Variance
4. Material Mix Variance, and
5. Material Sub-usage Variance.

Material	*Standard*		*Actual*	
	Qty.	*Price*	*Qty.*	*Price*
	Kg.	Rs.	Kg.	Rs.
A	10	8	10	7
B	8	6	9	7
C	4	12	5	11
	22		24	

[**Ans :** *MCV : Rs. 12 (A)*
MPV : Rs. 6 (F)
MUV : Rs. 18 (A)
MMV : Rs. 2 (A)
MSUV : Rs. 16 (A)

31. From the following data for May of a factory, calculate :

(*a*) Material Cost Variance
(*b*) Material Price Variance
(*c*) Material Usage Variance
(*d*) Material Mixture Variance
(*e*) Material Yield Variance.

Items of material	*Standard*	*Rate*	*Actual*	*Rate*
X	8,000 Kg	1.05	7,500 Kg	1.20
Y	3,000 Kg	2.15	3,300 Kg	2.30
Z	2,000 Kg	3.30	2,400 Kg	3.50

Also write a short note on the relationship among these different variances.

(*ICWA, Inter*)

[**Ans :** *MCV : Rs. 3,540 (A)*
MPV : Rs. 2,100 (A)
MUV : Rs. 1,440 (A)
MYV : Cannot be found out)]

32. Find out :
Material Cost Variance,
Material Price Variance,
Material Usage Variance,
Material Mix Variance and
Material Sub-usage Variance.

Material	*Standard*			*Actual*		
	Qty	*@*	*Amount*	*Qty*	*@*	*Amount*
	kg	Rs.	Rs.	kg	Rs.	Rs.
A	100	2	200	90	2.20	198
B	50	5	250	60	4.50	270
	150		450	150		468

(*B. Com., Madurai*)

Solution :

[**Ans :** *MCV : Rs. 18 (A)*
MPV : Rs. 12(F)
MUV : Rs. 30 (A)
MMV : Rs. 30 (A)
MUV : = MMV]

33. It is estimated that in the manufacture of a product, for each tonne of material consumed, 100 articles should be produced. The standard price per tonne of material is Rs. 10. During the first week of September 100 tonnes of materials were issued to production, the purchase price of which was Rs. 10.50 per tonne. The actual output for the period was 10,250 units. Calculate (*a*) Material Cost Variance, (*b*) Material Price Variance, (*c*) Material Usage Variance. (*M. Com., Madras*)

[**Ans :** *MCV : Rs. 25 (A)*
MPV : Rs. 50 (A)
MUV : Rs. 25 (F)]

34. A furniture manufacturer uses Sunmica tops for tables. From the following information, find out Price Variance, Usage Variance and Joint Variance.

Standard quantity of Sunmica per table	4 Sq. metre
Standard price per sq. meter of Sunmica	Rs. 5.00
Actual production of tables	1,000
Sunmica actually used	4,300 sq. metre
Actual purchase price of sunmica per sq. metre	Rs. 5.50

Who is responsible for the above Variances ? (*B. Com., Madurai*)

[**Ans :** *MPV : Rs. 2,150 (A)*
MUV : Rs. 1,500 (A)
JV or MCV : RS. 3,650 (A)]

35. Design a Material Cost Analysis Form and enter suitable figures from the details given below :

Production of the period 192 units

	Material X	*Material Y*
Standard price per tonne	Rs. 480	Rs. 640
Actual price paid per tonne	Rs. 455	Rs. 616
Actual weights	16 tonnes	13 tonnes

The standard production for the period represented by the above figures is 400 units, for which the standard quantity allowance for materials are 30 tonnes of X and 25 tonnes of Y. (*ICWA*)

[**Ans :** *MCV : Rs. 696 (A)*
MPV : Rs. 712 (F)
MUV : Rs. 1,408 (A)]

36. From the following information compute (*a*) Mix, (*b*) Price, and (*c*) Usage Variances :

	Standard			*Actual*		
	Quantity (kg)	*Unit Rs.*	*Total Rs.*	*Quantity (Kg)*	*Unit Price Rs.*	*Total Rs.*
Material A	4	1.00	4.00	2	3.50	7.00
Material B	2	2.00	4.00	1	2.00	2.00
Material C	2	4.00	8.00	3	3.00	9.00
Total	8		16.00	6		18.00

(*B. Com., Delhi*)

[**Ans :** *MMV : Rs. 4(A)*
MPV : Rs. 2(A)
MUV : Nil]

37. From the following data of a company, calculate the different material variances. Wherever necessary, suitable assumptions may be made to explain the point.

	Standard			*Actual*		
	Qty	*Price*	*Cost*	*Qty*	*Price*	*Cost*
		Rs.	Rs.		Rs.	Rs.
A	1,000	10	10,000	1,090	11	11,990
B	250	20	5,000	400	18	7,200
C	400	15	6,000	380	17	6,460
D	600	10	6,000	610	9	5,490
	2,250		27,000	2,480		31,140

(*I.C.W.A. Inter*)

[**Ans :** *MCA : Rs. 4,140 (A)*
MPV : Rs. 440 (A)
MUV : Rs. 3,700 (A)
MMV : Rs. 939 (A)]

38. From the following information, compute (*a*) Mix, (*b*) Price and (*c*) Usage variance.

	Standard			*Actual*		
	Quantity (Kilos)	*Unit Price Rs.*	*Total Rs.*	*Quantity (Kilo)*	*Unit Price Rs.*	*Total Price Rs.*
Material A	10	2	20	5	3	15
Material B	20	3	60	10	6	60
Material C	20	6	120	15	5	75
Total	50		200	30		150

[**Ans :** *MCV : Rs. 50 (F)*
MPV : Rs. 20 (A)
MMV : Rs. 10(A)
MUV : Rs. 70 (F)
MSUV : Rs. 80 (F)

39. From the following figures given to you, calculate material variances.
Production for the period, 192 units.

	Material X	*Material Y*
Standard price per tonne	Rs. 240	Rs. 320
Actual price paid per tonne	Rs. 227.50	Rs. 308
Actual weights	16 tonnes	13 tonnes

The standard production for the period represented by the above figures is 400 units for which the standard quantity allowance for material are 30 tonnes of X and 25 tonnes of Y. (*I.C.W.A.*)

[**Ans :** *MCV : Rs. 348 (A)*
MPV : Rs. 356 (F)
MSUV : Rs. 718.55 (A)
MUV : Rs. 704 (A)]

40. The standard cost of chemical mixture is as under :
4 tonnes of material X at Rs. 20 per tonne.
6 tonnes of material Y at Rs. 30 per tonne.
Standard yield is 90 per cent of input.
Actual cost for a period is as under :
4.5 tonnes of material X at Rs. 15 per tonne.
5.5 tonnes of material Y at Rs. 34 tonne.
Actual yield is 9.1 tonnes.
Compute : (*a*) Material Price Variance ;
(*b*) Material Usage Variance ;
(*c*) Material Mix Variance ; and
(*d*) Material Yield Variance.

[**Ans :** *MPV Rs. 0.50 (F)* *MUV = Rs. 7.90 (F)*
MMV : Rs. 5 (F)
MYV : Rs. 2,90 (F)]

41. The standard cost of certain chemical mixture is :
35% Material A at Rs. 25 per Kg.
65% Material B at Rs. 36 per Kg.
A standard loss of 5% is expected in production.
During a period there is used :
125 Kgs. of Material A at Rs. 27 per Kg. and 275 Kgs. of Material B at Rs. 34 per Kg.
The actual output was 365 Kgs.
Compute : (a) Material Cost Variance
(*b*) Material Price Variance
(*c*) Material Mix Variance
(*d*) Material Yield Variance (*A.C.S. Final*)

[**Ans :** *MCV : Rs. 373 (A)*
MPV : Rs. 300 (F)
MMV : Rs. 165 (F)
MYV : Rs. 508 (F)

42. S.V. Ltd manufacture BXE by mixing three raw materials. For every batch of 100 Kg of BXE, 125 Kg of raw materials are used. In April, 60 batches were prepared to produce an output of 5,600 Kg of BXE. The standard and actual particulars for April are as under :

Raw Material	Standard		Actual		Quality of Raw Material Purchased
	Mix (%)	Price per Kg (Rs.)	Mix (%)	Price per Kg (Rs.)	(Kg.)
A	50	20	60	21	5,000
B	30	10	20	8	2,000
C	20	5	20	6	1,200

Calculate the variances.

[**Ans :** *MCV :Rs. 17,500 (A)*
MPV : Rs. 3,000 (A)
MUV : Rs. 14,500 (A)
MMV : Rs. 7,500 (A)
MYV : Rs. 7,000 (A)

Labour Cost Variances

43. Calculate Labour Cost Variances :
Standard hours : 40 @ Rs. 3 per hour
Actual hours : 50 @ Rs. 4 per hour (*B. Com. Calicut, Madurai, Rajasthan*)
[**Ans :** *LCV : Rs. 80 (A)*
LRV : Rs. 50 (A)
LRV : Rs. 30 (A)

44. SV Ltd. has furnished you the following data :

	Budget	Actual (July)
No. of working days	25	27
Production in units	20,000	22,000
Fixed Overheads	30,000	31,000

Budgeted fixed overhead rate is Rs. 1.00 per hour. During the month the actual hours worked were 31,500.

Calculate : 1. Efficiency Variance
2. Capacity Variance
3. Calendar Variance
4. Volume Variance
5. Expenditure Variance
6. Total overhead Variance. (*C.A.*)

[**Ans:** *LEV = Rs. 1,500 (F); LCV = Rs. 1,500 (F); RCV = Rs. 900 (A)*
LCV = Rs. 2,400(F); LVV = Rs. 3,000 (F); LEV = RS. 1,000 (A);
Total = Rs. 2,000 (F)

45. Standard hour for manufacturing two products M and N are 15 hours per unit and 20 hours per unit respectively. Both products require identical kind of labour and the standard wage rate per hour is Rs. 5. In the year 2004, 10,000 units of M and 15,000 units of N were manufactured. Total labour hours actually worked were 4,50,500 and the actual wage bill came to Rs. 23,00,000. This included 12,000 hours paid for @ Rs. 7 per hour and 9,400 hours paid for @ Rs. 7.50 per hour, the balance having been paid @ Rs. 5 per hour. You are required to compute the labour variances. (*I.C.W.A.*)
[**Ans.** *LRV = Rs. 47,500 (A);*
LEV = Rs. 2,500 (A);
LCV = Rs. 50,000 (A)]

46. The following are the cost data for he Month of April

Actual number of working days in the Month	24
Actual man-hours worked during the Month	9,600
Units produced in the Month	800
Actual fixed overhead incurred in the Month	Rs. 4,200

The company's budget and standard cost data for the Month are as follows :

Budgeted number of working days per Month	22
Budgeted man-hours for the Month	8,800
Standard man-hours per unit produced	11
Standard fixed overhead rate per man-hour	Rs. 0.50

Calculate fixed overhead variances"

[**Ans :** *Expenditure variance Rs. 200(F); Capacity and Volume Variance Nil, Calendar variance Rs. 400(F); Overhead Variance Rs. 200(F); Efficiency Variance Rs. 400(A)*]

47. From the data given below, calculate labour variances for the two departments :

	Dept. A	Dept. B
Actual gross wages (direct)	Rs. 2,000	Rs. 1,800
Standard hours produced	8,000	6,000
Standard Rate per hour	30 paise	35 paise
Actual Hours worked	8,200	5,800

(*I.C.W.A. Inter*)

[**Ans** : *Dept A B*
LCV Rs. 400 (F), Rs. 300 (F)
LRV Rs. 460 (F), Rs. 230 (F)
LEV Rs. 60 (A), Rs. 70 (F)]

48. The Standard Cost for a product is :
Time : 10 hours per unit.
Cost : Rs. 5 per hour

The Actual performance was :

Production	1000 units
Hours taken :	
Production :	10,400 hours
Idle time	400 hours
Total time	10,800 hours

Payment made : Rs. 56,160 @ Rs. 5.20 per hour. Calculate :
(*a*) Labour Rate variance
(*b*) Labour Efficiency Variance
(*c*) Idle time Variance
(*d*) Labour cost variance (*B. Com., Meerut*)

[**Ans :** *(a)Rs. 2,160(A) ;*
(b) Rs. 2,000(A) ;
(c) Rs. 2,000(A) ;
(d) Rs. 6,160(A)]

49.

Items	Budget	Actual
No. of working days	20	22
Man-hours per day	8,000	8,400
Output per man-hour in unit	1.00	0.90
Overhead cost	1,60,000	1,68,000

From the data given above, calculate overhead variances such as :

(*i*) Overhead Cost Variance
(*ii*) Overhead Efficiency Variance
(*iii*) Overhead Capacity Variance
(*iv*) Overhead Calendar Variance. (*C.A.*)

[**Ans :** (*i*) *Rs.1,680(A)* ;
(*ii*) *Rs. 18,480(A)* ;
(*iii*) *Rs. 24,800(F)* ;
(*iv*) Rs. *16,000(F)*]

50. Following data are available from a card of a factory :

Standard labour rate	Rs. 2 per hour
Standard hours	2 per unit
Actual labour rate	Rs. 2.25 per hour
Actual units produced	1,000 units
Actual hours worked	1,950 hours

Calculate labour variances.

(*B. Com.*)

[**Ans :** *Labour Rate Variance* : *Rs.* 487.50 (A)
Labour Efficiency Variance : *Rs. 100.00 (F)*
Labour Cost Varinace : *Rs.* 387.50*(A)]*

51. Calculate standard labour time for machining part No. Z 235 from the following data :

Standard batch size	100 pieces
Set up time	64 minutes
Operating time (each piece) :	
Fixing job on machine	2 minutes
Cutting time	10 minutes
Removing from the machine	3 minutes

Allow 10% on total operation time for inspection during process and allow further 5% on total time for fatigue. (*I.C.W.A.*)

[**Ans :** *Std. time for 100 pieces is 1,800 minutes*]

52. Find out different Labour Variances, including Yield Variance.

Standard	*Actual*
Output : 1,000 Units	Output: 1,200 Units
Rate of Payment: Rs. 6 per unit	Wages paid with bonus : Rs. 8,000
Time Taken : 50 Hrs.	Time Taken : 40 Hrs. (*B. Com. Bombay*)

[**Ans** : *LCV : Rs. 800 (A)*
LRV : Rs. 3,200 (A)
LEV : Rs. 2,400 (F)
LYN : Rs. 2,400 (F)

53. Data relating to a job are thus :

Standard rate of wages per hour Rs. 10	
Standard hours	300
Actual rate of wages per hour	Rs. 12
Actual hours	200

You are required to calculate

(*i*) Labour Cost Variance,

(*ii*) Labour Rate Variance, and
(*iii*) Labour Efficiency Variance. (*B. Com. Hons. Delhi*)

[**Ans :** *LCV : Rs. 600 (F)*
LRV : Rs. 400 (A)
LEV : Rs. 1,000 (F)]

54. Using the following information calculate each of three labour variances for each department.

	Dept. X	*Dept. Y*
Gross wages direct	(Rs.) 28,080	19,370
Standard hours produced	8,640	6,015
Standard rate per hour (Rs.)	3	3.40
Actual hours worked	8,200	6,345

[**Ans :** *LCV : Rs. 1,079 (A)*
LRV : Rs. Rs. 1,277 (A)
LEV : Rs. 198 (F)]

55. The details regarding the composition and the weekly wage rates of labour force engaged on a job scheduled to be completed in 30 weeks are as follows :

Category of workers	*Standard*		*Actual*	
	No. of labourers rate	*Weekly wage per labourer*	*No. of labourers*	*Weekly wage rate per labourer*
Skilled	75	60	70	70
Semi-skilled	45	40	30	50
Unskilled	60	30	80	20

The work is actually completed is 32 weeks. Calculate the various labour variances. (*B.Com. Hons. Delhi*)

[**Ans :** *LCV : Rs. 13,000 (A)*
LRV : Rs. 6,400 (A)
LEV : Rs. 6,600 (A)
LMV : Rs. 9,600 (F)]

56. The budgeted labour force for producing 1,000 articles 'X' is

	Total Standard hours	*Total Standard Cost Rs.*
30 men @ 40 P. per hour for 50 hrs.	1,500	600.00
20 men @ 30 P. per hour for 30 hrs.	600	180.00
10 men @ 20 P. per hour for 20 hrs.	200	Rs. 40.00
	2300	Rs. 820.00

The actual data and related work force are as follows : Articles produced, 1,000

	Total actual hrs.	Total cost Rs.
25 men @ 45 P. per hour for 50 hrs.	1,250	562.50
30 men @ 30 P. per hour for 30 hrs.	900	270.00
10 men @ 20 P. per hour for 20 hrs.	150	30.00
	2,300	Rs. 862.00

Calculate: (*i*) Labour Cost Variance
(*ii*) Labour Rate Variance,
(*iii*) Labour Mix Variance.

[**Ans :** *LCV : Rs. 42.50 (A)*
LRV : Rs. 62.50 (A)
LMV : Rs. 20 (F)

57. Calculate variances from the standard for a particular month as disclosed from the following figures:

	Standard *Rs.*	*Actual* *Rs.*
Number of workers employed	600	550
Average wages per worker per month	250	264
Number of working days in a month	25	24
Output in units	30,000	28,000

(*B. Com., Delhi*)

[**Ans :** *LCV : Rs. 5,200 (A)*
LRV : Rs. 13,200 (A)
LEV : Rs. 8,000 (F)]

Overhead Variances

58. Calculate overhead variances from the following data :

	Standard	*Actual*
Fixed Overheads	8,000	8,500
Variable Overheads	12,000	11,200
Output in units	4,000	3,800

(*B. Com., Madurai*)

[**Ans :** *VOV : Rs. 200 (F)*
FOV : Rs. 900 (A)
FOVV : Rs. 400 (A)
FOEV : Rs. 500 (A)

59. In a factory the standard units of production for the year were fixed at 1,20,000 units and estimate overhead expenditures were estimated to be :

Fixed	Rs. 12,000
Variable	Rs . 6,000
Semi-Variable	Rs. 1,800

Actual Production during April of the year was 8,000 units. Each month has 20 working days.

During the month in question there was one statutory holiday. The actual overheads amounted to :

Fixed	Rs. 1,190
Variable	Rs. 480
Semi-Variable	Rs. 192

Semi-variable charges are considered to include 60 per cent expenses of fixed nature and 40 per cent of variable character.

Find out (*i*) Overhead Expenditure Variance
(*ii*) Overhead Volume Variance
(*iii*) Overhead Cost Variance (*C.A. Inter*)

[**Ans :** *OCV : Rs. 542 (A)*
OEV : Rs. 324 (A)
OVV : Rs. 218 (A)]

60. A factory has estimated its overheads for some year at Rs. 96,000. The factory runs for 300 days in a year, it works 8 hours a day. The total budgeted production for the year is 24,000 articles.

Actual data are also given to you as under for the month of April

Actual Overhead	Rs. 8,500
Output	2,100 articles
Idle time	4 hours.

Calculate :1. Overhead Cost Variance
2. Overhead budget Variance.
3. Overhead Efficiency Variance
4. Idle Time Variance.

[**Ans :** OCV : Rs. 100 (A)
OEV : Rs. 500 (A)
OEV : Rs. 560 (A)
ITV : Rs. 160 (A)

61. Calculate fixed overhead variances from the following information :

	Budgeted	*Actual*
Fixed Overhead for June	Rs. 5,000	Rs. 6,000
Production in June (units)	1,000	1,050
Standard time per unit	10 hours	
Actual hours worked	11,000 hours	

[**Ans :** *Exp. Variance* = *Rs. 1,000* (A)
Volume Variance = Rs. 250 (F)
Capacity Variance = Rs. 500 (F)
Efficiency Variance = Rs. 250 (A)]

62. Actual Overhead: Rs. 1,800

Budgeted Overhead	:	Rs. 2,000
Budgeted Period	:	4,000 labour hours
Standard per unit	:	10 labour hours
Budgeted number of days	:	20
Standard Overhead per hour	:	Rs. 0.50
Actual number of days	:	22
Actual hours	:	4,300
Actual production	:	425 units

Calculate : (*a*) Expenditure Variance
(*b*) Calendar Variance
(*c*) Capacity Variance
(*d*) Efficiency Variance
(*e*) Total overhead Variance and
(*f*) Volume Variance

[**Ans :** *Expenditure variance Rs. 200(F)*
Calendar variance Rs. 200(F)
Capacity variance Rs. 50(A) Efficiency variance Rs. 25(A)
Volume variance Rs. 125(F) Total variance Rs. 325(F)]

63. In department A the following data is submitted for the week ending 31st October :

Standard output for 40 hours per week	1,400 units
Standard fixed overhead	Rs. 1,400
Actual output	1,200 units
Actual hours worked	32 hours
Actual fixed overhead	Rs. 1,500

Prepare a statement of variance. (*C.A. Inter*)

[**Ans :** *FOVC : Rs. 300 (A)*
FOVV : Rs. 200 (A)
FOEV : Rs. 100 (A)
FOEV : Rs. 80 (A)
FOCV : Rs. 280 (A)]

64. A manufacturing company operates a costing system and showed the following data in respect of the month of November.

Actual No. of working days	22
Actual man hours worked during the month	4,300
Number of product produced	425
Actual overhead incurred (Rs.)	1,800

Relevant information from the company's budget and standard cost data are as follows :

Budgeted number of working days per month	20
Budgeted man hours per month	4,000
Standard man hours per product	10
Standard Overhead rate per man hour	50 P

You are required to calculate for the month of November.

(*a*) The Overhead Variance,
(*b*) The Calendar Variance,
(*c*) The Volume Variance. (*I.C.W.A. Inter*)

[**Ans :** *OCV : Rs. 325 (F)*
OCV : Rs. 200 (F)
OVV : Rs. 125 (F)

65. The following information was obtained from the records of a manufacturing unit using Standard Costing System :

	Standard	*Actual*
Production	4,000 units	3,800 units
Working Days	20	21
Fixed Overhead	Rs. 40,000	Rs. 39,000
Variable Overhead	Rs. 12,000	Rs.12,000

You are required to calculate the following Overhead Variances :

(*a*) Variable Overhead Variance
(b) Fixed Overhead Variance
(*i*) Expenditure Variance
(*ii*) Volume Variance
(*iii*) Efficiency Variance
(iv) Calendar Variance

[**Ans :** *VOV : Rs. 600 (A)*
FOV : Rs. 1,000 (A)
OEV : Rs. 1,000 (F)
OVV : Rs. 2,000 (A)
OEV : Rs. 4,000 (A)
OCV : Rs. 2,000 (F)]

66. A Company manufacturing two products operates a standard costing system. The standard overhead content of each product in cost centre 101 is.
Product A Rs. 240 (8 direct labour hours @ Rs. 0.30 per hour)

Product B Rs. 1.80 (6 direct labour hours @ Rs. 0.30 per hour)

The rate of 30 p. per hour is arrived at as follows :

Budgeted Overhead	Rs. 570
Budgeted direct labour hours	1,900

For the month of October the following data were recorded for cost centre 101.

Output of product A	100 units
Output of product B	200 units
No opening or closing stock	
Actual direct labour hours worked	2,320
Actual overhead incurred	Rs. 640

(*a*) You are required to calculate total overhead variance for the month of October.

(*b*) Show its division into

(*i*) Overhead Expenditure Variance.

(*ii*) Overhead Volume Variance

(*iii*) Overhead Efficiency Variance. (*I.C.W.A. Inter*)

[**Ans :** *OCV : Rs. 40(A)*
OEV : Rs. 70(A)
OVV : Rs. 30 (F)
OEV : Rs. 96 (A)]

67. A manufacturing company operating a standard costing system had the following data in respect of a month :

	Standard	*Actual*
Number of working days	25	27
Man hours per month	5,000	5,400
Output in units	500	525
Fixed Overheads	Rs. 2,500	Rs. 2,400

Calculate the fixed overheads variances for the month.

[**Ans :** *OCV : Rs. 200(F); OEV : Rs. 75(A)*] (*M. Com. Madurai*)

Sales Variance

68. The budgeted and actual sales of a concern manufacturing and marketing a single product are furnished below :

Budgeted sales	10,000 units at Rs. 4 per unit
Actual sales	5,000 units at Rs. 3.50 per unit
	8,000 units at Rs. 4 per unit.

Calculate : (*a*) Sales Price Variance.

(*b*) Sales Volume Variance. (*C.A. Inter*)

[**Ans :** *SPV : Rs. 2,500 (A)*
SVV : Rs. 12,000 (F)]

69. The Sales Manager of a Company engaged in the manufacture and sale of three products P, Q and R gives you the following information for the month of October.

Product	Budget Sales Units Sold	Selling Price per unit	Standard Contribution Margin per unit.
P	2,000	Rs. 12	Rs. 6
Q	2,000	Rs. 8.	Rs. 4
R	2,000	Rs. 5	Rs. 1

Actual Sales :

P	1,500 units for Rs. 15,000
Q	2,500 units for Rs. 17,500
R	3,500 units for Rs. 21,000

(a) You are required to calculate the following variances :

(*i*) The Sales Price Variance

(*ii*) The Sales Volume Variance

(*iii*) The Sales Quantity Variance

(*iv*) The Sales Mix Variance

(*b*) The cost of examining into the cause of the variances would be Rs. 200 and the corrective action to be taken, if needed, would be Rs. 300.

If there is 85% probability of the variances arising out of justifiable reasons and 15% probability of the situation going completely out of control, work out the total cost in carrying out a complete investigation. (*C.A. Final*)

[**Ans :** *SPV : Rs. 2,000 (A)*
SVV : Rs. 5,500 (F)
SQV : Rs. 12,500 (F)
SMV : Rs. 7,000 (A)]

70. Pioneer Plastic Ltd. operates a budgetary control and standard costing system. From the following data calculate :

Product	*Std. Cost of sales per unit*	*Std. Selling price per unit*	*Budget*		*Actual*	
			units to be sold	*Sale value*	*Units sold*	*Sale volume*
A	10.00	12.00	100	1,200	100	1,100
B	9.40	12.00	50	600	50	600
C	7.50	9.00	100	900	200	1,700
D	4.00	6.00	75	450	50	300
Total			325	3,150	400	3,700

(*C.A.*)

[**Ans :** *(i) 500(F) (ii) Rs. 750(F) (iii) Rs. 200(A)*]

71. From the following particulars, calculate

(*a*) Sales value variance,

(*b*) Sales price variance, and

(*c*) Sales volume variance.

The budgeted and actual sales for a period in respect of two products are :

Product	*Budgeted quantity (Units)*	*Price*	*Actual quantity (Units)*	*Price*
		Rs.		Rs.
A	1,000	20	1,300	21
B	2,000	15	2,300	14
	3,000		3,600	

(*B. Com., Madurai*)

[**Ans :** *SVV : Rs. 9,500 (F)*
SPV : Rs. 1,000 (A)
SVOV : Rs. 10,500 (F)]

Profit Variances

72. From the following particulars, calculate :
(*a*) Total sales margin variance.
(*b*) Sales margin variance due to selling price.
(*c*) Sales margin variance due to volume.

Product	*Standard*			*Actual*		
	Quantity units	*Cost per unit*	*Price per unit*	*Quantity units*	*Cost per unit*	*Price per unit*
X	3,000	10	12	3,200	10.50	13
Y	2,000	15	18	1,600	14.00	17

[**Ans :** *(a) Rs. 800 (F)*
(b) Rs. 1,600 (F)
(c) Rs. 800 (A)]

73. From the following budgeted and actual figures, calculate the variances on sales margin basis:

Budget:

Sales – 2,000 units @ Rs. 15 each	Rs. 30,000
Cost of Sales @ Rs. 12 peach	Rs. 24,000
Profit	Rs. 6,000

Actual :

Sales –1,900 units @ Rs. 14 each	Rs. 26,600
Cost of Sales @ Rs. 10 each	Rs. 19,000
Profit	Rs. 7,600

(*I.C.W.A.*)

[**Ans :** *Sales Margin Price Variance Rs. 1,900 (F)*
Sales Margin Quantity Variance Rs. 300 (A)
Total Sales Margin Variance Rs. 1,600 (F)]

74. From the following information relating to sales and profits, calculate the sales variance on the basis of profits :

Budget

Product	*Sales*			*Costs*		*Profit*	
	Units	*Per unit*	*Total*	*Per unit*	*Total*	*Per unit*	*Total*
		Rs.	Rs.	Rs.	Rs.		Rs.
A	12,000	5	60,000	4	48,000	1	12,000
B	8,000	10	80,000	8	64,000	2	16,000
	20,000		1,40,000		1,12,000		28,000

Actual

Product	*Units*	*Per unit*	*Total*	*Per unit*	*Total*	*Per unit*	*Total*
		Rs.	Rs.	Rs.	Rs.	Rs.	Rs.
A	15,000	4.50	67,500	3.50	52,500	1.00	15,000
B	7,500	12.00	90,000	8.50	63,750	3.50	26,250
	22,500		1,57,500		1,16,250		41,250

(*B. Com. Hons., Bangalore*)

[**Ans :** *Total Sales Margin Variance Rs. 13,250 (F)*
SPV : Rs. 11,250 (F)
SVV : Rs. 2,000 (F)
SMV : Nil
SQV : Rs. 2,000 (F)]

75. For a month, the budgeted and actual figures for sales in a company were as under :

Product	*Budget*			*Actual*		
	Qty	*Price Rs.*	*Value Rs.*	*Qty.*	*Price Rs.*	*Value Rs.*
I	20	2	40	15	2	30
II	10	1	10	15	1.50	22.50
III	5	3	15	10	2.50	25
IV	10	3.50	35	10	3	30
	45		100	50		107.50

The budgeted costs for the different products were :

I	Rs. 1.50
II	Rs. 0.80
III	Rs. 2.00
IV	Rs. 3.00

Calculate the sale variance based on :
(*a*) Turnover and
(*b*) Profits

Verify your calculations : (*SAS. Comml*)

[**Ans :** (*a*) *Sales Value Variance Rs. 7.50 (F)*
Sales Rate Variance Rs. 2.50 (A)
Sales Volume Variance Rs. 10 (F)
Sales Quantity Variance Rs. 1.1 (A)
(*b*) *Sales Profit Variance Re. 1 (F)*
Total SRPV: Rs. 2.50 (F)
Sales Volume Variance Rs. 3.50 (F)]

Miscellaneous

76. Calculate the efficiency and activity ratios from the following figures :

Budgeted production	88 units
Standard hours per unit	10
Actual production	75 units
Actual working hours	600

(*I.C.W.A.*)

[**Ans :** *Efficiency Ratio ; 125% ; Activity Ratio : 85.2%*]

77. The Standard Cost on 'Material' and 'Labour' for the making of a unit of a certain product are estimated as under :

Material 80 Kg. at Rs. 1.50 per Kg.
Labour 18 hrs at Rs. 1.25 per hr.

On completion of the production of a unit, it was found that 75 Kg. of material costing Rs. 1.75 per kg. has been consumed and that the time taken was 16 hours, the wage rate being Rs. 1.50 per hour.

You are required to (*a*) analyse material and labour variances, and (*b*) indicate their significance. (*M.Com. Madras*)

[**Ans.** *MCV : Rs. 11.25 (A) LCV : Rs. 1.50 (A)*
MPV : Rs. 18.75(A) LRV : Rs. 4 (A)
MUV : Rs. 7.50 (F) LTV : Rs. 2.50 (F)]

78. For unit of product A, the standard data are given below :

	Rs.
Material	
5 kg @ Rs. 40 per kg.	200
Labour	
40 hrs. @ Rs. 1.00 per hour	40
	240

Actual Data

Actual production 100 units	Total Rs.
Material 490 Kg. @ Rs. 42 each	20,580
Labour 3960 hrs. @ Rs. 1.10 per hour	4,356
	24,936

Calculate Variance. (*B. Com., Bombay*)

Ans : *MCV : Rs. 580 (A) LCV : Rs. 356 (A)*
MPV : Rs. 980 (A) LRV : Rs. 396 (A)
MUV : Rs. 400 (F) LEV : Rs. 40 (F)]

79. From the following information, compute the various variances :

Standards :

Materials quantity	1.00 per unit
Materials price	Rs. 1.40 per Kg.
Direct labour hours	1.5 hours per unit
Labour rate	Rs. 3 per hour
Overheads	Re. 1 per standard direct labour hour
Capacity	5,000 units

Actual :

Materials purchased	10,000 Kg.
Material Price	Rs. 1.50 per Kg.
Materials used	5,400 Kg.
Direct labour hour	8,000
Labour rate	Rs. 3.15 per hour
Overheads	Rs. 8,800
Units produced	5,000

(*M. Com., Bangalore*)

[**Ans :** *MPV : Rs. 540 (A) LRV : Rs. 1,200 (A) VOV : Rs. 1,300 (A)*
MUV : Rs. 560 (A) LEV : Rs. 1,500 (A) VOEV : Rs. 800 (A)
MCV : Rs. 1,100 (A) LCV : Rs. 2,700 (A) VOEV : Rs. 500 (A)]

80. From the following data you are required to calculate :

(*a*) Calendar Variance ;

(*b*) Efficiency Variance;

(*c*) Capacity Variance ; and

(*d*) Volume Variance.

	Budgeted	*Actual*
No. of working days	40	44
Standard direct labour hours per day	16,000	16,800
Standard Overhead rate per direct labour hour Rs. 2		
Total units of output	1,60,000	2,21,760

(*I.C.W.A.*)

[**Ans :** *(a) Rs. 1,28,000 (F)*
(b) Rs. 2,95,680 (F)
(c) Rs. 70,400 (F)
(d) Rs. 4,94,080 (F)]

81. R & Co. makes only one product, the standard variable costs of one Unit are :

	Rs.
Direct Material 1 unit @ Rs. 0.50	0.50
Direct Labour 1 hour @ Rs. 2	2.00
Variable Overhead 1 hour @ Rs. 1.50	1.50
	4.00

There are no initial inventories. Production for the month of September was 10,000 units. The costs for this production are as follows :

Materials purchased	15,000 units @ Rs. 0.40 ...	Rs. 6,000
Materials used	11,000 units	
Direct Labour	9,000 hours @ Rs. 2.10 ...	Rs. 18,900
Variable Overheads incurred		Rs. 16,000

The Overhead is recovered on Standard Direct Labour Hours.

You are required to compute :

(*a*) Materials — Price and Usage Variances.

(*b*) Labour — Rate and Efficiency Variances.

(*c*) Overhead-Spending and Efficiency Variances. (*A.I.M.A.*)

[**Ans :** *MCV : Rs. 600 (F) LCV : Rs. 1,100 (F)*
VOExpenditure V: Rs. 2,500 (A)
MPV : Rs. 1,100 (F) LRV : Rs. 900 (A) VOCV : Rs. 1,000 (A)
MUV : Rs. 500 (A) LEV : Rs. 2,000 (F)
VOEfficiency V : Rs. 1,500 (F)]

82. The following standards have been set to manufacture a product :

Direct Materials	Rs.
2 units of A at Rs. 4 per unit	8.00
3 units of B at Rs. 3 per unit	9.00
15 units of C at Re. 1 per unit	15.000
	32.00
Direct Labour 3 hours at Rs. 8 per hour	24.00
Total Standard Prime Cost :	56.00

The company manufactured and sold 6,000 units of the product during the year. Direct Material Costs were as follows :

12,500 units of A at Rs. 4.40 per unit
18,000 units of B at Rs. 2.80 per unit
88,500 units of C at Rs. 1.20 per unit

The company worked 17,500 labour hours during the year. For 2,500 of these hours the company paid at Rs. 12 per hours while for the remaining the wages were paid at the standard rate.

Calculate Material Price and Usage Variances and Labour Rate and Efficiency Variances.

(*C.A. Inter*)

[**Ans :** *MPV : Rs. 19,100 (A) LRV : Rs. 10,000 (A)*
MUV : Rs. 500 (A) LEV : Rs. 4,000 (F)

83. The Standard Cost Card for a product shows as thus :

	Per Units Rs.
Material Cost – 2 Kg. @ Rs. 2.50 each	5.00
Wages – 2 hours @ 50 p. each	1.00

The Actuals which have emerged from business operations are as follows :

Production	8,000 units
Material Consumed —	
16,500 Kg. @ Rs. 2.40 each	Rs. 39,600
Wages Paid —	
18,000 hours @ 40 p. each	Rs. 7,200

Calculate appropriate material and labour variances.

(*B. Com Hons. Delhi*)

[**Ans :** *MCV : Rs. 400 (F) LCV : Rs. 800 (F)*
MPV : Rs. 1,650 (F) LRV : Rs. 1,800 (F)
MUV : Rs. 1,250 (A) LTV : Rs. 1,000 (A)]

84. The Standard Cost for one unit of a product shows the following costs for material and labour :

Material : 4 pieces @ Rs. 5 per piece
Labour : 10 hours @ Rs. 1.50 per hour

5,700 units of the product were manufactured during the month of July with the following material and labour costs :

Material : 23,000 pieces @ Rs. 4.95 per piece
Labour : 56,800 hours @ Rs. 1.52 per hour

Calculate appropriate material and labour variances.

(*B. Com. Hons. Delhi*)

[**Ans :** *MCV : Rs. 150 (F) LCV : Rs. 836 (A)*
MPV : Rs. 1,150 (F) LRV : Rs. 1,136 (A)
MUV : Rs. 1,000 (A) LEV : Rs. 300 (F)

85. A Company produces a single product from a single material. It operates a standard cost system and furnishes you the following information :

Particulars	*Budget (Standard)*	*Actual*
Product Units	8,000	6,000
Materials :		
Total Quantity — Kg.	16,000	13,000
Total Amount — Rs.	32,000	27,300
Labour:		
Total hours	2,400	2,000
Total Amount	Rs. 3,000	3,000
Variable Overhead		
Expenses :		
Total Hours	2,400	2,000
Total Amount	Rs. 2,400	2,200

You are required to compute the following variances :

(*a*) Material Price Variance
(*b*) Material Usage Variance
(*c*) Labour Rate Variance
(*d*) Labour Efficiency Variance
(*e*) Overhead Efficiency Variance
(*f*) Overhead Budget Variance. (*C.A. Inter*)

[**Ans :** *MPV : Rs. 1,300 (A), OEV : Rs. 200 (A)*
MUV : Rs. 2,000 (A), OBV : Rs. 4,00 (A)
LRV : Rs. 500 (A) LEV : Rs. 250 (A)]

Chapter **10**

Budget And Budgetary Control

Definition; Forecast and Budget; Objectives of a Budget; Budgeting; Objectives of Budgeting; Budgetary Control; Characteristics; Advantages; Essentials of a Successful Budgetary Control; Limitations of Budgetary Control; Organisation; Master Budget; Classification of Budgets; Long Term Budgets; Short Term Budgets; Current Budgets; Fixed and Flexible Budgets; Preparation of Flexible Budget; Control Ratios; Calendar Ratio; Sales Budget; Production Budget; Material Budget; Labour Budget; Works Overhead Budget; Administrative Overheads Budget; Capital Expenditure Budget; Cash Budget; Zero Base Budgeting; Objective Type Questions; Theoretical Questions; Practical Problems.

Modern business world is full of competition, uncertainty and exposed to different types of risks. This complexity of managerial problems has led to the development of various managerial tools, techniques and procedures useful for the management in managing the business successfully. Budgeting is the most common, useful and widely used standard device of planning and control. The budgetary control has now become an essential tool of the management for controlling costs and maximising profit. Costs can be reduced, wastage can be prevented and proper relationship between costs and incomes can be established only when the various factors of production are combined in profitable way. The resources of a business can be effectively utilised by efficient conduct of its operations. This requires careful working out of proper plans in advance, co-ordination and control of activities on the part of management.

A proper planning and control are essential for an efficient management. A good number of tools and devices are available. Of all these, the most important device used is budget. Cost accounting aims not only at cost ascertainment, but also greatly at cost control and cost reduction. Thus the management aims at the proper and maximum utilisation of resources available. It is possible when there is a pre-planning. Modern management aims that all types of operations should be predetermined in advance, so that the cost can be controlled at every step. The more important point is that the actual programme is compared with the pre-planned programme and the variances are analysed and investigated. All are familiar with the idea of budget, at every walk of life—state, firm, business etc.

Definition

A budget is a detailed plan of operations for some specific future period. Many of us are familiar with the term 'Budget'. For instance, if we want to have a holiday trip to Kashmir, we are to estimate the cost of travelling, boarding, lodging etc. so as to have sufficient amount for the trip. On return from the trip, we may like to compare the actual amount spent with the estimated or budgeted figures. Similarly we can know the importance of budgets even from the household management. The word 'budget' is derived from a French term "Bougette" which denotes a leather pouch in which funds are appropriated for meeting anticipated expenses. The same meaning applies to the business management. A budget is a numerical statement expressing the plans, policies and goals of the enterprise for a definite period in the future. It is a plan laying down the targets to be achieved within a specified period. It is a final and approved share of a forecast. When forecasts are approved by the management as a tentative plan for the future they become budget. The following are some of the important definitions.

1. "Budget is an estimate of future needs arranged according to an orderly basis, covering some or all of the activities of an enterprise for definite period of time."
   —*George R. Terry*
2. "A Budget is a comprehensive and co-ordinated plan, expressed in financial terms, for the operations and resources of an enterprise for some specific period in the future."
   —*James*
3. "A budget is a pre-determined statement of management policy during a given period which provides a standard for comparison with the results actually achieved."
   —*Brown and Howard*
4. "A financial and/or quantitative statement, prepared prior to a defined period of time, of the policy to be pursued during that period for the purpose of a given objective."
   —*ICMA, England*

A study of the above definitions reveals the following basic elements of a budget :

1. Budget is a comprehensive plan of what the enterprise endeavours to achieve.
2. It is a statement in terms of money or quantity or both.
3. It is prepared for a definite future period.
4. It is prepared prior to the defined period.
5. It provides yardsticks and measures for the purpose of comparison.
6. It is prepared in advance and refers to the future course of action.
7. It indicates the business policy which has to be followed so as to achieve a given objective.

Forecast and Budget

Forecast is mainly concerned with probable events; but budget is concerned with planned events.

Forecast may be done for longer time; but budget is prepared for shorter periods.

Forecast is only a tentative estimate and can be revised; but budget remains unchanged for the budget period.

Forecast results in planning and the planning results in budgeting.

Forecast is a prediction or an estimate of changes, if any, in characteristics, economic phenomena which may affect one's business plans. It is a study into the future, when the forecasts are given a shape and approved by the management as a commitment, they become budgets. For example, sales forecast is an estimate for future sales, while a sales budget is a commitment with an objective to reach certain sales figures.

Forecast is the base while a budget is the structure built on the base.

Forecast is not used for evaluating the efficiency of performance while a budget is always used for this purpose.

Forecast refers to the events over which there is no control, (for example, forecast of restricted import) while a budget is an endeavour to control the events.

Objectives of a Budget

1. It directs the attention of all concerned to the attainment of a common goal.
2. It leads to the disclosure of organisational weakness. The budgets are compared with actual performance; and variances, if any, are investigated. This step helps in taking corrective and remedial measures.
3. It aims at careful control over the performance and cost of every function.
4. It contributes to co-ordinated efforts of all departments in order to achieve an integrated goal. Budgets grow from bottom and are controlled from top-level.

Budgeting

A budget is essentially a statement of the intention of management. Budgeting refers to the management action of formulating budgets. Preparation of budgets involves study of business situations and understanding of management objectives as also the capacity of the enterprise. It includes the entire processing of making the budget plans. Preparation of budgets or budgeting is a planning function, and their application or implementation is a control function.

When plans are embodied in a budget and the same is used as the basis for regulating operations, we have budgetary control. Budgetary control starts with budgeting and ends with control. Budgeting is defined as :

1. "The entire process of preparing the budgets is known as budgeting." —Batty
2. "Budgeting may be said to be the act of building budgets." —Rowland and Harr

Objectives of Budgeting

The main objectives of budgeting are :

1. To obtain more economical use of capital.
2. To prevent waste and reduce expenses.
3. To facilitate various departments to operate efficiently and economically.
4. To plan and control the income and expenditure of the firm.
5. To create a good business practice by planning for future.
6. To fix responsibilities on different departments or heads.
7. To co-ordinate the activities of various departments.
8. To ensure the availability of working capital.
9. To smooth out seasonal variations, by developing new products.
10. To ensure the matching of sales with production.

What is a Budget

1. Budgets are blueprint of the desired plan of action.
2. They are means of communications.
3. They indicate the business policies.
4. They serve as declaration of policies.
5. They provide a means of coordination of the business as a whole.
6. They are instruments of managerial control.
7. They are controlling tools.
8. They provide yardstick for comparison.
9. They set definite goals.
10. They fix responsibilities and direct to profitable direction.

Budgetary Control

"Budgetary control means the establishment of budgets relating to the responsibilities of executives to the requirements of a policy, and continuous comparison of actual with budgeted results either to secure by individual action the objective of that policy or to provide basis for its revision."

Budget, budgeting and budgetary control, according to Rowland and William H. Harr is that, "Budgets are the individual objectives of a department etc., whereas budgeting may be said to the act of building budgets. Budgetary control embraces all this and in addition includes the science of planning the budgets themselves and the utilisation of such budgets to effect an overall management for the business planning and control."

A budget is a numerical statement expressing the plans, policies and goals for a definite future period. Budgeting means the process of preparing budgets. Budgetary control is a system of controlling costs which includes the preparation of budgets, co-ordinating the departments and establishing responsibilities, comparing actual performance with the budgeted; and acting upon results to achieve maximum profitability.

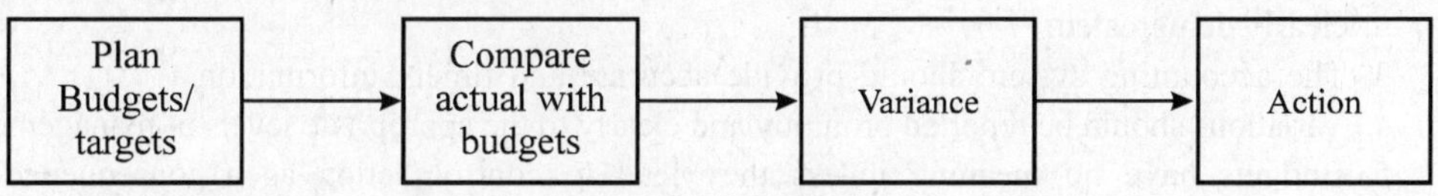

Budgetary Control

Characteristics

1. *Establishment*. Budgets are prepared for each department and then the plans and objectives are presented before the management.
2. *Co-ordination*. The budgetary control co-ordinates the plans of various departments and master budget is prepared.
3. *Continuous comparison*. The essential feature of budgetary control is to conduct continuous comparison of actual performance with budgeted figures, revealing the variations.
4. Revision. Budgets are revised, if necessary, according to changed conditions.

Advantages

The advantages and benefits of budgetary control are summarised below:

1. Budgets fix the goals and targets, without which operation lacks direction.
2. Reduction in cost and elimination of inefficiency is achieved automatically.
3. The budget facilitates to maintain ordered effort and brings about efficiency in results.
4. An effective system of budgetary control results in co-ordinated effort of all persons involved.
5. Budgetary control enables the management to decentralise responsibility without losing control of the business since it pin-points inefficiency.
6. The budgetary control and standard costing go hand in hand and the combination of the two gives the most effective results. It promotes mutual co-operation and team spirits among the persons involved.
7. Budgetary control ensures that the capital employed at a particular level is kept at a minimum level.
8. It facilitates an intelligent and planned forecast for future.
9. It is a good guide to the management for making future plans. It is on the basis of budgetary control, realistic budgets can be drawn.
10. It aims at maximisation of profit through cost control and proper utilisation of resources.
11. It brings to light the inefficiencies and weaknesses on comparing actual performance with budget. Thus management can take remedial measures.

12. It is a guide to the management in the field of research and development in future.
13. It evaluates the performance.
14. Since budget provides advance information, financial crisis can be avoided.
15. It acts as a safety signal for the management. It prevents wastages of all types.

Essentials of a Successful Budgetary Control

A budget is both a plan as well as a control tool. A business budget is a plan covering all phases of operations for a definite period in future. It is a formal expression of policies, plans, objectives and goals laid down in advance by the top management for the concern as a whole and for every sub-division thereof. For an effective system of budgetary control, certain pre-requisites must be present. These essentials are :

1. The budgetary control system should have full support of top management.
2. There should be well-planned organisational set-up, with responsibility and authority clearly demarcated.
3. The accounting system should provide accurate and timely information.
4. Variations should be reported promptly and clearly to the appropriate levels of management.
5. Budgets have no meaning unless they lead to control action as a consequence of feedback provided.
6. Staff should be strongly and properly motivated towards the system.
7. The budgets should lay down the targets which are realistic and attainable.
8. It is most desirable that there is full and meaningful participation of all concerned.
9. Budgets should actually aim as a co-ordinating device rather than control device.
10. The budgets should be flexible enough to permit the adjustments in the light of changed operational circumstances.

Limitations of Budgetary Control

Budgetary control is a sound technique of control. But it is not a perfect tool. Despite the appreciation, it has its own limitations which are as follows :

1. Budgets deal with future. Forecasting is necessary for budgeting. Forecasts and estimates are rarely cent per cent accurate. The success largely depends upon the degree of accuracy of the estimates.
2. Budgeting is time-consuming process. During the preparation period, the business conditions may change and estimates may go wrong by that time.
3. The successful operation and execution of budgets depends upon the efficiency of the executive personnel.
4. Budgetary control is essentially a tool of decision-making and it helps the management in taking sound decisions. But it cannot replace the management.
5. Budgeting necessitates the employment of specialised staff and this involves expenditure which small concerns may not afford.
6. A budget programme should be dynamic, capable of being adapted to changing conditions. But when budgets are prepared with pre-determined targets, there is a feeling that the budgeted figures are final. Thus budgetary programme is bound to become rigid.
7. The success of the budgetary control largely depends upon willing, co-operation or team-work of all concerned. If there is no co-operation, the whole system collapses.

Organisation

The following are the essentials for a sound system of budgetary control :

1. **Chart.** There must be an organisational chart to show the authority and responsibility of each executive of the firm. This will enable him to know his relationship with other executives. The budget director derives power from the chief-executive, helps in co-ordination and drawing up of

all budgets and suggests changes, if necessary. The sales manager, production manager, purchasing manager, personnel manager and accountant will prepare their budgets.

2. **Budget Centre.** For the purpose of effective budgetary control, budget centres are defined. A budget centre may be a department or a section of the undertaking. Separate budgets are prepared for each department and the departmental head is responsible for carrying out budgets. Departmental heads should have effective control over the execution of the budget, to prevent unfavourable variation.

3. **Budget.** In small firms, the chief accountant prepares the budgets and co-ordinates various activities. In big concerns, a committee is appointed for this task. The committee consists of various section heads, the chief executive and the budget controller. The budgets are prepared by section heads and submitted to the committee for approval; changes are made, if necessary, and approved.

4. **Budget Manual.** It is a document which sets out the responsibilities of persons engaged in the routine work. Budget manual lays down the objectives of the organisation, responsibilities of all executives and the procedure to be followed for budgetary control. Duties, authorities, powers of each official of the different departments are clearly defined, so as to avoid conflicts among the personnel. It also specifies different forms and records to be used for the purpose of budgetary control.

5. **Budget Period.** This is the period or time for which the budget is prepared and remains in operation. The length of period depends on the nature of business, the production period,the control aspects etc. There is no budget rule as regards the duration of a budget period. Generally, the budget is prepared for a year, which is preferred by most concerns. For example manufacturers of consumer goods may prepare budgets for a year, whereas in industries like ship-building the period of the budget may be 5 to 10 years.

6. **Key-Factor.** Key-factor is also known as 'limiting factor' or 'governing factor' which means this is the factor, the extent of whose influence must first be assessed, in order to ensure that the functional budgets are reasonably capable of fulfilment. The key factor may be, shortage of raw materials, non-availability of labour, limited sales, government restrictions etc. The key-factor is a limitation on production or sales. First locate the key-factor, before preparing the budget, as it influences all other budgets. For example, shortage of power supply leads to under-utilisation of plant capacity. Therefore, the concern will have to first prepare a budget for plant utilisation and later the other budgets say sales will be prepared.

Master Budget. A master budget is the summary budget for the entire enterprise and embodies the summarised figures for various activities. This is also known as summary budget or finalised profit plan. This budget includes the budgeted position of the profit and loss as well as balance sheet. Master budget is prepared by the committee and becomes a target for the company.

Classification of Budgets

On the basis of time	*On the basis of Flexibility*	*On the basis of Functions*
1. Long Term	1. Fixed	1. Sales
2. Short Term	2. Flexible	2. Production
3. Current	3. Materials	4. Labour
		3. Materials
		5. Overheads
		6. Plant Utilization
		7. Cash
		8. Capital expenditure.

There are various types of budgets. Some of the important budgets are discussed below :

A. CLASSIFICATION ACCORDING TO TIME

1. Long Term Budgets

The budgets are prepared to depict long term planning of the business. The period of long term budgets varies between five to ten years. Long term budgets are prepared for some sectors of the concern such as capital expenditure, research and development, long term finances etc. The long term planning is done by the top level management.

2. Short term Budgets

These budgets are generally for one or two years and are in the form of monetary terms. The consumer goods industries, like, sugar, cotton, textiles etc. use short term budgets.

3. Current Budgets

The period of current budgets is generally of months and weeks. The budgets are related to the current activities of the business. Current budget is a budget which is established for use over a short period of time and is related to current conditions.

B. CLASSIFICATION ACCORDING TO FLEXIBILITY

Fixed and Flexible Budgets

Fixed Budget. This is a budget which is designed to remain unchanged irrespective of the level of activity actually attained. This is prepared for definite production and capacity level. It is not adjusted according to activity level attained. The fixed budgets are not effective tools of cost control. These types of budgets have limited use.

A fixed budget has been defined by ICMA, England as "A budget which is designed to remain unchanged irrespective of the level of activity actually attained."

However, in practical life, conditions do not remain static. The main reason is that actual output is often different from the budgeted output. In such a case the budget cannot be used for the purpose of cost control. There may be internal or external factors which force the level of activity to change.

Flexible Budget. This is a dynamic budget. It is a budget which is designed to change in accordance with the level of activity. Actual output may differ from the budgeted output; and as such, it is necessary to modify the budget on the basis of changed output. The budget is prepared in such a way as to present the budgeted cost for different levels of activity, it is more realistic and practical, because changes expected at different levels of activity are given due consideration. It is also called variable budget or sliding scale budget. The expenses are divided into three categories—fixed, variable and semi-variable. It is an important tool of cost control, as it facilitates comparison of actual results with the budgeted figures.

ICWA, UK defines flexible budget as "a budget which, by recognising the difference between fixed, semi-fixed and variable costs, is designed to change in relation to the level of activity." Ascertainment of costs at various levels of activity becomes possible. Price fixation, sending quotations and tenders and finding out profit at changed capacities are facilitated.

Preparation of Flexible Budget

A budget prepared in a manner so as to give the budgeted cost for any level of activity is known as flexible budget. A flexible budget is the opposite of static budget. It is prepared for a range of activity instead of a single level. Fixed costs are related mostly to the period of time and are not concerned with the level of production or volume of sales. Variable costs vary directly and proportionately with the volume of activity. At zero level activity, the variable costs will not be in existence. The semi-variable costs occupy an "in-between" position between the fixed and variable costs. A part of these costs is variable and the rest is fixed. They are fixed to a certain level of activity and then rise with increase in the level of activity but not in the same proportion as the activity increases. As a matter of fact budget for each department can be prepared on the lines of flexible budget by classifying the costs into 'fixed' and 'variable'. In order to appropriately fix up the costs for different volumes, the degree of variability for each item cost at various levels of output could be evolved on the basis of past experience. This requires a close study of the individual items of expenditure, their nature and variability.

1. Decide the range of activity to develop a flexible budget.
2. Determine the cost behaviour–fixed, variable and semi-variable to each element of cost.
3. Select the activity level (generally in terms of output).
4. Prepare the budget at each activity level.

Illustration 1. The budgeted output of a factory specialising in the production of single product at the optimum capacity of 6,400 units per annum amounts to Rs. 1,76,048 as detailed below :

	Rs.	*Rs.*
Fixed cost		20,688
Variable costs :		
Power	1,440	
Repair etc.	1,700	
Miscellaneous	540	
Direct materials	49,280	
Direct labour	1,02,400	1,55,360
		1,76,048

Having regard to possible impact on sales turnover by market trends, the company decides to have a flexible budget with a production of 3,200 and 4,800 units (the actual quantity proposed to be produced being left to a later date before commencement of budget period). Prepare a flexible budget for production levels at 50% and 75%. Assuming the sale per unit is maintained at Rs. 40 as at present, indicate the effect on net profit.

Administration, selling and distribution expenses continue at Rs. 3,600.

(*B.Com., Madurai, C.A.*)

Solution :

Flexible Budget

	3200 units *50%*	*4800 units* *75%*	*6400 units* *100%*
Fixed Expenses	20,688	20,688	20,688
Variable costs :			
Direct materials (Rs. 7.70)	24,640	36,960	49,280
Direct labour (Rs. 16.00)	51,200	76,800	1.02,400
Power (0.225)	720	1,080	1,440
Repairs : (0.266)	850*	1275	1700
Miscellaneous (0.084)	270**	405	540
Total Cost	98,368	1,37,208	1,76,048
Selling & Distribution	3,600	3,600	3,600
Cost of Sales	1,01,968	1,40,808	1,79,648
Sales (Rs. 40.00)	1,28,000	1,92,000	2,56,000
Profit	26,032	51,192	76,352

$\frac{*1700}{6400} \times 3200 = 850 \quad \frac{**540}{6400} \times 3200 = 270$

Control Ratios

Ratios are used to determine the production efficiency and the costs. It tells the ratio of actual level of activity attained, degree of efficiency attained and the actual capacity utilised during a budgeted period. Three important ratios are commonly used by the management to find out whether the deviations of actuals from budgeted results are favourable or otherwise.

These ratios are expressed in terms of percentages. They are :

(*a*) **Activity Ratios :** It is a measure of the level of activity attained over a period. This ratio expresses relationship between standard hours for actual production and budgeted hours. The formula is :

$$\text{Activity Ratio} = \frac{\text{Standard hours for actual output}}{\text{Budgeted Standard hours}} \times 100$$

(*b*) **Capacity Ratio :** This ratio indicates whether and to what extent budgeted hours of activity are actually utilised. The object is to show whether or not the available hours are being fully utilised.

The formula is :

$$\text{Capacity Ratio} = \frac{\text{Actual Hours Worked}}{\text{Budgeted Hours}} \times 100$$

(*c*) **Efficiency Ratio or Productivity Ratio :** The ratio is an important measure of the level of efficiency attained by the productive processes. This ratio indicates the efficiency attained in producing a stated output. The formula is :

$$\text{Efficiency Ratio} = \frac{\text{Standard Hours for Actual Production}}{\text{Actual Hours worked}} \times 100$$

The results of the above ratios are interpreted as below :

Result	*Interpretation*
100%	No deviation
Above 100%	Favourable Deviation
Below 100%	Unfavourable Deviation

Calendar Ratio

This ratio indicates if the actual working days have been equal to, more than or less than the budgeted number of days in the period under study. The formula is :

$$\text{Calender Ratio} = \frac{\text{Actual working Days in the Period}}{\text{Working Days on the basis of budget during the period}} \times 100$$

Illustration 2. A factory manufactures two types of products X and Y. Product X takes 5 hours to make and Y requires 10 hours. In a month of 25 effective days of 8 hours a day, 1,000 units of X and 600 units of Y were produced. The company employs 50 workers in the production department. The budgeted hours are 1,02,000 for the year. Calculate Capacity ratio, Activity ratio and Efficiency ratio.

Solution :

$$\text{Budgeted hours for the month} = \frac{1,02,000}{12} = 8,500 \text{ hours}$$

$$\text{Actual hours worked : } 50 \text{ workers} \times 25 \text{ days} \times 8 \text{ Hours} = 10,000 \text{ hours}$$

Standard hours for actual production :

Product X : 1,000 × 5 =	5,000
Product Y : 600 × 10 =	6,000
	11,000

(*a*) Capacity Ratio $= \dfrac{\text{Actual Hours Worked}}{\text{Budgeted Hours}} \times 100$

$= \dfrac{10{,}000}{8{,}500} \times 100 = \mathbf{117.65\%}$

(*b*) Activity Ratio $= \dfrac{\text{Standard Hours for Actual Output}}{\text{Budgeted Hours}} \times 100$

$= \dfrac{11{,}000}{8{,}500} \times 100 = \mathbf{129.4\%}$

(*c*) Efficiency Ratio $= \dfrac{\text{Standard Hours for Actual Output}}{\text{Actual Hours Worked}} \times 100$

$= \dfrac{11{,}000}{10{,}000} \times 100 = \mathbf{110\%}$

Alternatively :

Activity Ratio = Capacity Ratio × Efficiency Ratio
= 1.1765 × 1.1 = 1.29415
= 1.294 is multiplied by 100, we get 129.4%

Illustration 3. Narang Ltd. produces two commodities, Good and Better, in one of its department. Each unit takes 5 hours and 10 hours as production time respectively. 1,000 units of Good and 600 units of Better were produced during March. Actual man-hours spent in this production were 10,000. Yearly budgeted hours are 96,000. Compute the various control ratios. (*C.S.*)

Solution :

Yearly Budgeted Hours = 96,000

Monthly Budgeted Hours $= \dfrac{96{,}000}{12} = 8{,}000$ Hours

Standard Hour for Actual Output
= 1,000 × 5 + 600 × 10 = 11,000 Hours

Actual Hours worked = 10,000 Hours

(*a*) Efficiency Ratio $= \dfrac{11{,}000}{10{,}000} \times 100 = 110\%$

(*b*) Activity Ratio $= \dfrac{11{,}000}{8{,}000} \times 100 = 137.5\%$

(c) Capacity Ratio $= \dfrac{10{,}000}{8{,}000} \times 100 = 125\%$

Alternatively :

Activity Ratio = Capacity Ratio × Efficiency Ratio
= 1.25 × 1.10
= 1.375
1.375 is multiplied by100, we get,
= **137.5%**

Illustration 4. Prepare a flexible budget for overheads on the basis of the following data. Ascertain the overhead rates at 50%, 60% and 70% capacity.

	At 60% capacity
	Rs.
Variable overheads :	
Indirect material	6,000
Indirect labour	18,000
Semi-variable overheads :	
Electricity (40% fixed 60% variable)	30,000
Repairs (80% fixed 20% variable)	3,000
Fixed overheads :	
Depreciation	16,500
Insurance	4,500
Salaries	15,000
Total Overheads	93,000
Estimated direct labour hours	1,86,000

(*B. Com., Madurai*)

Solution :

Flexible Budget and Overhead Rates

Items	*50% Capacity*	*60% Capacity*	*70% Capacity*
Variable overheads :	Rs.	Rs.	Rs.
Indirect material	5,000	6,000	7,000
Indirect labour	15,000	18,000	21,000
Semi-variable overheads :			
Electricity	(1)27,000	30,000	(1)33,000
Repairs and maintenance	(2)2,900	3,000	(2)3,100
Fixed overheads :			
Depreciation	16,500	16,500	16,500
Insurance	4,500	4,500	4,500
Salaries	15,000	15,000	15,000
Total overheads	85,900	93,000	1,00,100
Estimated direct labour hours	1,55,000	1,86,000	2,17,000
Overhead rate	Re. 0.55	Rs. 0.50	Re. 0.46

Notes. 1. Electricity. *Rs. 30,000 is the cost of electricity at 60% capacity, of which 40% is fixed overhead; i.e., Rs. 12,000 and variable is Rs. 18,000.*

For 60% capacity variable overheads; = Rs. 18,000

For 50% capacity variable overhead $= \left(\frac{18,000}{60} \times 50\right) = 15,000$

Therefore electricity cost at 50% capacity

= Rs. 12,000 + 15,000 = Rs. 27,000

For 70% capacity, variable overhead $= \frac{18,000}{60} \times 70 = Rs.\,21,000$

Therefore electricity cost at 70% = Rs. 12,000 + Rs. 21,000 + Rs. 33,000

2. Repairs and Maintenance. *Rs. 3,000 is the cost of repairs and maintenance at 60% capacity, of which 80% is fixed overhead, i.e. Rs. 2,400 and variable is Rs. 600.*

For 60% capacity variable overhead = *Rs. 600*

For 50% capacity variable overhead $= \frac{600}{60} \times 50 = \text{Rs.}500$

Therefore the total cost of repairs and maintenance at 50%

= Rs. 2,400 + Rs. 500 = Rs. 2,900

For 70% capacity, the variable overhead $= \frac{600}{60} \times 70 = \text{Rs.}\,700$

Therefore the total cost of repairs and maintenance

= Rs. 2,400 + Rs. 700 = **Rs. 3,100**

Illustration 5. A company working at 50% capacity manufactures 10,000 units of a product. At 50% capacity the product cost is Rs. 180 and sale price is Rs. 200. The break up of the cost is as below :

	Cost per unit
Material	Rs. 100
Wages	30
Factory	30 (40% fixed)
Administration overheads	20 (50%fixed)

At 60% working raw material cost goes up by 2% and sales price falls by 2%. At 80% working the raw material cost increases by 5% and sale price decreases by same percentage *i.e.*, 5%.

Prepare a statement to show profitability at 60% and 80% capacity. (*B. Com., Madurai*)

Solution :

Flexible Budget

Particulars Production (Units)	*at 50%* 10,000		*at 60%* 12,000		*at 80%* 16,000	
	Per unit	*Total*	*Per unit*	*Total*	*Per unit*	*Total*
Sales	200	20,00,000	196	23,52,000	190	30,40,000
Materials	100	10,00,000	102	12,24,000	105	16,80,000
Wages	30	3,00,000	30	3,60,000	30	4,80,000
Factory overhead:						
Variable (60%)	18	1,80,000	18	2,16,000	18	2,88,000
Fixed (40%)	12	1,20,000	10	1,20,000	7.50	1,20,000
Administration overhead :						
Variable (50%)	10	1,00,000	10	1,20,000	10	1,60,000
Fixed (50%)	10	1,00,000	8.33	1,00,000	6.25	1,00,000
Total	180	18,00,000	178.33	21,40,000	176.75	28,28,000
Profit	20	2,00,000	17.67	2,12,000	13.25	2,12,000

It is not advisable to increase the production to 80% capacity because the profits are the same at 60% and 80% capacities.

Illustration 6. For the production of 10,000 electric automatic irons; the following are the budgeted expenses :

	Per unit *Rs.*
Direct material	60
Direct labour	30
Variable overhead	25
Fixed overhead (Rs. 1,50,000)	15
Variable expenses (direct)	5

Selling expenses (10%) fixed	15
Administration expenses (Rs. 50,000 rigid for all levels of production)	5
Distribution expenses (20%) fixed	5
The total cost of sale per unit	160

Prepare a budget for the production of 6,000 and 7,000 and 8,000 irons, showing distinctly the marginal cost and the total cost. (*B. Com., Calicut*)

Solution :

Flexible Budget

Period :

	Capacity levels					
	6,000 units		*7,000 units*		*8,000 units*	
	Per unit	*Total*	*Per unit*	*Total*	*Per unit* unit	*Total*
	Rs.	*Rs.*	*Rs.*	*Rs.*	*Rs.*	*Rs.*
Expenses :						
Direct materials	60.00	3,60,000	60.00	4,20,000	60.00	4,80,000
Direct labour	30.00	1,80,000	30.00	2,10,000	30.00	2,40,000
Direct expenses	5.00	30,000	5.00	35,000	5.00	40,000
Variable overheads :						
Production	25.00	1,50,000	25.00	1,75,000	25.00	2,00,000
Selling	13.50	81,000	13.50	94,500	13.50	1,08,000
Distribution	4.00	24,000	4.00	28,000	4.00	32,000
Marginal Cost	137.50	8,25,000	137.50	9,62,500	137.50	11,00,000
Fixed overheads :						
Production	25.00	1,50,000	21.43	1,50,000	18.75	1,50,000
Administration	8.34	50,000	7.14	50,000	6.25	50,000
Selling	2.50	15,000	2.14	15,000	1.88	15,000
Distribution	1.66	10,000	1.43	100,000	1.25	10,000
Fixed Cost	37.50	2,25,000	32.14	2,25,000	28.13	2,25,000
Total Cost	175.00	10,50,000	169.64	11,87,500	165.63	13,25,000

Note: Selling expense is Rs. 15 for one unit and Rs. 1,50,000 for 10,000 units, of which 90% is variable; *i.e.* Rs. 1,35,000 and Rs. 15,000 (10%) are fixed. Therefore, the variable selling expense for one unit is Rs. 13.50 (90% of Rs. 15) and Rs. 15,000 is fixed for all level of activity. Hence, the fixed expenses of Rs. 15,000 at 6,000 unit level is Rs. 2.50 (15,000/6,000) at 7,000 unit level it is Rs. 2.14 (15,000/7,000) and at 8,000 unit level it is Rs. 1.88 (15,000 ÷ 8,000). Similarly distribution expenses are Rs. 5 per unit and Rs. 50,000 for 10,000 units, of which 20,000 is fixed *i.e.,* Rs. 10,000 and Rs. 40,000 are variable.

Therefore,

$$\text{at 6,000 units the fixed overhead} = \frac{10{,}000}{6{,}000} = 1.66$$

$$\text{at 7,000 units the fixed overhead} = \frac{10{,}000}{7{,}000} = 1.43$$

$$\text{at 8,000 units the fixed overhead} = \frac{10{,}000}{8{,}000} = 1.25$$

Illustration 7. S.M. Ltd. produces two products and budget for 60% level of activity for the year gives the following information.

Particulars	*Product A*	*Product B*
	Rs.	*Rs.*
Raw material cost per unit	7.50	3.50
Direct labour cost per unit	4.00	3.00
Variable overheads per unit	2.00	1.50
Fixed overheads per unit	6.00	4.50
Selling price per unit	20.00	15.00
Production and sales	4,000 units	6,000 units

The Managing Director, not being satisfied with the projected results as stated above, referred the Budget to the Marketing Director for improvement of the performance. The Marketing Director proposed that the sales quantities of products A and B could each be increased by 50% provided the selling price were reduced by 5% in case of product A and 10% in the case of product B. The price reduction should be made applicable to the entire quantity of sales of each of the products.

1. Present the overall profitability under the original budget and the revised budget after taking the increased sales into consideration.

2. Find out overall Break-even sales under original budget and the revised budget. (*C.A. Inter*)

Solution :

Statement of Overall Profitability

Particulars	*Original*			*Revised*		
	A	*B*	*Total*	*A*	*B*	*Total*
Production & Sales (units)	4,000	6,000		6,000	9,000	
Selling price (unit)	20	15		19	13.50	
Sales amount (*a*)	80,000	90,000	1,70,000	1,14,000	1,12,500	2,35,500
Raw Material cost	30,000	21,000	51,000	45,000	31,500	76,500
Direct labour cost	16,000	18,000	34,000	24,000	27,000	51,000
Variable overheads	8,000	9,000	17,000	12,000	13,500	25,500
(Variable) Total : (*b*)	54,000	48,000	1,02,000	81,000	72,000	1,53,000
Contribution : (*a*) – (*b*)	26,000	42,000	68,000	33,000	49,500	82,500
Less: Fixed Cost	24,000	27,000	51,000	24,000	27,000	51,000
	(It is assumed that there is no change in fixed cost)					
Profit	2,000	15,000	17,000	9,000	22,500	31,500

$$\text{P/V Ratio} = \frac{68,000}{1,70,000} \times 100 = 40\% \; ; \quad \frac{82,500}{2,35,500} \times 100 = 35.03\%$$

$$\text{BEP Sales} = \frac{\text{F}}{\text{P/VRatio}} = \frac{51,000}{40\%} = 1,27,500 \; ; \quad \frac{51,000}{35.03\%} = 1,45,590$$

Illustration 8. A factory engaged in manufacturing plastic buckets is working at 40% capacity and produces 10,000 buckets per month.

The present cost break up for one bucket is as under :

Material Rs. 10

Labour Rs. 3

Overheads Rs. 5 (60% fixed)

The selling price is Rs. 20 per bucket. If it is desired to work the factory at 50% capacity the selling price falls by 3%. At 90% capacity the selling price falls by 5% accompanied by a similar fall in the price of material.

You are required to prepare a statement showing the profit at 50% and 90% capacities and also calculate the break-even points at this capacity production. (*B. Com., Madras, Madurai*)

Solution :

Flexible Budget

Particulars	Capacity		
	40%	50%	90%
Production and sales units	10,000	12,500	22,500
Sales price per unit	20	19.40	19.00
Sales amount	2,00,000	2,42,500	4,27,500
Marginal Cost :			
Material : Rs. 10 per unit (at 90%—(Rs. 9.50 per unit)	1,00,000	1,25,000	2,13,750
Labour	30,000	37,500	67,500
Variable overhead	20,000	25,000	45,000
Total	1,50,000	1,87,500	3,26,250
Contribution	50,000	55,000	1,01,250
Less: Fixed	30,000	30,000	30,000
Profit	20,000	25,000	71,250
Contribution : Per unit	5	4.40	4.50
BEP (units)	30,000 ÷ 5 = 6,000	30,000 ÷ 4.40 = 6,818	30,000 ÷ 4.50 = 6,667

C. CLASSIFICATION ACCORDING TO FUNCTION

A functional budget is a budget which relates to any of the functions of an organisation. The following are the functional budgets commonly used.

1. Sales Budget. Generally sales factor becomes a key-factor in the majority of cases, and therefore, it is the starting point. This is the most important budget, as it is usually the most difficult to forecast. It is prepared by the sales manager. In the preparation, the sales manager should consider the following points :

(*a*) Analysis of the sales of the previous year.

(*b*) Salesman's assessment

(*c*) General trade conditions

(*d*) Availability of raw materials

(*e*) Availability of funds

(*f*) Plant capacity

(*g*) Seasonal fluctuations

(*h*) Restrictions imposed by the government

(*i*) Competition and consumer's preference

(*j*) Efficiency of advertising

Sales budget must show in terms of finished products, quantities and price; and it is prepared according to products, territories, periods, types of customer or salesman etc.

Illustration 9. A company produces and sells three items : (*a*) Snow Cream, (*b*) Talcum Powder and (*c*) Cold Cream. The Company has divided its market into two Zones : Zone A and Zone B. The actual figures for the previous year sales were as under :

	Zone A		Zone B	
	Units	Unit price Rs.	Units	Unit price Rs.
(*a*) Snow Cream	4,00,000	12.00	2,50,000	12.00
(*b*) Talcum Powder	2,50,000	15.00	3,50,000	15.00
(*c*) Cold Cream	3,00,000	16.00	3,00,000	16.00

For the Current year *i.e.* 2010, it is estimated that sale of snow cream will go up by 10% in Zone B and of cold cream by 25,000 units in Zone A. The company plans to introduce a publicity film for talcum powder in the T.V. network. The budgeted figures for talcum powder are to be increased by 20% in both the Zones.

The prices of the two creams are to be maintained but for talcum powder, a bonus cut of Re. 1 will be announced.

You are required to prepare quantitative-cum financial budget for sales in the current year *i.e.* 2010.

Solution :

SALES BUDGET (2010)

Products	*Snow Cream*		*Talcum powder*		*Cold Cream*		*Total*
Sales	*Rs.* 12		Rs. 14 (Rs.15 – 1)		Rs. 16		
price	*Units*	*Amount*	*Units*	*Amount*	*Units*	*Amount*	*Amount*
Zone A	4,00,000	48,00,000	3,00,000	42,00,000	3,25,000	52,00,000	1,42,00,000
Zone B	2,75,000	33,00,000	4,20,000	58,80,000	3,00,000	48,00,000	1,39,80,000
Total	6,75,000	81,00,000	7,20,000	1,00,80,000	6,25,000	1,00,00,000	2,81,80,000

2. Production Budget : It is a budget prepared by the production manager, showing the forecast of output. The objective is to determine the quantity of production for a budgeted period. It is in quantity of units to be produced during the budget period. It is based on the sales budget. It is in two parts — one part contains the volume of production and the other part shows the cost of production. Apart from the sales budget, optimum utilisation of plant, availability of raw materials, labour etc., are to be considered. It must avoid overwork in rush seasons. It must maintain a minimum stock of finished goods.

Cost of Production Budget : is divided into material cost budget, labour cost budget and overhead cost budget, because cost of production includes materials, labour and overheads. Therefore separate budgets are required for each item.

3. Material Budget : To carry out the production satisfactorily regular supply of materials during the budget period is ensured by preparing a budget. In this, the decision regarding the quantity of materials as shown at different times during that period is followed. Only direct materials are taken into account; indirect materials are not taken into account and they are considered under overheads. The material budget helps proper planning of purchases. It shows the estimated quantities as well as the cost of raw materials, required for production as per production budget.

4. Labour Budget : It is a part of the production budget. The budget is prepared by the personnel department and it shows an estimate of the requirements of labour to meet the production target, on the basis of previous records and budgeted production. This budget gives detailed information relating to the number of workers, rates of wages and cost of labour hours to be employed.

5. Works Overhead Budget : It sets out the estimated costs of indirect materials, indirect labour and indirect factory expenses, during the budget period in order to achieve the target. This is classified into fixed, variable and semi-variable. This facilitates preparation of budgets and further department-wise and sub-division to have effective control. The preparation of budget is based on the previous year's records for fixed overheads; and budget targets are verified for variable expenses, which are bound to change with the change of output.

Illustration 10. From the following particulars, prepare a Production Budget of a Company for the year ended June 30, 2010.

Product	*Sales (Units)* (as per sales Budgets)	*Estimated Stock (units)* 1 July 2009	30 June 2010
A	1,50,000	14,000	15,000
B	1,00,000	5,000	14,500
C	70,000	8,000	8,000

Solution :

PRODUCTION STATEMENT

PERIOD
YEAR ENDING ON
30TH JUNE 2010

	Product A Units	*Product B Units*	*Product C Units*
Sales as per Sales Budget	1,50,000	1,00,000	70,000
Add : Estimated Stock on 30.6.2010	15,000	14,500	8,000
	1,65,000	1,14,500	78,000
Less : Estimated Stock on 1.7.2009	14,000	5,000	8,000
BUDGETED PRODUCTION	1,51,000	1,09,500	70,000

Illustration 11. Draw a material procurement budget (quantitative) from the following information :

Estimated sales of a product 40,000 units. Each unit of the product requires 3 units of material A and 4 units of material B.

Estimated opening balances at the commencement of the next year :

	Units
Finished Products	5,000
Material A	12,000
Material B	20,000
Material on order :	
Material A	7,000
Material B	11,000

The desirable closing balances at the end of the next year :

Finished Product	7,000
Material A	15,000
Material B	25,000
Material on order	
Material A	8,000
Material B	10,000

(*B. Com. Madurai*)

Solution :

Total production should be worked out first.

Opening balance + Productions = Sales + Closing balance

5,000 + Production = 40,000 + 7,000

Thus, production = **42,000 units**

Material required : Material A = 42,000 × 3 = 1,26000 units

Material B = 42,000 × 4 = 1,68,000 units

MATERIAL PROCUREMENT BUDGET (Quantitative)

	A	B	*Material A Units*	*Material B Units*
Material required			1,26,000	1,68,000
Add : Closing stock :	15,000	25,000		
under order	8,000	10,000	23,000	35,000
			1,49,000	2,03,000
Less : Opening stock :	12,000	20,000		
Material on order	7,000	11,000	19,000	31,000
Units to be procured :			1,30,000	1,72,000

Illustration 12. From the following figures prepare raw materials purchase budget for January:

Materials (Units)

	A	B	C	D	E	F
Estimated Stock Ist January	16,000	6,000	24,000	2,000	14,000	28,000
Estimated stock 31st January	20,000	8,000	28,000	4,000	16,000	32,000
Estimated Consumption	1,20,000	44,000	1,32,000	36,000	88,000	1,72,000
Standard price per unit	25 paise	5 paise	15 paise	10 paise	20 paise	30 paise

(*B.Com. M.S.*)

Solution

Raw Materials purchase budget for January

	A	B	C	D	E	F
Estimated Consumption (Units)	1,20,000	44,000	1,32,000	36,000	88,000	1,72,000
Add: Estimated stock on 31st January (Units)	20,000	8,000	28,000	4,000	16,000	32,000
	1,40,000	52,000	1,60,000	40,000	1,04,000	2,04,000
Less: Estimated stock on Jan.1 (Units)	16,000	6,000	24,000	2,000	14,000	28,000
Estimated purchase	1,24,000	46,000	1,36,000	38,000	90,000	1,76,000
Rate per unit	0.25	0.05	0.15	0.10	0.20	0.30
Estimated price (Rs.)	31,000	2,300	20,400	3,800	18,000	52,800

Illustration 13. The Sales Director of a Manufacturing Company reports that next year he expects to sell 50,000 units of a particular product :

The Production Manager consults the store-keeper and casts his figures as follows :

Two kinds of raw materials A and B are required for manufacturing the products.

Each unit of the product requires 2 units of A and 3 units of B.

The estimated opening balances at the commencement of the next year are :

Finished Products :	10,000 Units
Materials A	12,000 Units
Materials B	15,000 Units

The desirable closing balances at the end of the next year are :

Finished Products :	14,000 Units
Materials A	13,000 Units
Materials B	16,000 Units

Draw up a quantitative chart showing materials purchase budget for the next year.

Solution :

Units to be produced = Sales + Desired Closing Stock – Opening Stock

= 50,000 + 14,000 – 10,000 = 54,000 Units

MATERIALS PROCUREMENT BUDGET (Quantity)

	Finished Product	Materials	
	Units	*A* Units	*B* Units
Budgeted Production	54,000	1,08,000	1,62,000
Estimated Opening Balance	10,000	(–) 12,000	(–) 15,000
	64,000	96,000	1,47,000
Estimated closing Balances	(–) 14,000	(+) 13,000	(+) 16,000
Estimated product for Sales	50,000		
Estimated materials to be Purchased		1,09,000	1,63,000

Illustration 14. The budget manager of Cosmetics Limited is preparing a budget for the accounting year starting from 1st July 2010.

As part of the budget operations, some items of factory overhead costs have been estimated by him under specified conditions of volume as follows:

Volume of Production (Units)	1,20,000	1,50,000
	Rs.	Rs.
Expenses:		
Indirect materials	2,64,000	3,30,000
Indirect labour	1,50,000	1,87,500
Maintenance	84,000	2,02,000
Supervision	1,98,000	2,34,000
Engineering Service	94,000	94,000

Calculate the cost of factory overhead items given above at 1,40,000 units of production.

(*B.Com. Delhi*)

Solution :

Factory overheads budget

	Production : 1,40,000
	Rs.
Indirect materials (Variable @ Rs. 2.20) (*a*)	3,08,000
Indirect Labour (Variable @ 1.25 per unit (*b*)	1,75,000

Maintenance : Fixed (*c*)	12,000
Variable @ Rs. 0.60 per unit	84,000
Supervision : Fixed (*d*)	54,000
Variable @ Rs. 1.20 per unit	1,68,000
Engineering services : Fixed (*e*)	94,000
TOTAL FACTORY OVERHEADS :	8,95,000

Workings :

(*a*) Variable Cost per unit $= \dfrac{\text{Change in Expense}}{\text{Change in Output}}$

$$= \frac{\text{Rs. } 66{,}000}{30{,}000} = \textbf{Rs. 2.20}$$

There is no fixed Expense in indirect materials.

Proof : for 1,20,000 units, the indirect materials

$= 120,\ 000 \times \text{Rs. } 2.20 = \text{Rs. } 2{,}64{,}000 = \text{Rs. } 2{,}64{,}000$

(*b*) Applying the above formula:

$$\frac{\text{Rs. } 37{,}5000}{30{,}000 \text{ units}} = \text{Rs. } 1.25$$

There is no fixed expense in indirect labour

Proof : 1,20,000 units @ Rs. 1.25 = 4,50,000

(*c*) $\dfrac{\text{Rs. } 18{,}000}{30{,}000 \text{ units}} = \textbf{Rs.0.60}$

Maintenance for 1,20,000 units @ Rs. 0.60 = Rs. 72,000

Therefore, fixed expense = Rs. 84,000 – 72,000 = Rs. 12,000

(*d*) $\dfrac{\text{Rs. } 36{,}000}{30{,}000 \text{ units}} = \textbf{Rs.1.20}$

Fixed Supervision Cost = 1,98000 – (1,20,000 × Rs. 1.20)

= Rs. 1,98,000 – Rs. 1,44,000

= **Rs. 54, 000**

(e) only fixed expense

6. (*a*)Administration Overheads Budget. This budget covers the expenditure of administrative office and management salaries. It is prepared with the help of past experiences and expected changes in future. The administration cost of each budget centre is drawn separately and incorporated in administrative cost budget.

(*b*) Selling and Distribution Overhead Budget. This budget relates to selling and distribution of products for the budget period and is based on sales budget. It is generally prepared territory-wise by the sales manager of each territory. The costs are divided into fixed, variable and semi-variable; and estimate is taken on the basis of past records.

7. Capital Expenditure Budget. This budget shows the estimated expenditure on fixed assets — land, building, plant, machinery etc. It is a long-term budget. The capital expenditure is necessitated on account of replacement of old machines, increased demand of products, expansion of industry, adoption of new technological progresses etc.

Illustration 15. The following information at 50% capacity is given. Prepare a flexible budget and forecast the profit or loss at 60%, 70% and 90% capacity.

	Expenses at 50% capacity
Fixed Expenses:	Rs.
Salaries	50,000
Rent and Taxes	40,000
Depreciation	60,000
Administrative Expenses	70,000
Variable Expenses:	
Materials	2,00,000
Labour	2,50,000
Others	40,000
Semi-variable:	
Repairs	1,00,000
Indirect Labour	1,50,000
Others	90,000

It is estimated that fixed expenses will remain constant at all capacities. Semi-variable expenses will not change between 45% and 60% capacity, will rise by 10% between 60% and 75% capacity, a further increase of 5% when capacity crosses 75%.

Estimated sales at various levels of capacity are:

Capacity	*Sales (Rs.)*
60%	11,00,000
70%	13,00,000
90%	15,00,000

(*M.Com. Madurai*)

Solution:

FLEXIBLE BUDGET

Particulars	*Capacities*			
	50% *Rs.*	60% *Rs.*	70% *Rs.*	90% *Rs.*
Fixed Expenses:				
Salaries	50,000	50,000	50,000	50,000
Rent and Taxes	40,000	40,000	40,000	40,000
Depreciation	60,000	60,000	60,000	60,000
Administrative Expenses	70,000	70,000	70,000	70,000
Variable Expenses:				
Materials	2,00,000	2,40,000	2,80,000	3,60,000
Labour	2,50,000	3,00,000	3,50,000	4,50,000
Others	40,000	48,000	56,000	72,000
Semi-variable Expenses:				
Repairs	1,00,000	1,00,000	1,10,000	1,15,000
Indirect Labour	1,50,000	1,50,000	1,65,000	1,72,500
Others	90,000	90,000	99,000	1,03,500
Total Cost	10,50,000	11,48,000	12,80,000	14,93,000
Profit		—	20,000	7,000
(Or) Loss		48,000	—	—
Estimated Sales		11,00,000	13,00,000	15,00,000

8. **Cash Budget.** This budget represents the amount of cash receipts and payments, and a balance during the budgeted period. it is prepared after all the functional budgets are prepared by the chief accountant either monthly or weekly giving the following hints (1) It ensures sufficient cash for business requirements. (2) It proposes arrangements to be made overdraft to meet any shortage of cash. (3) It reveals the surplus amount, and the effect of the seasonal fluctuations on cash position. The objective of cash budget is the proper co-ordination of total working capital, sale, investment and credit.

Illustration 16. From the following forecasts of income and expenditure prepare a cash budget for the three months commencing 1st June, when the bank balance was Rs. 1,00,000.

	Sales	*Purchases*	*Wages*	*Factory Expenses*	*Admin. and Selling expenses*
	Rs.	*Rs.*	*Rs.*	*Rs.*	*Rs.*
April	80,000	41,000	5,600	3,900	10,000
May	76,500	40,500	5,400	4,200	14,000
June	78,500	38,500	5,400	5,100	15,000
July	90,000	37,000	4,800	5,100	17,000
August	95,000	35,000	4,700	6,000	13,000

A sales commission of 5 per cent on sales, due two months after sales, is payable in addition to selling expenses. Plant valued at Rs. 65,000 will be purchased and paid for in August, and the dividend for the last financial year of Rs. 15,000 will be paid in July. There is a two month credit period allowed to customers and received from suppliers. *(I.C.W.A. Final)*

Solution :

Cash Budget
For three months to 31st August

	June *Rs.*	*July* *Rs.*	*August* *Rs.*
Receipts :			
Opening balance	1,00,000	1,11,400	1,03,075
Sundry debtors	80,000	76,500	78,500
	1,80,000	1,87,900	1,81,575
Payments:			
Sundry creditors	41,000	40,500	38,500
Wages	5,400	5,400	4,800
Factory expenses	4,200	5,100	5,100
Adm. & selling expenses	14,000	15,000	17,000
Sales commission	4,000	3,825	3,925
Purchase of plant	—	—	65,000
Payment of dividend	—	15,000	—
	68,600	84,825	1,34,325
Closing balance	1,11,400	1,03,075	47,250

Note : It is assumed that wages, factory expenses and administration and selling expenses are payable in the following month.

Illustration 17. A department of Company X attains sales of Rs. 6,00,000 at 80% of its normal capacity and its expenses are given below :

Administration Costs :

Office Salaries	Rs. 90,000
General Expenses	2% of sales

Depreciation	Rs. 7,500
Rates and Taxes	Rs. 8,750
Selling Costs :	
Salaries	8% of sales
Travelling Expenses	2% of sales
Sales office	1% of sales
General Expenses	1% of sales
Distribution Costs :	
Wages	Rs. 15,000
Rent	1 % of sales
Other Expenses	4 % of sales

Draw up flexible administration, selling and distribution costs budget, operating at 90%, 100% and 110% of normal capacity. *(CA Inter)*

Solution :

Flexible administration, selling and distribution costs budget

	80% Rs.	90% Rs.	100% Rs.	110% Rs.
Sales	6,00,000	6,75,000	7,50,000	8,25,000
Administration Costs :				
Office Salaries	90,000	90,000	90,000	90,000
General Expenses (2% of sales)	12,000	13,500	15,000	16,500
Depreciation	7,500	7,500	7,500	7,500
Rates and Taxes	8,750	8,750	8,750	8,750
Total (*a*)	1,18,250	1,19,750	1,21,250	1,22,750
Selling Costs :				
Salaries (8% of sales)	48,000	54,000	60,000	66,000
Travelling expenses (2% of sales)	12,000	13,500	15,000	16,500
Sales office (1% of sales)	6,000	6,750	7,500	8,250
General Expenses (1% of sales)	6,000	6,750	7,500	8,250
Total (*b*)	72,000	81,000	90,000	99,000
Distribution Costs :				
Wages	15,000	15,000	15,000	15,000
Rent (1% of sales)	6,000	6,750	7,500	8,250
Other Expenses 4%	24,000	27,000	30,000	33,000
Total (*c*)	45,000	28,750	52,500	56,250
Grand total (a + b + c)	2,35,250	2,49,500	2,63,750	2,78,000

Illustration 18. A company expects to have Rs. 37,500 cash in hand on 1st April, and requires you to prepare an estimate of cash position during the three months, April, May and June. The following information is supplied to you :

	Sales	*Purchases*	*Wages*	*Factory Expenses*	*Office Expenses*	*Selling Expenses*
	Rs.	*Rs.*	*Rs.*	*Rs.*	*Rs.*	*Rs.*
February	75,000	45,000	9,000	7,500	6,000	4,500

March	84,000	48,000	9,750	8,250	6,000	4,500
April	90,000	52,500	10,500	9,000	6,000	5,250
May	1,20,000	60,000	13,500	11,250	6,000	6,570
June	1,35,000	60,000	14,250	14,000	7,000	7,000

Other information :

1. Period of credit allowed by suppliers 2 months.
2. 20% of sales is for cash and period of credit allowed to customers for credit is one month.
3. Delay in payment of all expenses — 1 month.
4. Income tax of Rs. 57,500 is due to be paid on June 15th.
5. The company is to pay dividends to shareholders and bonus to workers of Rs. 15,000 and Rs. 22,500 respectively in the month of April.
6. Plant has been ordered to be received and paid in May. It will cost Rs. 1,20,000.

(B. Com. Madurai)

Solution :

Cash Budget

Particulars	*April* Rs.	*May* Rs.	*June* Rs.
Opening Balance (Cash)	37,500	11,700	(–)91,050
Receipts from :			
Cash Sales (20% of sales)	18,000	24,000	27,000
Debtors (80% of previous month sales)	67,200	72,000	96,000
Total : (*a*)	1,22,700	1,07,700	31,950
Payments :			
Creditors (2 months previous purchases)	45,000	48,000	52,500
Wages (previous month)	9,750	10,500	13,500
Factory expenses (previous month)	8,250	9,000	11,250
Office expenses (previous month)	6,000	6,000	6,000
Selling Expenses (previous month)	4,500	5,250	6,570
Dividend to shareholders	15,000	—	—
Bonus to workers	22,500	—	—
Purchase of plant	—	1,20,000	—
Income Tax	—	—	57,500
Total (*b*)	1,11,000	1,98,750	1,47,320
Closing Balance (a – b)	11,700	(–)91,050	(–)1,15,370

The company needs overdraft facilities in May and June to the extent of Rs. 91,050 and Rs. 1,15,370 respectively.

Illustration 19. Prepare a Cash Budget for the three months ending 30th June from the following information :

(*a*) Month	Sales *Rs.*	Materials *Rs.*	Wages *Rs.*	Overheads *Rs.*
February	14,000	9,600	3,000	1,700
March	15,000	9,000	3,000	1,900
April	16,000	9,200	3,200	2,000
May	17,000	10,000	3,600	2,200
June	18,000	10,400	4,000	2,300

(*b*) Credit terms are :
Sales/Debtors — 10% sales are on cash, 50% of the credit sales are collected next month and the balance in the following month.

(*c*) Creditors : Materials, 2 months
Wages, 1/4 month
Overheads, $\frac{1}{2}$ month.

(*d*) Cash and Bank balance on 1st April is expected to be Rs. 6,000.

(*e*) Other relevant informations are :

(1) Plant and Machinery will be installed in February at a cost of Rs. 96,000. The monthly instalments of Rs. 2,000 are payable from April onwards.

(2) Dividend @ 5% on Preference share capital of Rs. 2,00,000 will be paid on 1st June.

(3) Advance to be received for sale of vehicles Rs. 9,000 in June.

(4) Dividends from investments amounting to Rs. 1,000 are expected to be received in June.

(5) Income-tax (advance) to be paid in June is Rs. 2,000

(*ICWA Inter*)

Solution :

Cash Budget

Particulars	*April*	*May*	*June*
	Rs.	Rs.	Rs.
Balance	6,000	3,950	3,000
Receipts :			
Sales/Debtors	14,650	15,650	16,650
Dividend	—	—	1,000
Advance against vehicle	—	—	9,000
Total	20,650	19,600	29,650
Payments :			
Creditors for Materials (after 2 months)	9,600	9,000	9,200
Wages	3,150	3,500	3,900
Overheads	1,950	2,100	2,250
Capital expenditure	2,000	2,000	2,000
Dividend on Preference share	—	—	10,000
Income tax advance	—	—	2,000
Total	16,700	16,600	29,350
Balance	3,950	3,000	300

Amount against Sales/Debtors :

	April	*May*	*June*
	Rs.	*Rs.*	*Rs.*
February (14,000 –10%) × 50%	6,300	—	—
March (15,000 – 10%) × 50%	6,750	6,750	—
April (10% of 16,000)	1,600		
(16,000 – 10%) × 50%		7,200	7,200
May (10% of 17,000)		1,700	
(17,000 – 10%)			7,650
June : (10% of 18,000)			1,800
	14,650	15,650	16,650

Sales :

Toughened Glass Rs. 3,00,000
Bent Toughened Glass Rs. 5,00,000

Wages : 75% of the month + 25% of previous month

Overheads : 50% of the month + 50% of previous month.

Illustration 20. A Glass Manufacturing Company requires you to calculate and present the budget for the next year from the following information :

Direct materials cost : 60% of sales
Direct wages : 20 workers @ Rs. 150 per month
Factory Overheads :
Indirect labour :
Works Manager : Rs. 500 per month
Foreman : Rs. 400 per month
Stores and spares : $2\frac{1}{2}\%$ on sales
Depreciation on machinery : Rs. 12,600
Light and power : Rs. 5,000
Repairs and maintenance : Rs. 8,000
Other Sundries : 10% on direct wages.
Administration, selling and distribution expenses : Rs. 14,000 p.a. *(C.A. Inter)*

Solution :

Master Budget

	Rs.	*Rs.*
Sales : (*Sales budget*)		
Toughened Glass		3,00,000
Bent Toughened Glass		5,00,000
		8,00,000
Cost of production budget:		
Direct Materials: 60% of sales :	4,80,000	
Direct Wages	36,000	
Prime Cost	5,16,000	
Factory overheads :		
Variable :		
Stores and spares : $2\frac{1}{2}\%$ of sales:	20,000	
Light and power	5,000	
Repair and maintenance	8,000	
Fixed :		
Works manager's salary	6,000	
Foreman's salary	4,800	
Depreciation	12,600	
Sundries	3,600	
Works Cost	5,76,000	
Administration selling and distribution overheads	14,000	
Cost of sales :		5,90,000
Net Profit :		2,10,000

Zero base budgeting

In common practice building the functional budgets is to base the budget year's figures on the previous year's budget. Taking the previous figures as the base, the required adjustments are made for the impact of inflation, proposed increased or decreased level of activity etc. in the light of experience. Thus, in the traditional budgeting system, budgets are based on trends or historical level of expenditure. Thus a budget is developed on the concept of incremental basis. Mostly what is done is to add some percentage to the figures of previous year to determine the budget figures. That is, under the incremental budgeting system, the figures of the previous budget, on the basis of which future budget is drawn, are considered to be acceptable. It is the experience of many, particularly in the government departments and public undertakings that the actual expenditure should be in line with the budgeted amount otherwise the higher authorities will reduce the future budgeted and allocated amounts. The managers justify the need to spend more than that of the previous budget. But they do not review their past activities and thus expenditure and inefficiencies are brought forward to the subsequent period i.e. the incremental budgeting perpetuates inefficiency instead of promoting operational efficiency.

In order, therefore, to streamline the allocation, to curb this tendency of equalising the expenditure with budgeted figures and to control the costs, a new technique called "Zero Base Budgeting"or "Zero Base Budgeting" emerged. Under this technique, no special budget is prepared but the approach is changed.

The use of Zero-Base Budgeting (ZBB) as a managerial tool has become increasingly popular since the early 1970's. It first came into being when Ex-President Jummy Carter of the United States of America introduced it as a means of controlling state expenditure. The underlying idea of ZBB is that there is no given base figure for a budget. A fresh budgeted figure is to be determined keeping the circumstances and requirements. This basic concept of ZBB is simple : budgeting starts from scratch or zero. That is, every activity in an organisation must be examined and justified, any alternatives must be considered and the results evaluated. It is a method whereby all activities are re-evaluated each time when a budget is formulated :

It implies that :

1. Every budget starts with a zero base.
2. No previous figure is to be taken as a base figure for adjustments.
3. Each activity is to be examined afresh.
4. Every budget allocation is to be justified in the light of anticipated circumstances.
5. Alternatives are to be given due consideration.

Benefits

1. Effective cost control can be exercised.
2. Careful planning is facilitated.
3. Management by objectives becomes a reality.
4. Uneconomical activities are identified.
5. Inefficiencies are controlled.
6. Scarce resources are allocated and used beneficially.
7. Each activity is thoroughly examined and justified.

OBJECTIVE TYPE QUESTION

A. Choose the correct answer to the following :

1. Sales budget is :
   (a) Functional budget.
   (b) Master budget.
   (c) Expenditure budget.

2. In the case of plant the limiting factor may be :
   (a) Insufficient capacity.
   (b) Shortage of experienced hands.
   (c) Shortage of power.
3. In case of materials, the key factor may be :
   (a) Insufficient advertising.
   (b) Restrications imposed by quote.
   (c) Low market demand.
4. The budget that is prepared first of all is :
   (a) Cash budget.
   (b) Master budget.
   (c) Budget for the key factor.
5. The budget which commonly takes the form of budgeted Profit & Loss Account and Balance Sheet is :
   (a) Cash budget.
   (b) Master budget.
   (c) Flaxible budget.
6. The difference between fixed and variable cost has a special significance in the preparation of :
   (a) Flaxible budget.
   (b) Master budget.
   (c) Cash budget.

(Ans: 1. (a) ; 2. (a) ; 3. (b) ; 4. (c) ; 5. (b) ; 6. (a)

B. State State whether the following statements are ture or false :

1. There is no difference between a forecase and a budget.
2. A fixed budget is concerned with budgeting of assets.
3. Sales budget is the most important budget among all other budgets.
4. A fixed budget is preferable to flexible budget.
5. The budget key factor constitute the starting point for the preparation of various budgets.
6. A budget manual contains a summary of all functional budgets.
7. Cost centre and responsibility centres are not synonymous terms.
8. Efficiency ratio determines the capacity used by the factory.
9. Flexible budgets change with the level of activity.
10. Budgeting may be said to be an act of determining costing standards.

(Ans: 1. False ; 2. .False ; 3. True ; 4. False ; 5. True ; 6. False ; 7. True ; 8. False ; 9. True ; 10. False.

THEORETICAL QUESTIONS

1. Define budget and budgetary control. Give a description of important budgets. *(B. Com., Delhi)*

2. Define budgetary control and state its objectives. *(C.A.)*

3. What is 'budgetary control' and how is it exercised ?
Discuss variances, advantages and essentials for the success of budgetary control. *(B. Com., Panjab)*

4. What is master budget ? What are its components ? *(B. Com., Madurai)*

5. What are fixed and flexible budgets ? (*B. Com., Madurai, 1983*)
6. How and why cash budgets are prepared ? (*B. Com. Madurai, 1983*)
7. Write short notes on :
   (*a*) Budget officer and budget committee
   (*b*) Principal budget factor
   (*c*) Activity ratio and efficiency ratio.
8. Define and explain briefly, what you understand by
   (*a*) Sales budget (*b*) Materials budget
   (*c*) Labour budget (*d*) Overhead budget.
9. What is a sales budget and how is it prepared ?
10. Explain the difference between a forecast and a budget.
11. What is a Cash Budget ? What are its advantages ? How is it prepared ? (*B. Com., Punjab, Madurai*)
12. What do you understand by Zero Base budgeting ? How is it different from traditional budgeting ?
13. Explain any three control ratios.

PRACTICAL PROBLEMS

14. A factory engaged in manufacturing plastic buckets is working to 40% capacity and produces 10,000 buckets per month.

The present cost break-up for one bucket is as under :

Material — Rs. 10
Labour — Rs. 3
Overhead — Rs. 5 (60% fixed)

The selling price is Rs. 20 per bucket. If it is decided to work the factory at 50% capacity the selling price falls by 3%. At 90% capacity the selling price falls by 5% accompanied by a similar fall in the price of material.

You are required to prepare a statement showing the profit at 50% and 90% capacities and also calculate the break-even points at these capacity productions.

(*B. Com., Bombay*)

(**Ans.**	40%	50%	90%
Profit	Rs. 20,000	Rs. 25,000	Rs. 71,250
BEP	6,000	6,819	6,667)

15. ABC Ltd. has prepared a budget for the production of lakh units of the only commodity manufactured by them for a costing period as under :

	Rs.
Raw materials	2.52 per unit
Direct labour	0.75 per unit
Direct Expenses	0.10 per unit
Works Overheads (60% fixed)	2.50 per unit
Administration Overheads (80% fixed)	0.40 per unit
Selling Overheads (50% fixed)	0.20 per unit

The actual production during the period was only 60,000 units. Calculate the revised budgeted cost per unit. (*I.C.W.A. Inter*)

(**Ans.** Rs. 7.75)

16. With the following data for a 60 per cent activity, prepare a budget for production at 80% and 100% activity.

Production at 60% activity-600 units

Materials	Rs. 100 per unit
Labour	Rs. 40 per unit
Expenses	Rs. 10 per unit
Factory Expenses :	Rs. 40,000 (40% fixed)

Administration Expenses Rs. 30,000 (60% fixed) *(ICWA Inter)*

[**Ans.** *Rs. 1,60,000 (60%)*
Rs. 2,02,000 (80%)
Rs. 2,44,000 (100%)]

17. The cost of an article at a capacity level of 10,000 units is given under A below : For a variation in capacity above or below this level, the individual expenses vary as indicated in B below :

	A	B
	Rs.	
Material cost	50,000	(100% varying)
Labour	30,000	(100% varying)
Power	3,000	(80% varying)
Repairs and maintenance	3,500	(80% varying)
Stores	2,000	(100% varying)
Inspection	800	(25% varying)
Depreciation	10,000	(100% varying)
Administration Overhead	3,600	(25% varying)
Selling Overhead	4,500	(50% varying)
Total :	1,07,400	
Cost per unit	10.74	

Find out the unit cost of the product under each individual expense at production level of 8,000 units and 12,000 units. *(ICWA Inter)*

(**Ans.** *8,000 units* *Rs. 10.91 per unit*
10,000 units *Rs. 10.74 per unit*
12,000 units *Rs. 10.63 per unit)*

18. Prepare a flexible budget for overheads on the basis of data given below. Ascertain the Overhead rates at 50, 60 and 70 per cent capacity.

	At 50% Capacity	At 60% Capacity	At 70% Capacity
Fixed Overheads :	*Rs.*	*Rs.*	*Rs.*
Depreciation		16,500	
Insurance		4,500	
Salaries		15,000	
Variable Overheads :			
Indirect material		6,000	
Indirect labour		18,000	
Semi-variable Overheads :			
Electricity (40% fixed 60% variable)		30,000	
Repairs and maintenance (80% fixed) (20% variable)		3,000	
Total Overheads		93,000	
Extimated direct labour hours—1,86,000			

[**Ans.** *Rs. 85,900 (50%)*
Rs. 1,00,100 (70%)]

19. A factory is currently working to 50% capacity and produces 10,000 units. Estimate the profits of the company when it workes to 60% and 80% capacity and offer your critical comments.

At 60% working raw material cost increases by 20% and selling price falls by 5%

At 50% capacity working the product costs Rs. 180 per unit and is sold at Rs. 200 per unit., The unit cost of Rs. 180 is made up as follows.

	Rs.
Material	100
Labour	30
Factory Overhead	30 (40% fixed)
Administrative Overhead	20 (50% fixed)

At 50% capacity :

Factory Overhead Rs. 30 per unit.

Fixed cost is 40% of Rs. 30 or Rs. 12 per unit.

Production — 10,000 units.

Total fixed factory Overhead — 10, 000 × 18 or Rs. 1,80,000

Administrative Overhead — Rs. 20 per unit.

Fixed Cost is 50% of Rs. 10 per unit.

Total fixed administrative Overhead —10,000 × 10 or Rs. 1,00,000

It may be noted that the fixed overhead will normally remain constant up to 100% capacity, increase in raw material cost and decrease in selling price are to be calculated with reference to the figure given 50% capacity usage. (*I.C.W.A. Inter*) (*B. Com., Madurai*)

(**Ans.**	Capacity	Total	Cost per unit
	50%	Rs. 20,00,000	Rs. 200
	60%	Rs. 23,52,000	Rs. 196
	80%	Rs. 30,40,000	Rs. 190)

20. From the following particulars, prepare a production Budget of Sales Corporation for the year ended on 30th June 2009.

Product	Sales (units) (As per Sales Budget)	Estimated stock (units) 1 July 2009	30 July 2010
A	1,50,000	14,000	15,000
B	1,00,000	5,000	4,500
C	70,000	8,000	8,000

(*B. Com. Bharathidasan*)

(**Ans.** *Units to be produced* :
A — 1,51,000 Units
B — 99,500 Units
C — 70,000 Units)

21. Bright Limited have prepared the budget for the production of 1,00,000 units of product for a costing period as under :

	Per unit *Rs.*
Raw Materials	10.08
Direct Labour	3.00
Direct Expenses	0.40

Works Overhead (60% fixed)	10.00
Administration Overhead (80% fixed)	1.60
Sales Overhead	0.80

Actual production in the period was only 60,000 units. Prepare budgets for the original and revised levels of output. (*B. Com. Madurai*)

(**Ans.**	*Per Unit*	*Total*
	Rs.	*Rs.*
Original	25.88	25,88,000
Revised	31.00	18,60,000)

22. The following budget estimates are available from a factory working at 50% of its capacity :

Variable expenses	Rs. 60,000
Semi-variable expenses	Rs. 20,000
Fixed expenses	Rs. 10,000

Prepare a budget for 75% of the capacity assuming that semi-variable expenses increase by 10% for every 25%.

(**Ans.** *Rs.* 1,22,000) (*B. Com. Calicut*)

23. The expenses budgeted for production of 10,000 units in a factory are given below :

	Rs. per unit
Materials	70
Labour	25
Variable Overheads	20
Fixed Overheads (1,00,000)	10
Variable Overheads (Direct)	5
Selling Expenses (10% fixed)	13
Administration Expenses (Rs. 50,000)	5
Distribution Expenses (20% fixed)	7
	155

Prepare a budget of the production (*a*) 8,000 units (*b*) 6,000 units. Assume that the administration expenses are rigid for all levels of production.

(*B. Com., Jiwaji, Rohtak*)

(**Ans.** (*a*) Rs. 12,75,400 (*b*) Rs. 10,00,800)

24. The expenses of producing 1,800 units in a factory with a capacity to produce, 2,400 units are given below :

	Rs.
Materials	4 per unit
Labour	3 per unit
Factory Expenses :	
Fixed	720
Variable	900
Variable selling Expenses	450
Office and Administration Expenses	1,800 (fixed)

What will be the cost of production per unit if the actual output and normal capacity are taken into consideration ?

(**Ans.** *Rs. 9.15 and 8.80*) (*B. Com. Calicut*)

25. You are requested to prepare a Sales Overhead Budget from the estimates given below :

	Rs.
Advertisment	2,500
Salaries of the sales department	5,000
Expenses of sales department	1,500
Counter salesmen's salaries and dearness allowance	6,000

Commission to counter salesmen at 1% on their sales

Travelling salesmen's commission at 10% on their sales and expenses at 5% on their sales.

The sales during the period were estimated as follows :

Counter sales	*Travelling salesmen's commission*
Rs.	*Rs.*
80,000	10,000
1,20,000	15,000
1,40,000	20,000

(**Ans.** *Rs. 17,300;18,450;19,400*) (*C.A. Inter*)

26. A limited company is engaged in the business of manufacturing standard toys. It has prepared a six-monthly budget, which shows the following particulars :

Sales	80,000 units @ Rs. 20 per unit
Variable Costs :	
Manufacturing	Rs. 6 per unit
Selling	Re. 1 per unit
Distribution	Re. 0.25 per unit
Semi-Variable Costs :	
Manufacturing	Rs. 60,000
Selling	Rs. 30,000
Administration	Rs. 16,000
Fixed Costs :	
Manufacturing	Rs. 60,000
Selling	Rs. 40,000
Administration	Rs. 80,000

It is decided to provide a plastic tray alongwith sale of toys. It is estimated this gesture on the part of the company would boost up the sales from 80,000 units to 1,00,000 units. The above proposal would involve an additional expenditure estimated as under :

Semi-variable	Rs. 4,000
Selling	Rs. 4,000
Administration	Rs. 2,000
Fixed Costs :	
Manufacturing	Rs. 10,000

You are required to prepare a statement showing (*i*) comparative cost of production and (*ii*) profitability. (*C.A.*)

(**Ans.** *Cost Rs. 7,34,000 for 80,000 units, profit Rs. 7,34,000*
Cost Rs. 10,31,000 for 1,00,000 units, profit Rs. 9,69,000)

27. The following overhead expenses relate to a cost centre operating at 50% of normal capacity. Draw up a flexible budget for the cost centre for operating at 75%, 100% and 125% of normal capacity. Indicate the basis upon which you have estimated each item of expenses for the different operating levels.

	Rs.
Foreman	60
Assistant foreman	40
Inspectors	65
Shop labourers	40
Machinery repairs	100
Defective work	25
Consumable stores	20
Overtime bonus	—
Machine depreciation	110
	Rs. 460

(*I.C.W.A. Inter*)

(**Ans.** *75%, Rs. 565; 100%, Rs. 760; 125%, Rs. 950*)

28. Draw up a flexible budget for overhead expenses on the basis of the following data and determine the overhead rates at 70%, 80% and 90% capacity levels.

	At 80% capacity
	Rs.
Variable Overheads :	
Indirect labour	12,000
Indirect material	4,000
Semi-Variable Overheads:	
Power (30% fixed and 70% variable)	20,000
Repairs and maintenance (60% fixed and 40% variable)	2,000
Fixed Overheads :	
Depreciation	11,000
Insurance	3,000
Others	10,000
Total Overheads	62,000
Estimated direct labour hours	1,24,000 hours

(*ICWA Inter*)

(**Ans.** *Overhead Rate of recovery : Re 0.54 at 70%, Re. 0.50 at 80% and Re. 0.47 at 90%*)

29. A Company wishes to arrange overdraft facilities with its Bankers during the period April to June when it will be manufacturing most for stock. Prepare cash budget for the above period from the following data, indicating the extent of bank facilities the company will require at the end of each month :

	Sales	*Purchases*	*Wages*
	Rs.	*Rs.*	*Rs.*
February	1,80,000	1,24,800	12,000
March	1,92,000	1,44,000	14,000
April	1,08,000	2,43,000	11,000
May	1,74,000	2,46,000	10,000
June	1,26,000	2,68,000	15,000

50% of credit sales are realised in the month following sales and the remaining 50% in the second month following. Creditors are paid in the month following the month of purchase.

Wage are paid on the first of very next month.

Cash at bank on 1st April Rs. 25,000 *(ICWA)*

[**Ans.** *Cash on hand* *Rs. 53,000* *(April)*
Overdraft *Rs.* 51,000 (May)
Overdraft *Rs. 1,66,000* *(June)]*

30. The following data are available in a manufacturing company for a yearly period :

	Rs (in lakhs)
Fixed Expenses :	
Wages and salaries	9.5
Rent rates and taxes	6.6
Depreciation	7.4
Sundry administration expenses	6.5
Semi-Variable Expenses (At 50% of capacity)	
Maintenance and repairs	3.5
Indirect labour	7.9
Sales department salaries	3.8
Sundry administration salaries	2.8
Variable Expenses : (At 50% of capacity)	
Materials	21.7
Labour	20.4
Other Expenses	7.9
Total Cost	98.0

Assume that the fixed expenses remain constant for all levels of production; semivariable expenses remain constant between 45% and 65% of capacity, increasing by 10% between 65% and 80% capacity and 20% between 80% and 100% capacity.

Sales at various levels are :

	Rs. (lakhs)
50% capacity	100
60% capacity	120
75% capacity	150
90% capacity	180
100% capacity	200

Prepare a flexible budget for the year and forecast the profit at 60%, 75%, 90% and 100% capacity. *(ICWA Inter, B. Com. (Hons.) Delhi)*

[**Ans.** *Profit Rs. 2,00,000 (50%)*
Profit Rs. 12,00,000 (60%)
Profit Rs. 25,20,000 (75%)
Profit Rs. 38,40,000 (90%)
Profit Rs. 48,40,000 (100%)]

31. With the following data for a 60 per cent activity, prepare a budget for production at 80 per cent and 100 per cent activity. Production at 60 per cent activity : 600 Units.

Materials	*Rs.*	100 per unit
Labour	*Rs.*	40 per unit

Expenses Rs. 10 per unit
Factory Expenses Rs. 40,000 (40 per cent fixed)
Administration expenses Rs. 30,000 (60 per cent fixed) (*I.C.W.A*)
(**Ans.** 80% budget : Rs. 2,02,000 : 100% budget : 2,44,000)

32. A company is expecting to have Rs. 25,000 cash in hand on 1st April 2010 and it requires you to prepare an estimate of cash position during the three months, April to June 2010. The following information is supplied to you.

	Sales *Rs.*	*Purchases* *Rs.*	*Wages* *Rs.*	*Expenses* *Rs.*
February	70,000	40,000	8,000	6,000
March	80,000	50,000	8,000	7,000
April	92,000	52,000	9,000	7,000
May	1,00,000	60,000	10,000	8,000
June	1,20,000	55,000	12,000	9,000

Other Information :— (*a*) Period of credit allowed by suppliers two months (*b*) 25% of sale is for cash and period of credit allowed to customers for credit sale one month (*c*) Delay in payment of wages and expenses — one month (*d*) Income tax of Rs. 25,000 is to be paid in June 2010. (*B. Com. Madurai*)

[**Ans.** *Balance of cash in hand : Rs. 53,000 (April)*
Rs. 81,000 (May)
Rs. 91,000 (June)]

Chapter 11

Capital Budgeting

Meaning of Capital Budgeting; Importance of Capital Budgeting; Capital Budgeting Process; Evaluation of Investment Proposals; Pay-back Period Method; Acceptance or Reject Criterion; Advantages of Pay-Back Method; Disadvantages of Pay-Back Method; Improvement in Traditional Approach to Payback Period; Post Payback Profitability; Discounted Payback Period; Payback Reciprocal; Rate of Return Method; Time Adjusted Method; Merits of Net Present Value Method; Internal Rate of Return Method; Profitability Index Number; Capital Rationing; Objective Type Questions; Theoretical Questions; Practical Problems.

Meaning of Capital Budgeting

Capital budgeting is the process of making investment decisions in the capital expenditures. A progressive business firm always moves ahead, its fixed assets and other resources continue to expand or there comes a need for expanding them. Capital budgeting is actually the process of making investment decisions in capital expenditure, or fixed assets. A capital expenditure may be as an expenditure the benefits of which are expected to be received over a period of time exceeding one year. Capital expenditure is one which is intended to benefit future periods and normally includes investments in fixed assets and other development projects. It is essentially a long-term function. Capital budgeting is also known as Investment Decision Making, Capital Expenditure Decisions, Planning Capital Expenditure etc.

Capital budgeting is the most important and complicated problem of managerial decisions. Because it is concerned with designing and carrying out through a systematic investment programme. It involves the planning of such expenditures which provide yields over a number of years.

Charles T Horngreen has defined capital budgeting as, "Capital budgeting is long-term planning for making and financing proposed capital outlays."

According to Philippatos, "Capital budgeting is concerned with the allocation of the firm's scare financial resources among the available market opportunities. The consideration of investment opportunities involves the comparison of the expected future streams of earnings from a project, with the immediate and subsequent streams of expenditure for it."

Richard and Green have defined "Capital budgeting as acquiring inputs with long-run return."

According to Lynch, "Capital budgeting consists in planning development of available capital for the purpose of maximising the long-term profitability of the concern."

FEATURES OF INVESTMENT DECISIONS

1. Capital budgeting decisions are essentially a long-term function.
2. Huge funds are invested in long-term assets.
3. The future benefits will occur to the firm over a series of years.
4. They involve the exchange of current funds for the benefits to be achieved in future.
5. They have a significant effect on the profitability of the concerns.
6. They are 'strategic' investment decisions.
7. They are irreversible decisions.

Capital budgeting has a vital role to play in the broader process of strategic planning and budgetary control. Capital budgeting systems should strive to create an atmosphere which encourages the generation of new investment proposals and evaluates them as accurately as possible. However, loss-making proposals must be identified at the earliest possible moment.

Importance of Capital Budgeting

Capital budgeting means planning for capital assets. Capital budgeting decisions are among the most crucial and critical business decisions. It is the most important single area of decision-making for the management. Unsound investment decision may prove to be fatal to the very existence of the concern. The significance of capital budgeting arises mainly due to the following:

(1) Large Investment

Capital budgeting decisions, generally, involve large investment of funds. The funds available with the firm are always limited and the demand for the funds far exceeds the resources. These funds are raised by the firm from various internal and external resources at substantial cost of capital. A wrong decision prove disastrous for the continued survival of the firm. Hence it is very important for a firm to plan and control its capital expenditure.

(2) Long-term Commitment of Funds

The funds involved in capital expenditure are not only large but more or less permanently blocked also in long-term investment. The longer the time, the greater the risk involved. Greater the risk involved, greater is the need for careful planning of capital expenditure i.e. capital budgeting. The long-term commitment of funds increases the financial risk involved in the investment decision. Firm's decision to invest in long-term assets has a decisive influence on the rate and direction of its growth. An unsound investment decision may prove to be fatal to the very existence of the firm. Hence a careful planning is essential.

(3) Irreversible in nature

Most investment decisions are irreversible. Once the decision for acquiring a permanent asset is taken, it is very difficult to reverse that decision. It is difficult to find a market of such capital goods once they have been acquired. The only alternative will be to scrap the capital assets so purchased or sell them at a substantial loss in the event of the decision being proved wrong.

(4) Complicacies of Investment Decisions

The long-term investment decisions are more complicated in nature. The capital budgeting decisions require an assessment of future events which are uncertain. It is really a difficult task to estimate the probable future events. In most projects the investment of funds has to be made immediately but the returns are expected over a number of future years. Both returns as well as the length of the period over which they will accrue are uncertain.

(5) Long-term Effect on Profitability

Capital budgeting decisions have a long-term and significant effect on the profitability of a concern. Capital budgeting is of utmost importance to avoid over-investment or under-investment in fixed assets. An unwise decision may prove disastrous and fatal to the very existence of the concern. The future growth and profitability of the firm depends upon the investment decision taken today. Capital expenditure projects exercise a great impact on the profitability of the firm for a very long time.

(6) National Importance

Investment decision taken by individual concern is of national importance because it determines employment, economic activities and economic growth.

Capital Budgeting Process

Capital budgeting is a complex process as it involves decisions to the investment of current funds for the benefit to be achieved in future and the future is always uncertain. A capital budgeting process may involve a number of steps depending upon the size of the concern, nature of projects, their numbers, complexities and diversities etc. That is, capital budgeting decisions of a firm have a pervasive influence on the entire spectrum of entrepreneurial activities. Hence they require a complex combination and knowledge of various disciplines for their effective administration, such as economics, finance, mathematics, economic fore-casting, projection techniques and techniques of financial control. In order to tie all these elements, a financial manager must keep in mind the three dimensions of capital budgeting programme – policy, plan and programme. These three Ps constitute a sound capital budgeting programme.

Quinin G David has suggested that (*a*) project generation, (*b*) project evaluation, (*c*) Project selection and (*d*) Project execution are the important steps involved in a capital budgeting process. However, the following procedure may be adopted in the process of capital budgeting.

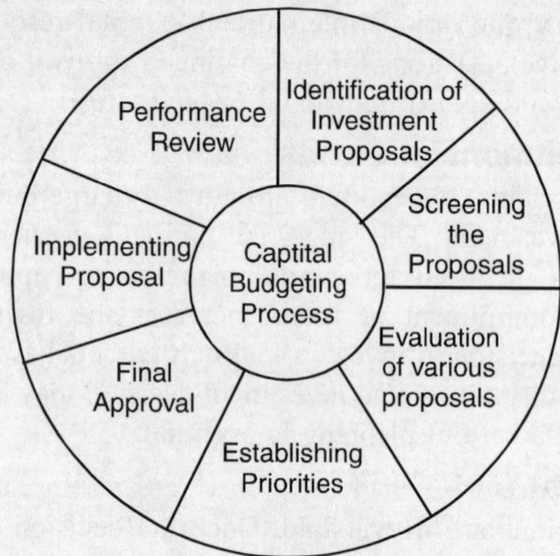

Capital Budgeting Process.

(1) Identification of Investment Proposals

Investment opportunities have to be identified or searched for: they do not occur automatically. The capital budgeting process begins with the identification of investment proposals. The first step in capital budgeting process is the conception of a profit-making idea. Investment proposals of various types may originate at different levels within a firm, depending on their nature. They may originate from the level of workers to top management level. Most of the proposals, in the nature of cost reduction or replacement or process for product improvement take place at plant level. The proposal for adding new product may emanate from the marketing department or from plant manager who thinks of a better way of utilising idle capacity. Suggestions for replacing an old machine or improving the production techniques may arise at the factory level. The departmental head analyses the various proposals in the light of the corporate strategies and submits suitable proposals to the capital expenditure planning committee in case of large organisation or to the officers concerned with the process of long-term investment decisions.

A continuous flow of profitable capital expenditure proposals is itself an indications of a healthy and vital businesss concern. Although business may pursue many goals, survivals and profitability are two of the most important objectives.

(2) Screening the Proposals

Screening and selection procedures would differ from firm to firm. Each proposal is then subjected to a preliminary screening process in order to assess whether it is technically feasible; resources required are available and the expected returns are adequate to compensate for the risk involved. In large organisations, a capital expenditure planning committee is established for screening of various proposals received from different departments. The committee views these proposals from various angles to ensure that these are in accordance with the corporate strategies or selection criterion of the firm and also do not lead to departmental imbalances. All care must be taken in selecting a criterion to judge the desirability of the projects. The criterion selected should be a true measure of the investment project's profitability, and as far as possible, it must be consistent with the firm's objective of maximising its market value. This stage involves the comparison of the proposals with other projects according to criteria of the firm. This is done either by financial manager or by a capital expenditure planning committe. Such criteria should encompass the supply and cost of capital and the expected returns from alternative investment opportunities.

(3) Evaluation of Various Proposals

The next step in the capital budgeting process is to evaluate the profitability of various proposals. If a proposal satisfies the screening process, it is then analysed in more detail by gathering technical, economic and other data. Projects are also classified, for example, new products or expansion or improvement and ranked within each classification with respect to profitability, risk and degree of urgency. There are many methods which may be used for this purpose such as pay back period method, rate of return method, net present value method etc. All these methods of evaluating profitability of capital investment proposals have been discussed in detail separately in the following pages of this chapter. The various proposals of investments may be classified as:

(*a*) Mutually exclusive proposals

(*b*) Independent proposals

(*c*) Contingent or dependent proposals.

Mutually exclusive proposals serve the same purpose and compete with each other in a way that the acceptance of one precludes the acceptance of other or others. Thus, two or more mutally exclusive proposals cannot both or all be accepted. Some technique has to be used for selecting the better or the best one. Once this is done, other alternatives automatically gets eliminated. A company may, for instance, propose to use semi-automatic machine or highly automatic machine for production. Here choosing the highly automatic machine precludes the acceptance of the semi-automatic machine.

Independent proposals are those which do not compete with one another and the same may be either accepted or rejected on the basis of minimum return on investment required. For instance, when there are two proposals, a firm can undertake both the proposals.

Contingent or dependent proposals are those whose acceptance depends upon the acceptance of one or more other proposals. For instance, a firm decides to build a factory in a remote area, it may have to invest in houses, hospitals, roads etc. for the staff. Thus, building a factory also requires investment in facilities for employees. The total investment will be treated as a single investment.

(4) Establishing Priorities

After evaluation of various proposals, the unprofitable or uneconomic proposals are rejected. The accepted proposals i.e. profitable proposals are put in priority. It may not be possible for the firm to invest immediately in all the acceptable proposals. Thus, it is essential to rank the various proposals and to establish priorities after considering urgency, risk and profitability involved therein.

(5) Final Approval

Proposals finally recommended by the committee are sent to the top management along with a detailed report, both of capital expenditures and of sources of capital. Financial manager will present several alternative capital expenditure budgets. When capital expenditure proposals are finally selected, funds are allocated for them. Projects are then sent to the budget committee for incorporating them in the capital budget.

(6) Implementing Proposals

Preparation of a capital expenditure budgeting and incorporation of a particular proposal in the budget does not itself authorise to go ahead with the implementation of the project. A request for authority to spend the amount should further be made to the capital expenditure committee which may like to review the profitability of the project in the changed circumstances. Further, while implementing the project, it is better to assign responsibilities for completing the project within the given time frame and cost limit so as to avoid unnecessary delays and cost over runs. Network techniques used in the project management such as PERT and CPM can also be applied to control and monitor the implementation of the projects.

(7) Performance Review

Last but not the least important step in the capital budgeting process is an evaluation of the performance of the project, after it has been fully implemented. It is the duty of the top management or executive committee to ensure that funds are spent in accordance with the allocation made in the capital budget. A control over such capital expenditure is very much essential and for that purpose a monthly report showing the amount allocated, amount spent, amount approved but not spent should be prepared and submitted to the controller. The evaluation is made through post completion audit by way of comparison of actual expenditure on the project with the budgeted one, and also by comparing the actual return from the investment with the anticipated return. The unfavourable variances, if any, should be looked into and the causes of the same be identified so that corrective action may be taken in future.

Evaluation of Investment Proposals

The funds available with the firm are always limited and it is not possible to invest funds in all the proposals at a time. Therefore, it is very essential to select from amongst the various competing proposals, those which give the highest benefit. A firm may face a situation where more investment proposals may be available than investible funds. Some proposals may be good, some moderate and some may be poor. The management has to select the most profitable project or to take up the most profitable project first. There are many considerations, economic as well as non-economic, which influence the capital budgeting decisions. Because of the utmost importance of the capital budgeting decision, a sound appraisal method should be adopted to measure the economic worth of each investment project. Capital expenditures represent long-term commitment in the sense that current investment yields benefits in future. The capital expenditure decisions assume great importance for the future development of the concern. The important factor that influences the capital budgeting decision is the profitability of the prospective investment. The risk involved in the proposal cannot be ignored because profitability and risk are directly related, that is, higher the profitability, the greater the risk and vice-versa. The goal of financial management of a firm is the worth maximisation of the firm, and in order to achieve this goal, the management must select those projects which deserve first priority in terms of their profitability. While evaluating, two basic principles are kept in mind, namely, the bigger benefits are always preferrable to small ones and that early benefits are always better than the deferred ones. The essential property of sound evaluation technique is that it should maximise the shareholders' wealth. The following other characteristic should also be possessed by a sound investment evaluation criterion:

1. It should provide a means of distinguishing between acceptable and unacceptable projects.
2. It should provide clear cut ranking of the projects in order of the profitability or desirability.
3. It should also solve the problem of choosing among alternative projects.
4. It should be a criterion which is applicable to any conceivable investment project.
5. It should emphasize upon early and bigger cash benefits in comparison to distant and smaller benefits.
6. The method should be suitable according to the nature and size of capital project to be evaluated.

Methods of Evaluating Capital Investment Proposals

A number of appraisal methods may be recommended for evaluating the capital expenditure proposals. The most important and commonly used methods are:

TRADITIONAL METHODS

1. Pay-back period Method or Pay-out or Pay-off Method.
2. Improvements in Traditional Approach to Pay-back period Method.
3. Rate of Return Method or Accounting Method.

Time Adjusted Methods or Accounting Methods

4. Net Present Value Method.
5. Internal Rate of Return Method.
6. Profitability Index Method.

Traditional Methods

(1) Pay-back Period Method

The term pay-back (or pay out or pay off or break-even period or recoupment period) refers to the period in which the project will generate the necessary cash to recoup the initial investment. Business units, while selecting investment projects, would consider the recovery of cost as the first and foremost concern even though earning maximum profits is their ultimate goal. This method describes in terms of period of time the relationship between annual savings (cash inflow) and total amount of capital expenditure (investment), pay-back period is defined as the number of years required for the savings in costs or net cash inflow (after tax but before depreciation) to recoup the original cost of the project. In simple sentence, it represents the number of years in which the investment is expected to "pay for itself". Under this method, various investments are ranked according to the length of their pay-back period in such a manner that the investment with a shorter pay-back period is preferred to the one which has longer pay-back period.

Calculation of pay-back period

(*a*) In the case of even cash inflows

If the annual cash inflows are constant, the pay-back period can be computed by dividing cash outlay (original investment) by annual cash inflows. For instance, if a project requires Rs. 10,000 as initial investment and it will generate an annual cash inflow of Rs. 2,500 for ten years, the pay-back period will be 4 years, calculated as follows:

$$\text{Pay-back period} = \frac{\text{Initial Investment}}{\text{Annual Cash Inflow}}$$

$$= \frac{\text{Rs. } 10,000}{\text{Rs. } 2,500} = 4 \text{ years}$$

(b) In the case of uneven inflows

If cash inflows are not uniform, the calculation of pay-back period takes a cumulative form. In such a case the pay-back period can be found out by adding up the figure of net cash inflows until the total is equal to initial investment. For instance, if a project requires an initial investment of Rs. 10,000 and the annual inflows for 5 years are Rs. 3,000; Rs. 4,000; Rs. 2,500; Rs. 2,000 and Rs. 2,000 respectively, the pay-back period will be calculated as follows:

Year	*Annual Cash Inflows* Rs.	*Cumulative Cash Inflows* Rs.
1.	3,000	3,000
2.	4,000	7,000
3.	2,500	9,500
4.	2,000	11,500
5.	2,000	13,500

The above workings show that in 3 years Rs. 9,500 has been recovered. Rs. 500 is left out of initial investment. In the fourth year the cash inflow is Rs. 2,000. It means the pay-back period is between 3 to 4 years, calculated as follows:

$$\text{Pay-back period} = 3 \text{ years} + \frac{\text{Rs. } 500}{\text{Rs. } 2,000}$$

$$= \mathbf{3.25 \text{ years}}$$

Illustration 1. Payoff Ltd. is producing articles mostly by manual labour and is considering to replace it by a new machine. There are two alternative models M and N of the new machine. Prepare a statement of profitability showing the pay-back period from the following information:

	Machine M	Machine N
Estimated life of machine	4 years	5 years
Cost of machine	Rs. 9,000	Rs. 18,000
Estimated savings in scrap	Rs. 500	Rs. 800
Estimated savings in direct wages	Rs. 6,000	Rs. 8,000
Additional cost of maintenance	Rs. 800	Rs. 1,000
Additional cost of supervision	Rs. 1,200	Rs. 1,800

(*M.Com. Madurai*)

Solution:

Statement showing annual cash inflows

	Machine M *Rs.*	*Machine N* *Rs.*
Estimated savings in scrap	500	800
Estimated savings in direct wages	6,000	8,000
Total savings (A)	6,500	8,800
Additional cost of maintenance	800	1,000
Additional cost of supervision	1,200	1,800
Total additional cost (B)	2,000	2,800
Net cash inflow (A) – (B)	4,500	6,000

$$\text{Pay-back period} = \frac{\text{Original Investment}}{\text{Annual Average Cash Inflow}}$$

$$= \frac{\text{Rs. } 9{,}000}{\text{Rs. } 4{,}500} = \textbf{2 years}, \quad \frac{\text{Rs. } 18{,}000}{\text{Rs. } 6{,}000} = \textbf{3 years}$$

Machine M should be preferred because it has a shorter pay-back period.

Acceptance or reject criterion

Many firms use the pay-back period as an accept or reject criterion as well as a method of ranking projects. If the pay-back period calculated for a project is less than the maximum pay-back period set by management, it would be accepted; if not, it would be rejected. As a ranking method, it gives highest ranking to the project which has shortest pay-back period and lowest ranking to the project with highest pay-back period. Thus, if the firm has to choose among two mutually exclusive projects, project with shorter pay-back period will be selected.

Advantages of pay-back method

1. It is easy to calculate and simple to understand.
2. It saves in cost, as it requires lesser times and labour as compared to other methods.
3. Under this method, a shorter pay-back period is preferred to the one having a longer pay-back period, and it reduces the loss through obsolescence and is more suited to the developing countries, like India, which are in the process of development and have quick obsolescence.
4. This method is useful to a concern which is short of cash and is eager to get back the cash invested in a capital expenditure project.
5. As the method considers the cash flows during the pay-back period of the project, the estimates would be reliable and the result may be comparatively more accurate.

Disadvantages of pay-back method

1. It does not take into account the cash inflows earned after the pay back period and hence the true profitability of the project cannot be correctly assessed.
2. This method does not consider the amount of profit earned on investment after the recovery of cost of investment.
3. It does not take into consideration the cost of capital which is a very important factor in making a sound investment decisions.
4. It may be difficult to determine the minimum acceptable pay-back period, it is usually, a subjective decision.
5. It ignores interest factor which is considered to be a very significant factor in taking sound investment decision.
6. Too much emphasis on the "liquidity of the investment", ignoring the "profitability of investment" may not be justified in a number of situations.
7. It ignores time value of money. Cash flows received in different years are treated equally.
8. It does not take into account the life of the project, depreciation, scrap-value, interest factor etc. Because, a rupee tomorrow is worth less than a rupee today.

(2) Improvement in Traditional Approach to pay-back period

One of the most commonly used techniques for evaluating capital investment proposal is the cash pay-back or pay-back method. Some authorities on accountancy, in order to make up the deficiencies of the pay-back period method, evolved new concepts. The improvements are discussed below.

(A) Post pay-back profitability

One of the limitations of the pay-back period method is that it neglects the profitability of investment beyond the pay-back period. This method is also known as Surplus Life over pay-back period. According to this method, the project which gives the greatest post pay-back period profits may be accepted. It has been explained in the following illustration:

Post pay-back profitability = Annual Cash Inflow (Estimated Life – pay-back period)

Further, post pay-back profitability index can also be calculated by multiplying the above formula with 100.

Illustration 2. A Concern is considering two projects X and Y. Following are the particulars in respect of them:

	Project X	*Project Y*
Cost (Rs.)	1,40,000	1,40,000
Economic Life (in years)	10	10
Estimated scrap (in Rs.)	10,000	14,000
Annual Savings	25,000	20,000

Ignoring income-tax, recommend the best of these projects using (*a*) pay-back period, (*b*) post pay-back profit, and (*c*) Index of post payback profit.

Solution

	Project X	*Project Y*
1. Cost	1,40,000	1,40,000
2. Savings	25,000	20,000
3. Pay-back period	5.6 years	7 years
4. Economic Life	10 years	10 years
5. Surplus Life	4.4 years	3 years
6. Post pay-back profit (2 × 5)	Rs. 1,10,000	Rs. 60,000
7. Index of post pay-back profit	$\frac{1,10,000}{1,40,000} \times 100$	$\frac{60,000}{1,40,000} \times 100$
	= **78.6%**	**42.9%**

Project *X* is the best one by all the methods of ranking.

(B) Discounted Pay-back Period

Another serious limitation of pay-back period method is that it ignores the time value of money. This method can be improved or modified to consider the time value of money. Under this method the present values of all cash outflows and inflows are computed at an appropriate discount rate. The number of periods taken in recovering the investment outlay on the present value basis is called the discounted pay-back period. The present values of all inflows are cumulated in order of time. The time period at which the cumulated present value of cash inflows equals the present value of cash outflows is known as discounted payback period.

Illustration 3. The following are the particulars relating to a project.

	Rs.
Cost of the project	50,000
Operating Savings:	
Ist year	5,000
2nd year	20,000
3rd year	30,000
4th year	30,000
5th year	10,000

Calculate pay-back period ignoring interest factor and (*b*) discount pay-back period taking into account interest factor at 10%.

Solution:

(*a*) Pay-back period

Year	*Annual Savings*	*Cumulative Savings*
	Rs.	*Rs.*
1	5,000	5,000
2	20,000	25,000
3	30,000	55,000

Upto second year, Rs. 25,000 recovered

$$\text{Therefore, pay-back period} = 2 \text{ years} + \frac{\text{Rs. } 50{,}000 - \text{Rs. } 25{,}000}{\text{Rs. } 30{,}000}$$

$$= 2 + \frac{\text{Rs. } 25{,}000}{\text{Rs. } 30{,}000}$$

= 2 years 10 months

(*b*) Discounted pay-back period at 10% interest factor

Years	*Savings*	*PV Factor*	*Discounted Savings*	*Cumulative Discounted Savings*
	Rs.		*Rs.*	*Rs.*
1	5,000	0.9091	4,546	4,546
2	20,000	0.8265	16,530	21,076
3	30,000	0.7513	22,539	43,615
4	30,000	0.6830	20,490	64,105

$$\text{Discounted pay-back period} = 3 \text{ years} + \frac{\text{Rs. } 50{,}000 - 43{,}615}{20{,}490}$$

= 3 years 4 months

(C) Pay-back Reciprocal

Sometimes, pay-back reciprocal method is employed to estimate the internal rate of return generated by a project.

$$\text{Pay-back Reciprocal} = \frac{\text{Annual Cash Inflow}}{\text{Total Investment}}$$

However, this method of ranking investment proposals should be used only when:

(*a*) Annual savings are even for the entire period.

(*b*) The economic life of the project is at least twice of the pay-back period.

(3) Rate of Return Method (Accounting Method)

This method is also known as Accounting Rate of Return method or Return on Investment or Average Rate of Return method. According to this method, various projects are ranked in order of the rate of earnings or rate or return. Projects which yield the highest earnings are selected and others are ruled out. The return on investment can be expressed in several ways, as follows:

(a) Average Rate of Return Method

Here, average profit, after tax and depreciation, is calculated and then it is divided by the total capital outlay or total investment in the project. This method establishes the ratio between the average annual profits to total outlay.

$$\text{Average Rate of Return} = \frac{\text{Average Annual Profit}}{\text{Outlay of the Project}} \times 100$$

Project giving a higher rate of return will be preferred over those giving lower rate of return.

(b) Return Per unit of Investment Method

In this method, the total profit after tax and depreciation is divided by the total investment. This gives us the average rate of return per unit of amount invested in the project.

$$\text{Return Per unit of Investment} = \frac{\text{Total Profit}}{\text{Net Investment}} \times 100$$

(c) Return on Average Investment Method

Under this method the percentage return on average amount of investment is calculated. To calculate the average investment, the outlay of the project is divided by two.

$$\text{Return on Average Investment} = \frac{\text{Total Profit after Depre. \& Taxes}}{\text{Total Net Investment/2}}$$

(d) Average Return on Average Investment Method

Under this method, average profit after depreciation and taxes is divided by the average amount of investment. This is an appropriate method of rate of return on investment.

$$\text{Average Return on Average Investment} = \frac{\text{Average Annual Profit}}{\text{Net Investment/2}} \times 100$$

Illustration 4. Calculate the average rate of return for projects A and B from the following:

	Project A	*Project B*
Investment	Rs. 20,000	Rs. 30,000
Expected Life (no salvage value)	4 years	5 years

Projected Net Income, after interest, depreciation and taxes:

Years	*Project A*	*Project B*
	Rs.	*Rs.*
1	2,000	3,000
2	1,500	3,000
3	1,500	2,000
4	1,000	1,000
5	—	1,000
Total:	6,000	10,000

If the required rate of return is 12% which project should be undertaken?

Solution:

	Project A	*Project B*
	Rs.	*Rs.*
Total profit, after interest, depreciation and taxes	6,000	10,000
Expected Life	4 years	5 years
Average Profit	Rs. 1,500	Rs. 2,000
Investment	Rs. 20,000	Rs. 30,000
Average Rate of Return	$\frac{1,500}{20,000} \times 100 = 7.5\%$	$\frac{2,000}{30,000} \times 100 = 6.6\,\%$
Average Return on Average Investment	$\frac{1,500}{20,000/2} \times 100 = 15\%$	$\frac{2,000}{30,000/2} \times 100 = 13.33\%$

The average return on average investment is higher in the case of project A, besides it is also higher than the required rate of return of 12%. Project A is suggested to be undertaken.

Merits of Rate of Return Method

The following are the merits:

1. It is simple to understand and easy to calculate.
2. It takes into consideration the total earnings from the project during its life time. Thus this method gives a better view of profitability as compared to pay-back period method.
3. It is based upon accounting concept of profit. It can be calculated from the financial data.

Demerits of Rate of Return method

This method suffers from the following demerits:

1. It ignores the time value of money. Profits earned in different periods are valued equally.
2. This method may not reveal true and fair view in the case of long-term investments.
3. It does not take into consideration the cash flows which is more important than the accounting profits.
4. It ignores the fact that profits can be reinvested.
5. There are different methods for calculating the Accounting Rate of Return. Each method gives different results. This reduces the reliability of the method.

Time Adjusted Method (Discounted Cash Flow Method)

Discounting is just opposite of compounding. In compound rate of interest, the future value of the present money is ascertained whereas in discounting, the present value of future money is calculated. The rate at which the future cash flows are reduced to their present value is termed as discount rate. Discount rate, otherwise called time value of money, is some interest rate which expresses the time preference for a particular future cash flow.

The discounted cash flow method is an improvement on the pay-back method as well as accounting rate of return. This method is based on the fact that future value of money will not be equal to the present value of money. That is, discounted cash flow technique recognises that Re. one of today (cash outflow) is worth more than Re.one received at a future date (cash inflow). The time adjusted or discounted cash flow method take into account the profitability and also the time value of money. The discounted cash flow method for evaluating capital investment Proposals are of three types:

1. Net Present Value Method

This method is also known as Excess Present Value or Net Gain Method or Time Adjusted methods. Under this method, cash inflows and cash outflows associated with each project are first worked out. The present values of these cash inflows and outflows are then calculated at the rate acceptable to the management. This rate of return is considered as the cut-off rate and is generally determined on the basis of cost of capital suitably adjusted to allow for the risk element involved in the project.

The present values of total of cash inflows should be compared with present values of cash outflows. If the present value of cash inflows are greater than (or equal to) the present value of cash outflows (or initial investment), the project would be accepted. If it is less, then proposal will be rejected.

Illustration 5. A Company is considering the purchase of the two machines with the following details:

Life Estimated	Machine I 3 years	Machine II 3 years
	Rs.	Rs.
Capital Cost	10,000	10,000
Net earning after tax:		
Ist year	8,000	2,000
2nd year	6,000	7,000
3rd year	4,000	10,000

You are required to suggest which machine should be preferred.

Solution:

Calculation of Net Present Value (10%)

Year	*PV Factor*	*Machine I*		*Machine II*	
		Cash Inflow Rs.	*Present Value Rs.*	*Cash Inflow Rs.*	*Present Value Rs.*
1	0.909	8,000	7,272	2,000	1,818
2	0.826	6,000	4,956	7,000	5,782
3	0.751	4,000	3,004	10,000	7,510
			15,232		15,110
Less: Cost of Net Present value			10,000		10,000
			5,232		5,110

Machine I should be preferred as net present value is Rs. 5,232 which is higher than Rs. 5,110 in case of Machine II.

Merits of Net Present Value Method

The merits of this method of evaluating investment proposal are as follows:

1. This method considers the entire economic life of the project.
2. It takes into account the objective of maximum profitability.
3. It recognises the time value of money.
4. This method can be applied where cash inflows are uneven.
5. It facilitates comparison between projects.

Demerits of this method are as follows:

1. It is not easy to determine an appropriate discount rate.
2. It involves a great deal of calculations. It is more difficult to understand and operate.
3. It is very difficult to forecast the economic life of any investment exactly.
4. It may not give good results while comparing projects with unequal investment of funds.

2. Internal Rate of Return Method

This method is popularly known as time adjusted rate of return method or discounted rate of return method. The internal rate of return is defined as the interest rate that equates the present value of the expected future receipts to the cost of the investment outlay. This internal rate of return is found by trial and error. First, we compute the present value of the cash-flows from an investment, using an arbitrarily selected interest rate. Then, we compare the present value so obtained with the investment cost. If the present value is higher than the cost figure, we try a higher rate of interest and go through the procedure again. Conversely, if the present value is lower than the cost, lower the interest rate and repeat the process. The interest rate that brings about this equality is defined as the internal rate of return. This rate of return is compared to the cost of capital and the project having higher difference, if they are mutually exclusive, is adopted and other one is rejected. As this determination of internal rate of return involves a number of attempts to make the present value of earnings equal to the investment, this approach is also called the Trial and Error Method.

Illustration 6. Initial Investment Rs. 60,000

Life of the Asset 4 years

Estimated net annual cash-flows:

Ist year Rs. 15,000

2nd year Rs. 20,000

3rd year Rs. 30,000

4th year Rs. 20,000

Calculate Internal Rate of Return.

Solution:

Calculation of Internal Rate of Return

Year	*Annual cashflow*	*PVF 10%*	*PV*	*PVF 12%*	*PV*	*PVF 14%*	*PV*	*PVF 15%*	*PV*
1.	15,000	0.909	13,635	0.892	13,380	0.877	13,155	0.869	13,035
2.	20,000	0.826	16,520	0.797	15,940	0.769	15,380	0.756	15,120
3.	30,000	0.751	22,530	0.711	21,330	0.674	20,220	0.657	19,710
4.	20,000	0.683	13,660	0.635	12,700	0.592	11,840	0.571	11,420
Total of PV of Cash inflow			66,345		63,350		60,595		59,285

Initial investment is Rs. 60,000. Hence internal rate of return must be between 14% and 15% (Rs. 60,595 and Rs. 59,285). The difference comes to Rs. 1,310 (Rs. 60,595 – Rs. 59,285).

For a difference of 1,310, difference in rate = 1% (Excess PV: 60595 – 60,000 = 595)

$$\text{Therefore, exact Internal Rate of Return} = 14\% + \frac{595}{1,310} \times 1\%$$

$$= 14\% + 0.45\%$$

$$= \mathbf{14.45\%}$$

3. Profitability Index Number

It is also a time adjusted method of evaluating the investment proposals. Profitability index also called Benefit Cost Ratio or Desirability factor. It is the ratio of the present value of cash inflows, at the required rate of return to the initial cash outflow of the investment. The proposal is accepted if the profitability index is more than one and is rejected in case the profitability index is less than one. By computing profitability indices for various projects, the financial manager can rank them in order of their respective ratio of profitability.

$$\text{Profitability Index} = \frac{\text{PV of Cash Inflows}}{\text{Initial Cost Qutlay}}$$

Illustration 7. The initial cash outlay of a project is Rs. 50,000.

Estimated cash inflows:

Ist year Rs. 20,000

2nd year Rs. 15,000

3rd year Rs. 25,000

4th year Rs. 10,000

Compute profitability Index

Solution:

Calculation of Profitability Index

Year	*Cash Inflows* *Rs.*	*PV Factor at 10%*	*PV* *Rs.*
1	20,000	0.909	18,180
2	15,000	0.826	12,390
3	25,000	0.751	18,775
4	10,000	0.683	6,830
		Total	56,175

Total Present Value = Rs. 56,175
Less: Initial Outlay = Rs. 50,000
Net Present Value = 6,175

$$\text{Profitability Index (gross)} = \frac{\text{PV of Cash Inflow}}{\text{Initial Cash Outflow}}$$

$$= \frac{56{,}175}{50{,}000} = \mathbf{1.1235}$$

Profitability Index is higher than 1, the proposal can be accepted.

$$\text{Net Profitability Index} = \frac{\text{NPV}}{\text{Initial Cash Outlay}} = \frac{\text{Rs. }6{,}175}{\text{Rs. }50{,}000} = \mathbf{0.1235}$$

Or NPI = 1.1235 – 1 = **0.1235**

Net Profitability Index is positive, the proposal can be accepted.

Capital Rationing

Capital rationing is a situation where a firm has more investment proposals than it can finance. Many concerns have limited funds. Therefore, all profitable investment proposal may not be accepted at a time. In such event the firm has to select from amongst the various competing proposals, those which give the highest benefits. There comes the problem of rationing them. Thus capital rationing may be defined as a situation where the management has more profitable investment proposals requiring more amount of finance than the funds available to the firm. In such a situation, the firm has not only to select profitable investment proposals but also to rank the projects from the highest to lowest priority.

Illustration 8. X Ltd. is considering the purchase of a machine. Two machines are available, A and B. The cost of each machine is Rs. 60,000. Each machine has an expected life of 5 years. Net profits before tax but after depreciation during the expected life of the machine are given below:

Year	*Machine A* *Rs.*	*Machine B* *Rs.*
1	15,000	5,000
2	20,000	15,000
3	25,000	20,000
4	15,000	30,000
5	10,000	20,000

Following the method of return on investment ascertain which of the alternatives will be more profitable. The average rate of tax may be taken at 50%.

Solution:

Computation of Profit After Tax

Year	Machine A			Machine B		
	Profit before Tax Rs.	*Tax at 50% Rs.*	*Profit after Tax Rs.*	*Profit before Tax Rs.*	*Tax at 50% Rs.*	*Profit after Tax Rs.*
1	15,000	7,500	7,500	5,000	2,500	2,500
2	20,000	10,000	10,000	15,000	7,500	7,500
3	25,000	12,500	12,500	20,000	10,000	10,000
4	15,000	7,500	7,500	30,000	15,000	15,000
5	10,000	5,000	5,000	20,000	10,000	10,000
Total	85,000	42,500	42,500	90,000	45,000	45,000

	Machine A	*Machine B*
Average profit after tax	$\frac{\text{Rs. } 42,500}{5} = \text{Rs. } 8,500$	$\frac{\text{Rs. } 45,000}{5} = \text{Rs. } 9,000$
Investment	Rs. 60,000	Rs. 60,000
Average Investment	$= \frac{\text{Rs. } 60,000}{2} = \text{Rs. } 30,000$	$\frac{\text{Rs. } 60,000}{2} = \text{Rs.} 30,000$
Average Return on Investment	$= \frac{\text{Rs. } 8,500}{60,000} \times 100 = 14.17\%$	$\frac{\text{Rs. } 9,000}{60,000} \times 100 = 15\%$
Average Return on Average Investment	$\frac{\text{Rs. } 8,500}{30,000} \times 100 = 28.34\%$	$\frac{\text{Rs. } 9,000}{30,000} \times 100 = 30\%$

Machine B is more profitable.

Illustration 9. A Ltd. Company is considering the purchase of a new machine which will carry out some operations performed by labour. X and Y are alternative models. From the following information, you are required to prepare a profitability statement and work out the pay-back period for each model.

	Model X	*Model Y*
	Rs.	*Rs.*
Estimated Life	5 years	6 years
Cost of Machine	1,50,000	2,50,000
Cost of indirect materials	6,000	8,000
Estimated savings in scrap	10,000	15,000
Additional cost of maintenance	19,000	27,000
Estimated savings in direct wages:		
Employees not required	150	200
Wages per employee	600	600

Taxation to be regarded 50% of profit before charging depreciation. Which model would you recommend? (*CA final*)

Solution:

Profitability Statement

	Model X Rs.		Model Y Rs.
Estimated saving per year			
scrap	10,000		15,000
Wages (150 × 600) (200 × 600)	90,000		1,20,000
Total Savings	1,00,000		1,35,000
Less: Additional Cost:			
Cost of indirect materials 6,000		8,000	
Cost of Maintenance 19000	25,000	27,000	35,000
Additional Earnings	75,000		1,00,000
Less: Tax @50%	37,500		50,000
Cash flow (annual)	37,500		50,000
Less: Depreciation: 1,50,000 ÷ 5	30,000	2,50,000 ÷ 6	41,667
Net Increase in earnings	7,500		8,333
Pay-back period: $\frac{\text{Cost of Machine}}{\text{Annual Cash flow}}$	$\frac{1,50,000}{37,500} = 4$ years		$\frac{2,50,000}{50,000} = 5$ years
Rate of Return on Investment	$\frac{7,500}{1,50,000} \times 100 = 5\%$		$\frac{8,333}{2,50,000} \times 100 = 3.3\%$

As pay-back period of Model X is less than that of Model Y, and also the return on Investment is higher in respect of X, Model X is recommended.

Illustration 10. A Company proposing to expand its production can go either for an automatic machine costing Rs. 2,24,000 with an estimated life of $5\frac{1}{2}$ years or an ordinary machine costing Rs. 60,000 having an estimated life of 8 years.

	Automatic Machine Rs.	Ordinary Machine Rs.
The annual sales and costs are estimated as follows:		
Sales	1,50,000	1,50,000
Costs:		
Materials	50,000	50,000
Labour	12,000	60,000
Variable Overhead	24,000	20,000

Compute the comparative profitability under pay-back method. (*M.Com. Madurai*)

Solution:

		Automatic Machine Rs.		Ordinary Machine Rs.
Annual Sales		1,50,000		1,50,000
Less: Variable Cost				
Materials	50,000		50,000	

Labour	12,000		60,000	
Overheads	24,000	86,000	20,000	1,30,000
Marginal Profit		64,000		20,000
Pay-back period:	$\frac{2,24,000}{64,000}$ =	$3\frac{1}{2}$ years	$\frac{60,000}{20,000}$	= 3 years
Post pay-back profitability		$64,000\left(5\frac{1}{2}-3\frac{1}{2}\right)$ = **Rs. 1,28,000**		20,000 (8 – 3 yrs) = **Rs. 1,00,000**

Illustration 11. The Tamil Nadu Fertilizers Ltd. is considering a proposal for the investment of Rs. 5,00,000 on product development which is expected to generate net cash inflows for 6 years as under:

Year	Net Cash Flows ('000)
1	Nil
2	100
3	160
4	240
5	300
6	600

The following are the present value factors @15% p.a.

Year	1	2	3	4	5	6
Factor	0.87	0.76	0.66	0.57	0.50	0.43

(*M.Com. Madras*)

Solution:

Calculation of Net Present Value

Year	*Cash Inflows ('000)* Rs.	*PV Factor*	*Present Values ('000)* Rs.
1	Nil	0.87	Nil
2	100	0.76	76.0
3	160	0.66	105.60
4	240	0.57	136.80
5	300	0.50	150.00
6	600	0.43	258.00
		Total	726.40
		Less: Cash Outlay	500.00
		Net Present Value	226.40

As the net present value is positive, the proposal is acceptable.

Illustration 12. The Financial Manager of a company has to advise the Board of Directors on choosing between two compelling project proposals which require an equal investment of Rs. 1,00,000 and are expected to generate cash flows as under:

	Project I Rs.	*Project II* Rs.
End of year 1	48,000	20,000
2	32,000	24,000

3	20,000	36,000
4	Nil	48,000
5	24,000	16,000
6	12,000	8,000

Which project proposal should be recommended and why? Assume the cost of capital to be 10% p.a. The following are the present value factors at 10% p.a.

Year	1	2	3	4	5	6
Factor	0.909	0.826	0.751	0.683	0.621	0.564

(*M.Com. Madras*)

Solution:

Calculation of Net Present Value

Year	*Project I Net Cash Inflows*	*Project II Net Cash Inflows*	*PV Factor @ 10%*	*PV of Project I*	*PV of Project II*
	Rs.	*Rs.*		*Rs.*	*Rs.*
1	48,000	20,000	0.909	43,632	18,180
2	32,000	24,000	0.826	26,432	19,824
3	20,000	36,000	0.751	15,020	27,036
4	Nil	48,000	0.683	Nil	32,784
5	24,000	16,000	0.621	14,904	9,936
6	12,000	8,000	0.564	6,768	4,512
			Total	1,06,756	1,12,272
			Less: Cash Outlay	1,00,000	1,00,000
			Net Present Value	6,756	12,272

Project II should be accepted as the NPV is more than that of Project I

Illustration 13. From the following information, calculate the net present value of the two projects and suggest which of the two profits should be accepted assuming a discount rate of 10%.

	Profit X	*Profit Y*
	Rs.	*Rs.*
Initial Investment	20,000	30,000
Estimated Life	5 years	5 years
Scrap Value	1,000	2,000

Profits before depreciation and after taxes are as follows:

Year	*Profit X*	*Profit Y*
	Rs.	*Rs.*
1	5,000	20,000
2	10,000	10,000
3	10,000	5,000
4	3,000	3,000
5	2,000	2,000

(*M.Com., Madras*)

Solution:

Year	*Cash Flows*		*PV of Re 1 @ 10%*	*Present Value of Net Cash Flow*	
	Project X	*Project Y*		*Project X*	*Project Y*
	Rs.	*Rs.*		*Rs.*	*Rs.*
1	5,000	20,000	0.909	4,545	18,180

2	10,000	10,000	0.826	8,260	8,260
3	10,000	5,000	0.751	7,510	3,755
4	3,000	3,000	0.683	2,049	2,049
5	2,000	2,000	0.621	1,242	1,242
(scrap) 5	1,000	2,000	0.621	621	1,242
				24,227	34,728
				20,000	30,000
				4,227	4,728

Project Y should be selected as NPV of Project Y is higher.

Illustration 14. A Firm is considering the purchase of a machine. Two machines A and B are available, each costing Rs. 50,000. In comparing the profitability of those machines a discount rate of 10% is to be used. Earnings after taxation are expected to be as follows:

Year	*Machine A Cash Inflow*	*Machine B Cash Inflow*
	Rs.	*Rs.*
1	15,000	5,000
2	20,000	15,000
3	25,000	20,000
4	15,000	30,000
5	10,000	20,000

You are also given the following data:

Year	*PV Factor @ 10% discount*
1	0.909
2	0.826
3	0.751
4	0.683
5	0.621

Evaluate the projects using:

(*a*) the pay-back period

(*b*) the accounting rate of return

(*c*) the net present value

(*d*) the profitability index (*M.Com. Madurai*)

Solution:

(*a*) Machine A

Year	*Cash Inflow*	*Cumulative cash Inflow*
	Rs.	*Rs.*
1	15,000	15,000
2	20,000	35,000
3	25,000	60,000
4	15,000	75,000
5	10,000	85,000

The above calculation shows that in two years Rs. 35,000 has been recovered. Rs. 15,000 is left out of initial investment. In the 3rd year cash inflow is Rs. 25,000. It means the pay-back period is between 2nd and 3rd year, thus:

$$\text{Pay-back Period} = 2 + \frac{15,000}{25,000} = \textbf{2.6 years}$$

(*b*) Machine B

Year	Cash Inflow	Cumulative Cash Inflow
	Rs.	*Rs.*
1	5,000	5,000
2	15,000	20,000
3	20,000	40,000
4	30,000	70,000
5	20,000	90,000

In three years, Rs. 40,000 has been recovered. The balance left out of initial investment is Rs. 10,000. It means the pay-back period is between 3rd and 4th year, thus:

$$\text{Pay-back Period} = 3 + \frac{10,000}{30,000} = \mathbf{3.33\ years}$$

Machine A should be purchased. Because pay-back period is less.

Accounting Rate of Return

Machine A

Total Returns = Rs. 85,000

Average Return = Rs. 85,000 ÷ 5 = Rs. 17,000

$$\text{Average Rate of Return} = \frac{17,000}{50,000} \times 100 = \mathbf{34\%}$$

Machine B

Total Returns = Rs. 90,000

Average return = 90,000 ÷ 5 = Rs. 18,000

$$\text{Average Rate of Return} = \frac{18,000}{50,000} \times 100 = \mathbf{36\%}$$

Machine B should be preferred as it gives a higher average rate of return.

Net Present Value

Calculation of Net Present Value

Year	PV Factor at 10%	Cash Inflows Machine A	Cash Inflow Machine B	PV Machine A	PV Machine B
		Rs.	*Rs.*	*Rs.*	*Rs.*
1	0.909	15,000	5,000	13,635	4,545
2	0.826	20,000	15,000	16,520	12,390
3	0.751	25,000	20,000	18,775	15,020
4	0.683	15,000	30,000	10,245	20,490
5	0.621	10,000	20,000	6,210	12,420
				65,385	64,865
			Less: Cash Outlay	50,000	50,000
			Net Present Value	15,385	14,865

The Net Present Value of Machine A is more than that of Machine B. So, machine A should be purchased.

Profitability Index

$$\textit{Machine A} = \frac{\text{Present Values}}{\text{Cost of Investment}} = \frac{65,385}{50,000} = \mathbf{1.308}$$

$$\textit{Machine B} = \frac{64,865}{50,000} = \mathbf{1.297}$$

Probability Index of Machine A is more than that of Machine B and therefore, machine A should be preferred.

Table I
Present Value of Re. 1

Years	5%	6%	8%	10%	12%	14%	%	16%	18%	20%	22%	24%	25%	28%	30%
1	0.952	0.913	0.926	0.909	0.893	0.877	0.870	0.862	0.847	0.833	0.820	0.806	0.800	0.781	0.769
2	0.907	0.890	0.857	0.826	0.797	0.769	0.756	0.743	0.718	0.694	0.672	0.650	0.640	0.610	0.592
3	0.864	0.840	0.794	0.751	0.712	0.675	0.658	0.641	0.609	0.579	0.551	0.524	0.512	0.477	0.450
4	0.823	0.792	0.735	0.683	0.636	0.592	0.572	0.552	0.516	0.482	0.451	0.423	0.410	0.373	0.350
5	0.784	0.747	0.681	0.621	0.567	0.519	0.497	0.476	0.437	0.402	0.370	0.341	0.328	0.291	0.269
6	0.746	0.705	0.630	0.564	0.507	0.456	0.432	0.410	0.370	0.335	0.303	0.275	0.262	0.227	0.207
7	0.711	0.665	0.583	0.513	0.452	0.400	0.376	0.354	0.314	0.279	0.249	0.222	0.210	0.170	0.159
8	0.677	0.627	0.540	0.467	0.404	0.351	0.327	0.305	0.266	0.233	0.204	0.179	0.118	0.139	0.123
9	0.645	0.592	0.500	0.424	0.361	0.308	0.284	0.263	0.225	0.193	0.167	0.144	0.134	0.108	0.094
10	0.614	0.558	0.463	0.386	0.322	0.270	0.247	0.227	0.191	0.162	0.137	0.116	0.107	0.085	0.073
11	0.585	0.527	0.429	0.350	0.287	0.237	0.215	0.195	0.162	0.135	0.112	0.094	0.087	0.066	0.056
12	0.557	0.497	0.397	0.319	0.257	0.208	0.187	0.168	0.137	0.112	0.092	0.076	0.069	0.062	0.043
13	0.530	0.469	0.368	0.290	0.229	0.182	0.163	0.145	0.116	0.093	0.075	0.061	0.055	0.040	0.033
14	0.505	0.442	0.340	0.263	0.205	0.160	0.141	0.125	0.099	0.078	0.062	0.049	0.044	0.032	0.025
15	0.481	0.417	0.315	0.239	0.183	0.140	0.123	0.108	0.084	0.065	0.051	0.040	0.035	0.025	0.020
16	0.458	0.394	0.292	0.218	0.163	0.123	0.107	0.093	0.071	0.054	0.042	0.032	0.028	0.019	0.015
17	0.436	0.371	0.270	0.198	0.146	0.108	0.093	0.80	0.060	0.045	0.034	0.026	0.023	0.015	0.012
18	0.416	0.350	0.250	0.180	0.130	0.095	0.081	0.069	0.051	0.038	0.028	0.021	0.018	0.012	0.009
19	0.396	0.331	0.232	0.164	0.116	0.83	0.070	0.060	0.043	0.031	0.023	0.017	0.014	0.009	0.007
20	0.377	0.312	0.215	0.149	0.104	0.073	0.061	0.051	0.037	0.026	0.019	0.014	0.012	0.007	0.005

TABLE II

Present Value of Re. 1 Received Annually for years

Years	5%	6%	8%	10%	12%	14%	%	16%	18%	20%	22%	24%	25%	28%	30%
1	0.952	0.943	0.926	0.909	0.893	0.877	0.870	0.862	0.847	0.833	0.820	0.806	0.800	0.781	0.769
2	1.859	1.833	1.783	1.736	1.690	1.647	1.646	1.605	1.566	1.528	1.492	1.457	1.440	1.392	1.361
3	2.723	2.676	2.577	2.487	2.402	2.322	2.283	2.246	2.174	2.016	2.042	1.981	1.952	1.868	1.816
4	3.546	3.465	3.312	3.170	3.037	2.914	2.855	2.798	2.690	2.589	2.494	2.404	2.362	2.241	2.166
5	4.330	4.212	3.993	3.791	3.605	3.433	3.352	3.274	3.127	2.991	2.864	2.745	2.689	2.532	2.346
6	5.076	4.917	4.623	4.335	4.111	3.889	3.784	3.685	3.498	3.326	3.167	3,020	2.951	2.759	2.643
7	5.786	5.582	5.206	4.868	4.564	4.288	4.160	4.039	3.812	3.605	3.416	3.242	3.161	2.937	2.802
8	6.463	6.210	5.747	5.335	4.968	4.639	4.487	4.344	4.078	3.837	3.619	4.421	3.329	3.076	2.925
9	7.109	6.802	6.247	5.759	5.328	4.946	4.772	4.607	4.303	4.031	3.786	3.566	3.463	3.184	3.019
10	7.722	7.360	6.710	6.145	5.650	4.216	5.019	4.833	5.494	4.192	3.923	3.682	3.571	5.269	3.092
11	8.306	7.887	7.139	6.495	5.937	5.453	5.234	5.029	4.656	4.327	4.035	3.776	3.656	3.335	3.147
12	8.863	8.384	7.536	6.814	6.194	5.660	5.421	5.197	4.793	4.439	4.127	3.851	3.725	3.387	3.190
13	9.394	8.853	7.904	7.103	6.424	5.842	5.583	5.342	4.910	4.533	4.203	3.912	3.780	3.427	3.223
14	9.899	9.295	8.244	7.367	6.628	6.002	5.724	5.468	5.008	4.611	4.265	3.962	3.824	3.459	3.249
15	10.380	9.712	8.559	7.606	6.811	6.142	5.847	5.575	5.092	4.675	4.315	4.001	3.859	3.483	3.268
16	10.838	10.106	8.851	7.824	6.974	6.265	5.954	5.669	5.162	4.730	4.357	4.033	3.887	3.503	3.283
17	11.274	10.477	9.122	8.022	7.120	6.373	6.047	5.749	5.222	4.775	4.391	4.059	3.910	3.518	3.295
18	11.690	10.828	9.372	8.201	7.250	6.467	5.128	5.818	4.273	4.812	4.419	4.080	3.928	3.529	3.304
19	12.085	11.158	9.614	8.365	7.366	6.550	6.198	5.877	5.316	4.844	4.442	4.097	3.942	3.539	3.311
20	12.462	11.470	9.818	8.514	7.469	6.623	6.259	5.929	5.353	4.870	4.660	4.110	3.954	3.546	3.316

OBJECTIVE TYPE QUESTIONS

A. Choose the correct answer to the following :

1. While evaluating capital investment proposals, the time value of money is considered in case of :
   (a) Pay back method.
   (b) Discounted cash flow statement.
   (c) Accounting rate of return method.
2. The return after the pay off pariod is not considered in case of :
   (a) Pay back method.
   (b) Internal rate of return method.
   (c) Accounting rate of return method.
3. Depreciation is included in costs in case of :
   (a) Pay back method.
   (b) Accounting rate of return method.
   (c) Present value index method.
4. The cash inflows on account of operations are presumed to have been reinvested at the cut-off rate in case of :
   (a) Pay back method.
   (b) Accounting rate of return method.
   (c) Discounted cash flow method.

(**Ans:** (1) (b); (2) (a) ; (3) (b) ; (4) (c))

B. State whether the following statements are true or false :

1. Internal rate of return and time-adjusted rate of return are the same.
2. Capital rationing and capital budgeting means the same thing.
3. Pay back period method measures the true profitability of a project.
4. The internal rate of return and net present value are synonymous terms.
5. Cash flows from a project can be worked out only on the basis of certain probabilities.
6. Depreciation is considered while calculating the return on a project according to the Accounting rate of return method.
7. Discounted cash flow technique takes into account the time value of money.
8. Tax concessions have no role to play in estimating the cash flows from a project.

Ans: (1) True; (2) False; (3) False; (4) False; (5) True; (6) True; (7) True; (8) False.

THEORETICAL QUESTIONS

1. What is a Capital Expenditure Budget?
2. Explain the nature and concept of Capital budgeting.
3. Explain the importance and features capital expenditure control.
4. What are the objectives of capital expenditure budgeting?
5. "Despite all limitations of the methods of pay-back period, it has still significance in project appraisal." Explain.
6. What does the profitability index signify?
7. "Investments alternative yielding the highest discount rate of return is the most acceptable." Will this always be true? Explain.
8. "Pay-back method is a test of liquidity and not profitability". Explain
9. What is capital rationing?

10. What do you understand by capital budgeting process?
11. Give comparative description of various methods of ranking investment proposals.
12. Explain briefly the following methods of capital budgeting:
    (*a*) Pay-back method (*b*) Accounting rate of return method
13. What are the distinct categories of investment decisions? Discuss the basic factors on which investment decisions depend?

PRACTICAL PROBLEMS

14. Calculate the net present value of a small sized project requiring an initial investment of Rs. 20,000 and which provides a net cash inflow of Rs. 6,000 each year for six years. Assume the cost of funds to be 8% p.a. and that there is no scrap value.

(**Ans:** NPV = Rs. 7,738) (*M.Com. Delhi*)

15. The Alpha Ltd. is considering the purchase of a new machine. Two alternatives (A and B) have been suggested, each having an initial cost of Rs. 4,00,000 and requiring Rs. 20,000 as additional working at the end of Ist year. Earnings after taxation are expected to be as follows:

Cash Inflow

Year	*Machine A*	*Machine B*
	Rs.	*Rs.*
1	40,000	1,20,000
2	1,20,000	1,60,000
3	1,60,000	2,00,000
4	2,40,000	1,20,000
5	1,60,000	80,000

The Company has a target of return on capital of 10% and on this basis, you are required to compare the profitability of the machines and state which alternative you consider financially preferable.

Note: The following Table gives the PV of Re. 1 due in 'n', Number of years.

Year	1	2	3	4	5
PV at 10%	0.91	0.83	0.75	0.68	0.62

(**Ans:** NPV = Rs. 1,00,200 (A) Rs. 1,05,000 (B)
Machine B is preferable (*M.Com. Madras*)

16. Payoff Ltd. is producing activities mostly by manual Labour and is considering to replace it by a new machine. Prepare a statement of profitability showing the payback period from the following information:

	Machine A	*Machine B*
Estimated life of Machine	4 years	years
Cost of the machine	Rs. 9,000	Rs. 18,000
Estimated Savings in scrap	Rs. 500	Rs. 800
Estimated Savings in direct wages	Rs. 6,000	Rs. 8,000
Additional Cost of maintenance	Rs. 800	Rs. 1,000
Additional Cost of supervision	Rs. 1,200	Rs. 1,800

Ignore Taxation

(**Ans:** Pay-back period: 2 years, (A) 3 years (B) (*M.Com. Madurai*)

17. Orient Trading Ltd. propose to increase their production. They are willing to purchase a new machine. There are three types in the market. The following are the details regarding them:

	X	Y	Z
	Rs.	*Rs.*	*Rs.*
Cost of Machine	17,500	12,500	9,000
Estimated Savings in Scrap	400	750	250
Wages per operative	250	300	250
Cost of indirect materials	—	400	—
Expected Savings in indirect materials	100	—	250
Additional Cost of Maintenace	750	550	500
Operatives not required	11 Nos.	20 Nos.	9 Nos
Estimated life of machine	10 years	6 years	5 years

You are required to advise the management which type of the machine is to be purchased.

(M.Com. Bombay)

	X	*Y*	*Z*
(**Ans:** Marginal Profit	Rs. 2,500	Rs. 5,000	Rs. 2,250
Net Savings after tax (50%)	Rs. 1,250	Rs. 2,500	Rs. 1,125
Pay-back period	14 yrs.	5 yrs.	8 yrs.
Pay-back profitability	Nil	Rs. 2,500	Nil

18. A Company has an investment opportunity costing Rs. 40,000 with the following expected net cash flow, after Tax but before depreciation:

Year	*Net cash Flow*
	Rs.
1	7,000
2	7,000
3	7,000
4	7,000
5	7,000
6	8,000
7	10,000
8	15,000
9	10,000
10	4,000

Using 10% as the rate of discount, find out the following:

(*a*) Pay-back period

(*b*) Net present value

(*c*) Profitability Index

(**Ans.** (*a*) 5 years $7\frac{1}{2}$ months (PBP)

7 years $6\frac{1}{2}$ months (DPBP)

(*b*) Rs. 8,961 (*c*) 122.4%)

19. The Directors of a Ltd. Co. consider a proposal to invest a sum of Rs. 1,00,000 on a plant that has an expected life of 5 years which at the end has no residual value.

The expected annual incomes during the life of the plant are:

	Rs.
Ist year	30,000
2nd year	40,000
3rd year	40,000
4th year	30,000
5th year	20,000
	1,60,000

Money is available at an interest of 10% p.a. Calculate rate of return and advise the Directors of the company.

(**Ans.** Average Return on Investment = 12%

Average Return on Average Investment = 24%.

20. A Ltd. Company is considering investing in a project, requiring a capital outlay of Rs. 2,00,000. Forecast for annual income after depreciation but before tax is as follows:

Year	*Rs.*
1	1,00,000
2	1,00,000
3	80,000
4	80,000
5	40,000

Depreiation may be taken at 20% on original cost and taxation at 50% of net income. You are required to evaluate the project according to each of the following methods.

(*a*) Pay-back method

(*b*) Rate of Return on Original Investment

(*c*) Rate of Return on Average Investment

(*d*) Discounted cash flow method, taking cost of capital at 10%.

(*e*) Excess Present Value Index.

(*M.Com. Madurai*)

Ans: (*a*) 2.25 years

(*b*) 20%

(*c*) 40%

(*d*) NPV = Rs. 1,08,130

(*e*) 154%

21. A choice is to be made between two competing profits which require an equal investment of Rs. 50,000 and are expected to generate net cash flows as under:

End of the year	*Profit I* Rs.	*Profit II* Rs.
1	25,000	10,000
2	15,000	12,000
3	10,000	18,000
4	Nil	25,000
5	12,000	8,000
6	6,000	4,000

The cost of capital of the company is 10% using discounted cash flow method, recommend which proposal is to be preferred.

(*M.Com. Bombay*)

(**Ans:** NPV : Rs. 3461 (I)

: Rs. 6819 (II)

Profit II is to be preferred)

22. A Ltd. Company is considering to purchase a new machine. Two alternative models, A and B, are available, each costing Rs. 80,000. Earnings after taxation are expected to be as follows:-

Year	Cash flows *Model A* *Rs.*	*Model B* *Rs.*
1	8,000	24,000
2	24,000	32,000
3	32,000	40,000
4	48,000	24,000
5	32,000	16,000

The Company has a target of return on capital of 10%. On the basis, you are required to compare the profitability of the models and state which alternative you consider financially preferable. *(M.Com. Bhopal)*

(**Ans:** NPV: Rs. 23,784 (A) Rs. 24,616 (B)
Model B is more profitable)

23. Using the information given below, compute the pay-back period under (a) Traditional pay-back method, and (b) discounted pay-back method and comment upon the result:

	Rs.
Initial outlay	80,000
Estimated life	5 years
Profit after Tax:	
I year	6,000
II year	14,000
III year	24,000
IV year	16,000
V year	Nil

Depreciation has been calculated under straight line method. The cost of capital may be taken at 20% and PV of Re. 1 at 20% p.a. is given below:

Year	1	2	3	4	5
PVF	0.83	0.69	0.58	0.48	0.40

(M.Com. Jabalpur)

(**Ans:** Pay-back period:
Traditional = 2 years 8.4 months
Discounted = 4 years 4.65 months)

Chapter 12

MIS and Reporting

Essentials of an Ideal Report; General Principles of a Good Reporting; Methods of Reporting; Types of Reports; MIS; Reporting Needs of Different Management Levels; Theoretical Questions.

One of the important functions of the management accountant is to keep the management informed of all facts relating to the business so as to assist the management in controlling the undertaking effectively and for the efficient management of the business. Information is life-blood of a business. The efficiency of an organisation is to a large extent governed by the pertinence and regularity of the information provided to those who perform the functions of management. As a matter of fact, the ultimate effectiveness of the information is itself dependent upon the form and timing of its presentations. A management reporting system can be defined as "an organised method of providing each manager with all the data and only those data which he needs for his decisions, when needs them and in a form which aids his understanding and stimulates his actions". The organisation can design such a system only after it has established its goal, policies and the basic organisation structure.

The business at present operates under an environment which is more difficult and complex as compared to earlier times. The growth of size of business has necessitated the delegation of authority of various levels of management. Therefore, there arises problems of control, coordination and communication. The term "information" means "data processed or evaluated for a specific purpose". It is necessary to evolve and operate an effective and efficient management information or reporting system. Without information, the managers, working at different levels in the organisation, cannot carryout the functions of planning, controlling and decision-making efficiently. Therefore, one of the main functions of accounting is to provide management with necessary information which may be communicated in the form of reports, statements, diagrams, graphs etc.

The accounting reports consist of financial statistics. The large scale production has rendered the business operations more complex in nature. Management to-day cannot analyse all significant facts regarding the entire operations. It is through accounting reports only it is possible to get a full insight into the entire operative activity of the firm. The reports are the basis for the management to make decisions. It is important to recall that management information system is designed to produce routine data and highlights the conditions to which management must react. Reporting may be defined as communicating the facts and data through reports and statements to the persons for whom such facts and data are compiled and collected. The function of reporting starts, when accounting function comes to an end.

The primary object of reporting to management is two fold : appraising the management with the actual performance, and secondly, to enable the management to make scientific and sound decisions. The efficiency of an organisation is to a certain extent governed by the pertinence and regularity of the information provided to those who perform the functions of management. The ultimate effectiveness of this information is itself dependent upon the form and timing of its presentation. The process of management reporting essentially involves :

1. Proper selection of financial and operating data and other relevant facts and figures which are to be communicated.
2. Organisation of data to put the information in a proper form that can be readily understood and appreciated by the management.
3. Selecting the appropriate method of reporting.

Thus, we observe that the process of management reporting is deeply concerned with the communication of financial and non-financial information to the management. The routine system of accounting does not cater this need. Hence, the management accountant is concerned with the task of obtaining, arranging, analysing and interpreting the necessary data and then communicating it to the management. The effectiveness with which relevant information is communicated to the management of–ten largely determines the success or failure of management at various levels in the organisation.

The term 'report' may be defined as a formal communication which moves upward. It differs from the word 'communication'. The superior communicates orders to the subordinate. The subordinate communicates the results. The word 'report' is generally used for factual communication by a lower level to a higher level of authority. Thus, orders are 'communicated', while results and performances are 'reported'.

ESSENTIALS OF AN IDEAL REPORT

A report is a vehicle carrying information to those who need it. The following are the essentials of a good management reporting or information system.

1. The system should yield information required for the *evaluation of each manager's area of responsibility* in relation to the goals of the organisation.
2. There should be a *proper flow of information*. It should originate from the right place and should be transmitted to the proper level of authority where decisions are to be made. *Complete and consistent* information should flow in a systematic manner.
3. Each decision's informational requirements should be anticipated so that all the relevant data are assembled and made *available at the decision point*.
4. The information should be communicated in a proper form so that management may appreciate it and use it in decision making without any difficulty.
5. The system should ensure furnishing of the information at the proper time, i.e. neither too late nor too early.
6. The system should be capable of being adjusted according to the requirements of the user–*flexibility*
7. The system should include some procedure for measuring and matching the cost of obtaining information and the value to be obtained from its use–*cost benefit analysis*.
8. The report should be presented in a simple, unambiguous and clear language - *simplicity*. The reader should be able to understand the report without any difficulty.
9. There should be a *consistency* in the presentation of reports. The comparability of reports will be possible only if they are consistent.

GENERAL PRINCIPLES OF A GOOD REPORTING

A good reporting system is helpful to the management in planning and controlling. Every level of management needs information relating to its activities centre so that effective planning may be undertaken and current activities may be controlled and necessary corrective measures may also be taken in time, if needed. Some general principles, in brief, are given below :

1. The draft of the report should be simple.
2. The report should be precise, specific and accurate.
3. It should bear a suitable title.
4. It must follow the organisational lines.
5. Report must contain up-to-date information.
6. Reports should be presented in time.
7. They should be specific and definite.
8. They should be economical.
9. It must suit to the end-user's requirements.
10. They must be consistent and correct as to information.
11. It must be attractive.
12. It must distinguish between controllable and uncontrollable costs.
13. The report should highlight the trouble spots.
14. It must provide for exceptional circumstances.
15. Report should cover broad trends only and not minute details.
16. Each report should be pertinent.
17. Report should contain unbiased and not personal opinions.
18. Reports should be directed towards those areas where variances are most significant.
19. Each report should have purpose to justify its preparation.

METHODS OF REPORTING

Reports may be presented in any of the following forms :

1. **Written Reports** :These include the following :
   (*a*) **Formal Financial Statements** : Such statements may deal with any one or more of the following :
      (*i*) Actuals against the budgeted figures.
      (*ii*) Comparative statements over a period of time.
   (b) **Tabulated Statistics** : The report may deal with statistical analysis of a particular type of expenditure over a period of time or sales of a product over a period in different territories etc.
   (*c*) **Accounting Ratios** : These may be a part of the formal financial statements prepared or may be given in the form of a separate statement. The various types of ratios have been explained in the chapter-Accounting ratios.
2. **Graphic Reports :** Sometimes information may be supplied in the form of charts, diagrams, pictures etc.
3. **Oral Reports :** Information may be communicated orally. Group meetings and conferences with individuals are most common forms of such communication.

TYPES OF REPORTS

There are several ways of classifying the reports. The following are the important types :

I According to Object or Purpose
   (*a*) External Reports
   (*b*) Internal Reports

II According to Functions
   (*a*) Operating Reports

(*b*) Financial Reports

III According to Frequency

(*a*) Regular or Routine Reports

(*b*) Special Reports

IV According to Contents :

(*a*) Production Reports

(*b*) Sales Reports

(*c*) Cost Reports etc.

I According to Object or Purpose

(*a*) **External Reports :** The reports meant for persons outside the business are known as external reports. Outsiders interested in company reports may be shareholders, creditors, bankers etc. A company publishes Income Statement and Balance Sheet at the end of every financial year. And these statements are filed with the Registrar of Companies and Stock Exchange authorities.

(*b*) **Internal Reports :** Internal reports refer to those reports which are meant for different levels of management. They are not public documents. They do not have to conform to any statutory standards. These reports may be meant for different level of management - top level, middle level and lower level of management.

II According to Functions

(*a*) **Operating Reports :**These reports provides information about operations of the concern. The operating reports may consist of control reports and information reports etc. Control reports are designed to measure the actual performance with the budgeted standards. They show the extent of variance. Current control reports indicate deviation of actual performance from planned performance of operations so that prompt action may be taken to stop further losses. Summary control reports summarise the deviation of actual performance from planned performance over a period of time.

***(b)* Financial Reports :** These reports highlight the financial position, strength and structure of the business enterprise. Again these reports may be static or dynamic.

III According to Frequency

(a) **Regular or Routine :** These are the reports that are rendered at periodic intervals. The intervals at which routine reports are to be presented should be fixed for each report, say, weekly, monthly, quarterly etc.

(*b*) **Special Reports :** These are the reports which are prepared and submitted to the management for any special purpose. Special reports are required for special purposes only. These reports are prepared according to the need of the situation. It may carry messages :

(*i*) Reasons for the report; (*ii*) Investigations made; (*iii*) Findings

(*iv*) Conclusions and recommendations.

Special reports may deal with the following topics :

(*a*) Market Analysis (*b*) Technological changes

(*c*) Problems of Raw materials (*d*) Political changes

(*e*) Buy or make decisions (*f*) Cost reduction schemes.

(*g*) Labour Dispute, etc.

IV According to Contents

According to the contents of reports they may be production reports, production cost reports, sales reports, cost reports etc. These reports are used by the management for planning and policy determination.

MANAGEMENT INFORMATION SYSTEM

Information is the basis for decision-making in an organisation. The efficiency of management depends, to a larger extent, upon the availability of regular and relevant information to those who exercise the managerial function. A regular system of reporting is considered as a better guarantee of efficiency and operation than reliance on personal qualities. Thus it is essential that an effective and efficient reporting system is developed as part of accounting method. The main object of management reporting is to obtain the required information about the operating results of an organisation regularly in order to use them for future planning and control. The term 'report' normally refers to a formal communication which moves upward, i.e. by a lower level to a higher level of authority in response to orders received from higher level. A person, who is issued with instructions to do certain things, should report back what he has done in compliance thereof.

The old techniques like intuition, rule of thumb, personal whim and prestige etc. are now considered useless in the process of decision-taking. Modern management is constantly on the look out for such quantitative and other information which can help in analysing the proposed alternative actions and choosing one as its decision. Thus, modern management functions are information-oriented more popularly known as 'Management by information'. And the system through which necessary information is communicated to the management is known as "Management Information System (MIS)." The management needs full information before taking any decision. Good decisions can minimise costs and optimise returns. Management Information System can be helpful to the management in undertaking management functions smoothly and effectively.

REPORTING NEEDS OF DIFFERENT MANAGEMENT LEVELS

Generally the reporting levels in the internal management fall in the following three categories:

(A) Top Management Level: The top level management comprises of Board of Directors, General Manager, Assistant Managers, Finance Directors, Production Directors, Sales Directors etc. The top management is primarily concerned with the policy formulations, planning and organisation. They are, therefore, interested in the overall efficiency or inefficiancy of the business. Generally, the top management should receive the following reports at different intervals:

1. Periodic report about Profit & Loss Account and Balance Sheet.
2. Statement of Funds Flow and Cash Flow at regular interval.
3. Report plant utilisation.
4. Report of cost of production.
5. Report on research and development activities
6. Periodic report on sales, credit collection, selling and distribution expenses etc.

(B) Middle Management Level: This comprises the heads of various departments such as Sales Manager, Production Manager etc. The report for this level should show the efficiency and cost data relating to respective areas or departments. The departmental managers are primarily concerned with the execution of plans, administration of policies, directing operating supervisors etc. The work of co-ordinating activities of different departments is also undertaken by middle management. They receive the following reports : weekly or fortnightly.

1. Reports on material price and usage variances
2. Reports on labour rate and efficiency variances
3. Report on idle time, wastage of materials etc.
4. Reports on stock levels
5. Reports on sales, production, etc.
6. Reports on orders booked, orders executed and orders still to be executed.

(C) Lower Management Level: The lower level management is assigned the work of executing various policies. They are in touch with the day-to-day performance of their section. They may need reports on daily or weekly basis. Supervisors, formen, section-chief, sectional incharge etc. come under this level. Reports are almost in the form of scrap of paper having no proper format. Reports are detailed and specific, restricted only to the activity with which they are concerned; Examples of such reports are:

1. Reports of over-time
2. Material usage variances
3. Labour efficiency variances
4. Material spoilage report
5. Accident report etc.

THEORETICAL QUESTIONS

1. What is meant by management reporting?
2. Explain the basic requisites of a good report. (*M. Com. Madras*)
3. Explain the usefulness of reporting to management.
4. Explain the different types of reports that are used for the internal management of an enterprise. (*B. Com. Bombay*)
5. "Accounting reports are a matter of necessity for the management and not a matter of convenience". Explain (*M. Com. M.S.*)
6. What are the objects of reporting?
7. Discuss the importance of a proper system of reports.
8. What do you mean by MIS? What are its important elements? (*M. Com. Madurai*)

Chapter 13

Responsibility Accounting

Definition; Steps; Responsibility Centres; Expense Centres; Revenue Centre; Profit Centre; Investment Centre; Advantages of Responsibility Accounting; Cost Centres Vs. Responsibility Centres; Transfer Prices; Theoretical Questions.

The systems of costing like standard costing and budgetary control are useful to management for controlling the costs. In those systems the emphasis is on the devices of control and not on those who use such devices. Responsibility accounting is a system of control where responsibility is assigned for the control of costs. The persons are made responsible for the control of costs. Responsibility accounting implies a system of accounting whereby the performance of various people is judged by assessing how far they have achieved the predetermined targets set for the divisions, departments or sections for which they are responsible. Each person is responsible for his area of operation. Responsibility accounting is similar to any other system of cost such as standard costing or budgetary control but with greater emphasis towards fixing of the responsibility of the persons entrusted with the execution of specific job. For example, if Mr. A has prepared the cost budget of his department, he will be made responsible for keeping the costs under control. Mr. A will be supplied with detailed information of actual costs incurred by his department. In case the costs are more than budgeted costs, then A will try to find out the reasons and take corrective measures. A will be personally responsible for the performance of his department.

Definition

Responsibility accounting is a system under which managers are given decision-making authority and responsibility for each activity occurring within a specific area of the company. Under this system managers are made responsible for the activities of segments. These segments may be called departments or divisions.

Eric Kohier defines responsibility accounting as "a method of accounting in which costs are identified with persons assumed to be capable of controlling them, rather than with products or functions. It differs from activity accounting, in that it does not in itself require an organisational grouping by activities and sub-activities or provide a systematic criterion of system design."

Charles T. Horngreen defines "Responsibility accounting is a system of accounting that recognizes various responsibility centres throughout the organisation and reflects the plans and actions of each of these centres by assigning particular revenues and costs to the one having the pertinent responsibility. It is also called profitability accounting and activity accounting".

Institute of Cost and Works Accountants of India defines responsibility account is "a system of management accounting under which accountability is established according to the responsibility delegated to various levels of management and a management information and reporting system instituted to give adequate feedback in terms of the delegated responsibility. Under this system divisions or units of an organisation under a specified authority in a person are developed as responsibility centres and evaluated individually for their performance."

David Fanning defines responsibility accounting is "a system or mechanism for controlling the wider freedom of action that executives – decision centre manager in other words – are given by senior management and for holding those executives responsible for the consequences of their decisions."

Robert Anthony defines responsibility accounting is "that type of management accounting that collects and reports both planned and actual accounting information in terms of responsibility centres."

Responsibility accounting focussed main attention on responsibility centres. The managers of different activity "centres are responsible for controlling the costs of their centres. Information about costs incurred for different activities is supplied to the persons incharge of various centres. The performance is constantly compared to the standards set and this process is very useful in exercising cost controls. Responsibility accounting is different from cost accounting in the sense that the future lays emphasis on cost control whereas the latter lays emphasis on cost ascertainment. Responsibility accounting is a system which makes every-one conscious and responsible for the job that is entrusted to him by his supervisor, i.e. a control by delegating and locating responsibility for cost. Each supervisory area in the organisation is charged only with the cost for which it is responsible or over which it has control. Not only the costs but also the revenues are assigned. That is why it is defined as "a system of accounting that recognises various responsibility centres throughout the organisation and that reflects plans and actions of each of these centres by assigning particular revenues and cost to one having pertinent responsibility". This system defines the specific responsibility of the departmental supervisor as well as functional managers which should be performed. Practically it is the management that has to chalk out the plan and control the activities relating to the responsibility centre. It follows the basic principle like any other control system, example, Standard Costing or Budget. The only difference is that the fixation of responsibility lies in the hands of individuals or departments.

The following inferences can be made from the above definitions:

(1) Responsibility accounting stresses on communication of information in general and accounting information in particular to various decisional centres.
(2) Responsibility accounting lays greater emphasis on persons (human factor management)
(3) Responsibility accounting is tailored to the organisational structure so that the process of communication of information follows principles of organisation.
(4) It is an accounting system which collects and report both planned and actual accounting data in terms of sub-units which are recognised as responsibility centres.

Steps Involved in Responsibility Accounting

Responsibility accounting is used as a control device. Following steps are necessary to effect control through the responsibility accounting:

(1) The organisation is divided into various responsibility centres. Each responsibility centre is put under the charge of a responsibility manager.
(2) The targets or budgets of each responsibility centre are set in consultation with the manager of responsibility centre so that he may be able to give full information about his department. The manager of responsibility centre should know as what is expected of him – each centre should have a clear set of goals. The responsibility and authority of each centre should be well defined.

(3) Managers are charged with the items and responsibility over which they can exercise a significant degree of direct control.

(4) Goals defined for each area of responsibility should be attainable with efficient and effective performance.

(5) The actual performance is communicated to the managers concerned. If it falls short of the standards, the variances are conveyed to the top management. The names of persons responsible for the variances are also conveyed so that responsibility may be fixed.

(6) The performance reports for each centre should be prepared highlighting the variances and items requiring management's attention. The corrective measures are suggested or taken and communicated to the concerned managers of the centres.

The purpose of all these steps is to assign responsibility to different individuals so that their performance is improved and costs are controlled. The personal factor in responsibility accounting is most important. The management may prepare the best plan or the budget and put up before its staff, but its success depends upon the initiative and the will of the workers to execute it. The essence of responsibility accounting is to communicate the right information to the right person at the right time. Responsibility accounting provides a means of control, it cannot control. Control is a personalised affair, people control, not the reports. Responsibility accounting will certainly act control device and it will help in improving the overall performance of the business.

Responsibility Centres

Responsibility accounting focuses attention on responsibility centres. A responsibility centre is a sub-unit of an organisation under the supervision of a manager who has the responsibility for the activities of that responsibility centre. Each sub-unit has certain activities to perform and its manager is assigned the responsibility and/or authority to carry out those activities. Responsibility centre is the segment of business with reference to which information will be communicated to pin point responsibilities. In the words of Anthony and Races, "A responsibility centre is like an engine in that it has inputs, which are physical quantities of material, hours of various types of labour, and a variety of services; it works with these resources usually; working capital and fixed assets are also required. As a result of this work, it produces output, which are classified either as goods, if they are tangible or as services, if they are intangile. These goods or services go either to other responsibility centres within the company or to customers in the outside world." Responsibility centres, for planning and control purposes, are classified into the following cases:

(A) Expense Centre: An expense centre is a responsibility centre in which inputs, but not outputs, are measured in monetary terms. Expense or cost centre is a segment of an organisation in which the managers are held responsible for the costs incurred in that segment. Responsibility accounting is based on financial information relating to input (costs) and outputs (revenues). In an expense centre of responsibility, the accounting system records only the cost incurred in/by the centre or unit but revenues earned (output) are excluded. In case of certain responsibility centres, it is neither possible nor necessary to measure the output in terms of monetary units. Most of the service departments come in this category. For example, it is almost impossible to measure the monetary value of the finance or the account department's contribution to the company. The accounting system, therefore, records the cost incurred in respect of these centres but not the revenue incurred. The performance of the responsibility centre managers is evaluated by comparing the costs incurred with the budgeted costs. Management focuses its attention on cost variances for control purposes.

(B) Revenue Centre: A revenue centre is a segment of the organisation which is primarily responsible for generating sales revenue. A revenue centre manager does not possess control over cost, investment in assets, but usually has control over some of the expenses of the marketing department. The performance of a revenue centre is evaluated by comparing the actual revenue with budgeted revenue. The marketing manager of a product line, or an individual sales representative are example of revenue centres.

(C) Profit Centre: A responsibility centre is called a profit centre when the manager is held responsible for both costs (inputs) and revenues (outputs) and thus for profit. A profit centre is a big segment of activity for which both revenues and costs are accumulated. A centre whose performance is measured in terms of both – the expense it incurs and revenue it earns, is termed as a profit centre. The output of a responsibility centre may either be meant for internal consumption or for outside customers. In the latter case the revenue is realised when the sales are made. That is, when the output is meant for outsiders, then the revenue will be measured from the price charged from customers. If the output is meant for other responsibility centre, then management takes a decision whether to treat the centre as profit centre or not. In fact, any responsibility centre can be turned into a profit centre by determining a selling price for its outputs. For instance, in case of a process industry, the output of one process may be transferred to another process at a profit by taking into account the market price. Such transfers will give some profit to that responsibility centre. Although such transfers do not increase the Company's assets, they help in management control process.

(D) Investment Centre: It is defined as a responsibility centre in which inputs are measured in terms of cost/expenses and outputs are measured in terms of revenues and in which assets employed are also measured. A responsibility centre is called an investment centre, when its manager is responsible for costs and revenues as well as for the investment in assets used by his centre. He is responsible for maintaining a satisfactory return on investment i.e. asset employed in his responsibility centre. The investment centre manager has control over revenues, expenses and the amounts invested in the centre's assets. The manager of an investment centre is required to earn a satisfactory return. Thus, return on investment (ROI) is used as the performance evaluation criterion in an investment centre. He also formulates the credit policy which has a direct influence on debt collection, and the inventory policy which determines the investment in inventory. It is a centre in which the manager is held responsible for the proper utilisation of assets. He is expected to earn a satisfactory return on the assets employed in his responsibility centre. Measurement of assets employed poses many problems. It becomes difficult to determine the amount of assets employed in a particular responsibility centre. Some of the assets are in the physical possession of the responsibility centre while for some assets it may depend upon other responsibility centres or the Head Office of the company. This is particularly true of cash or heavy plant and equipment. Whether such assets should be included in the figure of assets employed of the responsibility centre and if included at how much figure, is a difficult question. On account of these difficulties investment centres are generally used only for relatively large units which have independent divisions both manufacturing and marketing for their individual products.

Advantages of Responsibility Accounting

Management uses responsibility accounting as a control device. The aim of responsibility accounting is to help management in achieving organisational goals. It is an invaluable support to modern management. It contributes to the firm's management by providing relevant information on a continuous basis. The following are some of the advantages of responsibility accounting:

1. It introduces sound system of control – a system of closer control.
2. Each and every individual in the organisation is assigned some responsibility and they are accountable for their work.
3. Everybody knows what is expected of him. Nobody can shift responsibility to anybody else if something goes wrong.

4. It is effective tool of cost control and cost reduction applied with budgetary control and standard costing.
5. It facilitates the management to set realistic plans and budgets.
6. It is not only a control device but also facilitates decentralisation of decision-making.
7. It measures the performance of individuals in an objective manner.
8. It fosters a sense of cost-consciousness among managers and their subordinates.
9. It helps the management to make an effective delegation of authority and required responsibility as well.
10. Under the system of responsibility accounting, detailed information is collected about costs and revenues, on a continuous basis and the data is helpful in planning for future costs and revenues.
11. Timely corrective action can be taken and better control over costs can be achieved.

Cost Centres vs. Responsibility Centres

A cost centre is "a location, person or item of equipment (or group of these) for which costs may be ascertained and used for purposes of cost control". Thus, cost centre is used as a means of assembling items of cost, so that they can be assigned to goods and services. In the case of cost centre, emphasis is more on products, jobs or processes whose costs are to be ascertained. Thus here the emphasis is not on the persons who may be managing a level or product or process.

Responsibility centres, on the other hand, are established on the basis of responsibility delegated to responsible personnel of the organisation with a view to identify costs which can be controlled by each one of them. However, cost centres sometimes may be used as responsibility centres too. In that case cost reports are prepared both cost centre-wise and responsibility-centre-wise.

Transfer Prices

The measurement of profit in a profit centre type of responsibility accounting is also complicated by the problem of transfer prices. A transfer price is a price used to measure the value of goods/services furnished by a profit centre to other responsibility centres within a company. That is, when internal exchange of goods and services take place between the different divisions of a firm, they have to be expressed in monetary terms. The monetary amount for these inter-divisional exchanges/transfers is called the transfer price. That is, a transfer price is that national value at which goods and services are transferred between divisions in a decentralised organisation. The implication of the transfer price is that for the selling division (the division whose goods or services are being transferred) it will be a source of revenue whereas for the buying division (that division which is receiving the goods or services) it is an element of cost. The goods that are produced by the buying division and sold to the outside world are known as final products. A question arises as to how the transfer of goods and services between divisions should be priced. The transfer prices can have impact on the evaluation of each division's performance and measures applied for such measurements of performance. While determining transfer prices a number of criteria should be carefully considered:

1. Transfer prices should help in the accurate measurement of divisional performance (profitability) measurement.
2. Transfer prices should motivate the divisional managers into maximising the profitability of their divisions and making decisions that are in the best interest of the organisation as a whole.
3. Transfer prices should ensure that divisional autonomy and authority is preserved.

4. Transfer prices should allow goal congruence to take place, which in effect means that the objectives of divisional managers are compatible with the objectives of overall company.

Transfer price policies refer to the selection of policies/methods that would govern the calculations of such prices under various circumstances. The concern of transfer price policies is with developing a transfer pricing system that (*i*) allows a measure of performance to reflect the use of resources by a division, and (*ii*) allows the optimal allocation of the firms' resources. In other words, suitable transfer prices should be related to (*a*) management performance assessment, and (*b*) decision-optimisation.

Chiefly there are two methods of transfer pricing – cost based and market based. Based on these, there are many types of transfer pricing – cost price, marginal cost price, standard cost price, cost plus fixed margin, market price, negotiated price, opportunity cost price etc. Each type of transfer pricing have advantages and disadvantages too.

THEORETCIAL QUESTIONS

1. Define responsibility account. What are the advantages of responsibility accounting?
2. What do you mean by transfer pricing?
3. "Responsibility accounting is an important device for control." Explain.
4. Discuss various steps involved in responsibility accounting.
5. Explain clearly what do you understand by the term – Cost Centre and responsibility centre.

Chapter 14

Management Audit

Definition; Objectives of Management Audit; Difference between Financial Audit and Management Audit; Need for Management Audit; Conducting Management Audit; Theoretical Questions.

Management audit is a new concept in the sphere of auditing. The word 'Audit' takes its origine from Latin word 'audire' which means 'to hear'. The person who conducts audit is known as the auditor. In olden days, the original object of an audit was principally to see whether the Accountant had properly accounted for the receipts and payment of cash. In those days, audit was simply a comparison of records. That is, auditors are generally expected to detect errors and omissions in the books of accounts. In the context of financial accounting, the term auditing means examination of books of accounts to ensure that the financial statements are prepared in accordance with the statutory requirements and that they reflect a true and a fair view of the affairs of the concern. Cost audit which is concerned with the audit of cost accounts is a part of the work of the internal auditor. The principles underlying cost audit differs from financial audit not only in scope but objectives also. The term 'cost audit', according to ICWA, India, "It is an audit of efficiency of minute details of expenditure while the work is in progress and not a post-mortem examination. Financial audit is *a fait accompli*. Cost audit is mainly a preventive measure, a guide for management policy and decision, in addition to being a barometer of performance." The difference of the two is clear from the definition.

The management audit is an expansion of internal audit and which is now called Management Audit. It is the latest development of internal audit. Though, this concept is still in its infancy, yet it has caught world-wide attention of the Accountants, Management and Auditors. Management audit is concerned with management process as a whole. It covers review and appraisal of managerial policies and plans in comparison to pre-determined standards.

Definition

As its name signifies, the management audit means the audit of management process and functions. It is an independent appraisal activity for the review of control of managerial functions so as to ensure compliance with the organisational objectives, policies and procedures and the management methods and purposes.

William P Leonard defines Management Audit, as "A comprehensive and constructive examination of an organisational structure of a company, institution or branch of Government, or of any component thereof, such as a division or department, and its plans and objectives, its means of operations, and its use of human and physical facilities".

Leslie R Howard has given a comprehensive definition of Management Audit. According to him, Management audit is an investigation of a business from the highest level downward in order to ascertain whether sound management prevails throughout, thus facilitating the most effective relationship with the outside world and the most efficient organisation and smooth running of internal organisation."

According to Bhandari, "Management audit is a comprehensive examination of an organisational system which comprises a review of final results and an intensive examination of objectives, programmes, policies, procedures, organisational structure, decisions and internal controls."

Taylor and Perry has given another definition. According to them, "Management auditing is a method to evaluate the efficiency of management at all levels throughout the organisation, or more specifically, it comprises the investigation of a business by an independent body from the highest executive level downwards, in order to ascertain whether sound management prevails throughout, and to report as to its efficiency or otherwise, with recommendations to ensure its effectiveness where such is not the case".

In this regard, George A Terry states: "The periodic assessment of a company's managerial planning, organising, actuating and controlling compared to what might be called the norm of successful operation is the essential meaning of management audit. It reviews the company's past, present and future. The areas it covers are examined with a view to determine whether the company is receiving maximum results out of its endeavours."

Management audit may even be used to provide guidance on critical assessment of capital budgeting or profit performance, forecasting and planning activities on long-term and short-term basis. Management audit is thus concerned with evaluation of the control system and information system in various segments of the organisation. Thus it is clear that management audit is an evaluation, appraisal and review of managerial policies and programmes to ascertain whether they are carried out efficiently or not. If the work is not done satisfactorily then recommendations are made to take corrective actions.

Objectives of Management Audit

The basic objectives as contained in the above definitions are:

1. The management audit aims at achieving the efficiency of the management.
2. It suggests ways and means of increasing managerial efficiency.
3. It examines the organisational structure. If there are deficiencies then changes in organisations are suggested.
4. It studies the relationship of the concern with the outside world and the economic environment.
5. It is the main objective of management audit to see whether the business is managed efficiently or not.
6. It helps the management at all levels in the efficient discharge of duties and responsibilities.
7. It evaluates the performance of various management processes and functions.

Difference between Financial Audit and Management Audit

The following are the differences between the two, in brief:

Financial Audit	*Management Audit*
1. It is concerned with the certification of true and fair character of financial accounts.	It is not intended to certify the correctness of accounting data but is concerned with an appraisal of means and results.
2. It is simply a post mortem examination.	It is preventive as well as curative check up
3. It requires accounting expertise.	It requires inter-disciplinary expertise.
4. It is mainly based on internal financial data.	It is based on financial and non-financial data obtained from internal as well as external.

5. It is statutory in case of Joint Stock Company.	It is still voluntary.
6. Scope of audit is determined by laws.	Scope of management audit is based on mutual agreement.
7. It is well developed and professionally controlled activity.	It is in its infancy stage.
8. Motivation for audit comes from tradition and law.	It depends upon the consciousness of management.
9. It is useful for shareholders and other external parties.	It is mainly useful for management itself.
10. It is an annual feature	It depends on management and need not be annual - may be 2 or 3 or 4 yearly programme.

Need for Management Audit

Financial audit is concerned with the certification of true and fair character of financial accounts. It is not concerned with evaluation of either 'means' or 'results'. The financial auditor does not report whether the policies laid down by the concern are carried out properly or not. He looks only at the history of financial transactions. He is concerned with financial aspects of the organisation. He does not suggest ways and means to eliminate wastage or reduce the cost of production.

The management of business at present is becoming more and more complex. The Directors are not experts in every field of management. Management audit is a kind of internal audit which reveals defects in the working of the organisation and suggests improvements to obtain best result of the operations of the concern. It is a comprehensive examination — an appraisal of all functions of management, viz., planning, organising, motivating, controlling and co-ordinating undertaken by management auditor.

Some of the uses of management audit, in brief, are:

1. Management audit makes substantial contribution to systems of goal setting in the organisation.
2. It helps to avoid wasteful, unnecessary and extravagant use of resources.
3. It is a kind of internal audit which reveals defects in the working of the concern and suggests improvements to obtain best results.
4. It helps in the improvement of Management Information System to expedite flow of information among responsibility centres.
5. It guides the management in pin-pointing key functions or operations in the profit-making process.
6. It helps in establishing, reviewing and improving the planning system.
7. It facilitates the management in getting the adequate information for correct decisions.
8. It sees whether the management is properly using the information that it is getting.
9. It enables appraisal of performance of various managers.
10. It assists all members of management to overcome delays, wasteful expenditure, recurring losses, gaps between budgeted and actual achievements etc.

"Management Audit is performed with the object of examining the efficacy of the information control system, management procedures towards the achievement of enterprise goals."

"Management Audit can be defined as an objective and independent appraisal of the effectiveness of managers and the effectiveness of the corporate structure in the achievement of company objectives and policies. Its aim is to identify existing and potential management weaknesses within an organisation and to recommend ways to rectify these weaknesses."

Conducting Management Audit

Management audit is primarily concerned with evaluation of management functions and organisational functions keeping in view the overall organisational objectives. Management audit requires the review of all aspects of management. One man cannot be expert in every field of management. Therefore, there should be a team to conduct the management audit. It will be good, if the team of management auditors consists of an accountant, operational research specialist, industrial engineer, social scientist etc. All the members must have "ability to think like managers".

The following procedure may be followed:

1. The management audit team must have a clearly defined authority from the management of the enterprise.
2. Management auditor requires information for the appraisal of various managerial aspects. For this purpose, management auditor can make use of standard questionnaire, which may be specially designed.
3. The management auditor carefully examine the information collected by him. Whenever information is received from any source, the persons supplying it must put their signatures to authenticate it.
4. The management auditor, who consciously observes, will become aware of many problems that are not recorded or are incapable of analysis through data.
5. The management auditor should also evaluate the internal audit report, inspection report etc. to form his own opinion.
6. In the process of conducting a review of the various activities of the concern, management auditor can adopt and use a number of techniques of verificatory audit, such as enquiry, examination, confirmation, observation of an activity or condition etc.
7. He is concerned with the appraisal of performance in the various areas of management, such as planning, organisation, control, systems and procedures, inventory management, production and sales management etc.
8. In the last, management auditor has to prepare a report, which should be concise and free from ambiguity. He can criticise the management. The management auditor has to compare the actual performances with the standards laid down or performance in the various years. On the basis of the above analysis and evaluation, a useful course of action is to be suggested.

THEORETICAL QUESTIONS

1. What is management audit.
2. What are the objectives of management audit.
3. What is the need for management audit.
4. Distinguish between financial audit and management audit.
5. Appraisal of management functions is a must in India for correcting the problem arising out of weak management.

Chapter 15

Price Level Accounting (Inflation Account)

Introduction; Limitation of Historical Accounting; Methods of Accounting for Changing Prices; Current Purchasing Power Method; Determination of Profit; Current Cost Accounting Method; Features of CCA System; Current Cost Operating Profit; Depreciation Adjustment; Cost of Sales Adjustment; Monetary Working Capital Adjustment; Gearing Adjustment; Merits of Inflation Account; Demerits; Miscellaneous; Theoretical Questions; Practical Problems.

Introduction

Accounting is based on the traditional concept of cost and revenue. Money is the yardstick for measuring profits and losses and financial health of the business — operating results and financial position. The basic objective of accounting is the preparation of financial statements in a way that they give a true and fair view of the business. That is, the income statement should disclose the true profit or loss made by the business during a particular period while the balance sheet must show a true and fair view of the financial position of the business on a particular date. Financial statements are prepared in monetary units *i.e.*, rupee. The medium of expression is the money value. The value of money is itself fluctuating; any measurement with an unsteady scale cannot be finite and comparable. The recording of business transactions under the assumption that monetary unit is stable is known as historical accounting. However, it has been our experience that over a period of time, the prices have not remained stable. There have been inflationary as well as deflationary tendencies. Rise in general price level, termed *inflation* erodes the intrinsic value of money, conversely, fall in general prices called *deflation*, raises its purchasing power. Inflation is a concept which every human being is not only aware of, but also painfully experiencing. The direct effect of inflation is the erosion in the purchasing power of money. The root cause of the problem is the change in the value of money.

Monetary unit is never stable and all types of countries have been experiencing high rates of inflation. The prices change as a result of various economic and social forces and such changes bring about a change in the purchasing power of money. Unless the necessary adjustments are made, price level changes produce distortions in the financial statements and suffer serious limitations. Financial statements, prepared according to conventional or historical accounting system, do not reflect current economic realities. The assumption of stable money value subject to which the financial statements are prepared is fallacious in the context of rising prices. Inflation by which we mean a rise in general price level and a fall in the value of money. Because historical rupee is not comparable to the present day rupee. Unlike *physical units*, such as kilogram, metre etc. are stable units in measuring weight and distance, monetary units *i.e., rupee is an unstable unit of exchange value.*

Consider the following example :

Capital Employed	8,00,000	Fixed Assets	8,00,000
Current Liabilities	2,00,000	Less : Depreciation	2,00,000
			6,00,000
		Current Assets	4,00,000
	10,00,000		10,00,000

Profit after tax @ 50% and depreciation of Rs. 80,000 (10% of the original cost of assets), the profit is Rs. 2,00,000. The replacement cost of the fixed asset is Rs. 15,00,000 due to inflation.

In the above example, the rate of return on capital employed is 25% , $\left(\frac{2,00,000}{8,00,000}\times 100\right)$ under historical accounting system. But when the profit is compared to the real value of the fixed assets, being used *i.e.*, Rs. 15,00,000, it would be clear that the rate of return on capital employed is not 25% as shown below :

Net Profit	Rs 2,00,000
Add : 10% depreciation on Rs. 8,00,000	80,000
Add : Tax @ 50% of profit before tax	2,00,000
Profit before charging depreciation and tax :	4,80,000
Less : 10% of depreciation on replacement cost of asset : Rs 15,00,000	1,50,000
	3,30,000
Less : Tax @ 50%	1,65,000
Profit on the basis of price level accounting	1,65,000
Capital employed on the basis of replacement cost :	
Fixed Assets	Rs 15,00,000
Less : Depreciation (as in historical accounting system)	3,75,000
	11,25,000
Add : Current Assets	4,00,000
	15,25,000
Less : Current Liabilities	2,00,000
Capital Employed	13,25,000
Rate of Return on Capital Employed	
$\frac{\text{Rs. } 1,65,000}{\text{Rs. } 13,25,000}\times 100$	12.45%

Thus it is clear that the profit is over-stated and the fixed assets are under-stated, when the effect of inflation is ignored. In this example, when the asset has to be replaced, larger funds are required on account of inflationary conditions. The asset purchased for Rs. 8,00,000 and its life was expected to be 10 years, a sum of Rs 80,000 (10%) would be charged as depreciation every year. If after 10 years, the asset can be purchased for Rs. 13,00,000, the firm may have to face serious problems because of insufficiency of funds. Hence, the need for inflation accounting.

Limitations of Historical Accounting

In order to trace the impact of inflation on the financial statements, it becomes necessary to pin-point the limitations of the conventional statements conveying historical financial information for end-users within an organisation and also outsiders.

1. Changes in the price level are not taken into account. The financial statements prepared under the conventional system are merely statements of historical facts. They fail to give realistic

and correct picture of the state of affairs of a concern. Because monetary unit is never stable under inflationary conditions. This instability has resulted in a number of distortions in the financial statements and is the most serious limitation of historical accounting.

2. Fixed assets are shown in the position statement at the cost at which they were acquired. Further purchase of assets at different points of time are clubbed together as additions to the existing assets, without any regard to change in the purchasing power of rupee. For example, we constructed a building at a cost of Rs. 1,00,000 in 2009 and constructed a similar building in 2010 at a cost of Rs 2,50,000. The rupee value in 2009 is not the same as in 2010. The value is significantly less in 2010. These buildings are shown as follows :

Building (2009)	Rs. 1,00,000
Building (2010)	Rs. 2,50,000
	Rs. 3,50,000

3. Depreciation is charged on the historical cost of the asset. It is the charge of cost of the used up value of the asset against revenue. It is a mechanism of generating funds for the replacement of fixed assets when the replacement becomes due. The charge of depreciation of fixed assets is based on the original purchase price, and not the price at which the same asset could be acquired. The cost of replacement of an asset far exceeds the original cost at which the asset is acquired. The provision made by way of depreciation charge on the original cost will be insufficient for the purpose, on account of inflation. And the profit is overstated.

4. Financial statements contain non-comparable figures because of inflation. For example,

Year	*Sales (Rs.)*	*Price Index*
2008	20,000	100
2009	30,000	200
2010	40,000	300

The price index at the end of 2010 is 325.

By looking to the above, one will say that there is an increase in sales over the 3 years. But if they are adjusted for change in price level, the real situation would be different as shown below :

Year	*Sales (unadjusted) Rs.*	*Conversion Factor*	*Revised Sales Rs.*
2008	20,000	$\frac{325}{100}$	65,000
2009	30,000	$\frac{325}{200}$	48,750
2010	40,000	$\frac{325}{300}$	43,333

When adjusted for price level changes, the sales are constantly declining.

5. Tax is levied on money profits. The money profit under conventional accounting does not represent real profit. Since money profit is taken for taxation, a portion of capital is taken away by taxation. The reported profits are overstated and assets are understated under inflationary conditions.

6. In conventional accounting gains (or losses) on account of holding inventories may be mixed up with operating gains (or losses). To determine the true operating performance, holding gains (or losses) should be segregated from operating profits (or losses). The operating profit should be available for distribution while holding profit should not. For example, a businessman purchased 100 grams of gold @ Rs 1,400 in 2008 and sold 50 grams of gold in the year. In 2009 purchased another 100 grams of gold @ Rs 1,600 and sold all 150 grams of gold @ Rs 1,800. In such case, the profit in 2009 is :

Sales (150 grams × Rs. 1,800)	Rs. 2,70,000
Less : Cost 50 gms × 1,400 = Rs. 70,000 +	
100 gms × 1,600 = Rs. 1,60,000	Rs. 2,30,000
Profit	Rs. 40,000

The holding profit is Rs.10,000 (50 gms × Rs. 200) and the operating profit is Rs. 30,000. This is because if all the units sold has been purchased in 2009, the profit would have been only Rs. 30,000 (150 gms × Rs. 200).

7. Balance Sheet consists of monetary as well as non-monetary items. Monetary items-cash, debtors, creditors etc, are shown at their current money value. Non-monetary items—building, inventories etc. are shown at their unexpired historical cost, and not at real current value. In other words, the non-monetary items are understated. Thus Balance Sheet fails to present a fair value of financial position.

Methods of Accounting for Changing Prices

The following are the generally accepted methods of accounting for price level changes :

1. Current Purchasing Power Method (or) General Purchasing Power Method (CPP or GPP Method)
2. Current Cost Accounting Method (CCA Method)
3. Hybrid Method i.e. mixture of CPP and CCA Methods.

Current Purchasing Power Method (CPP)

Institute of Chartered Accountants in England and Wales recommended that changes in the price level should be reflected in the financial statements through the current purchasing power method (CPP). For measuring changes in the price level and incorporating the changes in the financial statements we use index numbers, which may be considered to be a barometer meant for the purpose. Under this method any established and approved general price index is used to convert the values of various items in the Balance Sheet and Profit and Loss Account. This method takes into consideration the changes in the value of items as a result of the general price level, but it does not account for changes in the value of individual items. For example, a particular machine may have become cheaper over the last few years, whereas the general price level may have risen; the value of the machine will also be raised in accordance with general price index. Thus general price level adjustment restates financial data by bringing past rupee amounts in line to current rupee purchasing power by general index multiplier.

The preparation of the financial statements according to CPP method, needs understanding of the following steps :

(i) Conversion Factor

CPP method involves the restatement of historical figures at current purchasing power. For this purpose, historical figures must be multiplied by conversion factors and the formula for the calculation of conversion factor is :

$$\text{Conversion Factor} = \frac{\text{Price Index at the date of revaluation}}{\text{Price Index at the date of existing figures}}$$

Illustration 1. A Company purchased a machine on 1.1.2008 for Rs. 60,000. The retail price index on that date stood at 150. You are required to restate the value of the machine according to CPP method on 31.12.2009 when the price index stood at 200.

Solution :

$$\text{Conversion Factor} = \frac{\text{Price Index at the date of revaluation}}{\text{Price Index at the date of existing figures}} = \frac{200}{150} = \frac{4}{3}$$

Value of machine on

31st December 2009 = Existing Value Conversion Factor = $\text{Rs. } 60,000 \times \frac{4}{3} = \text{Rs. } 80,000$

In case one desires to know only the difference between existing value and the converted value of an item, it can directly be known by applying the following formula :

Difference = Existing Value × (Conversion Factor – 1)

$$= \text{Rs. } 60,000 \times \left(\frac{4}{3} - 1\right)$$

$$= \text{Rs. } 60,000 \times \frac{1}{3} = \text{Rs. } 20,000$$

(ii) Mid-Period Conversion

In case of transactions occurring throughout a period, it will be advisable to convert them according to the average index of the period. Such transactions generally include revenue items such as sales and purchases of goods, payment of expenses etc. In case the information regarding average index is not available, it may be calculated by taking the average of the index numbers at the beginning and at the end of the period.

(iii) Monetary and Non-Monetary Items

Monetary items are those assets and liabilities the amount of which are fixed by contract or otherwise, and expressed in units of money, regardless of changes in general price level. These cover cash, bank, bills receivable, bills payable, debtors, creditors, outstanding expenses, pre-paid expenses etc., represent specific monetary claim which is receivable or payable in specified number of rupees regardless of price level changes. For example, a person lends to a company a sum of Rs. 10,000 on 1st Jan. 2010 and payable on 31st Dec. 2010. The price index on 1st Jan. 2010 was 100 while it is 150 on 31st Dec. 2010. If the creditor is to be compensated for loss in purchasing power on account of increase in the price level, he should be paid Rs 15,000 $\left(\text{Rs.} 10,000 \times \frac{150}{100}\right)$. However, he will be paid as per contract only a sum of Rs. 10,000. Similarly the company is gaining Rs. 5,000 while the lender is losing Rs. 5,000. Monetary items need no conversion since they are already stated in current rupees at the end of the period to which the accounts relate.

Contrary to monetary items, non-monetary items denote such assets and liabilities that do not represent specific monetary claims and include land, buildings, machinery, investments, stocks, etc. For example, a land costing Rs. 50,000 in 2009 may sell for Rs. 1,00,000 in 2010. This is due to change in the general price level. The non-monetary items do not carry a fixed value like monetary items. Therefore, under CPP method, all such items are to be restated to represent current general purchasing power.

Monetary assets lose their value during a period of inflation since they are expressed in fixed monetary value : similarly, there is a gain in holding monetary liabilities. Accordingly, the loss by holding monetary assets is offset to a little extent by the gain on monetary liabilities. The difference between the loss and gain indicates the extent to which the concern is exposed to inflation.

Illustration 2. Compute the net monetary result of X Company Ltd. as at 31st December 2010. The relevant data are given below :

	1.1.2010	*31.12.2010*
	Rs.	*Rs.*
Cash	5,000	10,000
Book Debts	20,000	25,000

Creditors	15,000	20,000
Loan	20,000	20,000
Retail Price index Numbers :		
Ist January	200	
31st December	300	
Average for the year	240	

(*B. Com., (Hons) Delhi*)

Solution :

Statement showing the Net Monetary Result on account of Price Level Changes

	Rs.	
Monetary liabilities as on Ist Jan. 2010 should have gone up with increase in price indices (Rs. 35,000 × 1.5)	52,500	
Increase in monetary liabilities during 2010 which should have gone up with increase in price indices (Rs. 5,000 × 1.25)	6,250	
Monetary liabilities on 31st Dec. 2010 should have stood at :	58,750	
However the liabilities on 31st Dec. 2010 stood at	40,000	
Gain on holding of monetary liabilities		18,750
Monetary assets as on Ist Jan. 2010 should have gone up with increase in price indices (Rs. 25,000 × 1.5)	37,500	
Increase in monetary assets during 2010 should have gone up with increase in price indices (Rs. 10,000 × 1.25)	12,500	
Monetary assets on 31st Dec. 2010 should have stood at	50,000	
However the monetary assets on 31st Dec. 2010 stood at	35,000	
Loss on holding monetary assets		15,000
Net gain on monetary items		3,750

Working Notes :

Conversion Factor :

For items as on Ist Jan. 2010 $\frac{300}{200} = 1.5$

For items arising during 2010 $\frac{300}{240} = 1.25$

Increase in monetary assets and liabilities during 2010 :

	as on 1.1.2010	as on 31.12.2010	Increase during the year
	Rs.	*Rs.*	*Rs.*
(*a*) Monetary assets	25,000	35,000	10,000
(*b*) Monetary Liabilities	35,000	40,000	5,000

It is not necessary to find out monetary gain or loss for each item separately.

(*iv*) Cost of Sales and Inventories

Cost of sales and inventory value vary according to cost flow assumptions, *i.e.*, FIFO or LIFO. Under FIFO method cost of sales comprise the entire opening stock and current purchases less closing stock. And closing stock is entirely from current purchases.

Under LIFO method cost of sale comprise current purchases only. However, if the current purchases are less than cost of sales, a part of the opening inventory may also become a part of cost of sales. And closing stock comprises purchases made in the previous year.

The following indices are used under CPP method for restating the historical figures :

(*i*) For current purchases : Average index of the year.

(*ii*) For opening stock : Index at the beginning of the year.

(*iii*) For purchases of the previous year : Average indices for the year.

Illustration 3 From the following data calculate (*a*) cost of sales and cost of inventory under CPP method presuming that the firm is following LIFO method for inventory valuation:

		Rs.
Inventory as on 1.1.2010		8,000
Purchases during 2010		48,000
Inventory as on 31.12.2010		12,000
Price Index as on 1.1.2010	100	
Price Index as on 31.12.2010	140	
Average Price Index for 2010	125	

(*B. Com. (Hon). Delhi*)

Solution :

Cost of Sales and Closing Inventory (LIFO)

	Historical Cost *Rs.*	*Conversion Factor*	*Converted Amount under CPP* *Rs.*
Inventory as on 1.1.2010	8,000	140/100	11,200
Add : Purchases	48,000	140/125	53,760
	56,000		64,960
Less : Closing Inventory (*b*)			
From opening inventory	8,000	140/100	11,200
From current purchase	4,000	140/125	4,480
Cost of goods sold (*a*)	44,000		49,280

Determination of Profit

Under Current Purchasing Power Method, the profit can be determined in two ways :

(*i*) Net Change Method

This method is based on the normal accounting principle that profit is the change in equity during an accounting period. In order to determine this change the following steps are taken:

(*a*) Opening Balance Sheet prepared under historical cost accounting method is converted into CPP terms as at the end of the year. This is done by application of proper conversion factors to both monetary as well as non-monetary items. Equity share capital is also converted. The difference in the balance sheet is taken as reserves. Alternatively, the equity share capital may not be converted and the difference in balance sheet be taken as equity.

(*b*) Closing Balance Sheet prepared under historical cost accounting is also converted. Of course, monetary items are not restated, as explained earlier. The difference between the two sides of the balance sheet is put as reserves after converting the equity capital. Alternatively, the equity capital may not be restated in CPP terms and the balance be taken as equity.

(*c*) Profit is equivalent to net change in reserves (where equity capital has also been converted) or net change in equity (where equity capital has not been restated).

(*ii*) Conversion or Restatement of Income Statement Method

In case of this method, the income statement prepared on historical cost basis is restated in CPP terms, generally on the basis :

(*a*) Sales and operating expenses are converted at the average rate applicable for the year.

(*b*) Cost of sales is converted as per cost flow assumption (FIFO or LIFO) as explained in the preceding pages.

(*c*) Fixed assets are converted on the basis of the indices prevailing on the dates they were purchased. The same applies to depreciation.

(*d*) Taxes and dividends paid are converted on the basis of indices that were prevalent on the dates they were paid.

(*e*) Gain or loss on account of monetary items should be calculated and stated separately in Restated Income Statement to arrive at the overall figure of profit or loss.

Illustration 4. Following is the comparative Balance Sheet of a Company as on 31st December 2009 and 2010.

	2009	*2010*
	Rs.	*Rs.*
Assets :		
Cash and Receivables	2,00,000	2,60,000
Inventories (FIFO)	1,50,000	1,30,000
Land	40,000	40,000
Equipments	2,10,000	2,70,000
Less : Accumulated Depreciation	(Nil)	(24,000)
	6,00,000	6,76,000
Liabilities and Capital :		
Current Liabilities	80,000	90,000
Long-term Liabilities	1,00,000	1,16,000
Equity Share Capital (Rs.10)	1,40,000	1,40,000
Retained Earning		6,76,000
Share Premium	2,80,000	2,80,000
	6,00,000	6,67,000

The income statement of the company for the year 2010 disclosed the following information :

Income Statement for the year ended 31st Dec. 2010

Net Sales		8,00,000
Less : Cost of goods sold :		
Opening Inventories (FIFO)	1,50,000	
Purchases (Net)	5,00,000	
	6,50,000	
Less : Closing Inventory (FIFO)	1,30,000	
		5,20,000
Gross Profit		2,80,000
Less : Operating expenses (excluding depreciation)	96,000	

Depreciation	24,000	
		1,20,000
Profit before Tax		1,60,000
Less : Income Tax		70,000
		90,000
Less : Dividends paid		40,000
Retained Earnings		50,000

Equipment costing Rs. 60,000 was acquired on 1st July 2010 when the general price index was 157.5. The amount of depreciation has been calculated as follows :

10% on Rs 2,10,000	Rs 21,000
10% on Rs. 60,000 (for 6 months)	3,000
	24,000

Sales, purchases, operating expenses (excluding depreciation) took place evenly throughout the year. Inventories are priced according to first-in-first-out method. Goods in closing inventories were acquired evenly throughout the year. The dividend of Rs. 40,000 was declared and paid at the end of 2010. Income Tax accrued evenly throughout the year.

You are required to recast the above statement taking into account the price level adjustments under CPP method. The general price indices are as follows :

At the end of 2009/beginning of 2010	150
Average for the year 2010	157.5
At the end of the year 2010	163.8

Solution :

Conversion factors for restating the figures under CPP Method :

For items to which Price Index in the beginning of 2010 is applicable

$$= \frac{163.8}{150} = 1.092$$

For items to which Average Index is applicable $= \dfrac{163.8}{157.5} = 1.04$

For items to which Price Index at the end of 2010 is applicable $= \dfrac{163.8}{163.8} = 1.00$

Income Statement for the year ended 31st Dec. 2010

	As per historical basis	*Conversion factor*	*Restated under CPP Method*
	Rs.		*Rs.*
Sales (A)	8,00,000	1.04	8,32,000
Cost of goods sold :			
Opening inventory	1,50,000	1.092	1,63,800
Add : Purchases	5,00,000	1.040	5,20,000
Goods available for sale	6,50,000		6,83,800
Less : Closing Inventory	1,30,000	1.04	1,35,200
Cost of Goods sold (B)	5,20,000		5,48,600
Gross Profit (C)	2,80,000		2,83,400

(A) – (B)			
Operating Expenses	96,000	1.04	99,840
Depreciation	24,000	Rs. 21,000 × 1.092 Rs. 3,000 × 1.040	26,052
Total Operating Expenses (D)	1,20,000		1,25,892
Net Profit before General Price level gain or loss (C) – (D)	1,60,000		1,57,508
General price level Loss			4,800
Net Profit after General Price level loss			1,52,708
Less : Income Tax	70,000	1.04	72,800
Net Profit	90,000		79,908
Less : Dividends paid	40,000	1.00	40,000
Retained earnings at the end of 2010	50,000		39,908

Computation of General Price Level Gain or Loss
for the year ended 31st Dec. 2010

Net monetary items on 1.1.2010				
Cash and Receivables		2,00,000		
Less : Current liabilities	80,000			
Long Term Liabilities	1,00,000			
		1,80,000		
		20,000	1.092	21,840
Add : Source of Net monetary items during 2010:				
Sales		8,00,000	1.04	8,32,000
Total Sources		8,20,000		8,53,840
Uses of net monetary items during 2010 :				
Purchases		5,00,000	1.04	5,20,000
Operating Expenses		96,000	1.04	99,840
Income Tax		70,000	1.04	72,800
Dividends Paid		40,000	1.00	40,000
Purchase of Equipments		60,000	1.04	62,400
Total uses		7,66,000		7,95,040
Net monetary items as should have been if there were no general price level gain or loss				
Net monetary items actually existing as on 31.12.2010 :				
Cash and Receivables		2,60,000		
Less : Current liabilities	90,000			
Long Term Liabilities	1,16,000			
		2,06,000		54,000
General Price level loss during 2010 (Rs. 58,800 – Rs. 54,000)				4,800

Comparative Balance Sheet

	As on 31st Dec. 2009			As on 31st Dec. 2010		
	Historical Cost Basis Rs.	Conversion Factor	CPP Method Rs.	Historcal Cost Basis Rs.	Conversion Factor	CPP Method Rs.
Assets :						
Cash and Receivables	2,00,000	1.092	2,18,400	2,60,000	—	2,60,000
Inventories	1,50,000	1.092	1,63,800	1,30,000	1.04	1,35,200
Land	40,000	1.092	43,680	40,000	1.092	43,680
Equipment	2,10,000	1.092	2,29,320	2,70,000	1.092	2,91,720
Less Accumulated Depreciation	—		—	(24,000)	(21,000 × 1.092 + 3,000 × 1.04)	(26,052)
	6,00,000	—	6,55,200	6,76,000	—	7,04,548
Liabilities and Capital :						
Current Liabilities	80,000	1.092	87,360	90,000	—	90,000
Long term Liabilities	1,00,000	1,092	1,09,200	1,16,000	—	1,16,000
Equity Share Capital	1,40,000	1.092	1,52,880	1,40,000	1.092	1,52,880
Share Premium	2,80,000	1.092	3,05,760	2,80,000	1.092	3,05,760
Retained Earnings	—		—	50,000		39,908
	6,00,000		6,55,200	6,76,000		7,04,548

The net profit for 2010 will be the excess of Reserves in 2010 over that in 2009 as stated in CPP terms as shown below :

Assets in CPP terms as on 31.12.2010	Rs. 7,04,548
Add: Dividends paid on 31.12.2010	40,000
	7,44,548
Less: Liabilities in CPP terms as on 31.12.2010	6,64,640
Reserves as on 31.12.2010	79,908
Less: Reserves (Opening)	Nil
Net Profit for 2010 (after tax but before dividends)	79,908

Current Cost Accounting Method

The current cost accounting method is an alternative to the current purchasing power method. Price changes may be general or specific. Changes in the general level of prices which occur as a result of a change in the value of the monetary unit, are measured by index numbers. Specific price changes occur if prices of a particular asset held change without any general price movements. Under this method, assets are valued at current cost. Current cost is the cost at which the assets can be replaced as on a date. While the current purchasing power method is known as the general price level approach, the current cost accounting method is known as the specific price level approach or replacement cost accounting.

This method has been suggested by the Sandilands Committee of U.K. The Sandilands Committee published its report in September 1975 recommending the adoption of current cost accounting for dealing with the problem of inflation accounting. In this method, historic values of items are not taken into account; rather current values of individual items are taken as the basis for preparing profit and loss account and balance sheet. Thus items are not adjusted as a result of the change in the general price level as they are adjusted in the CPP method.

Features of CCA System

The following are the important features of the CCA Method :

(*a*) Fixed Assets are to be shown in the Balance Sheet at their *value to the business* and not at historical cost as reduced by depreciation. That is assets are shown in terms of what such assets would currently cost.

(*b*) Similarly, inventories are shown in the Balance Sheet at their value prevailing on the date of the Balance Sheet. These are not shown at cost or market price whichever is lower, as in case of historical accounting.

(*c*) Depreciation is to be computed on the current value of fixed assets.

(*d*) The cost of goods sold during the year has to be ascertained on the basis of prices prevailing at the date of consumption and not at the date of purchase.

(*e*) The difference between the current values and the depreciated original cost of fixed assets and of stocks, the increased requirements for monetary working capital and the under provision of depreciation in the past years may be adjusted through Revaluation Reserve Account.

(*f*) The fixed assets are shown at their "value to the business". The "value to the business" can be defined in one of the following three ways :

(*i*) *Replacement cost* is the estimated cost of acquiring new asset of the same productive capacity at current prices adjusted for estimated depreciation since acquisition.

(*ii*) *Net Realisable value* is the estimated selling price in the ordinary course of business less reasonably predictable costs of completion and disposal.

(*iii*) *Economic Value* is the sum of the discounted future cash flows expected from the use of an asset during its useful life.

Current Cost Operating Profit

Three main adjustments to trading account, calculated on the historical cost basis before interest, are required to arrive at current cost operating profit. These are called the Depreciation Adjustment, Cost of Sales Adjustment and Monetary Working Capital Adjustments.

Depreciation Adjustment

The depreciation adjustment allows for the impact of price changes when determining the charge against revenue for the part of fixed assets consumed in the period. It is the difference between the value to the business of part of fixed assets consumed during the accounting period and the amount of depreciation charged on historical cost basis. The resulting total depreciation charge thus represents the value to the business of the part of fixed assets consumed in earning the revenue of the period.

Illustration 5. A plant was purchased on 1st Jan. 2006 for Rs. 2,00,000 and is depreciated at 10% p.a. on straight line basis. By the end of 2010, the price of the same went upto Rs. 4,00,000. Show how the plant account would appear in the Balance Sheet as at 31st Dec. 2010.

Solution :

	Historical Cost	*Current Cost*
	Rs.	*Rs.*
Plant	2,00,000	4,00,000
Less : Depreciation for five years	1,00,000	2,00,000
	1,00,000	2,00,000

The increase in the value *i.e.* Rs. 2,00,000 less increased depreciation *i.e.* Rs. 1,00,000 = Rs. 1,00,000 would be shown on the lability side of the Balance Sheet as Current Cost Reserve.

Cost of Sales Adjustment

The important principle to be remembered is that current costs must be matched with current revenues. As far as sales is concerned, it needs no adjustment as it is a current revenue. One of the features of current cost accounting is to show inventories in the Balance Sheet on the basis of their value to the business, and not at cost or market price, whichever is lower. If there are stocks, certain adjustment are to be made to cost of sales. If there are no stocks, then cost of sales will comprise only current purchases and cost of sales adjustment is not necessary.

Illustration 6. From the following information calculate the Cost of Sales under Historical and Current Cost Accounting System :

Opening Stock of materials on 1.1.2010	
(1,000 kilos @ Rs 30 per kilo)	30,000
Purchases during the year 2010	Nil
Materials consumed during the year 2010	800 kilograms
Price of materials on 1.1.2010	Rs 35 per kilo
Average price during 2010	Rs 40 per kilo
Price of materials on 31.12.2010	Rs 45 per kilo

Solution :

Historical Cost Accounting system :	
Cost of Sales (800 kilos × Rs 30)	Rs 24,000
Closing Stock (200 kilos × Rs 30)	Rs 6,000
Current Cost Accounting System :	
Cost of Sales (800 kilos × Rs 40)	Rs 32,000
Closing Stock (200 kilos × Rs 45)	Rs 9,000

The increase in stock of Rs 3,000 in CCA method over Historical Cost basis will be credited to Current Cost Account Reserve. The closing stock in Balance Sheet will be shown at Rs. 9,000. The cost of Sales Adjustment amounting to Rs. 8,000 (Rs. 32,000 – Rs. 24,000) will be charged to Profit and Loss Account and credited to Current Cost Accounting Reserve.

Monetary Working Capital Adjustment

Most businesses have other working capital besides stock involved in their day-to-day operating activities. For example, when sales are made on credit the business has funds tied up in debtors. Conversely, if the suppliers of goods and services allow a period of credit, the amount of funds needed to support working capital is reduced. This monetary working capital is an integral part of the net operating assets of the business. Thus, the standard provides for an adjustment in respect of monetary working capital when determining current cost operating profit. This adjustment should represent the amount of additional (or reduced) finance needed for monetary working capital as a result of changes in the input prices of goods and services used and financed by the business.

In a business which holds stocks, the monetary working capital adjustment (MWCA) complements the COSA and together they allow for the impact of price changes on the total amount of working capital used by the business in its day-to-day operations. For example, the relationship between the MWCA made in respect of trade debtors and trade creditors and the COSA is as follows :

(*a*) When sales are made on credit the business has to finance the changes in its input prices until the sale results in a receipt of cash. The part of the MWCA related to trade debtors, in effect, extends the COSA to allow for this; and

(*b*) Conversely, when materials and services are purchased from suppliers who offer trade credit, price changes are financed by the supplier during the credit period. To this extent extra funds do not have to be found by the business and this reduces the need for a COSA and in some cases for a MWCA on debtors. The part of the MWCA related to trade creditors reflects this reduction.

Gearing Adjustment

The net operating assets shown in the Balance Sheet have usually been financed partly by borrowing and the effect of this is reflected by means of a gearing adjustment in arriving at current cost profit attributable to shareholders. No gearing adjustment arises where a company is wholly financed by shareholders' capital. While repayment rights on borrowing are normally fixed in monetary amount, the proportion of net operating assets so financed increases or decreases in value to the business. Thus, when these assets have been realized, either by sale or use in the business, repayment of borrowing could be made so long as the proceeds are not less than the historical cost of those assets.

Illustration 7. From the data given below calculate the gearing adjustment required under CCA method :

Current Cost		*Opening*	*Closing*
		Rs.	*Rs.*
Convertible Debentures		1,00,000	1,20,000
Bank Overdraft		60,000	80,000
Cash		10,000	20,000
Paid up Share Capital		1,50,000	2,00,000
Reserves		30,000	50,000
COSA	Rs. 20,000		
MWCA	15,000		
Depreciation	5,000		
	40,000		

Solution :

	Opening	*Closing*
	Rs.	*Rs.*
Calculation of net borrowing :		
Convertible Debentures	1,00,000	1,20,000
Bank Overdraft	60,000	80,000
Total of the borrowing	1,60,000	2,00,000
Less : Cash which does not enter MWCA	10,000	20,000
Net borrowings (L)	1,50,000	1,80,000
Shareholders funds (S)	1,80,000	2,50,000
Total of borrowings and shareholders funds (L + S)	3,30,000	4,30,000

The gearing adjustment is calculated by the application of the formula :

$$\text{Gearing Adjustment} = \frac{L}{L+S} \times A$$

L = Average net borrowing

S = Average shareholders interest

A = The total of the current cost adjustments.

$$\text{The gearing proportion equals } = \frac{1,50,000 + 1,80,000}{3,30,000 + 4,30,000} = 43.5\%$$

Gearing Adjustment = 43.5% × Rs. 40,000 = Rs. 17,400

Merits of Inflation Account

The following are the advantages :

1. Since assets are shown at current values, Balance Sheet exhibits a fair view of the financial position of a firm.
2. Depreciation is calculated on the value of assets to the business and not on their historical cost—a correct method. It facilitates easy replacement.
3. Profit and Loss Account will not overstate business income.
4. Inflation accounting shows current profit based on current prices.
5. Profit or loss is determined by matching the cost and the revenue at current values which are comparable—a realistic assessment of performance.
6. Financial ratios based on figures, adjusted to current value, are more meaningful.
7. Inflation accounting gives correct information, based on current price to the workers and shareholders. In the absence of this, workers may claim for higher wages and shareholders too claim for higher dividends.

Demerits

1. The system is not acceptable to Income tax authorities.
2. Too much calculations make complications.
3. Changes in prices are a never ending process.
4. The amount of depreciation will be lower in times of deflation.
5. The profit calculated on the system of price level accounting may not be a realistic profit.

MISCELLANEOUS

Illustration : 8. Mr. X purchased a machine in 2008 for Rs. 1,00,000 when the general price index was 180. He sold the machine in 2010 for Rs. 1,65,000 when the general index was 270.

Calculate the profit or loss on the sale of the machine, keeping aside the price level changes.

(B. Com. Madurai)

Solution :

Purchase price of the machine	Rs. 1,00,000 (2008)
Sales price in 2010	Rs. 1,65,000 (2010)
Profit	Rs. 65,000

The converted value of the machine at 2010 = Rs. $1{,}00{,}000 \times \frac{270}{180}$

= Rs. 1,50,000

Therefore, Profit is = Rs. 1,65,000 – Rs. 1,50,000 = Rs. 15,000

Illustration 9. A Company has the following transactions at the given dates and price indices for the first quarter of 2010.

		Price Index
Opening Balance (Jan. 1)	Rs. 6,000	100
Cash Sale (Feb. 1)	Rs.17,500	105
Payment to Creditors (Mar.1)	Rs.12,000	108
Cash Purchase (Mar. 1)	Rs. 2,000	108
Payment of Expenses (Mar. 31)	Rs. 2,000	110
Closing Balance (Mar. 31)	Rs. 7,500	110

Calculate monetary gain or loss.

(B. Com. Chennai)

Solution :

Statement of Cash

	Conventional Accounting	*Conversion Factor*	*Converted Values*
	Rs.		*Rs.*
Opening Balance	6,000	110/100	6,600
Add : Cash Sales	17,500	110/105	18,333
(A)	23,500		24,933
Less : Payments :			
Creditors	12,000	110/108	12,222
Purchases	2,000	110/108	2,037
Expenses	2,000	110/110	2,000
(B)	16,000		16,259
Closing Balance (A) – (B)	7,500		8,674

	Rs.
Expected Balance	8,674
Actual Balance	7,500
Monetary Loss :	1,174

Illustration 10. The information given below relates to monetary account of Ram and Company. Compute the general price level of gain or loss :

	As on 1.1.2010		*As on 31.12.2010*
	Rs.		*Rs.*
Monetary Assets	80,000		1,00,000
Monetary Liabilities	1,00,000		1,00,000
Retail Price Index	200		300
Average Index for the year		240	

(*M. Com. chennai*)

Solution :

(*a*) Computation of Monetary gain on account of holding monetary liabilities :
Converted Value of Monetary liabilities on 1.1.2010 :

$$\text{Rs. } 1,00,000 \times \frac{300}{200} = \text{Rs. } 1,50,000$$

Less : Historical Value of liabilities on 31.12.2010 Rs. 1,00,000

Gain on holding Monetary liabilities : 50,000

(*b*) Computation of Monetary loss on account of holding of monetary assets :
Converted Value of Monetary assets on 1.1.2010

$$\text{Rs. } 80,000 \times \frac{300}{200} = \text{Rs. } 1,20,000$$

Add : Converted Value of Monetary assets :

$$\text{Rs. } 20,000 \times \frac{300}{240} = \text{Rs. } 25,000$$

= 1,45,000

Less : Historical Value of Monetary assets on 31.12.2010 — 1,00,000

45,000

(*e*) Net Monetary Gain *i.e.* (a) – (b)

That is, Rs. 50,000

Rs. 45,000

Rs. 5,000

Illustration 11. A Summary of Balance Sheet of Sun Ltd is given below :

Cash and Accounts Receivable	Rs. 13,00,000
Plant and machinery	Rs. 14,00,000
(Net of Depreciation)	Rs. 27,00,000
Current Debts	Rs. 6,00,000
Long-term Debts	Rs. 10,00,000
Owner's Equities	Rs. 11,00,000
	Rs. 27,00,000

The current price index is 280. The plant and machinery and Long-term debt were acquired when the price index was at 180.

You are required to revise the Summary Balance Sheet to restate assets and equities in terms of current rupees. How will you treat the monetary gain or loss, if any ?

(*M. Com. Delhi*)

Solution :

BALANCE SHEET

Liabilities	Historical Values	Conversion Factor Rs.	Current Values	Assets Rs.	Historical Values Rs.	Conversion Factor	Current Values Rs.
Current Debts	6,00,000	280/280	6,00,000	Cash & Accounts Receivable	13,00,000	280/280	13,00,000
Debts Long-term	10,00,000	280/280	10,00,000				
Owner's Equity	11,00,000	280/280	17,11,111	Plant & machinery	14,00,000	280/180	21,77,778
Gain (balancing figure)	—	—	1,66,667				
	27,00,000		34,77,778		27,00,000		34,77,778

Monetary gain is to be owner's equity

Rs. 17,11,111 + Rs. 1,66,667 = Rs. 18,77,778

THEORETICAL QUESTIONS

1. Discuss the shortcomings of conventional accounting based on historical cost during inflation.
2. Distinguish between holding gain and operating gain.
3. What do you mean by Inflation Accounting ?
4. What are the limitations of historical accounting in a period of inflation ?

PRACTICAL PROBLEMS

1. Mr. X purchased a piece of land for Rs. 40,000 when the general price index was 120. Five years later he sold this piece of land for Rs. 60,000 when the price index stood at 200.

Find out the profit or loss on this transaction.
[**Ans :** Loss Rs. 6,667]

2. A company had the following monetary items on 1st January.

	Rs.		*Rs.*
Debtors	50,000	Bills Payable	12,000
Bills Receivable	15,000	Creditors	23,000
Cash	15,000		
	80,000		35,000

The transactions affecting monetary items during the years were :

(*a*) Sales of Rs. 1,98,000 made evenly throughout the year.
(*b*) Purchases of goods of Rs. 1,32,000 made evenly during the year.
(*c*) Operating expenses of Rs. 33,000 were incurred evenly throughout the year.
(*d*) One machine was sold for Rs. 24,000 on 1st July
(*e*) Dividend of Rs. 13,000 declared on 31st Dec.

The general price index was as follows :

On Ist January	90
Average for the year	110
On Ist July	120
On 31st December	120

You are required to compute the general purchasing power gain or loss for the year stated in terms of the current year and rupee.
[**Ans:** Purchasing power loss Rs 18,000]

3. Following information has been extracted from the financial statements of a company.

Plant and machinery	Rs 36,000	
Less : Accumulated Depreciation	6,000	30,000
Buildings	1,00,000	
Less : Accumulated depreciation	40,000	60,000
		90,000

The plant was purchased when the general price index was 120 and building was acquired when it was 100. Restate the amount of the assets when the present price index is 150.
[**Ans.** Plant & Machinery Rs 37,500; Buildings 90,000]

4. The Balance Sheet of a company, reveal the following among other things:

	31.3.2009	*31.3.2010*
Inventories	Rs. 5,50,000	6,10,000
Book Debts	4,50,000	5,50,000
Cash at Bank	60,000	80,000
Advances for supply of materials	1,00,000	1,26,500
Due to suppliers	2,50,000	3,22,000

During 2009-2010 material prices rose by 15% and those of finished goods by 10%. Calculate the Monetary Working Capital Adjustments to be made under the Current Cost Accounting system.
(**Ans.** Rs. 23,500) (*B.Com. MS*)